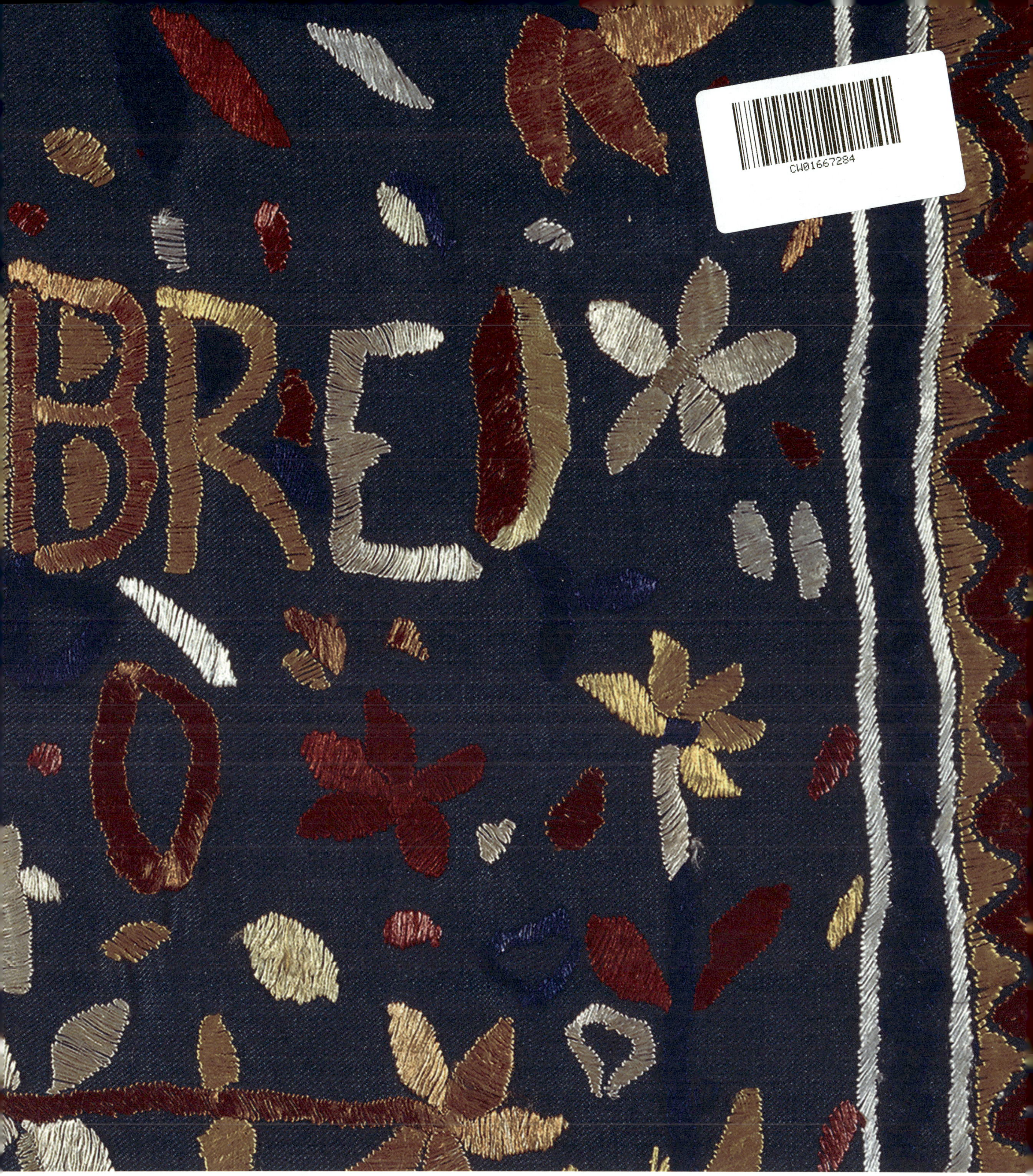

16 DICEMBRE 2040 – 11 LUGLIO 2023 (December 16, 2040 – July 11, 2023), 1971 (detail)

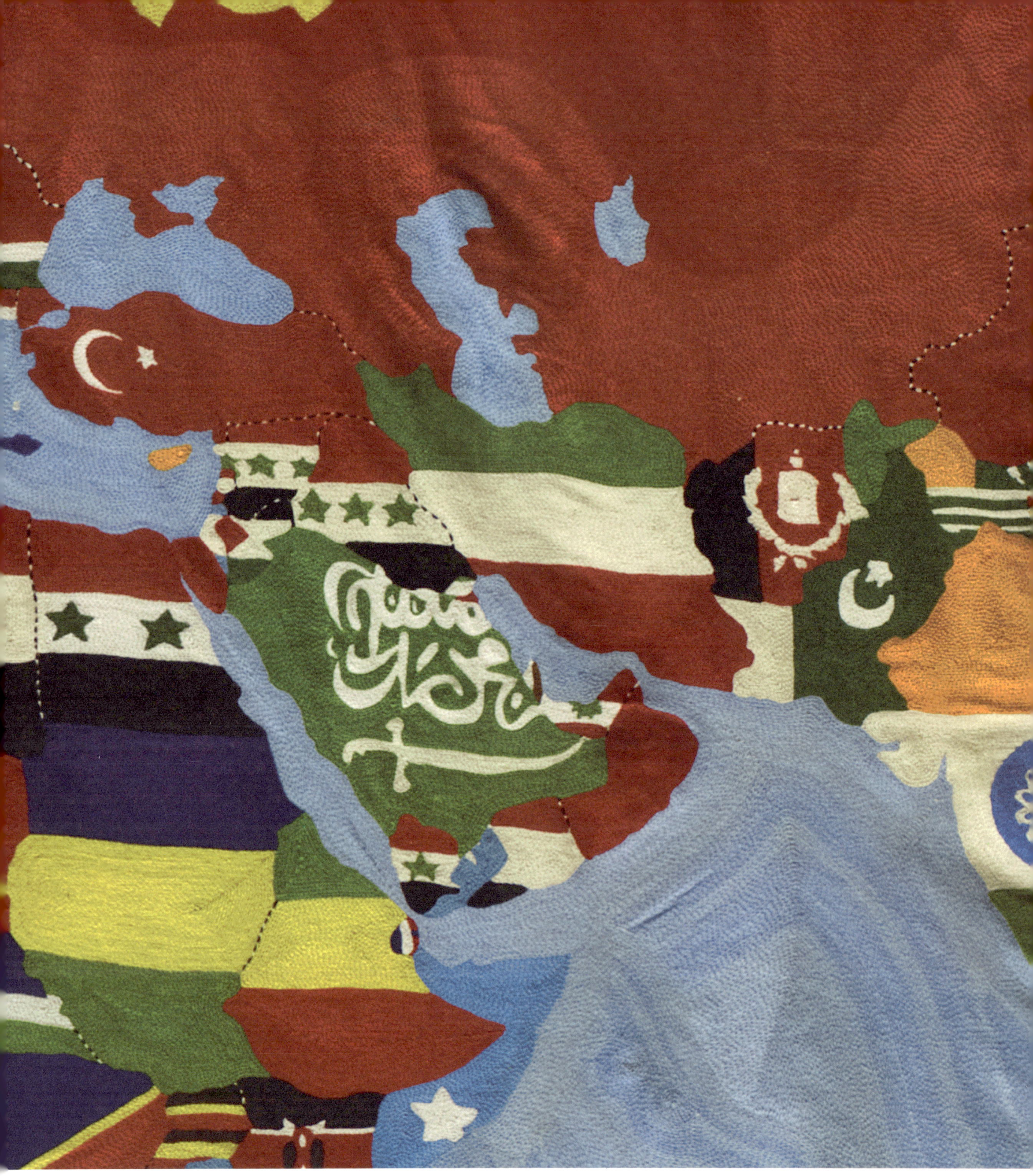

Mappa (Map), 1971–72 (detail)

alighiero

boetti

-

game

plan

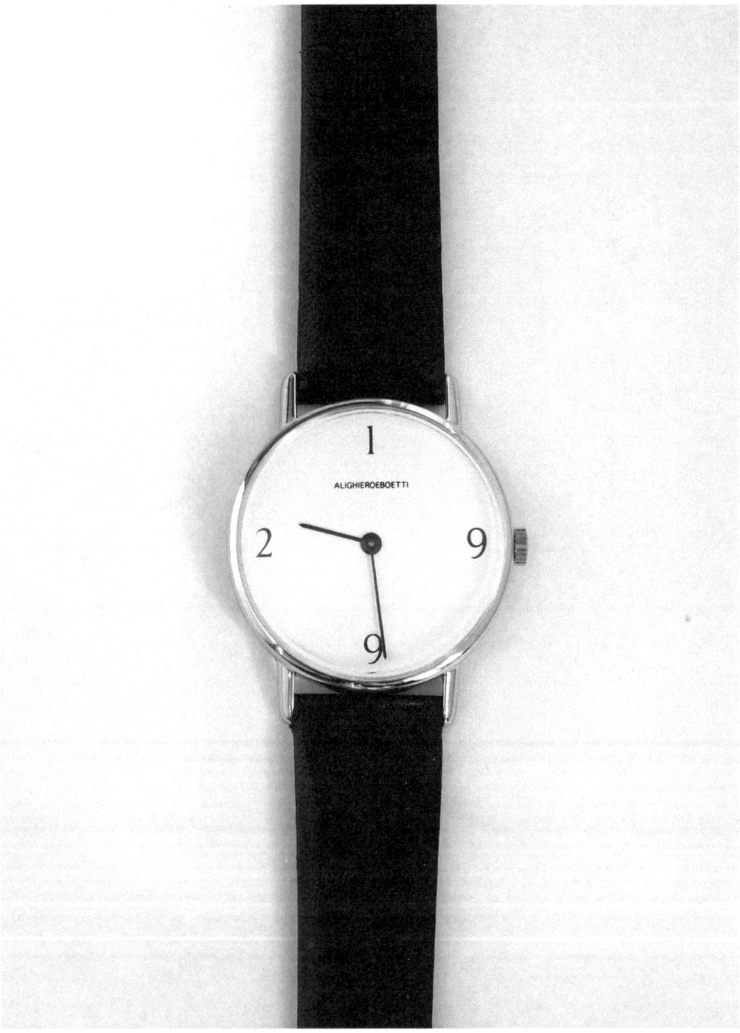

Orologi annuali (Annual Watches), 1977–94 (detail)

alighiero boetti – game plan

Edited by
Lynne Cooke
Mark Godfrey
Christian Rattemeyer

With texts by
Lynne Cooke
Claire Gilman
Mark Godfrey
Christian Rattemeyer
Jason E. Smith

and an interview by
Bruno Corà

Tate Publishing

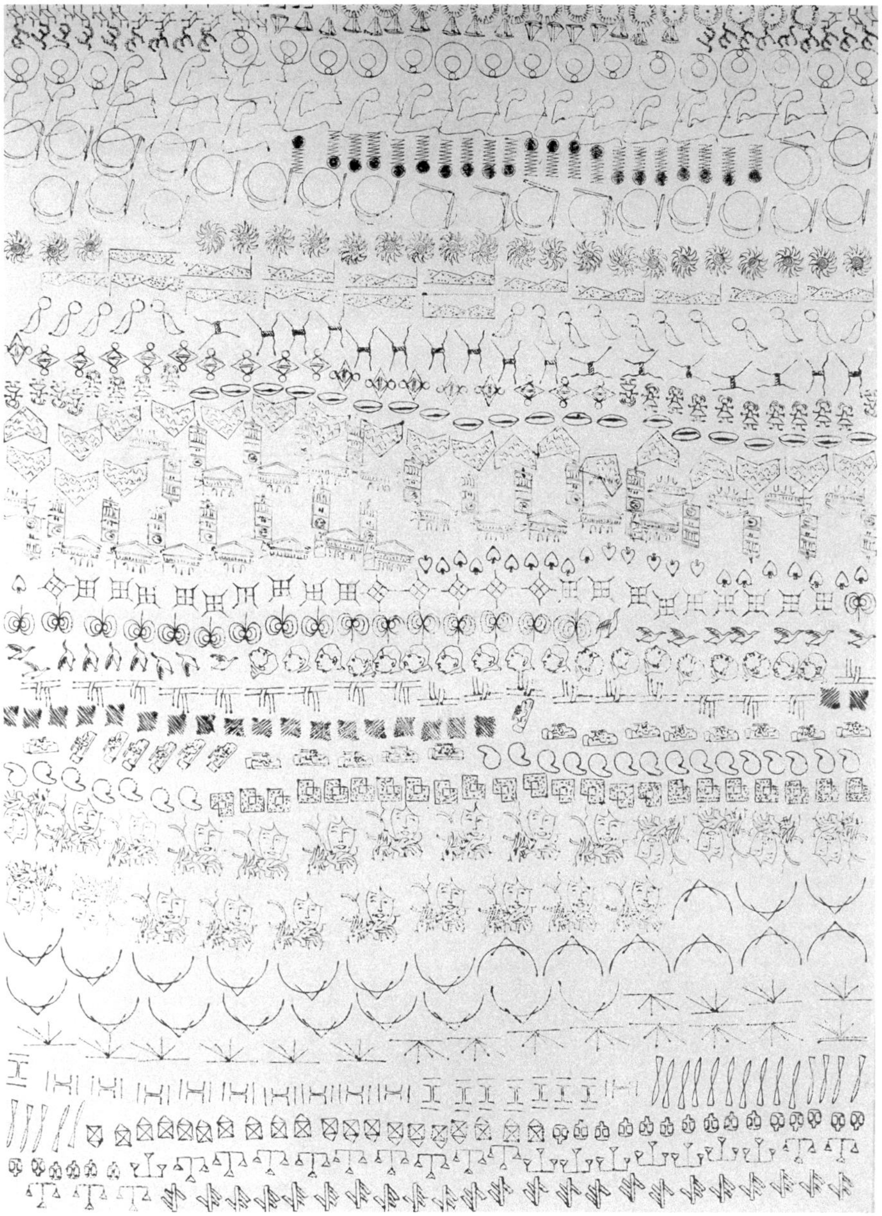

Gli anni della mia vita (The Years of My Life), 1976

Introduction

The burden of orthodoxies, categorizations and generations fixed in time and sanctioned by art criticism and institutional discourse during the 20th century calls upon a renewed approach to art history. This approach demands a profound reappraisal of artists who, one way or another, both consciously and spontaneously, defy typecasting or labeling. Alighiero Boetti emerges from the retrospective exhibition *Game Plan* as an artist occupying a central place in art history, paradoxically on account of his *eccentricity*—in its purest etymological sense, meaning a lack of (or a distance from) the center—but also, because of the multiplicity of starting points and voices from which he draws diverse itineraries, diverse worlds.
Boetti was born in wartime Turin, a city that was subsequently reclaimed as the model for the industrial development of the entire country. The disquiet following the mild storm of '68 in Italy—the *anni di piombo* (years of lead)—marked the new Italy as a country living in the fallout from the economic boom of the previous decade: it is a era marked by the disintegration of the only openly combative left-wing party in postwar Western Europe, by a form of terrorism of murky connections with power, and by the triumph of TV consumption as a laboratory for the political future of a whole country and as a substitute of the Italian collective projects, for which the ephemeral and belated *Autumn of '69* seems to represent little more than a melodramatic end of the party. The "anthroplogical mutation" that the Italian writer, poet and film director Pier Paolo Pasolini spoke of—that consumerism rather than an ancient notion of citizenship and compromise gave the new Italian his reason for being—is at the core of many of the decisions that Boetti took from the 1970s onwards.
So after "attitudes became form" and promptly froze in the transformation, Boetti was able to survive the subsequent collapse that duly followed *Arte Povera* attaining the height of its creativity and popularity: in other words, the demise of the strategy of construction of a group mathematically designed by Germano Celant. Boetti's position regarding artistic creation distanced him from any form of authorial self-absorption. Instead, he sought obsessively to create diverse forms of collaborative activity, through which he contested age-old notions of authorship, right at the time when contemporary thinkers Roland Barthes, Michel Foucault, Jacques Derrida and others were in the process of killing off the author. The way Boetti made this progressive disappearance of the creator-as-demiurge his own, provides the key to much of his work: from his collaboration with artisan embroiderers in Afghanistan, to his postal works that require the presence of an "other"—someone who participates after the time lapse between the delivery and the reception. These works escape the control of the artist in much the same way that the Persian and Afghan rugs only become complete and attain their proper status when their knots are tightened by the daily tramplings of an unknown person.

It is not by accident that Boetti finds in Afghanistan the most efficient way to neutralize the spectre of authorship. Within the domain of the Islamic art and architecture of Central Asia, the dissolution of authorship and collective work are undisputed facts of a centuries-old tradition. It is significant, that in this part of the world, Boetti felt more attraction for this possibility of creative cooperation than in searching for the historical roots of non-representative art, and that he should see in this distant environment, above all, a world of profoundly communicative symbols, whose message is only made complete in the act of their being read. This was a gesture very much in tune with the paradigmatic shift that, since the 1960s, sent into crisis the individualistic vision of the world that had been sustained by a lack of formal conventions, and in its place put in play different modes of participation and action with—and within—diverse environments. In this sense, this book analyzes Boetti's work as connected to relational aesthetics, the theory according to which it is not the image that has the job of representing or reconstructing, but the actual relationship between us all. It is inevitable that we insist on the nascence of Boetti's sense of association as rooted in the above-mentioned disappearance of the Italian collective movement (a process that preceded the emergence of different types of conservatism in the 1980s). A disappearance which takes place not just in the political arena, but also and especially, in the sphere of the everyday. To return again to Pasolini: "I wander [...] searching for brothers that are no longer there."

Immersed in this constant examination of reality that an artist is obliged to undertake, and having exhausted all possible attempts to eliminate singularity, he decides to split himself into Alighiero e Boetti (Alighiero *and* Boetti), thereby rejecting the distinction between the intimate (the given name) and the social (the surname). We are reminded here of how in Italian a name is accompanied by a "co-name" (*cognome*: surname), that is to say, that the author is indissolubly bound together with a co-author. There are echoes to be heard in this reflection, coming from both Rimbaud's "Je est un autre" [I is another] and from the *Gestalt* system of thought, according to which a number of different voices combine to form one's character.

This searching for doubles, for team-mates and collaborators, allowed Boetti to draw up his own map of the world—the real world of his own ambulatory wanderings and peripatetic journeys to distant lands, and the constructed world—which, from one of his earliest works, *Rotolo di cartone ondulato*, to his various "mappe," does not attempt to portray a reassuring compression of the world into one single image, but rather depicts, respectively, a tower of Babel and representations of the planet composed with the means of its identity signs (its national flags). By playing with the proliferation of languages and symbols, the things that create national identity, he embarks on a game whose rules are never completely revealed. He also returns to this game playing in his well-known work using a grid to deconstruct words and then splitting (or linking back together) their constituent letters to give them, paradoxically, greater order and less meaning. His intentions are only slightly revealed in some of the works' titles, associated at times with the passing of time (or the lapse of time between two parts of the process), the imagined date of death, etcetera. Are they not perhaps ways of mocking—or possibly respecting—the inevitability of a real death, therefore different from Barthes's "death of the author"? Alternatively, do they not perhaps constitute an ironic vision of the disappearance of the I, the transcendence of which is one of the demands of Sufi poetry, one of the fundamental and least studied keys to understanding Boetti?

For *Game Plan*, the retrospective and transnational project of Alighiero Boetti, we have decided to unite the forces of three institutions that are dedicated to modern and contemporary art and that originate from different places and contexts, with trajectories, histories and proposals that, in their convergences and divergences, trace interwoven lines that, like the threads of Boetti's rugs, remain permanently connected even if they are out of reach, and can only be fully realised with the participation of the viewing public.

We are extremely grateful to the curators at our respective institutions, Lynne Cooke, Mark Godfrey, and Christian Rattemeyer. They have brought their individual perspectives to their conversation: Lynne worked with Boetti in the last year of his life, creating a beautiful exhibition in dialogue with Frédéric Bruly Bouabré, his last important collaborator, at the Dia Center for the Arts in New York; Mark has recently completed a monograph on the artist; and prior to the exhibition, Christian finished a book which looked in part at Boetti's role in *When Attitudes Become Form*. Lynne, Mark, and Christian have also edited this catalogue, to which each has contributed a significant essay. Their dialogue has been exemplary and they have been ably supported by Soledad Liaño, Kasia Redzisz, and Maura Lynch.

We would like to extend our deepest gratitude to the Boetti family for their assistance during the research and organization of this exhibition. At the Fondazione Alighiero e Boetti, Caterina Boetti has been extraordinarily generous with her time, discussing Boetti's work with the curators and assisting with several loans. At the Archivio Alighiero Boetti, Annemarie Sauzeau Boetti has been instrumental to the success of the project in many ways, providing detailed information about, and images of, the work; and also discussing the significance of various pieces. These two organizations provide essential assistance to scholarship on Boetti's complex practice: we are grateful to the staff of both the Fondazione and Archivio, in particular Elena Salza, Ilaria Giaccone, Simone Cresci and Arianna Mercanti. The curators are also indebted to Boetti's three children, Matteo, Agata, and Giordano, who have helped them think about Boetti's work in new and fruitful ways.

Manuel J. Borja-Villel, Director, Museo Nacional Centro de Arte Reina Sofía, Madrid
Chris Dercon, Director, Tate Modern, London
Glenn D. Lowry, Director, The Museum of Modern Art, New York

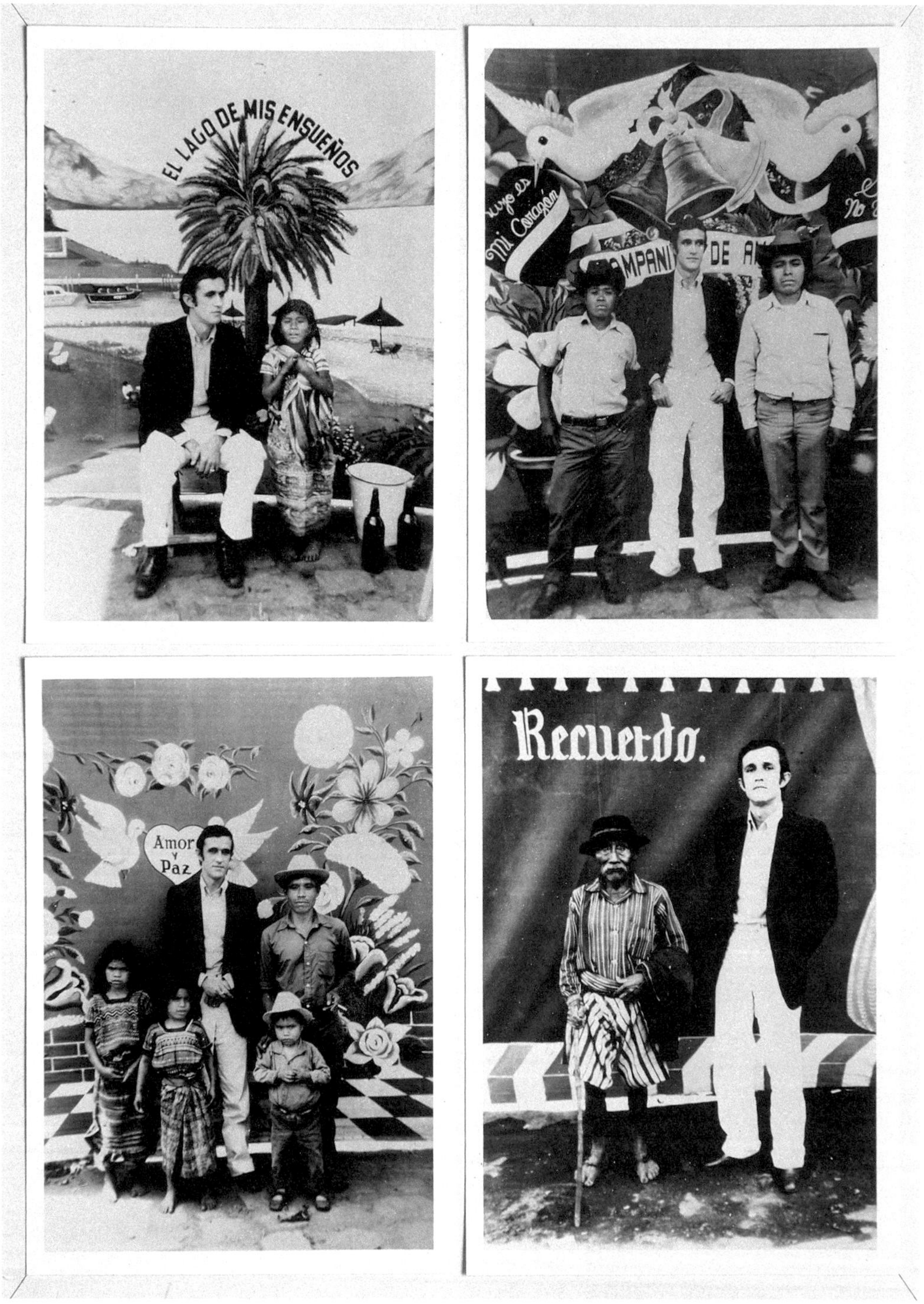

Guatemala, 1974

CONTENTS

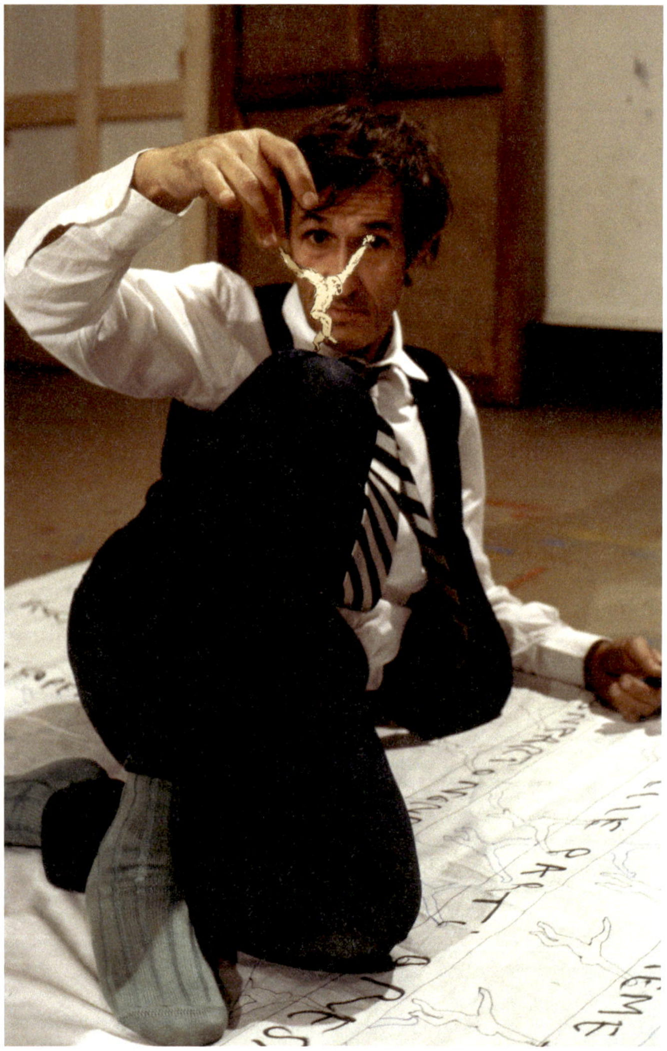

Alighiero Boetti in his studio, 1989

Boetti's Game Plan

Lynne Cooke

the sixth sense

> "In effect, there are five senses, and thought is the sixth. That is the most important thing that humankind possesses."

By early 1969 Alighiero Boetti had roundly condemned what he considered the excesses of Arte Povera and repudiated object making.[1] This emphatic rejection followed three years of frenetic art-making during which the critic Germano Celant had embraced him as a defining member of the new Italian movement. For Boetti, distancing himself from the work that had established his reputation did not mean a withdrawal from future Arte Povera shows in Italy and abroad. Rather, it meant that he would assume a radically different public stance as he realigned his practice in accordance with his shifting aesthetic.[2]

For his debut show at Christian Stein Gallery in Turin in early 1967, Boetti had grouped a number of objects theatrically, juxtaposing them so closely that the room took on the appearance of a hardware-store display.[3] Almost all the heterodox materials used in these works could have been sourced from a building supplier's storage: plastic piping, concrete, corrugated cardboard, cork, timber, sheet metal, printed cloth, lighting fixtures, and mirrors, among others. Several pieces were made by stacking, rolling or propping modular units: *Catasta* (1967), *Rotolo di cartone ondulato* (1966), and *ill. pp. 42/43,149* *Mazzo di tubi* (1966). *ill. p. 45* Others required basic joinery at the level that a handyman might provide: *Lampada annuale* *ill. p. 31* (1966), *Ping Pong* (1966), *Mancorrrente a squadra* *ill. pp. 49, 50/137* (1966).[4] As visitors negotiated the narrow aisles separating one object from another, they were offered resting points in the guise of sculptures that doubled as handrails, from which they could view favored pieces. For his solo show in April 1968 at Franco Toselli's De Nieubourg Gallery in Milan, Boetti created an even more dramatic context. In an environment resembling a dry stream bed, a field of rounded stones gathered from the river Po, he installed various works made that year including *Cubo*, *Colonne*, *Legnetti colorati*, and the *ill. pp. 54/134/55* now lost stone self-portrait *Autoritratto negativo*.

1 "With *Shaman/Showman*," Boetti told an interviewer, referring to his contribution to the exhibition/performance project in Amalfi in October 1968, "I quit. The Amalfi exhibition was really the nausea of the end of it all." Mirella Bandini, "Interview with Alighiero e Boetti," 1972, reprinted in Achille Bonito Oliva (ed.), *Alighiero & Boetti: Bringing the World into Art*, 1993-1962, (Naples: MADRE and Milan: Electa, 2009), p. 168.

2 Except for Emilio Prini, Boetti was the only artist to participate in all the Arte Povera shows, from the first, which took place in September 1967, to the last in Munich, 1971.

3 When conceiving an earlier body of work, a series of drawings of cameras, a desk lamp, and a microphone, Boetti had been keen to create what he deemed a theatrical presentation that would involve the spectator. See Annemarie Sauzeau, *Alighiero e Boetti: Shaman/Showman* (Cologne, Walther König, 2003), p. 37.

4 The invitation card for the show, *Untitled* (1966–67), resembled a sampler on which the various materials were laid out in a grid. When the works appeared in a subsequent catalogue, they were represented by drawings conceived in the diagrammatic technical style employed by an industrial draftsman—that is, in profile and section. It is worth noting that in 1964, Duchamp signed technical drawings for the remade readymades produced by Arturo Schwarz in Milan.

By early 1969 Boetti had manifested his disdain for the material excesses of his past practice by adopting the most basic of art materials—graphite and paper—and deploying them in rudimentary fashion. Painstakingly, he retraced the gridded lines on a sheet of ordinary notepaper, creating new squares and shapes little by little until he had covered the whole surface. Differences between sheets result from the alternate courses he followed as he constructed and divided rectangles in myriad ingenious ways; so inventive were these meticulous systems that there is remarkably little uniformity among the pages. Boetti gave the title
ill. pp. 80, 81 *Cimento dell'armonia e dell'invenzione* (Contest of Harmony and Invention) to this studied exercise because, he declared:

> You have to set yourself a rule, decide whether you want to cover the whole surface or just half. This is where the "test" comes in: because even if the space is small, the possibilities are vast. You could do it a hundred thousand different ways . . . it reveals how you felt and your state of mind while working [so it] is also a test of attitude.[5]

An alternative title for the first among this group of related works—*42 ore* (42 Hours)—refers to the surprisingly long period of time that he dedicated to its creation.[6]

"Attitude" was critical in this droll exercise, which might be likened to an elaborate form of doodling. When absorbed in his solitary game, Boetti found that "everything conceivable . . . happened": "I've inscribed both terrible and marvelous things into them," he confessed.[7] Attitude was also very much in evidence in his radically ascetic presentation at Sperone Gallery in Turin that spring. Three recent works were on show: a small
ill. p. 67 portrait of Walter de Maria (since destroyed); *Io che prendo il sole a Torino il 19 gennaio 1969*, comprised of balls of concrete fashioned by hand and set out in the form of a human figure (near whose breast/lapel a yellow butterfly was attached); and *Una vetrata*, a large gridded panel of glass that rested against two walls of the room [fig. 1].[8] In its self-reflexivity *Una vetrata* recalls

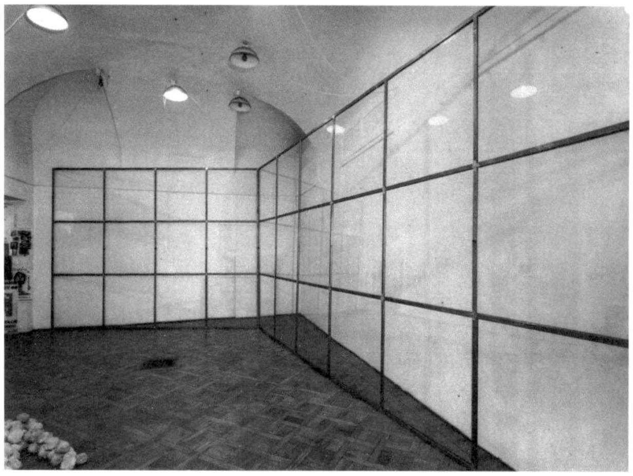

[fig. 1] Una vetrata (A Window), 1969 at Sperone Gallery, Turin, 1969

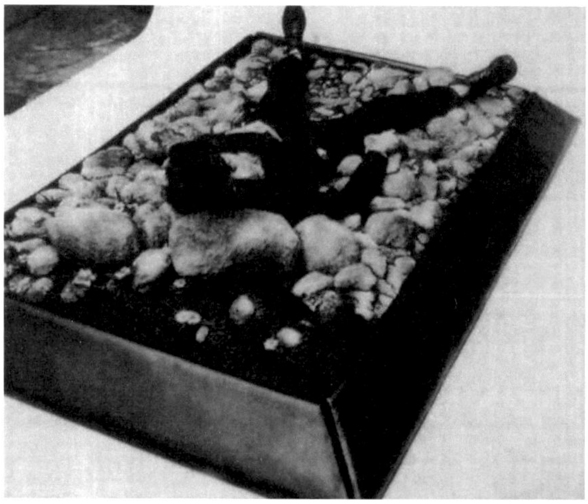

[fig. 2] Gilberto Zorio lying on Stones-bed, in Piero Gilardi's Turin studio, 1967

5 "Alighiero Boetti interviewed by Mirella Bandini in 1972," in *Che Fare? Arte Povera—The Historic Years* (Heidelberg: Kehrer and Liechtenstein Kunstmuseum, 2010), p. 89.

6 Its title was taken from the subtitle to Vivaldi's "Four Seasons." When shown in "Prospect 69" it was supplemented by a recording of silence mixed with quiet sounds conjuring the ambience in which it was produced.

7 *Che Fare?*, p. 89.

8 *Io che prendo*... underwent several modifications in its title, including a change of date: it was first dated "24-2-1969."

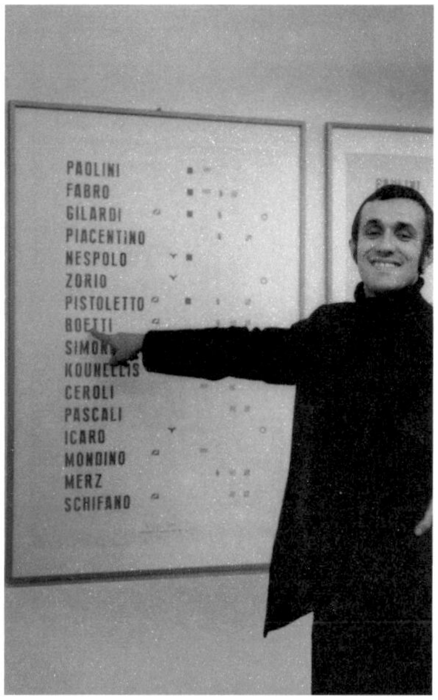

[fig. 3] A Performance by Alighiero Boetti in 1970 in front of *Manifesto*, 1967

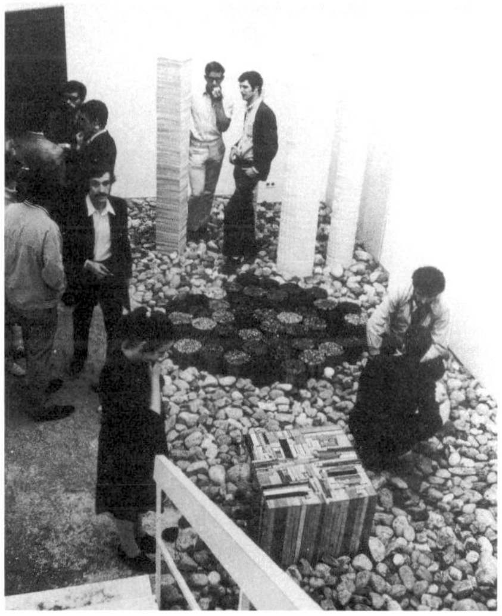

[fig. 4] The opening of "Shaman/Showman" at De Nieubourg Gallery, Milan, April 23, 1968

works by Boetti's close friend and fellow Arte Povera affiliate Giulio Paolini, though its deeper roots lie in the art and aesthetic of Marcel Duchamp. In Boetti's own oeuvre it was prefigured by a now lost piece, a sheet of smoke-colored Plexiglas that he had suspended from the ceiling in that first show at Christian Stein. There, it served as a device to frame whatever could be glimpsed through its cloudy surface. *Una vetrata* similarly provokes questions of representation, contesting the traditional model of painting as a window onto the world. Yet, unlike its translucent predecessor, *Una vetrata* did not merely frame whatever was beyond—nothing but the wall, in this case—it also acted as a screen: its internal grid recalling the device that painters traditionally use for squaring up and transferring onto the picture surface their subject of study. Here however, as the work's later title—*Niente da vedere niente da nascondere* (Nothing to *ill. p. 69* See, Nothing to Hide)—makes evident, there was no subject. Coupling the self-evidently clear (its material structure) with the tautologically elusive (the word-play in the title), Boetti introduced the first of several mind-teasing formulations through which he would articulate the principal thematics governing his oeuvre. Some years later, he elucidated the thinking underlining this and many subsequent works when he stated:

> Decisive . . . is the fact that structures (systems) have replaced pictures and that pictures obtain their meaning from structures (systems). The goal is to convey structures (systems) by constantly rediscovering them and to create pictures in such a way as to forget the structures within them.[9]

With the exception of *Lampada annuale*, Boetti's Arte Povera works elicited an active visceral engagement by foregrounding the act of physically confronting the object.

The three works in the spare show at Sperone, by contrast, inhabited a more cerebral register. The mise-en-scene of the exhibition at Toselli's Milan gallery, held during October of the following year, was again restrained. Hung in a tight line around the gallery's walls were some fifty of the 800 posters titled *Manifesto* that *ill. p. 63*

[9] Quoted in Jean-Christophe Ammann, "Anmerkungen zu einem Werk, das schwer in den Griff zu bekommen ist", in *Alighiero Boetti* (Basel: Kunsthalle Basel, 1978), n.p.

Boetti had printed in four different colors in 1967 then mailed to friends and colleagues. An offset print, *Manifesto* is comprised of a list of some sixteen artists broadly connected with Arte Povera: beside each name are several of the eight symbols that appear to encode relations among the group's members. No key was appended to decipher the cryptic chart. Notice was given, however, that its code was contained in an envelope that could be purchased from a local lawyer's office, where it had been deposited for safekeeping. In its original design, the poster manifestly failed to fulfil its self-proclaimed function: it neither declared the objectives of its adherents nor revealed the relations among them. The initial mailing largely passed unnoticed. Reconfigured three years later, the work took on a markedly different character. In the wake of Boetti's public distancing of himself from the manner of working defined by Celant as proper to Arte Povera—materially experimental, process-oriented, and physically immanent—the project could be read as a thinly veiled lampoon. Slyly mocking the idea that a coherent and intelligible collectivity bound the artists together, it suggested that whatever secret set of relations purportedly unified the group could now be made public, albeit for a price.[10] Once money, rather than any purported theoretical framework, became the vehicle that could unlock the hermetic cabal, then the way would be open for the market to play a central role in determining future relations among the disparate coterie. In pillorying the obscure, not to say obfuscating, terms in which the notion of Arte Povera had been constructed and disseminated, Boetti did not spare himself. His complicity in Celant's strategic fabrication of a movement from what was closer to a confederation of mutually supportive artists is revealed in a short performance that he made in 1970. Standing in front of *Manifesto*, he hams for the camera, pointing out with inflated pride the inclusion of his name among its list of artists [fig. 3]. This insouciant repurposing of the posters, now signed, numbered and framed, also served more constructive ends. It points to a revision of traditional hierarchies among art forms and genres to which Boetti would hold throughout his career. It also underlines the fact that, for him, the uniqueness of the artwork was never of primary importance—most of his works exist in series or as multiples, editions, and replicas.[11] Similarly, he did not regard the authorial hand as in itself a valued signifier. Increasingly, he would employ others to execute his artworks, privileging the thought process over the act of making.[12]

The spirit of playful subversion that informed his handling of *Manifesto* in 1970 was presaged in *Io che prendo il sole a Torino il 19 gennaio 1969*, which must have seemed an anomaly when it first debuted at Sperone the previous year. Taking an autobiographical turn, it explored the possibility of self-fashioning in ways that were soon to become of primary concern. Given the chilly, inclement weather in Turin in mid-winter, sunbathing is bound to be a futile activity. The attempt, in effect, is tantamount to a declaration that the artist is an idle layabout. Key to establishing the ludic tone in which Boetti here sports with his audience is the yellow butterfly. Its presence conjures a fin-de-siècle milieu, more specifically, the arch aestheticism that permeated the London art world inhabited by Oscar Wilde, Aubrey Beardsley, and James Abbot McNeill Whistler in the 1890s. Whistler, whose moniker was a butterfly, had become notorious for making art by what, Wilde charged, was nothing more than "flinging a pot of paint in the face of the British public." While admitting that his

10 Boetti's own relation to the market could be described as ambivalent, not to say conflicted. The works he showed in a jumbled ensemble in the four-day exhibition/performance jamboree "Arte Povera + Azioni Povera" at the Arsenale in Amalfi in October 1969 all bore price tags and the name of his gallery.

11 Within a year of his first solo show, Boetti had become a "hot property"; his response was to make small-scale versions of his three-dimensional works in an edition of ten. He also began the practice that he continued thereafter of making multiple variants of almost all his key works, whether the sprayed monochrome panels with text that he worked on between 1966 and 1972, the dozen or so checkerboards known as "dama," or the sticker pieces that began modestly with small pieces of paper in 1968 and culminated in the vast 20-metre piece *Estate '70*.

12 Note the trajectory in the monochrome spray paintings from cryptic idiomatic phrases ("frou-frou") to a playful self-reflexivity as the colors tautologically and indexically refer to the names of the titles which were spray-painted onto the metal surfaces as in a carbody shop: *beige sabbia fiat 583* (Beige Sahara Fiat 583) or *Rosso Palermo 511 52 27*. See Briony Fer, "Color Manual," in *Color Chart: Reinventing Color, 1959 to Today* (New York: The Museum of

working methods did not reveal evidence of technical virtuosity, the painter countered that his practice was nonetheless predicated on years of experience. The fractious critical debate centered not only on the relation between conception and resolution, but on the role of craft, skill, and by extension, deskilling. Its echoes haunt Boetti's laconic self portrait; they also resonate with the concurrent series of works, *Cimento dell'armonia*... As a studied nonchalance became the public face of Boetti's practice, the question of work—or its converse, idling—came increasingly to the fore.

Duchamp, the forefather of Conceptual art, presented himself as the quintessential dandy. In 1967 Boetti had paid fealty to the French master in a work that had something of the status of a manifesto in the form of an *ill. p. 60* equation: "AB:AW=MD:L" (Alighiero Boetti: Andy Warhol=Marcel Duchamp: Leonardo). Emulating his mentor's notorious gesture, the young Italian drew a goatee and moustache on a revered icon—this time the target was not the *Mona Lisa*, but a serigraphic reproduction of a Warhol silkscreen painting of Jackie Kennedy. Although prompted in part by a sense of rivalry with the Pop art imported from the United States that was then flooding the vanguard gallery scene in Northern Italy, Boetti's defacing of the Warhol was ultimately less a competitive gesture than a signal of where his allegiances really lay: a deepening engagement with Duchamp was to reshape the character and course of his career.[13] Formally, *AB:AW=MD:L* spoke to his privileging of print media, editions, performance, and other modes that inverted conventional hierarchies and valuations. Conceptually, it signalled his growing understanding of the role that self-fashioning might play in guiding the reception of his work: for, as Duchamp's example attested, the crafting of a public persona could prove critical to the governing and framing of an artist's oeuvre, and to the priority given to conceptual modes in conceiving and generating art works. With the nom de plume of Rrose Sélavy, Duchamp had adopted a cross-dressing alter ego, one of many aliases within his oeuvre that explored the means by which the self, like language, was both constructed and shared. Devoting himself to chess, for which he developed an almost consuming passion, he ostensibly gave up art. By stopping working, he staged a withdrawal that was not a withdrawal. Boetti, in turn, adopted a mode of self-fashioning based on twinning or duplication, which he formalized in the early 1970s by changing his name to Alighiero *e* Boetti (Alighiero *and* Boetti). Doubling himself, he created an identity grounded in dualistic relations whereby two sides of the self could be brought into relation as complementary principles rather than as opposites to be subsumed into each other: "It would be nice if there were two worlds, one completely conscious, the other unconscious, that could hold hands without getting confused, instead of having them both crammed together with no boundaries in the oppressive container of the subject," he declared.[14] Just as fundamental to his evolving aesthetic as this dual identity and his privileging of thinking over working manually, was his new-found focus on being idle. Though Boetti shared Duchamp's intense devotion to play as a means to while away time, and to games as vehicles for exploring metaphysical questions, his taste was more eclectic, running the gamut from the infantile to the sophisticated. And while he proclaimed that he too was inherently lazy, echoing the Frenchman's stated preference for "living [and] breathing, better than working," Boetti never overtly renounced the making of objects.[15] His strategy was to hire others as needed—professionals of various kinds, as well as craftspeople and the untrained—to carry out the manual and technical labor required to produce the artefacts that embodied his thinking.

Boetti first limned his burgeoning identity in 1968, in the lost self-portrait (*Autoritratto in negativo*): a photograph that he commissioned of himself lying beside the sculpture of his head in negative was reproduced in the catalogue to "When Attitudes Become Form: Live in

Modern Art, 2008), pp. 28–38.

13 Following Duchamp's lead with his *Boîte-en-valise* (1935–41), Boetti began compiling *Insicuro noncurante* in 1966. This portfolio, completed in 1975, is a compendium of his more significant previous projects from 1965 onwards, produced with the assistance of printmaker Rinaldo Rossi.

14 1968, Quoted in *Che Fare?*, p. 86.

15 Quoted in Helen Molesworth, "Work Avoidance: The Everyday Life of Marcel Duchamp's Readymades," *Art Journal*, Winter 1998, p. 51.

your Head," a landmark group show curated by Harald Szeemann and held in March 1969 in Bern. Then followed by a poster in which he assumed the guise of a tarot-card image in order to play the dual roles of Shaman and Showman, which was fly-posted in the streets of Milan in 1968 at the time of his show at the De Nieubourg Gallery.[16] Most memorably, his self-construction took the form of a postcard titled *Gemelli* (1968), in which he is photographed holding hands with his second self. The artist mailed the cards, printed in an edition of fifty, to friends, inscribing them with terse messages such as the warning "Nonmarsalarti"—don't become too sweet.[17] In 1969, the invitation card for his solo show at Sperone Gallery was an image shot two years earlier in which he is seen with his arms outstretched, the right hand open, the left closed into a fist, a photograph that became the basis for yet another poster work in 1978, *San Bernardino*. Over and over again, Boetti deployed these carefully crafted images in exhibitions, catalogues, and publications to reinforce and cement certain tenets of his identity, and thereby establish the terms in which his art would be received.[18] As a group, they complement the more sculptural *Ghise (ABoetti)* (1968), which is similarly involved with establishing identity. Comprised of two large metal plates that lean against the wall, *Ghise* features the artist's name, written into a sheet of corrugated cardboard then cast so that in one iron surface the signature reads positively and in the other it appears as mirrored writing. *Ghise* was first shown with *Io che prendo…* in "When Attitudes Become Form: Live in Your Head." It marked the first significant occasion on which Boetti's work was seen in a broad international context of like-minded artists who, as the cover to the show's catalogue indicated, were engaged with "concepts, processes, situations, [and] information."

ill. pp. 65/66
ill. p. 77
ill. p. 71

Issues of verification and hence of authenticity are crucial to the acts of self-presentation in all these works. Whether photograph, signature, negative mold (a kind of death-mask), or fingerprints (in the concrete balls in *Io che prendo…*) each bears an indexical relation to its maker. Turning to the relation between self-fashioning and self-positioning in 1974 while travelling in Central

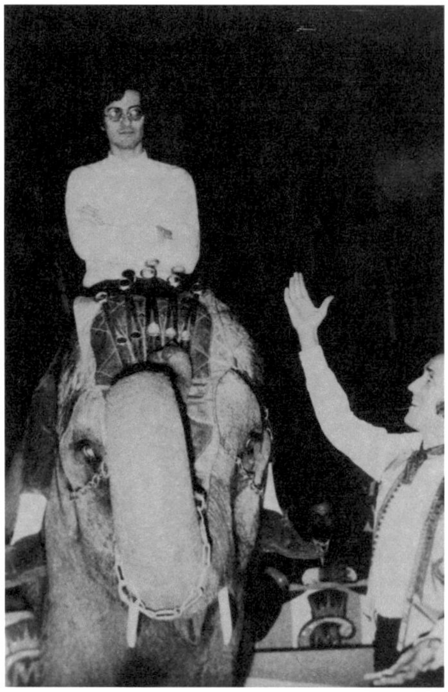

[fig. 5] Giulio Paolini and Alighiero Boetti, Turin, 1968

16 *Shaman / Showman* could be deemed another manifesto-like work, in the sense that in Italian *manifesto* can mean poster or billboard as well as a public statement.

17 Related works include *Strumento musicale* (1970), a photograph in which he holds a double-ended banjo, and the performance for Gerry Schum's Video Television Program, in which he wrote double-handed, in a remarkable feat of coordination, "Today is Thursday September 24, 1970."

18 The untitled artwork-cum-catalogue for his second show, at La Bertesca Gallery, Genoa, in 1967, reproduces the first images of the artist. Devoid of any commentary, the photographs show Boetti being shaved in a barber's shop, a series of images that may be linked, obliquely, to the famous image made by Man Ray of Duchamp as a satyr, his face and head covered in shaving cream, for *Obligation Pour la Roulette de Monte Carlo* (Monte Carlo Bond, 1924). Among the last direct references that Boetti made to Duchamp, who had recently died, was his citing as one of the participants—friends and colleagues in large part—whom Boetti sent on imaginary journeys in *Viaggi postali* (1969-70).

America, Boetti produced *Guatemala*. For this work, he hired a professional photographer to record him posing with children and local residents in four different "sites"—exotic scenarios depicted on painted backcloths. These studio props complicate the question of who might be native to the place and who the temporary visitor, since the photographs could have been taken anywhere. *Guatemala* postulates identity in terms of agency: either it is a construction or a form of alterity (the consequence of an act of conscription and objectification). Whichever, subject formation, as *Guatemala* demonstrates, is necessarily a function of collective identification.

The self-imposed task of shaping a public persona preoccupied Boetti alone among his peers in the late 1960s and early 1970s. Although it set him apart from even his close friend Paolini, it did not undermine the relationship they had forged during their formative years in Turin, in fact, Paolini's precocious Conceptualism, which had long distinguished him from other Arte Povera artists, finds its closest echoes in Boetti's works from the later 1960s. While the sense of dandyish wit that began to permeate Boetti's art has no direct counterpart in Paolini's cool practice, this did not prevent them from conspiring to create a fictional artist whose practice would consist in making toys. Pranks were clearly part of the texture of their friendship, as is evident in a memorable photograph that Boetti staged in 1968, which shows "the Master" Paolini astride an elephant and his companion in the role of impresario or "devout patron."[19] Boetti's delight in inspired intellection, strategic ploys, elaborate and complex structural systems, wordplay, and a studied lightness of touch would over time distance him from Paolini's orbit while reinforcing his affinities with Duchamp [fig. 5].

Alongside *Io che prendo*... and *Ghise*, Boetti had exhibited a third work in "When Attitudes become Form," *La Luna* (1968), later destroyed. Essentially a blackboard, its slate surface was covered with short vertical lines, as if the artist were a delinquent student whose punishment involved spending time in rote mark-making. Such repetitive gestures soon formed the basis of his series of Biro works. When accompanied by letters arranged along the upper edge of the paper, as seen, for example, in *AELLEIGACCAEIEERREOBIOTITII* (1973), these works *ill. p. 101* bring to mind the kind of blackboard, headed by an alphabet, once ubiquitous in primary schools. Another source for the Biro works lies in those studies in which the artist explored ways of reformulating his name; for example, by grouping its letters together in alphabetical order as in *ABEEGHIIILOORTT* (1971), or by employing *ill. p. 102* commas to tick off each letter in a phrase, such as *Mettere* *ill. p. 105* *al mondo il mondo* (1971), so that the viewer must parse them one by one like a child trying to decipher an unfamiliar word by spelling it out letter by letter. From these exploratory studies, Boetti devised ever more expansive versions, which he farmed out to others—a male and a female draftsperson in each instance—to realize. As the Biro works grew larger, they took on a gorgeous chromatic sensuality: "Beauty is an expression of thought," he contended, "and of the urge to express it."[20] In these monumental monochrome drawings he gives linguistic form to ideas that would henceforth shape his larger purpose, above all, *Mettere al mondo il mondo* (Putting the world in the world). Equally fundamental to his maturing aesthetic is a phrase that appears in several of the most ambitious (and hence the most time-consuming to make) of the Biro pieces: *I sei sensi* *ill. pp. 106–107* (The Six Senses).

For Boetti, thought—which he called the sixth sense—was pre-eminent among the senses: "the most important thing that humankind possesses," he declared. It had, moreover, "nothing to do with Nature."

[19] Placing this photograph among "the very first 'artistic experiments' of Alighiero," Annemarie Sauzeau Boetti quoted an interpretation offered by the critic Giovan Battista Salerno, Boetti's close friend, of this image, which she called an "authentic metaphorical situation": "It's beautiful to see the subtle intellect, sharp and enigmatic, in the person of Paolini hoisted up like an obelisk on the back of an enormous beast like the elephant, symbol *par excellence* of fortitude: together they can achieve great things. The one completes the other, they are invincible. Boetti stands a bit apart but grins, because it was he who invented this composite being, made up of brute strength and fine intelligence." Sauzeau, *Alighiero e Boetti*, p. 48. Paolini was the first of the twenty-five participants to be sent on an imaginary journey in *Viaggi postali* (1969–70).

[20] In *Alighiero e Boetti, Bringing the World into the World*, p. 215.

"That is why," he argued:

> if I were to tell you the great emotions and feelings of my life, I'd have to confess that none of them have been stirred by Nature. A petal, a butterfly, a sunset—these can all be beautiful. However, in my opinion, the great emotions come from listening to a work by Mozart, from reading a poem. Because in those there is thought made up of thousands of coincidences, synchronicities . . . [and] memories.[21]

In Italian, as in English, the term *il sesto senso* implies a keenly intuitive, as opposed to analytic, mode of thought: a poetic as opposed to a deductive analytical or scientific approach. These qualities would become the hallmark of much of Boetti's work. The last of his embroidered word squares (and the sole example in German), involved a phrase that, translated into English, reads, "Synchronicity, an acausal connecting principle," borrowed from the title of an essay by Carl Jung.[22] The happy coincidences that synchronicity implies are based in psychic rather than material events (the field proper to causality); they involve perceiving as meaningful what might otherwise be read as mere coincidence. Such happy accidents depend on a kind of intuitive, or inventive insight, and an openness to the telling improbability of aleatory occurrences, and therefore pertain to the province of the sixth sense. Alongside distraction and idling, Boetti welcomed improbability and chance as aids in galvanizing this singular species of thought, for it generates a mental frisson that in turn opens the door to deeper insights and speculation.

Among the more ambitious of Boetti's works from the early Seventies is a fantastical project *Viaggi postali* (1969–70) in which he sent twenty-five art-world friends and colleagues on imaginary trips courtesy of the postal system. This syntactically complex venture involved mailing letters addressed to each participant to one after another non-existent location: one individual, for example, was sent to places whose names began only with the letter "Z," another to destinations whose names began with the word "Acqua," and a third only to cities named after saints. The project risked failure at many levels—the misaddressed letters might not be returned to the sender, who would place them in new envelopes and then re-address them so that they could continue on their itineraries. Chance could easily have marooned his travellers in limbo, yet, miraculously, Boetti's gamble paid off: all of the voyagers returned safely. Xeroxes of the myriad documents recording their travels were then assembled, with all the appurtenances of a research project, into hundreds of folios. Laconically titled *Dossier postale* (1969–70), *ill. p. 117* this meticulous compendium of data records his fanciful defiance of the logic on which network communications depend.

Shortly afterwards, Boetti embarked on another vast undertaking that depended in many ways on the converse of *Viaggi postali* methodology. Ostensibly a *ill. p. 116* simple straightforward exercise in classification that involved the ordering of data according to a single criterion, it soon, however, proved alarmingly complex. Following the artist's directive to catalogue in descending order the thousand longest rivers in the world, his wife, Annemarie Sauzeau Boetti, in 1971 undertook the scholarly research needed to complete the exercise. Six years later, after she had navigated mountains of confoundingly contradictory data, a book was published tabulating the results. It was titled *Classifying* and subtitled *The Thousand Longest Rivers in the World*; that is, the *ill. p. 213* conceptual system itself is the real subject of study, the geographical feature an instance of its application. As the information that Sauzeau collected from multiple sources worldwide revealed, far from an objective, neutral scientific methodology, the act of classifying often involves arbitrary and aleatory decision-making, due to the unreliability of data, changing political and climactic situations, imprecise mensuration, outdated

21 Ibid., p. 34.

22 Rendered in German, it is also used on the cover of the publication accompanying Boetti's 1992 show in Bonn and Munich. See Sauzeau, *Alighiero e Boetti*, p. 208.

records and the like. Hence more valuable for this undertaking than a degree in advanced disciplinary methodologies would be a sixth sense that guided the researcher in figuring out how to arbitrate between competing claims and contradictory information and so produce a consistent, cogent, and convincing document.

The kinds of structures and thought processes entailed in these two very different schemes bear little affinity with the canonical forms of Conceptualism then emerging in the work of Boetti's peers. Thus, although he developed a friendship with Sol LeWitt, Boetti had little in common with the model of a mystic follower of irrational thoughts that the American artist had defined in his "Sentences of Conceptual Art," published in 1967.[23] Equally foreign to Boetti's maverick engagement with thought in the guise of a sixth sense were the analytic, deductive methodologies that inform Joseph Kosuth's linguistically based practice, and Lawrence Weiner's immaterial text-based works that leave the very question of their realization open. And while Boetti shared with Mel Bochner an interest in systems of diverse kinds, the dry, analytical investigatory procedures that underpin Bochner's fastidious practice are antithetical to the Italian's playful ventures. Nowhere are these differences more clearly evidenced than in their contradictory addresses to mensuration. Bochner's *Axiom of Indifference* (1973), for example, verges on the didactic in its elucidation of the principle at stake, whereas *Per una storia naturale della misurazione* (1970), which Boetti titled with tongue in cheek, is symptomatically quirky. A disarmingly modest work, it is comprised of Polaroid photographs that record the various attempts Boetti made to measure the dimensions of a simple object: an envelope. Foregoing standard devices such as rulers, tape-measures and yardsticks, he improvised. Among his happenstance tools were his own hand, a pair of scissors, a match, an eraser, and a playing card. He then mailed the envelope with the photographic evidence to his gallerist, who was charged with framing the data. Successive efforts to measure additional envelopes of different sizes required ever more images; the solutions devised to frame those experiments became in turn increasingly aberrant and comically awkward.[24] In contrast to the heavy intellectualizing evident in certain types of Conceptualism, Boetti's was always grounded in an intuitive lightness of touch and a playful élan that masks ideation in effects of beauty: the mental frisson was inextricable from its ludic and aesthetic pleasures.

ill. p. 114

Among Conceptual artists, Boetti's closest affinities remained with Duchamp. Yet even as he internalized his mentor's example, crucial distinctions came to light. While thinking was the well-spring of their practices, and they both revelled in word play, linguistic jokes, and verbal games, Duchamp was also drawn to arcane alchemical systems. Boetti, for his part, favoured cryptic tautological formulations with metaphysical import, whether temporal signatures, notions of order and disorder, classificatory systems or mundane conceptual structures. His enduring commitment to the preeminence of thought was wryly reprised at the end of his life in *Autoritratto* (1993), a fountain that doubles as a self-portrait. A life-size figure of the artist holds a tube from which a jet of water spurts intermittently onto his head. Clouds of steam rise from the heated cranium. With his suit hanging in folds on his thin frame, his body seems worn and aged, but his mind, as these misty thought-bubbles attest, is still vigorously active. Notable paradigms for the motif of the thinker in the annals of art history include Jean-Antoine Houdon's salute to Voltaire, seated and swaddled in classical robes, and Rodin's generic reworking of the subject as a heroic male nude grasping his head in his hands. Boetti's poignant work departs tellingly from these ubiquitous prototypes. As he cools his overheated brain, he celebrates the continuing fecundity of his sixth sense.

ill. p. 256

23 Cited in ibid., p. 147.

24 Again, there is a precursor in Duchamp's *Three Standard Stoppages* (1913–14). But whereas Duchamp's process wittily depends on chance to fix the standard gauges of measurement, Boetti's methodology is grounded in humorous forms of improvisation.

gaming/gambling

"He who plays alone never loses."

To Boetti, thought was humankind's highest accomplishment and play the arena in which he exercised it most fully; sometimes this took the form of games, and sometimes of leisure. In giving up work, he put others to work—among those in his service at various times were skilled professionals, including graphic designers and print-makers, traditional craftsmen and women, burgeoning artists (students in art schools and universities) and novices, amateurs, and children. In adopting a public stance based on the renunciation of work, whether in order to court idleness or to indulge in games, Boetti could be seen to position himself in relation to politically based refutations of works in Northern Italy at that moment, as Jason E. Smith argues in his stimulating essay in this volume.[25] For many theorists, and Marxists in particular, play has an idealistic, almost utopian dimension; it is posited to exist outside the rules and regulations of everyday life. Thus for Herbert Marcuse, play is a dimension of freedom, "a self-distraction, relaxing oneself, forgetting oneself and recuperating oneself"; it is therefore the Other of work, and only enabled or made possible by work.[26] Boetti, however, did not instrumentalize play as a reprieve from work, but concurred with anthropological theories that postulate that it pre-exists work in cultures of accumulation. If in the evolutionary chain of human social activity play precedes work, then its manifestations in childhood may also prove of seminal importance to adult experience. Among the familiar everyday structures, fundamental forms, and basic organizing systems that construct our mental universe—alphabets, numbers, maps, names—most are first encountered in childhood, often in the guise of games. Others are discovered in vernacular staples like checkers, as well as in simple puzzles and jigsaws: in short, for the young child play is an essential and primary vehicle for expressing thought, and may remain so in adulthood.[27]

Games figure prominently among Boetti's early works. For example, the "dama" or wooden checkerboards (1967–68), invite the viewer to spill the blocks out of their frames into a disorderly pile, and then reorder them, aligning them according to the simple codes imprinted along the edges of their principal faces. Somewhat related is the series of untitled works (1969–70) comprised from small circular stickers, placed whole, halved, and quartered on sheets of gridded paper, so that the configurations of colored elements start to read as some kind of encrypted abstract system, the bright decorative hues creating an all-over patterning that disarms the solemnity of the exercise. As a game-board *Iter-vallo* (1969/86), is more challenging than the various "dama" in that setting it up requires the interweaving of small iron blocks with a sheet of tissue paper: anticipating the pressures that the introduction of each subsequent metal form will exert on the paper as the checkerboard takes shape requires keen foresight.[28] Given that the heavy, sharp-edged metal blocks frequently cause the paper to rip as they settle into place, concentrated patience, a delicate touch, and a measure of good luck are needed. Once the checker board is completed, the game is essentially over, for the paper that describes the white squares is too fragile to

ill. p. 90
ill. p. 91
ill. p. 93

25 This fascination with play was, shared by many artists at that time, ranging from those who, like Pistoletto, had a formative background similar to Boetti's, to others such as Robert Morris and Joan Jonas whose work originated in quite different aesthetic realms. According to Boetti, his preoccupation with play was not politically motivated. He engaged with socio-cultural situations "as a citizen, not as an artist." See Mirella Bandini, p. 178.

26 Herbert Marcuse, "On the Philosophical Foundation of the Concept of Labor in Economics," *Telos*, Summer 1973, p. 15, quoted in Molesworth, "Work Avoidance," p. 56. I am indebted to Molesworth's insightful text for this reference.

27 Boetti's enthusiasm for projects with children is seen in a number of photographs from his later career in which he appears to be absorbed in the pursuits of the young artists who surround him. By contrast, very few of the many images taken of him show him at work in the context of his studio.

28 First titled *La Tritella* (1969), it was comprised of sixteen largish squares and illustrated in "When Attitudes Become Form" (Bern: Kunsthalle, Bern, 1969), n.p. Other variants followed. In its final form, the checkerboard is comprised of sixty-four small units, the same configuration as that found on a chess board.

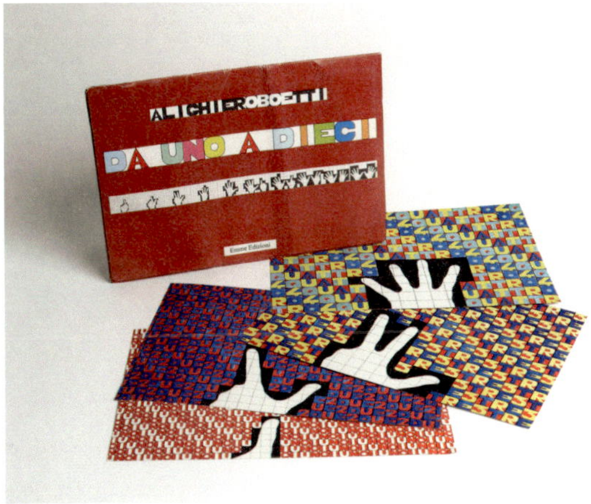

[fig. 6] Da uno a dieci (From One to Ten), 1980

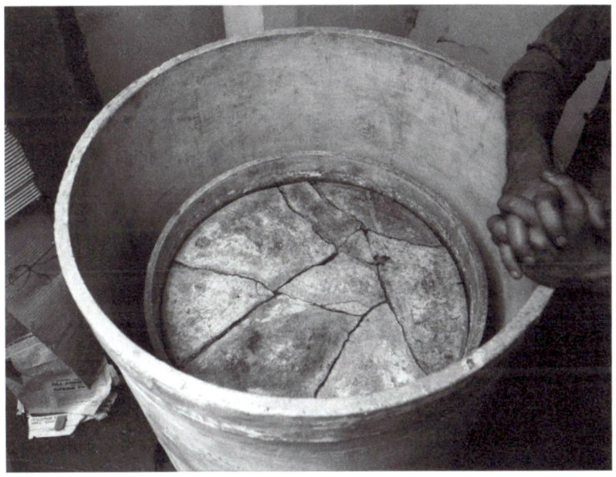

[fig. 7] Pack, 1967

sustain interaction.[29] Drawing on skills similar to those needed to construct an elaborate house of cards, *Intervallo* is best suited to the solitary player.

Boetti's delight in commonplace, even childish games was generated not only by the evident enjoyment they offer to audiences of all ages, but by the opportunities they provided for engaging, sometimes directly, and sometimes vicariously with others. *Contatore* (1967), for *ill. p. 128* example, references a commonplace game that the artist played with his family. It involves watching for that momentous instant when the numbers on the car's odometer change from, say, all nines to all zeroes as it hits the million kilometer mark. In several projects making up *Alternando da uno a cento e viceversa*, which is based on in- *ill. pp. 251–255* serting black and white units into 100 squares, each of which contains 100 squares, Boetti elicited the support of groups of art students. One of his few public artworks, the mosaic commissioned in 1984 by the State University of California at Northridge for its campus, was designed and carried out according to his instructions by students enrolled in the institution's Fine Arts Department. Boetti proposed that the students should first make the designs for the hundred squares, and then realize them, in the form of ceramic tiles.[30] A related scheme, launched in France during the early-1990s, and involving some fifty art schools, provided the basic designs from which fifty kilims were produced for an exhibition at Grenoble in 1993.

Boetti especially welcomed the participation of younger children, including his own daughter and son who were central to the creation of *Zoo* in 1979. For the artist, as well as his off-spring, the studio was a site of play rather than of labor, where drawings would be made by adopting a spectrum of juvenile techniques: blowing pigment through a straw, spraying over stencils, writing with the left-hand so it became a form of drawing, applying stamps and other logos, and throwing blindfold onto the paper's surface rubber-bands dipped in paint. Other projects were designed for a broader youthful audience. *Faccine* (1979), incorporates the work of young *ill. pp. 186, 187* children who gave vivid expression to schematically outlined interlocking heads. The multiple based on *Da uno a dieci* (1980), took the form of visual/verbal game-book *ill. pp. 184–185*

29 From at least 1937, a chess board hung on the walls of Duchamp's studio at 11, rue Larrey in Paris. According to Robert Lebel, Duchamp used the board to play "mental chess games." Robert Lebel, in Arturo Schwarz, *The Complete Works of Marcel Duchamp*, New York: Delano Greenidge Editions, 1997, p. 189.

30 See *Il mondo italiano*, Regione Piemonte: LAICA, Los Angles, 1984, pp. 24–26.

comprised of a sequence of loose tables. Created as a tool for children learning to count, read numbers, and identify colors, it parses the cardinals simultaneously in four different modalities: figure, letter, color and image. Also included in the folio are additional tables with white grounds that invite the children to make their own versions [fig. 6].[31] Less obviously pedagogical were the
ill. pp. 238-243 simple jigsaws based on Boetti's series of "Aerei", produced by Austrian Airlines for fledgling travelers unaccustomed to the longueurs of flight [fig. 8]. Jigsaws had long resonated in Boetti's imaginary. Though he
ill. pp. 232-237 claimed his "Tutto" series originated in the cracked residue of mud at the bottom of a bucket, they recall the iconic examples that Italian designer Enzo Mari created from the 1950s onwards [figs. 7, 9].

Boetti's fascination with games was clearly multiply determined. They were not only the principal vehicle through which he speculated on substantive issues, they were even crucial to his formation, constituting his first artistic endeavors. In an interview in 1983 he recounted his biography specifically in these terms. Rather than acknowledging the Turin milieu in which he had matured and first exhibited and, more specifically, the impact on his nascent practice of such close friends as Paolini, Pistoletto, and Piero Gilardi, he referenced some seminal moments in his childhood:[32]

> In 1948 I tore up a big brown sheet of paper making small quadrangular pieces, which I stacked up and used to erect a rather unstable column [a clear precursor of *Colonna* (1968)] . . . In 1950 I had about twenty small ice-cream glasses, which I'd collected laboriously, and I fitted them one inside the other so as to form an arch. In the same year I filled a small plastic box with about a dozen match boxes [see *Tubi Eternit* (1967), now destroyed] . . . In 1949 I rolled up a yellow tape measure and pushed my little finger into it forming a kind of tower of Babel [*Rotolo di cartone ondulato*] . . . The first pile of matches and the first bundle of pencils date back to 1947 [*Mazzo di tubi*].[33]

By locating many of the processes and forms central to his Arte Povera works from the later 1960s in preco-

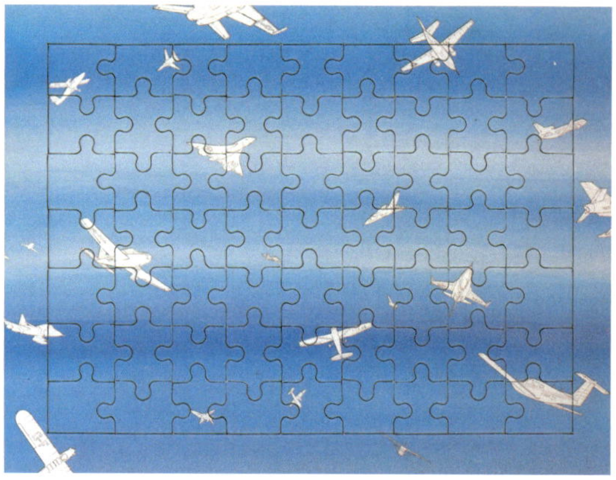

[fig. 8] Jigsaws produced in 1994 for Austrian Airlines based on the works Cieli ad alta quota (High Skies), 1993

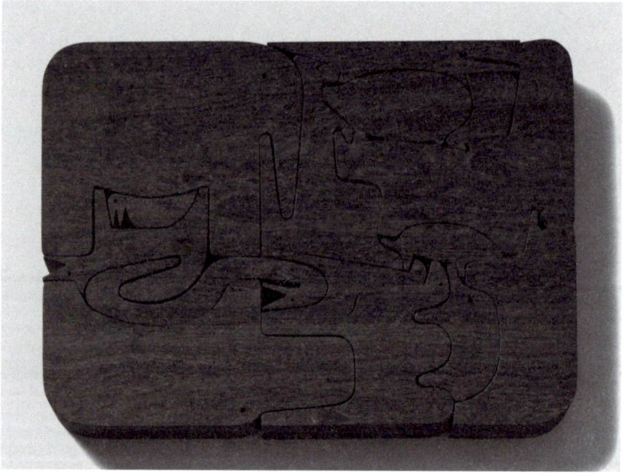

[fig. 9] Enzo Mari, 16 animali (16 Animals), 1957

31 The multiple also included a text by Gianni Jervis, whose academic field was teaching and social psychiatry, in which he argues that "Numbers are beautiful because they help us to think." In a 1991 interview, Boetti stated, "I always had didactic projects in mind . . . yet I realized just one . . . some copies [were distributed] in schools and it proved to be an incredible success." Mariuccia Casadio, "Concept Boetti", in *Alighiero Boetti 1965–1994*, Galleria Civica d'Arte Moderna e Contemporanea, Torino, 1996, p. 205.

32 Compare, for example, the bed of stones used to create an environment in Boetti's 1968 show at De Nieubourg with Gilardi's *Nature Carpets* (1967), or Boetti's *Mancorrente a squadra* (1966) with Pistoletto's *Struttura per parlare in piedi* (1965–66).

33 See "Untitled," 1983, in Sauzeau Boetti, *Alighiero e Boetti: Bringing the World into the World*, p. 199.

cious games, Boetti not only played down the influence of his peers, and of the signature Arte Povera techniques and methodologies, but also of contemporary critical theory. Designed to contest orthodox histories, Boetti's recital foregrounds the seminal role that games, toys, and other forms associated with play would assume in his practice and aesthetic. More cerebral versions of games, he believed, are central to an understanding of how the world works. "I have often worked with the concepts of order and disorder," he stated in 1988:

> I have done a lot of work on the concept of *order and disorder*; disordering order or putting order into certain kinds of disorder, or again presenting a visual disorder that was actually the representation of a mental order. It's just a question of knowing the rules of the game. Someone who doesn't know them will never see the order that reigns in things. It's like looking at a starry sky. Someone who does not know the order of the stars will see only confusion, whereas an astronomer will have a very clear vision of things.[34]

Many of Boetti's key works were based in language, in his predilection for such vernacular forms as puzzles, palindromes, puns, proverbs, and oxymorons, as well as in certain forms of poetry, and even sign language.[35] Sometimes banal, more often stimuli to philosophical speculation, as in *Dare tempo al tempo* (Giving time to time), his magic squares provided the basis for a plethora of embroidered works. Some are overtly cryptic, others aphoristic, while still more were made in tribute to friends and family—Annemarie Sauzeau was the subject of some of the earliest hand-drawn versions, and his second family figured among his last productions: notably, *Alighiero, Caterina e Giordano Boetti*, a subtle white on white embroidery from 1992. Not surprisingly, many of the phrases used in these works were discovered in conversation, as well as in reading and study.

Though Boetti employed a host of different professionals and amateurs to create his works, ultimately chance was his primary collaborator: he was a "born gambler."[36] Serendipity had played a vital role in his practice from his earliest years, as seen in *Lampada annuale*. Lighting up randomly for only eleven seconds each year, this work is most often experienced by audiences in a state of expectancy or frustrated anticipation. Boetti's faith in serendipity exercised on a more complex level also proved well founded. In his experience of the postal service there were no such things as "dead letters": all 5,040 envelopes (franked with 32,580 stamps), deployed in *Untitled—Victoria Boogie Woogie* (1972), reached their appointed destinations. More fatalistic are those works in which he speculated on his artistic future and fortunes.[37] *16 DICEMBRE 2040—11 JUGLIO 2023* both celebrates his immortality and predicts his death: the first date marks the centennial anniversary of his birth (only the famous are honoured with such commemorative recognition), while the second tempts fate by anticipating the day on which he will die. The superstitious artist then reprised this disturbing work on three occasions: as a pair of spray-painted monochrome blue panels with raised letters (1969), *ill. pp. 122–125* as engraved metal plates (1971), and as decoratively embroidered cloths (1971). The variations chart a

34 Alighiero Boetti, "From Today to Tomorrow," 1988, *in Alighiero e Boetti*, op cit. pp. 205–6.

35 Among his most ingeniously playful works is *Autorittrato* (1969), in which, by recourse to "an infantile memory and a scholastic one: that of sign language," he "tried to communicate with a machine that sees but does not listen": a Rank Xerox copier. The resulting work is comprised of "twelve portraits of myself . . . spelling with my hands the different letters that compose the word AUTORITTRATO." See Mariuccia Casadio, "Concept Boetti," p. 205.

36 Francesco Clemente, "Apricots and Pomegranates," in *Worlds Envisioned. Alighiero e Boetti and Frédéric Bruly Bouabré* (New York: Dia Center for the Arts, 1995), p. 61: "To be a gambler is so consistent with your worldview: a permutating field of possibilities, a chaotic weave of contrasting colors, a grid of lucky and unlucky chances." See also Sauzeau Boetti, *Alighiero e Boetti*, p. 72: "A juggler and diviner . . . Alighiero played with numbers all his life, with the Monza lottery, with [the] *I Ching* . . . and the numbers of letters in words.

37 According to astrologer Mariangelica De Gaetano, who supervised the outsourcing of the Biro pieces to many different draftspersons, Boetti was very superstitious. He would want to hear his fortune told or have her read the tarot, but soon after she had started he would invariably interrupt her, asking her to stop. Personal communication, May 30, 2011.

trajectory from industrial modes of manufacturing with ready-made colors to the traditional handiwork on which his later projects would greatly depend;[38] and from a pictorial mode (painting) to a readymade (functional signage) to traditional forms of craftsmanship.

Boetti's jousting with the date of his own demise is curiously reprised in his preoccupation with the fate of Gary Gilmore. In 1977, the convicted killer finally achieved his execution by firing squad in defiance of the forces and codes of the American state that had condemned him to death but then proved unwilling to carry
ill. p. 146 out the sentence. In *Gary Gilmore* (1977), Boetti juxtaposed sketches and texts relating to this infamous saga with outline drawings of the bodies of anonymous victims of contemporary political unrest. All were based on material culled from daily newspapers. The anonymity of the victims who randomly died in service to collective ideals resonates uncomfortably with the celebrity accorded the pathological criminal whose will to die garnered him a measure of immortality.

The French theorist Roger Caillois divides games into four basic types, defined by skill, chance, mimicry (forms of simulation and pretence), and "ilinx" (or vertigo, that is, forms of collective turbulence). The latter two categories involve the performative and what the sociologist calls "collective occasions for merry-making and jollity." Drawn to all these forms early on, as seen in his engagement with the festivities at Amalfi in the autumn of 1968, and with various forms of self-fashioning in the late Sixties and early Seventies, Boetti thereafter began to narrow his focus to forms of play that centered on skill and chance. Games are inherently social: even the solitary player at some level presumes the presence of others.[39] Curiously, the aphorism "*Chi gioca da solo non perde mai*" (He who plays alone never loses) appears in one of Boetti's magic squares[40]—curiously because collaborations of many kinds were fundamental to his practice; and because he was anything but risk averse.

Games and related forms of play enabled him to explore the larger metaphysical structures that subtend existence: "Time is something really fundamental; it underlies everything . . . [It] is the only thing that is really magical," Boetti contended: "Everything has its own time."[41] In his aesthetic, laziness came to operate as a third term, triangulating work and play. In a short interview titled "Dare to be Lazy," Roland Barthes differentiates between two kinds of laziness: one arises out of the struggle to get something done, a kind of marinating that allows a solution eventually to appear. Opposed to what he calls "this shameful laziness," Barthes postulates "the glorious and philosophical form of laziness."[42] Noting the difficulty of achieving that rare state—"I wonder whether there is such a thing as *doing nothing* in the modern Western world"—Barthes acknowledges its attendant dangers, its potential nihilism: "In a situation of idleness the subject is almost dispossessed of his consistency as a subject. He is decentered, unable even to say 'I'. That would be true idleness. To be able, at certain moments, to no longer have to say 'I'.[43] In his quest for "wasting time," Boetti devised a number of ingenious systems. After notating each quarter hour as chimed by the bells of the neighbourhood church; he produced a diagram which in turn generated the mysterious image that he titled *L'albero delle ore*
(1979). And in the absurdly tautological *Ammazzare il* ill. p. 131
tempo (Killing Time) (1981), he conscientiously worked out an elaborate system to ensure that each letter of the phrase would be represented by a combination of two colors, (one for the figure and one for the ground) that never recurred again in the piece. Above all, the series of "mappe" seemed to him to be the perfect works, because, he said, they required nothing of him: he chose nothing (the design already existed) and he did nothing

38 On the border on his first Mappa, 1971–73, is written "BETWEEN DECEMBER SIXTEENTH ONE THOUSAND NINE HUNDRED FORTY AND JULY ELEVENTH TWO THOUSAND TWENTY-THREE ALIGHIERO E BOETTI CAME TO KABUL PABLO PICASSO DIED DURING THAT PERIOD."

39 See: Johan Huizinga, *Homo Ludens* (1938), and Roger Caillois, *Man, Play and Games* (1958; Illinois: Simon and Schuster, 2001).

40 For an account of the origins of this phrase in his work see Sauzeau, *Alighiero e Boetti*, p. 120.

41 Achille Bonito Oliva, "Alighiero Boetti Interview," in *Alighiero Boetti* (Milan 1973; Vienna: Museum moderner Kunst Stiftung Ludwig, 1997), p. 208.

42 Roland Barthes, "Dare to be Lazy," in *The Grain of the Voice: Interviews, 1962–1980* (New York: Hill and Wang, 1985), p. 339.

43 Ibid, p. 341.

(they were executed by others). Far from disingenuous, his claim points to a goal in which he ceded all activity, mental and physical, to others and, since he never knew what colors the embroiderers would chose to render the oceans, to chance. Here he seems to have achieved the ideal, "a glorious and philosophical form of idleness."

Such efforts to waste time, or do nothing, are nonetheless feints. His freehand tracings of the squares that make up a gridded sheet of paper, notations recording each quarter hour as the minutes ticked on, and cartographic projections deployed as readymades are all *representations*. Trophies celebrating an alternative existence, they evidence Boetti's attempts to master his "own time," to shape it according to his will by spending it as he saw fit. Gambling with time, he both won and lost: he did not live to see July 11 2023, as he had predicted, but the centenary of his birth, December 16 2040, will be widely celebrated.

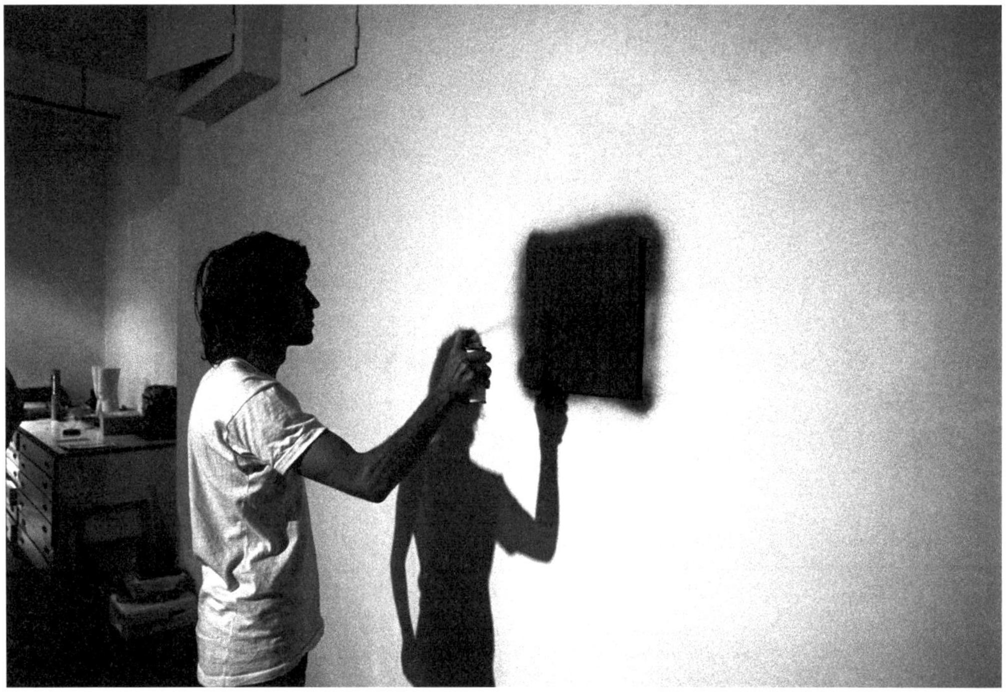

Alighiero Boetti spray painting the cast iron version of EMME I ELLE ELLE E ... MILLENOVECENTOSETTANTA (EMME I ELLE ELLE E ... Onethousandninehundredandseventy), 1970

From Alighiero to Boetti

Christian Rattemeyer

Alighiero Boetti's protean and multi-faceted career has most commonly been described through the major themes and groups of works for which he has been best known. Even though he ventured into many different areas and was at any given moment thinking about several different themes, making different bodies of work and garnering inspiration from different places, his work seemed to cohere around a few basic, almost philosophically profound concepts, such as time and its passing, singularity and duality, plenitude and difference, order and disorder, the familiar and the unfamiliar. And yet, while these concepts traverse his oeuvre like a thread, his work seems peculiarly resistant to more conventional readings of intrinsic development and logic. Rather than constructing an analysis that proceeds from one body of work to the next, accounts of Boetti's work have often highlighted how certain core principles preoccupied him from the start and simply fluctuated in their expression as he discovered new materials and visited new places.

At the same time, writers have sometimes struggled to separate the work from the man: a significant body of analysis has been created from the narration of Boetti's life, his genial and mesmerizing persona, his intuitive and emotional intelligence, his belief in the mystical and alchemic aspects of creation, and his frequent travels to faraway places such as Afghanistan. By all accounts, Boetti was a rare and beautiful individual who had a vivid and generous imagination, a keen intuition, and an emotional grasp of things. He worked quickly and was prolific, and embraced collaboration and chance—the "*felici coincidenze*" (happy coincidences) that often colored his work.

Born in 1940 in Turin, Boetti emerged as an artist in his hometown in the mid-1960s through association with a new direction in sculpture termed "Arte Povera" by the Italian critic Germano Celant in 1967. Boetti at first embraced the logic of arranging untraditional and often mass-produced materials into simple, process-based installations presented in temporary, non-institutional venues and the new, radical commercial galleries. But unlike many of his colleagues who have become firmly associated with Arte Povera for the better part of their careers, he shifted soon after his initial successes to a different style of working, developing an unpredictable, highly inventive, playful, and poetic oeuvre that spanned drawing, painting, and sculpture, mail art and conceptual practices, embroidery and weaving, and engaged with an ever-broadening global perspective. He cherished collaboration with assistants and colleagues, as well as with artisans in remote parts of the world, and he evolved a system of creative thought that embraced the dual principles of rule and chance, logic and indeterminacy, order and disorder, singularity and multitude, similarity and difference, classification and boundlessness, male and female, seeing and not-seeing.

In January 1967, a movement in Italy began to consolidate around the critics Germano Celant and Piero Gilardi, who each proposed terminology to name and claim it, with Celant's term "Arte Povera" winning historical favor. The same year, the twenty-six year old artist Alighiero Boetti staged his first solo exhibition at the Christian Stein Gallery in Turin, his hometown. The exhibition brought together work from the previous eighteen months and marks the beginning of Boetti's public career as a visual artist, after early private experiments with gestural paintings and drawings stenciled with machine parts scoured from the regional automobile industry. Consisting mainly of objects fabricated from common materials sourced from local hardware stores, at first sight Boetti's early work appeared to be in line with the sculptural sensibilities of Arte Povera in their preference for elemental materials, simple constructions and an anti-classical stance—in the classical tradition of Italy, still a provocation. But in many ways, Boetti's was not typical Arte Povera work: it was playful and humorous, it was devoid of metaphor, and it was concerned with concepts more than materials, since the directness of the material gesture was meant to speak of the object's existence in the world rather than function as a commentary on traditional concepts of sculpture; in fact, he never considered his works "sculptures" and always called them "objects."

Boetti presented works that employed materials in direct, nearly unaltered ways, except for basic forms of *ill. pp. 42, 149* selection and arrangement: *Catasta* (1967), a cubic grid of rectangular Eternit (a kind of asbestos-concrete) *ill. p. 44* tubes; *Mimetico* (1966) a "painting" made from stretched *ill. p. 43* camouflage fabric; *Rotolo di cartone ondulato* (1966), a cardboard roll with the core pushed out to form a con- *ill. p. 51* ical shape; *Colonna* (1967), a column constructed from *ill. p. 45* hundreds of stacked cake doilies; and *Mazzo di tubi* (1966), a vertical stack of PVC pipes. Even where he constructed or altered some of the objects on view, such *ill. p. 46* as *Scala* (1966), for which he nailed strips of wood onto the sides of a wooden standing ladder, rendering it useless while emphasizing its basic pyramidal shape, or *ill. p. 47* *Mancorrente metri 2* (1966), for which he elevated a wooden railing with a metal understructure to suggest a banister or barrier, Boetti was not so much concerned with their formal qualities as with their elemental necessity. Closer in spirit to Carl Andre's notion that "A man climbs a mountain because it's there. A man makes a work of art because it isn't there,"[1] Boetti in fact made objects precisely because their elements were already there, and their choice and assembly constituted only the smallest act of creation.

Two objects from his 1967 debut stand out because they introduce a different idea into the sculptural thinking of the late 1960s. *Ping Pong* and *Lampada annuale* *ill. pp. 49, 50/5* (both 1966) could at first sight be seen as riffs on the use of electricity and industrial light sources (such as neon and fluorescent light) so prevalent at the time, a smart commentary on light objects such as Dan Flavin's *Icons* (1961–63). *Ping Pong* consists of two wall-mounted cases, each half a meter square, and covered with a red glass front that encloses a light source. The words "ping" and "pong" emerge in each respective box at intervals as the electric current alternates between the two. For *Lampada annuale*, Boetti constructed a simple wooden plinth, painted dark blue, with a glass window on top that reveals a light bulb inside the box. A timing mechanism hidden in the structure regulates the electrical supply so that the lamp should light at a random moment once a year for eleven seconds. Both objects introduce time, and sequence, into the vocabulary of Boetti's objects, and suggest a preoccupation with games and mysteries as well as with duality and opposition that would remain central to all of his subsequent work.

But the most radical work may have been the easiest to overlook: the invitation card for the exhibition, which *ill. p. 32* Boetti arranged like a sample booklet containing swatches of PVC pipe, cork letters, Eternit, camouflage fabric, copper wire, and other materials used to construct the objects on view. Not only does this piece suggest a conceptual rather than sculptural understanding of materials, but it also prefigures a series of works beginning in 1969 that use the postal service as well as the arrangement of stamps as medium. The use of systematic classification that is the formal organizing principle of the invitation returns in multiple subsequent works, most prominently perhaps in the monumental work *I mille fiumi più lunghi del mondo* (1972– *ill. pp. 214–217* 77), two embroideries that list the thousand longest rivers of the world, and its companion publication *Classifying: The* *ill. p. 213* *Thousand Longest Rivers in the World* (1972–82).

1 Handwritten statement in "When Attitudes Become Form" (Bern: Kunsthalle Bern, 1969), n.p.

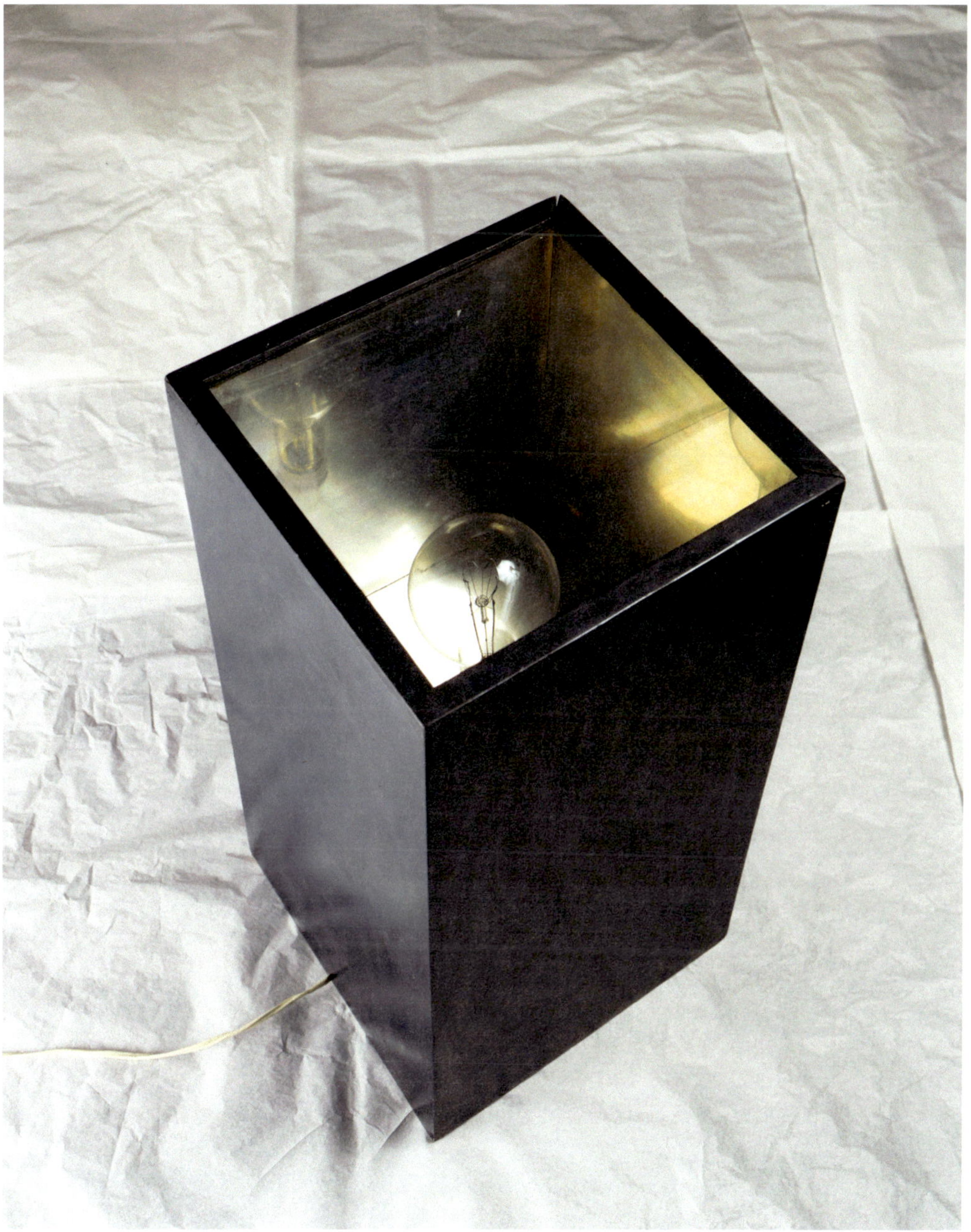

Lampada annuale (Annual Lamp), 1966

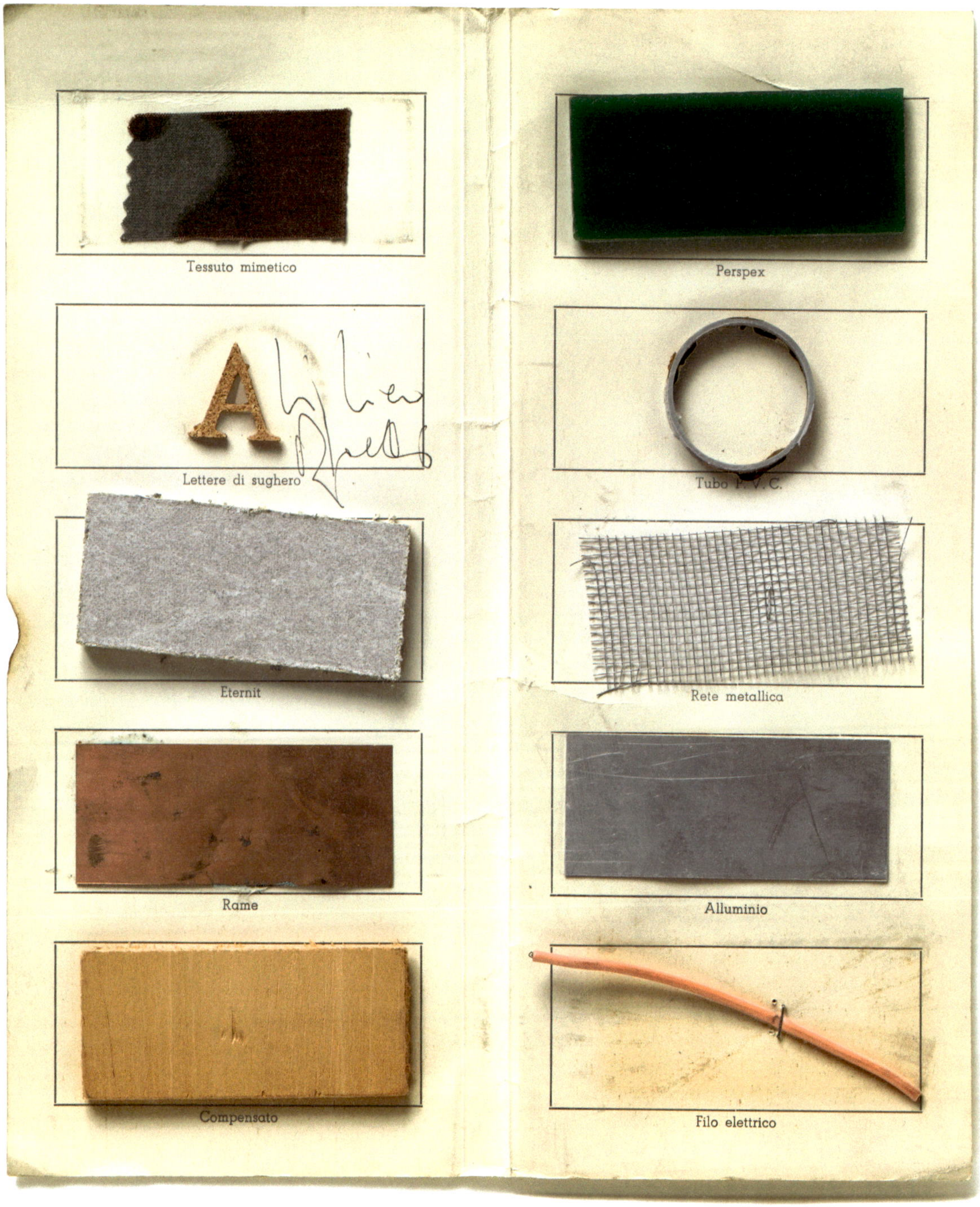

Untitled (Invitation), 1966–67

Over the course of 1968, Boetti participated in several group exhibitions and festivals associated with Arte Povera, where he presented works that incrementally broke with the forming orthodoxies of the movement by foregrounding humor and a child-like delectation in play and discovery through works such as *Legnetti colorati*, ill. p. 55 ill. p. 54 bundles of sticks sorted by color, or *Cubo*, an acrylic cube measuring one meter squared filled with a densely arranged assortment of wooden sticks, copper pipes, and strips of building material in almost geologically stratified density.

The student protests that took place in Paris during May 1968 came to Turin in the "Hot Autumn" of 1969,[2] and Boetti understood the radical social and political changes that these events facilitated. Yet unlike Gilardi, for instance (who took the implications for social change to heart and soon afterwards left the art world for the more politically minded open psychiatry movement), Boetti did not embrace politics. In a much-quoted interview with Mirella Brandini from 1972, he expresses his disgust with the monumental claims of the Arte Povera movement in 1968, no doubt triggered by the world outside: "This got so exaggerated in 1968 that it ended in nausea, then that was it—finished!"[3] Boetti's response was one of remove, rather than radicalization, and the following year, he would produce and present only a few slender works. I would argue, however, that 1969 represents one of the most significant shifts in his entire oeuvre, as these works move away from the objecthood of Arte Povera sculpture and, in two subsequent steps, reset the artist's vocabulary to a degree zero and introduce subject matter, fabrication techniques, and systematic ordering principles that would shape his oeuvre for the coming decades.

In March 1969, Boetti participated in the group exhibition "When Attitudes Become Form" in Bern, Switzerland, where he exhibited the work ill. p. 67 *Io che prendo il sole a torino il 19 gennaio 1969* (1969), which consists of the outline of his figure, composed from small clumps of concrete, topped by a single butterfly. The title points to an ironic gesture of leisure—sunbathing in mountainous Turin in the middle of winter—but it also suggests non-action and inefficiency as modalities of creative work. Shown in the same room as works by Bruce Nauman, the work echoed the latter's commentary on the function of the artist—the resolute belief that everything an artist produces is art. This attitude of non-action would manifest itself most directly in Boetti's solo exhibition of April 1969 at Sperone Gallery in Turin. It contained three works: *Io che prendo il sole...*, ill. p. 14 a small portrait of Walter de Maria, drawn in carbon powder onto a sheet of glass (the work is now lost) and an object at first titled *Una vetrata* and today known as *Niente da vedere niente da nascondere*. ill. p. 69 A simple grid of twelve panes of glass in a metal frame, it resembled a casement window or a shop front, and was shown leaning against a wall as if temporarily stored. This work could be considered an endpoint to the material experiments of Boetti's Arte Povera years, a turn away from the literal presentation of objects meant not to signify, but simply "be." The work scoffs at visuality and immediacy and instead demands an ability to focus on the "mental" inner vision of imagination and intellect. Executed by a metal shop instead of the artist himself, it was also a gesture of refusal to produce, a gesture that becomes particularly clear in relation to another series of works by Boetti also executed during 1969. The group *Cimento dell'armonia e dell'invenzione* ill. pp. 80, 81 consists of simple sheets of squared paper on which Boetti retraced the printed grid in pencil. On each sheet, he would try to change the way in which the tracing was done, arriving at more and more cumbersome, imprecise, and labor-intensive solutions. The whole series could be read as an exercise in exhaustion, unproductiveness, and ill-applied attention, as the grid becomes less exact and the drawing methods, even at their most expressive, fail to provide what one might term obvious virtuosity.

Seen together, the three works of *Niente da vedere niente da nascondere*, *Cimento dell'armonia e dell'invenzione*, and *Io che prendo il sole...* show an artist at a moment of extreme vulnerability and pause as he resets his vocabulary,

2 For a more detailed discussion of Italy's "Hot Autumn" and "Creeping May," see Jason E. Smith's essay in this volume, [pp. 142–153].

3 Mirella Bandini in conversation with Alighiero Boetti (1972). Originally published in NAC, No. 3, March 1973, reprinted in English in: *Zero to Infinity*, eds. Richard Flood and Frances Morris (Minneapolis: Walker Art Center, 2001), p. 188.

approach, and intention. But in the summer of 1969, just a few months after his pensive exhibition at Sperone Gallery, Boetti produced three works (or work series) ill. p. 79 that presage a decade or more of creative production. *Territori occupati* (Occupied Territories) is a cross-stitch embroidery about four feet in diameter showing the outline of Israel and the occupied territory of the Sinai peninsula captured during the Six-Day war of 1967. The embroidery is the first iteration of works using the schematic outlines of maps displaying zones of conflict (taken from the pages of the Turin newspaper *La Stampa*) in the time between the Six-Day war in 1967 and the secession of Bangladesh from Pakistan in 1971. In its final form, the ill. p. 78 work *Dodici forme dal 10 giugno 1967* (1971), is a set of twelve copper engraving plates the size of the newspaper, with the isolated outline of a territory placed where the original map would appear on the printed page.

Territori occupati and *Dodici forme dal 10 giugno 1967* testify to Boetti's growing interest in geography, both as a form of organization and abstraction as well as a source of real political conflict and cultural difference. Executed by Boetti's partner and collaborator Annemarie Sauzeau Boetti, *Territori occupati* is the first embroidery in Boetti's oeuvre, a technique of great importance in subsequent works. The geographical selection of this work is countered by two drawings that introduce the motif of the world map ill. p. 161 for the first time. Drawing on a *Planisfero politico*, a printed schematic world map common in school atlases or other textbooks that outlines the borders of every country on the planet, Boetti colored in each country with the design of its national flag and thus created the prototype for the ill. pp. 164-165/ 218-229 series of "mappe", which from 1971–72 onwards would translate this gesture into embroideries made by Afghan women, first in Afghanistan and after 1979 in Pakistan. In 1974, Boetti would say of the "mappe":

> For me, the work on the embroidered Map achieved the highest form of beauty. For the finished work, I myself did nothing, chose nothing, in the sense that the world is as it is (I didn't draw it) and the national flags are as they are (I didn't design them). In short, I did absolutely nothing. What emerges from the work is the concept: the rest is a matter of choice.[4]

Toward the end of 1969, Boetti began another work, *Viaggi postali*—finished the following year—that en- ill. p. 116 acted for the first time his desire for exploration, travel, and adventure, albeit in purely conceptual form. For the work, Boetti sent letters to twenty-five friends and colleagues (from collectors such as Count Panza di Biumo and Corrado Levi to artists such as Bruce Nauman and Marcel Duchamp, who had died the previous year) using imaginary addresses. When the envelopes were returned by the postal service, Boetti would put them in a new envelope and resend them to the same person, using a different fictive address of a similar poetic type (for one recipient, all the street names contained the word *acqua*—water—for instance). *Viaggi postali* creates an invisible conceptual network spanning the globe that connects Boetti with colleagues and friends. It also further explores the postal system as a means of creative production, a process begun two years earlier with the mailing of *Manifesto* (1967), a poster describing relation- ill. p. 63 ships between artists of the Arte Povera movement mailed to fifty recipients, and *Gemelli* (1968), a set of ill. pp. 65, 66 postcards showing Boetti holding hands with himself that the artist mailed to friends.

In retrospect, 1969 can be seen as a crucial year, slender in production yet rich in new directions, that rely on games and humor as much as on systems and networks. Language, a crucial "material" of conceptual practices of the time, also moves into the center of Boetti's practice around this time. A few years previously, he had executed some smaller works where he incised text into quick-drying square plaster panels, writing first the words *I VEDENTI* (1967) and later ill. p. 70 quotes by Marcuse (*Per un uomo alienato*, 1968) and Rim- ill. p. 73 baud (*Ma chère*, 1968). And yet these tablets were still as much concerned with the reduced palette and minimal appearance of Boetti's objects as with the linguistic elegance and wordplay of his subsequent works; by 1970, he had found a valid form for his word games. He

[4] Annemarie Sauzeau Boetti, "The Adventurous Life of Alighiero Boetti," in Achille Bonito Oliva (ed.), *Alighiero & Boetti: Bringing the World into Art, 1993–1962*, Naples: MADRE and Milan: Electa, 2009, pp. 233–34.

first took the phonetic spelling of the year's date (1970) and turned the resulting sequence of letters into a ill. p. 85 square (*Millenovecentosettanta*, 1970) executed in decorative lace. Subsequently he found the most universal and versatile expression in a small grid of four-by-four letters that spelled out short phrases such as *ordine e disordine*. These "word squares" in grids of four-by-four and five-by-five letters, and later in large, complex arrangements of six-by-six four-letter squares, would become one of the signature objects in Boetti's oeuvre from the mid-1970s onward. They serve as the repository for many of his aphoristic inventions: short koan-like sentences that summarize some of his concepts of duality ill. pp. 94/231 and opposition, time and space. *Ordine e disordine*, *Fare* ill. p. 152 *quadrare tutto*, *Dare tempo al tempo*, as well as the artist's amended name 'Alighiero e Boetti', all became microtreatises in his expanding philosophy. First executed as stencils and sprayed directly onto gallery walls, the word squares, like nearly every series on which he had been working, changed in 1971, when Boetti traveled for the first time to Afghanistan, to which he would regularly return, usually twice a year, until the Soviet Union invaded the country on Christmas Eve, 1979.

On March 15, 1971, apparently rather spontaneously, Boetti set off for Kabul, Afghanistan, where he stayed about a month. Here, he had two modest embroideries made: against a green background decorated with flowers and surrounded by a jagged border, the embroi- pp. 124-125 deries each laconically list a date, 11 Luglio 2023—his assumed death date—and 16 Dicembre 2040—his 100th birthday. Dates, a simple yet profound meter of the passing of time, fascinated Boetti. As he said to Bandini:

> Do you know why dates are important? Because . . . if you write "1970" for example on a wall, it looks like nothing much, nothing at all, but in thirty years' time . . . With every day that goes by, this date becomes more beautiful. It's time that works, it's all that works.[5]

On his return from Kabul, Boetti continued his play with dates by sending a telegram on May 4, pronouncing "Two days ago was May 2." A second telegram was sent four days after May 2, another eight days after that date, and so the series of telegrams continued like the Chinese legend of the chessboard and the grain of rice,[6] and was intended to conclude in 2017, the last date before his assumed day of passing. Systems, measure, time, play, poetry, the use of existing modes of communication: all the elements of Boetti's art were now in full force, even in his seemingly most private, ephemeral works.

In the fall of 1971, Boetti returned to Kabul, where he opened the One Hotel with the help of Gholan ill. pp. 154, 158 Dastaghir, who became its manager. The hotel followed the destiny of the country and ceased operation with the Soviet invasion in 1979. Dastaghir also helped Boetti connect with a group of Afghani women, who would embroider maps, word squares, "tuttos," and many other works for Boetti, even after they had to leave the country and set up shop in Peshawar, Pakistan, during the early 1980s. For his next trip, in the fall of 1971, Boetti brought two canvases, prepared with the outlines of the world map and the countries' national flags, which would take a year to finish.

Mappa (1971–72) began a series of embroidered ill. pp. 164-165 world maps that by the time of his death in 1994 numbered well above 200 and that, despite his claim that he had to "invent nothing" show an extraordinary range and diversity in color, size, and most importantly, political geography. Undoubtedly Boetti's most iconic work, the "mappe," as Luca Cerizza asserts, "is a work which time and history have acted upon and altered to an enormous degree. Recent history, for instance, has given *Mappa* a new and unexpected relevance."[7] Following the development of the series is to follow world politics in timelapse—one sees revolutions, independence movements, and the fall of the Iron Curtain changing the appearance of entire continents. But it is also to see other, more subtle changes in our perception. As the Mercator and Robinson map projections come in and out of use, the controversies surrounding the representation of the world according to, or in opposition to, Eurocentric parameters gently flare up, and one of the most striking

5 Ibid., p. 170.
6 For a description of the legend, see www.youtube.com/watch?v=rlZ-uhf9wUk
7 Luca Cerizza, *Alghiero e Boetti: Mappa*, (London: Afterall, 2008), p. 3.

aspects of the ongoing design choices—the color of the oceans—takes an increasingly autonomous role. Instead of leaving color choices to chance, Boetti sourced a thread that he knew was widely available in Afghanistan (the "Anchor" brand) and designated the colors in his prepared canvases. Once, he forgot to specify the color of the oceans, and the embroiderers, who had probably never seen the ocean, chose green instead of blue (*Mappa*, 1978). This error opened the door to color variations that produced silver and yellow, purple and black waters, and did in fact render the design of the *Mappa* very much an aesthetic decision. In subtle but precise ways, Boetti used the ongoing production of *Mappa* to express his political views, such as when he decided to leave the outline of Afghanistan white during the years of Soviet occupation, or allow the artisans in Kabul and Peshawar to add their own writings in the borders, which range from Sufi poetry to activist expressions of oppression and exile. The following major ill. pp. 94-97 body of work, the 100-part embroidery *Ordine e disordine*, completed in 1973, must thus not only be understood in light of Boetti's interest in wordplay and difference, random order and chance, but also in terms of its geo-political dimension: order and disorder are realities that structure the world in ways that have serious, and often bloody, consequences.

The border around the second *Mappa* that Boetti had embroidered in Kabul begins with another wordplay, which spelt out letter by letter in colorful squares the term "*mettere al mondo il mondo*" (bringing the world into the world). Few sentences could be more succinct in describing Boetti's interest in bringing forth—and thus creating—that which is already in existence, a genesis through duplication. The border inscription of the *Mappa* continues with location and date, grounding it in reality: "In Afghanistan negli anni settanta" (In Afghanistan during the Seventies). The sentence would reappear in a ill. pp. 101-111 new series of works that Boetti began around 1972–73. For these "Biro" works, he used a ball-point pen as the primary design element, filling entire sheets of paper with the blue (and later green, red, and black) ink of this ill. p. 105 most common of writing utensils. In *Mettere al mondo in mondo* (1972–73), two panels are covered in the iconic ball-point-pen blue, save for an alphabet of outlined letters on top of each sheet, and white commas, also spared from the overall fill of dense blue line, that, when read sequentially from top to bottom, spelled out the work's title. This way, Boetti would produce many variations on his best known wordplays, such as "*mettere al mondo il mondo*," "*dare tempo al tempo*," "*far quadrare tutto*," as well as his name and the names of others (it became an effective way to produce portraits, sometimes as gifts), and, second in prominence perhaps only to *Mettere al* ill. p. 103 *mondo in mondo*, a series of works called *I sei sensi* (The ill. pp. 106-1 Six Senses, 1972–73). On eleven panels, Boetti spelt out these senses "*vedere, udire, odorare, gustare, toccare, pensare*" (to see, to hear, to smell, to taste, to touch, to think), leaving five panels blank for senses yet to be developed.

Most important, although not immediately apparent, is the fact that each Biro work contains panels done by a man and a woman, usually not the artist himself. Enlisting assistants to help with the coordination and production of the drawings—the coordinator Mariangelica De Gaetano supervised up to thirty men and women who worked on several series simultaneously, a labor that could take months to produce a finished work—Boetti encouraged and embraced the uncertainty of a drawing's final appearance, the range in cross-hatches and hue, shading and evenness of each drawn panel. The Biro drawings, which he continued to produce until his death, became a repository for his thoughts and concepts, much like the word squares, while being able to encapsulate the poetic possibilities of language without being beholden to the strict metric order of those works.

Boetti's concern to make time and its passing visible and to measure the world, finds its expression in a group of different works that he began in the early 1970s and would occupy him for most of the decade. At first, he directed his encyclopedic interest toward his own work with the print portfolio *Insicuro noncurante* (1975), which he developed with the printmaker Rinaldo Rossi, who had drawn some of the outlines for his earliest *Mappa*. *Insicuro noncurante* is a retrospective of almost all ill. pp. 178-1 of Boetti's significant works since 1965, a *Boite-en-valise* of sorts, and besides being an obvious homage to Duchamp, a tour-de-force of printmaking techniques.

Much like Duchamp, who spent a considerable amount of energy and effort in handcrafting miniature models of most of his oeuvre, Boetti, with Rossi's help, added hand-applied touches to almost every sheet, drawing a *ill. p. 60* mustache onto a print of Andy Warhol's *Jackie* (his take on Duchamp's alteration of the *Mona Lisa*), or using vinyl stencils for more complicated outlines.

Almost simultaneously, Boetti and Sauzeau began a vastly more ambitious project, embarking on a correspondence with scientists and volunteers around the world that would continue for several years, and which would eventually result in two monumental embroideries and a book (which they hoped would be used as *ill. p. 213* a teaching tool): *Classifying: The Thousand Longest Rivers in the World* (1976–82; and 1977). For this project, Boetti and Sauzeau tried to determine, with some verifiable certainty, a list of the thousand longest rivers in descending order, complete with their actual length. Given the lack of precision over where one body of water begins and another ends, where tributaries change names and the frequent border crossings that must be made by nearly all long rivers, and the resultant changes in measurement, this enterprise seems almost poetically impossible. And yet, after several years, a book listing all thousand rivers in descending order of length, with as much scientific data as could be gathered, appeared in print in a limited edition of five hundred copies. Two large embroideries, the first in a rich emerald green and the second in a silvery white, celebrate the finished project. This project, certainly the most ambitious, research-intensive and symbolically far-reaching of Boetti's work so far, further shifted the artist's interest in plenitude and its organization, in the relationship between the unclassifiable multitude of the world around us and our continued attempt to impose order, narrative, sequence, and relations between them.

One of Boetti's sculptural experiments of the 1960s consisted of a bucket containing a shallow layer of plaster, hardened and then fractured into a jigsaw puzzle of in- *ill. p. 23* terlocking forms. This work, *Pack* (1967) did not survive, but the outlines of its image, a group of tightly fitting interlocking random forms contained within the circle of the round vessel, continued to fascinate him. In several mail works made during the 1970s, as well as in an early embroidery from 1975 that repeats the early work's name, Boetti developed the idea of a multitude of interlocking forms into new constellations. Beginning in 1982, after the completion of the Thousand Rivers project, he added another series to his repertoire of embroi- *ill. pp. 232-237* deries, "tutto" (Everything), which he would continue to develop until his death in 1994. For "tutto," Boetti designed fields of densely interlocking forms and objects, some recognizable, like tools or plants, others more vaguely reminiscent of elements of the visible world, comparable to the way in which we sometimes see animal forms in cloud formations. Executed in a riot of color and on an increasingly monumental scale—the largest *Tutto* (1994) *ill. pp. 236-237* measures more than 18 feet in width—these works are celebrations of the sheer diversity and difference of things on earth. They show Boetti at his most joyous, generously embracing all that surrounds us.

Two final works would conclude Boetti's oeuvre, cut short by his illness and death at only fifty-four years of age. The kilims (1993) are fifty carpets designed in collaboration with fifty student classes across many art schools in France and woven by master carpet-weavers in Pakistan—a collaborative work of enormous complexity and tremendous generosity toward his collaborators. The design of the kilims explores the mutation *ill. pp. 251-257* of white square into a black one: the carpet is made up of 100 squares, the first one all white, the last all black, with each intervening square changing one pixel at a time from light to dark. In the process, the figure-ground relationship shifts from a dark figure on a light ground to its reverse, and the growing number of pixels allows for ever different formations and graphic forms.

The final work of Boetti's life, perhaps fittingly, is a self-portrait: a life-size bronze cast of the artist holding *ill. p. 256* a water hose, which releases a small steady fountain onto the sculpture's head, which is heated from within so that a small puff of steam emanates from it on contact with the water. Sometimes nicknamed "*Mi fume il mio cervello*" (My brain is smoking), the sculpture casts an elegiac glance onto an interrupted life, with so many things not yet done, so many ideas unexecuted, so much of the great plenitude of the world yet to be explored.

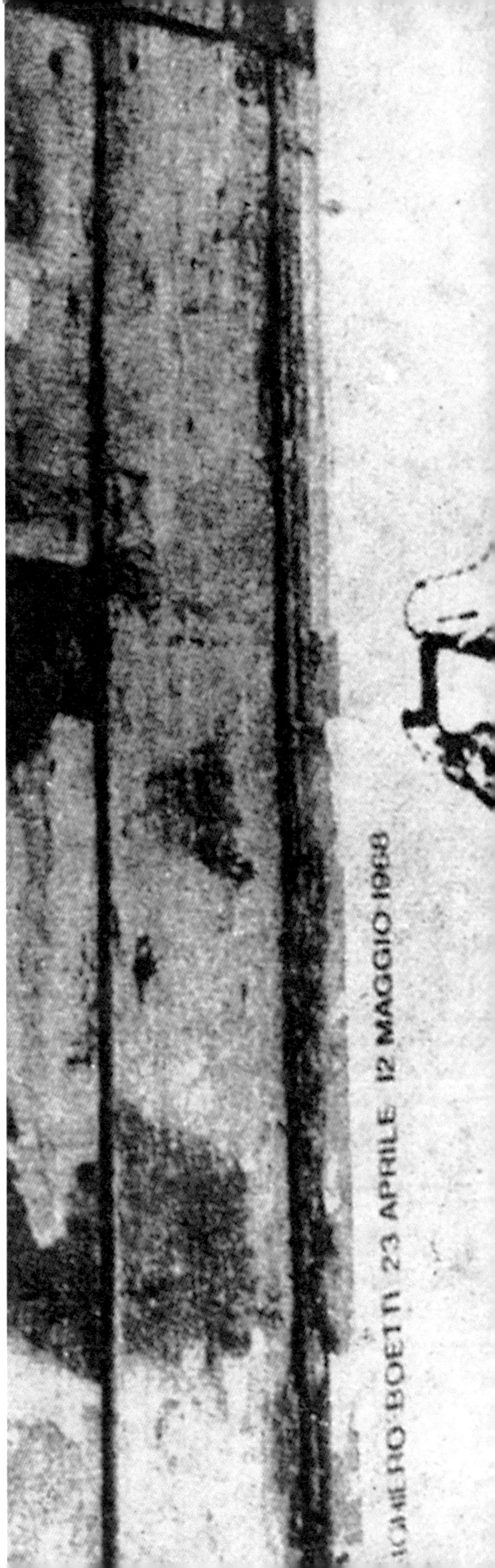

Shaman/Showman fly-posted in a street in Milan, April 1968

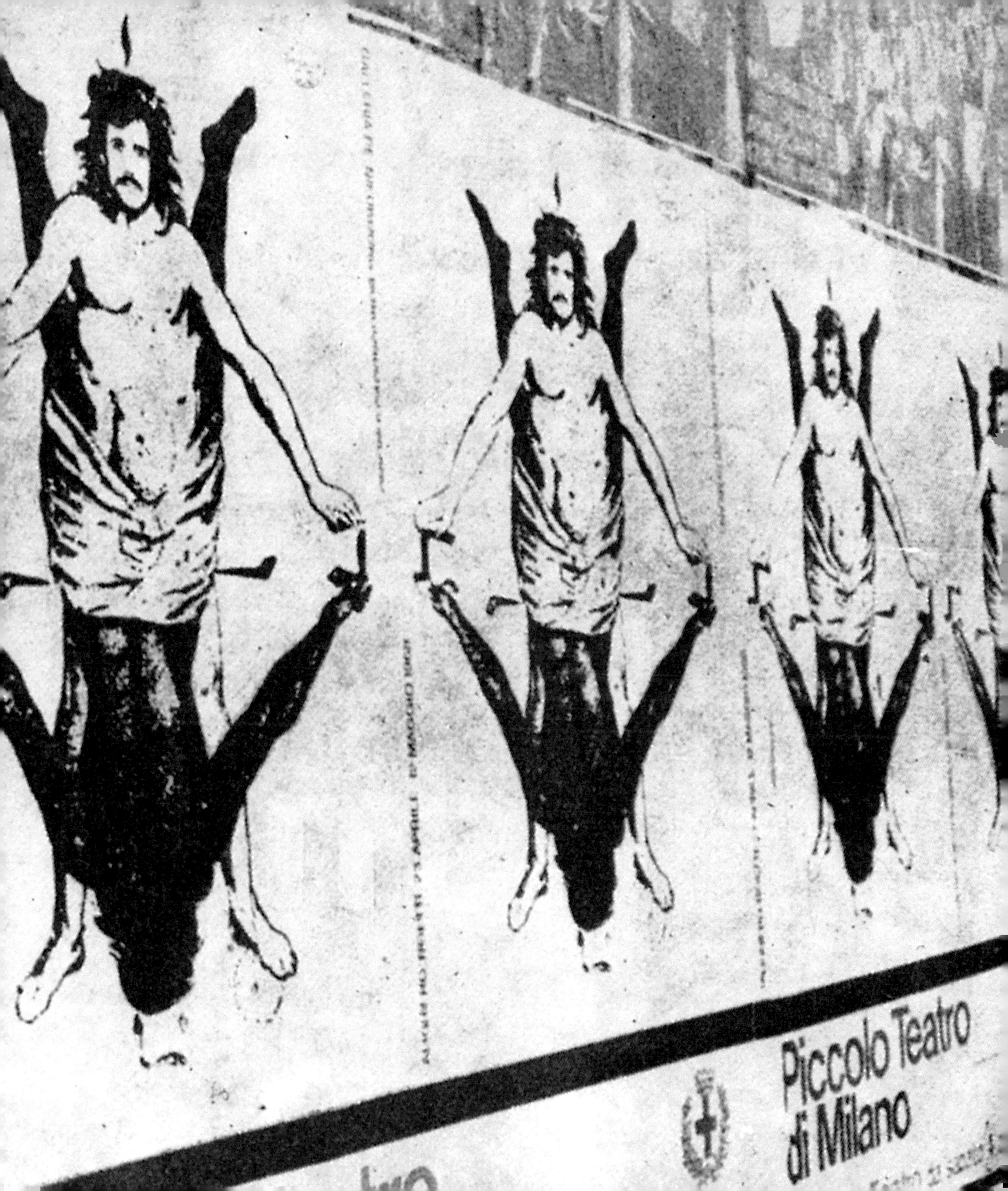
Piccolo Teatro
di Milano

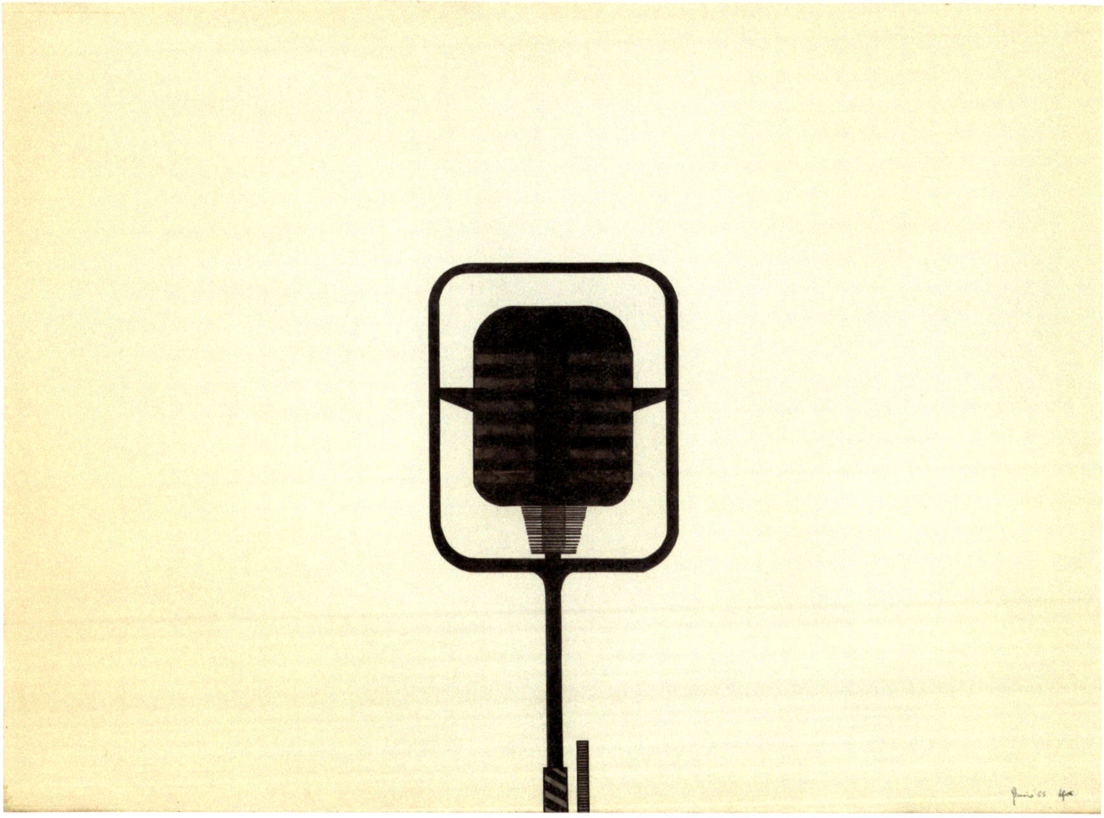

Untitled, 1965

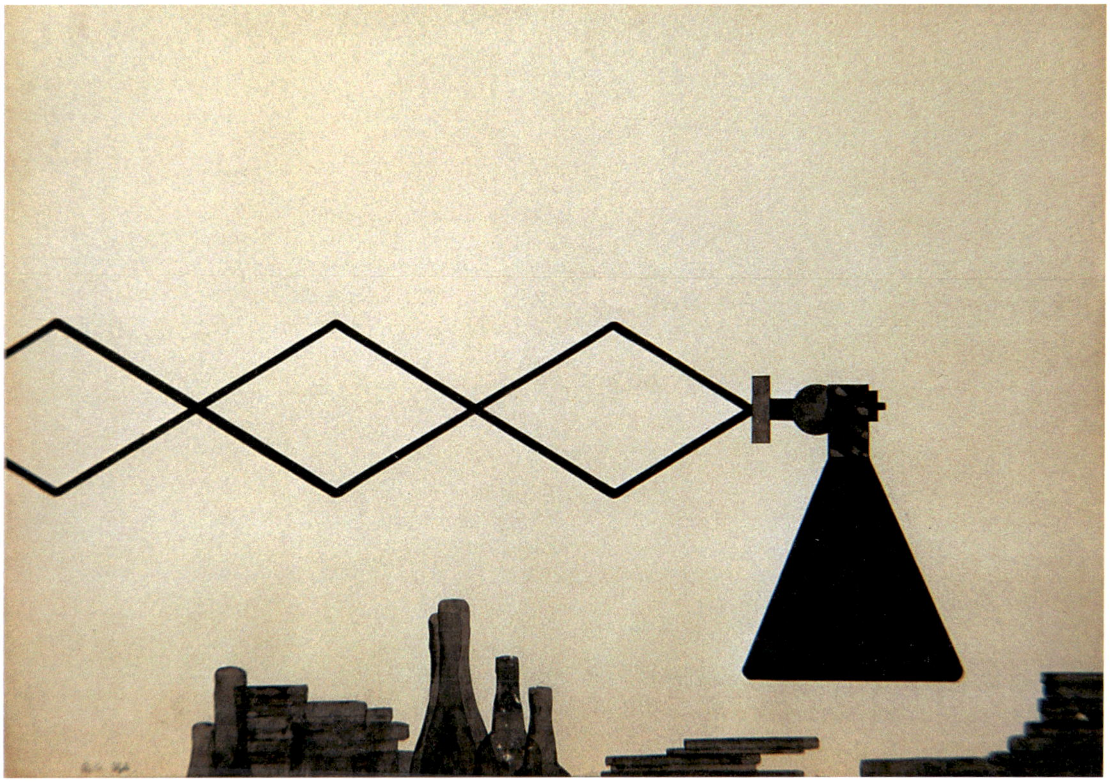

 Untitled, 1965

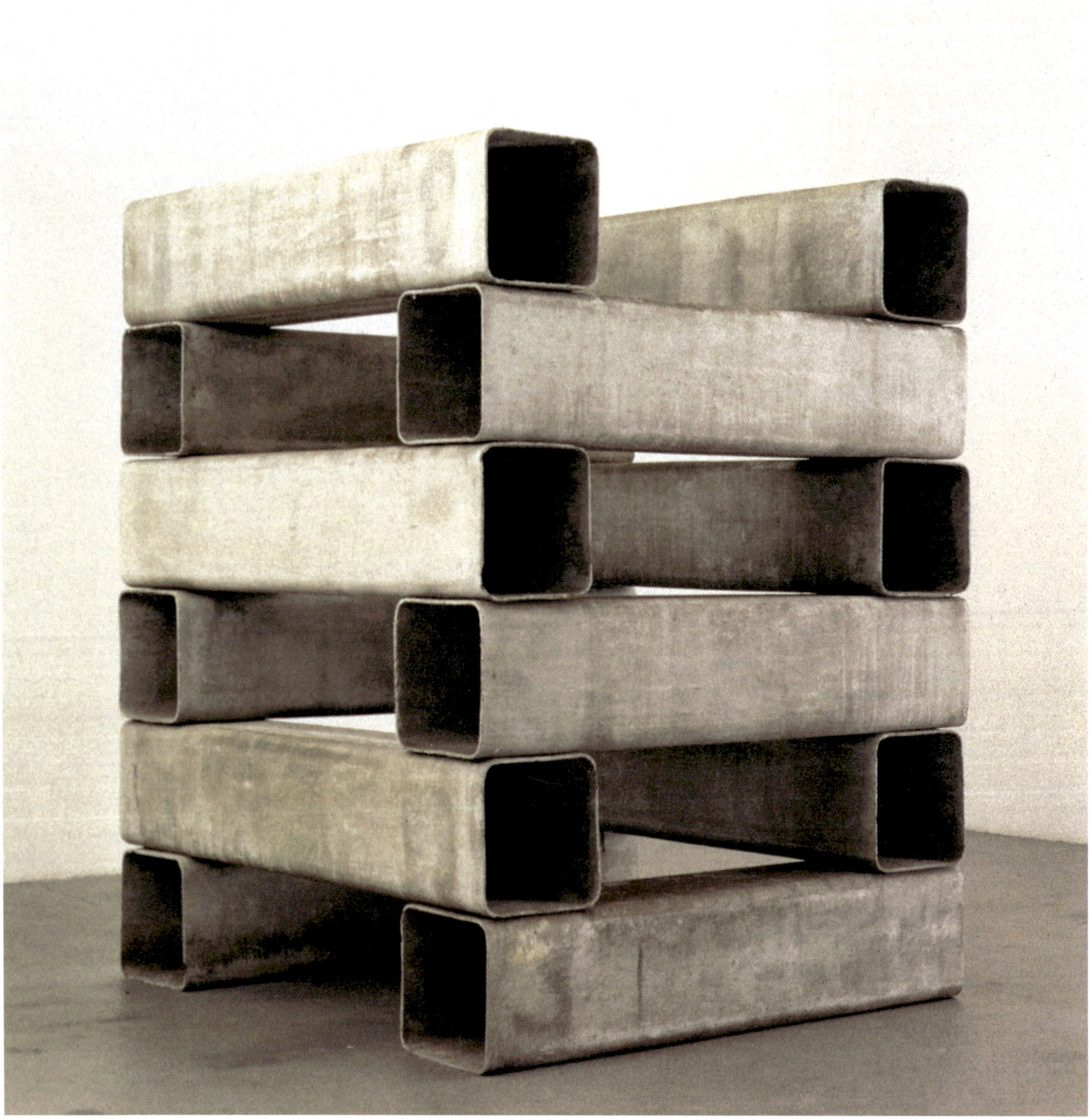

Catasta (Stack), 1967 / Rotolo di cartone ondulato (Roll of Corrugated Cardboard), 1966

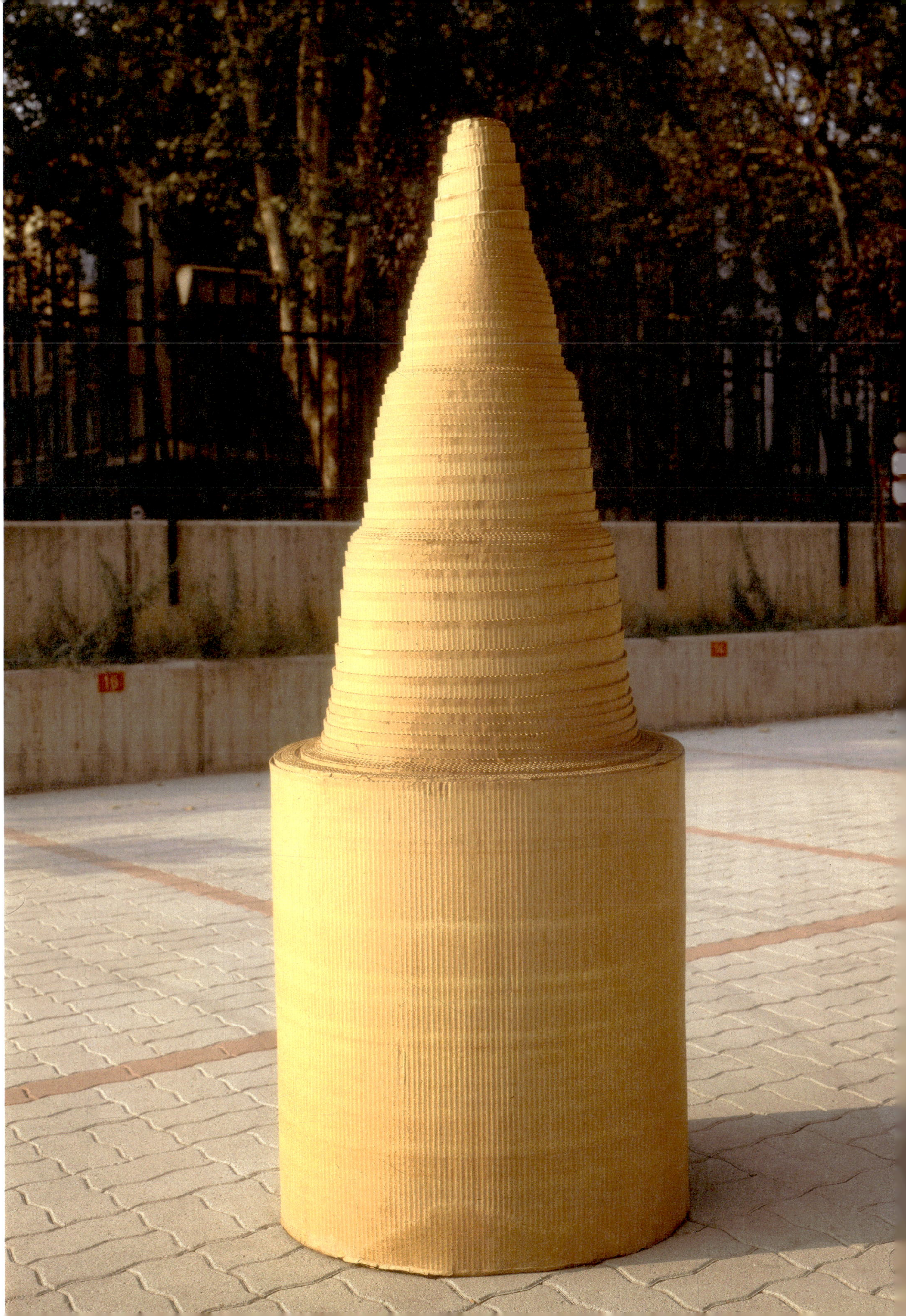

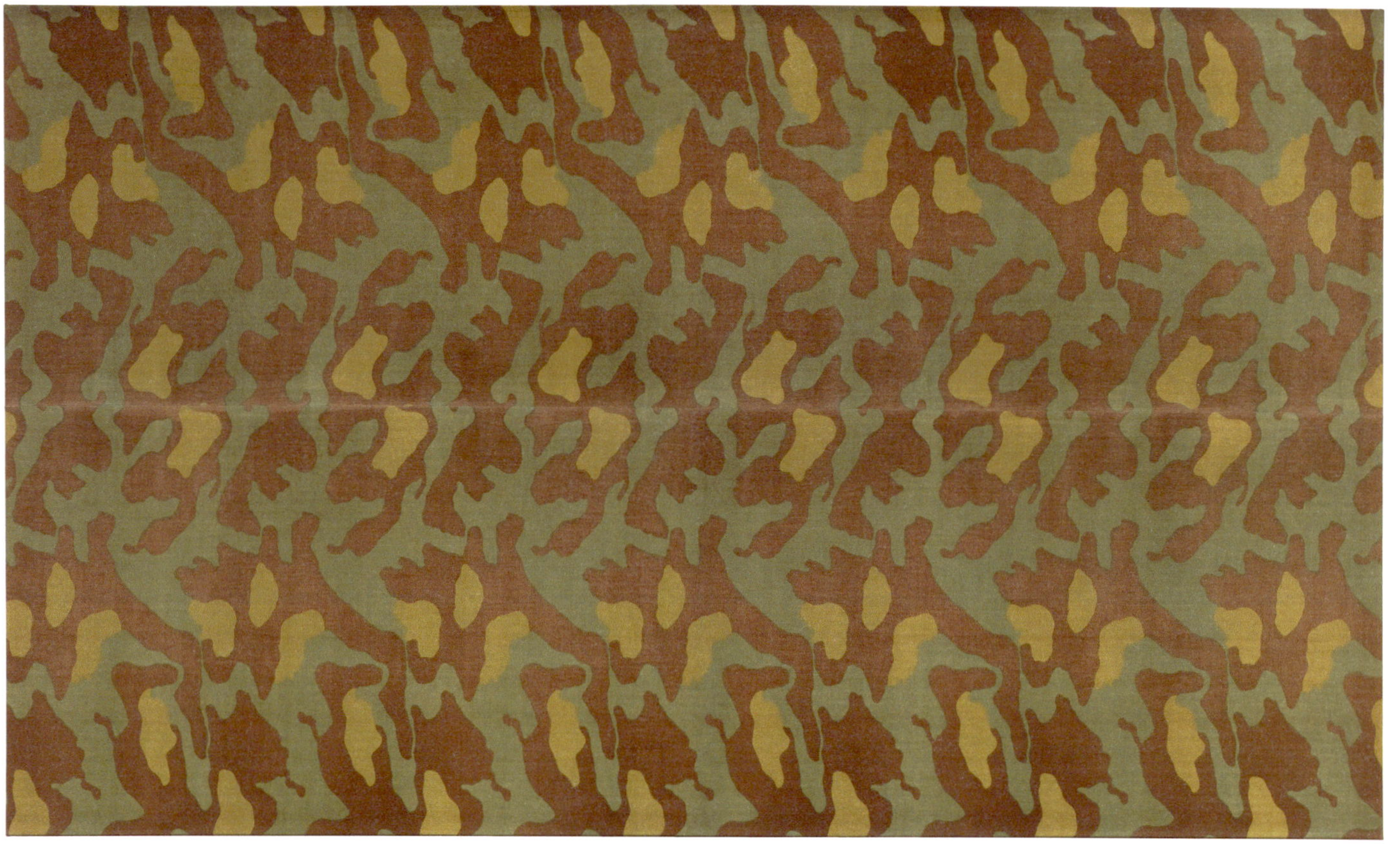

Mimetico (Camouflage), 1966

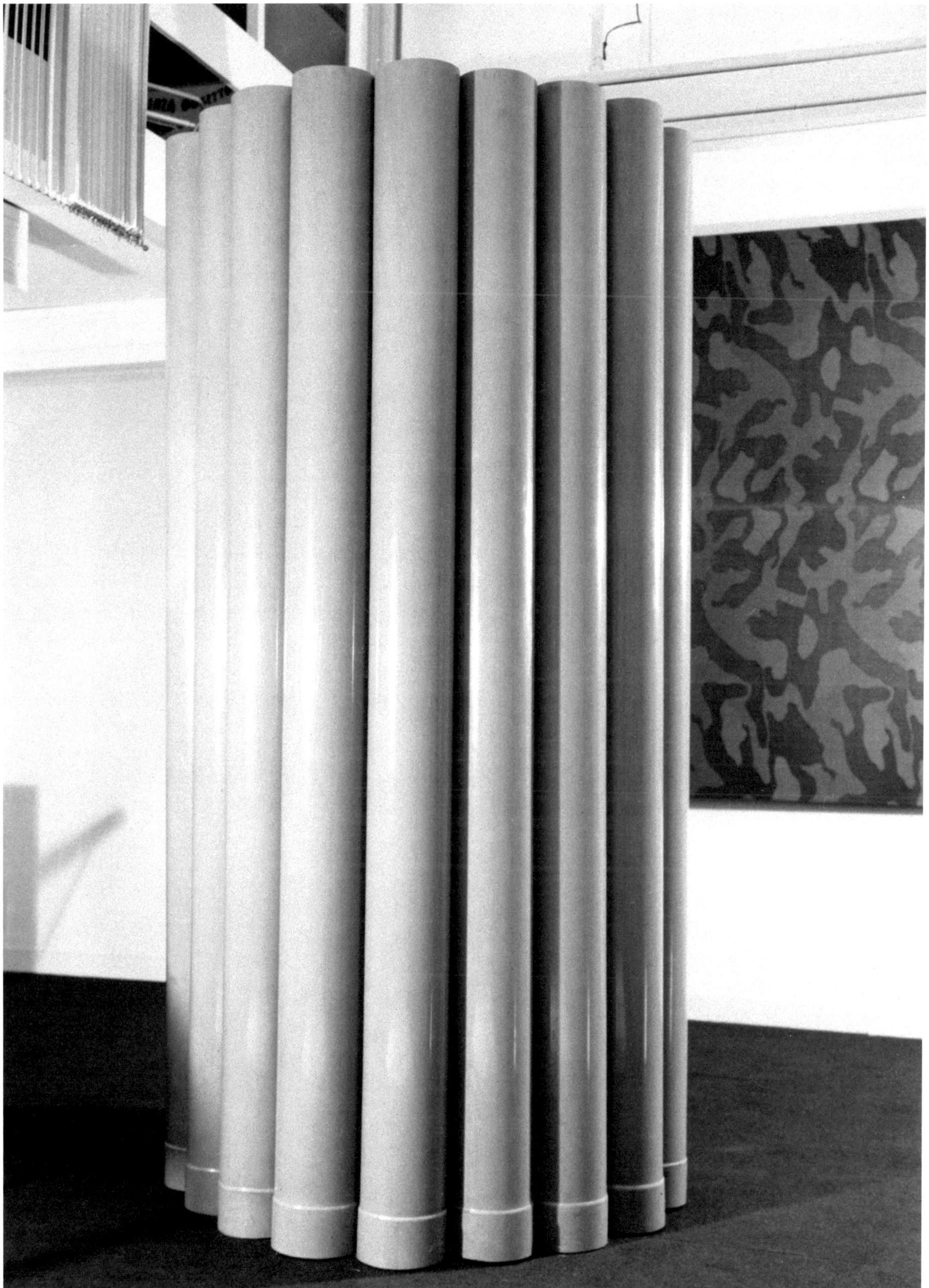

Mazzo di tubi (Cluster of Tubes), 1966

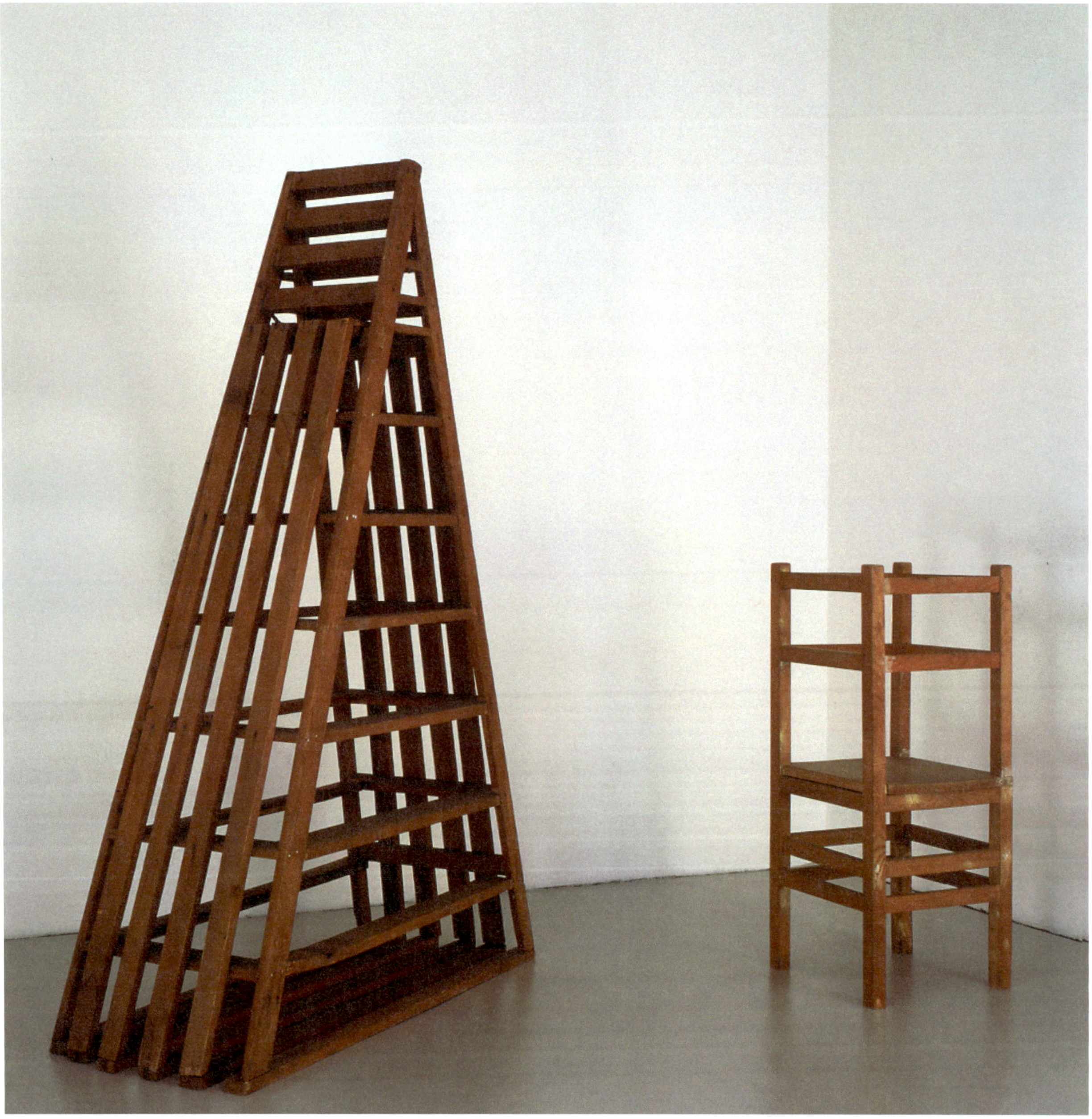

Scala (Ladder) and Sedia (Chair), 1966

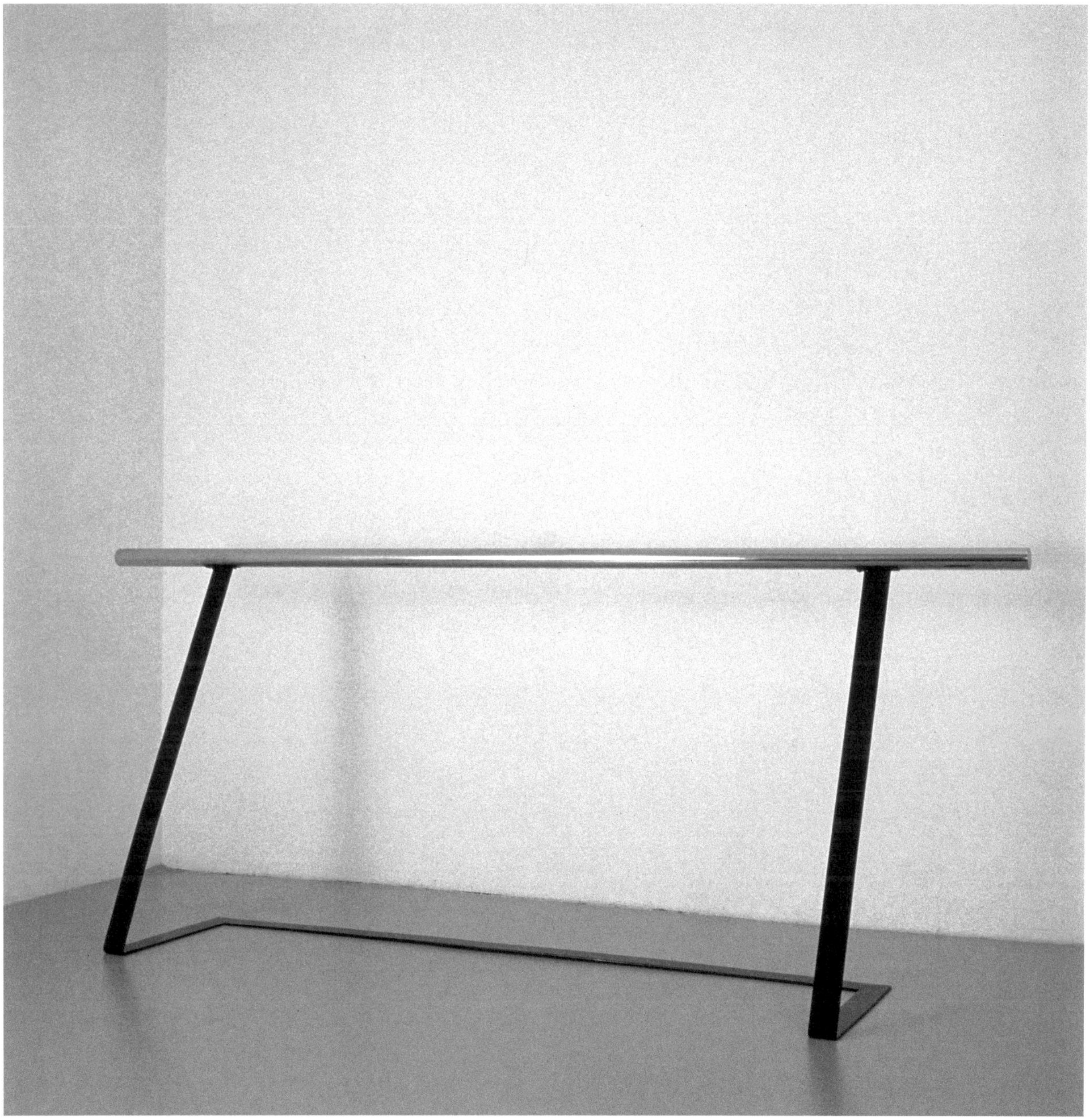

 Mancorrente metri 2 (2 Meter Handrail), 1966

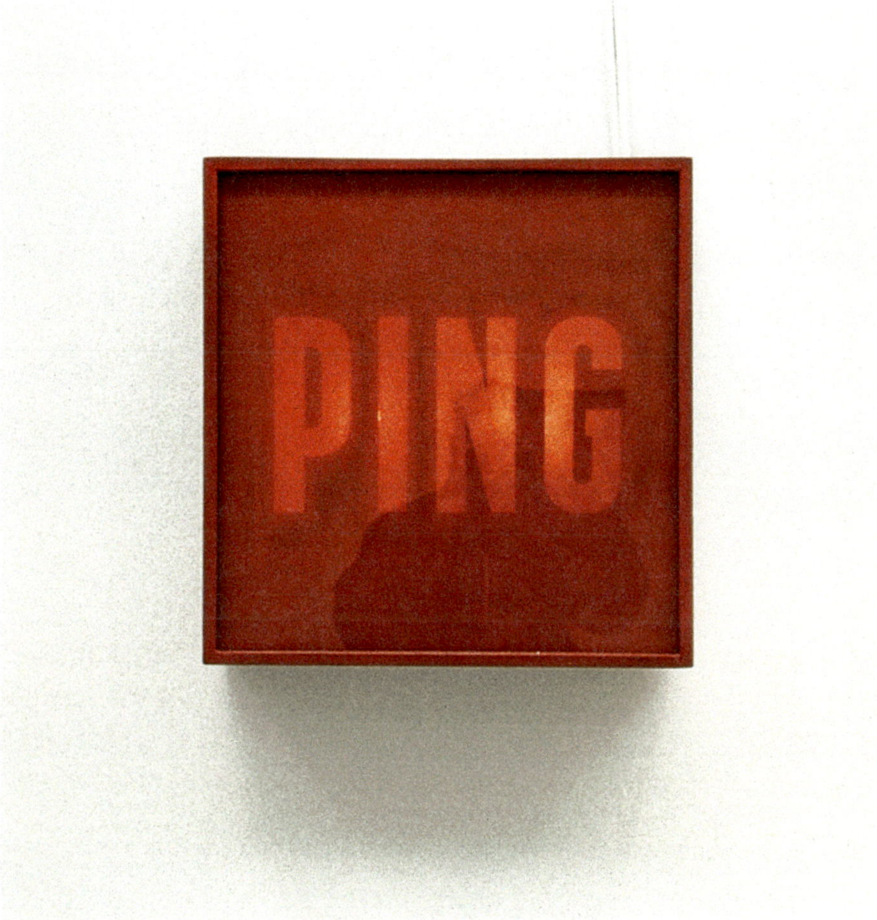

Ping Pong, 1966 (detail)

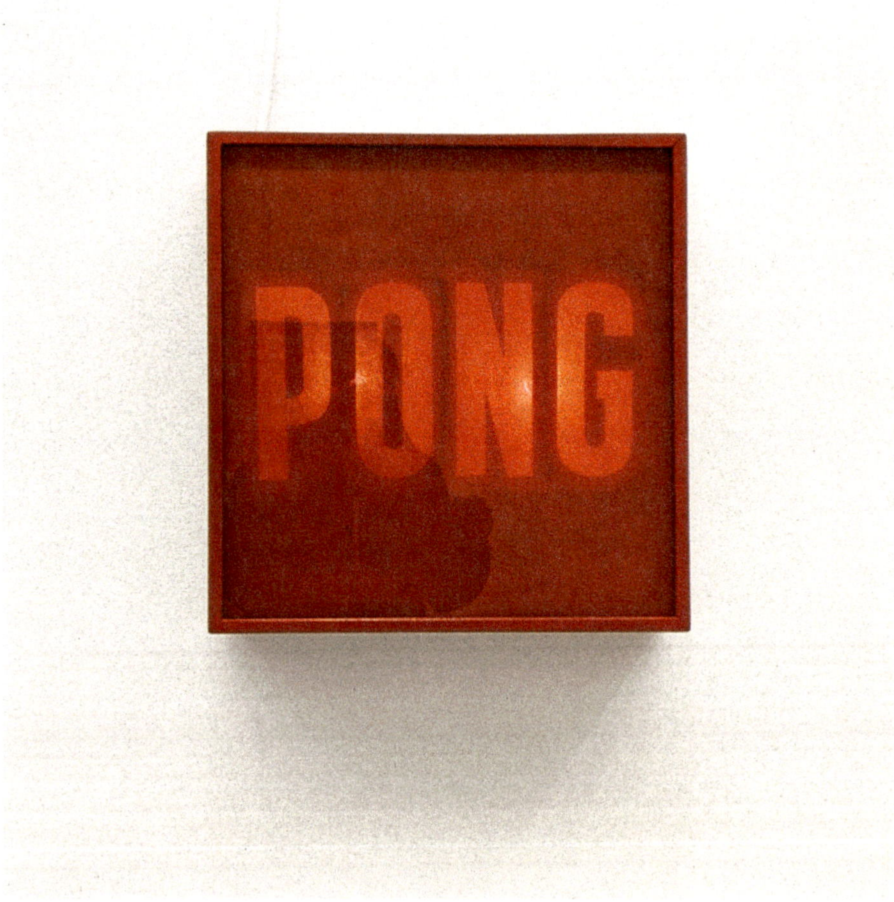

Ping Pong, 1966 (detail) / Colonna (Column), 1968

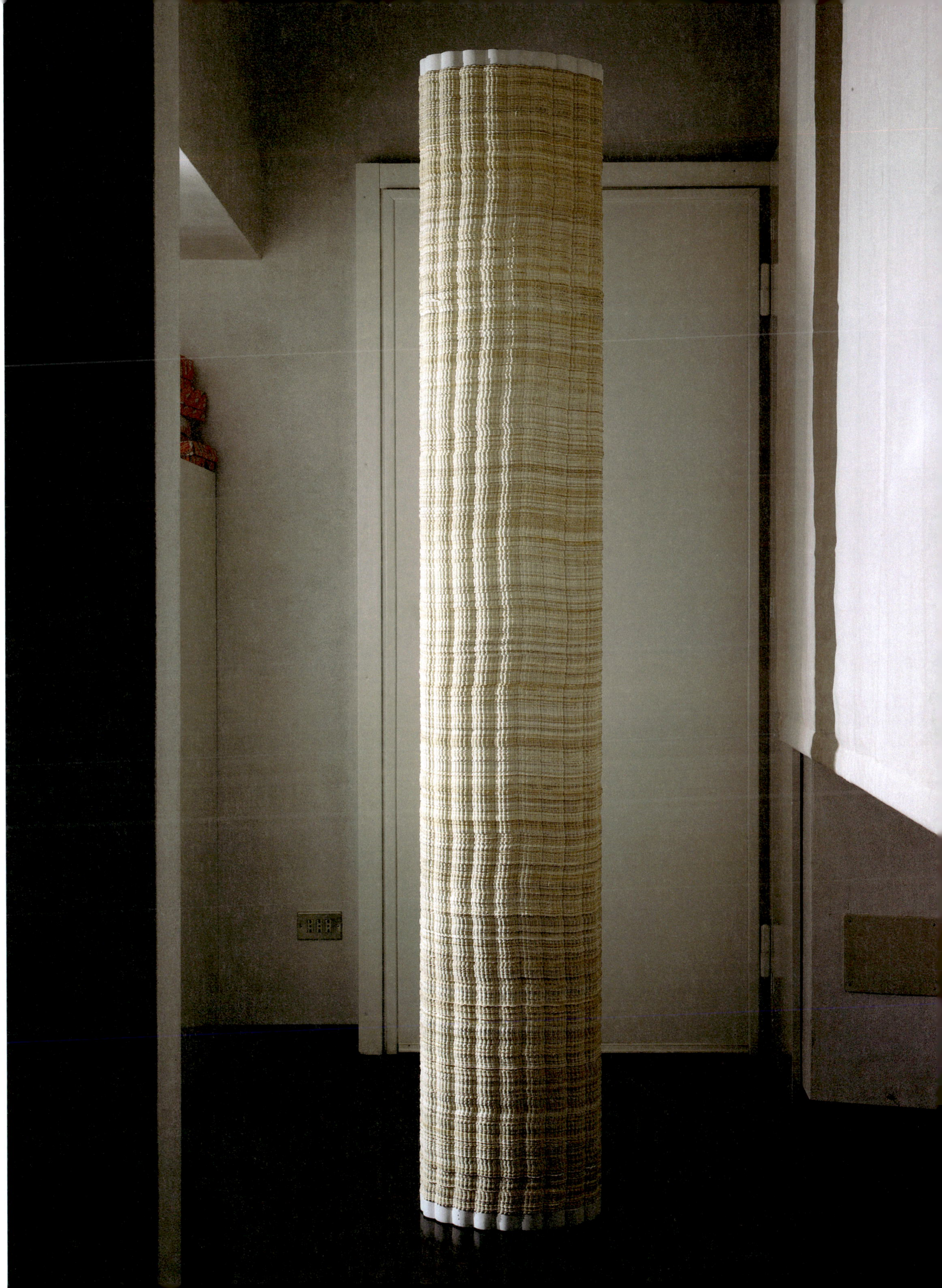

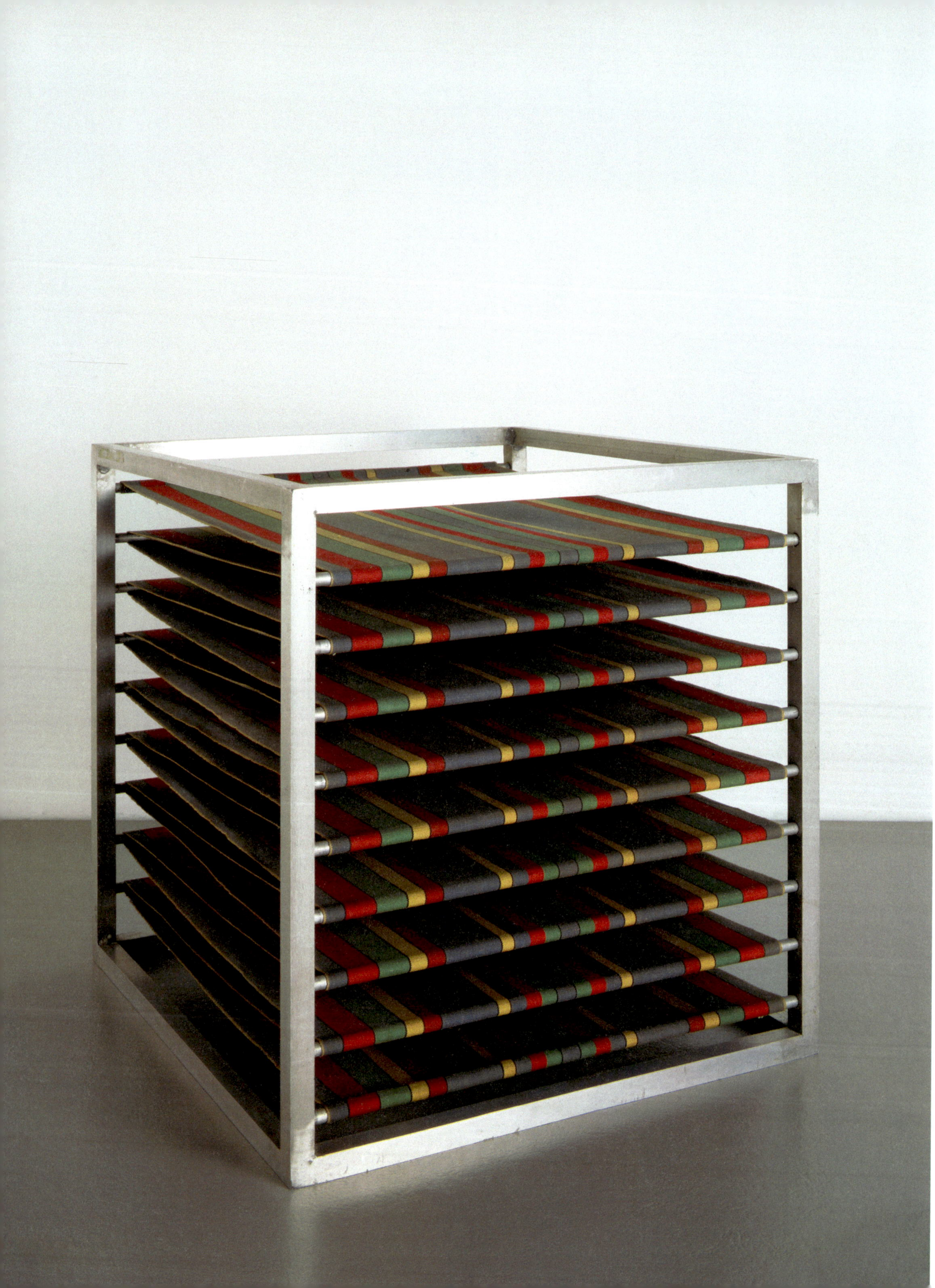

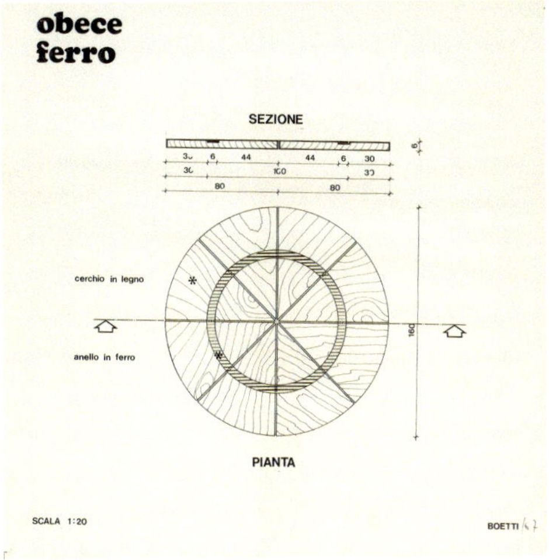

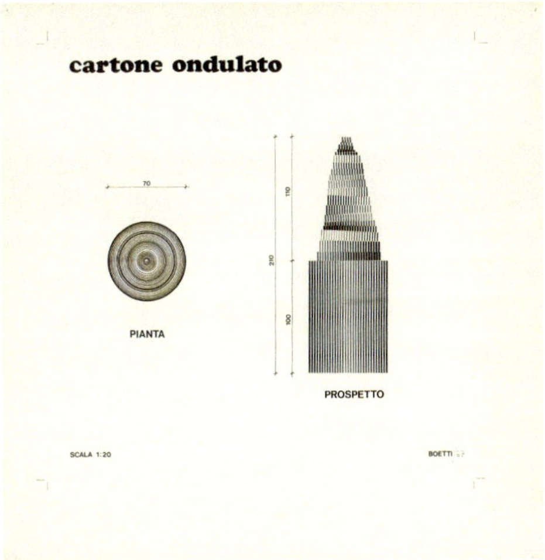

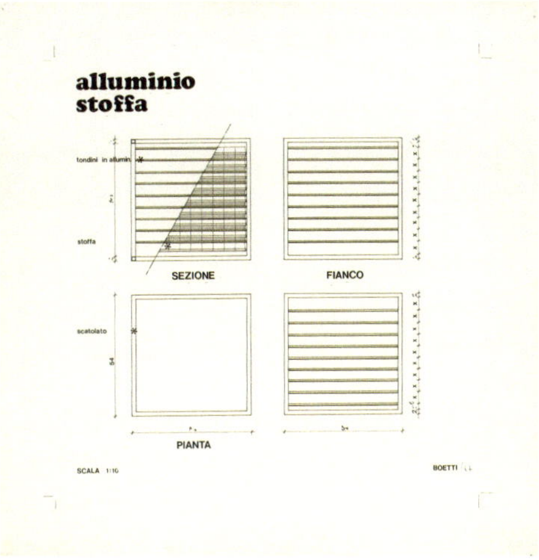

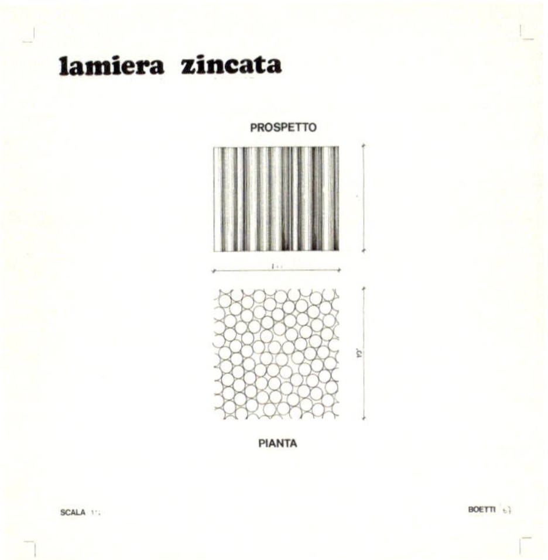

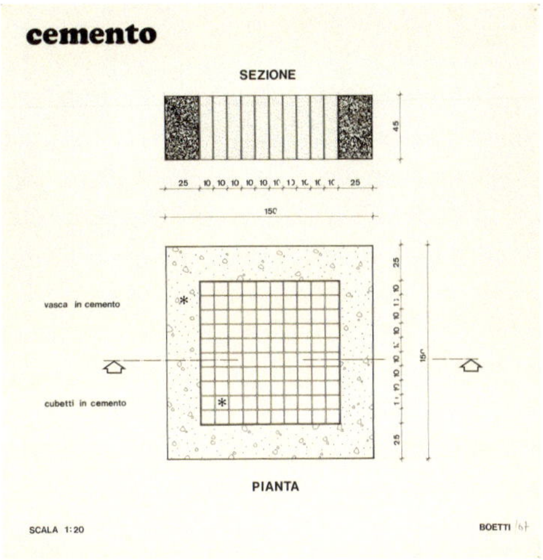

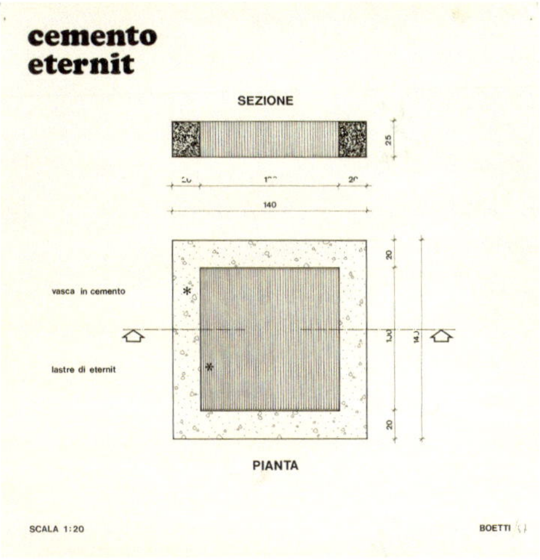

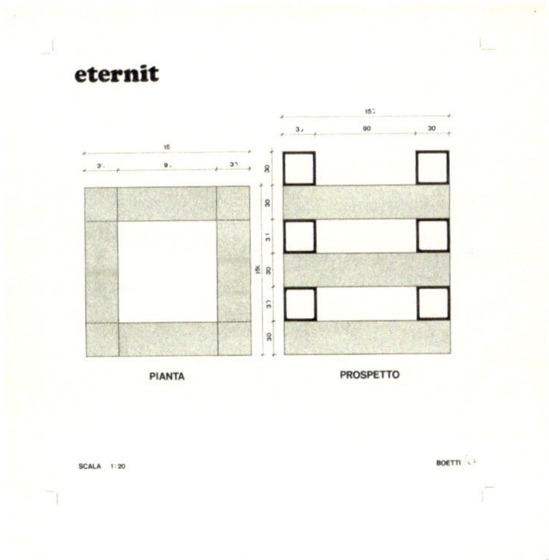

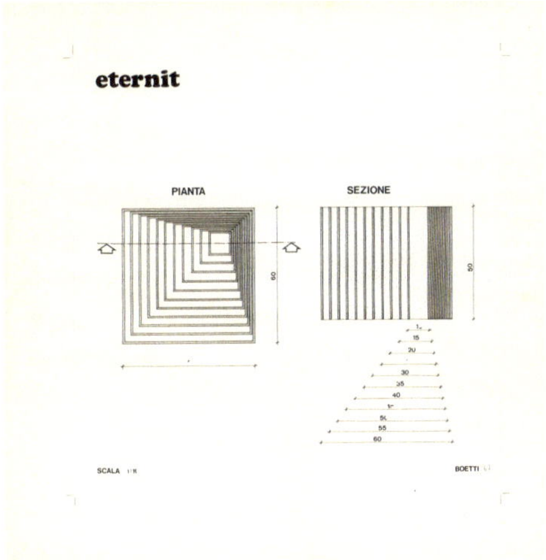

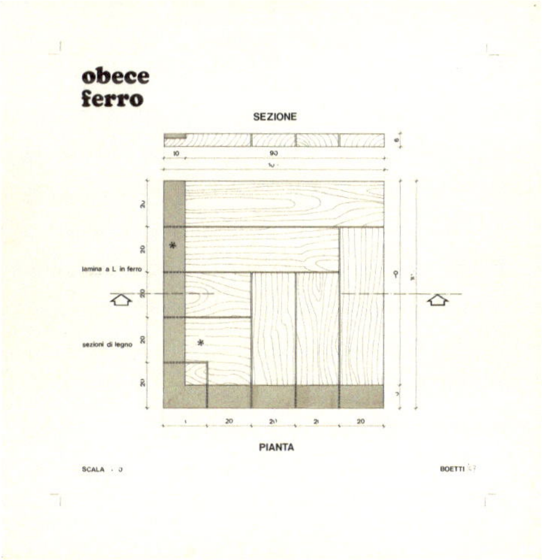

 8,50 (Zig Zag), 1966 / Prefissi e progetti (Prefixes and Projects), 1967

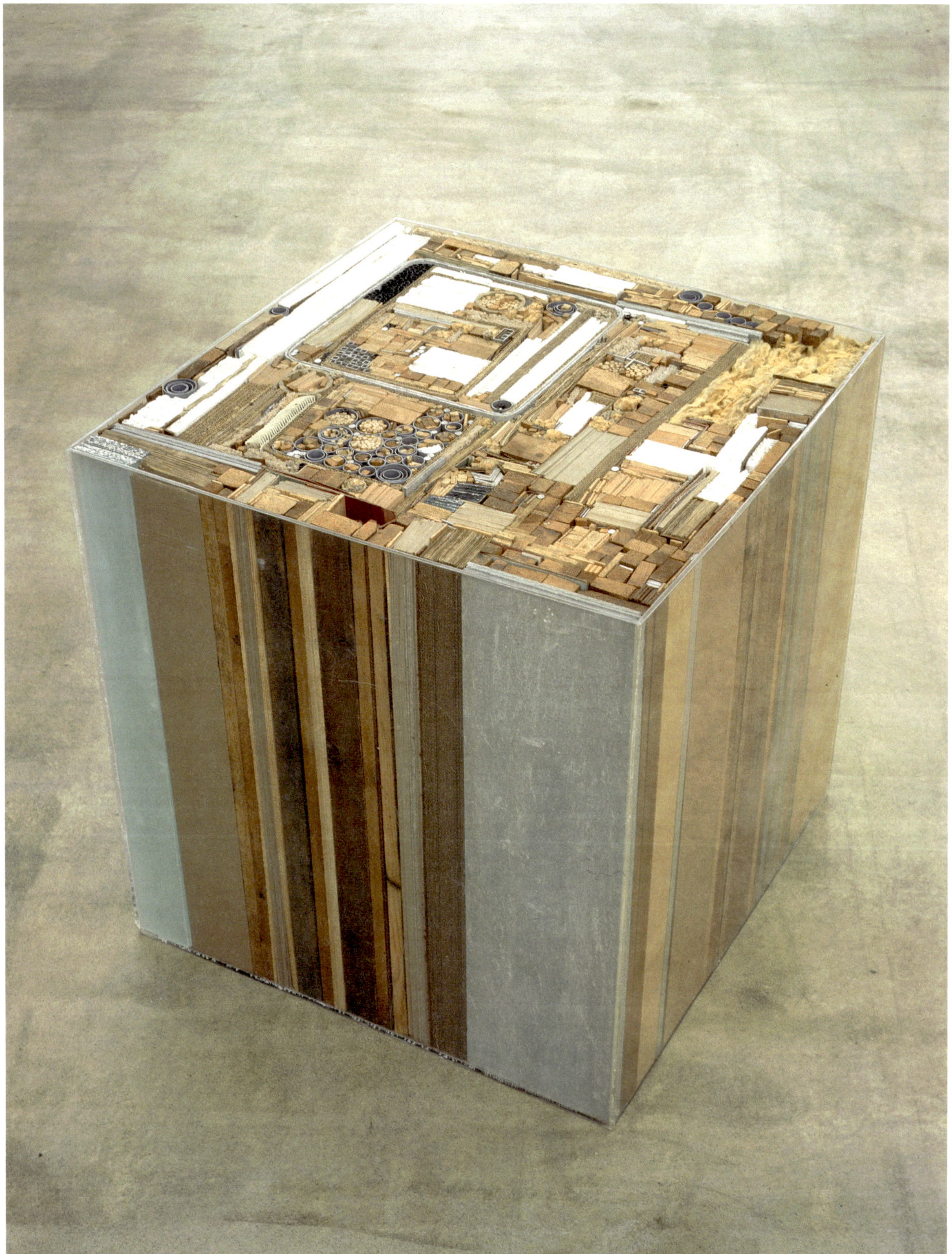

Cubo (Cube), 1968

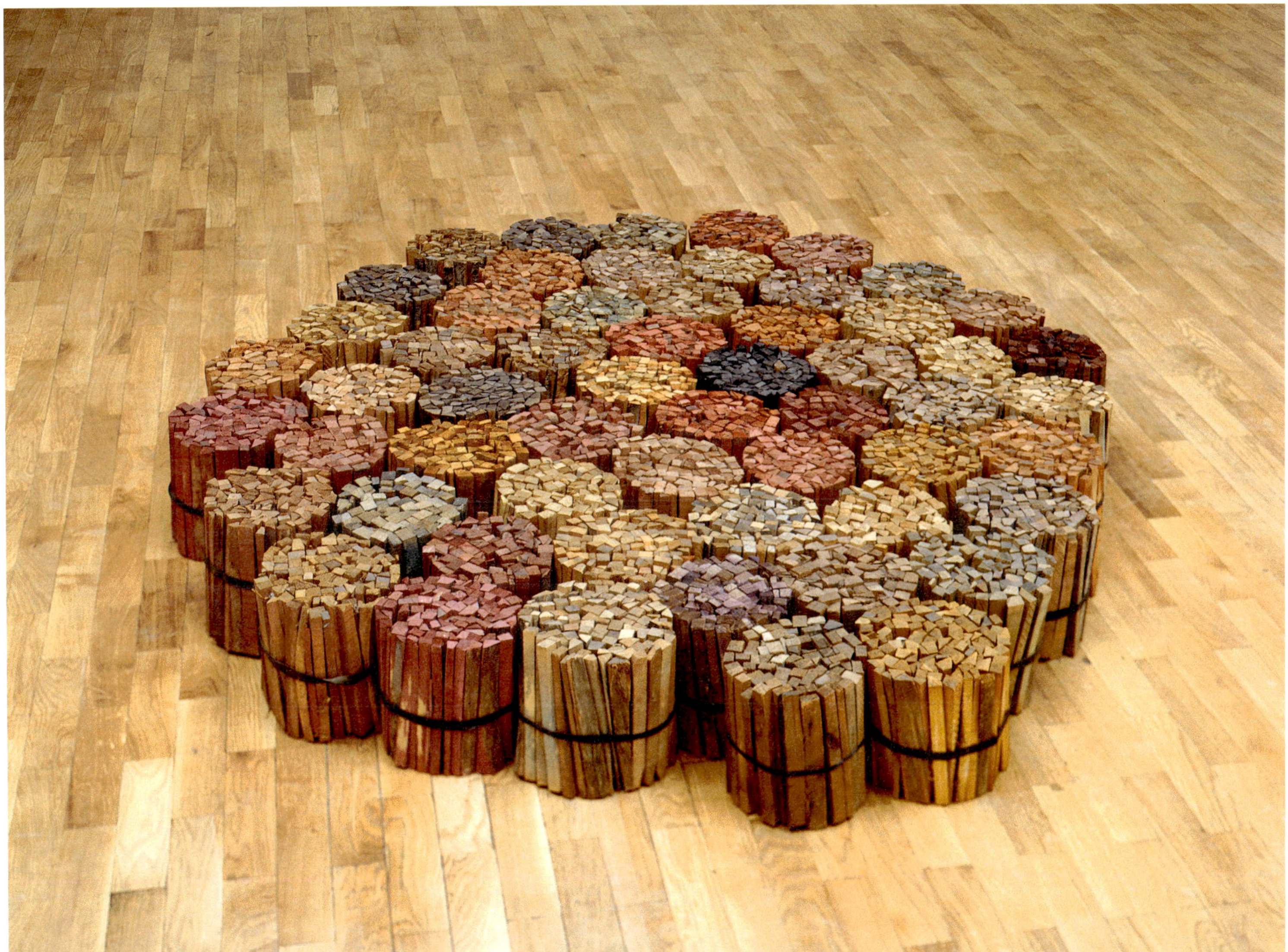

55 Legnetti colorati (Little Colored Sticks), 1968

Pannello luminoso (Light Panel), 1966

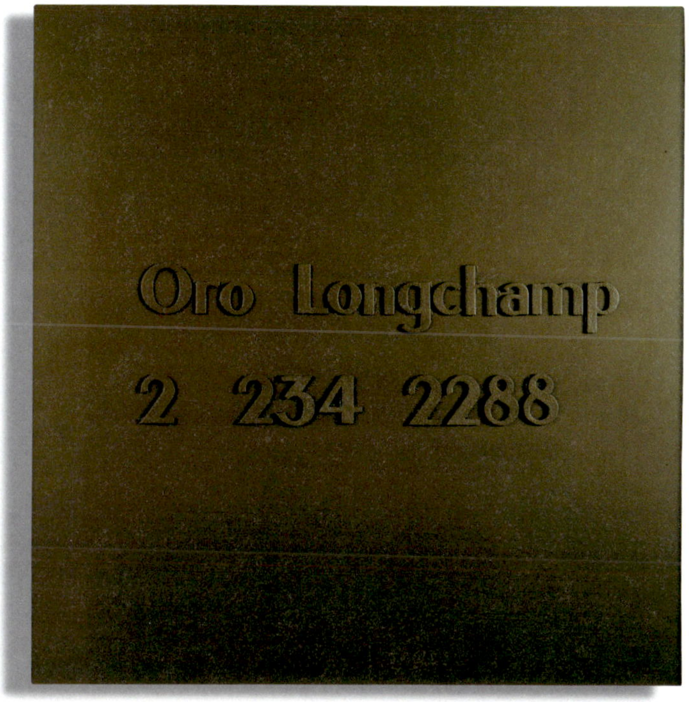

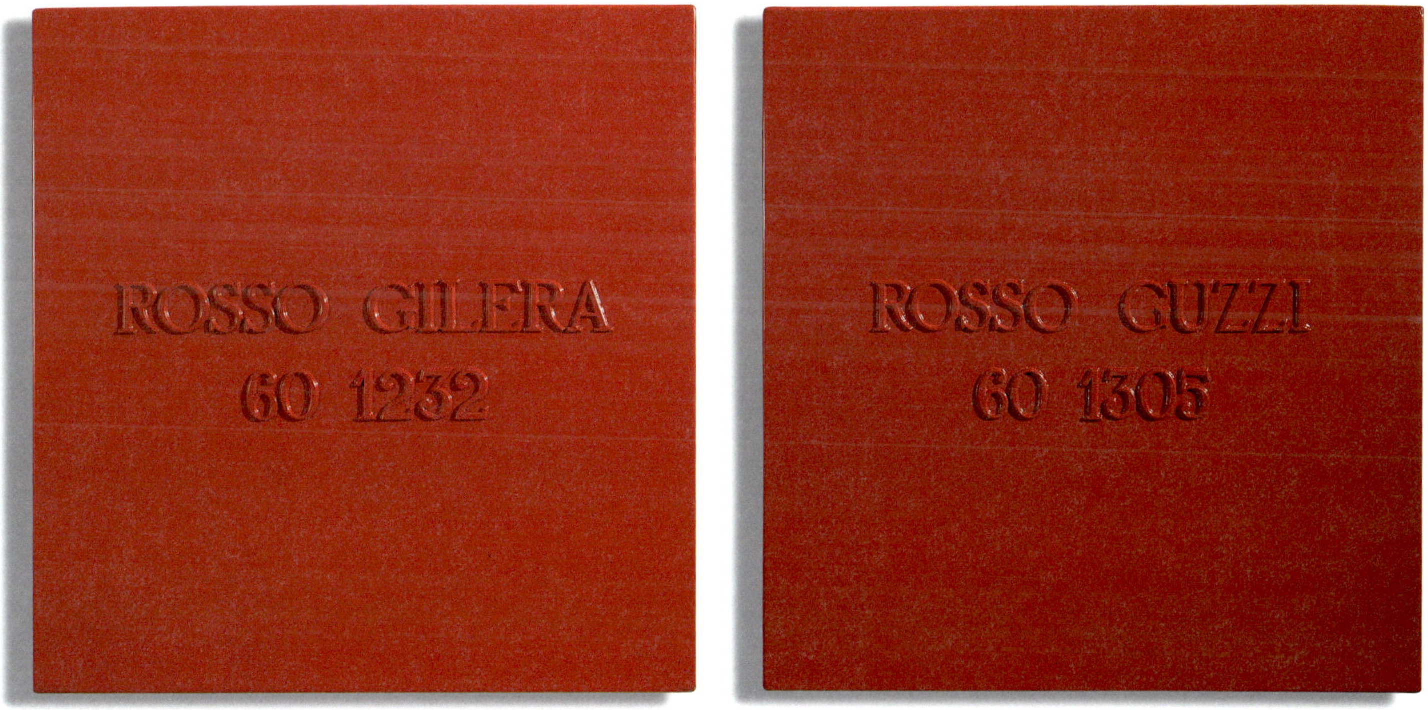

Rosso Palermo 511 52 27, 1967 / Oro Longchamp 2 234 2288, 1967
ROSSO GILERA 60 1232 ROSSO GUZZI 60 1305, 1967

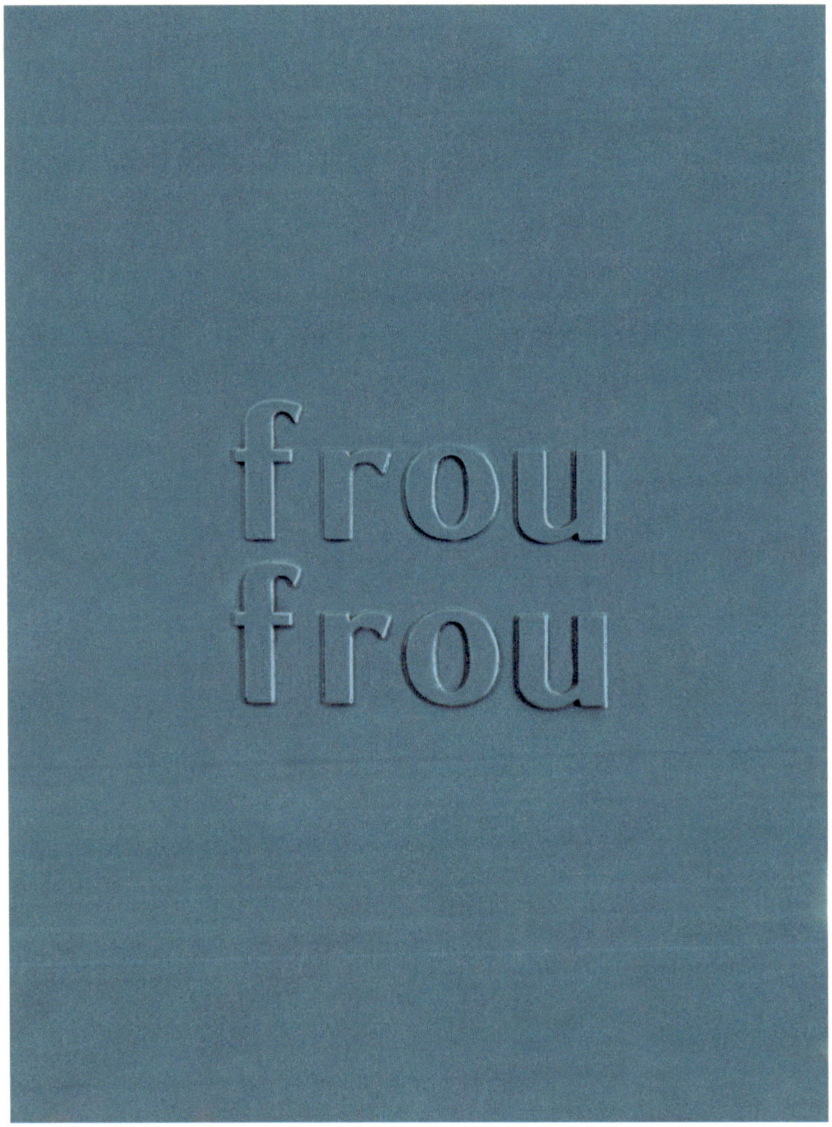

frou frou, 1966

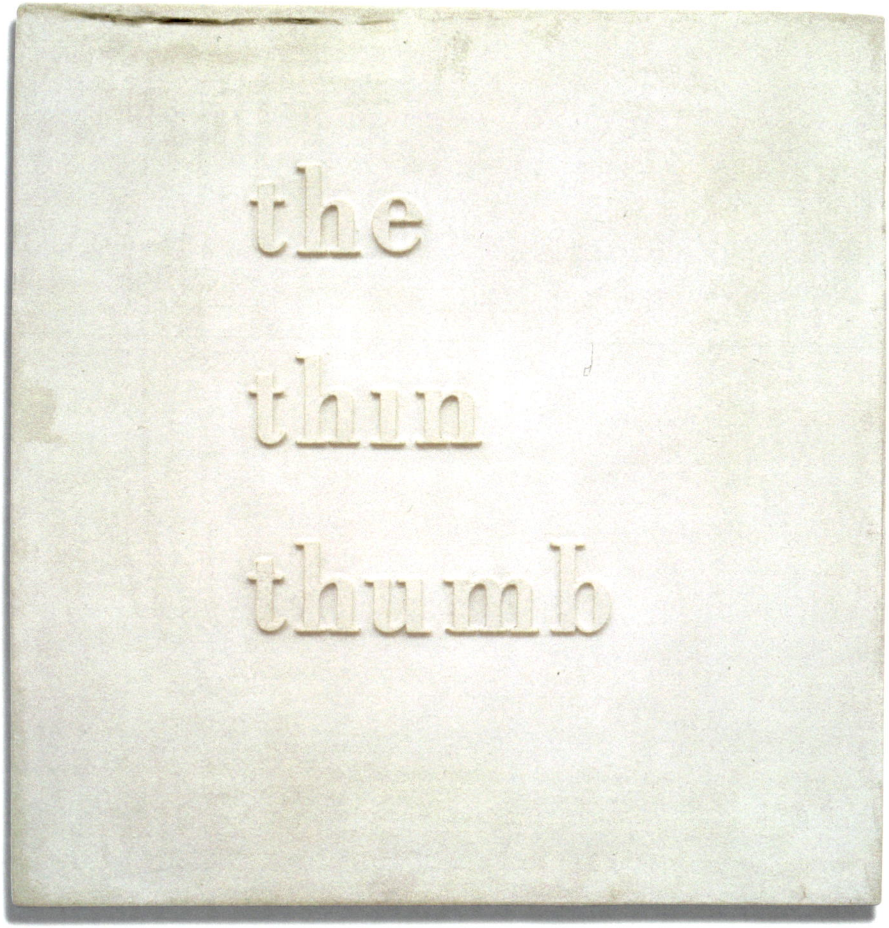

the thin thumb, 1966

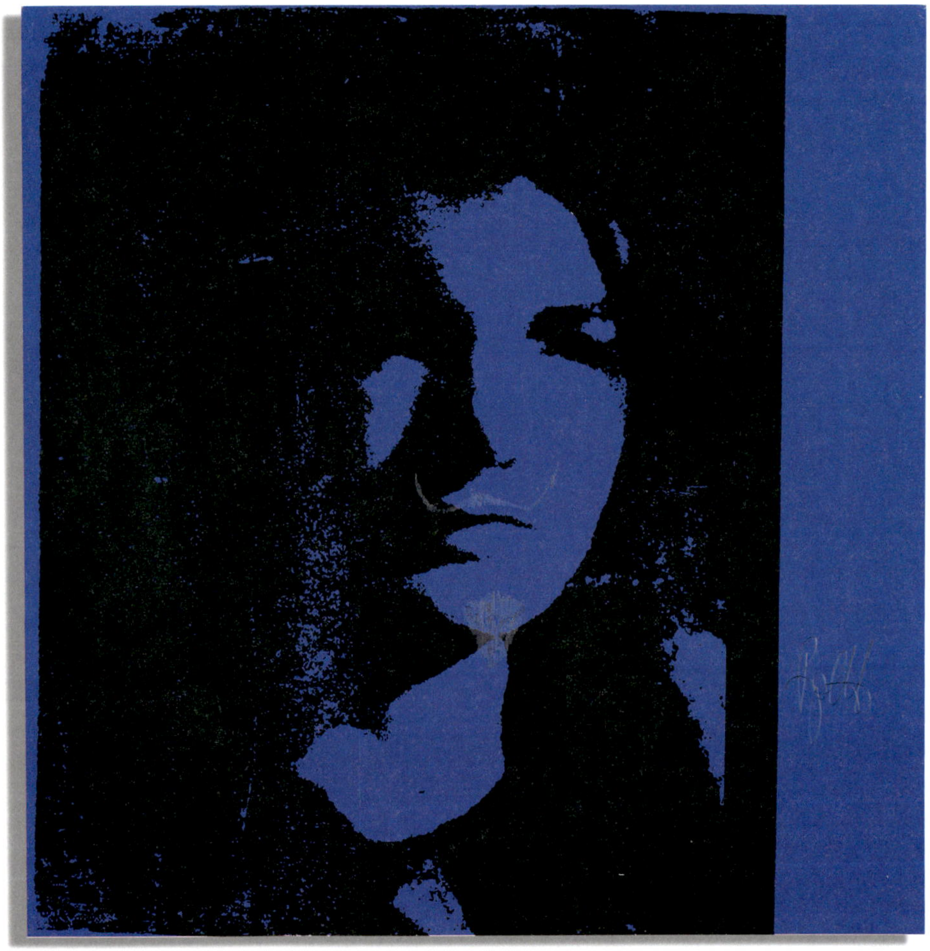

AB : AW = MD : L, 1967

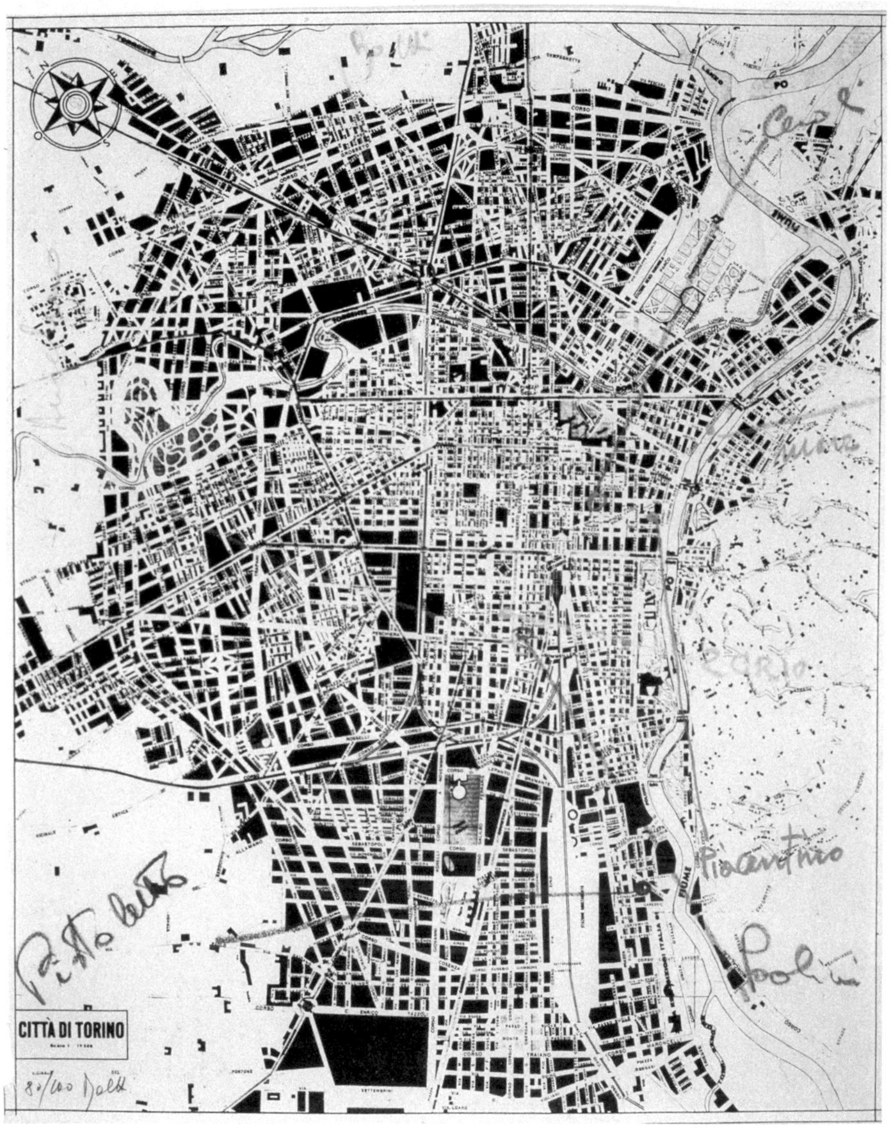

Città di Torino (City of Turin), 1968

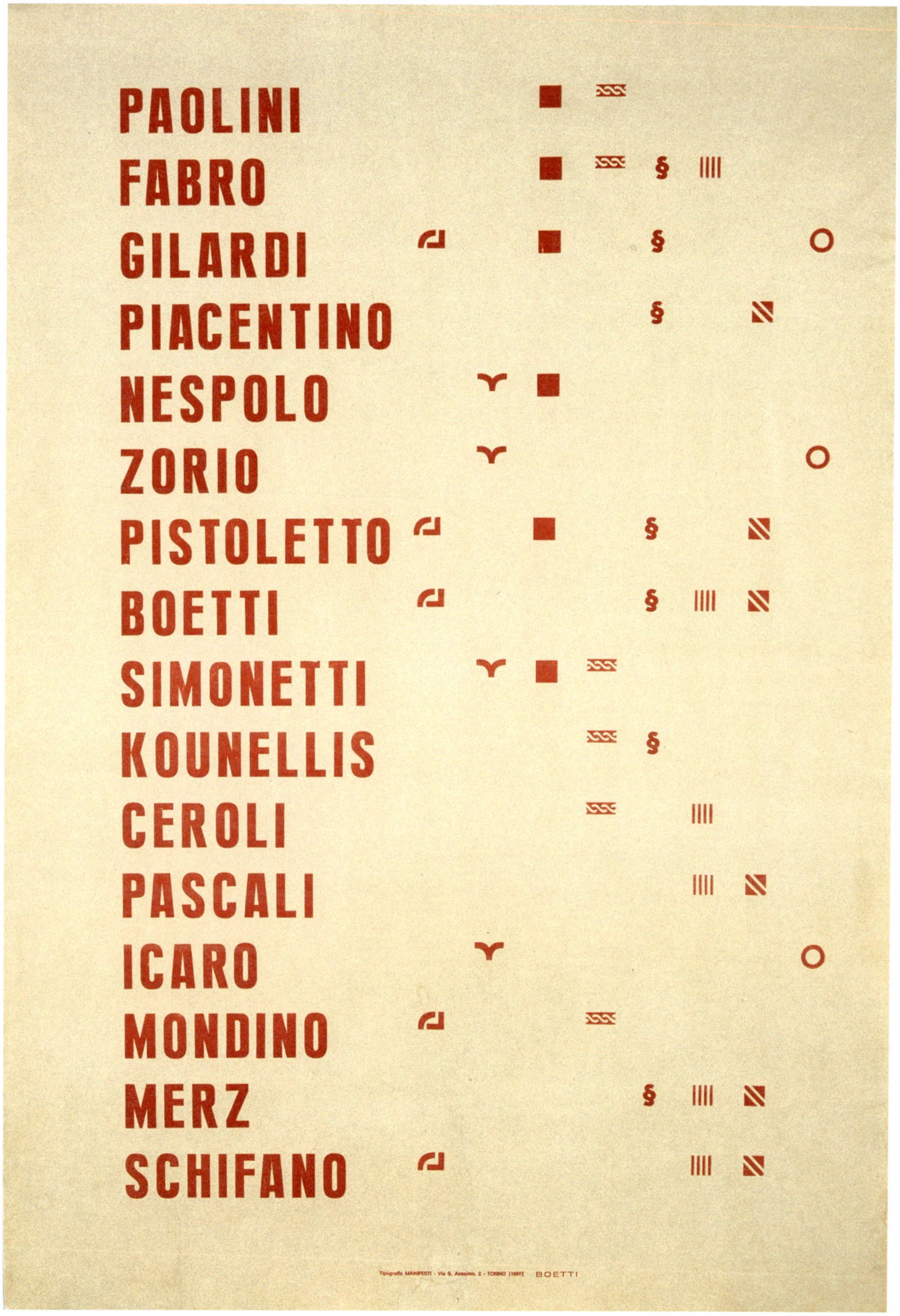

 Manifesto, 1967

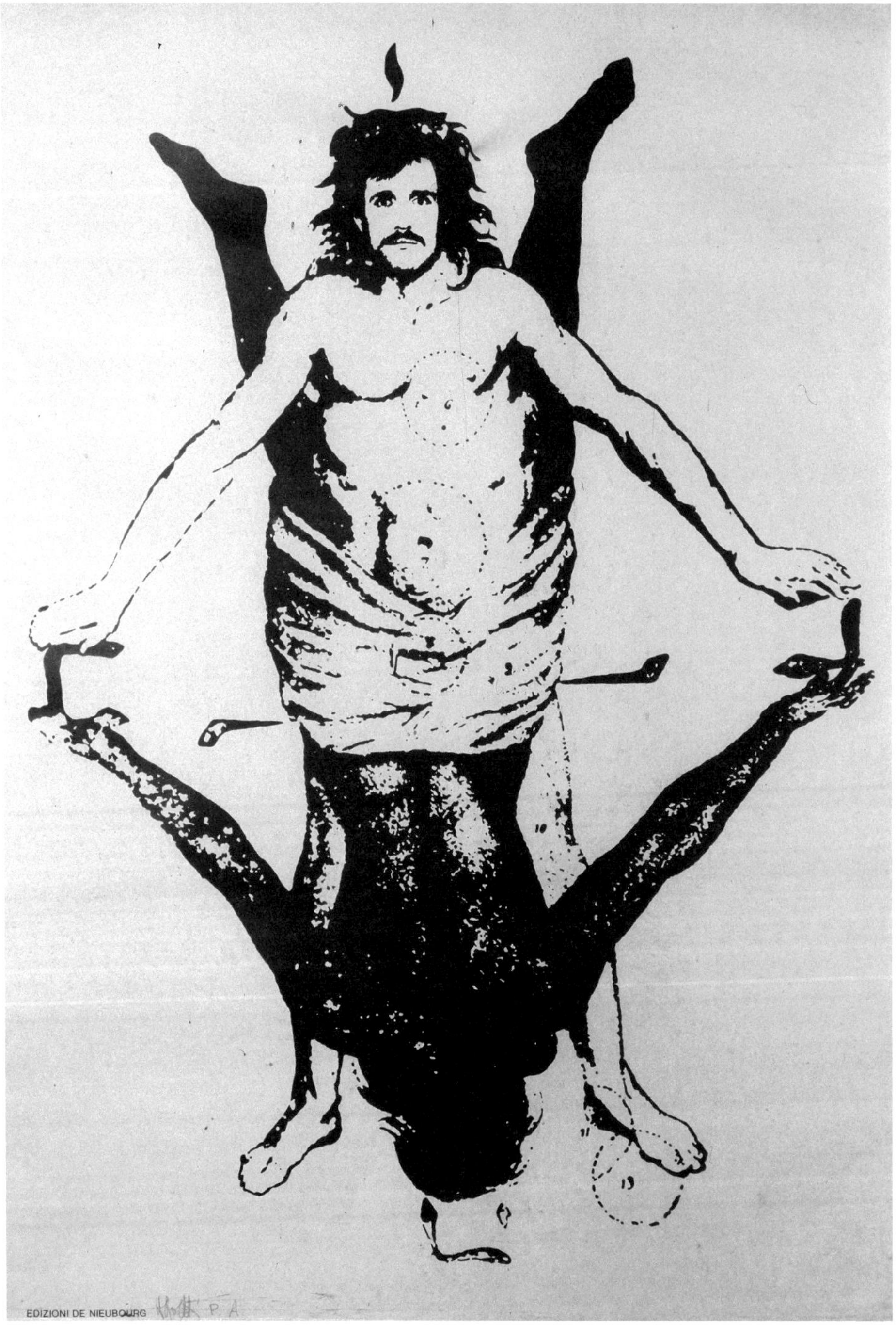

Shaman/Showman, 1968

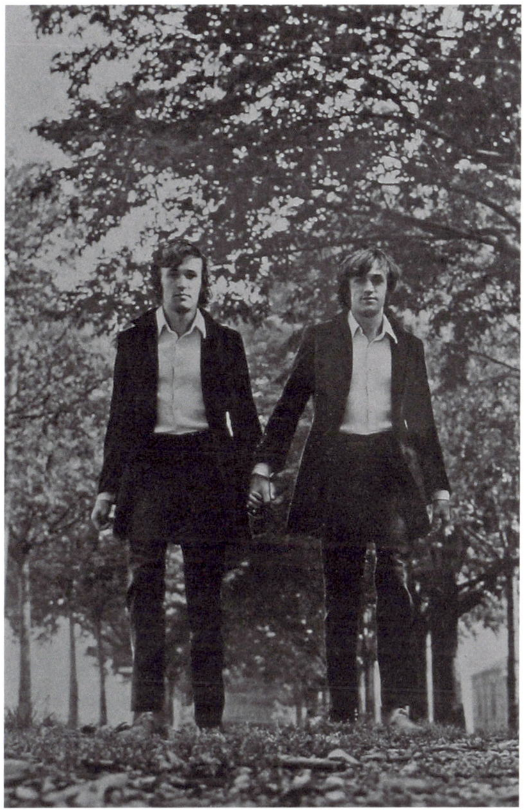

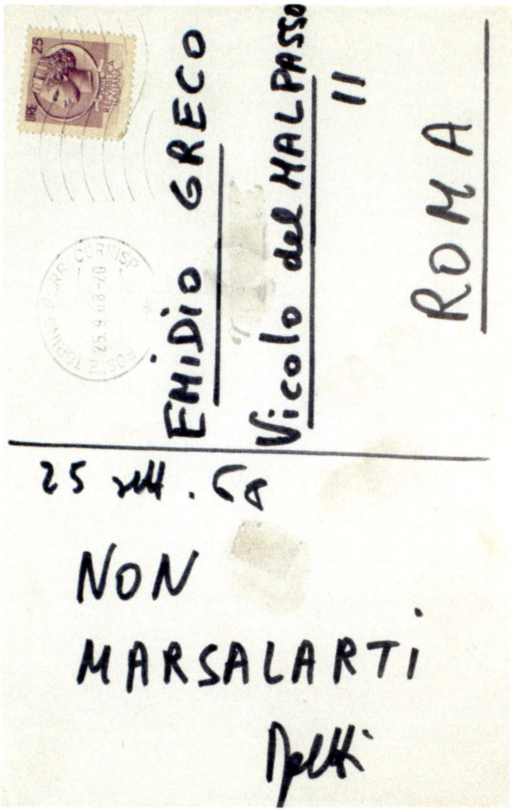

65 Gemelli (Twins), 1968 (recto, verso)

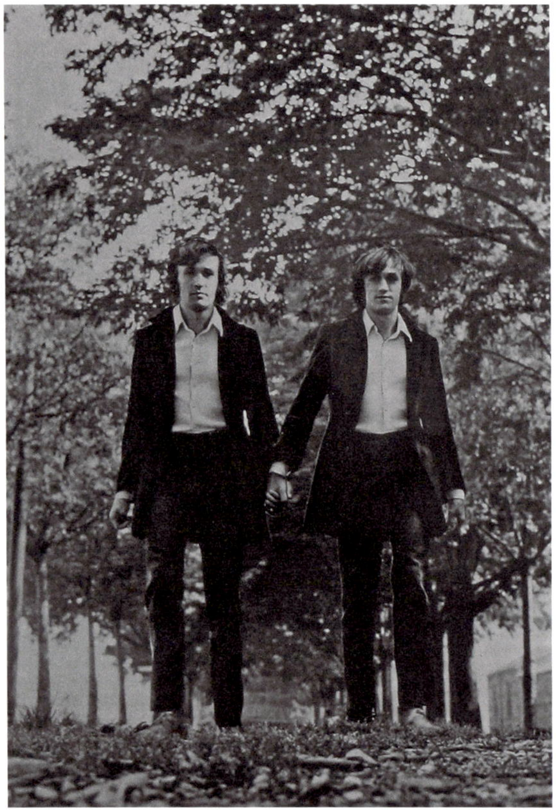

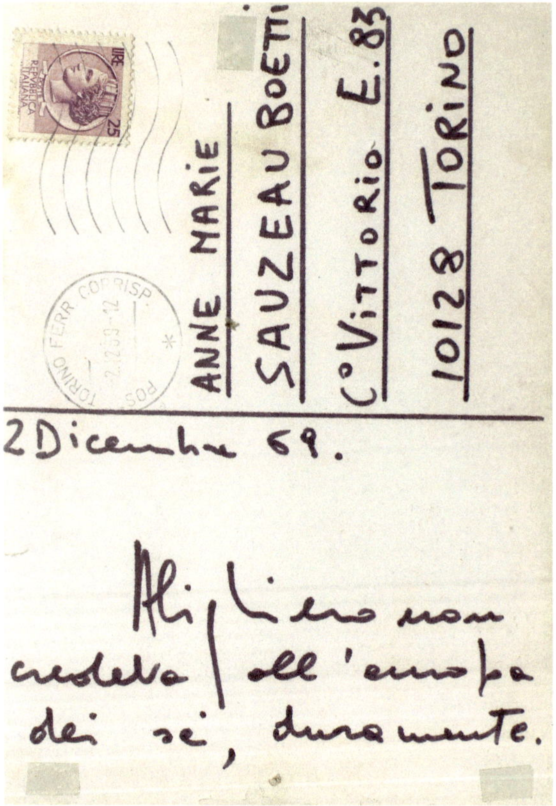

Gemelli (Twins), 1968 (recto, verso) /
Io che prendo il sole a Torino il 19 gennaio 1969, (Me Sunbathing in Turin January 19, 1969), 1969

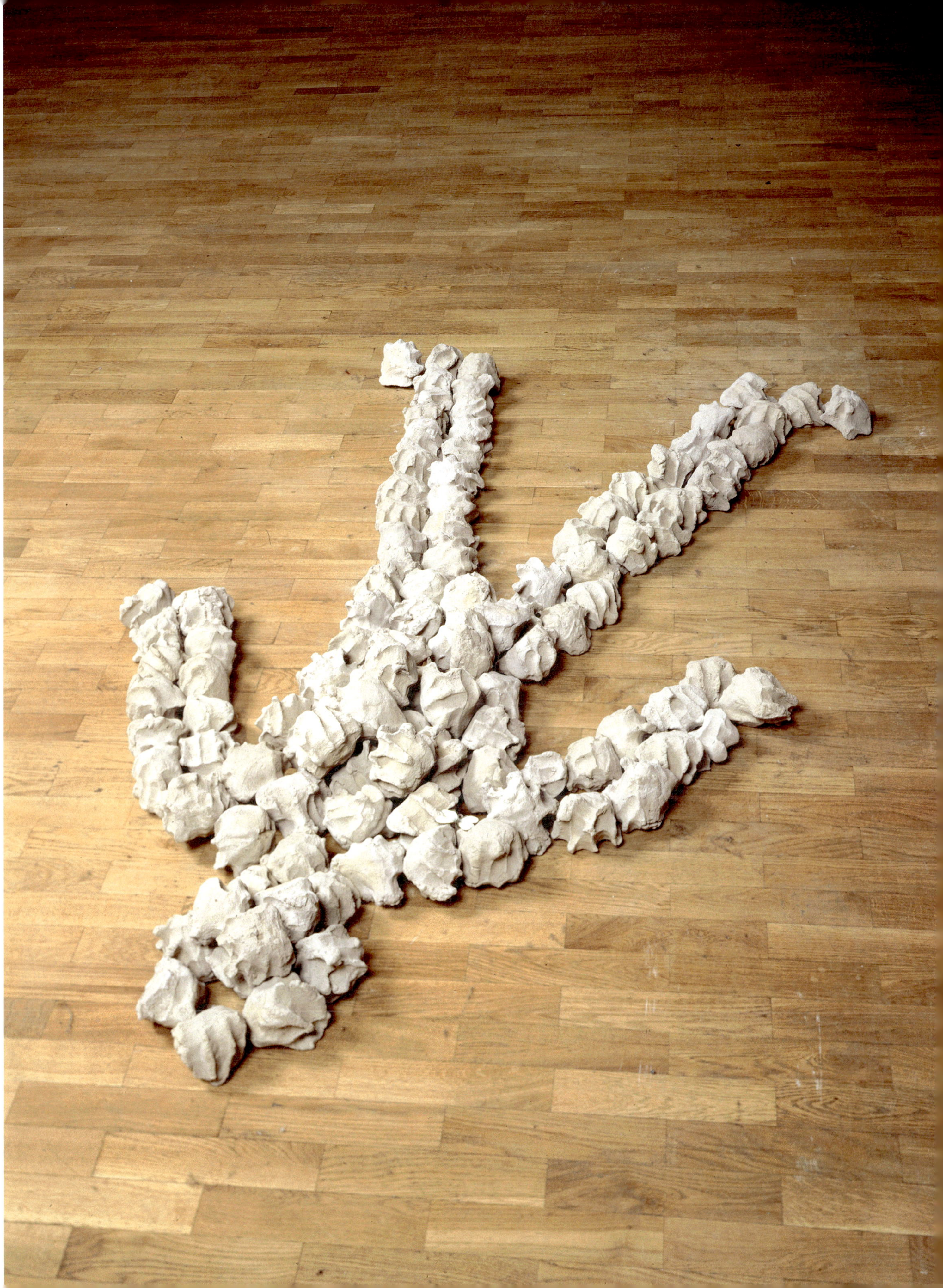

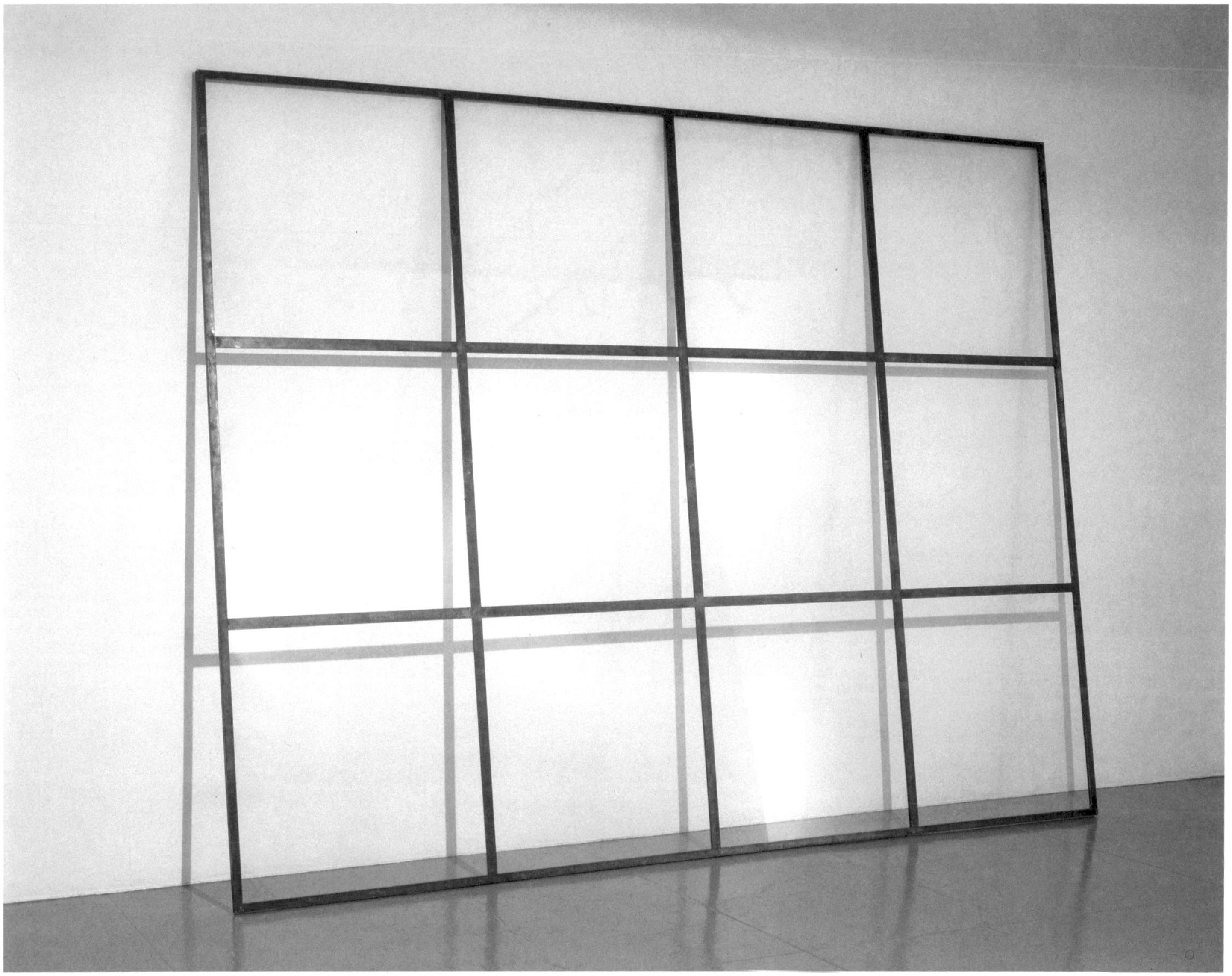

69 Niente da vedere niente da nascondere (Nothing to See Nothing to Hide), 1969

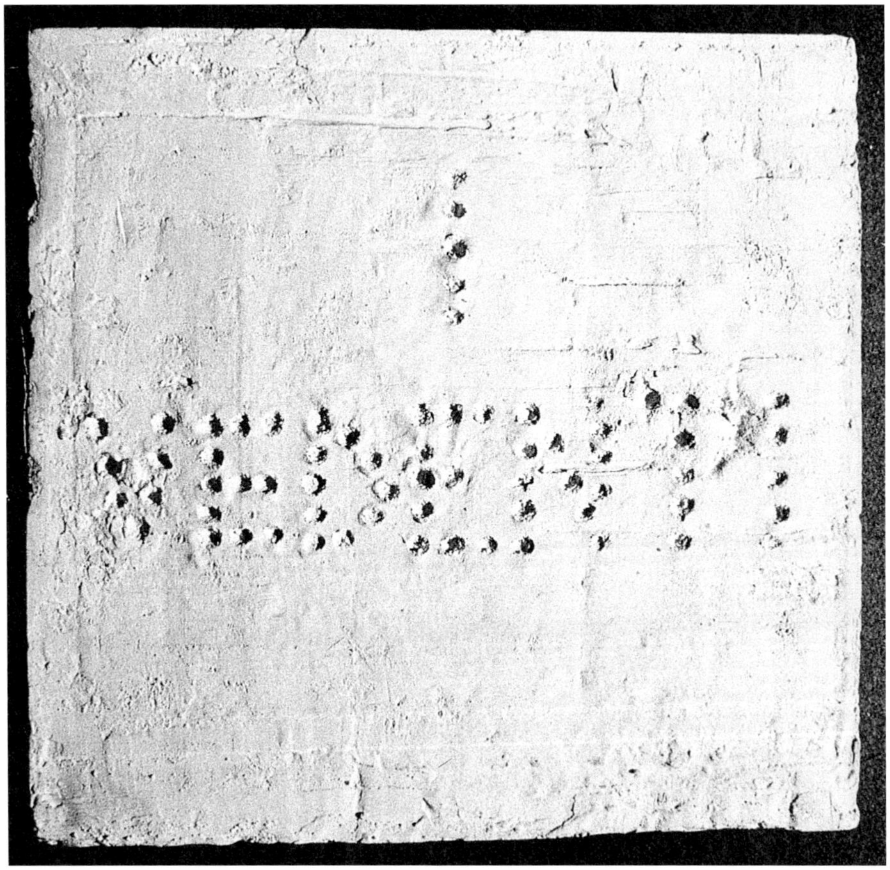

IVEDENTI (The Sighted), 1967 / Ghise (ABoetti) (Cast Iron [ABoetti]), 1968

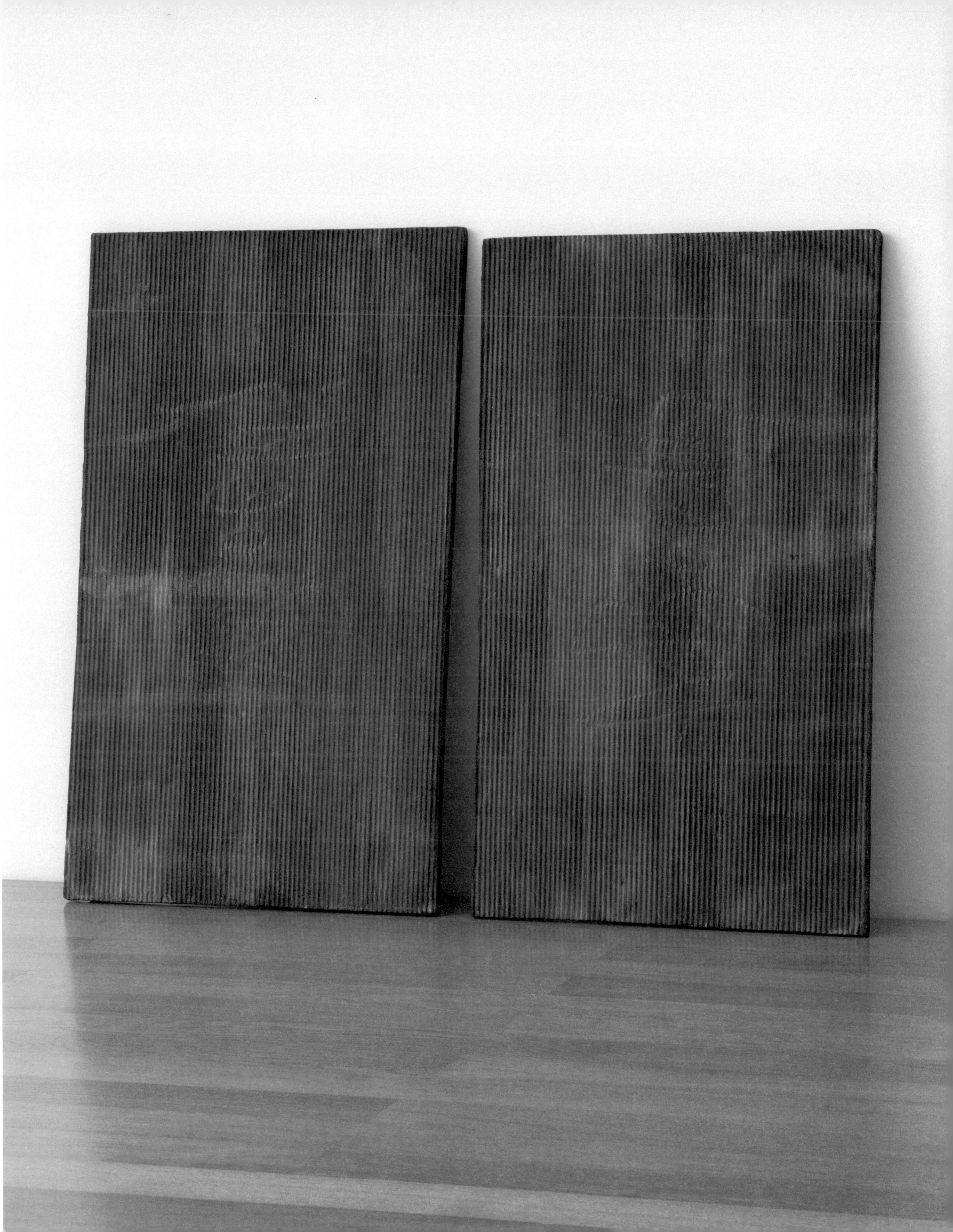

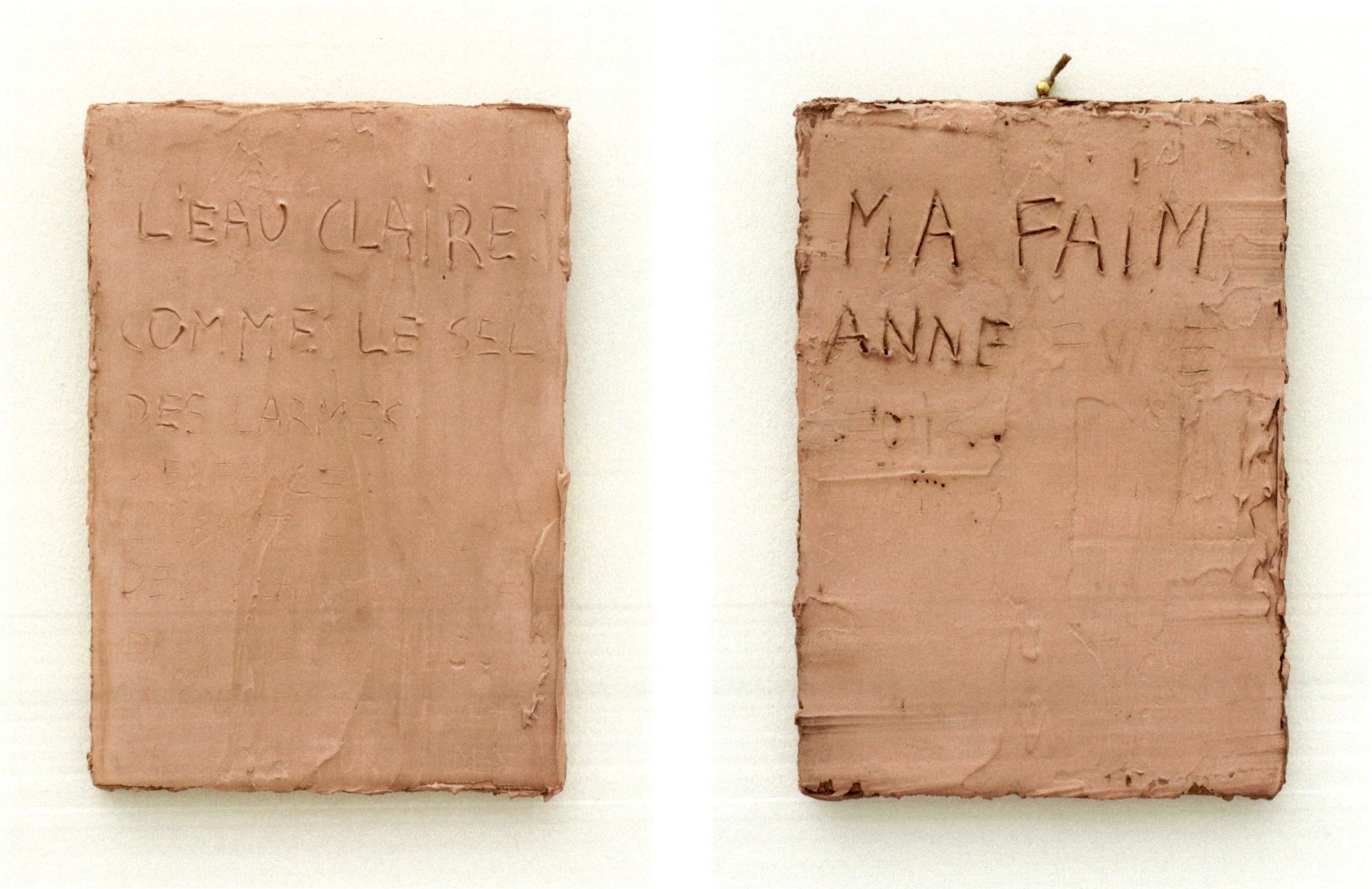

Scrittura graffita (Graffito), 1968

73 Per un uomo alienato (For an Alienated Man), 1968

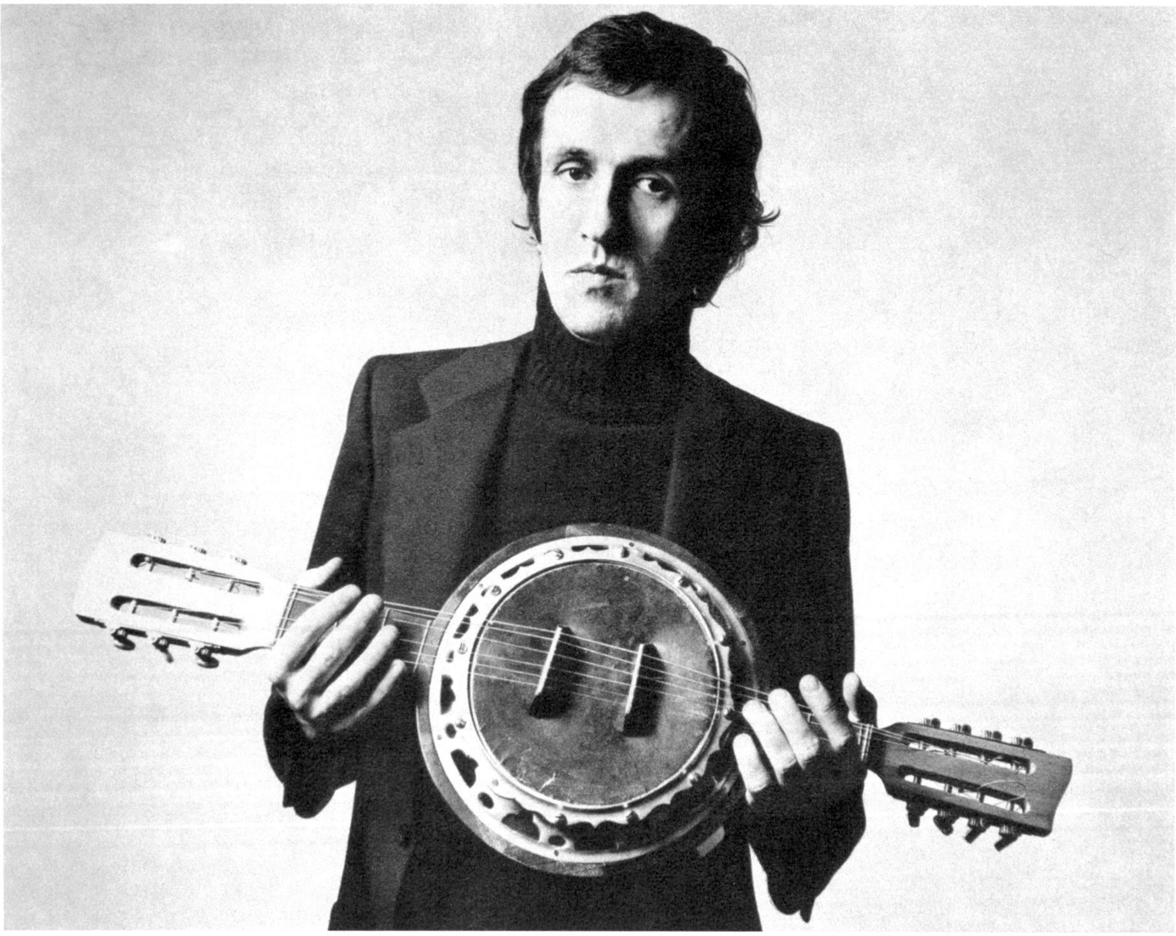

Strumento musicale (Musical Instrument), 1970

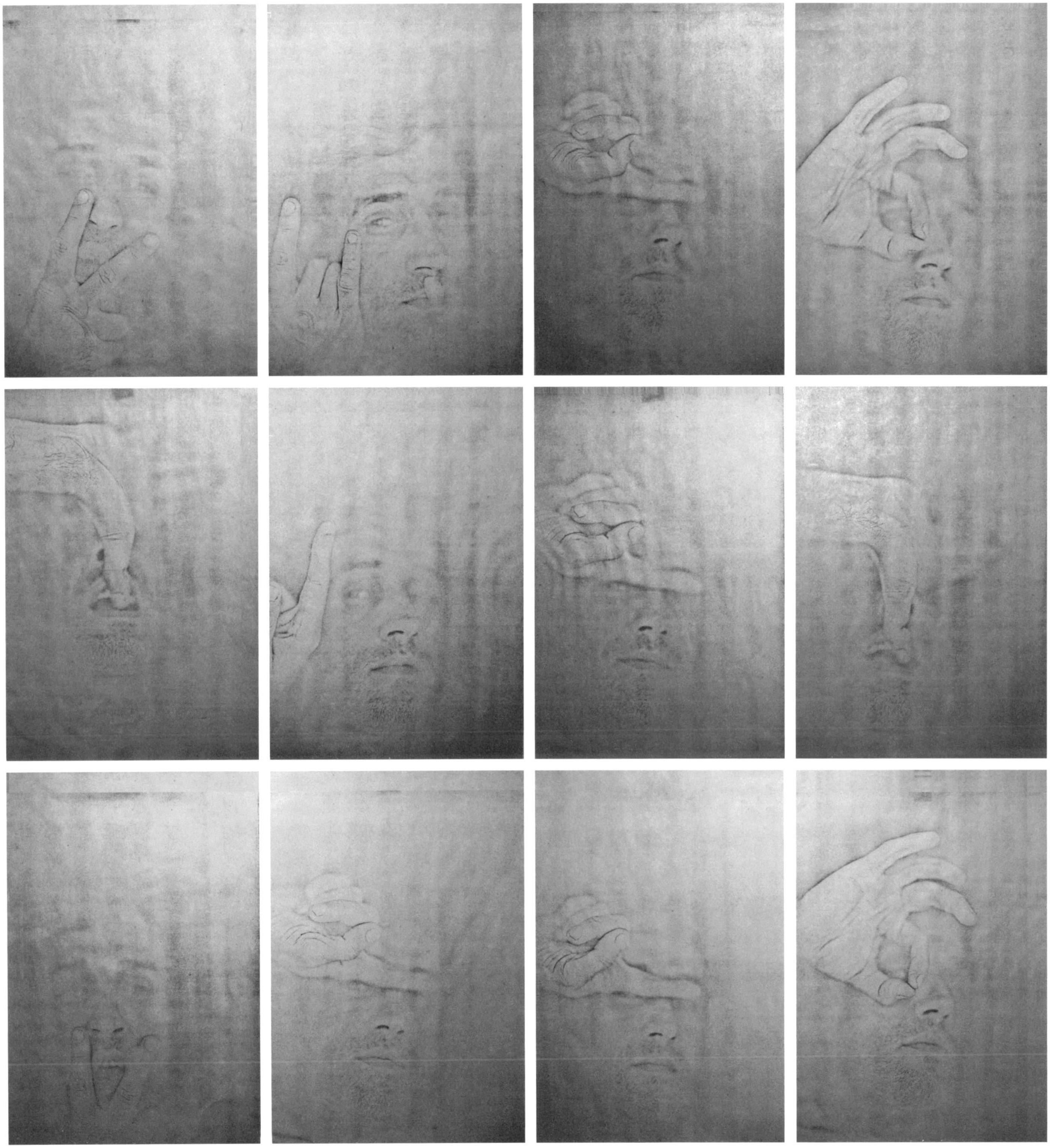

Autoritratto (Self-Portrait), 1969

 San Bernardino, 1968/1978

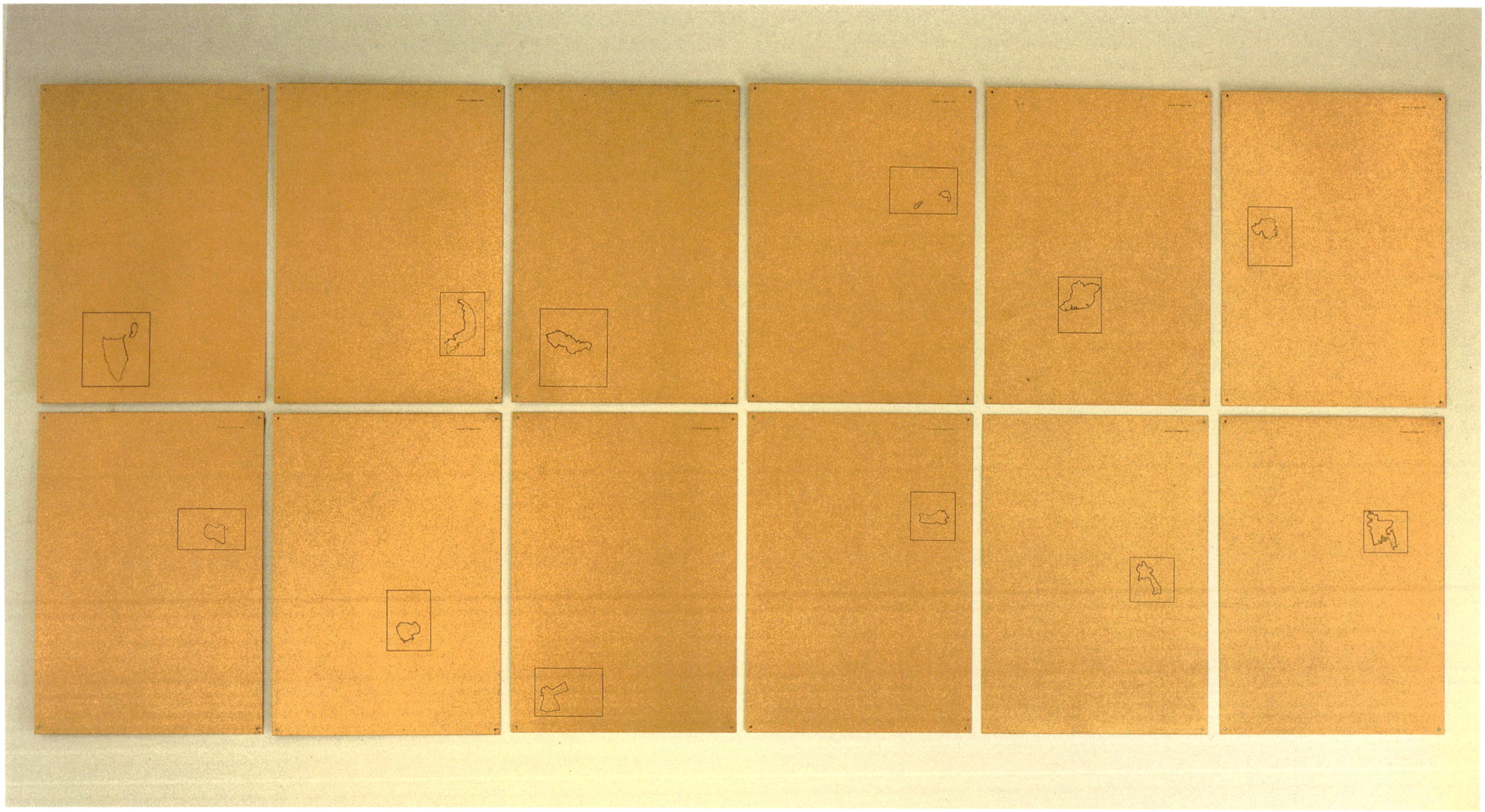

Dodici forme dal 10 giugno 1967 (12 Forms from June 10, 1967), 1971

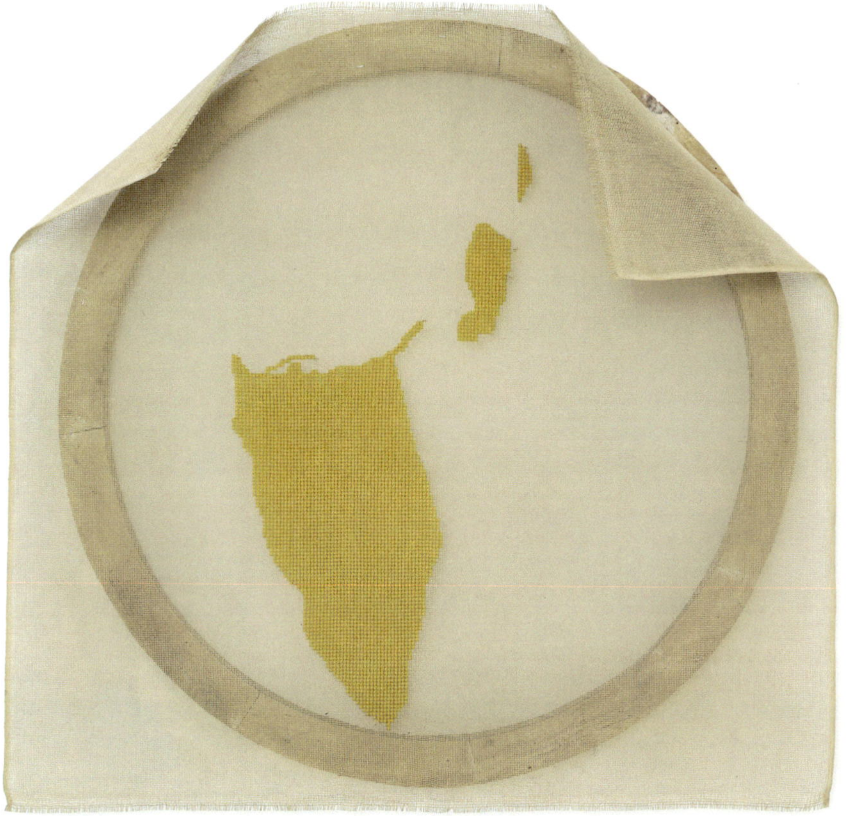

79 Territori occupati (Occupied Territories), 1969

Cimento dell'armonia e dell'invenzione (Test of Harmony and Invention), 1969 (detail)

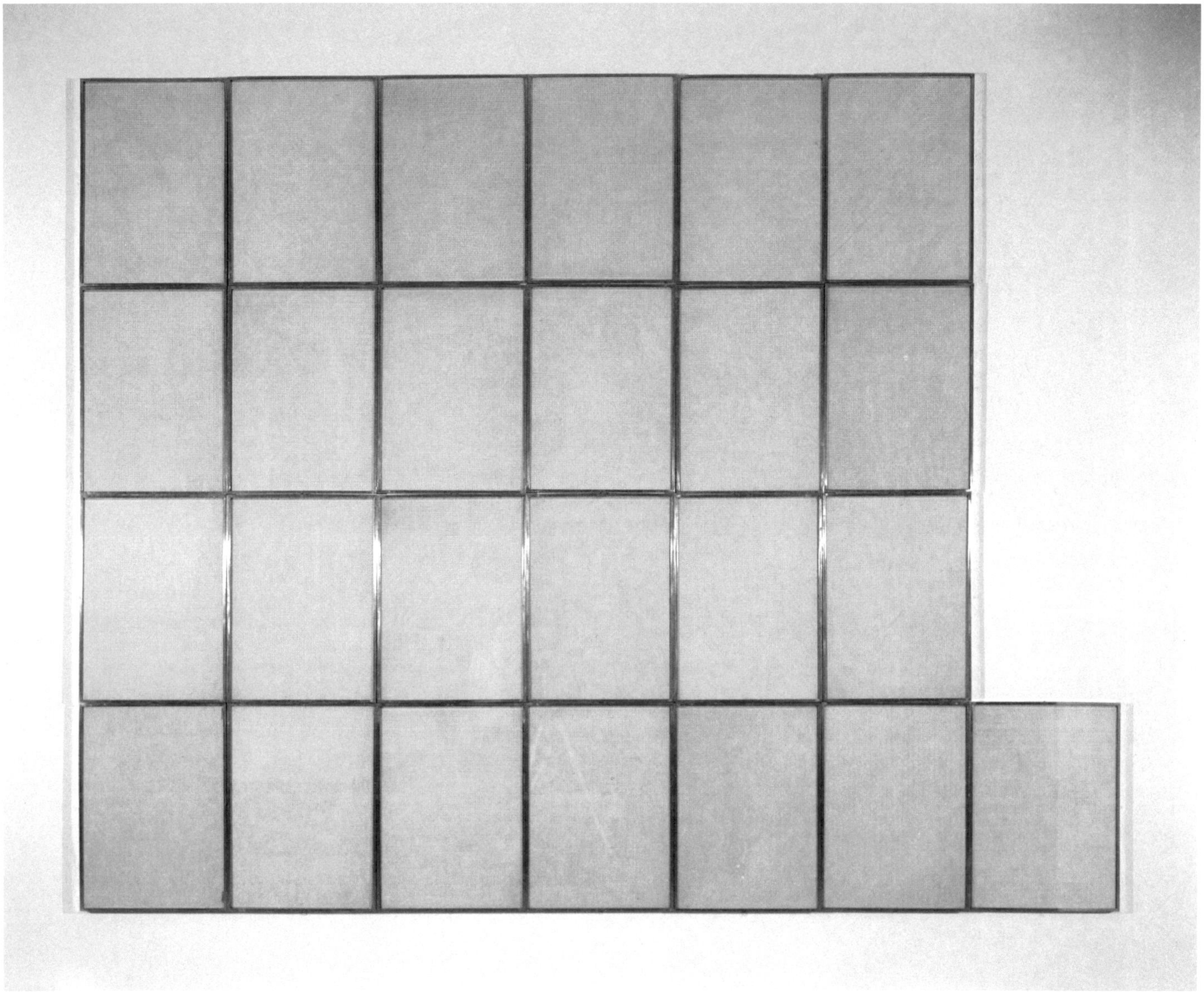

81 Cimento dell'armonia e dell'invenzione (Contest of Harmony and Invention), 1969

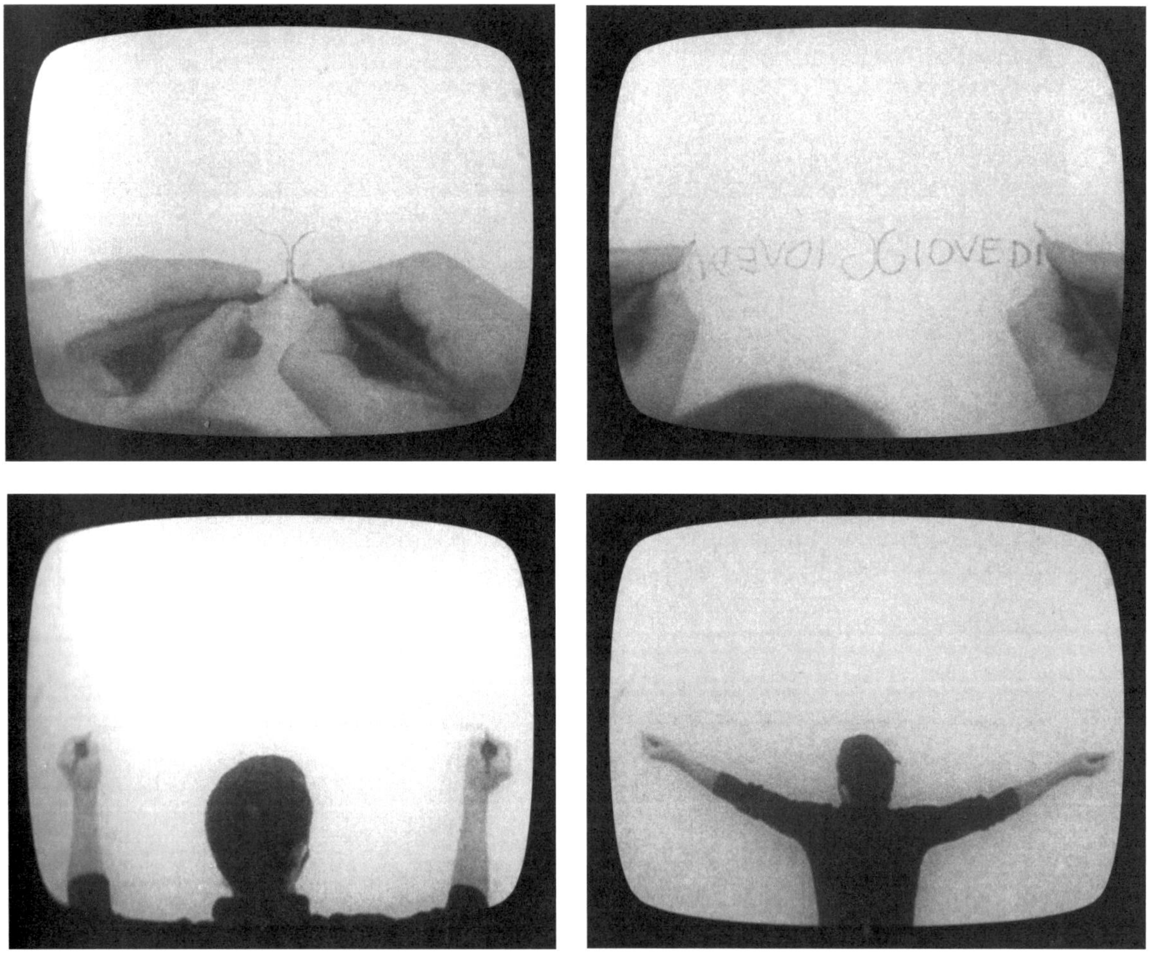

Gerry Schum, Identifications: Alighiero Boetti, Untitled – Turin, September 24, 1970

Alfabeto (Scrittura a due mani) (Alphabet [Writing with Two Hands]), 1970

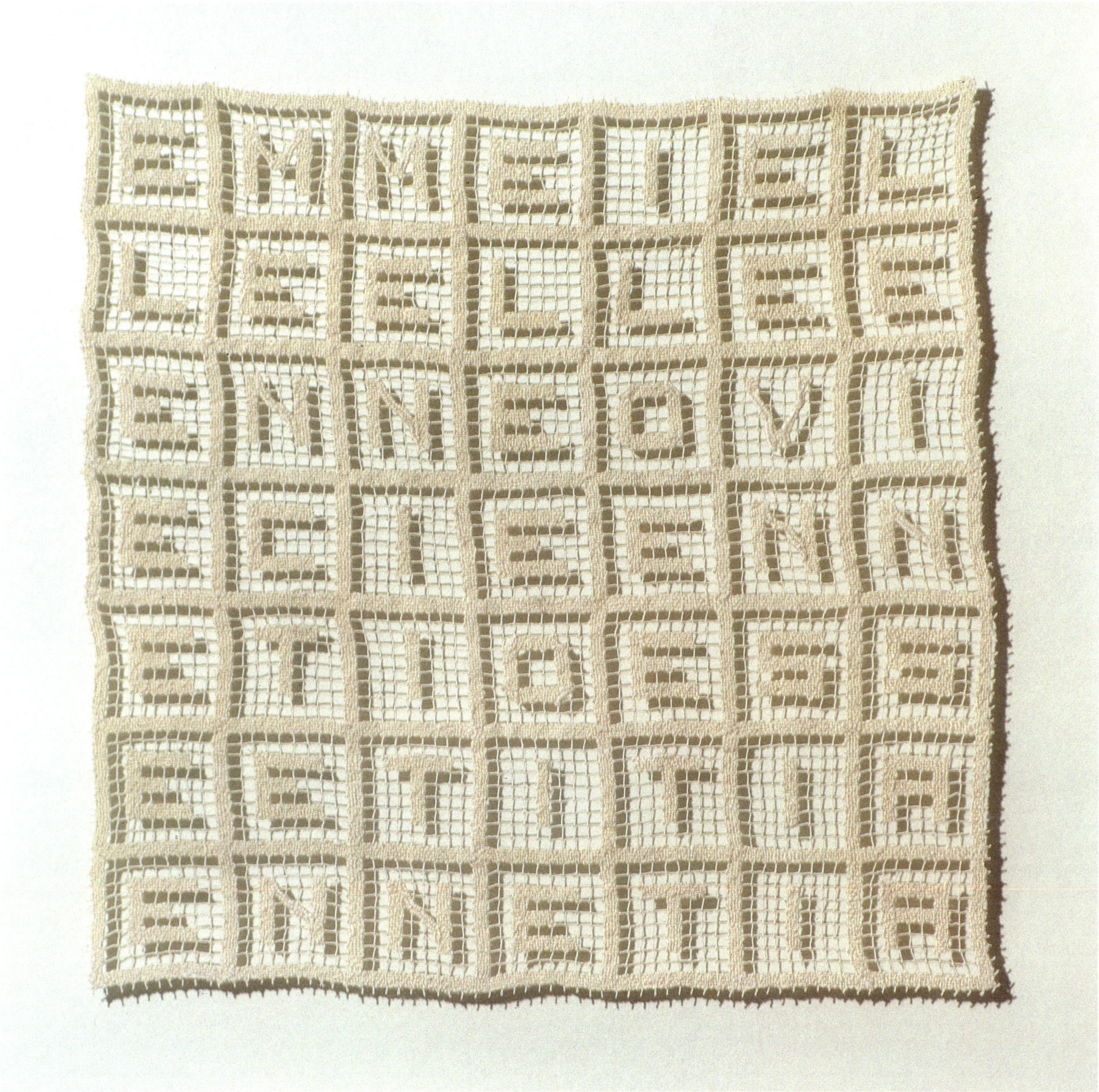

 EMME I ELLE ELLE E …, 1970

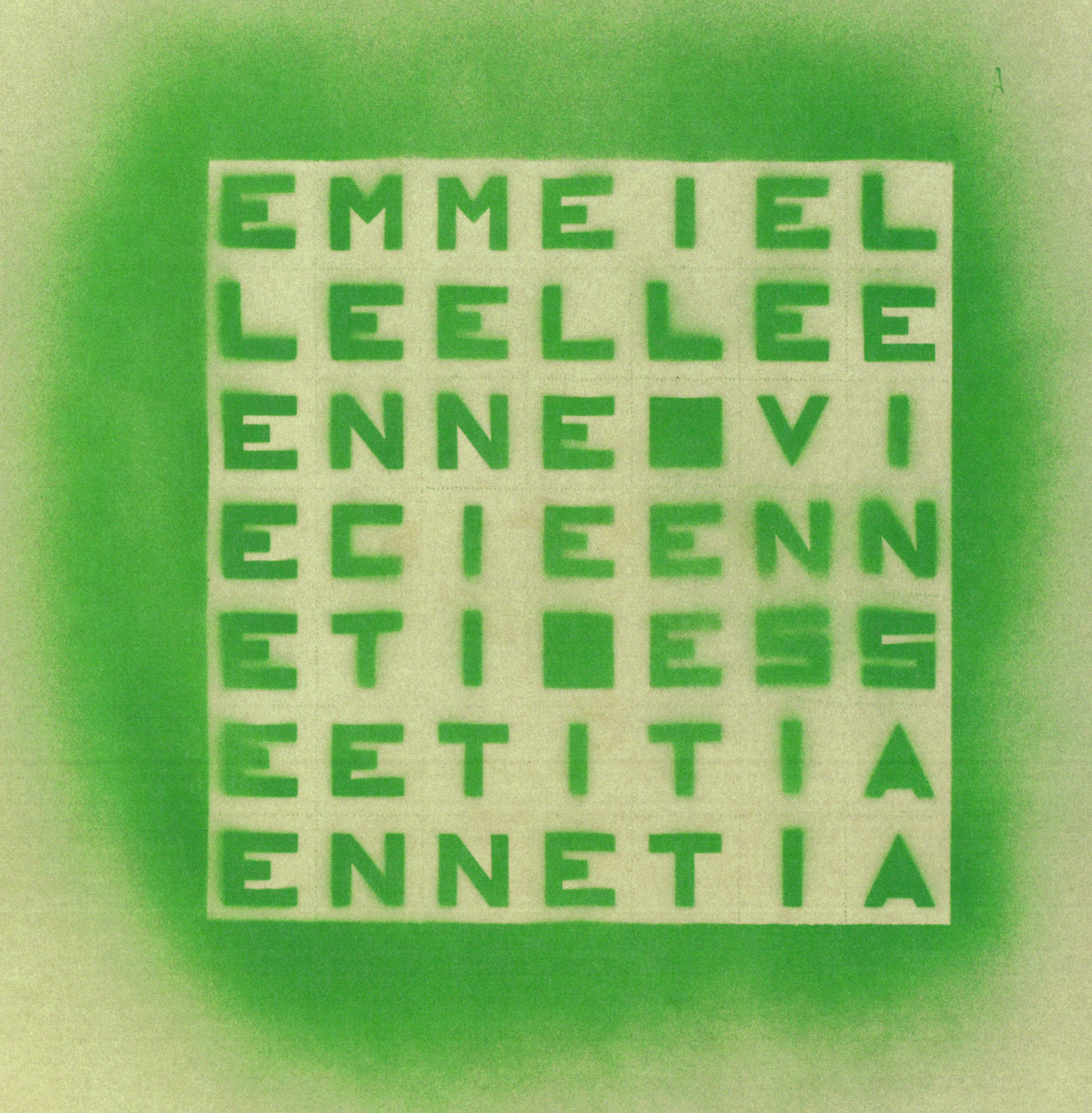
EMMEIEL
LEELLEE
ENNE■VI
ECIEENN
ETI■ESS
EETITIA
ENNETIA

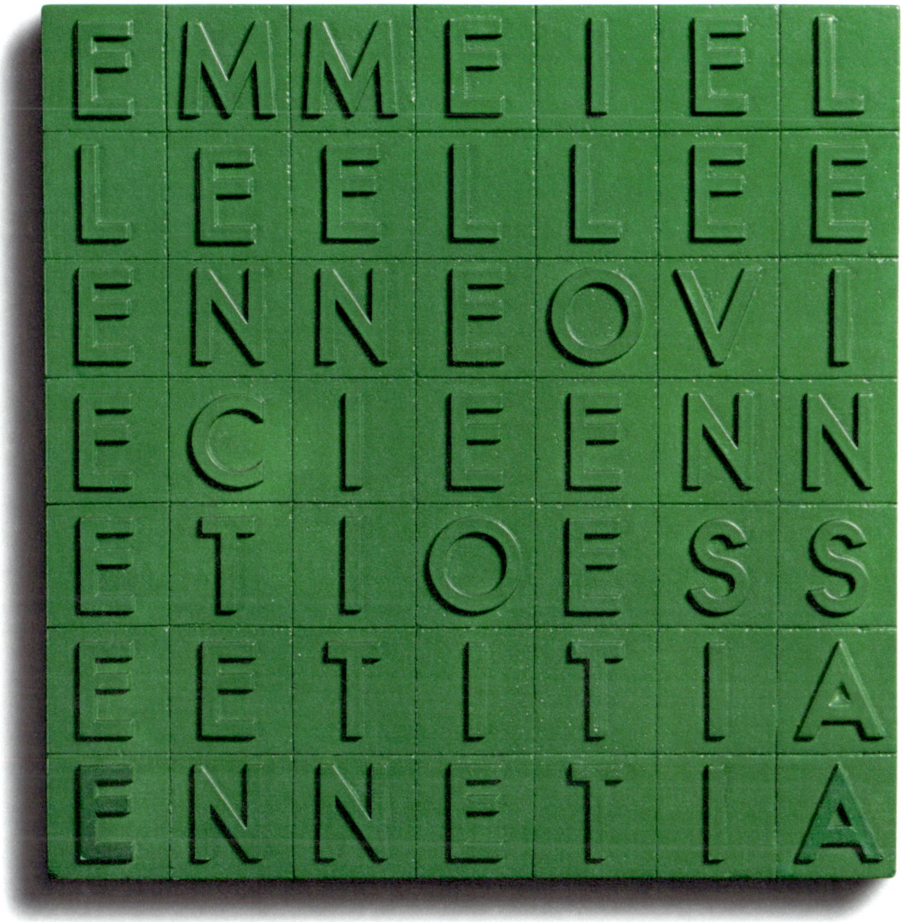

EMME I ELLE ELLE E … (Green on Green), 1970 / EMME I ELLE ELLE E … , 1970

Venticinque × venticinque seicentoventicinque lettere
(Twenty-five × Twenty-five Six Hundred and Twenty-five Letters), 1988

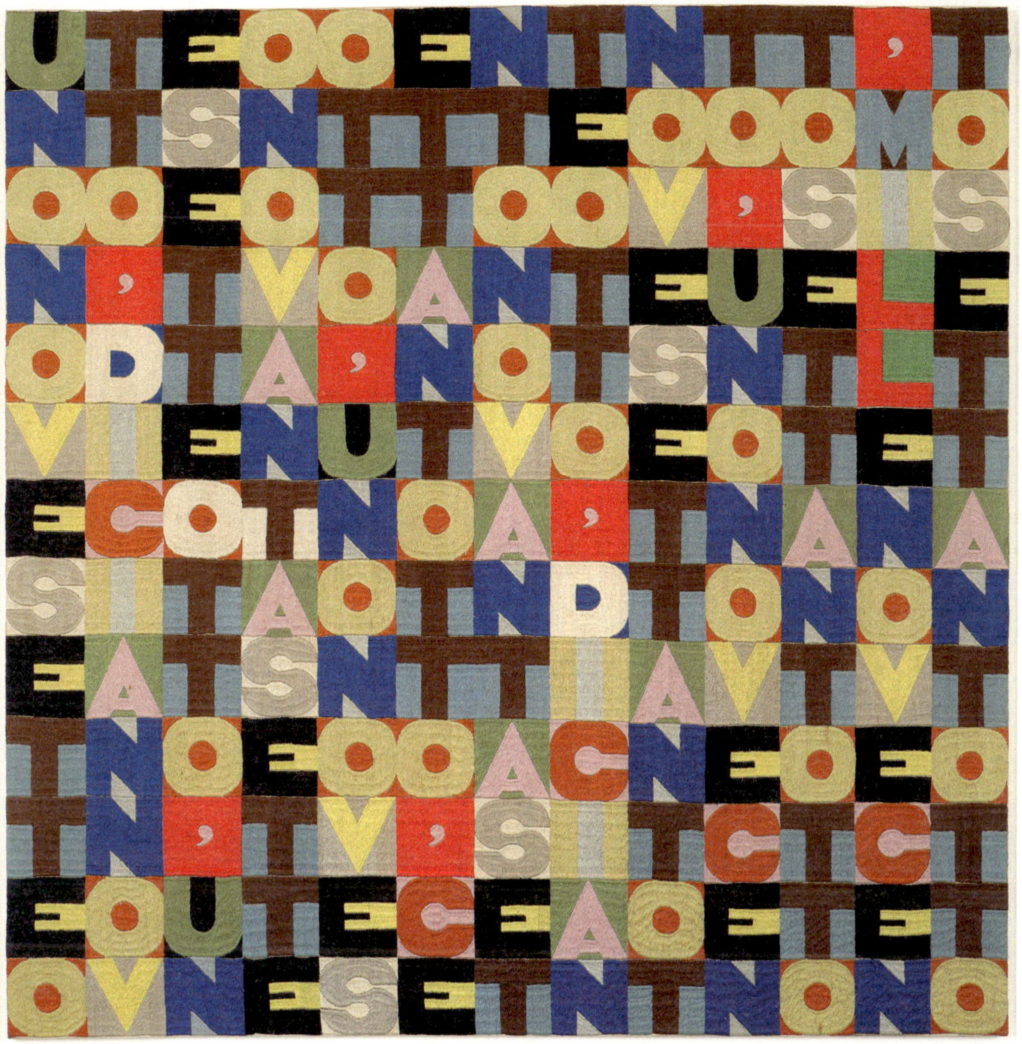

89 Untitled, 1978

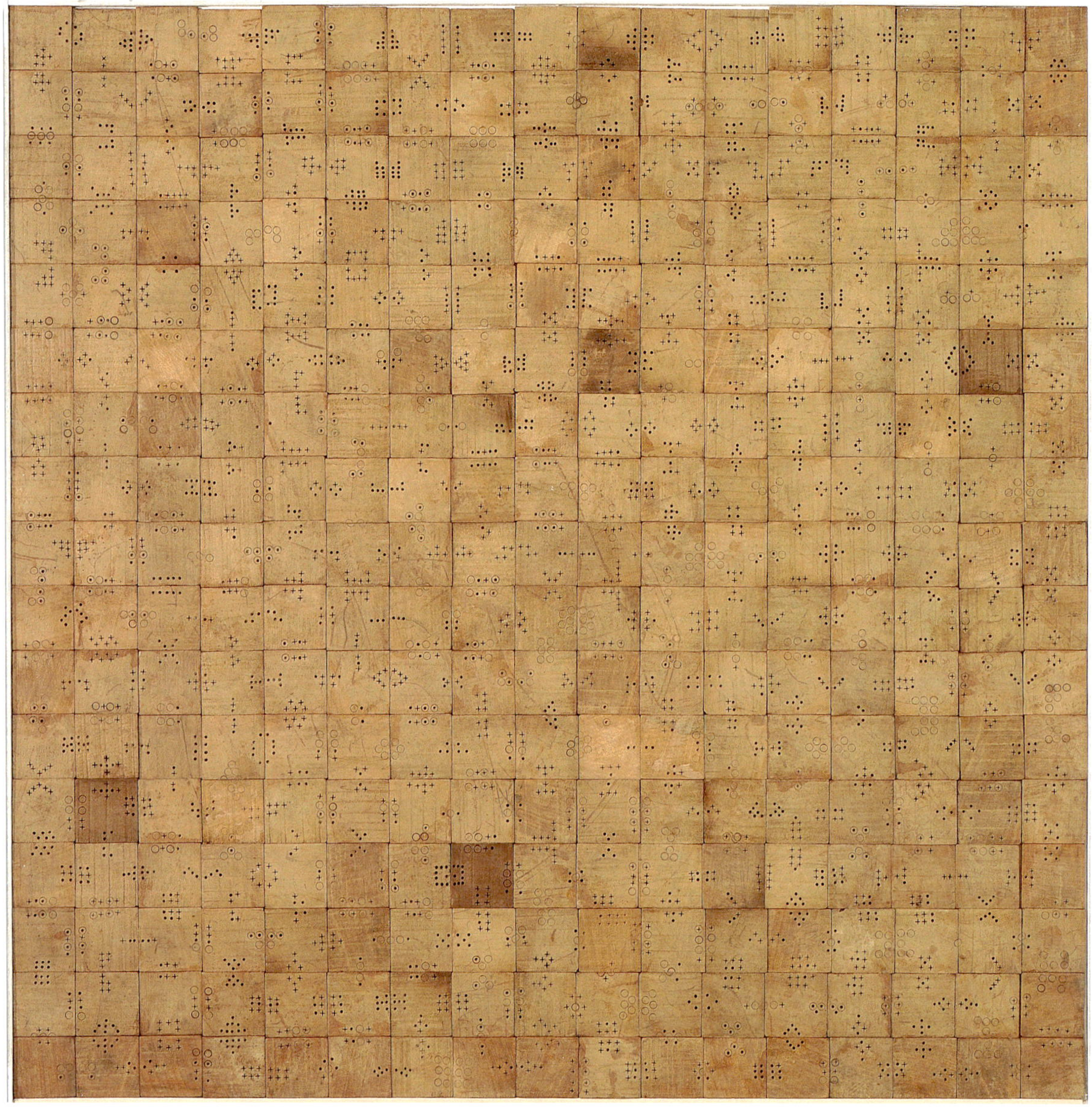

Dama (Checkerboard), 1967

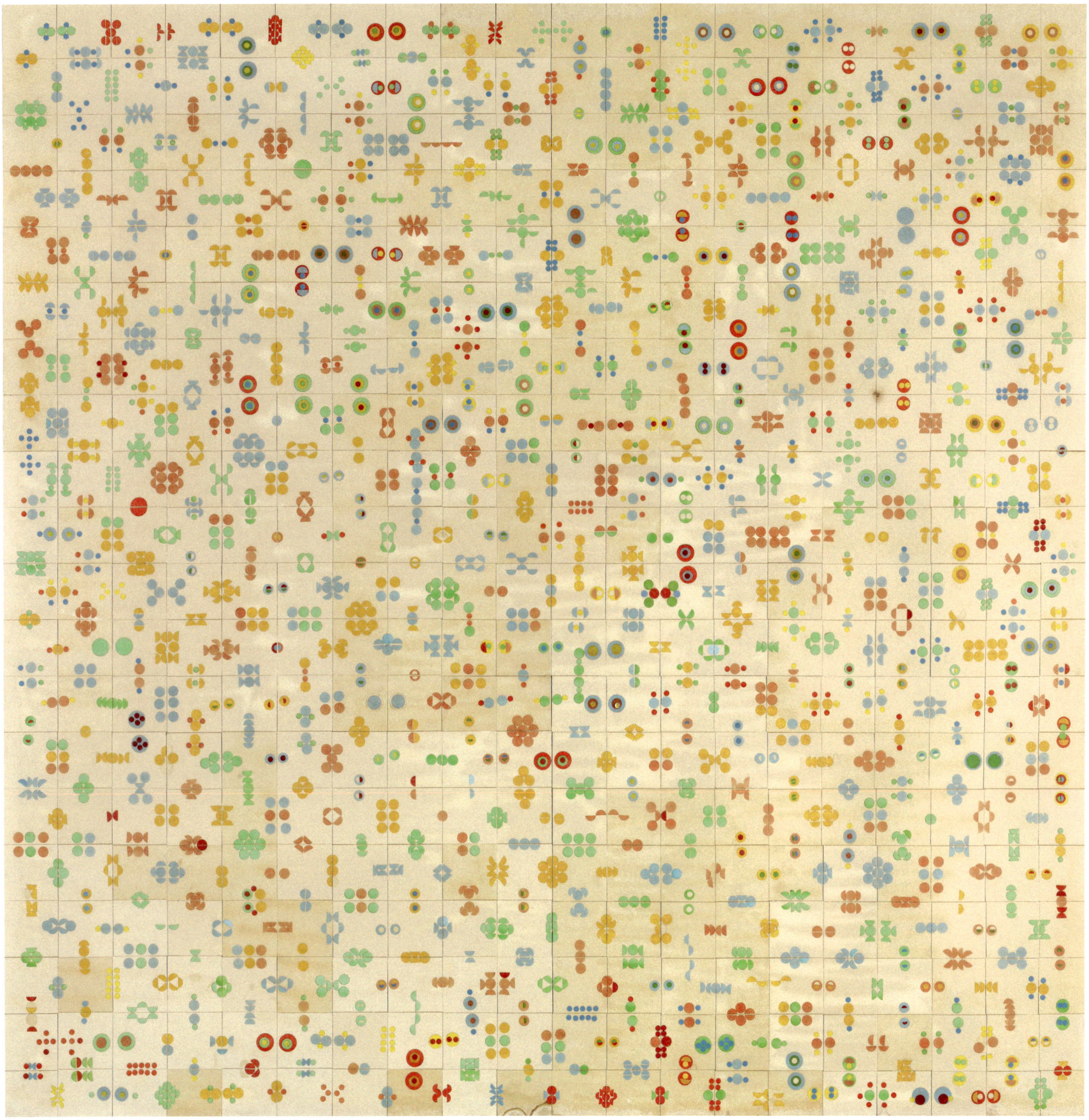

Untitled, 1969

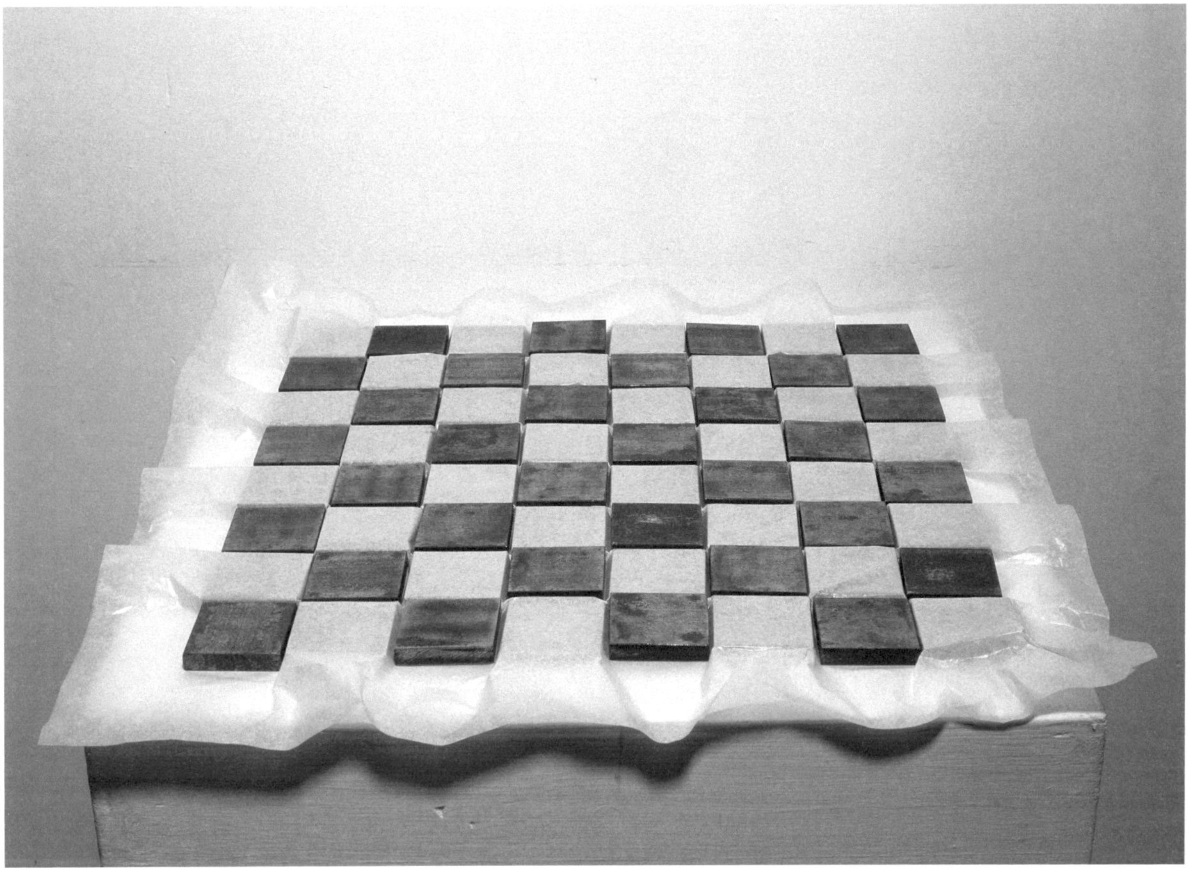

93 Iter-vallo, 1969/1986

Ordine e disordine (Order and Disorder), 1979

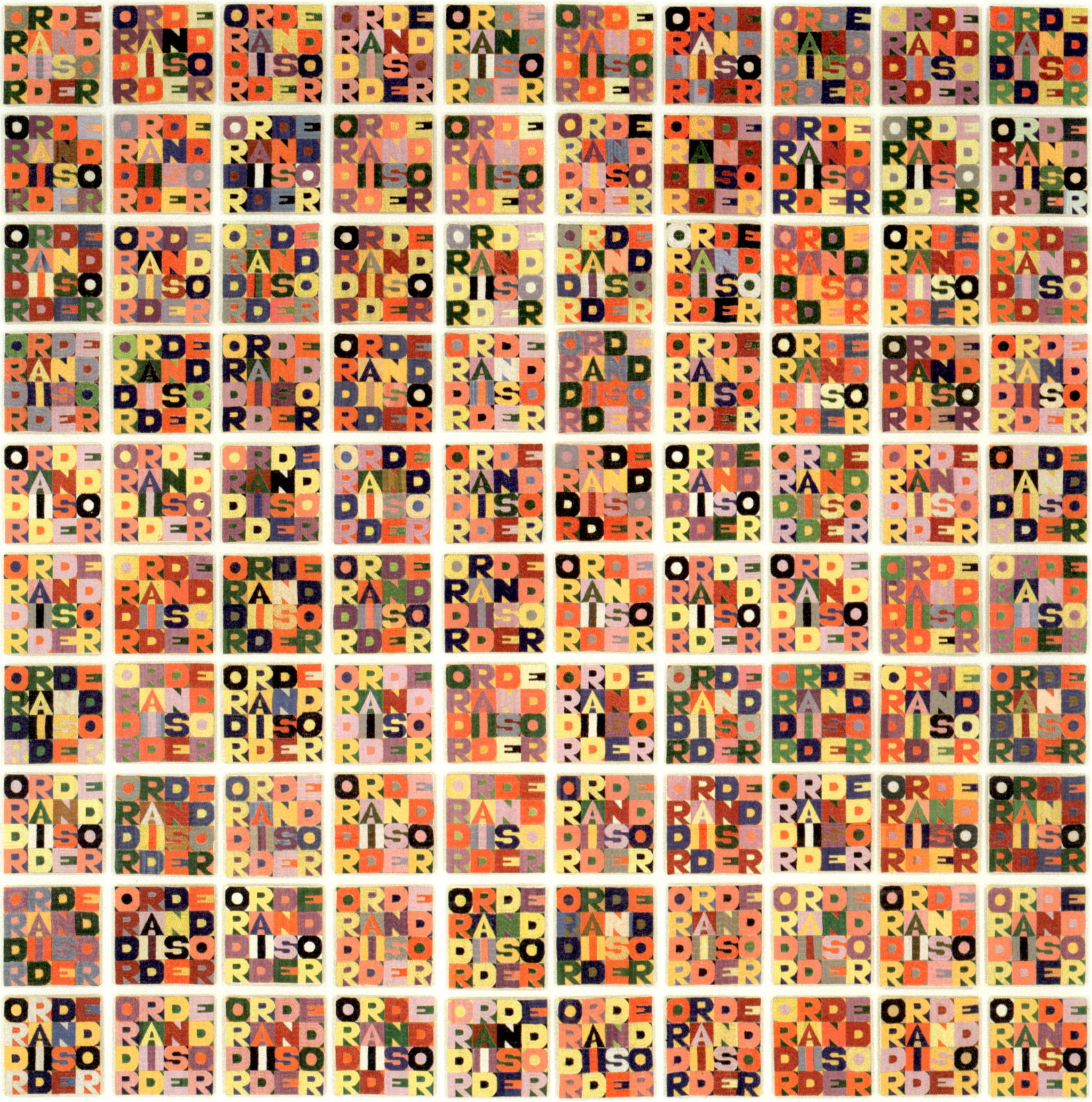

 Order and Disorder, 1985-86

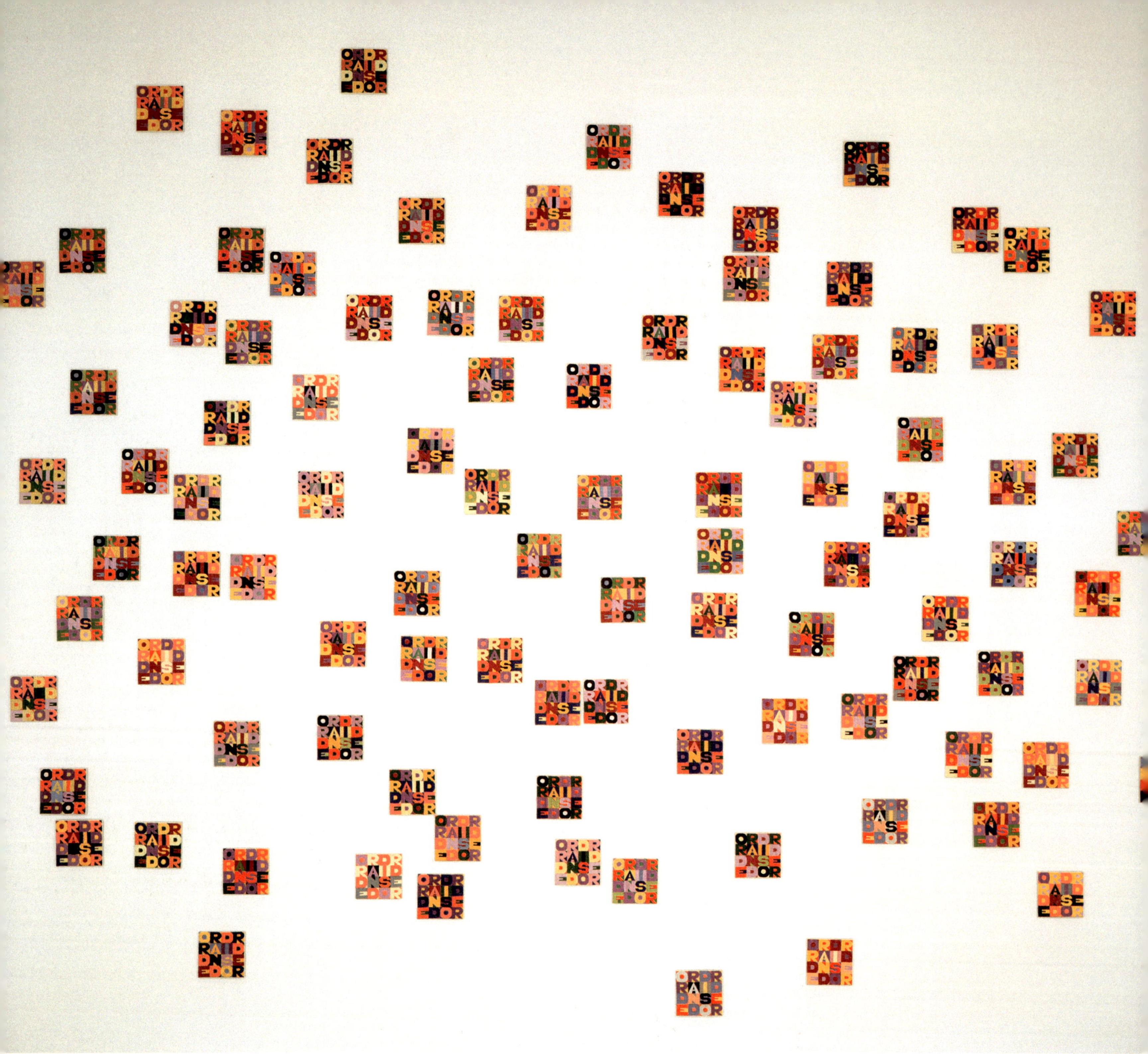

Order and Disorder, 1985-86

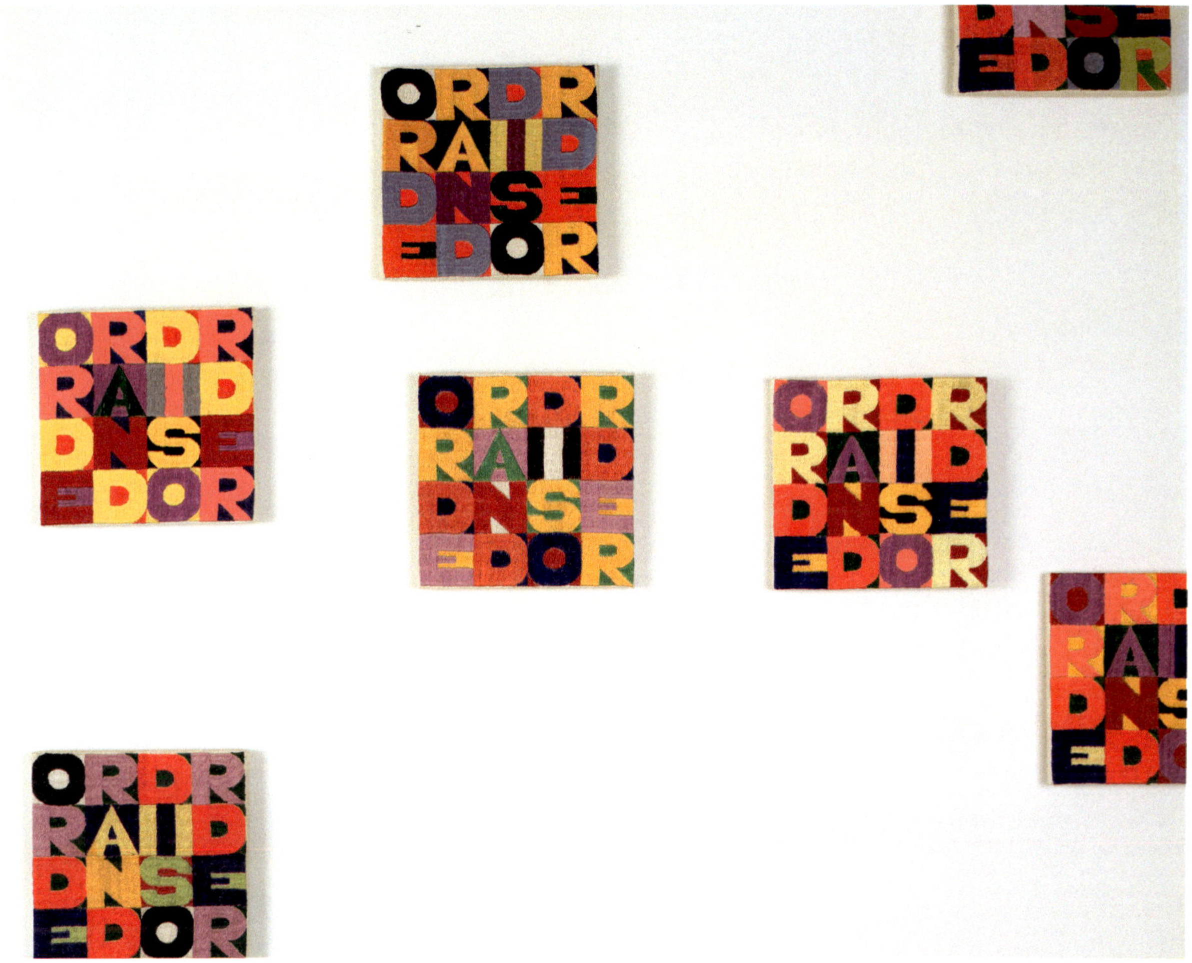

Order and Disorder, 1985-86 (detail)

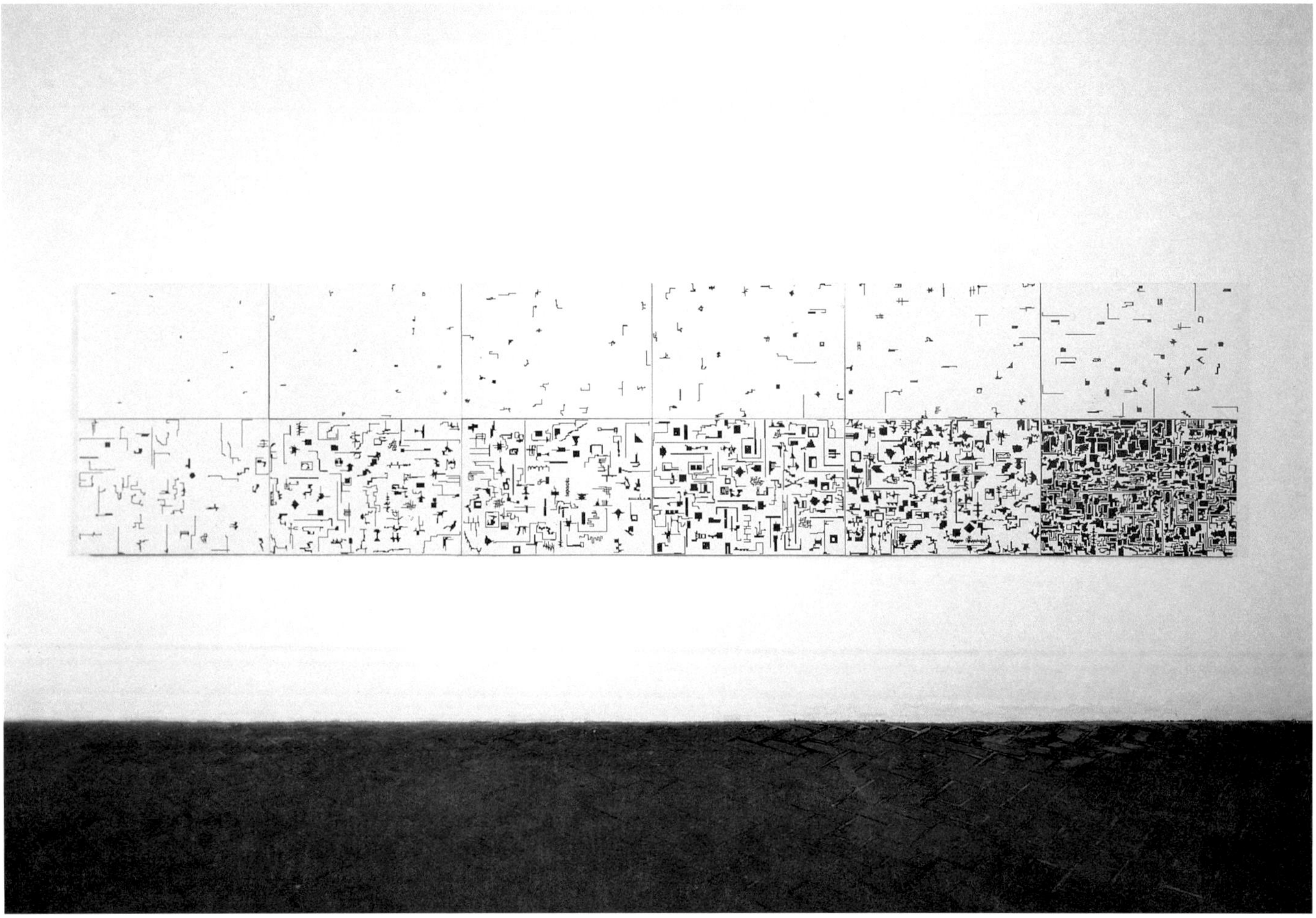

Storia naturale della moltiplicazione (Natural History of Multiplication), 1975

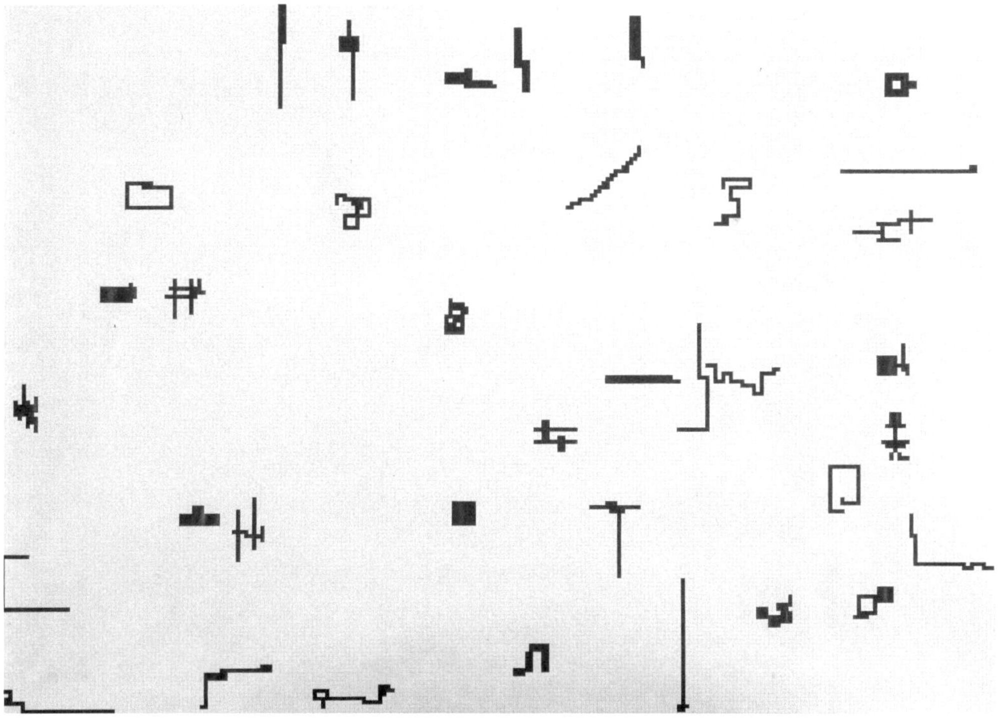

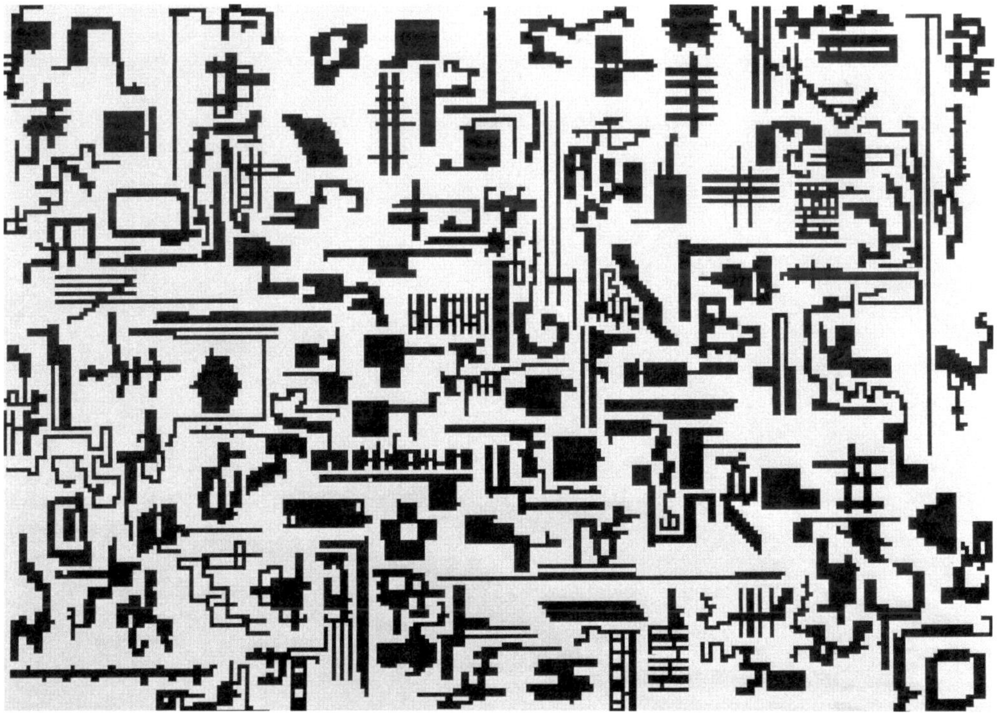

Storia naturale della moltiplicazione (Natural History of Multiplication), 1975 (details)

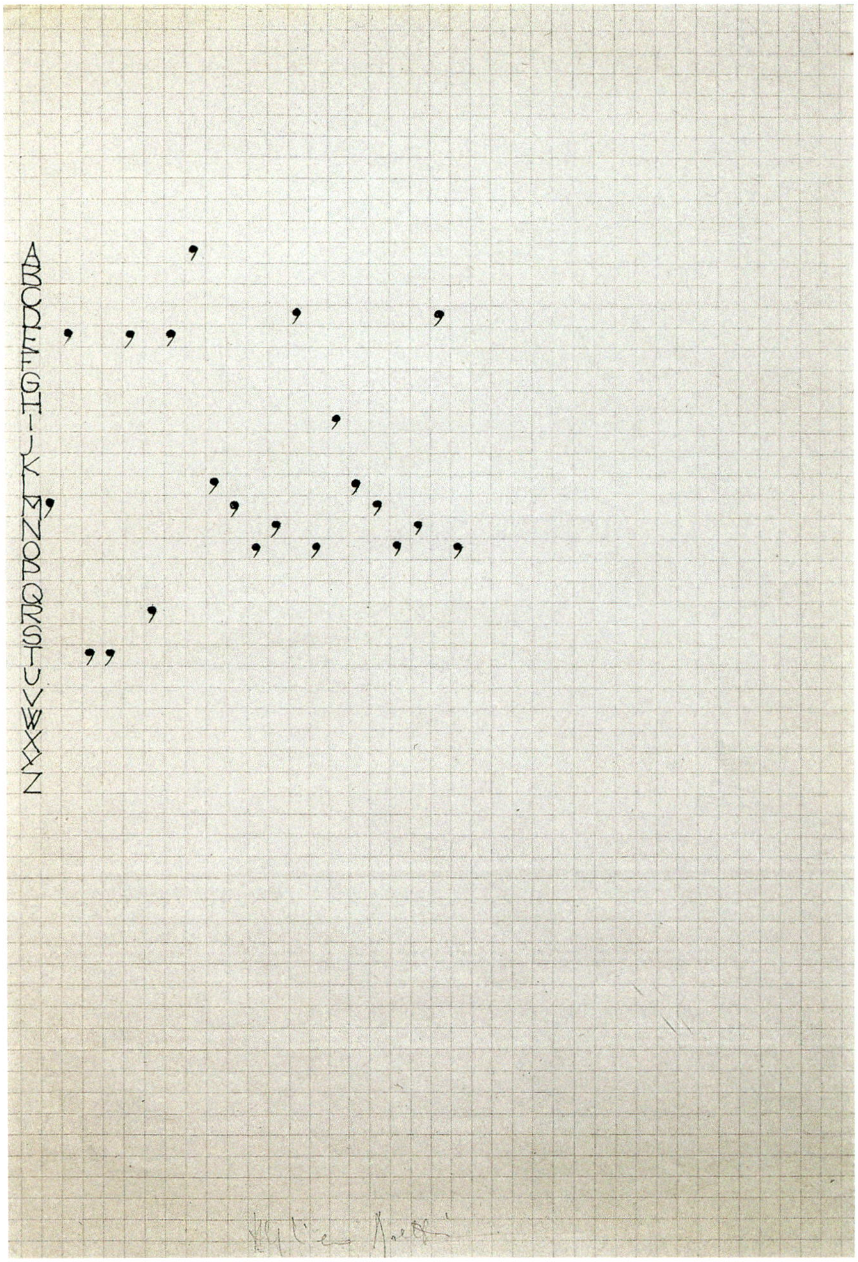

Mettere al mondo il mondo (Putting the World into the World), 1973

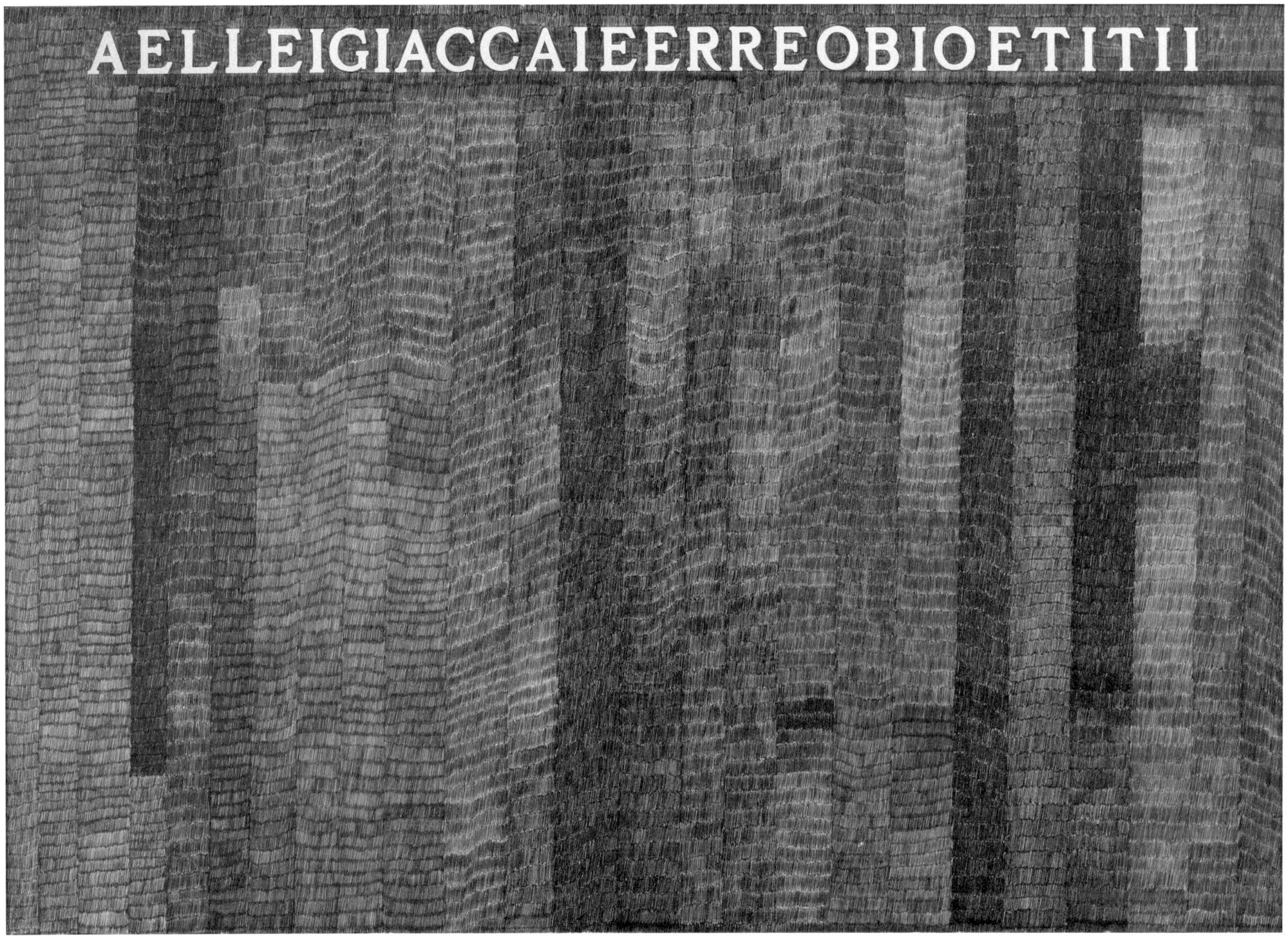

AELLEIGIACCAIEERREOBIOETITII, 1973

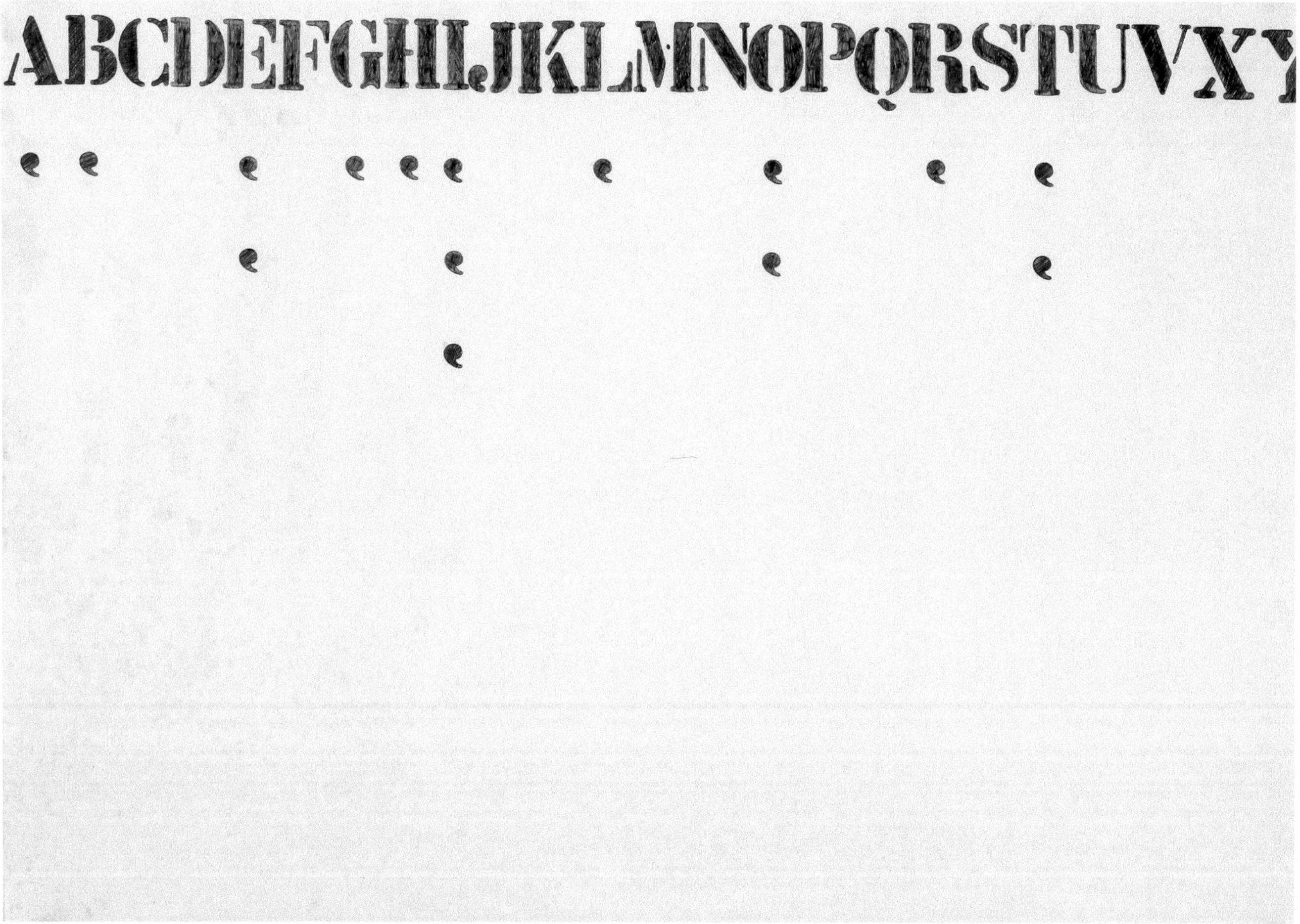

ABEEGHIIILOORT, 1971

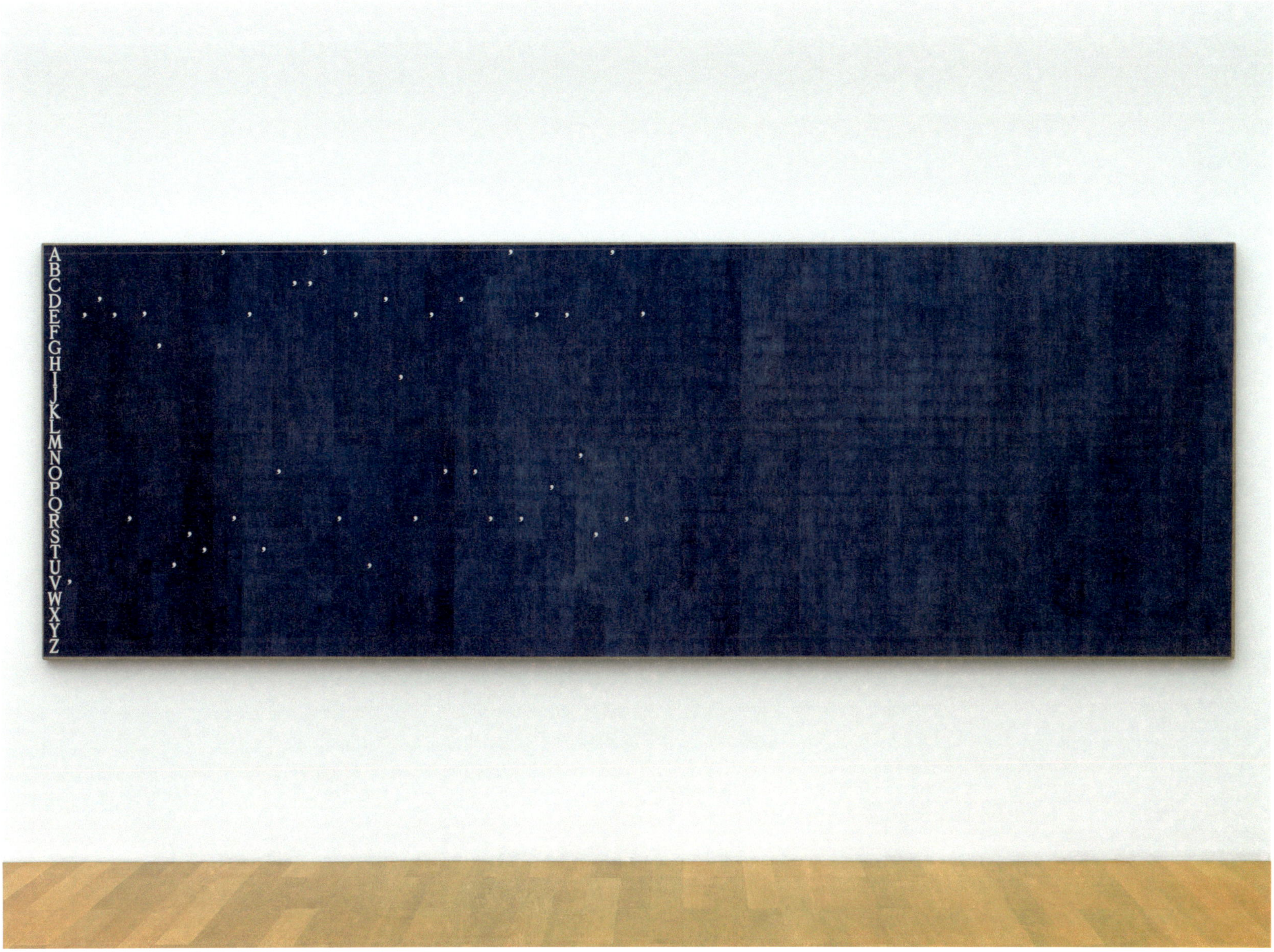

 I sei sensi (The Six Senses), 1974

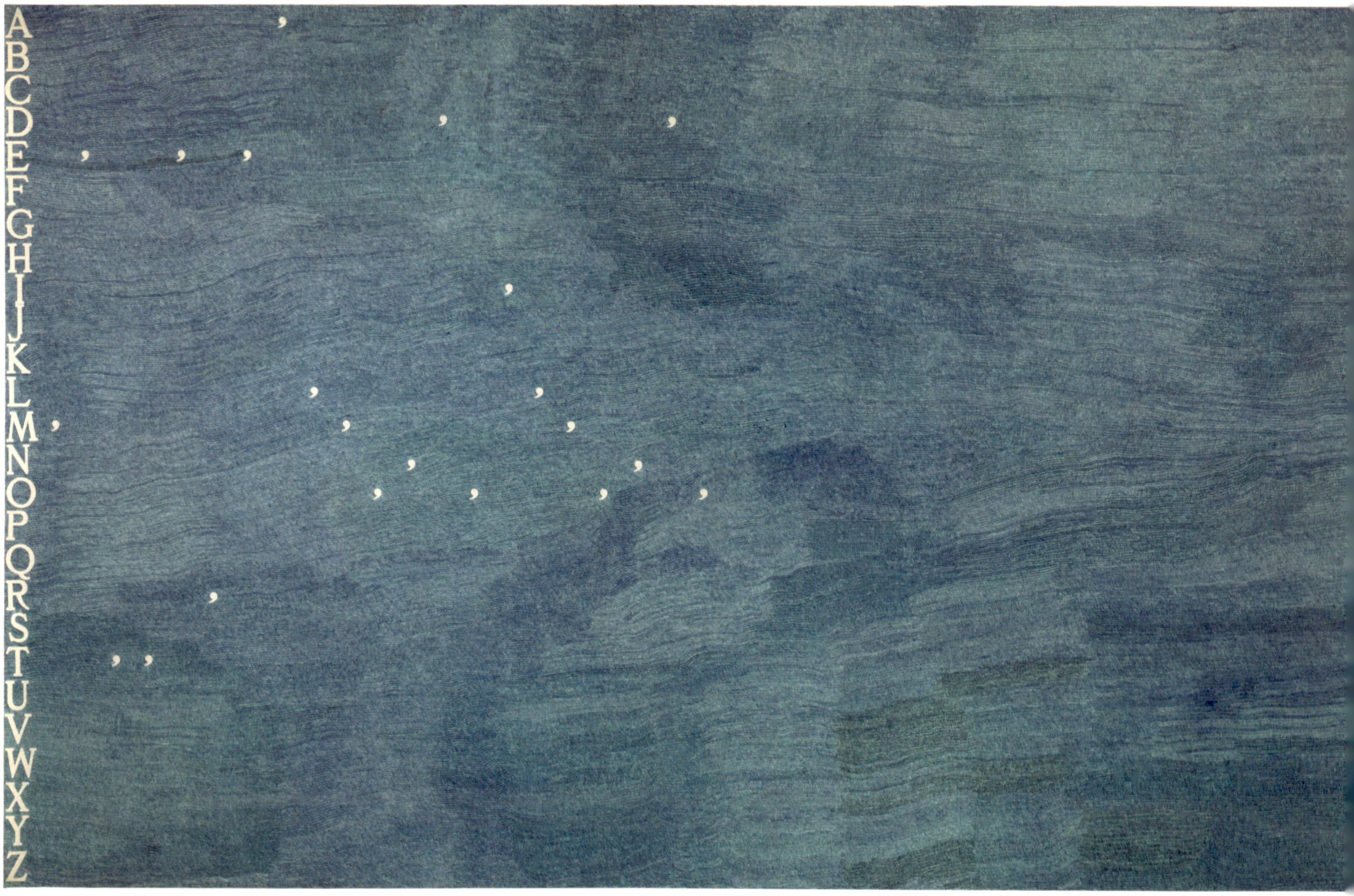
ABCDEFGHIJKLMNOPQRSTUVWXYZ

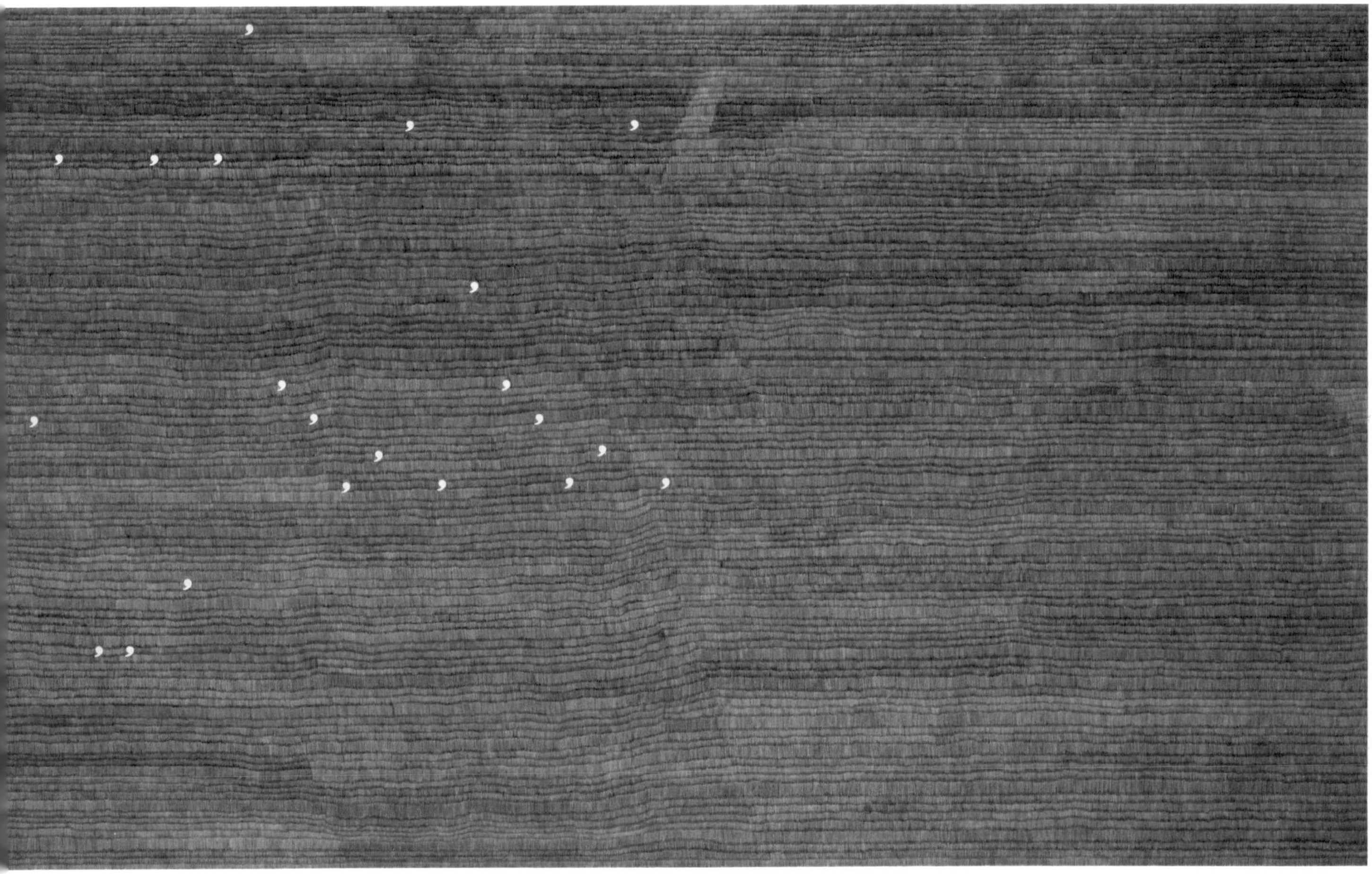

105 Mettere al mondo il mondo (Putting the World into the World), 1973–75

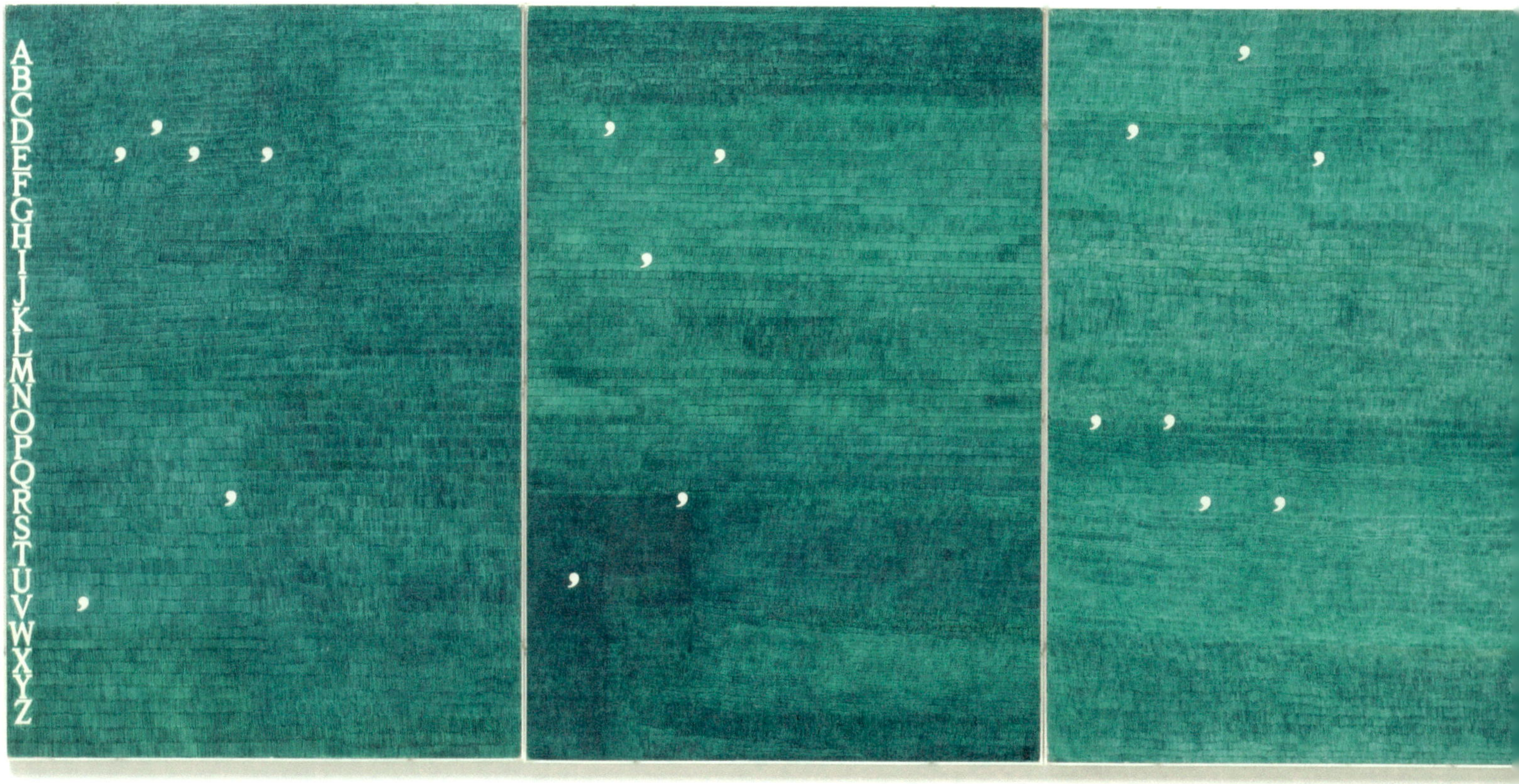
ABCDEFGHIJKLMNOPQRSTUVWXYZ

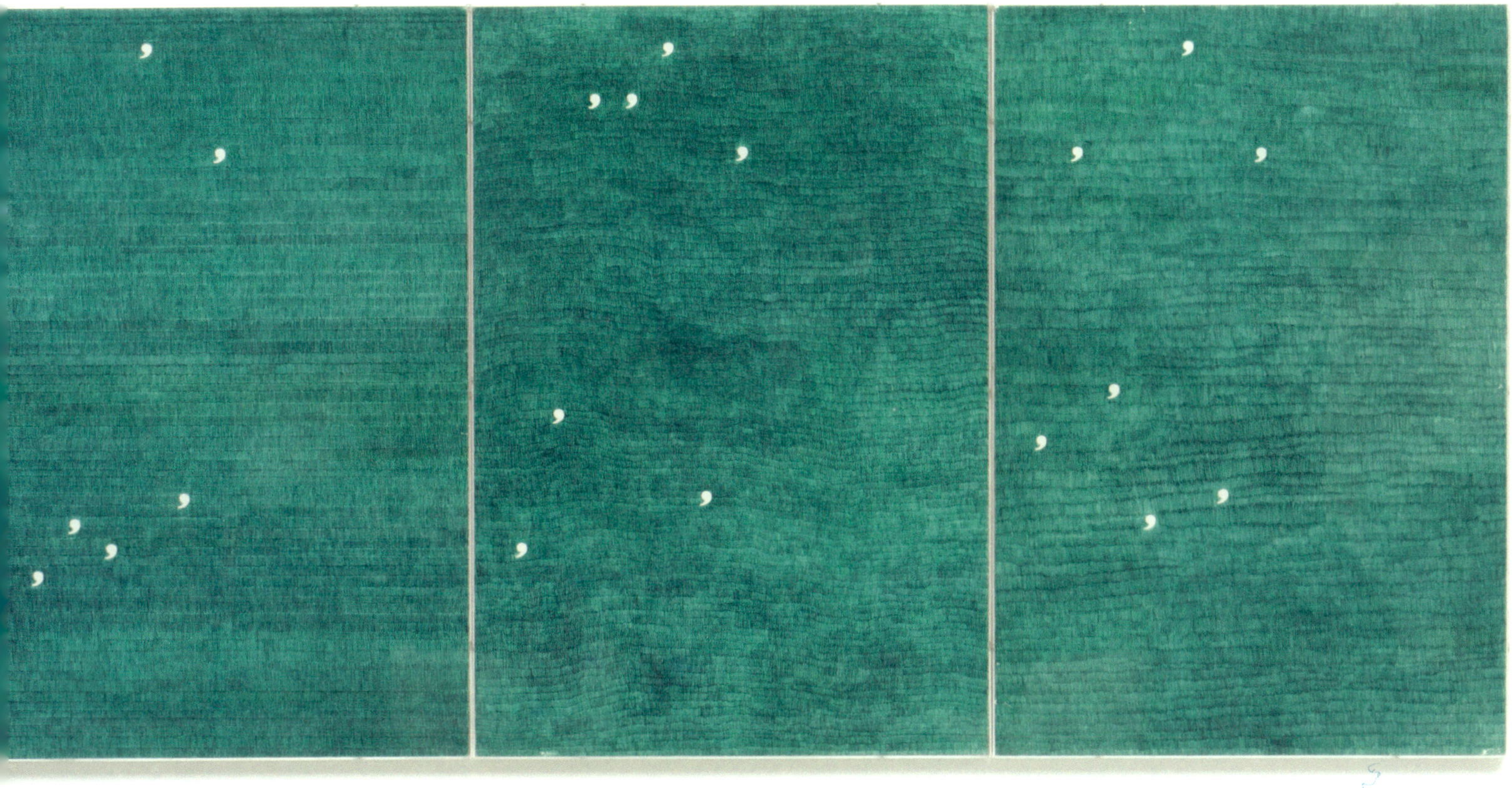

 I sei sensi (The Six Senses), 1974–75

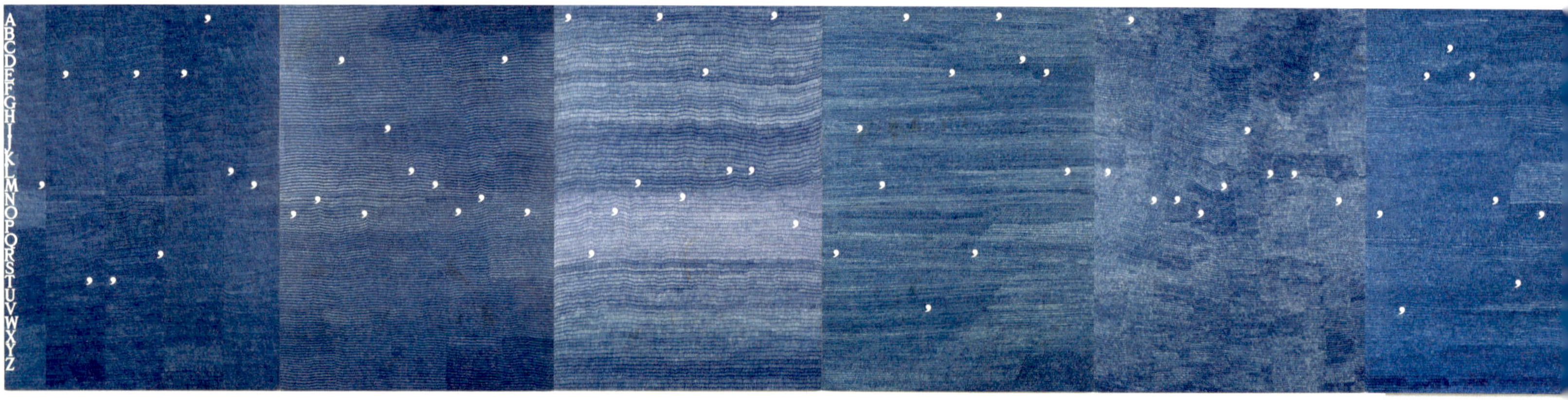
ABCDEFGHIJKLMNOPQRSTUVWXYZ

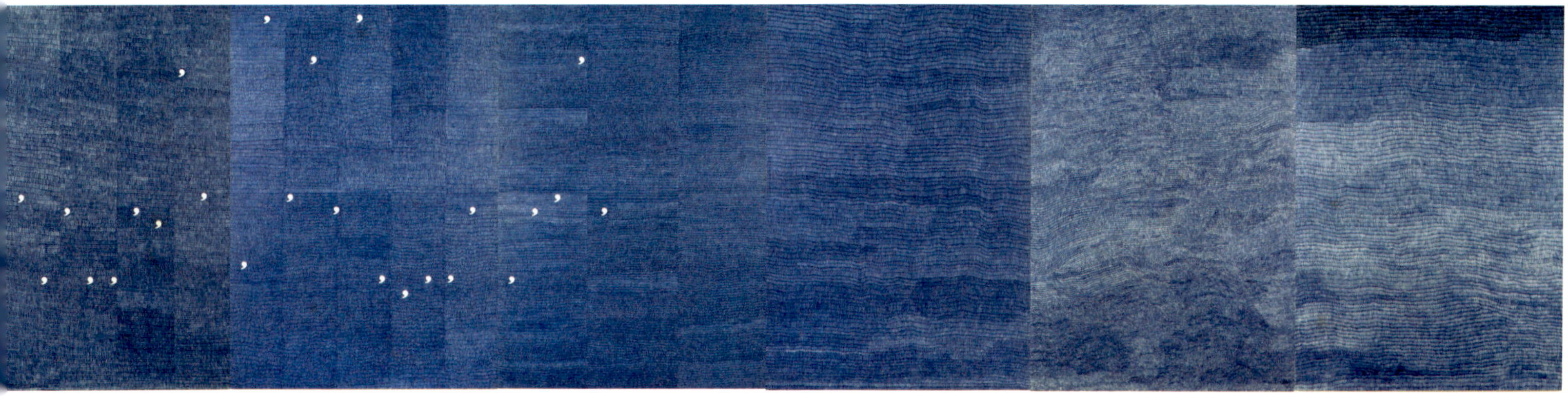

Mettere al mondo il mondo a Roma nella primavera dell'anno mille novecentosettantotto pensando a tutto tondo (Putting the World into the World in Rome in the Spring of the Year Nineteen Hundred and Seventy-eight Thinking in the Round), 1978

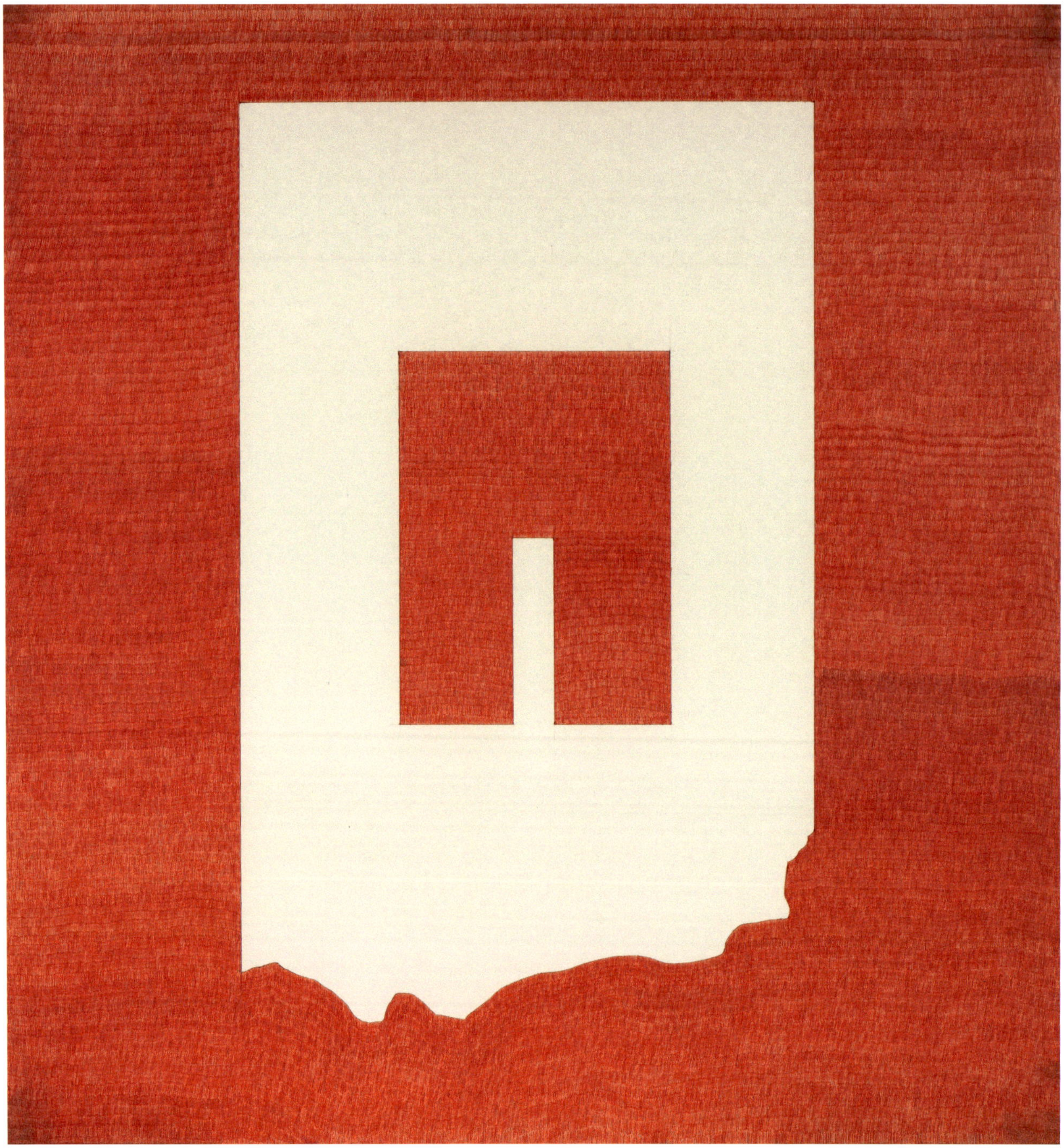

Pier/Piet, 1982 (detail)

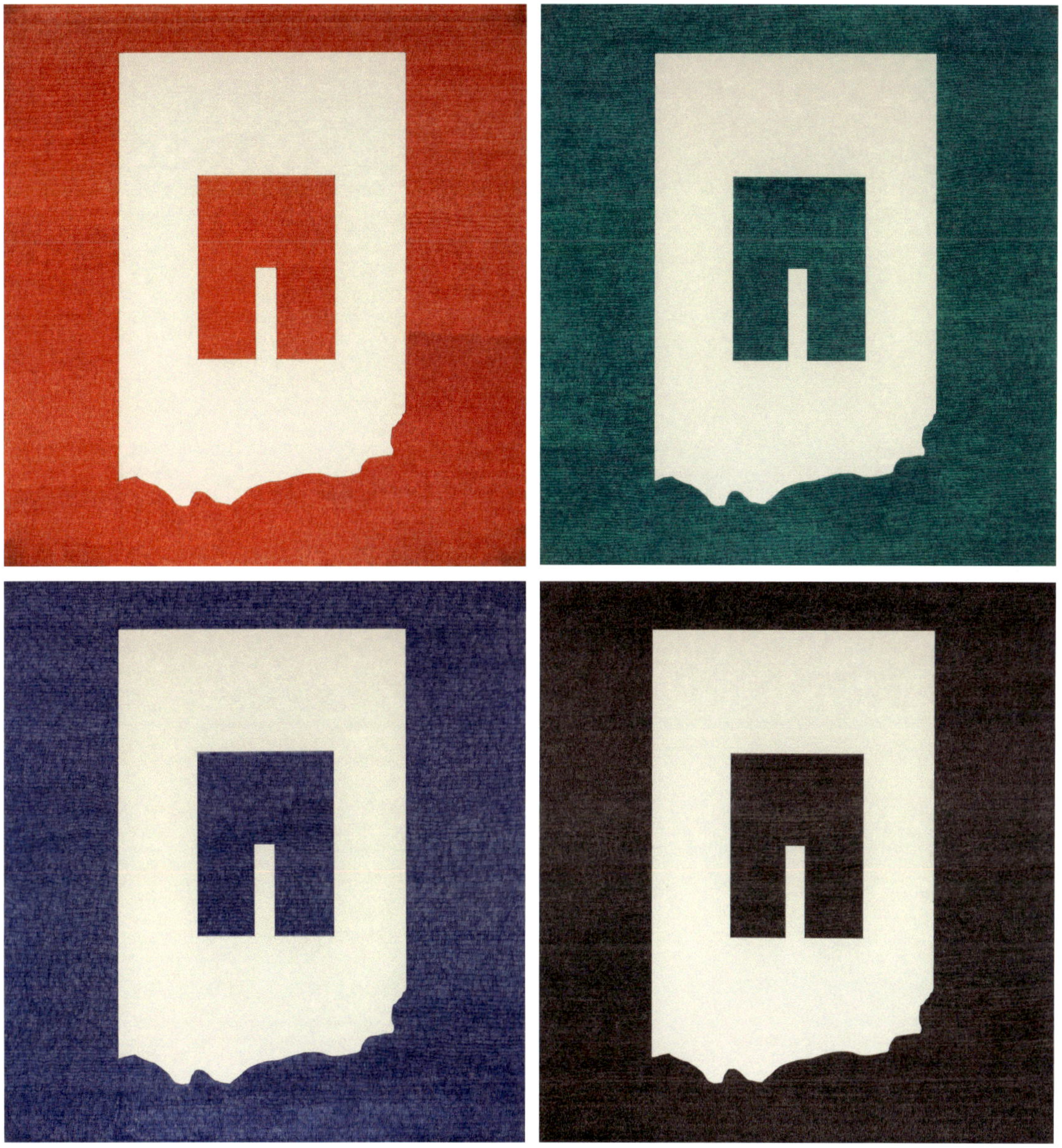

 Pier/Piet, 1982

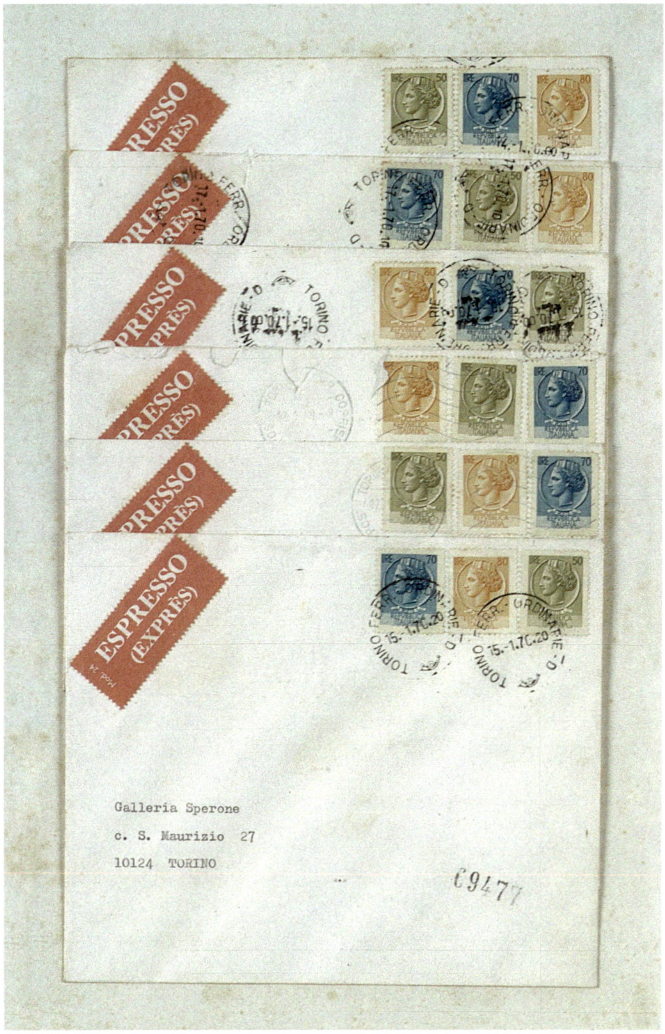

Lavoro postale (permutazione) (Postal Work [Permutation]), 1970

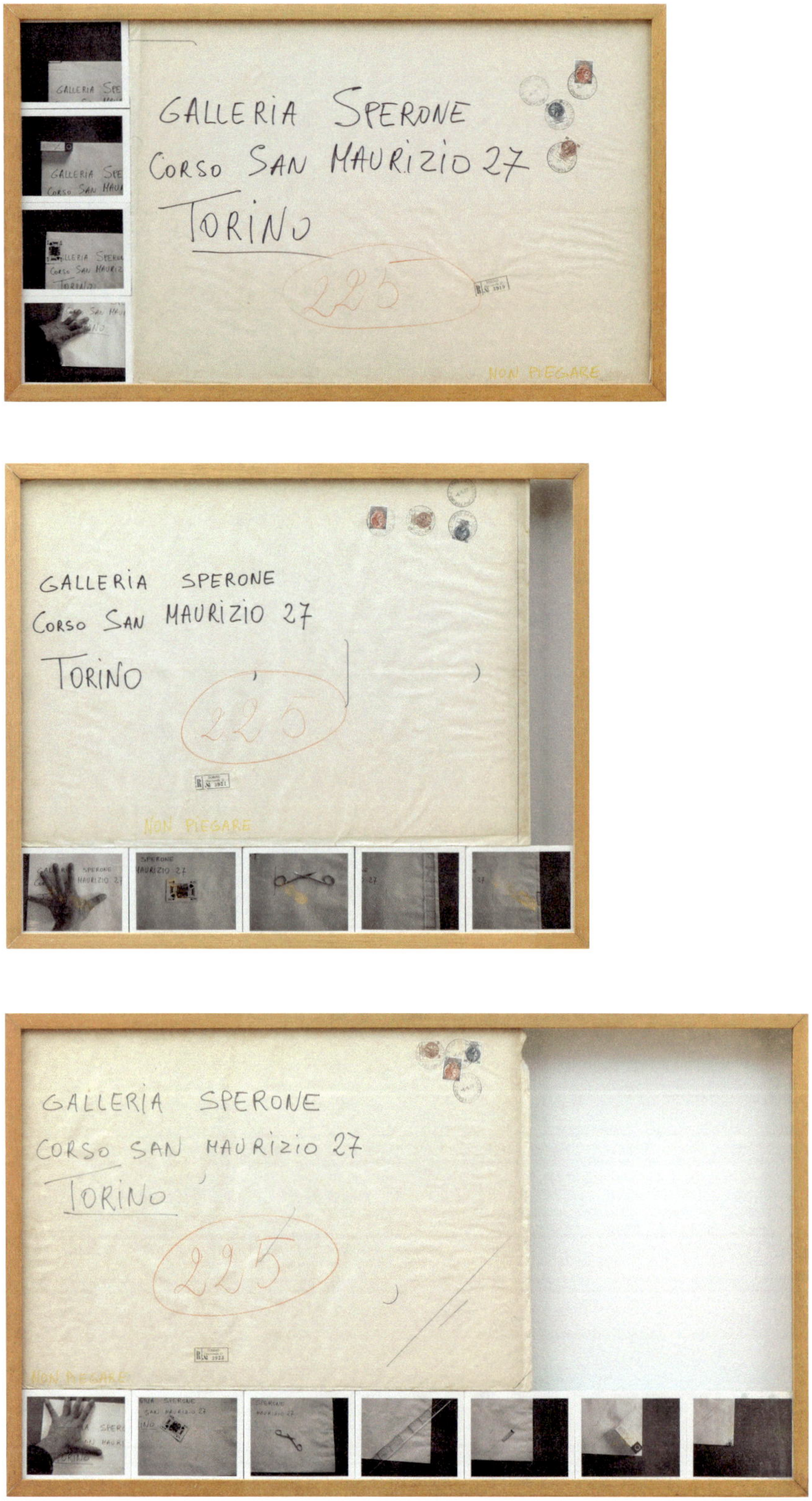

Per una storia naturale della misurazione (Towards a Natural History of Measurement), 1970

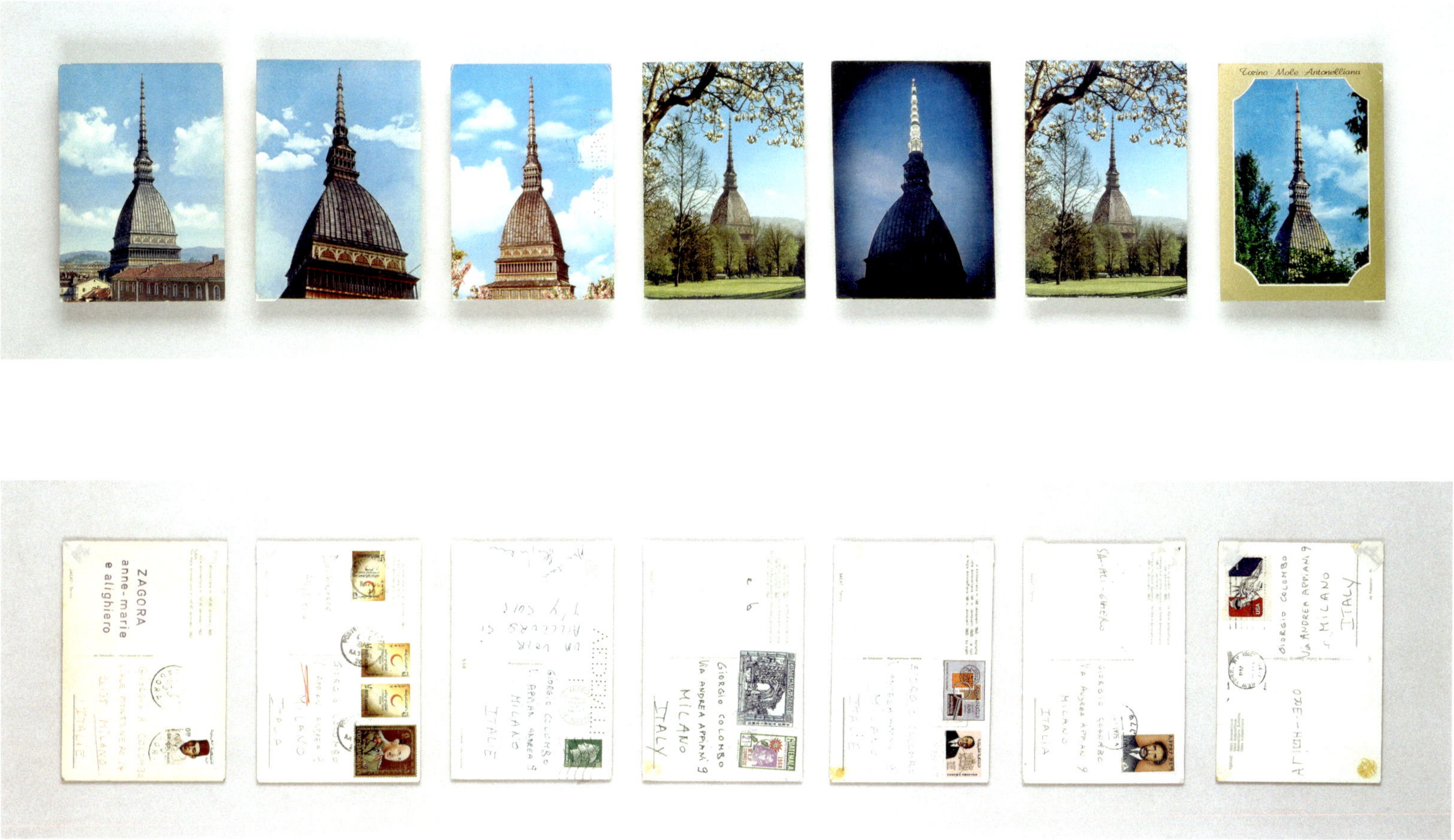

La Mole Antonelliana, 1970–75 (recto/verso)

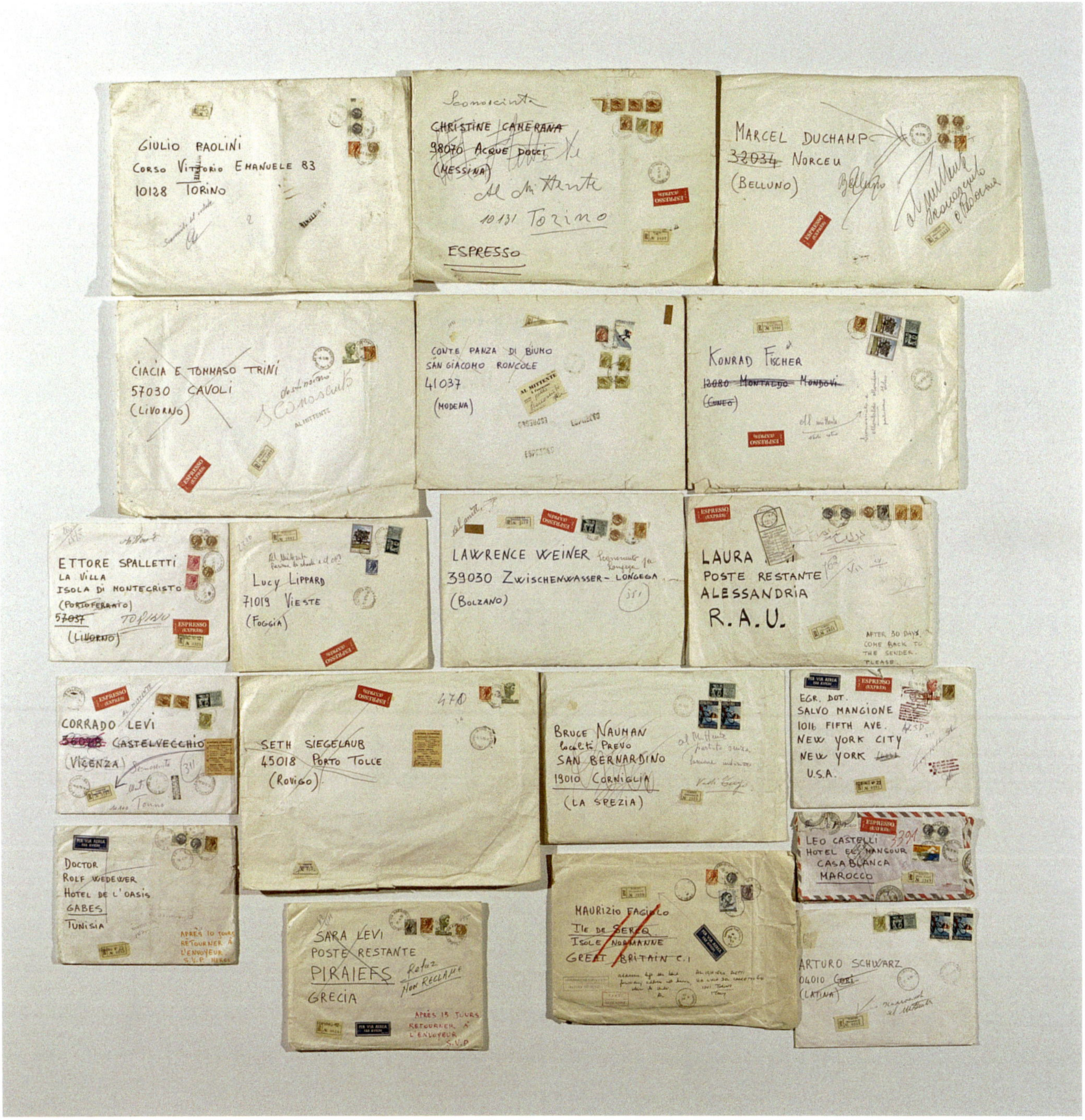

Viaggi postali (Postal Voyages), 1969–70

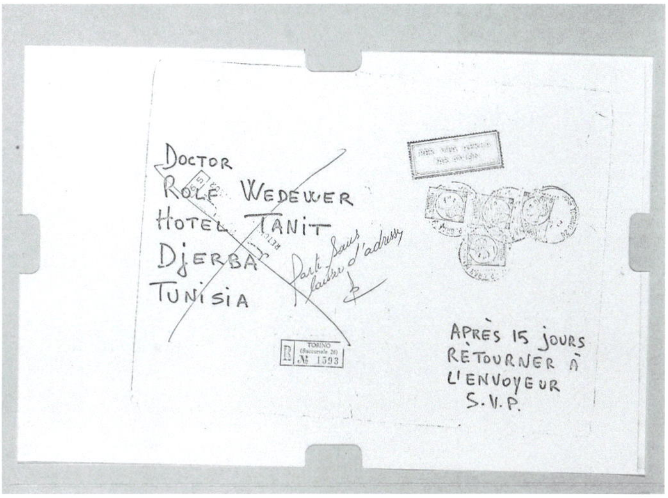

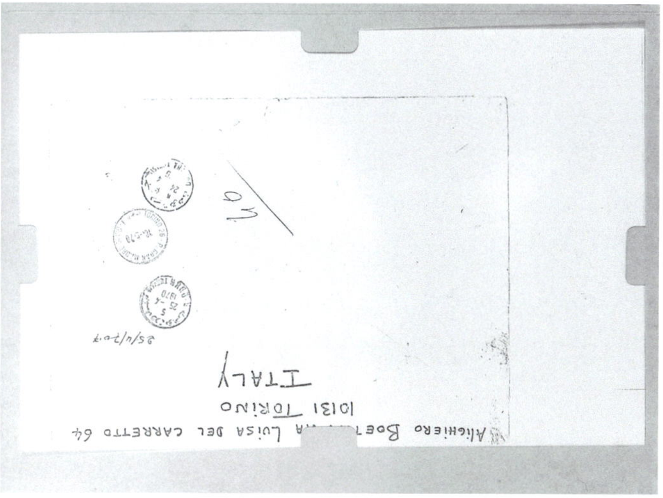

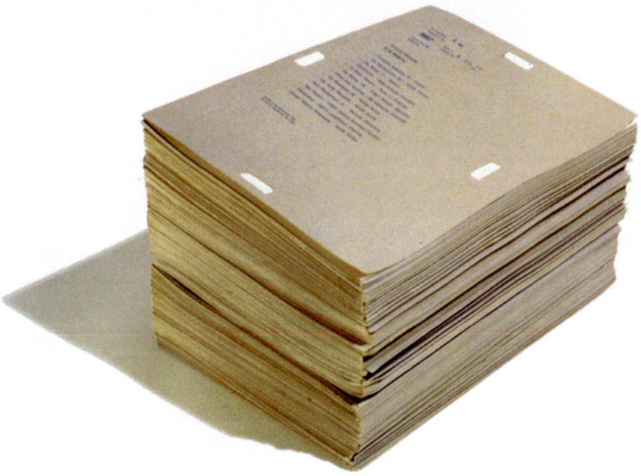

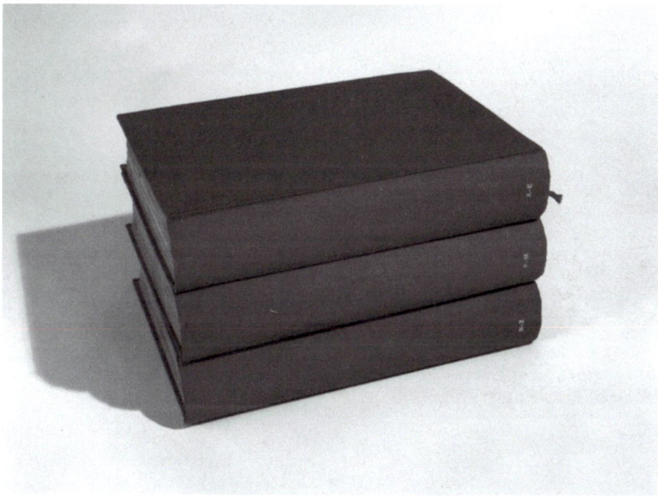

 Dossier postale (Postal Dossier), 1969–70 (details)

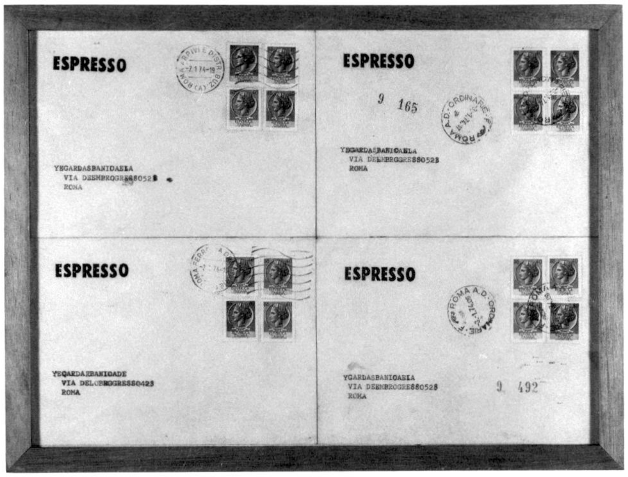

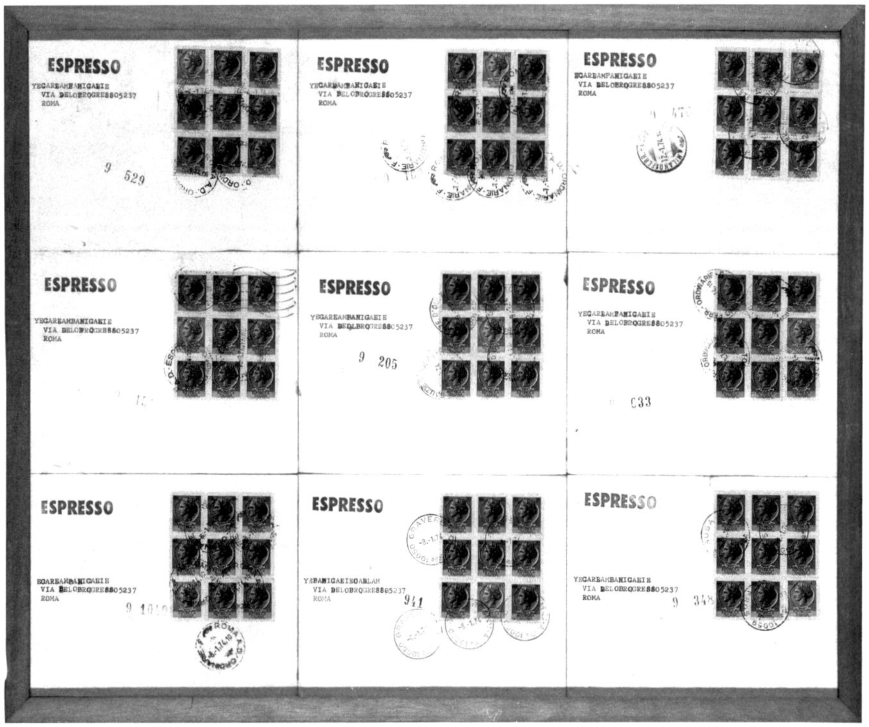

Lavoro postale (Postal Work), 1974 (details)

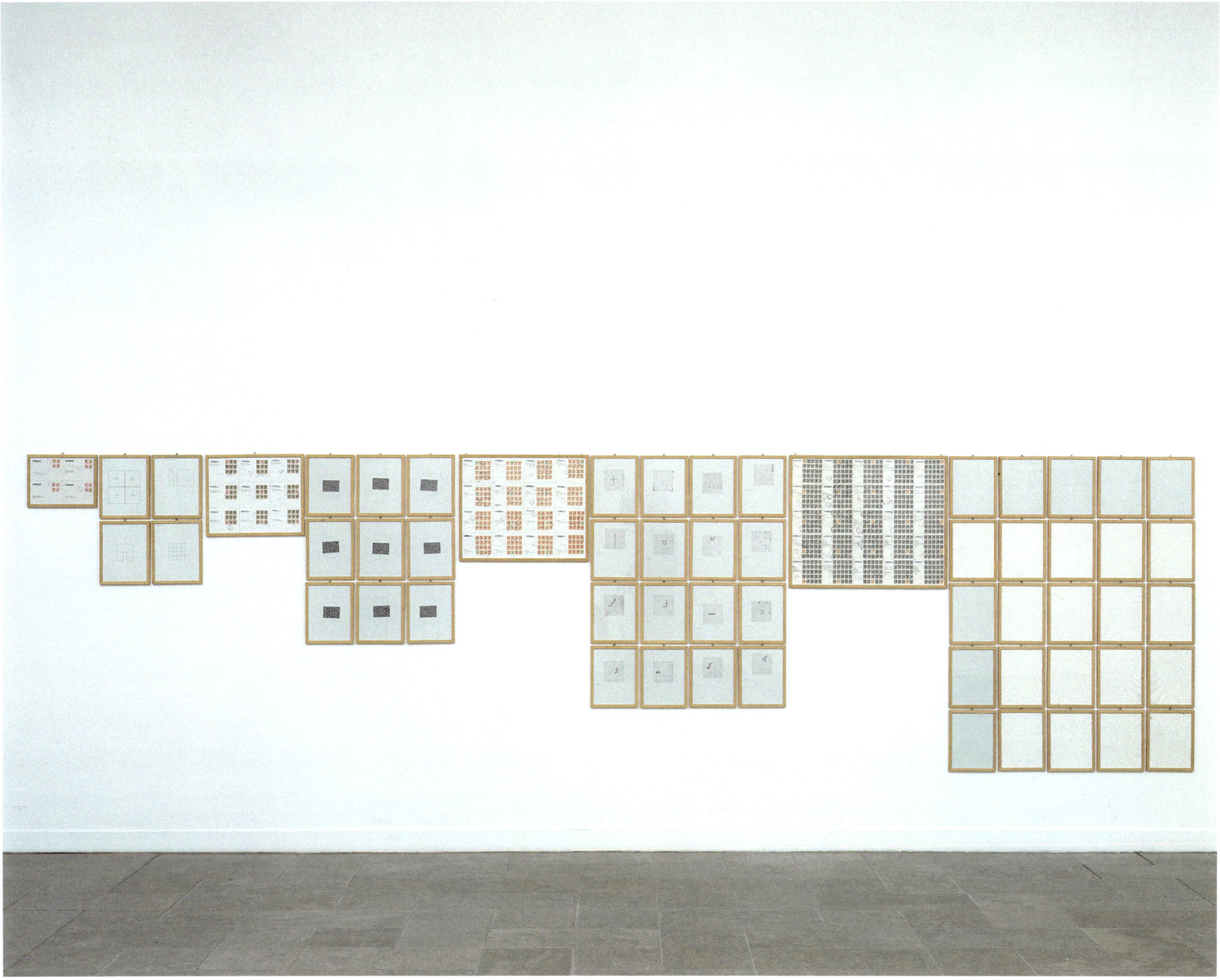

 Lavoro postale (Postal Work), 1974

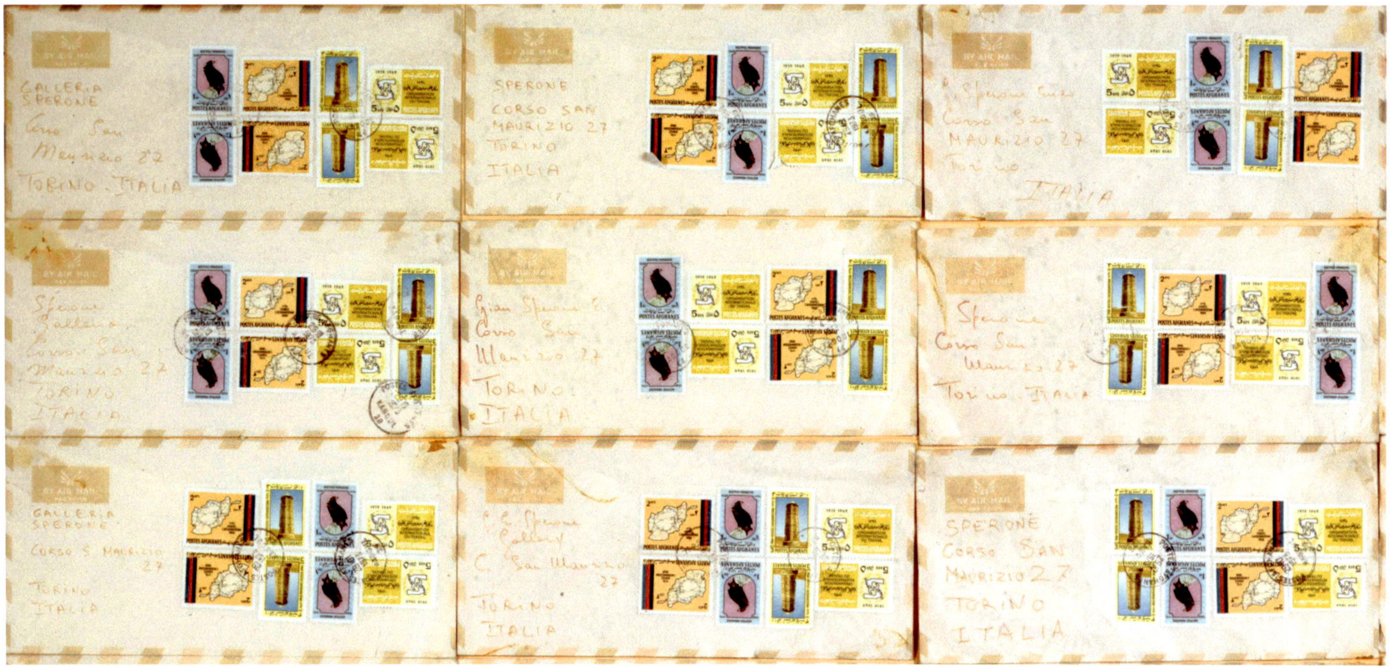

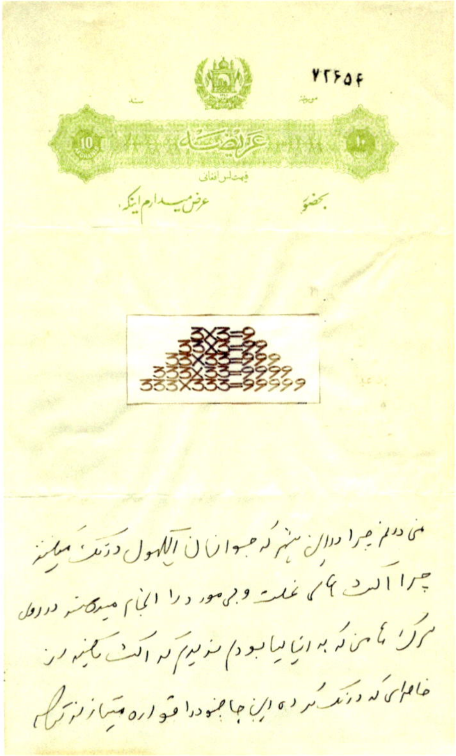

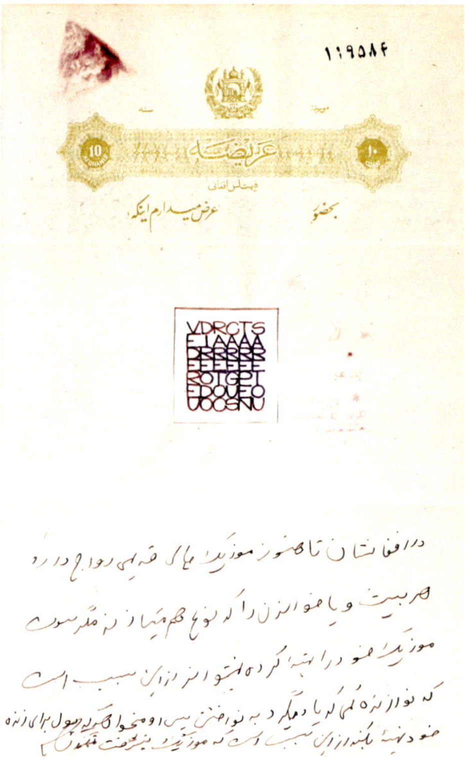

24 lettere dall'Afghanistan (24 Letters from Afghanistan), 1973 (details)

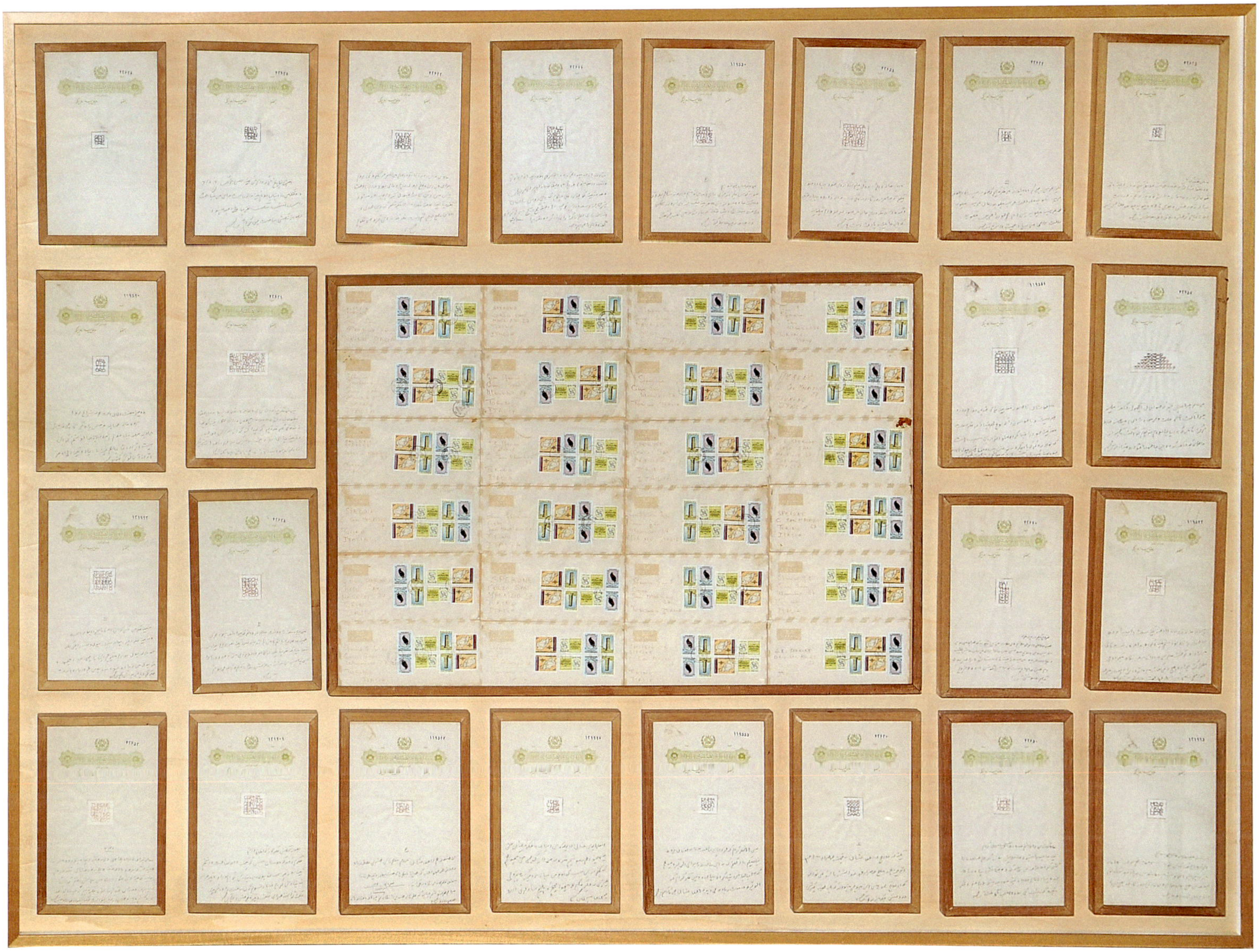

24 lettere dall'Afghanistan (24 Letters from Afghanistan), 1973

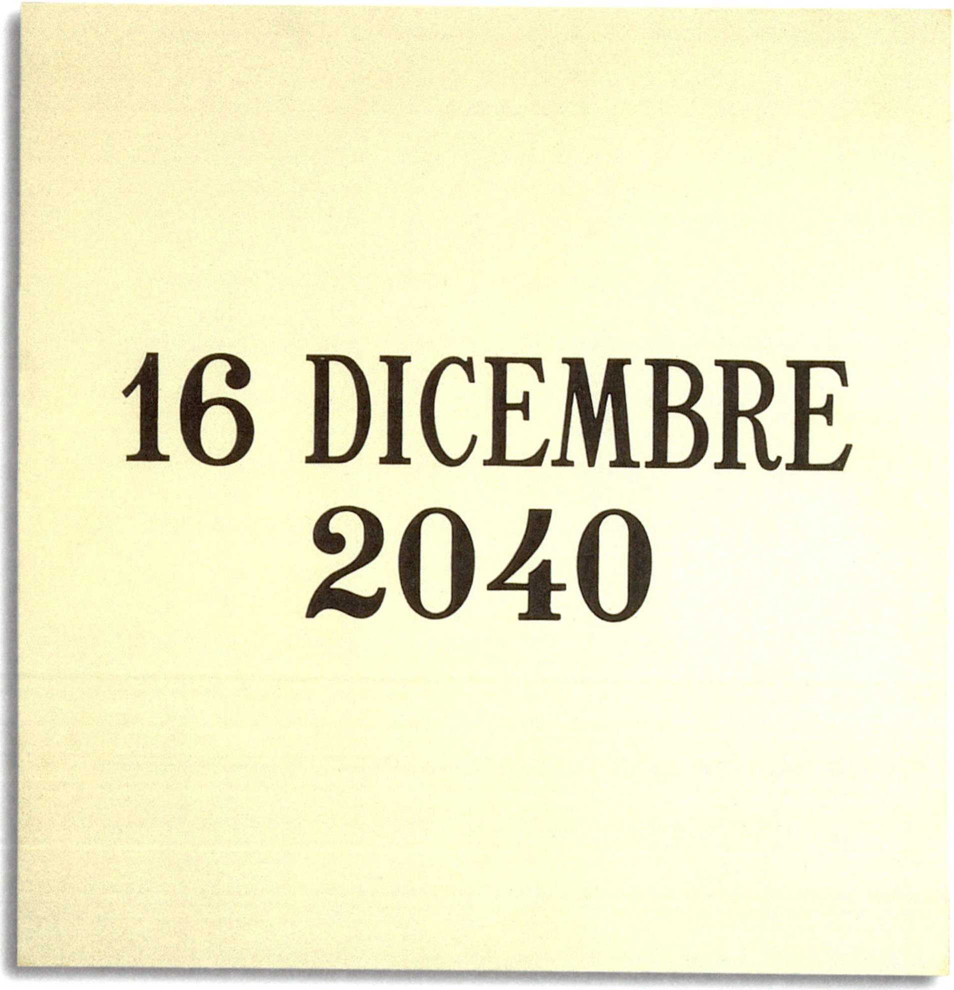
16 DICEMBRE
2040

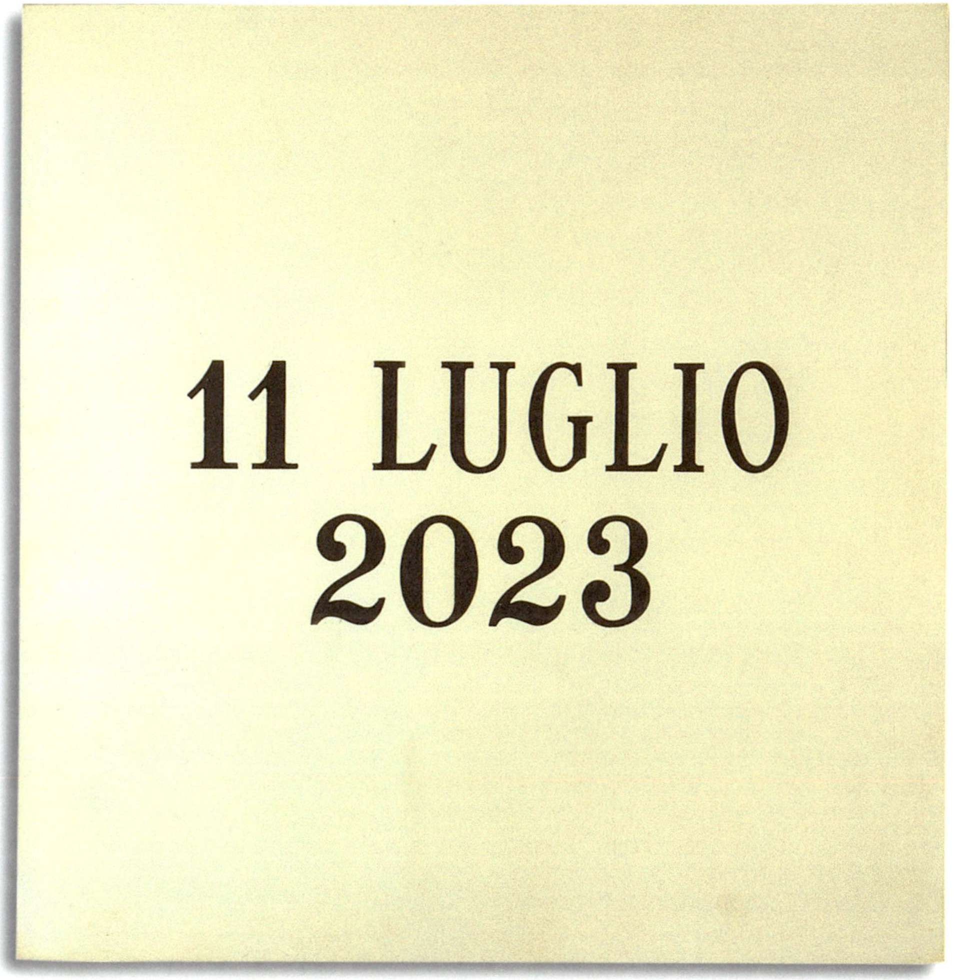

16 DICEMBRE 2040 – 11 LUGLIO 2023 (December 16, 2040 – July 11, 2023), 1971

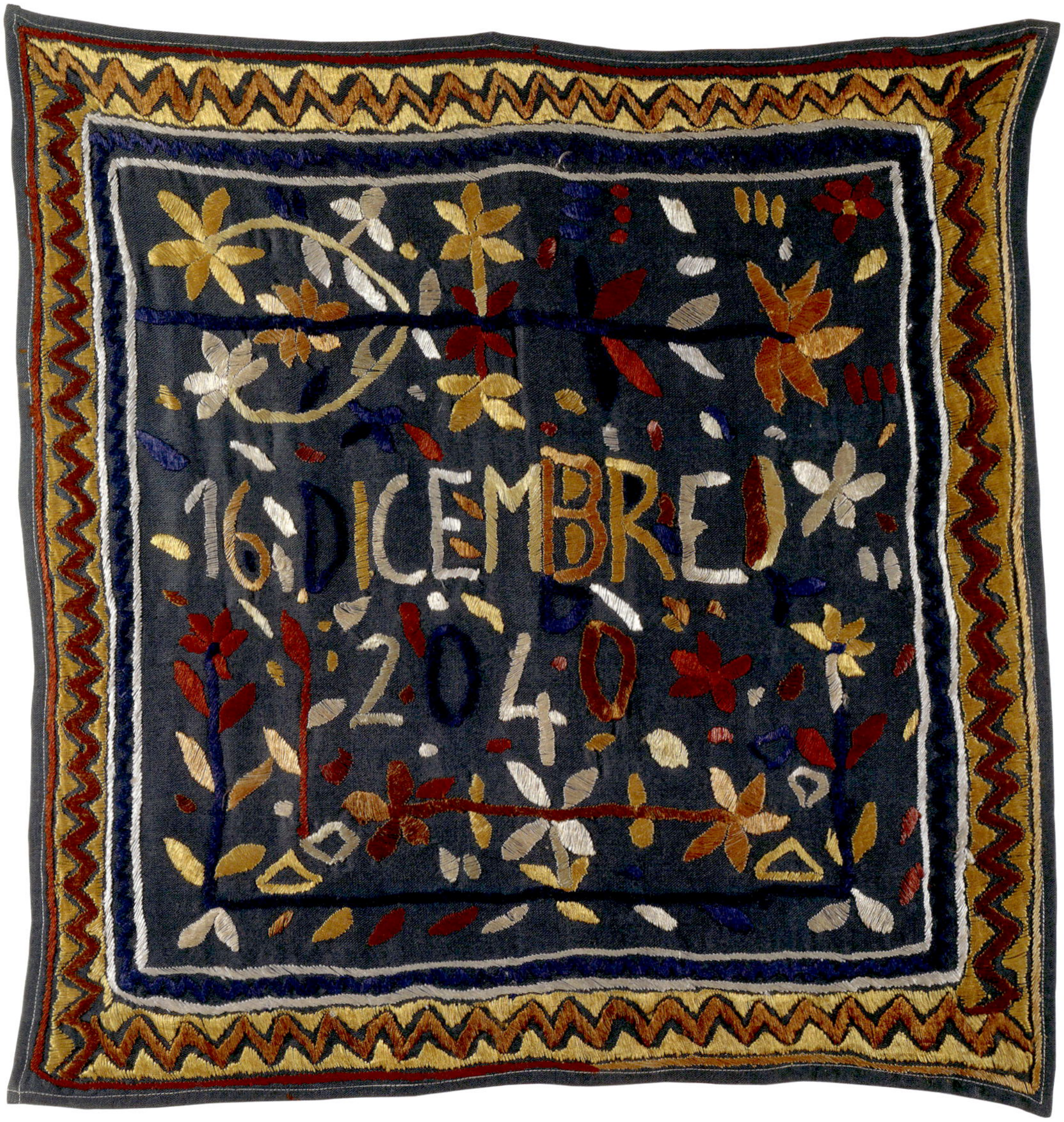
16 DICEMBRE
2040

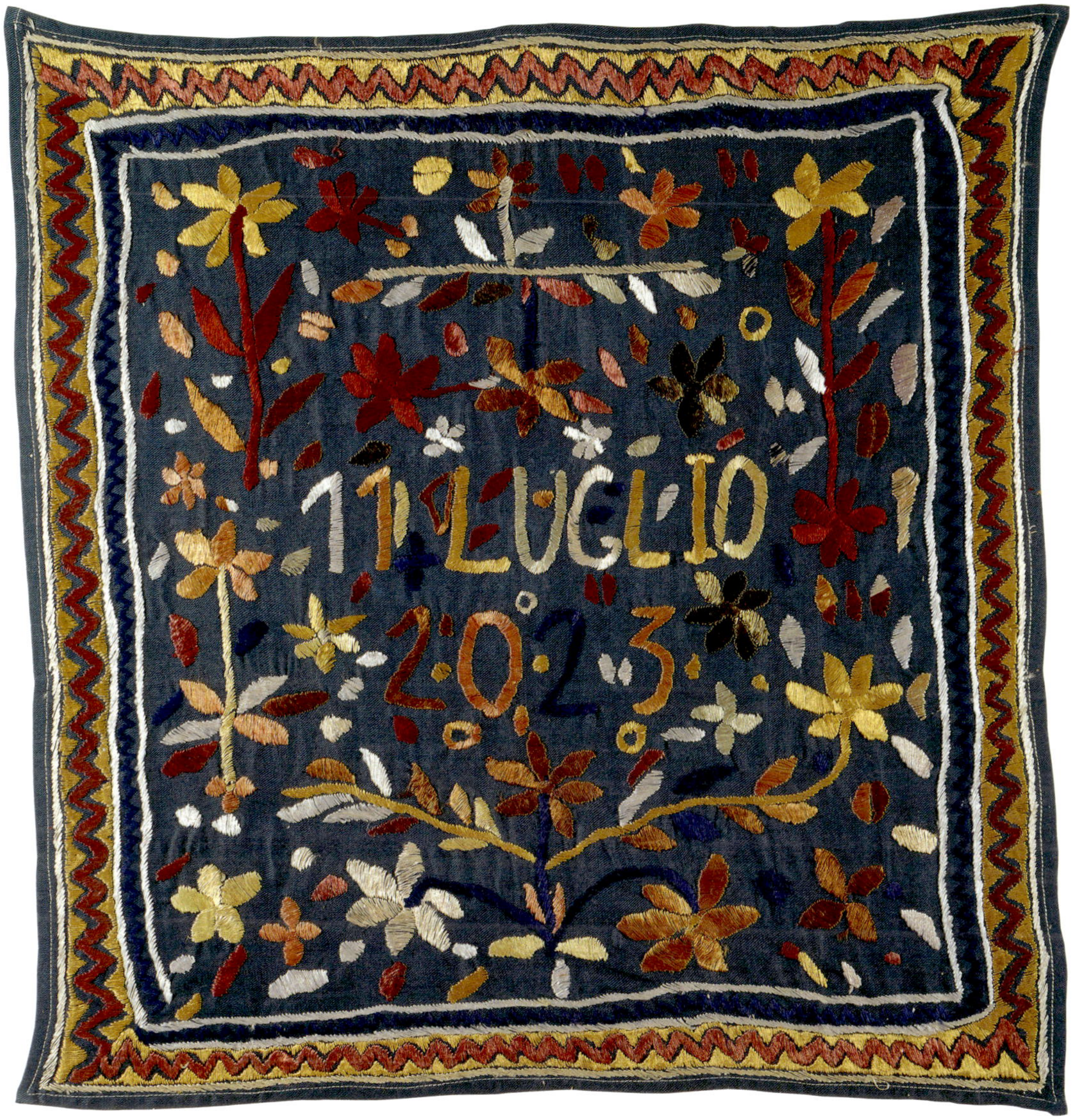

 16 DICEMBRE 2040 – 11 LUGLIO 2023 (December 16, 2040 – July 11, 2023), 1971

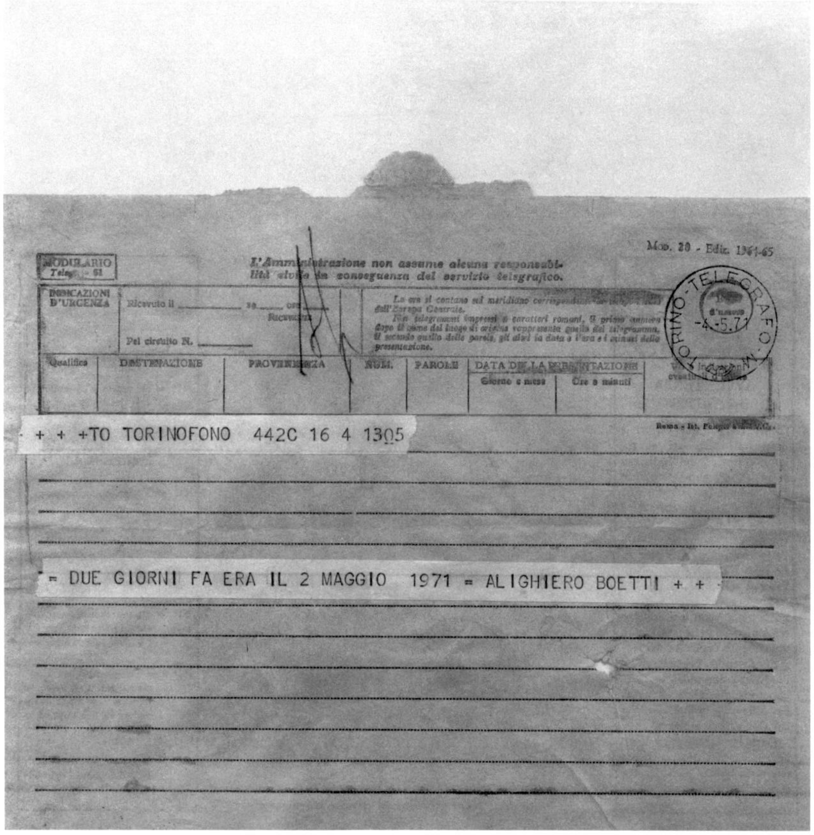

Mod. 20 - Ediz. 1964-65

L'Amministrazione non assume alcuna responsabilità civile in conseguenza del servizio telegrafico.

TORINO - TELEGRAFO

-4-5.71

Qualifica | DESTINAZIONE | PROVENIENZA | NUM. | PAROLE | DATA DELLA PRESENTAZIONE | Giorno e mese | Ore e minuti

+ + +TO TORINOFONO 442C 16 4 1305

= DUE GIORNI FA ERA IL 2 MAGGIO 1971 = ALIGHIERO BOETTI + +

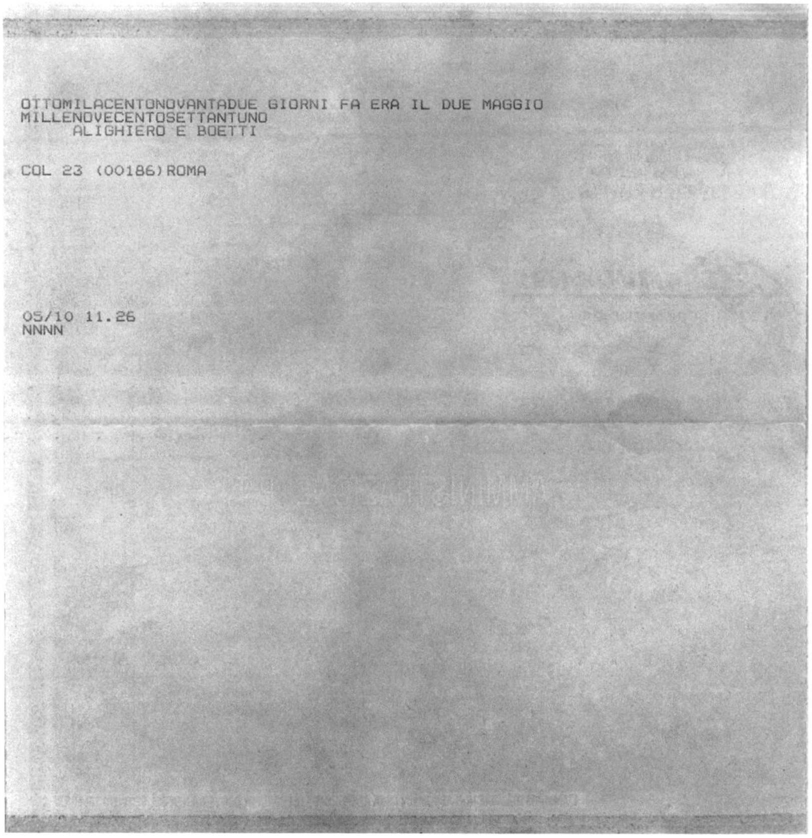

OTTOMILACENTONOVANTADUE GIORNI FA ERA IL DUE MAGGIO
MILLENOVECENTOSETTANTUNO
ALIGHIERO E BOETTI

COL 23 (00186) ROMA

05/10 11.26
NNNN

Serie di merli disposti a intervalli regolari lungo gli spalti di una muraglia (A Row of Merlons Set at Regular Intervals Along the Ramparts of a Wall), 1971–93 (details)

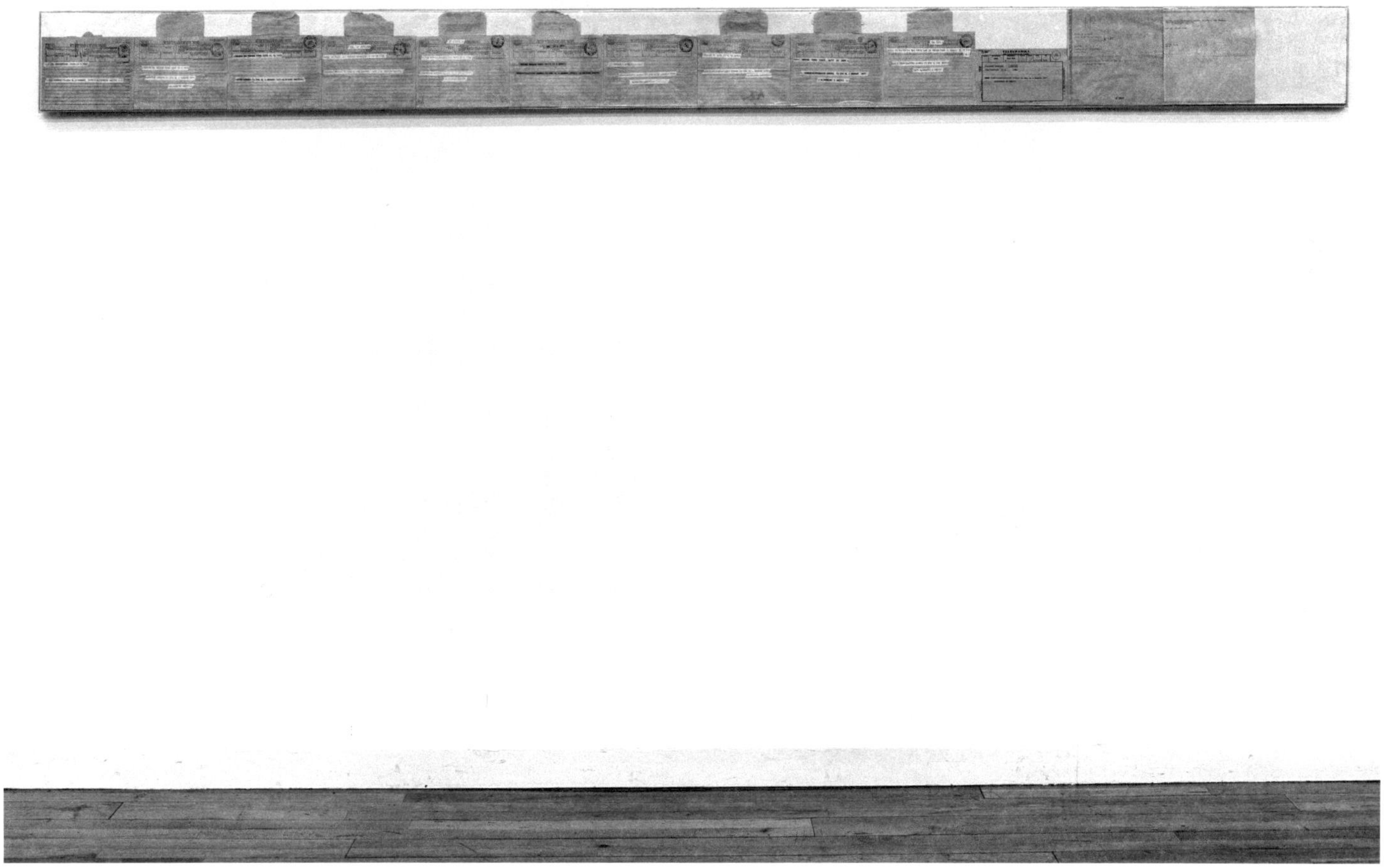

Serie di merli disposti a intervalli regolari lungo gli spalti di una muraglia (A Row of Merlons Set at Regular Intervals Along the Ramparts of a Wall), 1971–93

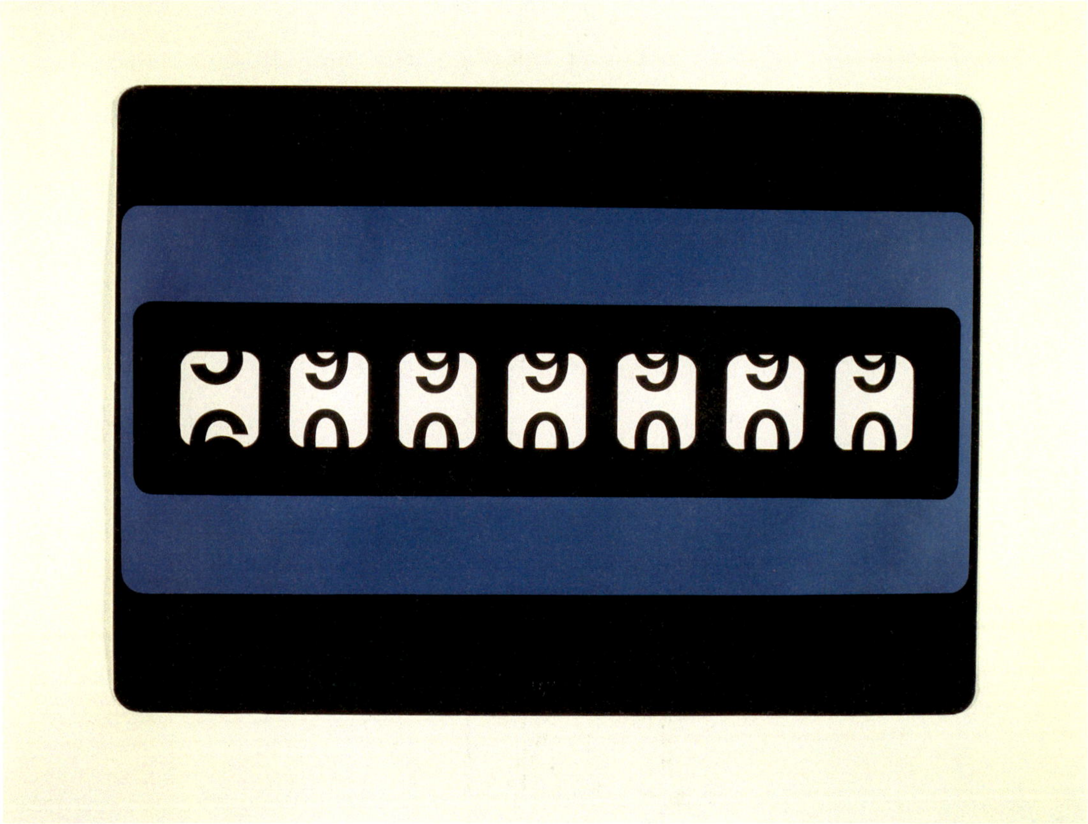

Contatore (Counter), 1967

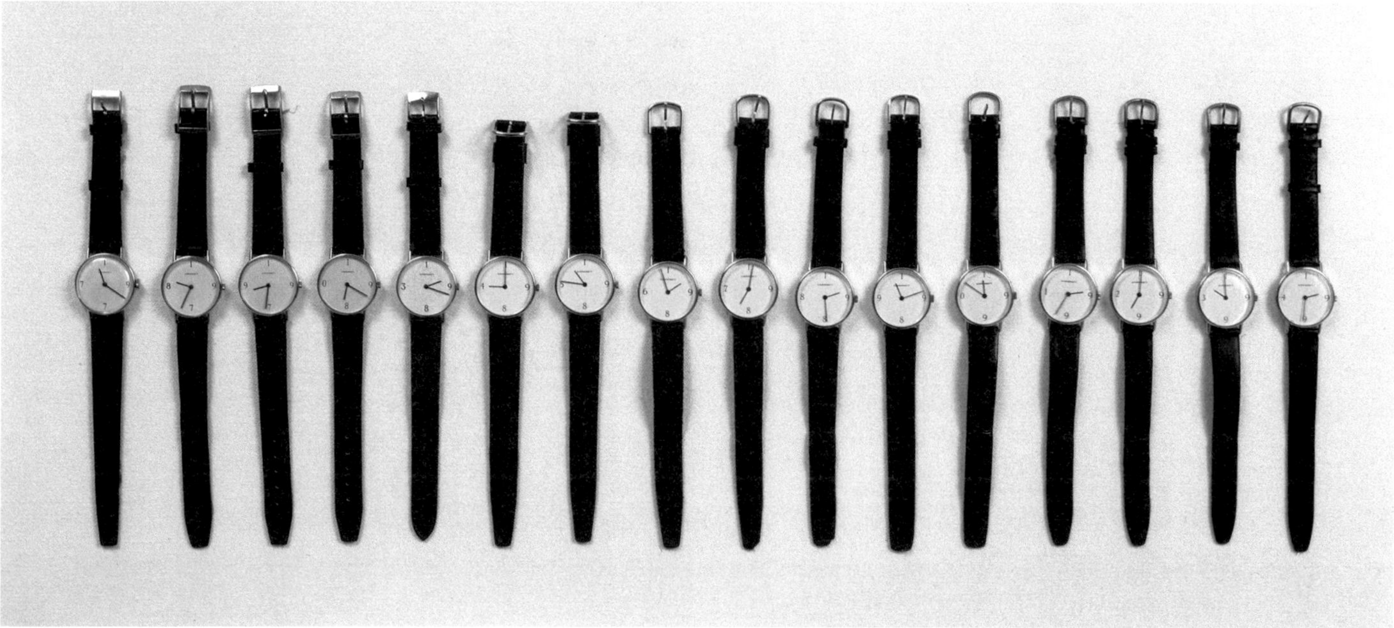

 Orologi annuali (Annual Watches), 1977–94

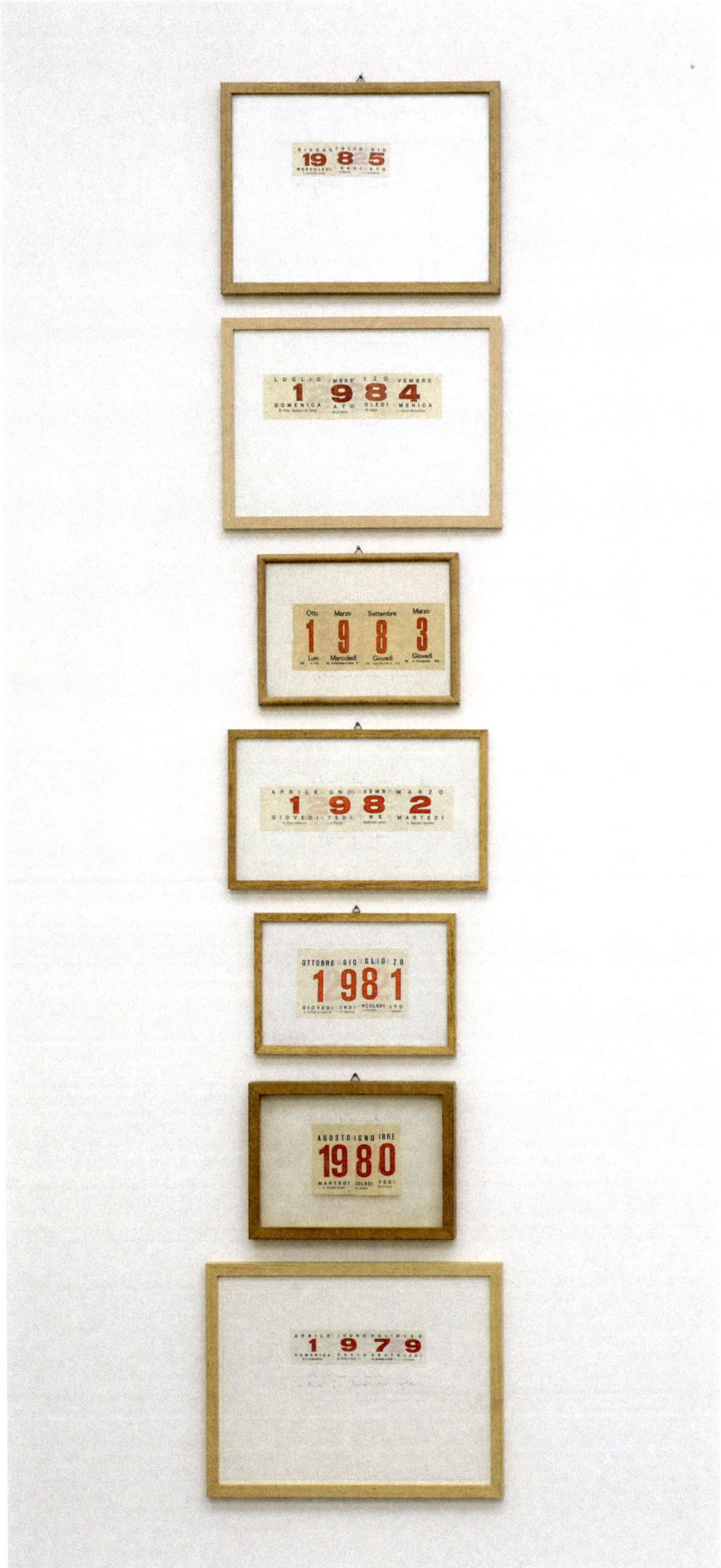

Calendari (Calendars) 1978–94

131 L'albero delle ore (The Hour Tree), 1979

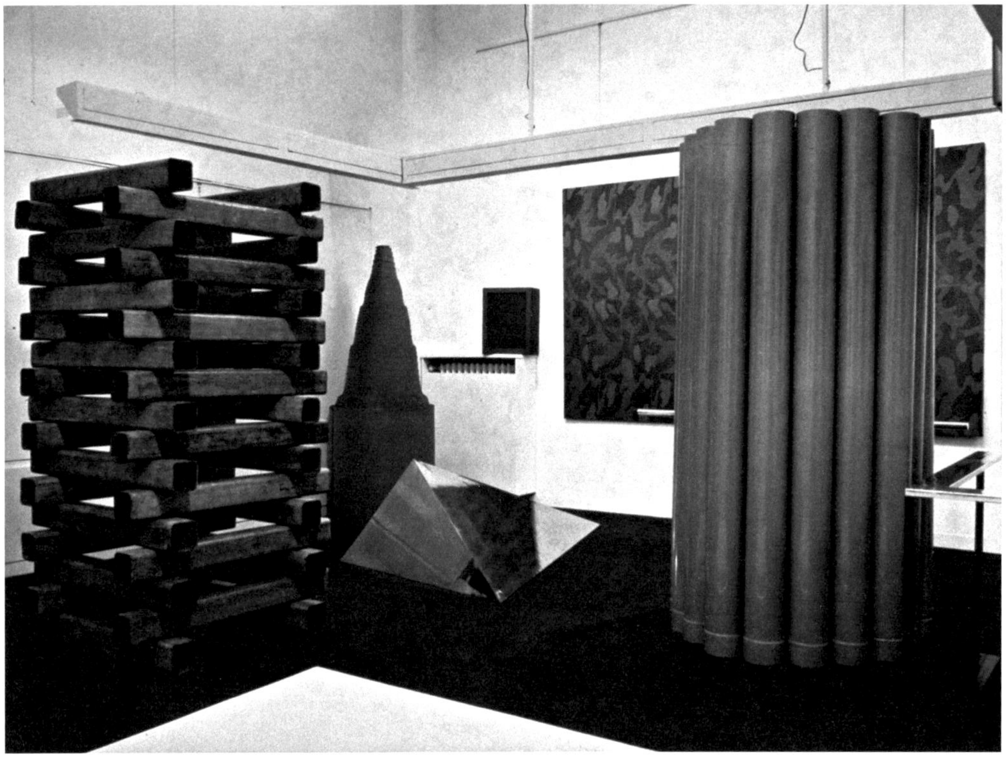

[fig. 1] Alighiero Boetti's first solo show at Christian Stein Gallery, Turin, 1967

Figuring Boetti

Claire Gilman

> I remember having exhibited *Colonne di carta* (made of paper from a cakeshop) in *Il percorso* [*Itinerary*] an exhibition of Arte Povera in 1968 at Arco d'Alibert Gallery in Rome [fig. 2]. On exactly the same day an exhibition by Pascali opened at the Attico: his *Bachi da setola* [*Bristle-worms*] were on show, made with brushes—the same sort of thing really. Pino and I were amazed by the story: on the very same day, I went to the cake shop to buy paper and he went to the hardware shop to buy the brushes, which he put together in a group. We had reached the limits of certain possibilities, and then Pascali died.[1]

Alighiero Boetti's declaration to Mirella Bandini in 1972 is generally taken as marking a fortuitous moment in Italian art history; a moment in which artists hailing from different cities and backgrounds came together to form the Arte Povera movement. As framed by Germano Celant, the Genoese critic who identified the group and organized its early exhibitions, Arte Povera was the Italian variant of a more international trend—reflected in tendencies like Postminimalism, Process, and Land Art—to reject artifice and illusionism in favor of essential material facts and behavioral conditions. Hence Arte Povera's penchant for unrefined, commonplace materials in opposition to Minimalism's hard-edged forms; its deliberate rejection of figuration for immediate, elemental "presence." With Boetti hailing from Turin and Pino Pascali from Rome, the artists' near simultaneous decision to purchase everyday objects at supply stores and to arrange their prefabricated materials through rote stacking seemed amply to demonstrate Arte Povera's geographical ubiquity as Celant defined it.

Boetti was one of Celant's favored artists: the curator selected him for the first Arte Povera group show at Genoa's La Bertesca Gallery in September 1967 and for every official exhibition thereafter. At La Bertesca, Boetti showed a version of *Catasta*, an object made of hollow bars of Eternit—a company-manufactured material used in building construction—stacked crosswise. *ill. p. 42* Another version of *Catasta* had premiered earlier that year in Boetti's first solo exhibition, at Turin's Christian Stein Gallery [fig. 1], and similar pieces made with Eternit tubes featured in his second solo show held at La Bertesca in December. *ill. p. 149* Of this work and others, Celant wrote: "Boetti's gestures . . . appear as an immediate apprehension of every gestural archetype . . . the cut as cut, the heap as heap, mathematical equations of real=real, action=action. A univocal sign language that expresses 'all the possible formative and organization processes' freed from every historical and worldly contingency."[2] Boetti is here positioned as the quintessential Arte Povera artist, intent on eliminating uncertainty and connotation in pursuit of the inviolability of materials and rudimentary gesture.

1 Mirella Bandini, interview with Alighiero Boetti (1972), trans. in *Zero to Infinity: Arte Povera 1962–1972*, eds. Richard Flood and Frances Morris (Minneapolis and London: Walker Art Center and Tate Modern 2001), p. 190. A portion of this interview was originally published in *NAC*, no. 3 (March 1973).

2 Germano Celant, "Arte Povera," reprinted and trans. in *Arte Povera / Art Povera*, ed. Germano Celant (Milan: Electa, 1988), p. 33. Originally published in *Arte Povera –IM spazio* (Genoa: Galleria La Bertesca, 1967).

ill. p. 52 Executed in 1968, *Colonne* followed two years of production in which Boetti experimented with everyday materials like cardboard, glass, cement, electric light, PVC tubes, steel, plywood, Eternit, and found fabric. His intervention was typically minimal—such as stacking doilies, piling Eternit bars or, in *Rotolo di cartone ondulato* (1966), pushing up the center of a roll of corrugated paper—and it is fundamental to the finished works that the materials remain unaltered. For example, *Mimetico* (1966) is nothing but a stretched panel of readymade military fabric, and *Mazzo di tubi* (1966) is a group of upright PVC tubes bunched together in a circle. *Scala* and *Sedia* (both 1966), a found ladder and chair respectively, remain unmolested save for the addition of extra wood strips following the objects' readymade contours. Similarly, *Catasta's* Eternit bars proudly display their company logo and date of manufacture as if refusing to accept their newfound aesthetic configuration. All of these works shared the space at Christian Stein, where they came together like a veritable catalogue of diverse building materials and methods. Supporting this impression was the official invitation to which Boetti attached samples of the materials employed. Wood, Eternit, PVC, Perspex, electric wiring—each was precisely positioned and labeled in frank testament to the objects' humble origins.

ill. p. 43 *ill. p. 44* *ill. p. 45* *ill. p. 46*

It may seem paradoxical therefore that, in likening his work to Pascali's, Boetti chose to align his intervention with one that assembled pre-found objects and overtly transformed them into *something else*. As I have argued elsewhere, there is in fact a resolutely figurative dimension throughout Pascali's brief career that, regardless of the materials employed, renders his affiliation with Arte Povera problematic to say the least.[3] From his 1965 trompe l'œil cannons made of found machine parts, through his animal sculptures including his "bristleworms," which the artist whimsically arranged climbing up gallery walls and across the floor, Pascali's sculptures consistently exploit the split between material substance and imagistic form. Scholars have reconciled Pascali's work with the standard account of Arte Povera by focusing on select works in which the artist incorporated everyday materials like scrubbing brushes and

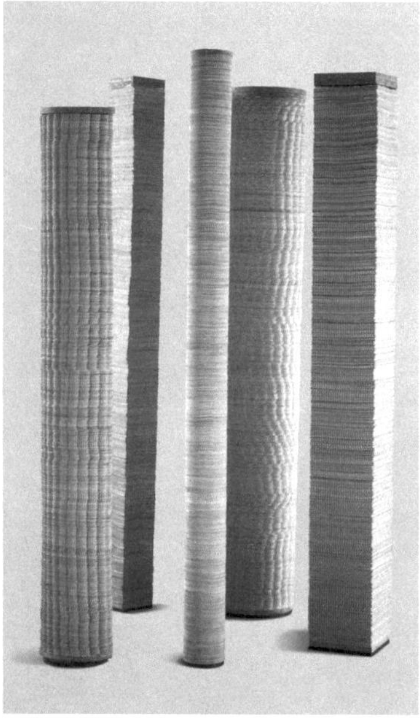

[fig. 2] Colonne (Columns) 1968

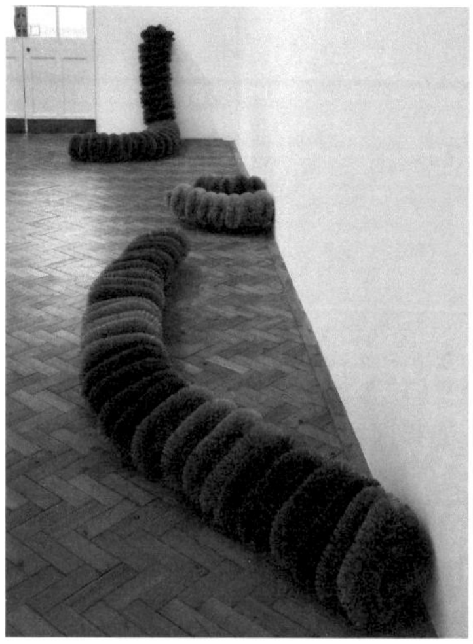

[fig. 3] Pino Pascali, *Bachi da setola* (Bristleworms), 1968

3 See my unpublished Ph.D. dissertation *Arte Povera's theatrical Impulse: Artifice and Anti-Modernism in Italian Art of the 1960s* (Ann Arbor, MI: UMI Research Press, 2006), Chapter 4. See also my "L'Arte Povera a Roma," in *La Confine evanescente: Arte italiana 1960–2010*, ed. Anna Mattirolo and Gabriele Guercio (Milan: Electa, 2010), pp. 52–57.

steel wool, as well as on his consistently exotic subject matter, as if his penchant for depicting prehistoric animals, seas, and waterfalls signaled a restoration of premodernity against the threat of consumer alienation. But what Pascali's sculptures evidence above all is the absurdity of Arte Povera's own pursuit of pure essence, a pursuit that underlies Modernism's dream of self-sufficiency more generally. His schematic creatures, all made out of white canvas stretched over visibly perceptible wooden frames, foreground the representational process itself. These are figures of convention, figures that have passed through an organizing consciousness and that are by no means fixed or necessary. Implicit here is an acknowledgment that images are not simply found; they are received, reconstructed in and through the act of perception [figs. 3–5].[4]

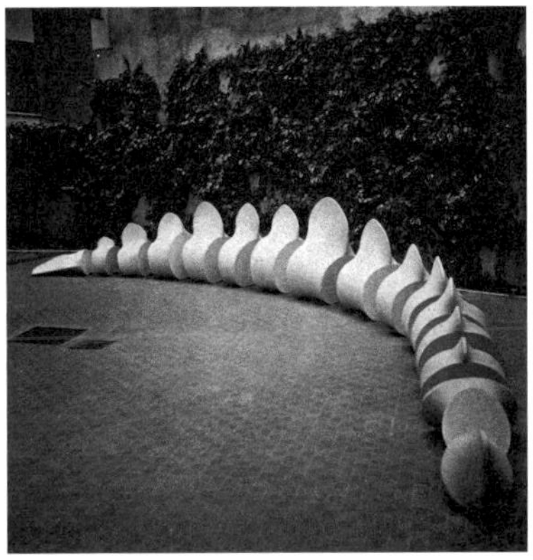

[fig. 4] Pino Pascali, *Ricostruzione del dinosauro* (Reconstruction of the dinosaur), 1966

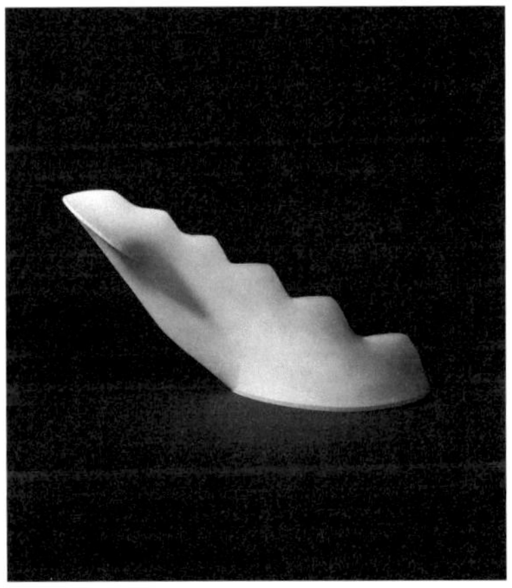

[fig. 5] Pino Pascali, *Testa di drago* (Dragon's Head), 1966

Boetti's own inappropriateness to the Arte Povera aesthetic is often acknowledged as well, but such discussions generally target his later more "conceptual" work (including the maps and language pieces), which follows his self-professed fatigue with the Arte Povera movement in late 1969. But his early affinity with Pascali suggests that it may be time to reconsider Boetti's Arte Povera period, and even the movement as a whole. Indeed, the artists to whom Boetti felt closest, both personally and professionally—Pascali, Giulio Paolini, Michelangelo Pistoletto, and Piero Gilardi to name a few—are without exception artists who have never quite fit the Arte Povera mold. These individuals did not necessarily hail from the same city or work in the same medium, but they shared an investment in art's representational function and, with it, the precise necessity of maintaining art's separation from real life.

Consider, for example, Pistoletto's mirror paintings (1961–62) in which he translated photographs of individuals via oil-stick crayon onto thin onionskin paper, which he then collaged, back-to-front, on reflective stainless steel grounds. In writing about the mirrors, critics have emphasized the element of live behavior, downplaying in turn the dialogue between painting, photography, and the reflecting surface. Whether an effect of the individuals' semi-turned-away poses or of the stillness produced by their abrupt isolation against

4 Notably, Pascali's public comments championed the artifice central to his work: "I do not want the feigned sculptures to become the sculptures that they seem to be," the artist explained in a 1967 interview. "What I hope is that they are not weighty... the canvases on their skeletons, resembling sculptures.... I have chosen not to concern myself with what is inside. The important thing is the layer of fiction that constitutes them all around." "Pino Pascali and Carla Lonzi: Discorsi," *Marcatré*, nos. 30–33, 1967, n.p.

active grounds, the cut-out figures manifest a kind of self-conscious posturing that in turn compels the viewer to reflect on his or her own behavior. Pistoletto reinforced this dynamic when he showed the mirror paintings in 1968 at Rome's L'Attico Gallery in a cinematic landscape complete with folding film chairs, period costumes, and props culled from *Cinecittà*. A strong film light accosted entering viewers while, in the next room, they were invited to dress up and pose for roving cameramen. Despite the common view that the mirror works activate free, mobile perception, the L'Attico installation showed them to be rooted in convention, in the way in which people pose, gesture, and take up positions within public space [fig. 6].

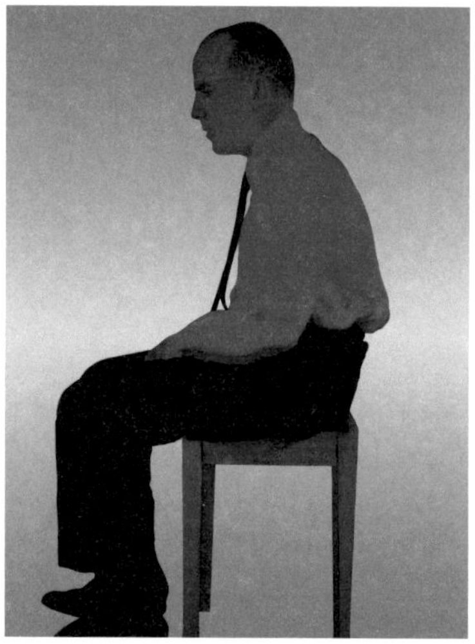

[fig. 6] Michelangelo Pistoletto, Uomo in camicia (Man with Shirt), 1962

A similar investment in the conventions that structure perception grounds the work of Paolini who, despite his persistent association with Arte Povera, was and remains an outlier due to his sustained preoccupation with painting. As early as 1960, he established the course his work would take with *Disegno geometrico*, a canvas empty but for the crossed ink lines traditionally used in measuring perspectival space [fig. 7]. Twelve years later, Paolini returned to this canvas, using it as a template for seven new paintings whose dimensions, horizon lines, and figures took their form from the structural geometry of the early work. In direct opposition to Arte Povera's emphasis on material immediacy, he explained his procedure as one of self-conscious transformation and removal: "If I place objects in the work, they are not there to place themselves in evidence in their objectness, but paradoxically, they are there in order to annul themselves, to make visible the space in which they come to be formed."[5]

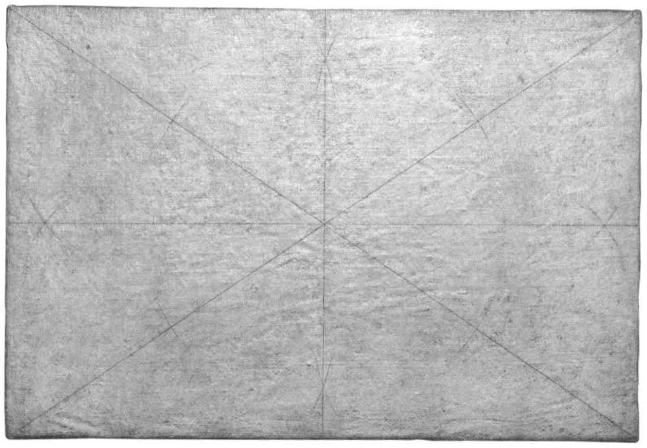

[fig. 7] Giulio Paolini, Disegno geometrico (Geometric Drawing), 1960

There is then in the work of Paolini, Pascali and Pistoletto what one may call a theatrical sensibility that, when considered as a whole, begins to present a very different picture of art in 1960s Italy from the one provided by the standard account. Boetti has referred to his own work in similar terms on more than one occasion, observing of a series of ephemeral interventions from 1966 (which ranged from arranging lines on the ground, to interspersing two flashing lights, to suspending a Plexiglas panel from the ceiling), that they

5 Giulio Paolini, "Luogo e contrade," interview by F. Pasini in *L'illustrazione italiana*, no. 24, May, 1985, quoted in Peter Weibel, *Giulio Paolini: Von heute bis gestern; Da oggi a ieri* (Stuttgart: Cantz, 1998), pp. 71–73. Unless otherwise noted, all translations are mine.

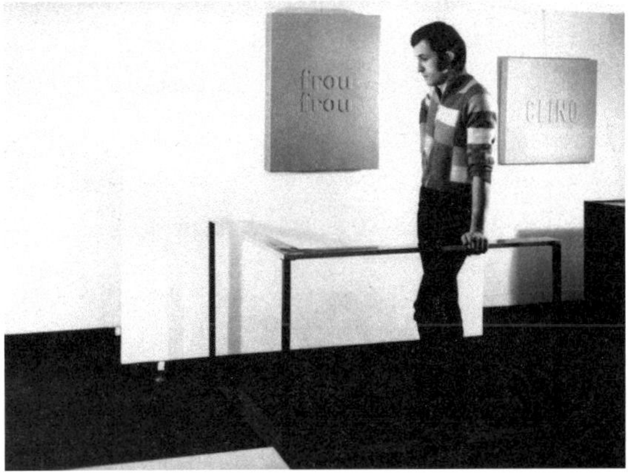

[fig. 8] Mancorrente a squadra (Right-angled Handrail), 1966

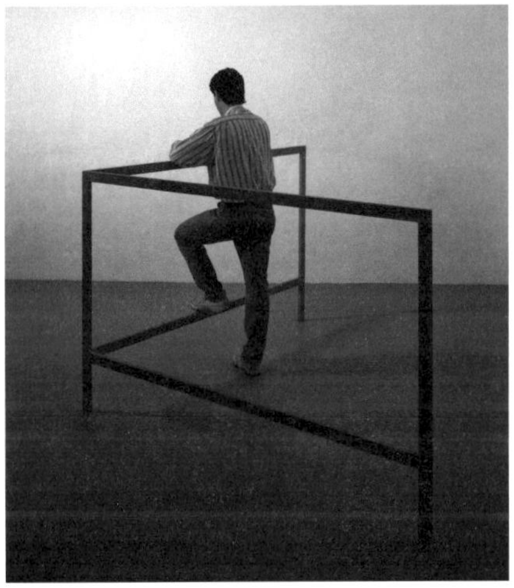

[fig. 9] Michelangelo Pistoletto, Structure for Talking Standing Up – Minus Objects (Struttura per parlare in piedi – Oggetti in meno), 1965–66

were motivated by "the need to place people in a situation, even to position them in a way that is typically theatrical."[6] Mature works like *Lampada annuale* (1966),—a *ill. p. 31* metal box containing a giant bulb programmed to light up for eleven random seconds a year—and *Ping Pong* (1966)—an installation consisting of two light boxes flashing the title words back-and-forth, have their root in these early interventions, and they are strikingly reminiscent in turn of Pistoletto's own *Lampada a mercurio, Minus Objects* (1965–66), positioned at his studio entrance when it was first exhibited in order to place the viewer in a heightened state of anticipation vis-a-vis the other work on view. It is also in this sense that we must understand Boetti's 1966 handrail-cum-sculpture *Mancorrente a squadra* [fig. 8] and Pistoletto's *Struttura per parlare in piedi, Minus Objects* (1965–66) [fig. 9]. In each case, artfully staged period photographs show onlookers (including, in Boetti's case, the artist himself) leaning on the respective sculptural supports and gazing into the distance. The relationship suggests a coordinated testament to the separation between viewer and viewed that necessarily structures aesthetic (and theatrical) contemplation.[7]

As I have observed elsewhere, this theatrical impulse was hardly a matter of geographic or historic accident. Where someone like Celant heralded a new art that would throw off the burden of history and embrace an essential reality, many of his Italian peers were skeptical of this position. The memory (and lingering effects) of Fascism's culture of consensus remained palpable for the 60s generation. Acutely aware of the facility with which the quest for objectively verifiable truths falls back on the mystical and the authoritarian, artists joined writers and philosophers in promoting an aesthetic of uncertainty and contradiction. Heterogeneity, separation, artificiality: these were the terms that defined the contemporary landscape, and as such, they had to be accepted not ignored. Writing about the need to escape the claustrophobic immanence of immediate postwar abstraction (Art Informel), art historian Marisa Volpi defined the new terrain: "It was evident only after a time that the urgency of exiting from the Informel meant liberating oneself from the ultimate convention on

6 Boetti, from an untitled declaration in 1967, excerpted in *Alighiero Boetti 1965–1994* (Milan: Gabriele Mazzotta / Turin: Galleria Civica d'Arte Moderna e Contemporanea), 1996, p. 199.

7 For a more detailed discussion of theatricality in Pistoletto's work and, in particular, his formation of the theater troupe Lo Zoo in the late 1960s, see my "Pistoletto's Object Theater," in *Michelangelo Pistoletto: From One to Many, 1956–1974* (Philadelphia: Philadelphia Museum of Art / Rome: Museo Nazionale delle Arti del XXI Secolo, 2010), pp. 81–107. In this essay, I discuss the difference between Lo Zoo's brand of theater, rooted as it is in disguise, narrative, and traditional scenic devices, and the anti-illusionistic trend in 1960s theater and performance art as represented by, for example, American Happenings.

which the Informel pivoted: that of *authenticity*, understood as the total and romantic gift of oneself."[8]

It is noteworthy in this context that so many of Italy's cultural critics to emerge after the war were also fiction writers: people like Umberto Eco, Italo Calvino, and Primo Levi, each of whom embraced narrative as a way of mediating recent history. In a series of retrospective essays published in the 1970s and 80s, Calvino maintained that the particular urge to tell stories in postwar Italy was motivated by the country's hyper-rapid economic and social development, which in turn prompted a need for personal forms of control and construction.[9] As Calvino describes it, storytelling served to counter the public passivity that had characterized the Fascist years by mobilizing the individual's forming capacity and concomitant accountability. The goal, he explains in his 1976 preface to his first novel *The Path to the Nest of Spiders*, was not descriptive accuracy so much as the urgency to express via the exercising of *style* and *craft*: "Language, style, pace had so much importance for us, for this realism of ours which was to be as distant as possible from naturalism."[10] In a surprising take on the notion of "engaged literature," Calvino asserts that in the wake of the war, commitment had nothing to do with illustrating a determined thesis. Instead, commitment was understood as a matter "first of all, [of] image and word, attitude, pace, style, contempt, defiance."[11]

In citing Calvino, I do not mean to imply that Boetti and his fellow artists were self-consciously impelled by similar political aspirations. On the contrary, Boetti has denied any interest in the revolutionary events circa 1968, and has claimed that he was too preoccupied with his artistic career to concern himself with world affairs. Boetti's own emphasis on fiction and theatricality nevertheless resonates with an alternative aesthetic sensibility prevalent among 1960s Italian artists and intellectuals, and provides another way of approaching his work. Consider again *Catasta* with its blatantly-registered manufacturing logo. If self-disclosure appears to confirm the material's resolute facticity, it is also this precise over-determination of materials that allows the viewer to perceive what is at stake in Boetti's transformation. Much like a child's game of blocks or Lincoln Logs, *Catasta* operates by ensuring that the viewer remains continually cognizant both of the individual elements and of the novel whole that they compose. In other words, in a manner akin to Pascali's trompe l'œil sculptures, *Catasta* stages a palpable (and unresolvable) back and forth between material and image; between real-world identity and aesthetic configuration.

There is, in short, an imaginative sensibility that pervades Boetti's work even at its most anti-representational, and that fundamentally distinguishes his objects from the material self-sufficiency conventionally attributed to Arte Povera or, for that matter, to the work of his Minimalist peers. For it is with the latter as much as the former that a work like *Catasta* is in dialogue. The relationship between *Catasta* and an early Carl Andre wood piece such as *Timber Piece (Well)* (1964–70), in which wooden beams are stacked cross-wise is, for example, immediately apparent. The difference between these sculptures may be slight but it is intentionally so. It consists in the subtle shift between material and image described above and that is reinforced in later more resolutely figurative objects. These include *Colonne*, as well as *Mazzo di tubi, Collina* (1967), a non-extant work consisting of metal tubes stacked to resemble rolling hills, and *Rotolo di cartone ondolato* (1966), the aforementioned roll of yellow cardboard pushed up in the center to form a Ziggurat-type shape. According to Boetti, these works have their roots in childhood experiments in which the artist tore up sheets of cardboard to make columns, arranged ice-cream glasses to form an arch, and "rolled up a yellow tape measure and pushed my little finger into it, forming a kind of tower of Babel."[12]

What is crucial in each case is the manifest imperfection that characterizes Boetti's makeshift "representations." Indeed, in referencing childhood make-believe, the artist invokes a form of making that is incomplete,

8 Marisa Volpi (1965) in *Tano Festa*, Achile Bonito Oliva ed. (Milan: Electa, 1988), p. 23.

9 Italo Calvino, "The Written and the Unwritten Word," *The New York Review of Books* (May 12, 1983).

10 Calvino, "Preface," in *The Path to the Nest of Spiders*, trans. William Weaver (New Jersey: The Ecco Press, 1976), pp. VII–VIII.

11 Ibid., p. XII.

12 Boetti, Untitled statement (1983) in *Alighiero Boetti 1965–1994*, p. 206.

adaptable, and distinctly temporary. It is this approach that connects a suggestively illusionistic work like *Rotolo* to an ostensibly formal enterprise like *Catasta*. In each case, Boetti foregrounds the fictive basis of artistic production—the fact that as soon as something is put on view, it is immediately rendered figurative, subject as it is to design and intentionality.

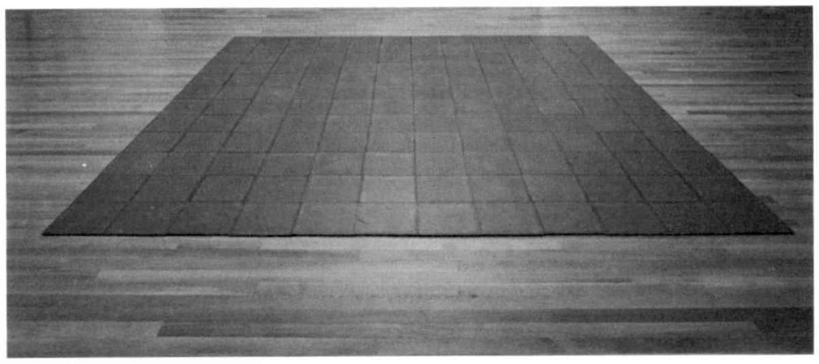

[fig. 10] Carl Andre, 144 Square Lead Unit, 1969

This is nowhere so evident as in a series of discreet objects comprised of wooden floor boards arranged in diagonal patterns that Boetti executed in 1967 and 1968. Ranging from 100 to 400 square inches, the individual works are differently patterned with alternating kinds and lengths of wood and occasional iron borders. Again, the comparison with Andre is illuminating. Like fellow Minimalist Donald Judd's stacked boxes or Sol LeWitt's open cubes, Andre's floor squares are both utterly tautological and self-generating. As Pamela Lee has observed, it is the conjunction between banal specificity and infinite spatial and temporal extension that impelled Michael Fried to term the new sculpture "inexhaustible" in his landmark 1967 essay.[13] The sculptures of Andre and Judd may be contained in each particular instance, but their replicating units give the impression that they could go on and on [fig. 10]. By contrast, Boetti's floor squares are carefully separated from their surroundings both by their frames and by the boards' shifts in orientation. This shift can be minimal—in the case of *Legno ferro (pavimento)* (1967) [fig. 11], the floor boards are placed ever so slightly off axis—but no more is required to insert a pause into the everyday. This is the physical world rendered picture—literally framed, bounded, and subject to the organizing impulse of pictorial form.

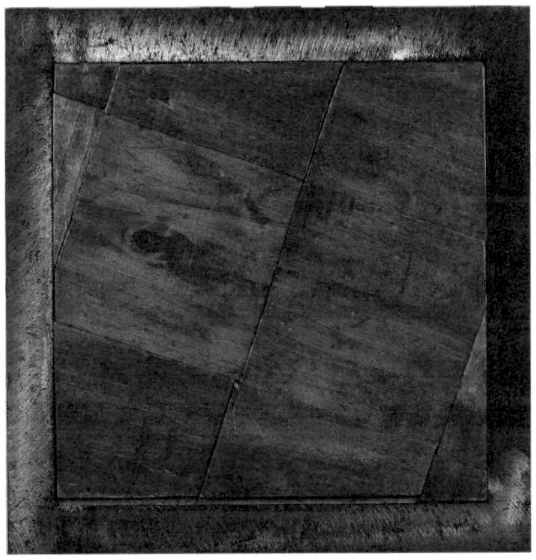

[fig. 11] Legno Ferro (pavimento), (Wood Iron [Floor]) 1967

It is in this context that we can understand a peculiar series of prints that Boetti produced on the occasion of his December 1967 solo show at La Bertesca. For the series, he commissioned the Genoese printmaker Rinaldo Rossi to make seriagraphs of many of the works that he had completed the previous year, including *Rotolo di cartone ondulato* and *Tavelle*, a variant on *Legno ferro (pavimento)*. The prints are technical in nature. They depict blueprint-type cross-sections complete with notations listing measurements and ratios, and they are accompanied by occasional hand-drawn sections that,

13 Pamela Lee, *Chronophobia: On Time in the Art of the 1960s* (Cambridge, Mass: MIT Press, 2004), pp. 37–48.

rendered without notations and measurements, are much looser in style.

Writing in hindsight, Boetti's close friend Giovan Battista Salerno has hypothesized that Boetti made the diagrams to provide guidelines for remaking his work in later years. However, as Mark Godfrey points out, the formal transparency of Boetti's objects would seem to render such instructions unnecessary.[14] Indeed, it is difficult to conceive that planar dissections would assist in the rudimentary act of pushing up the center of a roll of construction paper or laying out floor boards. What such diagrams do indicate is that Boetti's objects—no matter how simple—are nonetheless designed. And, as Boetti's penchant for making multiple versions of his works confirms, they can be redesigned. "Take the couple natural/artificial," Boetti observed in an appeal to craftsmanship that recalls Calvino. "A bamboo basket, is it natural or artificial? The truth is when man enters into things and natural things enter into human culture, all the antitheses are overturned . . . We have an enormous power in our hands. It is that of inventing the world."[15]

In 1969, shortly after having participated in the international exhibition *Arte Povera + Azioni Povere* in Amalfi, Boetti's art underwent a definitive turn. The artist abruptly abandoned object-making and began working in two-dimensions. He remembers the moment this way:

> I had been going in one direction, finishing with the exhibition at Amalfi. Then I began to doubt this direction. It had become too much about the materials. In the end, they were becoming more important than anything else. It had become the situation of the cornershop. For this reason, I remember how in the spring of 1969 I left the studio in Turin. It had become a depot for materials from Eternit to cement to stones. I left all of this as it was and began again from zero with a pencil and a sheet of paper.[16]

Scholars have tended to portray this shift as signaling Boetti's dissatisfaction with Arte Povera's rapid institutionalization, and certainly there is some truth to this depiction. Despite its emphasis on ephemeral projects and collaboration, the international scope of the Amalfi exhibition—and the art-world luminaries it attracted—proved that Arte Povera had finally achieved canonical status. To reject the homespun object for the blank piece of paper then becomes an act of purification, a way of thwarting market-driven production. This, for instance, is the way in which a transitional piece like *Una vetrata* ill. p. 24 (1969) is often understood. Later renamed *Niente da* ill. p. 69 *vedere niente da nascondere*, *Una vetrata* consists of nothing but an iron-framed, plate-glass window propped against the wall. As Godfrey observes, *Una vetrata* stands as a rebuke to a history of pictorial illusionism. Instead of Renaissance painting's window onto the world, it provides a real window onto nothing.[17] And yet, once again, the nature of this rejection is very different from the drive for self-sufficiency embraced by American Minimalism. Consider Boetti's later title for this work—which translates as "Nothing to See, Nothing to Hide." What might at first seem to be an homage to artistic purity is in fact subtly but directly opposed to the Minimalist ethos embodied in Frank Stella's famous dictum "What you see is what you see." Boetti's title, by contrast, implies that were there something to see, there would also be something to hide: i.e. nothing is complete unto itself. Rather, there is always another side to or behind of the image.

According to Boetti's first wife Annemarie Sauzeau Boetti, during this same period the artist began collecting personal "icons," including notes and sketches, cutouts and letters—essentially anything that caught his fancy—which he framed under glass and affixed to a wall in his home. Of this obsession, she writes: "I believe

14 Mark Godfrey, *Alighiero e Boetti* (London and New Haven: Yale University Press, 2011), pp. 41–42. Godfrey also notes the significance of Boetti's decision to flaunt the transformation of his objects into designs, but he comes to a somewhat different conclusion. According to Godfrey, Boetti's gesture reveals the ease with which even "artless constructions" can be appropriated by consumer or design culture. While I do not disagree with Godfrey, I am interested in the way in which the prints position Boetti's sculpture squarely within the realm of the aesthetic, quite apart from what they suggest about the ubiquity of consumer culture.

15 Boetti, "Dall'oggi al domani" (1988) in *Alighiero Boetti 1965–1994*, p. 212.

16 Antonella Soldaini, "Chronologia," in *Alighiero Boetti* (Milan: Skira, 1994), pp. 21–22.

17 Godfrey, p. 68–69.

I know when Alighiero became certain that fixing a piece of paper to the wall was a primordial and civilized act."[18] It was in 1971, she recalls, and the couple were in a teahouse in the otherwise deserted mountains west of Kabul, Afghanistan. Hanging on the wall was a plastic-covered page ripped from a magazine showing a spacecraft and an astronaut walking in space. Sauzeau Boetti recounts how Boetti turned to her and whispered that "the essential thing in art was the flat, two-dimensional image: photo or ex-voto, calendar, calligraphy or mandala, whether extravagant or simple, eternal or fragile, a chosen icon." "What is extraordinary," Sauzeau concludes, quoting Boetti, "is the value images assume in a society like that. The photo of a garden found in a copy of *Time* magazine will be cut out and framed with sticky tape under a sheet of glass."[19]

One might be tempted to dismiss these reflections as romantic indulgence, the sentimental ruminations that occur while sipping tea in a café in Afghanistan, but there is an impassioned appeal to individual agency here that recalls Calvino's plea for creative responsibility in the wake of a culture of consent. To frame a painting is a "civilized act" because it reveals the undifferentiated world to have passed through consciousness. Someone selects something, takes it out of the stream of everyday life and renders it meaningful. The same might be said of Boetti's objects, which, far from liberating art in the spirit of an egalitarian oneness with material reality, foreground the inventive transposition—and inherent separation—that grounds all artistic gestures however slight. In the process, they posit a notion of freedom rooted in intentionality. Like Calvino's stories, or Pascali's feigned sculptures, Boetti makes a fiction of reality with all the uncertainty, irresolution, and subjectivism that this term implies.

18 Annemarie Sauzeau Boetti, *Alighiero e Boetti Shaman/Showman* (Cologne: Verlag der Buchhandlung Walther König / Turin: Umberto Allemandi, 2003), p. 20.

19 Ibid., p. 22.

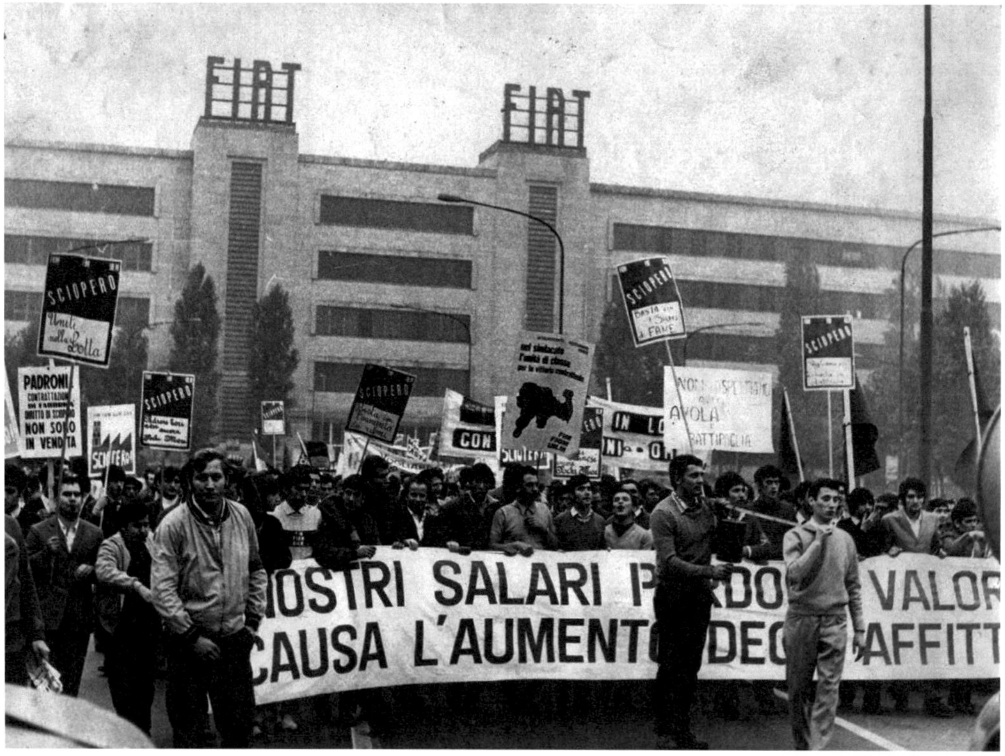

[fig. 1] FIAT strike in the "Hot Autumn" of 1969, Turin

Giving Time to Time: Boetti and Italy's "Creeping May"

Jason E. Smith

"Tracing is another way of seeing like the blind, by following the edges."[1] This is how Alighieri Boetti described the process he adopted for a series of drawings made during the tumultuous year of 1977, when the forces of Italian society—the "movement of '77" on the one side, the Italian State with the complicity of the Italian Communist Party (PCI) on the other—came into confrontation in increasingly violent fashion. The drawings are less drawings than, as Boetti underlines, literal transcriptions of images taken from the print media, the tracing out of bodies, many of them fallen militants left in the streets after clashes with the forces of the State. (They also include the lifeless body of Pier Paolo Pasolini, the cause of whose death was at the time enveloped in political speculation.)

Boetti had used this procedure before, for example in his series *Dodici forme dal 10 giugno 1967*, consisting of *ill. p. 78* the outlines, transposed from the pages of *La Stampa*, of territories torn by political violence between June 1967 and March 1971.[2] These tracings were then incised onto copper plates that preserved the dimensions of the newspaper's front page, as well as the position of the images within the text on the date in question. The images are abstracted and isolated from any discursive framing or context, making them at once more immediate and more arbitrary, since the contours of the territories in question were almost meaningless without some understanding of the movements and conflicts between peoples and states that originally produced and drew them out. The tracings of the slain bodies, in their turn, retain the specificity not simply of the shape of the body as it lies lifeless, struck, in the streets of Milan or Rome, but the details of the clothing as well. The tracing of the bodies represents another deployment of these poles—order and disorder—so important to the production of Boetti's work during the 1970s: the disordered edges of the fallen body and the order of political discourse itself, its reasons, its deductions, its syntax.

Why proceed like the blind—through the immediacy of contact rather than through the strategic vision of politics—in a political context marked by ramping levels of violence that were drawing out fronts through the body of Italian society? On the one hand, the forces of

1 Cited in Annemarie Sauzeau, *Alighiero e Boetti: Shaman-Showman* (Cologne: Walter König, 2003), p. 164.

2 It should be underlined that this work, consisting of twelve copper plates of tracings from newspapers, assumed more than one form. The first "diptych" made from these tracings—the original newspaper page juxtaposed with the framed tracing derived from it—was titled *Formazione di forme (territori occupati da Israeli)*, suggesting that the genesis of both the production aesthetic and political form emerges through violent acts of isolation, redaction, and "occupation." The assimilation of the tracing of the occupied territories—areas captured in the Six Day War in 1967—with other sites of political and postcolonial conflict during the period 1967–71 blunts the specificity of Boetti's gesture in these initial works, which is no doubt precisely why he made the decision to do so.

supposed order were known to have recourse to what was called a "strategy of tension," in which acts of violence were carried out by the State and its neo-fascist allies in order to sow disorder and terror, and to provide a rhetorical pretext for imposing "order," that is, for implementing emergency measures that in fact suspended the normal rule of law. On the other hand, 1977 also witnessed an increase in acts of violence by certain factions of the political movement called Autonomia that emerged in the early to mid-1970s and were in full force in the Bologna insurrection and "march" on Rome in March of that year. These factions perceived the failure of the events in Bologna and Rome—where in each case, through the collusion of the Italian Communist Party and the Italian state, what seemed like breaches in the political order were suppressed with violence—as a call for an intensification of the response, including the formation of armed groups capable of meeting the military force of the State. These groups, some of which (like the Red Brigades and Prima Linea) had existed alongside the movement for years, took an increasingly spectacular role in the media's portrayal of the social conflicts, with armed actions like kidnappings and political murders allowing these conflicts to become increasingly militarized, and to be portrayed by the political classes as a mere contest for State power, a sort of civil war between two forces that mirrored each other in their ambitions. This drift of the conflict represented a betrayal of the very logic of the movement before 1977, which had assumed a strategy of local autonomy and separation from the dynamics and logic of State power, and whose ambitions were less confrontation and victory over the state than what Paolo Virno has called a process of "exodus," the crystallization of autonomous forms of life outside the circuits of capital—work, value, money—and State sovereignty and its distribution of power.[3]

To "trace" this situation blindly, by "following the edges," would amount it seems, to blindly registering the "shocks of society," like a seismograph, a simple accumulation of corpses repeating the same pile-up as that witnessed by readers of the dailies. The situation in 1977 was confused enough—with the forces of State order sowing chaos, and certain factions of the forces of subversion increasingly mirroring the logic of the State—to motivate an artist in Boetti's situation merely to retrace, make immediate, provide blind contact and register the shock with this cruel convergence of *ordine e disordine*. But what to make of the recontextualization of these images in a work titled after, and devoted to, Gary Gilmore, the first American executed in the US after the lifting of the suspension of the death penalty in 1976? The fallen bodies of militants are presented side by side with the figure of Gilmore, the murderer who, after receiving his death sentence, demanded to be executed by firing squad, and received his bullet with an eagerness rare among the subjects of sovereign power. Such treatment renders Boetti's response to the images of the dead from Italy's more or less hidden civil war even more ambiguous. It simultaneously criminalizes them, identifies their corpses as the object and production of the sovereign power over life and death, and counters their serial anonymity with the dark luminosity of what Walter Benjamin, in his "Critique of Violence," called "The Great Criminal"—the criminal who is not content simply to break this or that law, but who challenges law and order as such, and who identifies himself in the process with the source of a new law, even if this law is the law of chaos, the relentless, diabolical application of disorder.[4]

Boetti's engagement with the political and social conflicts tearing at the seams of his country in the 1960s and 70s is difficult to situate. The practice of tracing, of making a seismographic registration, doesn't quite sort things out. While it amounts to the most direct form of contact with these confrontations imaginable, by the same token, it is also perhaps the most blind: the images are as abstract and arbitrary as they are immediate,

[3] See in particular Paolo Virno, "Virtuosity and Revolution: The Political Theory of Exodus," in *Radical Thought in Italy: A Potential Politics*, ed. Michael Hardt and Paolo Virno (Minneapolis: University of Minnesota Press, 1996), pp. 189–212. But also see Paolo Virno, *Esercisi di Esoda: Linguaggio e Azione Politica* (Verona: Ombre Corte, 2002).

[4] See Walter Benjamin's remarks in "Critique of Violence," in *Reflections*, trans. Edmond Jephcott (New York: Schocken, 1978), pp. 280–81.

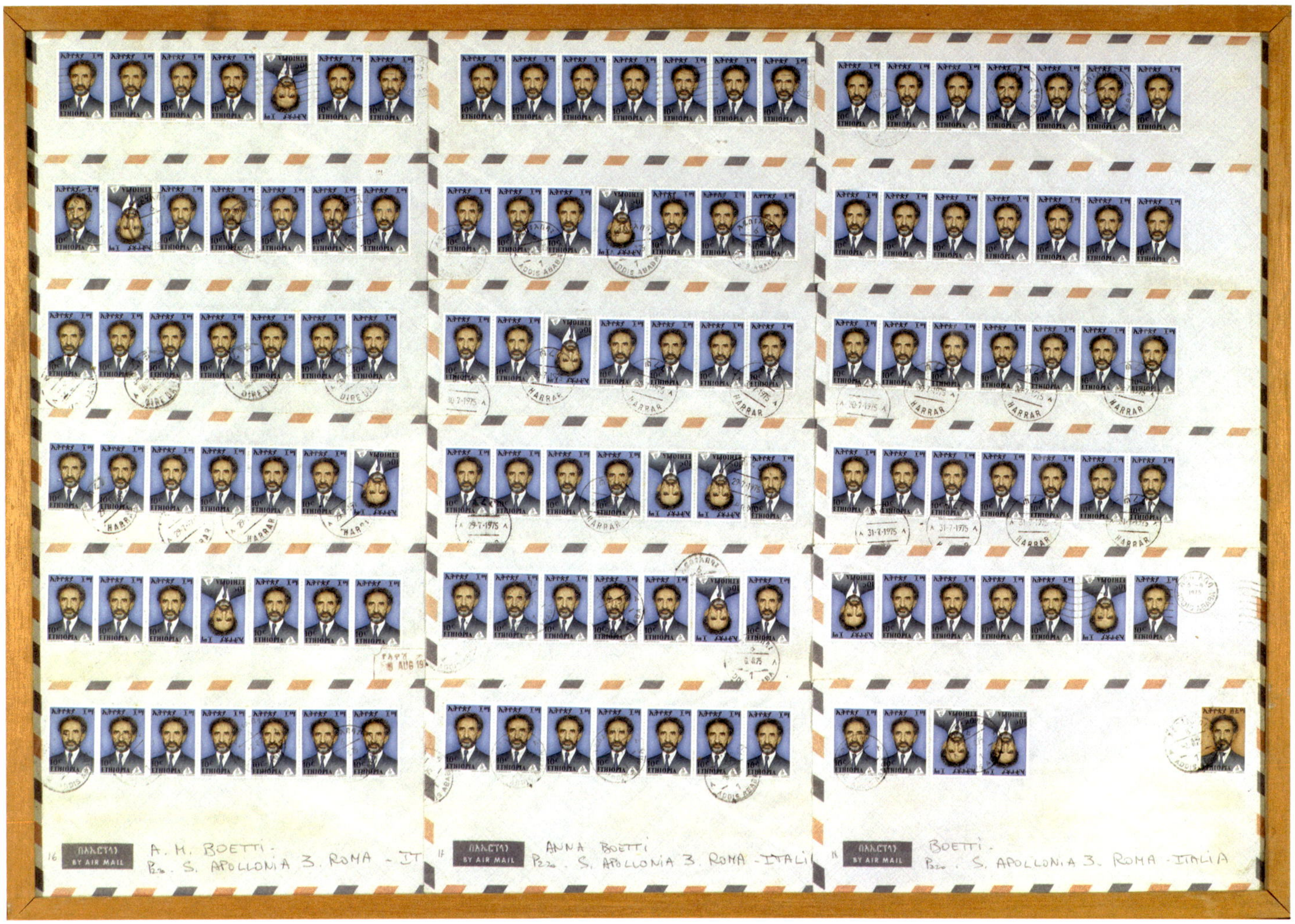

Codice: Eritrea libera (Codex: Free Eritrea), 1975

Gary Gilmore, 1977

forceful and irrefutable in their self-evidence (the obviousness of violence, of a fallen body). Boetti's work is instead a more mediated, more oblique manner of "following the edges" of this period in Italian history, which can be characterized as both the most innovative and most brutal period in postwar Europe. Such an obliqueness will, I want to suggest, even pass over, as these conflicts intensify and widen, into a seeming flight from politics, into what might seem more metaphysical territory: "time" and "world," to use Boetti's terms. But this flight from politics represents, in a certain sense registered by Virno's use of the term "exodus," the very specific and paradoxical nature of radical Italian politics in the 1970s: it is the abandonment of the political itself, in its classical contours, that is the most radical ambition of the movements of the 1970s. For this flight from the political—this "post-political politics"[5]—aims its sights not on the ownership of the means of production or the seizure of State power and its apparatuses, but on the making of worlds and the construction of autonomous temporalities. In Boetti's precise, tautological, syntax: "putting the world into the world," "giving time to time."

*

In July 1969, Turin was the site of an unprecedentedly large worker insurrection at the Fiat plant on the city's outskirts, a confrontation that spilled out of the factory gates into the city itself and resulted in a day's worth of running street battles between workers and police [fig. 1]. These street battles, in which the slogan "*Vogliamo tutto!*" (We Want Everything!) emerged as the demand—emphatically absolutist, and unmeetable—brought together different sectors of the working class, students, and militants from the extra-parliamentary left, and ushered in what came to be called the "Hot Autumn" of 1969, which witnessed the largest and most intense standoff between the Italian working class and contemporary capitalism since the conclusion of the World War II and the launching of the Italian economic "miracle."[6] This confrontation, which in 1969 was still centered in the factory and on the Italian industrial working class of the North, slowly spiraled out of the sphere of production into the realm of everyday life, with confrontations over rent, housing, public utilities, and transportation. From 1969 to 1977—that is, what came to be called Italy's "creeping May," in contrast to the punctual nature of France's May 1968 events—the locus of worker struggles gradually moved from the work place, where wage demands represented the fundamental lever of pressure, to the metropolitan fabric itself. Out of this shift a new slogan emerged, "*Prendiamoci la città*!" (Let's Take the City!), which registered this migration from the site of production to the space of circulation, consumption, and everyday life. This change was in turn occasioned by an increasingly adamant "refusal of work," as it came to be called within the most radical elements of the anti-capitalist struggles of the 1970s, by younger workers and workers who had recently emigrated from the rural, largely unindustrialized south. It represented a decisive displacement of the political center of gravity in Italy. If the 1969 worker insurrection at Fiat still assumed the classical schema of struggle inherited from the history of the workers' movement, with a priority placed on worker struggles at the point of production, by 1977 the key confrontations with the Italian State and capital were organized around questions of everyday life, and led not by the working class but by those who refused work, that is, as much by students as by the unemployed and precariously employed. The confrontations at Fiat in 1969 slowly gave way to what came to be called Autonomia, a loosely structured network of struggles flaring up outside of the factory and the sphere of work, and having as its fundamental stakes not wages (less work, more pay), but questions of pleasure, of free time, of life outside of the world of work and its system of mediations (money, commodities, exchange-value, and so on). The

5 This is the title of the magnificent issue of the journal *Semiotext[e]* devoted to Italian radical politics in the 1970s.

6 Nanni Balestrini's beautiful novel *Vogliamo tutto* (Milan: Feltrinelli, 1971)—recounting the experience of a southern worker in the Turin Fiat plant, in a trajectory beginning with his emigration to the city and concluding with a strike that spins out into a two-day insurrection in its streets—takes its title from this slogan.

radical politics of Italy in the 1970s had, by 1977, organized themselves around the production of autonomous worlds and the construction of novel temporalities, outside of society and its distribution and management of time through the imposition of work. These are questions registered, I want to argue, by Boetti's use of the terms "world" and "time."

As the home of Fiat, the most emblematic Italian firm of the postwar period, Turin was the site at which all of the dynamic forces of Italian society converged. It was the center of gravity of the so-called Italian economic "miracle," in which the development of the productive forces and industrial infrastructure in the North of the country—in Turin, but also Milan and the Venice region, for example—led to the emergence of a society of "abundance," that is, a society in which the working class, through wage increases negotiated by union representatives, were able to consume the very commodities they produced. This situation was made possible by a political consensus that emerged after the war, cemented between the PCI on the left and the Christian Democrats of the center-right, which argued that it was in the best interests of both the working class and the bourgeoisie to raise productivity levels. Worker organizations, acting within the framework of the PCI's own strategy for assuming power through peaceful means, negotiated these productivity increases by keying them to higher wages, raising in turn the "standard of living"—a very dubious concept, to be sure—of a working class that now had the capacity to consume the new, and increasingly available, commodities turned out by Fiat, among so many others. The actions undertaken by the workers at Fiat in 1969 marked the key point at which this "truce" began to fray, as workers organized their struggles outside of union oversight and began to demand an unlinking of wage levels from production levels.[7] The working class had begun to act outside of its organizations and institutional frames, breaking the postwar pact engineered by left-wing parties and unions, and a capital that was ready to take whatever steps necessary (including terrorist bombings by Fascists in co-ordination with the State) to bring them back into line.

It should be noted that these struggles, which began in 1969 and continued until 1977, were not waged against consumption as such, or the society of material abundance, unlike many critiques being posed within art and culture at the time. In Pasolini's 1975 *Lutheran Letters*, for example, one finds just such a critique of consumption, a jeremiad against the new "society" that entailed, Pasolini argues, not simply a quantitative increase in material abundance, but nothing less than an anthropological mutation in which the very physiognomy of Italian youth was affected, a decomposition writ large in the very flesh of the children of the Italian miracle.[8] (For this reason, Pasolini would renounce his early 1970s "trilogy of life" films, where he was able to witness, a few years after their making, this mutation in the body of the boys he hired to "act" in those films.) The struggles that emerged in the 1970s in Italy were, Pasolini notwithstanding, not struggles against consumption per se, or against the so-called society of consumption, but rather against the postwar articulation between consumption and productivity levels, that is, between work and consumption. The slogan "We Want Everything!" came to mean not only a demand for higher wages and less work—wages no longer tied to productivity levels—but, by the mid-1970s, an assertion of the "right" to consume without work or even money. This included an affirmation of the right or the capacity, on the part of radical youth, unemployed and others, to *directly* appropriate (through, for example, the organized looting of grocery stores or the mass theft of consumer luxury goods like jeans, among other less flamboyant practices) the material abundance represented by this "miraculous" society.

Unlike many of his contemporaries in what came to be called Arte Povera, Boetti never openly articulated political positions through his work, and he does not appear to have had much personal interest in the social

7 Perhaps the best account of the events of July 1969 at Fiat is the "fictional" account presented by Nanni Balestrini in *Vogliamo tutto*.

8 Pier Paolo Pasolini, *Lutheran Letters*, trans. Stuart Hood (Manchester: Carcanet New Press, 1983).

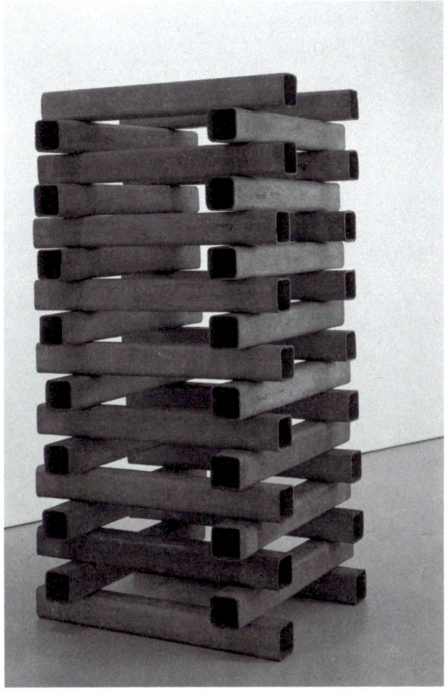

[fig. 2] Catasta (Stack), 1966

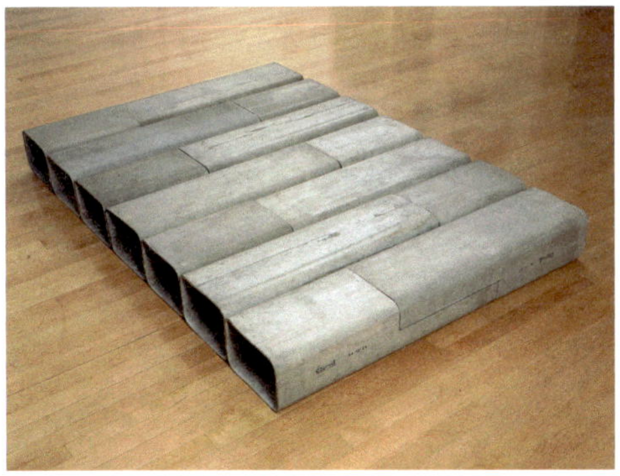

[fig. 3] Eternit (pavimento) (Eternit (Floor)), 1967

struggles occurring around him. And yet this monumental convergence of social and historical forces, a more or less open war—between labor and capital, between the spaces of Autonomia and the State— broke out at the very moment when Boetti's artistic career began. How did he register this turn in contemporary Italian politics and social struggles? Perhaps it is possible to locate something like a political "unconscious" in his work—that is, a series of formal and operational mutations that occur in response to, or in anticipation of, the twists and turns of the larger historical drama playing itself out in Italy. Formal and operational mutations that occur, in other words, without Boetti consciously identifying his own motivations and decisions explicitly with social dynamics which nevertheless must be channeled, refused, or managed by any artist operating in a moment of historical crisis. Such mutations, because they materialize at the level of the actual structure of the works themselves, or through the types of operations and actions that they set in motion, might more powerfully—but also more ambiguously—register these social conflicts than an artistic practice that addresses them at the thematic level alone.

Between 1966 and 1969 Turin was not only the site of the clashes at Fiat, but also of Boetti's first solo show at Christian Stein gallery. This was an era marked by the emergence of a sphere of activity—an orientation, movement, or mere curatorial grouping—dubbed by the critic and curator Germano Celant "Arte Povera." In the first phase of Boetti's work, exemplified by this show in early 1967, we witness a fascination with industrial materials of the sort that would be used by workers in northern Italian factories and cities, such as the PVC tubing of *Collina*, the asbestos tubing—called Eternit to emphasize its timelessness, its durability—used in *Catasta* and *Eternit (pavimento)* [figs. 2–3], or the trademarked factory colors borrowed from Fiat, Moto *ill. p. 57* Guzzi, and Vespa for the wall pieces from the same period (*I colori*) [fig. 4]. For the announcement of the show, *ill. p. 32* Boetti presented a panel with small samples of the various types of building materials, often new and synthetic, used in the exhibition, suggesting that the configurations assumed by these materials—whether the suggested natural formation of hills or, with the Eternit stack, the sheer, "abstract" act of accumulation itself—are themselves arbitrary or contingent, and can be reduced to mere samples or examples of possible forms these materials might assume. In an interview, Boetti humorously notes that "some of the best moments in Arte Povera were hardware shop moments, there's so much in a hardware shop." It was, he continues, "thrilling to see the wonderful things that were there! There was everything, from refractory bricks (which are stunning), to glass wool, to polysterene, everything."[9] This send-up was accompanied by a language that would have been completely at home in the American discussion around "primary structures," or what came to be called Minimalism. Boetti's early pieces, and *Catasta* in particular, are made in a manner recalling Carl Andre or early Richard Serra, using modular units that are configured not through welding—or "stitching" as Serra had it, deliberately regendering the macho welding of, say, David Smith, into an act of sewing, of domestic repair—or other forms of attachment, but through arrangements that relied solely on the physical properties of the materials themselves, first and foremost mass [fig. 5]. While Boetti's "hardware" pieces suggested, through the materials they used, architecture, plumbing and, in *I colori*, the palette of industrial design, he argued at the time that these constructions induced the "collapse" of all "analytical superstructures," with the result that the aesthetic focus was on "the elementary and non-signifying action."[10] Celant spoke in similar terms, affirming that these pieces—despite their apparent illusions to landscape, say—ultimately refused to resolve themselves into compositions or even shapes in the strongest sense of the term, that is, a unified field of components or elements that would have produced a certain effect of interiority, refusing to frame off a virtual space that would have set them apart from the actual space of the room and the body, from the architectural environment (immediately referenced by using building materials) and from the viewer, to whom *Catasta* was all the same scaled (it is approximately six feet tall; in principle, a stack can proceed upward with no limit).

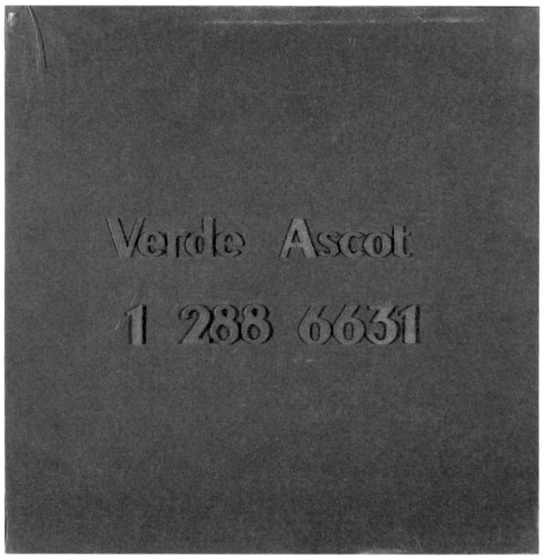

[fig. 4] Verde Ascot 1 288 6631, 1967

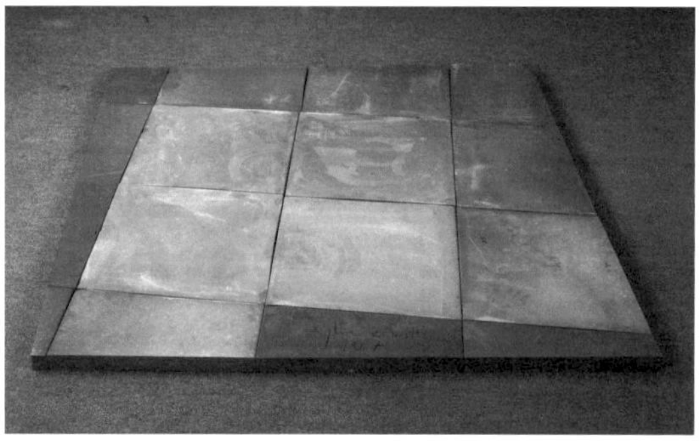

[fig. 5] Pavimento (Floor), 1967

[9] See the interview in *Zero to Infinity*, ed. Richard Flood and Frances Morris (Minneapolis: Walker Art Center, 2001): p. 188.

[10] Cited in Richard Cork, *Breaking Down the Barriers: Art in the 1990s* (New Haven: Yale University Press, 2003): p. 444.

This emphasis on modular units, materials with no artistic associations, and "non-signifying action"—the nominal form of the construction indexing the verbal, yet referentless "stacking" not of an artist, but of an anonymous operator or function, a completely abstract "labor" not unlike certain types of labor in industrial contexts—placed Boetti apart from many of the concerns current in Arte Povera. The other artists often used not the industrial materials of the sort that so "thrilled" Boetti, but organic materials with various time signatures or scales: the slow inhuman eternity of stone and earth, the age rings of Giuseppi Penone's tree works, the emphatic ephemerality of Giovanni Anselmo's lettuce. The almost instantaneous buzz of an electrical current, widely used among Arte Povera artists, when utilized in Boetti's work, slowed down to *ill. p. 49, 50* either the alternating back and forth of *Ping Pong* or the *ill. p. 31* once yearly, and aleatory illumination of *Lampada annuale* (both 1966). The limitations posed by this way of working—a variant of Italian minimalist practice, where the emphasis on non-composition, industrial materials and simple, anonymous or everyday actions like stacking channeled and reinvented an earlier twentieth-century integration of art and industry, scientific experimentation, and artistic practice, but without the charge of ideological commitment—were clearly felt by Boetti, whose initial enthusiasm for this aspect of his practice eventually deflated: "Seeing all these materials filled me with such crazy enthusiasm . . . This got so exaggerated in 1968 that it ended in nausea, then that was it—finished!"[11]

Why nausea? Perhaps it was due to the sheer abundance of newer, synthetic materials available to the artist, who needed only to procure them at a hardware store and arrange them according to simple, repeatable, non-signifying actions. Perhaps these actions were too non-signifying, reducible in a certain sense to a set of infinitives, impersonal and without tense or time: not "I stack" or "we stack," but "to stack," echoing Serra's own list of infinitives. Does this rejection, this nausea, have any relation to the refusal of work that began to resonate in the factories and industries of northern Italy? The answer is not clear. But just around 1969, at the very moment when the most intense social conflict since World War II flared up in the factories of Turin, Boetti renounced this practice and began working with extremely simple materials, pen and paper, and with various sorts of systems, primarily compositional systems that complicated the one-plus-one of the stacks. Often these were mathematical sequences and combinatories based on linguistic systems, or systems of social time like calendars and dates, or communication systems and grids, like telephone and postal networks. In a work such as *Cimento dell'armonia e dell'invenzione* *ill. pp. 80, 81* (1969), which consisted of the freehand retracing of gridded paper, the commitment to "non-signifying action" is retained. But in a work like *Dossier postale*, from *ill. p. 117* 1969–70, we witness an artistic practice that does away almost entirely with materiality in favor of networks and of action: the artist merely addresses twenty-five empty envelopes, often to other artists, who are not to be found at the deliberately false address, resulting in the return of the envelope to Boetti, who then places it in another envelope and sends it to another false address, so that an accumulation or piling up occurs.

This shift away from industrial materials and elementary actions to works in which the "site" referenced is no longer the factory or the built environment but the webs of circulation and address might be seen to accompany the broader movement, within the political and social dynamics of contemporary Italy, away from the industrial infrastructure toward the space of the city itself, in which questions of life in its broadest sense—whether it is a matter of pleasure or time, of communication and speech, of personal identity (including sexuality and gender)—assume a novel importance. Where, in a piece like *Castata*, the artist's identity was reduced almost entirely to a set of anonymous actions—artistic activity is no longer that of "composing" relationships with conventional artistic materials, but of arranging configurations based on the physical properties of non-artistic materials—we find the reassertion of identity in works as early as the famous double self-portrait *Gemelli* (1968). We also find it in Boetti's *ill. p. 65, 66*

[11] *Zero to infinity*, p. 188.

equally famous "performance" of separating his personal name from his family name with the word "and." Such actions are symptomatic of a kind of larger shift in the way social struggles and historical conflict was drifting during this period. But identity is here, to be sure, not identity at all, but the site of a gap, or split—between at least two, but often unequal sides, as when Boetti makes drawings with his left and right hands, emphasizing in this way their asymmetry, and a kind of internal distance. This split can be exploited in order to introduce new spaces, and time signatures in the otherwise of-a-piece present of contemporary social history.

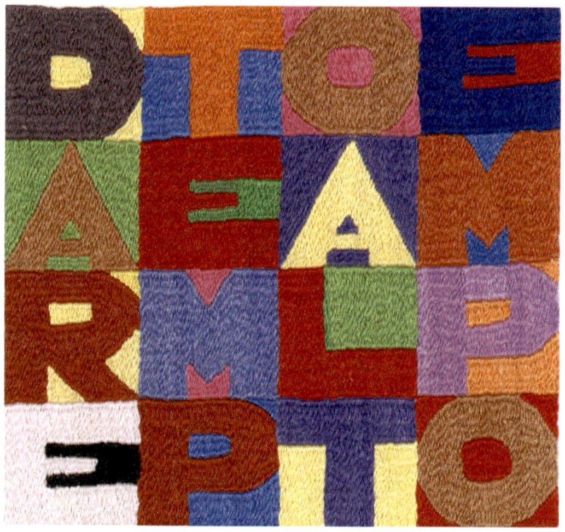

[fig. 6] Dare tempo al tempo (Giving Time to Time), 1989

By the early 1970s, Boetti's work underwent another shift that began to exemplify more clearly, if indirectly, the broader changes in the conception and practice of politics in Italy between 1969 and 1977. If already we note a certain movement away from the sphere of production to that of circulation and communication—indexed, if obliquely, by Boetti's bracketing (his "nausea") of the three-dimensional work of 1967-68, and the move into social systems—we might speculate that his "Biro" drawings mark a shift in the site of the political once again. In these works, what is essential is no longer even productive processes or communication, but what in the title of two of the works from this group Boetti simply, and enigmatically, calls "time" and "world." And not simply time and world, for what is really at stake is something like a process, an operation, that on the surface appears tautological: *Dare tempo al tempo* (1979) "Giving Time to Time," and *Mettere al mondo il mondo* (1972), "Bringing the World into the World." Painstakingly produced over the course of weeks or months by a man and a woman hired for the task, using ball-point pens (blue, black, green, red) on panels (typically 100 x 70 cm), these works can be seen as the counterpoint or twin of the well-known embroidered "mappe." This is true both in terms of their collaborative and relatively rudimentary mode of production and in terms of their apparent themes, with the "mondo" of the Biro drawings doubling the cartographic mapping of geopolitical shifts in the embroideries. But, as Mark Godfrey has underlined, there is a seeming "disconnection" between the "world" as it is addressed in these Biro drawings, which

ill. pp. 104–105, 108, 109

ill. pp. 218–229

[12] Mark Godfrey, "Divided Interests," *Artforum*, May 2009, p. 210.

consist entirely of pulsing, more or less monochrome fields of color, framed on one edge by a sequence of letters (often arranged alphabetically) and interrupted only by the apparently aleatory dissemination of commas, and the shifting flows of power, the "geography, politics and history" addressed by the "mappe."[12] Where the latter document changing power blocs, regime turnovers and territorial reconfigurations over the course of two decades, the Biro works seem to present only the smooth space of the sea or ocean, or the deep space of the sky, the commas sitting on their surface like stars or flotsam, seemingly placed at random, but spelling out, if time is given to time, a phrase or a constellation that makes up a world.

This remains rather abstract, or at least mysterious. And yet there is, in Italy's "creeping May," a transformation of politics that increasingly took on these fundamental issues of time, of worlds: it was no longer a question of producing a new society, but of making a new world, woven together with the threads of more than one time. The tautological nature of Boetti's titles reveals both the simplicity and the difficulty of these ambitions. If the sculptural work of the Arte Povera period employed "non-signifying action," here the nature of artistic and political action is characterized as the strangely paradoxical operation not of producing a world or a new use of time, but of giving the world to the world, giving time to time. World and time are posed, then, not as already given frames of action. Action consists, to the contrary, in the short pause between world and itself, the brief moment between time and itself; it is non-signifying action, like the interpolation of a comma, the punctuation of a breath.

As Italy's political and social conflicts evolved between 1969 and 1977, Boetti's work underwent a decisive mutation as well. This mutation was registered not simply in the types of materials and procedures he developed, but also in the manner in which his decisions reflected—in however mediated a way—with the social dynamics of the period. In the drawings of 1977 with which I began, we see the eruption of political violence puncturing the trajectory of a certain flight from politics that occurs in many of Boetti's works of this period. Such a flight seems to be actualized, for example, in his sojourns in Afghanistan and his enlistment of networks of Afghan women to produce his most famous works from this period, the "mappe," and but also captured by his turn toward certain figurations of worldhood and temporality that seem to strain at the conceptual and political limits imposed by geopolitical concepts of history. I want to suggest then, a certain flight from politics occurs in many of the works of this period—politics understood not as geopolitical distributions of power, but what happens when the state and its correlate, history, no longer govern the movements and moods of peoples. The politics of Autonomia amounted to just such a flight, an "exodus," in which action took place outside of the signifying networks of politics in its dominant representations. This is when the flight from politics becomes, in a sense, hyper-political; what was at stake is nothing less than a world, and all the time it takes to make one. Such worlds disorder the syntax of state power. It is in these caesuras, when power catches its breath, that the worlds that flee it form.

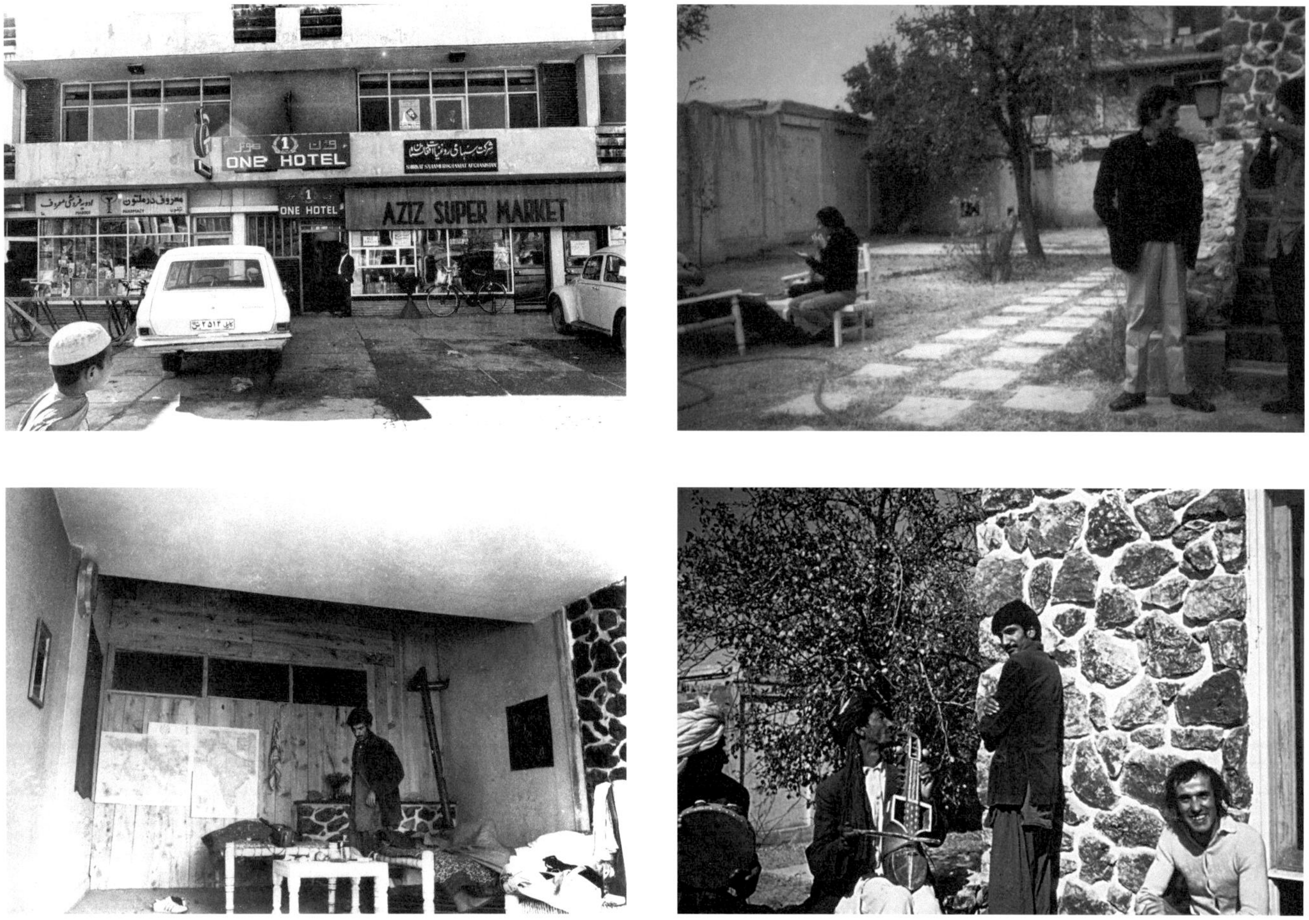

[fig. 1] One Hotel, Kabul, c. 1971–77 (clockwise: street-side entrance; two garden views; Dastaghir in a room)

Boetti and Afghanistan

Mark Godfrey

Why Afghanistan?

Alighiero Boetti's last wish, according to his first wife Annemarie Sauzeau Boetti, was that "his ashes should be dispersed at the earliest opportunity over the lapis lazuli waters of the lakes of Bandi a Mir—seven lakes in seven craters, high in the desert mountains in western Afghanistan."[1] In the years since Boetti's passing, fulfilling this wish has seemed less and less possible as Afghanistan has undergone successive tragedies. More and more artists, however, have become fascinated by Boetti's connection to the place: Jonathan Monk organized for an Afghan photographer to make the trip to Bandi a Mir and used the images in a work; Mario Garcia Torres has made a number of works about Boetti's *One Hotel*; and Francis Alÿs, as his contribution to the Chechen biennale, sent one of Boetti's small "arazzi" or word-squares, embroidered in Afghanistan by craftswomen, accompanied by a text expressing Alÿs's hope that Boetti would find it appropriate for these works to be seen in Chechnya, given his fascination with his ancestor Giovan Battiste Boetti, who had led the Chechen people against Catherine the Great. Countless other artists and curators see Boetti as one of the first artists to think more expansively about geography and about the production of art. Occasionally, the more romantic aspects of Boetti's attraction to Afghanistan are underlined, which is not surprising, given that a European artist basing himself in Kabul has become such an unlikely proposition over the years. Undoubtedly, Boetti was attracted to Afghanistan because of its beauty—Sauzeau Boetti writes of his arrival in Kabul that "he discovered a bare, pink landscape bathed in a crystal clear light that made distances seem to shrink"[2]—but there were many other reasons why he spent so much time there.

Boetti first traveled to Afghanistan in March 1971. He continued to visit Kabul twice a year until 1979, when the Soviet invasion made entry to the country impossible. By 1971, he had become ambivalent about Arte Povera and had rejected the hardware-store materials that many of the group would continue to exploit. Conceptual artists between 1969 and 1971 were looking for ways to make "dematerialized" art, but Boetti had been trying out new materials—postal stamps, copper panels, Biro pen, embroidery—and traveling to distant places might have opened up further possibilities for him. Equally, he distrusted the fact that Arte Povera was being marketed abroad as an Italian movement, and travel was tantamount to distancing himself from the group. It was also a way of removing himself from Italy—a country that over the following years would be characterized by political violence and by the disintegration of the left into antagonistic factions.

Boetti's decision to make work abroad connected him to other itinerant international artists—Douglas Huebler, On Kawara, Robert Rauschenberg, and Sigmar Polke—yet he also had personal reasons to go to

1 Annemarie Sauzeau Boetti, *Alighiero e Boetti: Shaman / Showman* (Cologne: Walther König, 2003), p. 216.

2 Ibid., p. 101.

Afghanistan. He had long been fascinated by the story of his ancestor Giovan Battista Boetti, an eighteenth-century Dominican monk who had converted to Islam on a mission to Constantinople. Giovan Battista became a leader of the Chechen people against Catherine the Great, changed his name to Sheikh Mansur, and eventually died in prison. In the catalogue for the exhibition "Formulation" at the Addison Gallery of American Art in January 1971, Boetti's first group show in the US, he created a double-page spread "self-portrait" pairing a painting of himself by the Italian artist Pietro Gallina with an oil portrait of the monk-turned-sheik [fig. 2]. This contribution, made only weeks before his first trip to Kabul, suggests that Boetti saw Mansur as his other half, and presages his determination not only to travel East, but to work with the peoples whom he met rather than to represent them as exotic others.

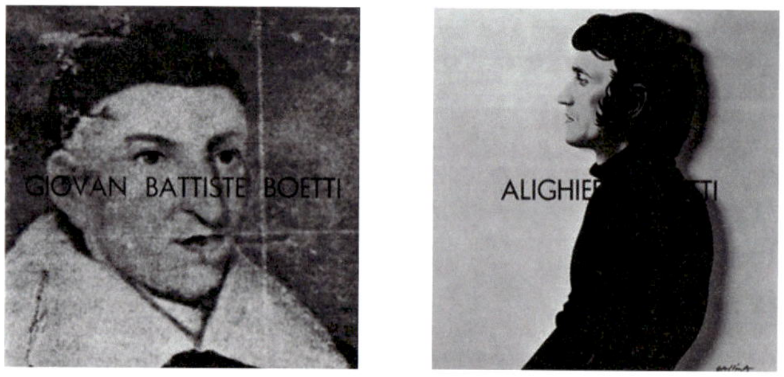

[fig. 2] Boetti's pages from the catalogue Formulation, 1971: Left, Giovan Battista Boetti, 1769. Right, Portrait of Alighiero Boetti by Pietro Gallina, 1970.

Why Boetti chose this country over Turkey, India or Iran remains unclear, since Sheikh Mansur never traveled as far as Afghanistan. It was a popular destination for Boetti's generation, however, and at the time, a stable country even after Mohammed Daoud Khan's coup of 1973. European visitors were attracted by the cheap travel, narcotics, the Buddhas of Bamiyam, and the towers of Herat, local traditions like *buzkashi* (a type of polo game) and by the presence of Sufi poets and mystics. Boetti loved Afghanistan for all of these reasons and also—as Francesco Clemente later recalled—because the country "was devoid of the cacophony of capitalism."[3] Late in his life, Boetti explained to Nicholas Bourriaud:

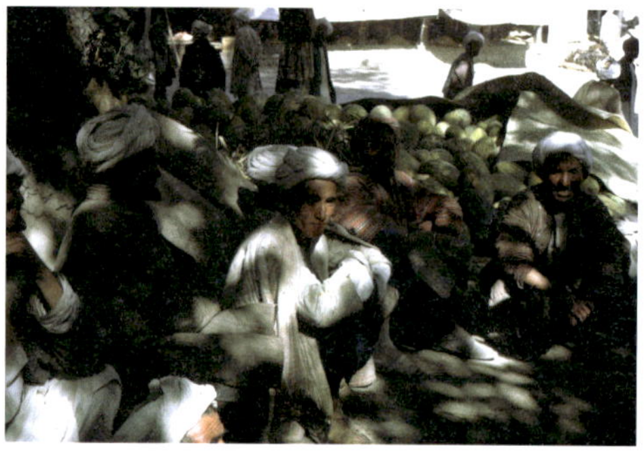

[fig. 3a] Bruce Chatwin, Man in shadows, Afghanistan, n.d.

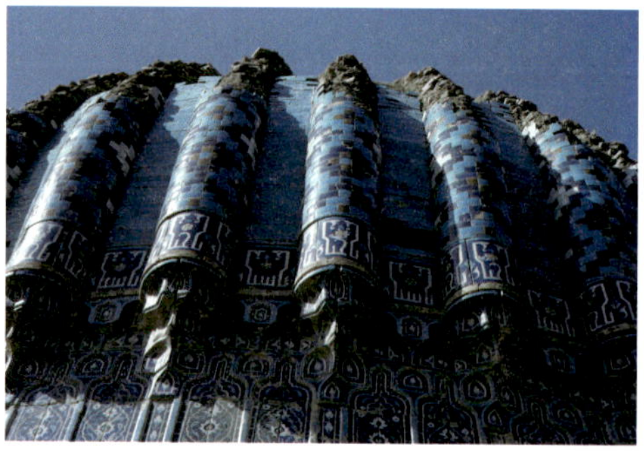

[fig. 3b] Bruce Chatwin, The shrine of Gohar Shad, Herat, Afghanistan, n.d.

> I was fascinated by the desert, and not just the natural desert. In an Afghan house there is nothing. Not a stick of furniture, so none of the things people place on their furniture either. Just carpets and rugs, and small mattresses, cushions, where you sit and drink, smoke and eat. I also like the way Afghan people keep the same clothes on night and day. So what fascinates me most is the bareness, the civilization of the desert.[4]

Given other contemporary descriptions of Afghanistan, such as Peter Levi's 1972 account of the streets of Kabul: "The flies swarm on everything, particularly in

3 Francesco Clemente and Louise Neri, "A Fugue for Alighiero e Boetti," in *Alighiero e Boetti* (New York: Gagosian, 2001), p. 85.

4 Alighiero Boetti, "Afghanistan" (interview with Nicolas Bourriaud), *Documents* no. 1, October 1992, p. 50.

the food shops and on children's faces, and it was odd to see swallows swooping idyllically over a pea soup sewage pond,"[5] Boetti could be accused of romanticizing the poverty of these households, but such criticism would be misplaced. In fact, underpinning his words was a connection between Boetti's own ideas of *Mettere al mondo il mondo*—the principle of making things without invention, of creating works with pre-existing images and materials—and the resourcefulness of Afghans: "Afghanistan is a mountainous country," he explained:

> and the villages are built on mountain-sides, so as not to fritter the rare areas of fertile land in the valleys. Nothing is added to the landscape, either. Rocks are moved, and used to build cube-houses (as in Klee's watercolors). Trees are felled to make the frame.[6]
>
> The valleys end in a wall of stones: the same stones that were removed to make the ground cultivable and serves as protective walls. It's all a perfect balance.[7]

Most importantly, Boetti understood Afghan culture as resistant. "The degree of resistance put up by the Afghans to our civilization, in this day and age, has always amazed me," he said.[8] With these simple words the artist was signaling his clear conviction that Afghanistan should be understood neither as some "other" place untouched by Western civilization nor as a culture somehow underdeveloped or ahistorical. Afghanistan, Boetti recognized, was a place that had always been in contact with other countries and that had maintained its culture through active choice and effort. This is why he was upset by the Westernizing ambitions of the Afghan royalty during the 1970s, when a nightclub had opened in Kabul. It had "two poor Afghan women in mini-skirts serving whiskies," he lamented: "The joint closed down after three or four months."[9] Although he opposed this Westernization, he was equally adamant about maintaining his own identity as a Western visitor rather than trying to blend in. "I always dress with a jacket and tie."[10] Just as he would never presume to appear like an Afghan, he determined never to picture Afghans in the work he would make in their country, unlike other travelers such as Sigmar Polke and Bruce Chatwin, who would return to Europe with images of bear fights and turbaned men and richly tiled shrines [figs. 3a, 3b].

During the time when Boetti was able to travel to Kabul, Edward Said was researching his 1978 book *Orientalism*, which he defined in his introduction as "a style of thought based upon an ontological and epistemological distinction made between 'the Orient' and 'the Occident'." For Said, "the relationship between Occident and Orient is a relationship of power, of domination."[11] It is clear that Boetti was not interested in maintaining such a relationship of power, but following Said's account, he could be accused of producing a problematic distinction between Italy and Afghanistan. For all his reluctance to picture Afghans, did Boetti essentialize Afghanistan by treating it as an ideal, an object of desire, a concept rather than as a complex place? If he was exhausted by the fissuring of Italian society in the 1970s, did he put to one side the fact that Afghanistan was also internally divided, with bitter hostility between different political and religious groups, and ingrained animosity between people from different ethnic sectors, including Pashtuns, Tajiks, Hazaras, Uzbeks and Turkmen?

It would be misguided to expect that any artist visiting the country during the 1970s could or would make an analysis of Afghanistan's situation at the time. Nonetheless, Boetti still saw Afghanistan as radically different from Italy, and it *did* serve him (at least in the early 1970s) as an ideal and as an "Other" culture to which

5 Peter Levi, *The Light Garden of the Angel King: Travels in Afghanistan with Bruce Chatwin* (1972; London: Pallas Athene, 2000), p. 16.
6 Alighiero Boetti, "Afghanistan', op. cit., pp. 50–51.
7 Alighiero Boetti in conversation with Maurizio Fagiolo, *Il Messaggero*, 23 March 1977; repr. in Achille Bonito Oliva (ed.), *Alighiero & Boetti: Bringing the World into Art, 1993–1962* (Naples: MADRE and Milan: Electa, 2009), p. 189.
8 Alighiero Boetti, "Afghanistan', p. 51.
9 Ibid.,p. 52.
10 Alighiero Boetti interviewed by Achille Bonito Oliva in 1973, first pub. in Achille Bonito Oliva, *Dialoghi d'artista: incontri con l'arte contemporanea 1970–1984*, trans. Paola Morsiani in Paola Morsiani, *When 1 is 2: The Art of Alighiero e Boetti* (Houston: Contemporary Arts Museum, 2002), p. 93.
11 Edward Said, *Orientalism* (London: Penguin, 2003), pp. 2, 5.

he could return from time to time. But if one considers his approach through the account of Victor Segalen's Exoticism rather than through Said's Orientalism, any criticisms that Said's position suggests begin to diminish. In his *Essay on Exoticism* composed between 1904 and 1918, Segalen defined and defended exoticism when he wrote that it is:

> not that kaleidoscopic vision of the tourist or of the mediocre spectator, but the forceful and curious reaction to a shock felt by someone of strong individuality in response to some object whose distance from oneself he alone can perceive and savor . . . Exoticism is the keen and immediate perception of an eternal incomprehensibility.[12]

Edouard Glissant has written that Segalen "experienced passionately the call of Diversity" and that his "crucial idea was that encountering the Other superactivates poetic imagination and understanding." Segalen, he continues, "does not merely describe recognition of the other as a moral obligation, but he considers it an aesthetic constituent, the first edict of a real poetics of Relation. The power to experience the shock of elsewhere is what distinguishes the poet."[13] Glissant allows one to understand that it was precisely Boetti's appreciation of Afghanistan's otherness that led him, right from the beginning of his time there, to open his work to the voices of Afghans. A powerful sense of its difference meant that it would be impossible and indefensible to represent Afghanistan or to speak on behalf of Afghans. Of course, this did not preclude communication—which is why, as we shall see, Boetti always worked with Afghans—but it did mean committing himself to making works in which Afghans could articulate their own experience and concerns.

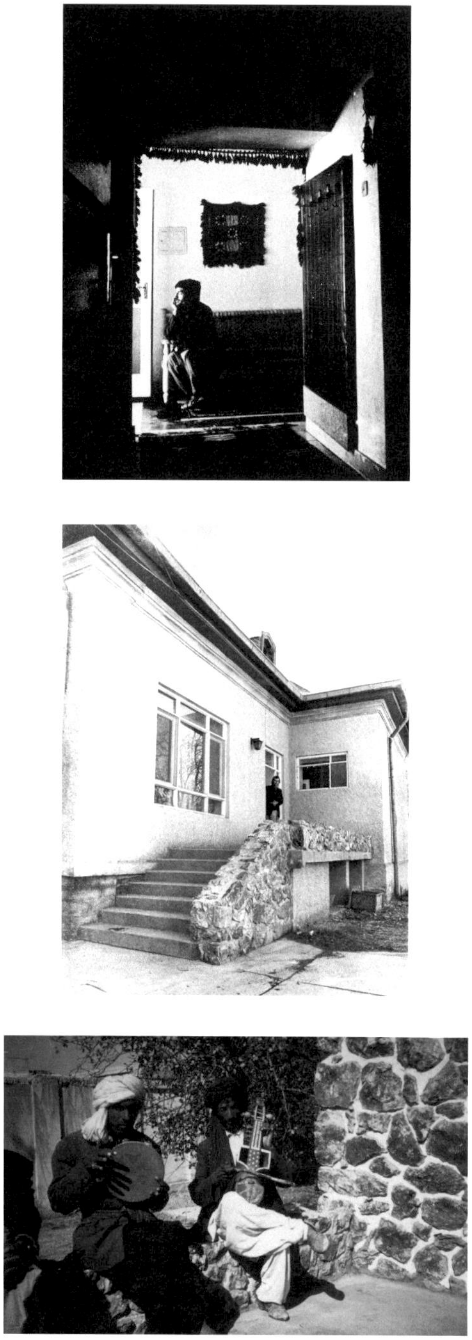

[fig. 4] One Hotel, Kabul, c. 1971–77 (top to bottom: Dastaghir in the hall; garden steps; musicians in the garden)

One Hotel and Postal Works

The embroideries and kilims are by far the most celebrated outcomes of Boetti's collaborations with Afghans, but other projects initiated in Kabul should also be considered, starting with the near-legendary *One Hotel*

12 Victor Segalen, *Essay on Exoticism* (Durham, N.C: Duke University Press, 2002), pp. 20–21. Annemarie Sauzeau Boetti has also turned to Segalen's defence of exoticism (and his critique of bad exoticism) in *Sauzeau Boetti, Shaman/Showman*, p. 104.

13 Edouard Glissant, *Poetics of Relation* (Ann Arbor, Michigan: University of Michigan Press, 2007) p. 29.

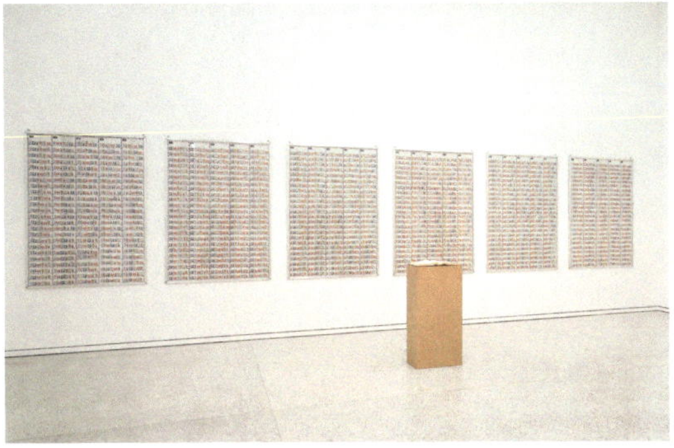

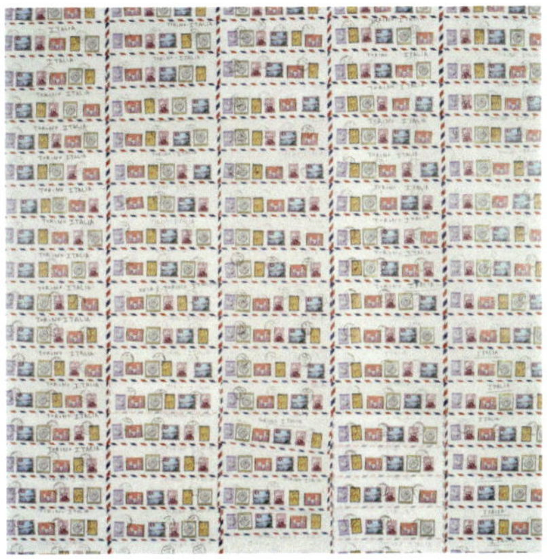

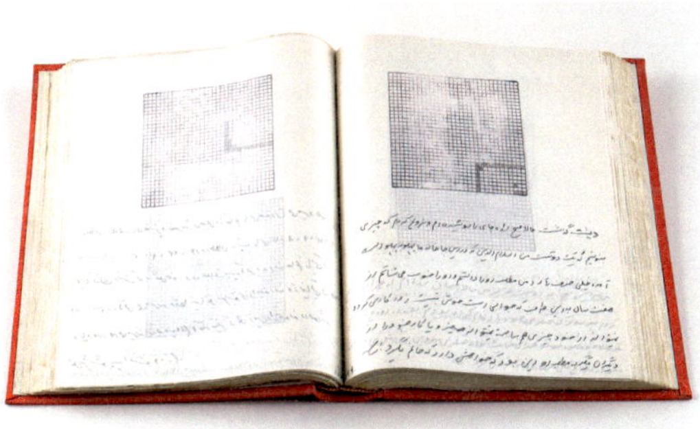

[fig. 5] 720 lettere dall'Afghanistan (720 Letters from Afghanistan), 1973–74

[figs. 1, 4a–c]. Boetti set up and provided five years' rent for *One Hotel* after meeting on his first visit to Kabul Gholam Dastaghir, whose ambition it was to own a hotel. As sketches reveal, Boetti tried out several names for the hotel, including El Mansour Hotel (a homage to his ancestor) and Letohotel (a palindrome suggesting the name of the river Lethe, representing "oblivion" in Greek mythology) but chose *One Hotel* on Dastaghir's suggestion. Sited in the Sharanaw residential quarter, but flanked by shops, the building was "a pleasant bungalow with a garden and a clientele of hippies and Indian and Pakistani carpet traders."[14] Boetti divided the building into eleven rooms—a number to which he was attracted as a kind of double and that he had used in many drawings; he stayed in Room 11 whenever he returned to the country, sometimes bringing friends, and lived there for a month with his son Matteo in 1977. In 1973, he insisted that the hotel should be seen as part of his practice, rather than as a subsidiary business project, asserting that "creativity also means opening a hotel."[15] *One Hotel* was identified and represented as an art project both in his 1975 portfolio of works *Insicuro noncurante*, which contained a sheet with the hotel's ink stamp, and in the catalogue for his 1978 show at the Kunsthalle Basel, where he inserted a photograph of the hotel between pictures of other works, recording it as just another outcome of his practice. The decision to create a hotel was testament to Boetti's gregariousness and to his interest in working with others. Synchronous with projects like Allen Ruppersberg's *Al's Hotel* and Gordon Matta-Clark's *Food*, *One Hotel* is now feted as a precursor for "Relational Aesthetics" and the inclusive, participatory activities of many artists of the 1990s. But we should beware of over-emphasizing its importance to Boetti. There are no records in his archive indicating that he took much notice of its day-to-day running during his absence. As much as it was a utopian outpost, it was also a convenience, a studio/accommodation where Boetti could base himself to organize his production.

Boetti's postal works and associated drawings, despite occasionally being overlooked in accounts of his Afghan projects, reveal how he questioned what it meant to make work in Afghanistan, and indeed elsewhere. The

14 Tom Francis, "One Star is Enough to Make a Cosmos: Alighiero e Boetti and the One Hotel," *Bidoun* 19, 2009.

15 Ibid.

ill. p. 115 various versions of *La Mole Antonelliana* (1970–75) comprise a row of postcards of this well-known Turin landmark. Each postcard contains the address of one of his friends in Italy, along with a different stamp from each country that Boetti visited in the early 1970s—the US, Morocco, Guatemala, Ethiopia, and Afghanistan. Refusing to produce objectifying images of these places or to send back souvenirs, he mailed his friends pictures of his hometown, not only showing how Italy marketed itself, but also giving a sense of how other countries employed similar images—architectural landmarks, religious symbols, and political leaders—on their stamps. Other postal works comprised envelopes sent from *One Hotel*. In many cases, he simply arranged the stamps in all possible permutations according to serial systems, similar to works made in Italy, implying that he wanted to represent Afghanistan as a country whose systems of communication were not entirely different to those of his own. Just as he would play with the paperwork of his home country (office calendars, postage stamps, phonebooks) so he would (mis)use Afghan stamps, postmarks and official forms. In some cases, Boetti would insert drawings based on the recurrent motifs of his work inside envelopes; the drawings would be shown alongside a set of the framed envelopes. He used the experience of willed displacement to condense and refine his thoughts in these works, determining how to distil his proliferating ideas into small groups of drawings.[16]

ill. pp. 120–121 The work *24 lettere dall'Afghanistan* (1973) comprises a set of envelopes in which four pairs of colored stamps appear in all possible combinations, surrounded by twenty-four drawings made on official forms. Boetti pasted number drawings and word squares on gridded paper onto each drawing, and at the bottom, asked Dastaghir to compose four lines of Persian text. The following winter, Boetti prepared the more ambitious *720 lettere dall'Afghanistan* (1974) [figs. 5a–c]. Six Afghan stamps were arranged in all combinations, requiring 720 envelopes. Each envelope contained a unique drawing based on a favorite numeric conundrum—that to make a grid of 1,000 squares, one needed to add thirty-nine units to a 31 x 31 grid or erase twenty-four squares from a 32 x 32 grid. Boetti then asked Dastaghir to compose a text for the bottom of each drawing describing the Afghan winter and to post them to a friend in Turin. No full translation of Dastaghir's writings in the larger work exists; the first set of twenty-four letters however, contain a bizarre array of texts. Dastaghir laments the high cost of marriage in Kabul,[17] mentions the popularity of Indian films,[18] and describes how Afghan musicians were held back in their ambition to make innovations by financial needs.[19] In one passage he seems to complain about the workload in the *One Hotel*[20] but in another expresses gratitude to Boetti because of the employment and money he provided.[21] These postal works might be seen as something of a light-hearted game, with Boetti setting a task, and Dastaghir playing with the idea that Boetti could not understand the messages that were this task's outcome, but there is also a more radical side to both postal works. Refusing to speak on behalf of others, or to send back his own descriptions of their culture, Boetti asked his Afghan friends to express themselves. The resulting works become a site of dual authorship. As for the

16 This impulse in Boetti's work, to archive his own production in the manner of Duchamp's *Boîte-en-valise*, continued in 1975 with *Insicuro noncurante* (1966–75) and culminated in his last kilim of 1994.

17 "A marriage in Afghanistan would cost one hundred thousand Afghanis. If a young person does not have this much money he cannot get married. So what should this young man do when there is always a beloved on his mind making him dizzy?" Translation by Gelare Khoshgozaran, 2011.

18 "People in Afghanistan still like Indian movies a lot. Everyone always wants to go to an Indian movie. People are not interested in other movies like the Indian ones. I, too, like watching Indian movies because there are ancient myths in them." Translation by Gelare Khoshgozaran, 2011.

19 "Oldies music is still popular in Afghanistan. They would match the lyrics with the melody when they cannot create their own tunes, but not every musician is able to do that. That is why the musician, after a short while after he has learned to play, wants to make some money. That is why music in Afghanistan does not improve." Translation by Gelare Khoshgozaran, 2011.

20 "Now I am having hardship. I do not know where to go and what to do. This much money was really good for me and I accepted to do this job. It has been a couple of days, almost a week now since I began to think this was little money for too much labor. Thinking what I should say to Alighiero…" Translation by Gelare Khoshgozaran, 2011.

21 "Alighiero told me he would give me 20,000 Afghanis to write 720 letters like this. It made me so happy since I am living a difficult life with no money or job. May God make the life of no human being miserable and hard." Translation by Gelare Khoshgozaran, 2011.

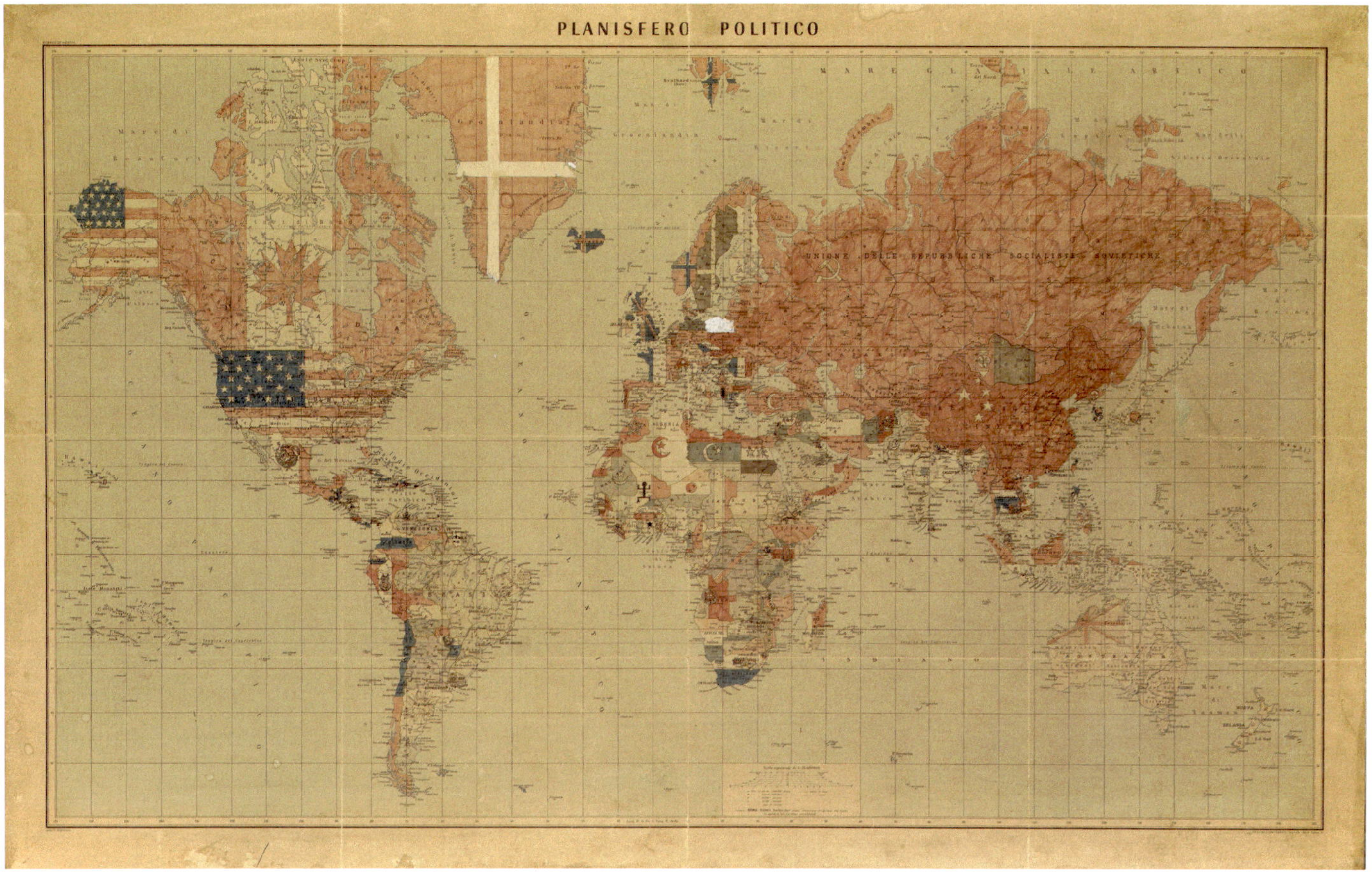

 Planisfero politico (Political Planisphere), 1969–70

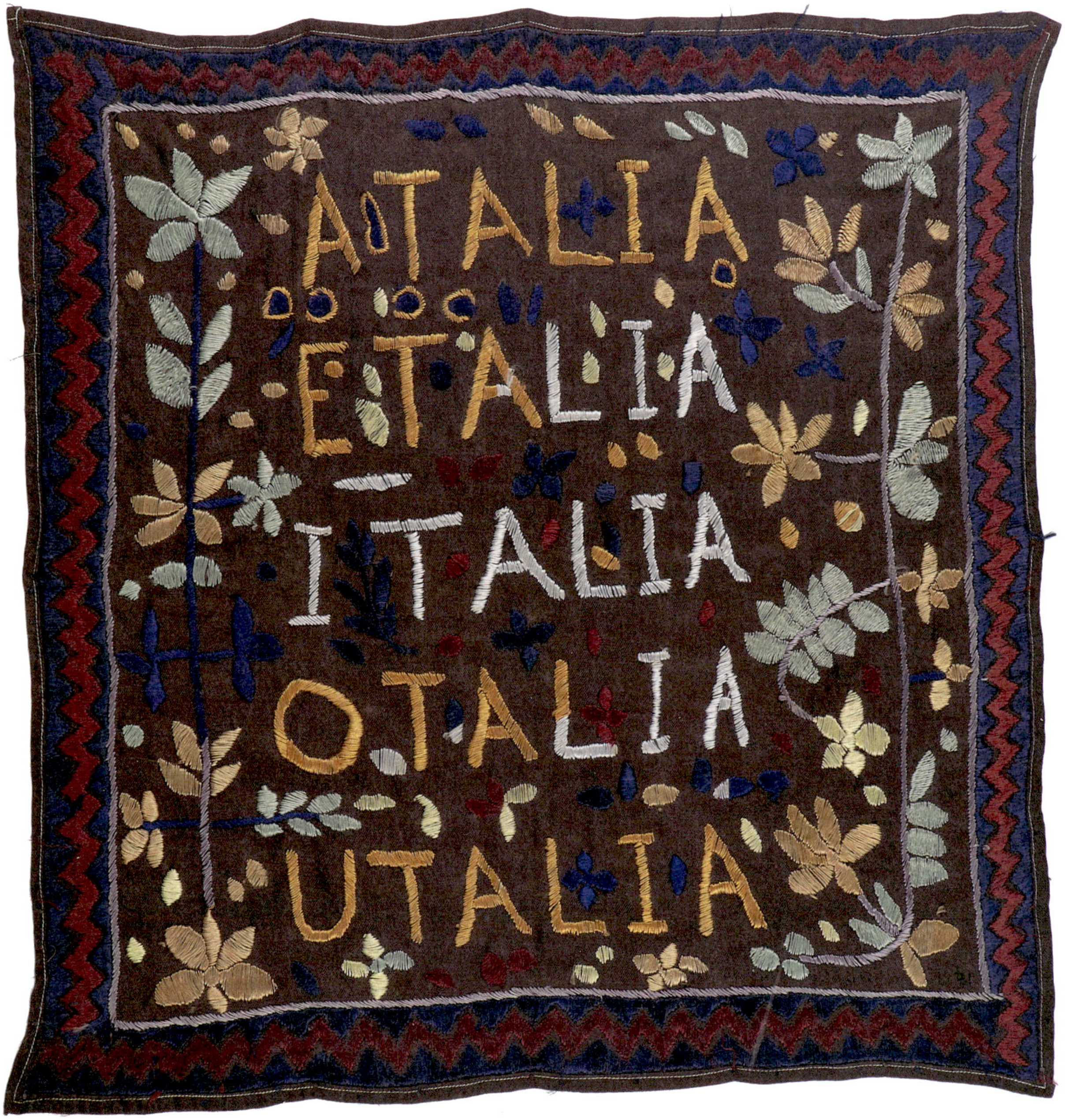

AEIOU, 1971

recipients of the works (in the first instance, the addressee of the letters, and later, museums visitors), viewers unable to speak Persian are forced to recognize that they have limited access to its meanings. As a consequence, they sense the limitations of their own ability to understand a distant culture. Meanwhile, the Afghan viewer in Europe or America (and we should consider that communities of Afghan exiles were forming at this time) will receive welcome news from home. Today, these texts might stand as a powerful testimony to the richness of life in Kabul before the Soviet, Taliban and coalition invasions.

Embroideries

One of Afghanistan's well-known exiles, the author Khaled Hosseini, has recently published a novel partly set in Kabul during 1974. In *A Thousand Splendid Suns*, Mariam, recently arrived from Herat, is taken for her first walk around Kabul, including the very street in which *One Hotel* was located: "The street was lined with shops and little stalls that sold lambskin hats and rainbow-colored *chapans* . . . Carpet shops, handicraft shops, pastry shops, flower shops, and shops that sold suits for men and dresses for women." Mariam is asked to "wait outside an embroidery shop" and from there:

> watched the cars crawling up Chicken Street, threading through the horde of hawkers and pedestrians, honking at children and donkeys who wouldn't move. She watched bored-looking merchants inside their tiny stalls, smoking, or spitting into brass spittoons, their faces emerging from the shadows now and then to peddle textiles and fur-collared *poostin* coats to passersby.[22]

Though fictional, Hosseini's account gives a vivid sense of the area around *One Hotel*, where Boetti could easily work with local craftspeople and embroiderers and collect *ikats*, rugs, and other textiles (which later adorned his country house in Todi). Prior to this, Boetti had used embroidery in two very different projects, as if in anticipation of his first trip to Kabul: in 1969 the work *Territori occupati* was his first attempt to find a way to *ill. p. 79* respond to the map on the cover of *La Stampa* during the "Six-Day War" of 1967. He asked Sauzeau Boetti to stitch the shapes of the Sinai desert, the West Bank, and the Golan heights onto a cloth, replicating a map of a war-zone with embroidery, as if a nineteenth-century keepsake (later, this map would be used again in the first copper plate for the *Dodici formi dal giugno 67.*) Then in *ill. p. 78* 1970, Sauzeau Boetti again used her needle to set out the phonetic transliterations of the Italian word for the date 1970, "EMMEIELLEELLEEENNEOVIECIEEN- *ill. p. 85* NETIOESSEETITIAENNETIA," celebrating the arrival of a new decade in the latter part of the twentieth century with a delicate embroidery on two white lace squares. In both cases, the medium and the image or text seem deliberately discordant, anticipating some important aspects of Boetti's later work.

The first two embroidered works fabricated in Kabul in early 1971 on Boetti's initial visit were on small square cloths. On the first work, two dates appear, "16 DICEMBRE 2040" and "11 LUGLIO 2023"; on the *ill. p. 124–125* second, a list of words: "ATALIA, ETALIA, ITALIA, OTALIA, UTALIA". The dates were the hundredth anniversary of Boetti's birth and his anticipated death date—dates also used in an earlier work made in Italy on brass plaques. In all likelihood, Boetti supplied these texts to the embroiderers without further direction. The resulting works would have pleased and surprised him for many reasons. The cloths came back with the texts surrounded by ornate borders. Boetti was interested in the idea that an artwork might be produced by different parties without collaboration or discussion, and that authorship could be split rather that shared. Some aspects of these embroideries were very clearly the contribution of Boetti, while others were down to the sensibilities of their fabricators. Boetti was also interested in how chance might determine the final appearance of a work. In "ITALIA," the embroiderers ran out of gold and silver thread halfway through a letter, but apparently without much concern, carried on stitching in another color.

[22] Khaled Hosseini, *A Thousand Splendid Suns* (London: Bloomsbury Publishing, 2007) p. 67.

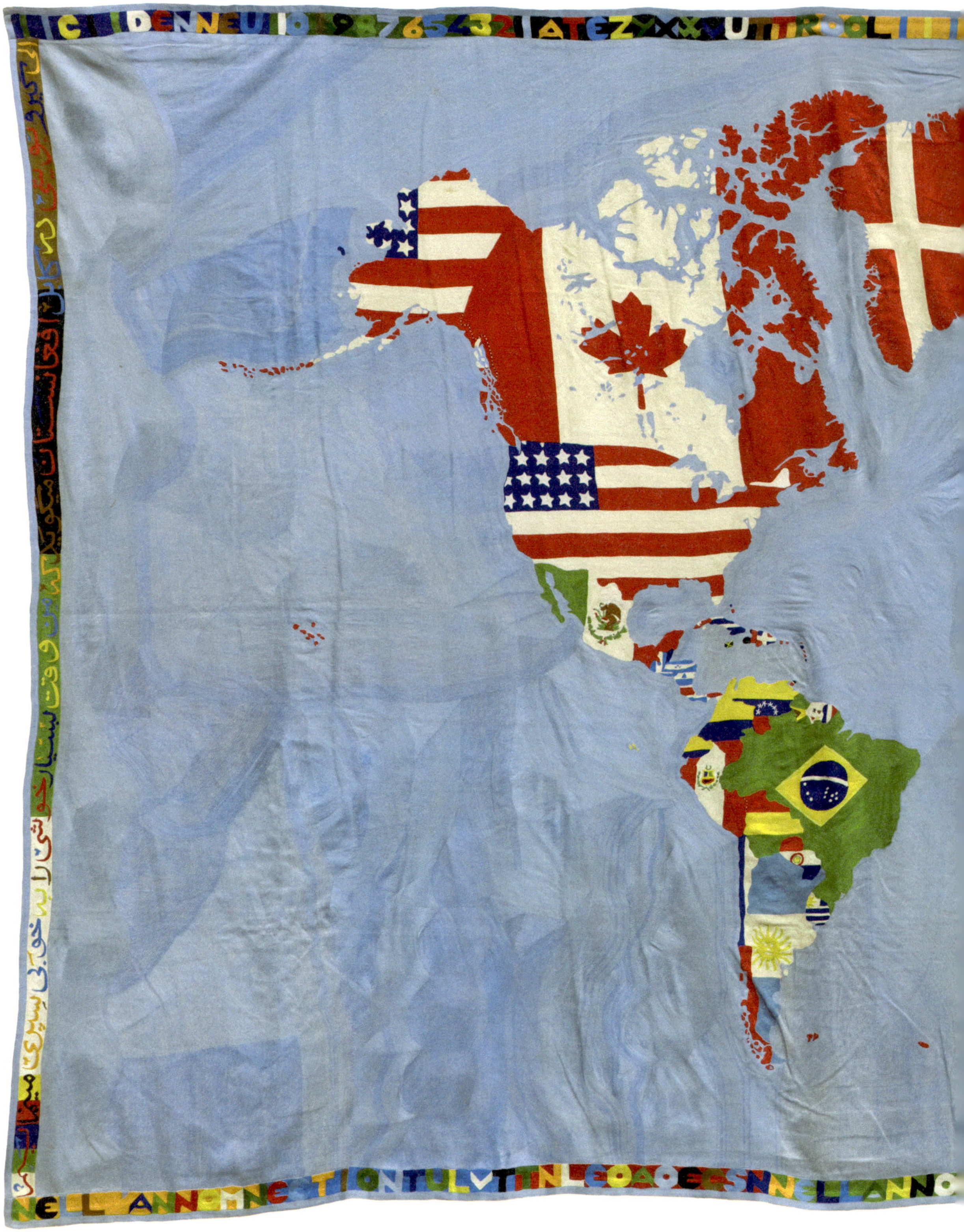

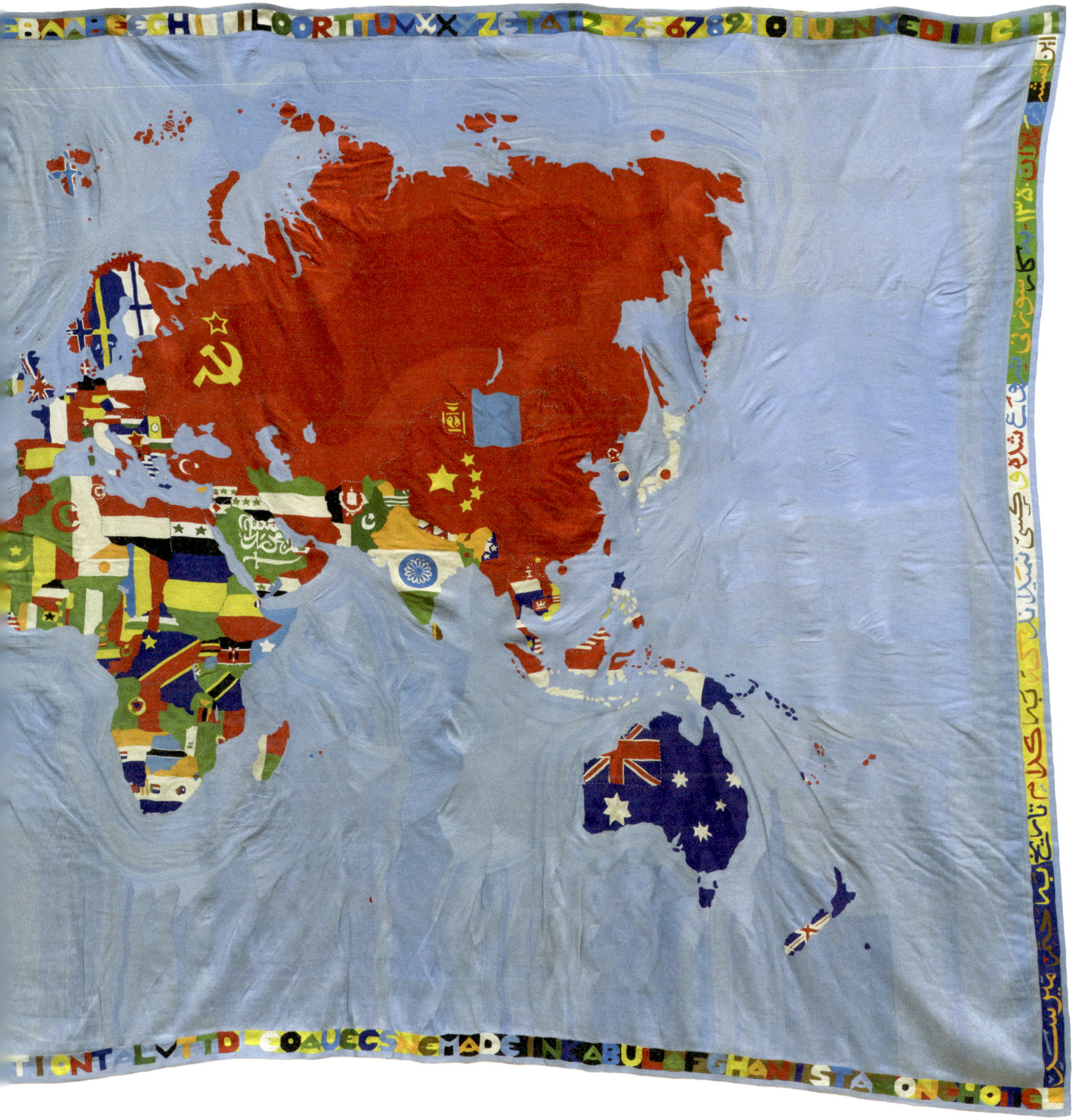

Mappa (Map), 1971–72

Boetti returned to Italy excited by the possibilities of the small embroideries. Later that year, he went back to Kabul with a number of large canvases in his luggage. Each was printed with the contours of the world map, and the countries marked with their flags in felt-tip pen *ill. p. 161* to indicate the colors: a design used in the drawing *Planisfero politico* two years earlier. From Turin, Sauzeau Boetti made contact with the Royal School of Embroidery in Kabul, and on his arrival in the city, Boetti handed over the canvases to be embroidered as he instructed. The work was time-consuming because the Royal School used a particularly fine Bokhara stitch and very thin threads, and because of the intricacy of stitching *ill. pp. 164–165* very thin borderlines between countries. Boetti soon decided to move production to a more versatile set-up organized through Dastaghir, working with a less delicate stitch and less refined threads. Dastaghir would relay Boetti's instructions to two women, Fatimah and Habibah, who employed teams of women to make the embroideries. In other words, Boetti never came into contact with the people who actually stitched his works. At this stage (the early 1970s) his Afghan output was relatively modest (in the late 1980s, as we shall see, there was an escalation of production), yet this way of working certainly raises questions, since Boetti's *modus operandi* could be seen as a precursor to the practices of major multinational corporations today, and clothing manufacturers in particular. But whereas businesses running on the principle of maximum profit pay workers as little as possible, Boetti rewarded his fabricators very generously.[23] Because of codes of behaviour in Afghan society at the time, there could be no dialogue with the women, but there was certainly extensive interaction with the male intermediaries. The affection that the producers felt for Boetti—the man commissioning their labor—was often expressed in the works through Persian texts surrounding the four sides of the "mappe" or within the "arazzi."

The embroideries signaled a new direction for Boetti on many levels. This medium enabled him to approach color in an entirely new way. During his Arte Povera years, he had been interested in the branding of color, making monochrome panels announcing the industrial name of the paint pigment, which suggested that color could only be understood in relation to commerce. By *ill. pp. 52, 59, 57, 150* 1969, the colors of Boetti's works were determined by other pre-existing factors: the hues of postage stamps or of flags. In both instances, he steered away from composing colors and creating harmonies. When it came to working with color in Afghanistan, however, Boetti took a new approach: he left the embroiderers to choose the threads in many works, and results were sometimes fascinating, as can be seen in the 1973 work *IVEDENTI*, *ill. p. 200* where each line is a different thread color. He admired the Afghan women for their great sense of color: "Their choices of color from the designs of my color schemes resulted in the combinations of color possibilities that were impossible to predict. The element of surprise is like the disorder invading the formal order of the grid."[24]

Boetti's method of production, of working with Afghan embroiderers, had other important implications. At this time, he later recalled, "not many artists had their work made by artisans."[25] To the Italian audience of the period, embroidered cloths from Afghanistan were a difficult proposition. "Initial reaction was awful," Boetti said. The embroideries were "at once conceptually troubling and too pretty."[26] This statement implies that it was not Boetti's hands-off approach to production, nor embroidery's association with "craft" rather than fine art per se that was problematic. In a context where Italian artists of the day were working with raw materials such as rock, glass, sacking, and coal, Boetti's embroideries could be seen as overtly feminine, perhaps more closely allied to the stitched works of Marisa Merz. The embroideries challenged some of the sexist biases of the Italian art world. They also troubled

23 So recalls Salman Ali, who worked at *One Hotel* and later came to work for the artist in Rome. Conversation with the author, 2011.

24 Alighiero Boetti interviewed by Kazuo Akao Art Agency, Tokyo, in 1980, first pub. in *Alighiero e Boetti*, exh. cat., Loggetta Lombardesca, Ravenna, 1990, repr. in Achille Bonito Oliva (ed.), *Alighiero & Boetti: Bringing the World into Art, 1993–1962* (Naples: MADRE and Milan: Electa, 2009), p. 195.

25 Alighiero Boetti, "Afghanistan," p. 52.

26 Ibid.

the implicit nationalism of Italian art, of Italy's flourishing tradition of sculpture and painting, and its sense of its own historical authority. The embroideries are a subtle reminder of another place, another tradition, and a reminder that other art forms have always existed side by side with Italian ones.

With the encouragement of dealers like Gian Enzo Sperone, Boetti's audience began to accept the embroidered works, but before long, they became challenging for other reasons. Boetti set out to disrupt the existing art market categories of the "unique work" and the "multiple"—categories that dealers knew how to cope with and to which Boetti himself had previously adhered. Although he was critical of the industrial society's obsession with identical consumer objects, and was pleased that each of his embroideries was unique,[27] Boetti was also delighted by the fact that their means of fabrication facilitated "profusion, mass production."[28] Sometimes he would commission 100 small word squares, each with the same phrase, and sell them separately:

> I've made 100 copies . . . but each one is different, with different colors, and depending on the style of the woman making it. So it's neither an original work, nor a multiple. These works are part of a new category. And they are for a market which is also quite different from the market for my other pieces. Someone told me I'd produced the first popular conceptual image.[29]

Boetti had a large range of works embroidered in Afghanistan: small and large "arazzi" or word squares, including those forming the 100-part work *Ordine e disordine*, the two large *I mille fiumi*, the first *Alternando da uno a cento e viceversa* grids of 1977, the monumental *L'albero delle ore*, based on a drawing recording the pattern of the chimes of Santa Maria in Trastevere, and the earliest precursors of the "tutto" works called *Pack*. However, he is most famous for the "mappe," and this body of work raises interesting questions concerning the disconnection between the image and the conditions of its production in Afghanistan. Boetti was always interested in making art without invention, and his schema for the maps—of coloring each country with the design of its map—accorded with this principle. He also recognized how popular the "mappe" could be: a "mappa" was "one of the few things I could see outside an art gallery, and that amuses me a lot!"[30] "For me the embroidered 'mappa' couldn't be more beautiful," he later said, "I did nothing for this work, chose nothing myself, in the sense that: the world is shaped as it is, I did not draw it; the flags are what they are, I did not design them. In short I created absolutely nothing."[31] As attractive as it is, Boetti's comment belies the number of decisions that he made about the "mappe": when and how frequently he should produce them, which map projection to work from, how to change borders and flags in war-torn countries, and which texts should appear on the borders of the maps.

ill. pp. 95–97
ill. pp. 214–217/249
ill. p. 131

Boetti did not have a fixed system to determine when to commission new "mappe" (for instance, he did not make a new one each time a border changed). They were made from time to time, but first, Boetti would ask his collaborator Rinaldo Rossi to obtain the latest maps and flags from a cartographer in London. This meant that from one batch of embroideries to the next, the results of independence struggles and civil wars are visible (for example, Mozambique and Angola dropping Portuguese insignia, and Namibia remaining blank without a flag for most of the 1980s because of its ongoing civil war). To draw the maps, Boetti initially used the Mercator projection. In the late 1980s, he changed to the Robinson projection, which provided a more

27 As Clemente commented in Clemente and Neri, "A Fugue for Alighiero e Boetti," p. 89, "If you consider Alighiero's works in the present context of mass-produced objects, there is certainly an evident utopian impulse in utilizing communities which will never make one thing exactly like the next—because happiness resides in difference and not in sameness."

28 Alighiero Boetti, "Afghanistan," p. 52.

29 Ibid., p. 54.

30 Alighiero Boetti interviewed by Mirella Bandini in 1972, first pub. in *NAC* no. 3, March 1973, trans. Caroline Beamish, in Richard Flood and Frances Morris (eds), *Zero to Infinity: Arte Povera 1962–1972* (London: Tate Publishing, 2001), p. 190.

31 Alighiero Boetti, "Artist's Statement, 1974"; first published in *Alighiero e Boetti: Insicuro noncurante* (Nouveau Musée de Villeurbanne, 1986); trans Liz Heron and Gilda Williams in Carolyn Christov-Bakargiev (ed.), *Arte Povera* (London: Phaidon, 1999), p. 237.

accurate visualization of land areas, whereas the Mercator, with its northern bias, severely diminished the size of southern continents.[32]

Boetti could have made his maps as a series of prints, or he could have asked Italian assistants to hand-color maps in the manner of other works like his participatory "Biro" drawings. Had he done this, the "mappe" as a series would still have formed an ongoing account of the changes in international history during the late twentieth century. I would argue, however, that by being embroidered by hand, first in Afghanistan and afterwards in Pakistan, Boetti's series creates a crucial and generative disconnection between the image of the map and the conditions and materials of its production, a disconnection that puts the idea of western cartography under critical pressure. No matter what cartographic projection he employed, the images Boetti used for his maps were Greenwich-centred western representations of the world, in which geography was understood as a flat terrain divided into nation states. These images, however, were produced by people who did not see the world from this perspective, and who often did not even recognize the image they were fabricating *as* an image of the world.

The perspective of the producers made itself evident in different ways. There is a powerful sense of how slowly the "mappe" must have been made; a sense of a culture that approaches time in a very different way from Northern Italy in the 1960s, where time (at least as Boetti sensed it) was always controlled, divided, and measured in order to serve the needs of economy and efficiency. The first "mappe" were hung over poles rather than stretched over a frame, mimicking the ways in which other embroideries might be hung in an Afghan home, and this means of display creates the look of a mutable and wobbly world that counters the emphasis that the image places on static territorial borders and the fixed geometrical designs of flags. We also feel the perspective of the Afghans in the Persian texts bordering the embroideries, alongside those by Boetti, that detail the circumstances of each map's production.

In contemplating the perspectives of the fabricators, one appreciates that the map is neither the objective nor universally used form of representation that we in the West often assume it to be. It is an image forged in a specific historical and ideological context; consequently, its claim to provide an authoritative representation of the world collapses. Yet more than each "mappa" being a site where the authority of the West erodes, it is a space where dialogue emerges. And there is another kind of utopian space in the "mappe": the oceans. On receipt of a delivery of "mappe," Boetti discovered that the embroiderers, not recognizing the image of the oceans, had used whatever color thread was in surplus: delighted by this error, and by the unexpected workings of chance, he let it stand. From then on, oceans were colored by the choices of the embroiderers, and maps would arrive with pink, silver, purple, orange, green, and gold waters. In contrast, the colors of flags were always determined by nationalist struggles. The polychrome waters are another sign of the dual origins of the maps, but might also be read as spaces beyond the control of nationalism, and spaces in which a new visionary geography is imagined.

Exile and Longing

One of the first unusually colored map dates from 1979. *ill. p. 219*
The continents appear against extraordinarily beautiful rose oceans, and looking to the area of Afghanistan, one discovers that the black, red, and green stripes of its flag have been replaced with a red background and a Persian text. The text reads "Khalq," naming the Communist-inclined government that took power after a coup in April 1978. Boetti could still visit Afghanistan during its reign, but when it failed to implement its revolutionary Marxist policies, the USSR, unwilling to countenance the collapse of a Communist government on its doorstep, took matters into its own hands and invaded Afghanistan. In the words of the anthropologist Thomas

[32] For another account of the "mappe," placing them in the context of Boetti's work, see Luca Cerizza, *Alighiero e Boetti: Mappa* (London: Afterall, 2008).

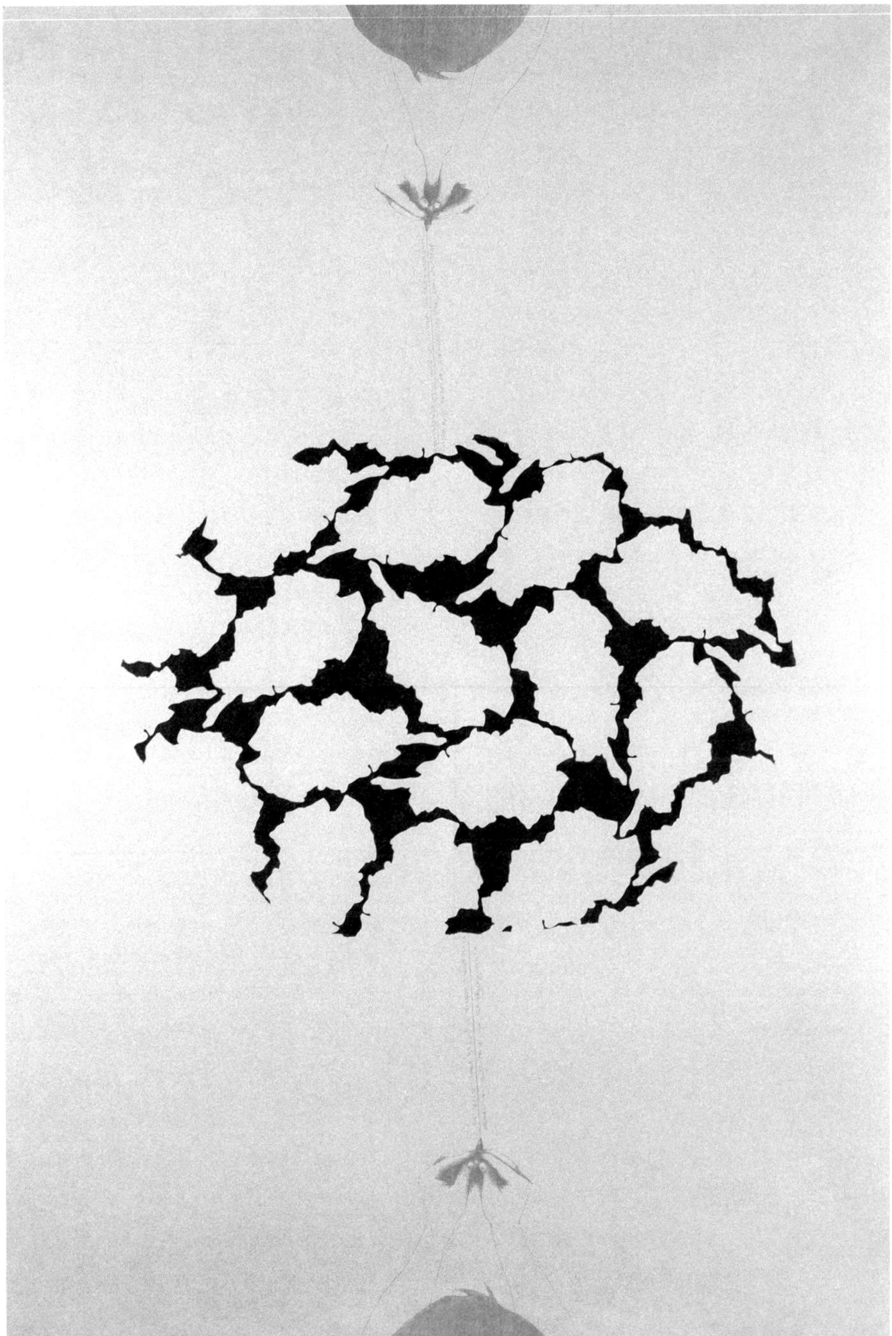

 Afghanistan, 1980

Barfield, who published a history of the country in 2010, the "intervention marked the beginning of a decade-long occupation that would result in the death of one million Afghans, the flight of four million refugees to Pakistan and Iran, and the displacement of millions of others internally."[33] The invasion put an end to Boetti's visits, and for a while, to his ability to work with middle-men and embroiderers. Over the next few years, the production of embroideries almost came to a halt. The "mappe" that do date from this period record the compromised circumstances of their own production. Earlier maps had been shipped direct from Kabul to Rome; one map from this time, however, contains a bordering text in Persian describing that it had been *ill. p. 220, top* passed hand-to-hand from Afghanistan through Iran to Europe. Some maps from 1979 did not reach Boetti until 1985, when he resumed contact with their makers. In testament to their displacement, he left these few ex- *ill. p. 220* amples without a border, perpetually incomplete.

A rare map from 1983 contains a Persian text that records that "I, Alighiero e Boetti dream about Afghanistan." and another from this time laments that it was composed in "Rome with nostalgia."[34] As these texts indicate, back in his studio in Rome, Boetti was *ill. p. 191* mourning the loss of Afghanistan. In some of the *La natura, una faccenda ottusa* collages from that period, he pasted fragments of news articles about the fate of the country next to the other components of the drawings. Earlier, in 1980, he had also made the drawing *ill. p. 169* *Afghanistan*. It uses a format that recurs in many of Boetti's late drawings: bird's-eye views of his head and of both hands holding a single pencil appear at the top and bottom of the image. A column extends down a central axis between these points. Here, a narrow line of letters extends from Boetti's hands to an irregular oval form in the centre. The Italian text translates as "Afghanistan, beloved country where 85,000 Russian soldiers entered to wrest power in December 1979. Now, during the last days of October 1980 sunshine, it is more than a year ago since Alighiero e Boetti departed." The oval is made up of a group outlines of Afghanistan in various orientations, with black ink filling the space between them. Boetti repeats the image of Afghanistan in the drawing no fewer than twenty-three times, but also presents it in disarray and disarticulation, as a form that is often incomplete. The drawing evokes violence without providing any images of warfare. It is Boetti's representation of the importance of Afghanistan to him—as if he was trying to conjure up its shape from memory again and again and to hold it between his hands; the clustered "Afghanistans" form a brain shape, suggesting a representation of his mind filled with its memory.[35] *Afghanistan* is therefore a complex articulation of violence as well as a representation of the experience of loss and of the capacities and inadequacies of memory in the face of loss. Yet, for all these qualities, it remains a work focused on the artist's response to the invasion of Afghanistan rather than a work that allows Afghans to communicate their own reactions to this event.

Boetti made his first trip to Japan in 1980, the same year in which he made *Afghanistan*. Japan grew in his affections and he traveled there again in 1985. Just as he had been taken by Afghan embroidery, so he looked at Japanese materials and traditions, as many works he made in the mid-1980s indicate. We find red ink strokes across the 1987 five-part frieze; printed marks made *ill. p. 194–195* from Japanese seals and rings; and origami elements in *ill. p. 192, 193* collages. The most interesting of the Japanese works were made with the calligrapher Enomoto San. Boetti approached him because of his fascination with this tradition of mark-making that, while gestural, had little to do with the angst and sentimentality re-emerging in Neo-Expressionist work across the United States and Europe and in the paintings of the Transavantguardia group in Italy. Boetti asked Enomoto San to draw the Japanese for "wind" on a sheet of folded paper, which

33 Thomas Barfield, *Afghanistan: A Cultural and Political History* (Princeton and Oxford: Princeton University Press, 2010) p. 234.

34 See *Alighiero e Boetti: Mappa* (New York, Gladstone Gallery, 2010) The first of these "mappe" is reproduced on page 37 and the second on page 36.

35 Sauzeau Boetti, in *Shaman / Showman*, p. 181, has read the work a little differently, suggesting that Boetti creates a form that can be seen as "the cosmic brain of a lost country": since its freedom has been destroyed, it exists as a mental image rather than as reality.

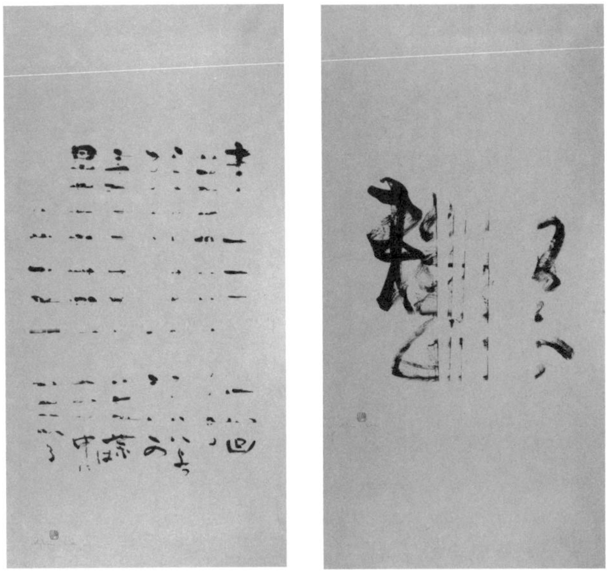

[fig. 6] Vento (Wind), 1985

he subsequently unfolded to complete the work, producing what he called the "decomposition of the initial calligram."[36] [figs. 6a, b] There is a contrast between the idea of a rush of wind, conveyed by the original word and by the fluidity of the original calligraphic ink strokes, and the stuttering brokenness of the final image. As well as working with Enomoto San, Boetti also took the opportunity to make a witty and charmingly subversive intervention with another aspect of Japanese culture. Knowing that Japanese fans present legible images only when unfurled, he created a work in which a word was only legible when the paper was folded. "For Enomoto, it was as if he had painted on a closed fan, whereas in Japan, fans are painted open, then afterwards closed, so as to hide the image."[37]

Around this time, Boetti traveled to Zanzibar, Morocco, and other destinations, yet he longed to re-establish his connection with Afghanistan, and by the mid-1980s, this became possible, albeit in very different circumstances. Using contacts made through Salman Ali and others (Ali had worked at the *One Hotel* and subsequently worked for Boetti in Rome), he started working with communities of exiled Afghans in Quetta and Peshawar, Northern Pakistan. Through the late 1980s, three characteristics developed in his work: there was a rapid escalation of production, an engagement with Sufi mysticism, and an expression within the embroideries of the political struggles of the exiled Afghans. These three conditions shaping the works from this period can be linked: Boetti increased production to sell more works for personal financial reasons, but also because his commissions were supporting the impoverished people who had been displaced from their lands. Sufism was also often taken up by the resistance fighters—historically, it had been embraced by those resisting wealthy Islamic leaders and more generally the more orthodox strains of Islam.

Boetti had begun to read Sufi poetry in the late 1960s in Turin, but over the course of his travels to Afghanistan and later Pakistan, he grew more and more attracted to Sufism because of the association with resistance and also because Sufi devotional ceremonies involved various methods of intoxication. In Pakistan during the late

36 Alighiero Boetti, "From Today to Tomorrow," in Sandro Lombardi, *Dall'oggi al domani* (Brescia: Edizioni L'Obliquo, 1988), repr. in Achille Bonito Oliva (ed.), *Alighiero & Boetti: Bringing the World into Art, 199—1962* (Naples: MADRE and Milan: Electa, 2009), p. 208.

37 Sauzeau Boetti, *Alighiero e Boetti: Shaman / Showman* (Cologne: Walter König Books, 2003), p. 195.

1980s he attended some of these ceremonies himself and worked closely with Sufi poets, and these collaborations culminated in his fifty-part *Poesie con il Sufi Berang* made on the occasion of the 1989 exhibition "Les Magiciens de la terre" at the Centre Georges Pompidou in Paris [fig. 7]. Whatever the nature of his personal spirituality, it nonetheless remains hard to assess the impact of Sufism on Boetti's works. It was important to him that his works should be capable of being appreciated on various levels and certainly this came out of his readings of Sufi poems, which could be understood in terms of their literal, lyrical meanings and of their allegorical, esoteric content. He believed that while most people could enjoy the beauty of a work (understanding it on the first level) only a few would grasp its "most secret, most hidden" meanings.[38] Yet, the works that actually included Sufi poems, such as the *Poesie con il Sufi Berang*, were not particularly compelling, and Boetti apparently found Berang's tendency to eulogise him as the "Poet of Rome," playing on the name of the thirteenth-century Sufi poet Rūmī, embarrassing.

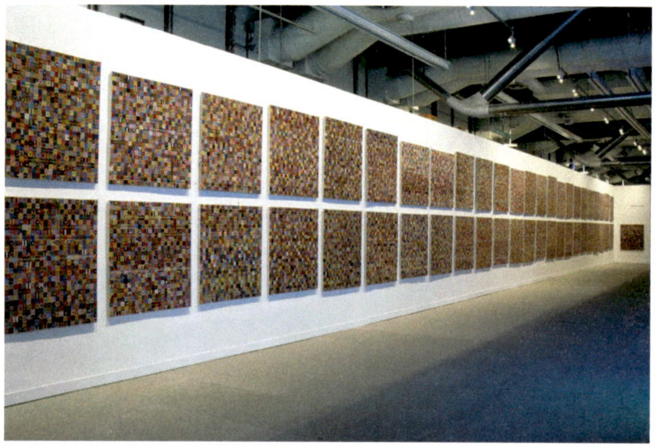

[fig. 7] *Poesie con il Sufi Berang* (Poems with Sufi Berang), installed in the exhibition "Les Magiciens de la terre," Centre Georges Pompidou, Paris, 1989

The most fascinating aspect of the late 1980s embroideries is instead the way in which the political sorrows and aspirations of their makers are articulated within and spread by the works. The Persian texts in the borders of most "mappe" express the conditions of exile. For example, in *Mappa* (1989) part of the text reads:

> The needlework of Alighiero e Boetti an Italian artist was produced in collaboration with Shahvali Afghan in the city of Peshawar in Pakistan. It is important to note that this work was hand-crafted by unnamed women who had immigrated from their beloved country Afghanistan to the Islamic country of Pakistan. These women have been living in these conditions for the past ten years.

ill. pp. 222–223 In one monumental map, an English text bluntly, but movingly, states that the work was "made in Peshawar by Afghan people." In this respect, however, the most *ill. pp. 245–250* complex works are the distinct body of "arazzi" that also date from 1988–89. Boetti drew up large grids on canvas, and supplied texts for approximately half the squares, reserving the rest to be filled with texts in

[38] Sergio Givone, "Dialogue with the Artist," in Achille Bonito Oliva (ed.), *Alighiero & Boetti: Bringing the World into Art, 1993–1962* (Naples: MADRE and Milan: Electa, 2009), p. 41.

Persian script written by the embroiderers themselves. He composed the grids in different ways—for instance, in a series of alternating horizontal rows of Italian and Persian, or in a complex checkerboard where little four-by-four grids of Persian were surrounded by Italian squares. Some texts are mournful, pining for the "beautiful landscapes" of Afghanistan plundered by the Russians,[39] some militant, declaring an intention to embark on a "Holy War" until the "last drop of the blood of their life's energy has been spent."[40] Another "arazzo" starts with words from the Sufi poetry of Hafiz: "I will not cease to strive until I have reached my goal. Either I will reach my goal or I will lose my life," and continues with a text that combines Sufi imagery with words describing the ongoing fighting:

> Muslim mujahadin have lost their lives like butterflies at the front and resisted the brutality of the cruel Russians and thousands of groups have suffered direly. They did this for the satisfaction of God and in order to found a society based on the Islamic faith. In order to achieve this they have embarked on the Holy War. For this holy goal they have sacrificed all. And we hope that they reach their goal and it will not be much longer before the flag of the Islamic faith flies in a free independent Afghanistan.[41]

Boetti's determination to split authorship reached a new degree of complexity in these works. The artwork is the outcome of widely different contributions and all its authors are present in the finished product, albeit in different ways. Boetti supplied the grid and the Italian text, his exiled Afghan contacts wrote the Persian messages, and finally the women embroiderers chose the colors and stitched the texts into the canvases. In the "arazzi," Boetti shared space with his fabricators and even allowed their contribution to break the rules of the system he had set up: unlike the Italian letters, each of which fits into its allotted square, the Persian script does not adhere to the order of the squares of the grid, since characters flow from one square to the next. Boetti clearly supported the cause of the *mujahidin* against the Soviet army at this time, and on trips to oversee production in Peshawar he would travel into the mountains to hold meetings with resistance leaders such as Ahmad Shah Massoud.[42] He saw his support for the Afghans as an echo of his ancestor Sheikh Mansur's work on behalf of the Chechens, who had fought a Russian army two centuries before. Yet, returning to his works rather than his acts, what was most important was that in setting up the production of the work, the artist, acknowledging the limits of his own self-expression, opinion, and indeed knowledge of a given political situation, created a space for a political message to be articulated clearly by the fabricators and their associates. No longer monovocal, the resulting work became a site where different political voices are present.

We might well read these works as representing not only the political desires of the exiled Afghans but also the conditions of language and speech in exile: The Persian text might have been authored by Afghan exiles, but it was never presented alone and instead appeared in the grids in such a way that sections of Persian were broken up by sections of Italian. The exiled subject cannot often speak at length, and sends his words to a distant audience with no knowledge of how they will be received. The visual cacophony of the "arazzi," with their buzzing colors, might itself be a representation of the fate of language and communication during a time of war. However, a more optimistic reading would be to note

39 "Our dear homeland, Afghanistan, has not only very pleasant weather but also large mines and all sorts of wonderful fruit. Except for now, because of bombardments and gunfire of the Russian infidels, its beautiful landscapes are destroyed and its pleasant weather is poisoned by the application of dangerous gases. The Russians are plundering its oil and gas resources and taking away its agricultural products." Translation of Persian text in embroidery *Nella primavera dell'anno millenovecentoottantanove* in Paulo Morsiani (ed.), *When 1 is 2: The Art of Alighiero e Boetti* (Houston: Contemporary Arts Museum, 2002), p. 98.

40 "The Afghan people consist mainly of Muslims. Their Holy Book is called the Koran. They are willing to sacrifice themselves for their Holy belief and home. For this reason they have embarked on the Holy War and will persist until the last drop of the blood of their life's energy has been spent." Translation of Persian in embroidery *Mese di marzo dell'anno mille nove 100 ottantanove* in Rolf Lauter (ed.), *Alighiero Boetti: Mettere al Mondo il Mondo* (Frankfurt: Museum für Moderne Kunst, 1998), p. 256.

41 Translation of Persian text in embroidery *Oggi dodicesimo giorno sesto mese anno mille novecento ottantanove*, in ibid., p. 244.

42 Alessandra Bonomo in conversation with the author, 2011

how these works became a vehicle by which to transport the messages from one place and time—Peshawar in the late 1980s—to another. That the authors of the Persian texts recognized this potential is demonstrated by their clear descriptions of the situation of Afghanistan to an imagined reader who would have no prior knowledge of its geography or customs. They knew that the works, from their inception, were part of a system of distribution (the Western art world) that although unknown to them could be useful to their cause.

It was just as these "arazzi" were being made that Edouard Glissant was reflecting on the legacy of Victor Segalen in the text discussed earlier, and they return us now to the discussion of Glissant, especially to what he called the "Poetics of Relation." He distinguishes "relation" from "relationships," because to speak of relation, it is not essential to define "relation between what and what."[43] Relation is a more general consciousness of the intertwining of peoples, languages, and thoughts. "Relation rightfully opposes the totalitarianism of any linguistic intent,"[44] Glissant continues, and the "Poetics of Relation interweaves and does not project." This is "a Poetics that is latent, open, multilingual in intention, directly in contact with everything possible."[45] Glissant was imagining the poetics that might emerge in the Caribbean, but one could also say that Boetti's encounter with Afghanistan produced works that contained the seeds of a similar poetics. We might recall the postal works, where Boetti's language games were coupled with handwritten texts by Dastaghir, or the Persian inscriptions surrounding the maps, but it is with these large "arazzi" of 1988–89 especially that we see one language interweaving with another, and the dominance of the European language being undone. From his first visit, Boetti recognized that Afghanistan had historically been (like the Caribbean) "one of the places in the world where Relation presents itself most visibly . . . a place of encounter and connivance, and at the same time, a passageway."[46] Boetti's achievement, in sum, was to build on his attraction to this place by creating new possibilities for a "Poetics of Relation" to emerge, and to persevere even when his partners were exiled and when Afghanistan was thrown into war.

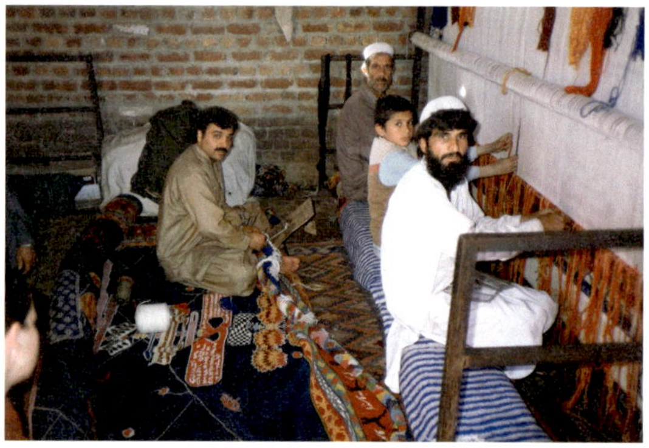

[fig. 8] Afghan weavers working on Boetti's carpets, Peshawar, Pakistan, 1994

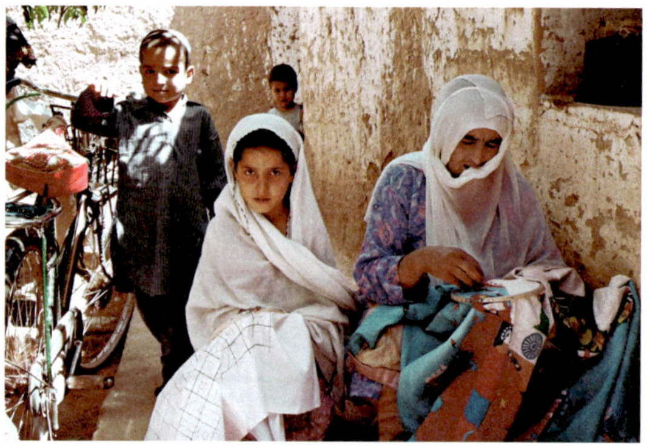

[fig. 9] Randi Malkin Steinberger, Afghan embroiderers working on Boetti's "mappe," Peshawar, Pakistan, 1990.

43 Edouard Glissant, *Poetics of Relation*, p. 27.
44 Ibid., p. 19.
45 Ibid., p. 32.
46 Ibid., p. 33.

Flying Carpets

The early 1990s—the last years of Boetti's life—saw the production in Peshawar of some of his most monu-
ill. pp. 232–233, 236–237 mental embroideries—two six-metre wide "tutto" works; three similarly-sized "mappe" (one made after
ill. pp. 226–227, 228, 229 the break-up of the USSR); and hundreds of small "arazzi." All these works were embroidered by women, but in the early 1990s, he turned to a new material and workforce: carpets and rugs (kilims) woven by men. This division of labor, women embroidering and men weaving, was rigorously maintained in Afghan society. The kilims were based on a numeric system that derived from drawings made by Boetti in the mid-1970s titled
ill. pp. 251–253 *Alternando da uno a cento e viceversa*. Boetti established a fixed schema, but within the rules, there were countless ways of producing a design. In 1993, on the occasion of an exhibition in Grenoble, he asked students in a number of French art schools to work with the schema, and their solutions were sent to Peshawar and turned into kilims. Boetti had never included photographs of the women embroiderers in his exhibition catalogues, but in the publication for the Grenoble show, for the first time, he allowed images of men at their looms to be published [fig. 8]. The photographer Randi Malkin Steinberger independently took photographs of women at work on Boetti's embroideries [fig. 9].

ill. p. 199 One of Boetti's very last works was also a carpet, and with this work he attempted to bring together many of the motifs that he had used throughout his life: the shape of an open violin case, which he had employed in the
ill. p. 189 drawing *Regno musicale* (1979), a word square featuring the letters of his name, two sections of "tutto" designs, and the gibbons that swing around his 1980s friezes. Sauzeau Boetti once described her husband returning back from Afghanistan and unfurling before his children embroideries, "still smelling of goat, curry and other spices . . . The tapestries would float like distant oceans, like mountains higher than the Appenines. These flying carpets were offered to our little girl."[47] Her language echoes the words used by Boetti's friend Giovan Battista Salerno to describe the 1994 carpet: a "carpet for flying in time."[48] The work sends one's thoughts flying back to all the moments of Boetti's life, back to the *Pack* object of 1967, to the 1969 word games with his name, to the drawings of the 1970s. But since he conceived it while sick in Rome just before he died, one can guess where Boetti would have flown his carpet: back to Kabul in the 1970s. For within this very work, along the spine, filled in with the design of its pre-1979 flag, can be found the shape of Afghanistan.

47 Sauzeau Boetti, *Shaman/Showman*, p. 153.

48 Giovan Battista Salerno, "A Carpet for Old Children," in Achille Bonito Oliva (ed.), *Alighiero & Boetti: Bringing the World into Art, 1993–1962* (Naples: MADRE and Milan: Electa, 2009), p. 60.

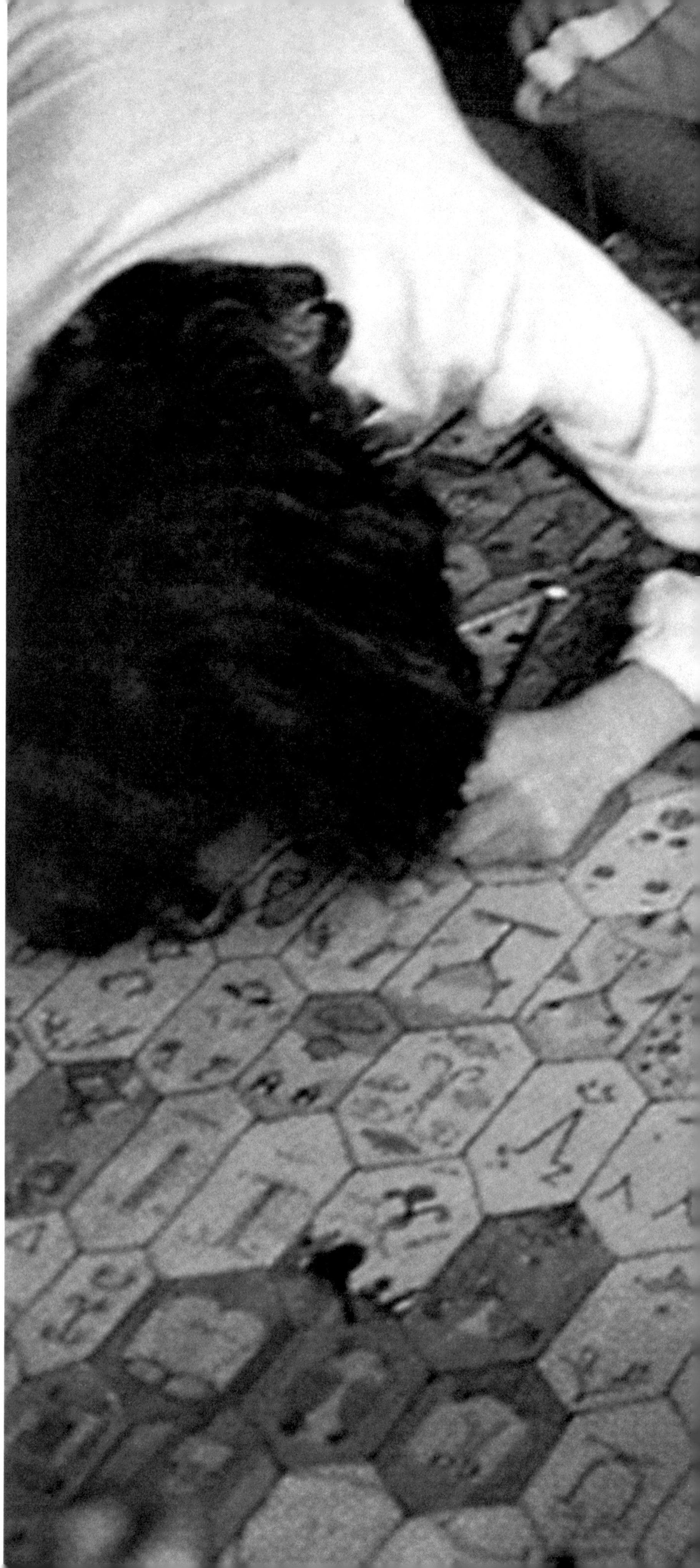

Children coloring Faccine (Little Faces), c. 1980

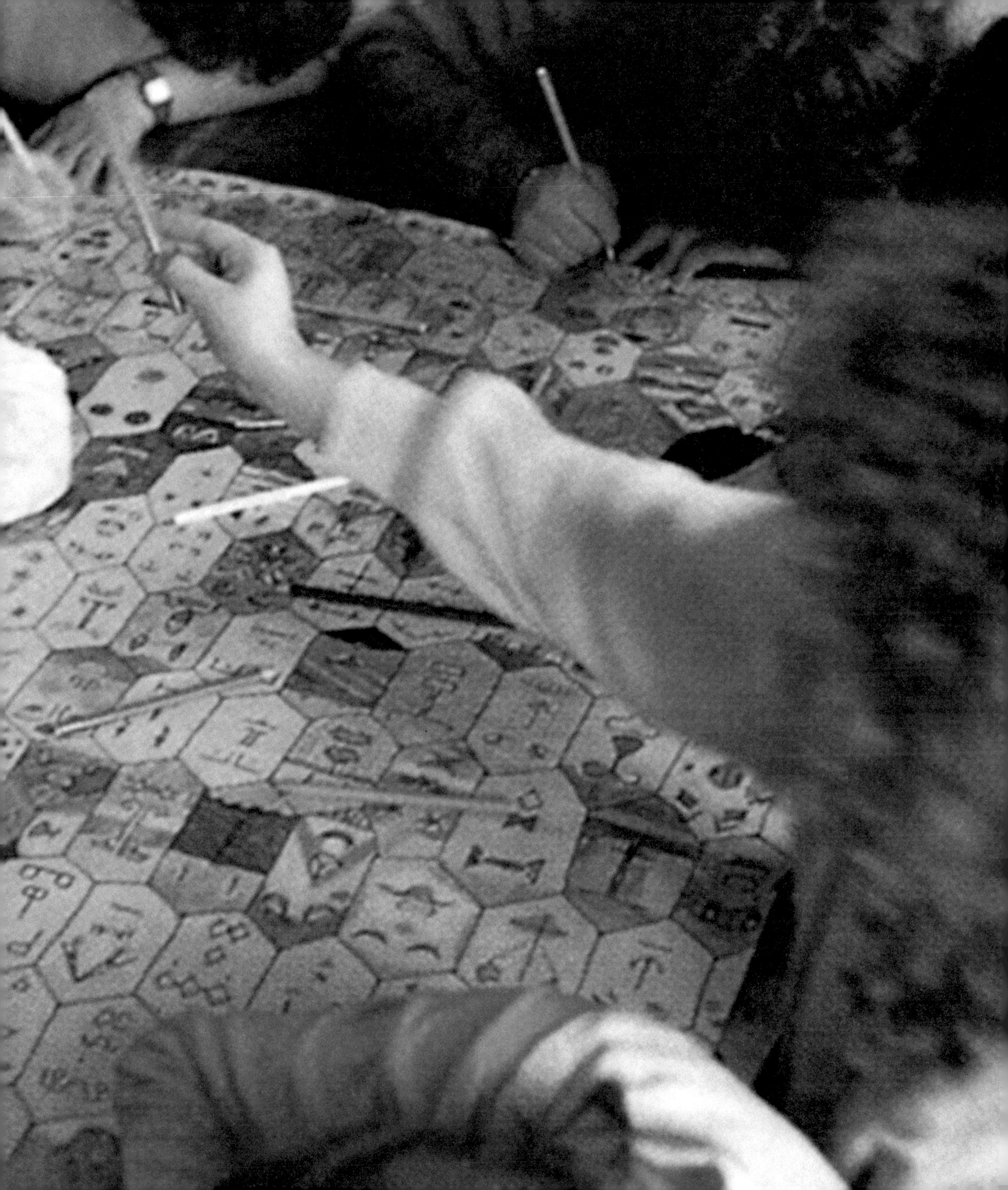

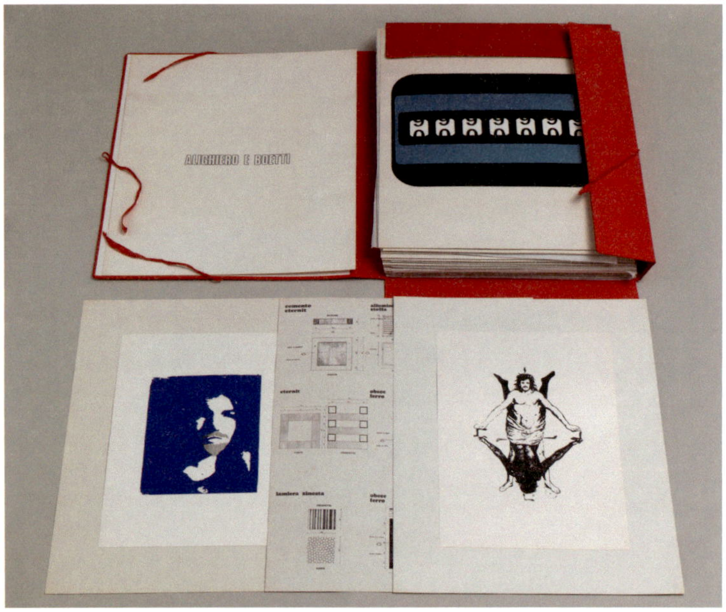
ALIGHIERO E BOETTI

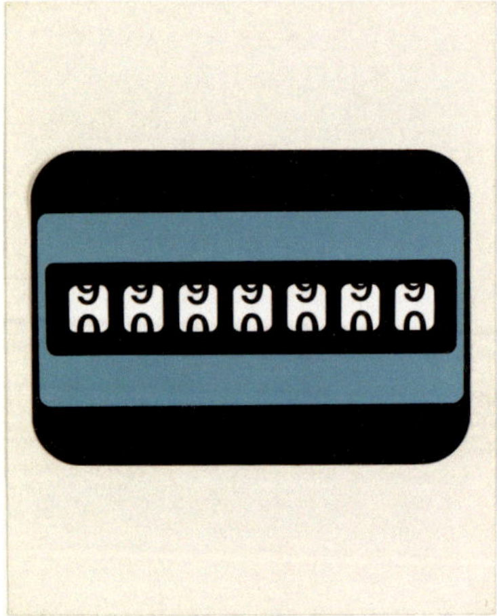

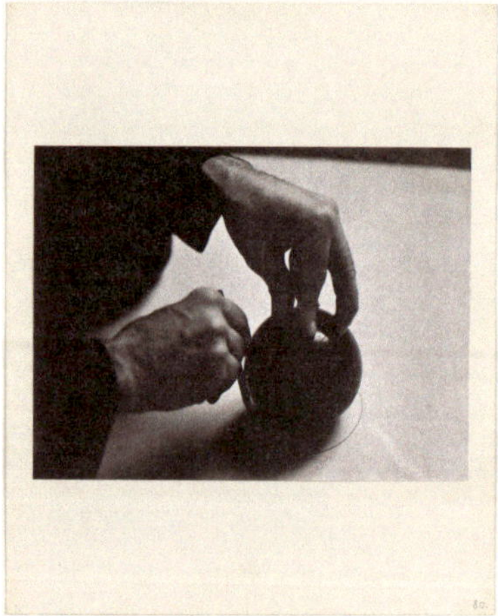

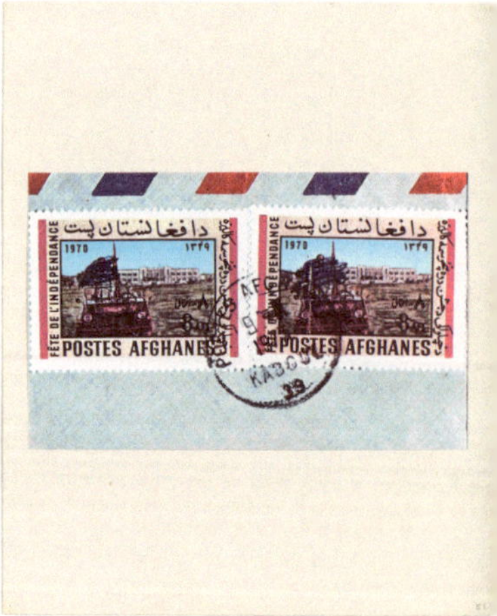
FETE DE L'INDEPENDANCE
1970
POSTES AFGHANES
FETE DE L'INDEPENDANCE
1970
POSTES AFGHANES

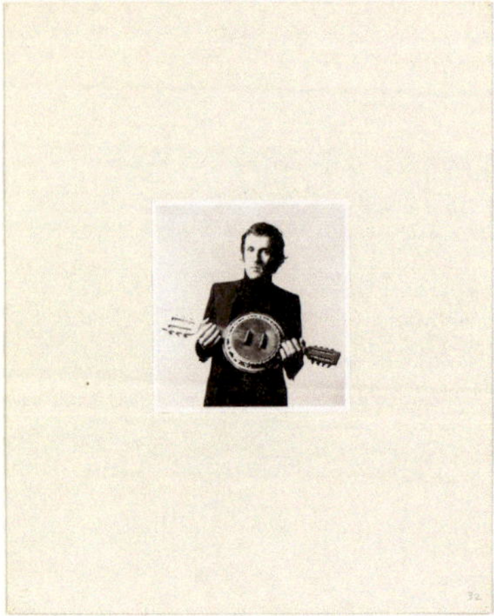

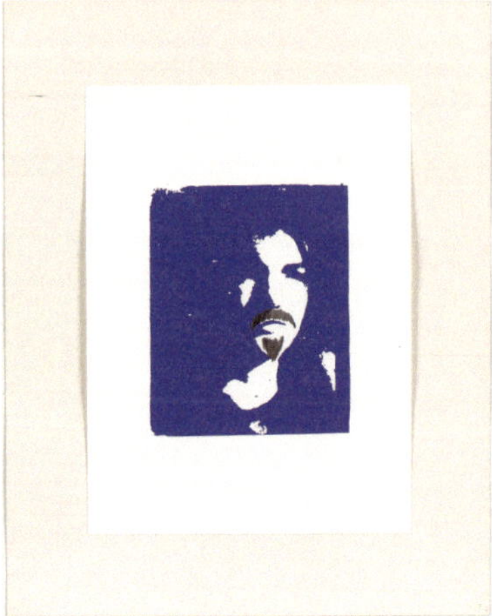

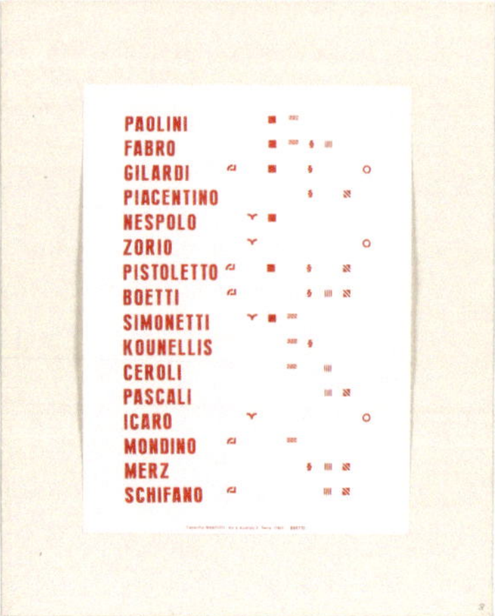
PAOLINI
FABRO
GILARDI
PIACENTINO
NESPOLO
ZORIO
PISTOLETTO
BOETTI
SIMONETTI
KOUNELLIS
CEROLI
PASCALI
ICARO
MONDINO
MERZ
SCHIFANO

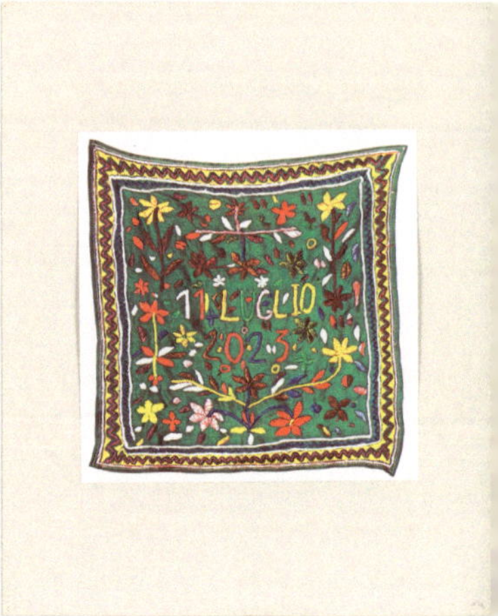

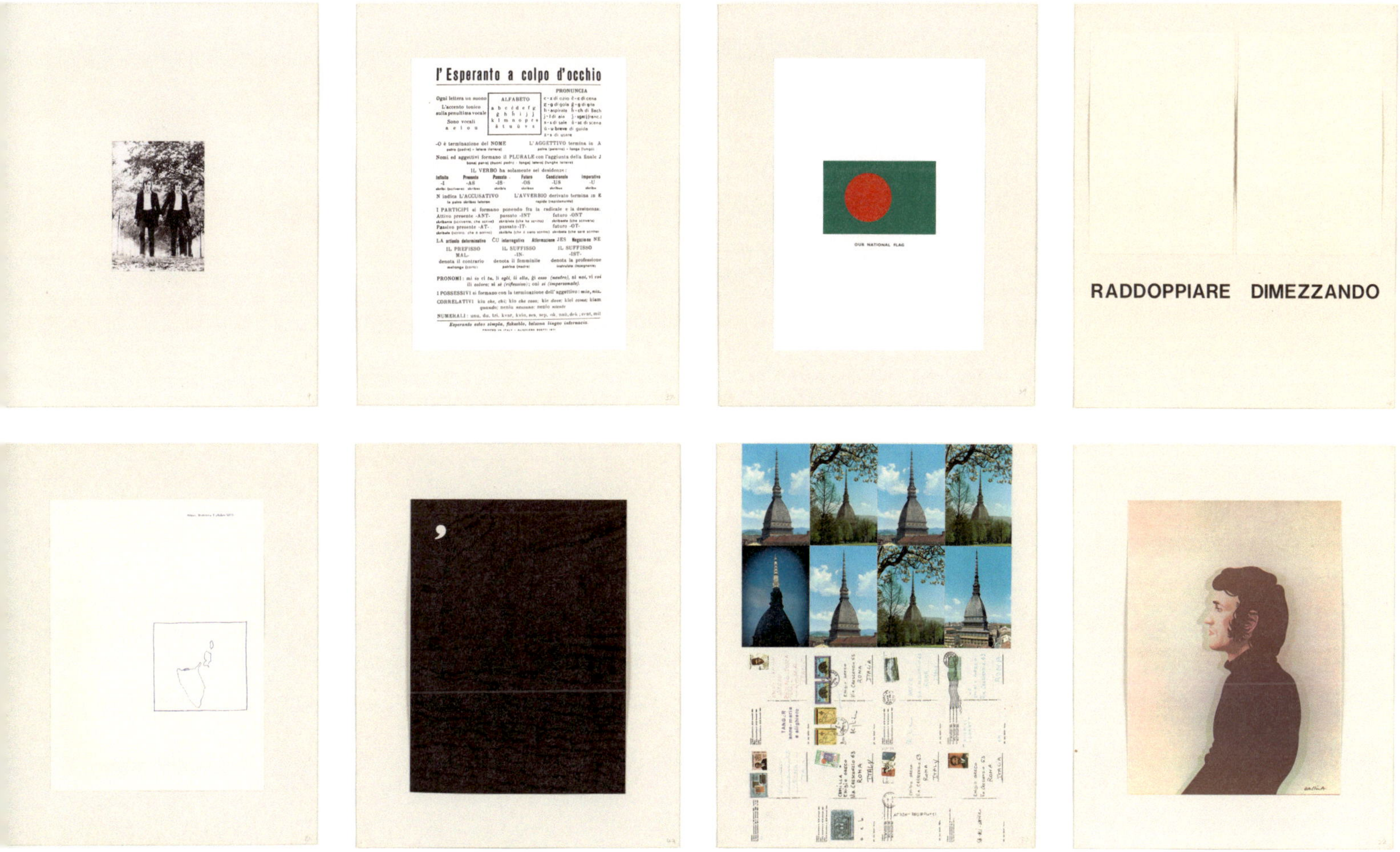

 Insicuro Noncurante (Insecure Careless), 1975 (1966–1975)

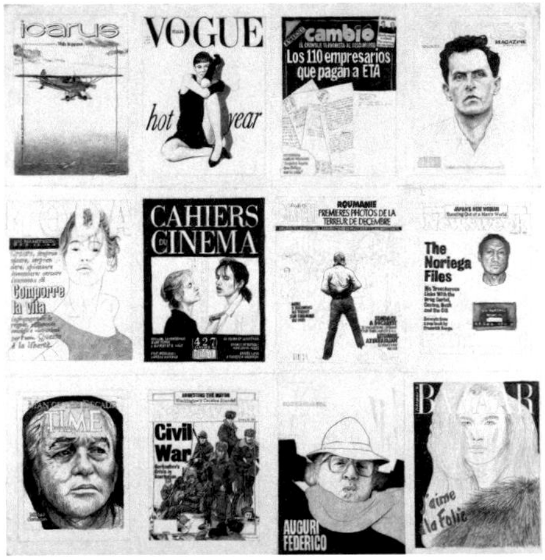
icarus
VOGUE
hot
wear
cambio
Los 110 empresarios que pagan a ETA
CAHIERS CINEMA
ROUMANIE
The Noriega Files
TIME
Civil War
AUGURI FEDERICO
BAZAAR

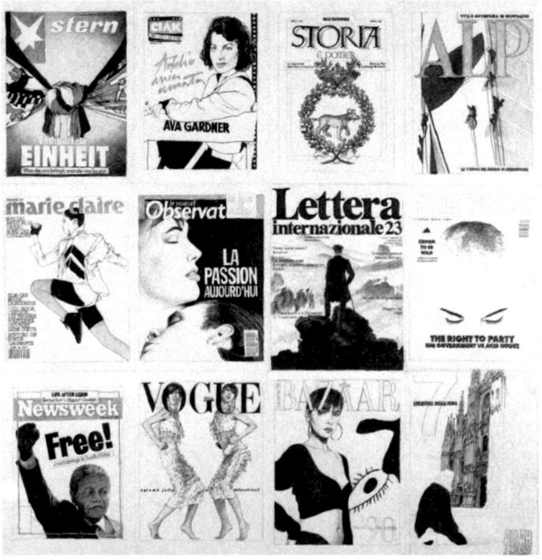
stern
EINHEIT
AVA GARDNER
STORIA
marie claire
Observat
LA PASSION AUJOURD'HUI
Lettera internazionale 23
THE RIGHT TO PARTY
Newsweek
Free!
VOGUE
BAZAAR

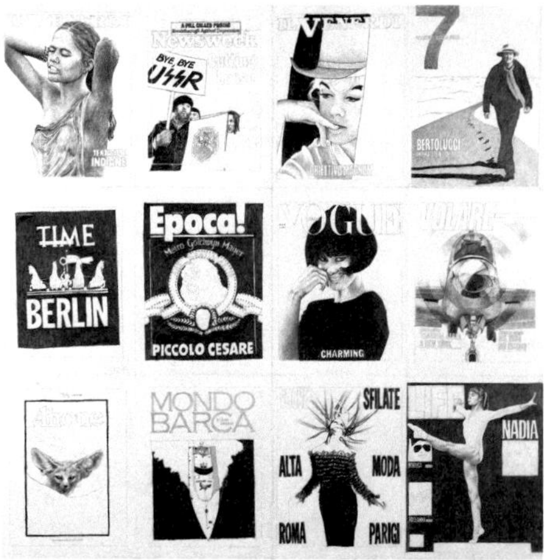
Newsweek
BYE BYE USSR
7
BERTOLUCCI
TIME
BERLIN
Epoca!
PICCOLO CESARE
VOGUE
CHARMING
MONDO BARCA
SFILATE
ALTA
MODA
ROMA
PARIGI
NADIA

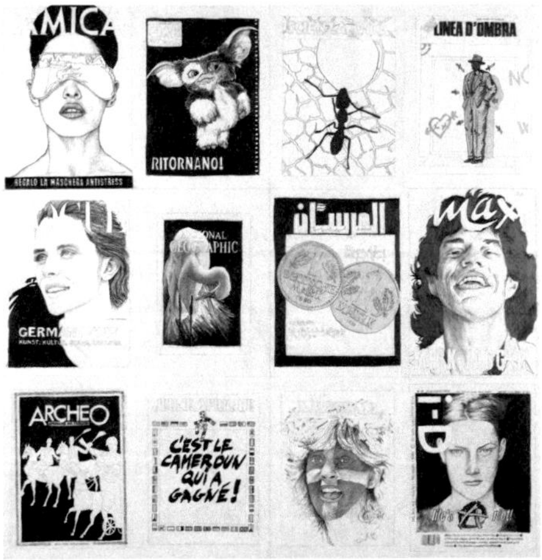
AMICA
RITORNANO!
LINEA D'OMBRA
GERMA
max
ARCHEO
C'EST LE CAMEROUN QUI A GAGNÉ!

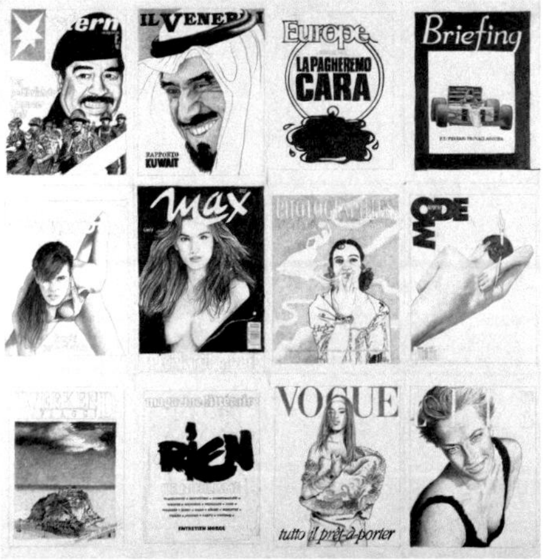
stern
IL VENERDI
KUWAIT
Europeo
LA PAGHEREMO CARA
Briefing
max
MODE
RIEN
VOGUE
tutto il prêt-à-porter

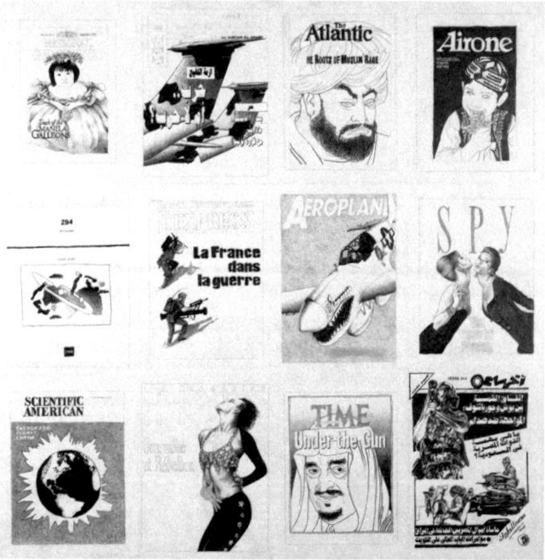
Atlantic
Airone
294
La France dans la guerre
AEROPLANI
SPY
SCIENTIFIC AMERICAN
TIME
Under the Gun

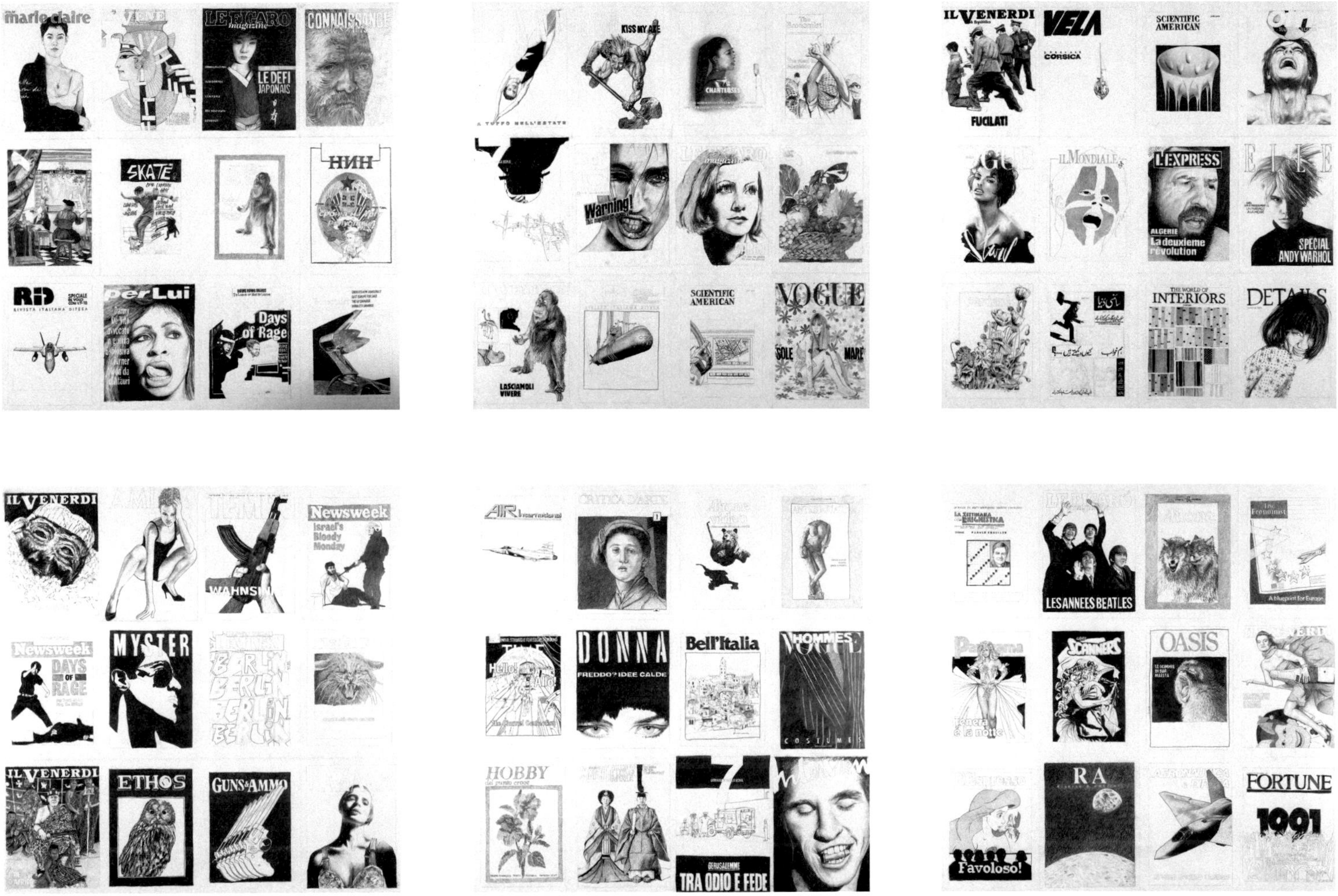

 Anno 1990 (The Year 1990), 1990

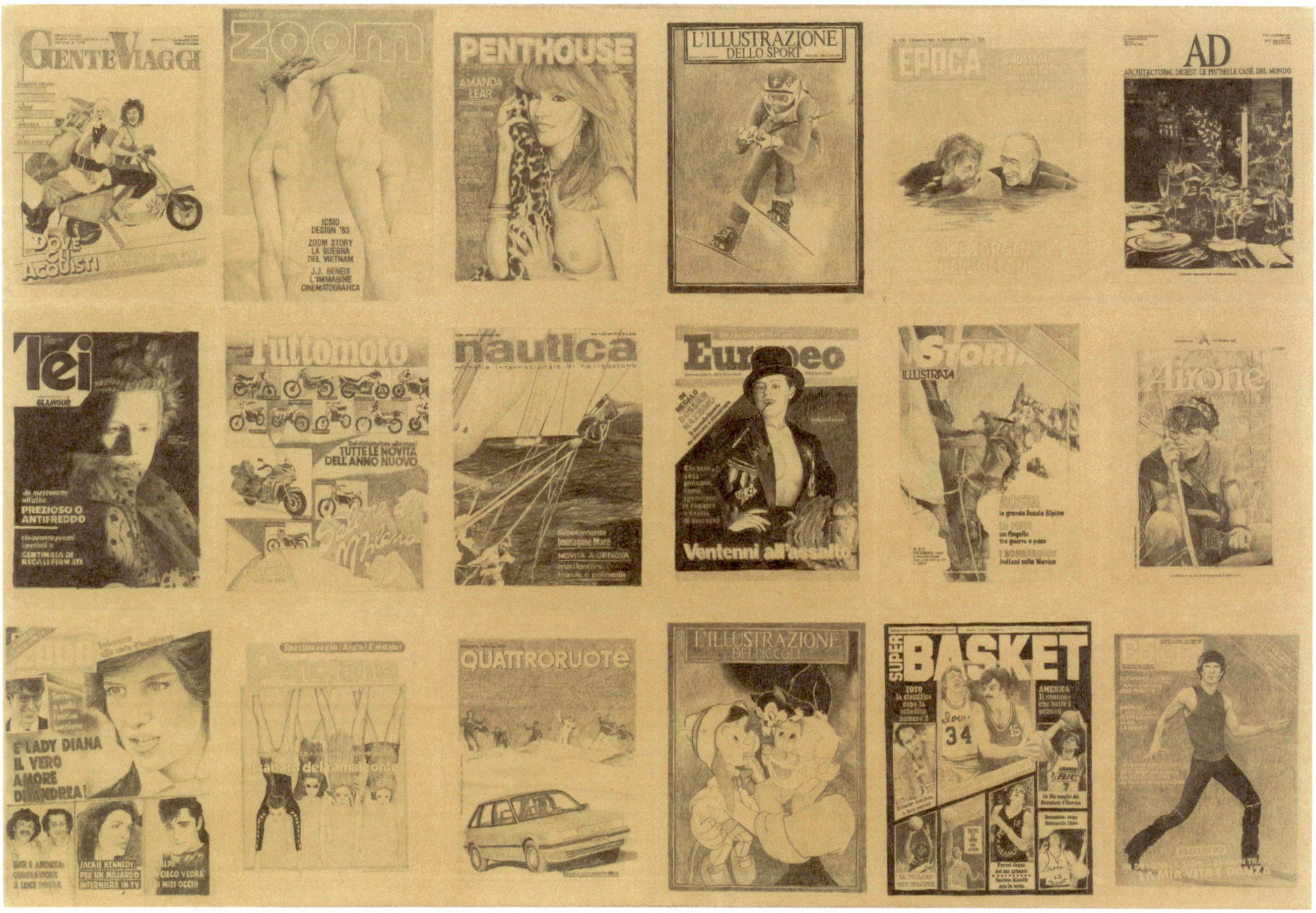

Dicembre 1983 (December 1983), 1983

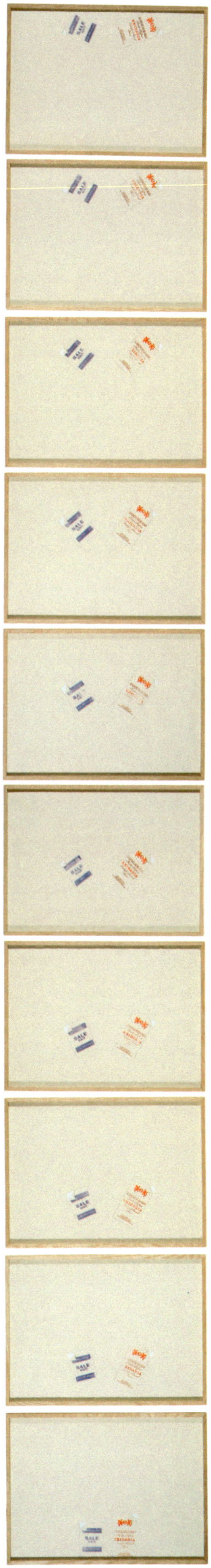

183 Sale e zucchero (Salt and Sugar), c. 1973

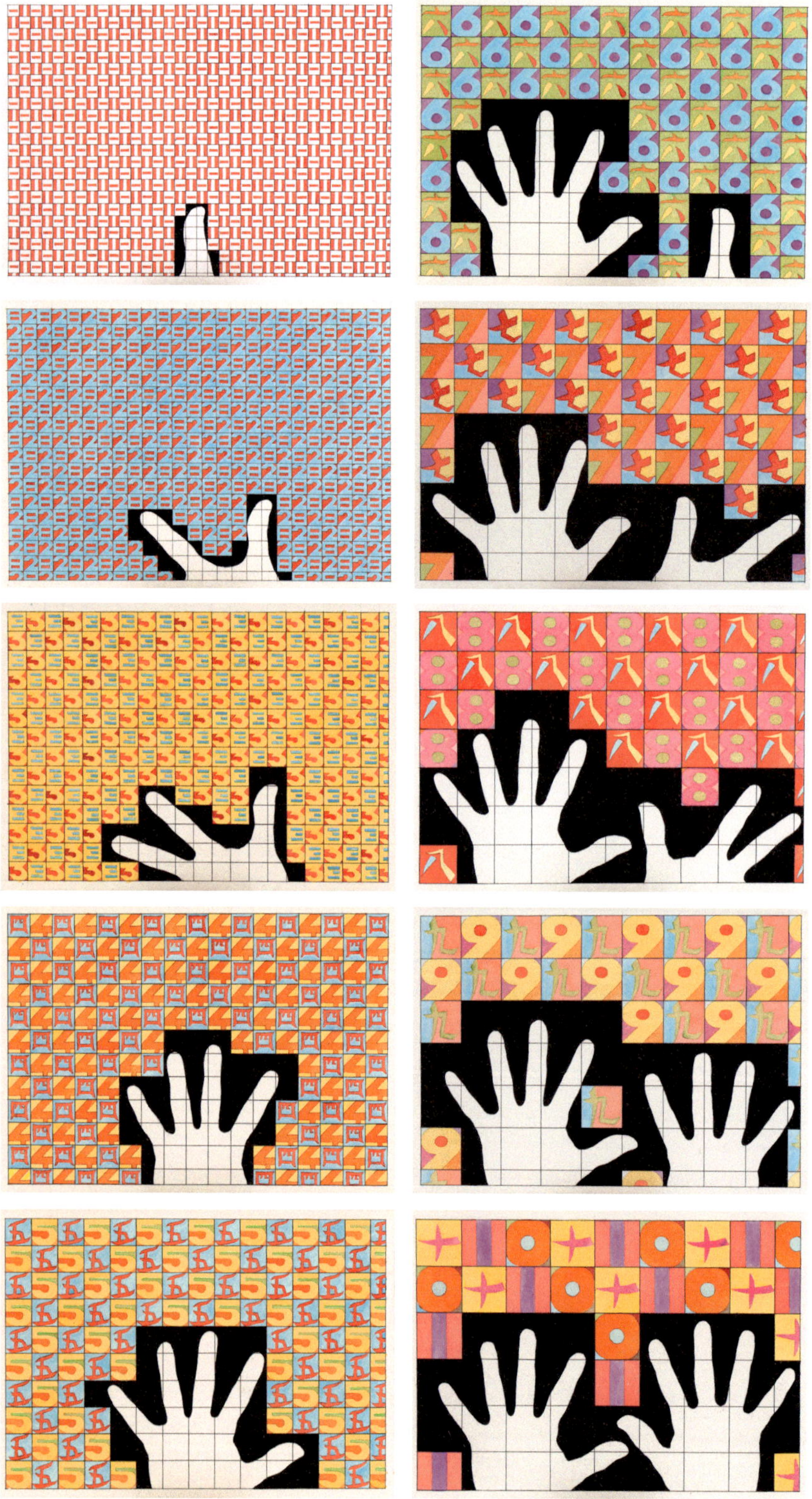

Da uno a dieci (giapponese) (From One to Ten [Japanese]), 1981

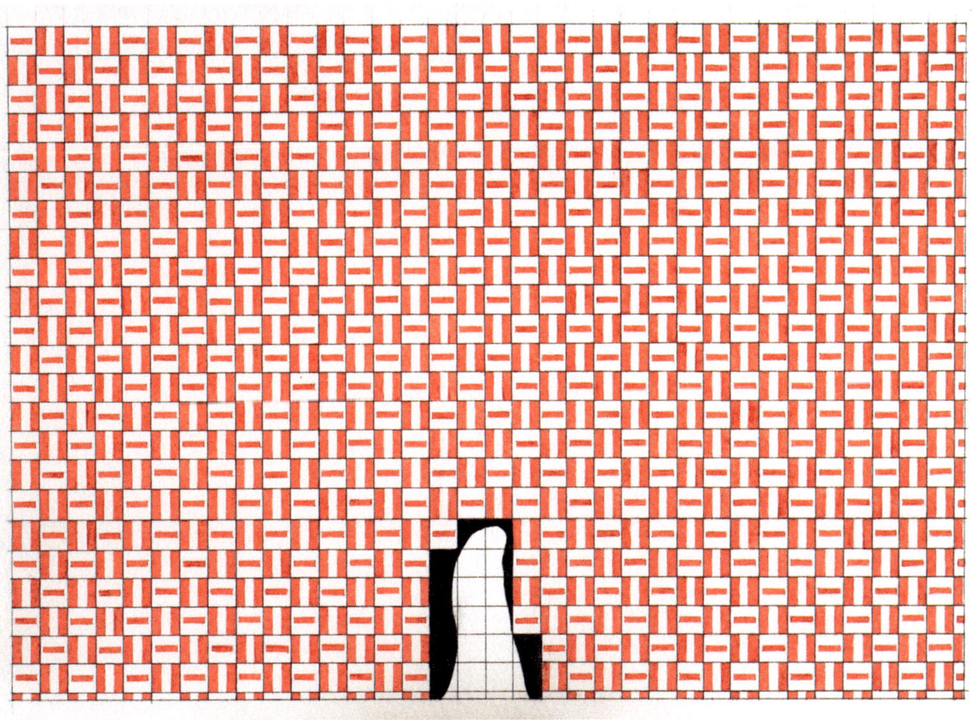

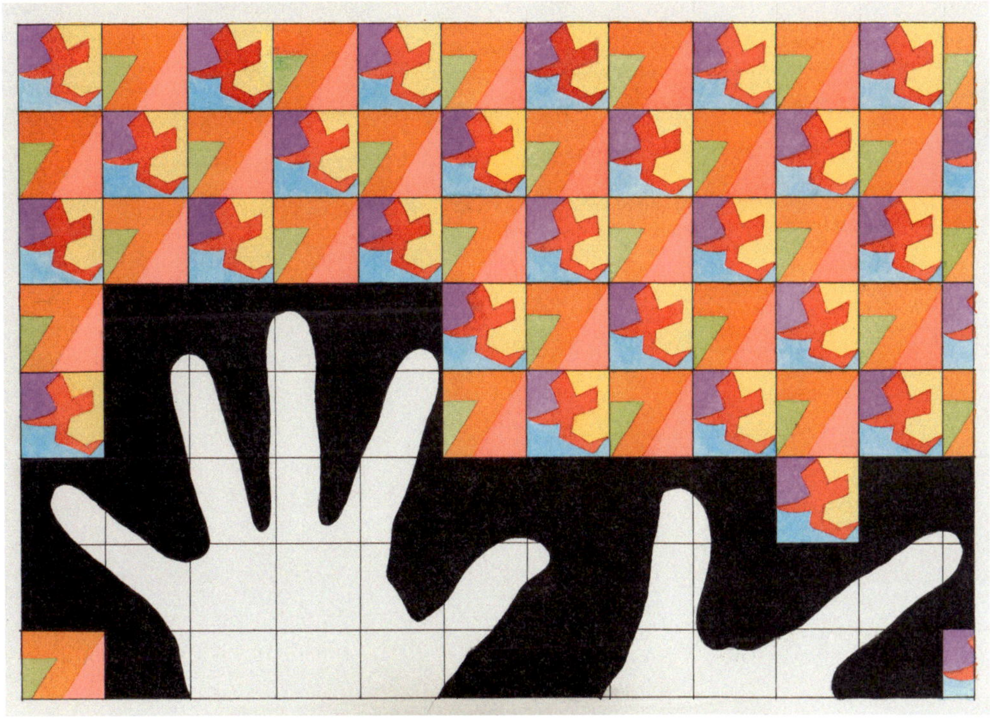

 Da uno a dieci (giapponese) (From One to Ten [Japanese]), 1981 (details)

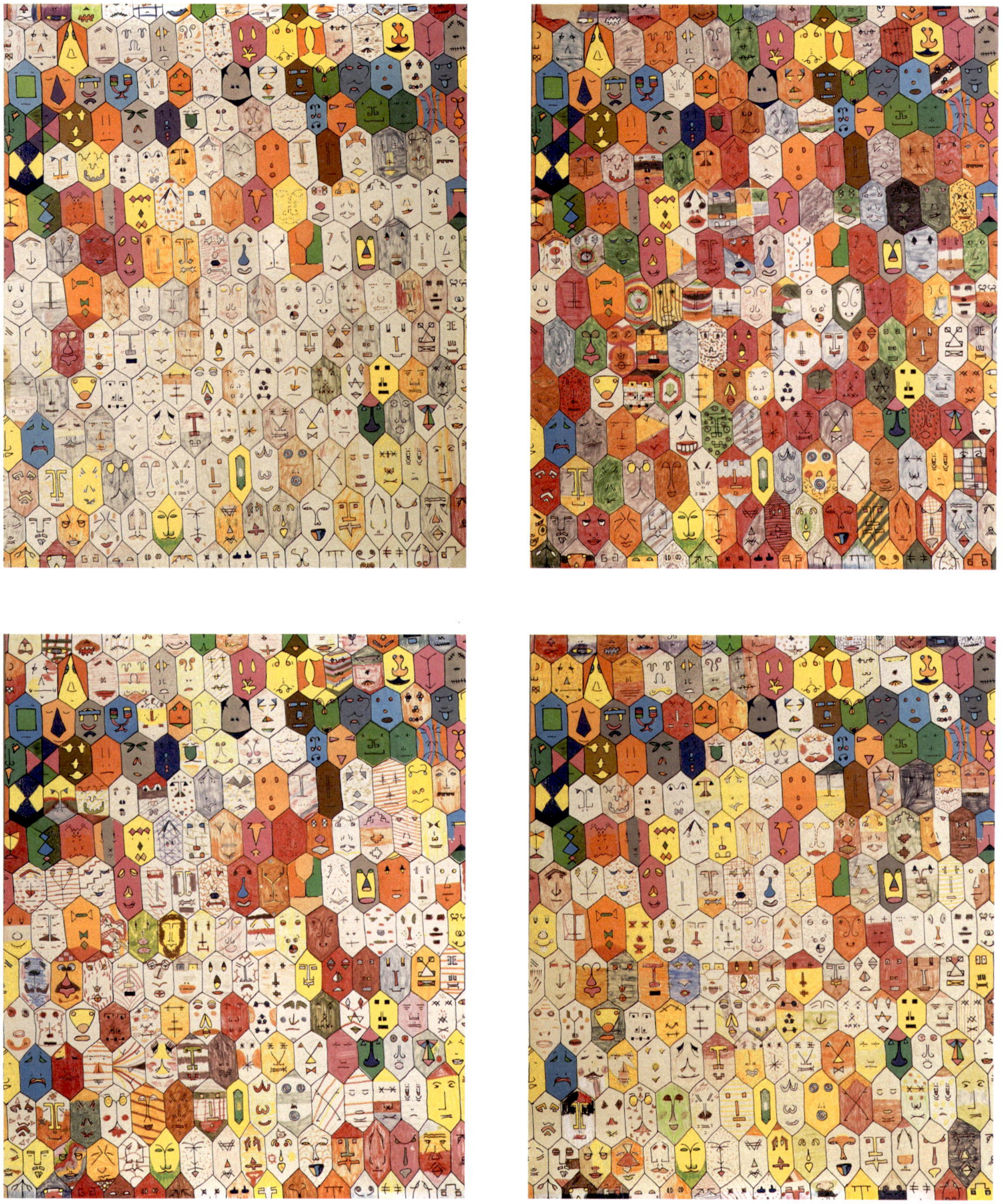

Faccine (Little Faces), 1979

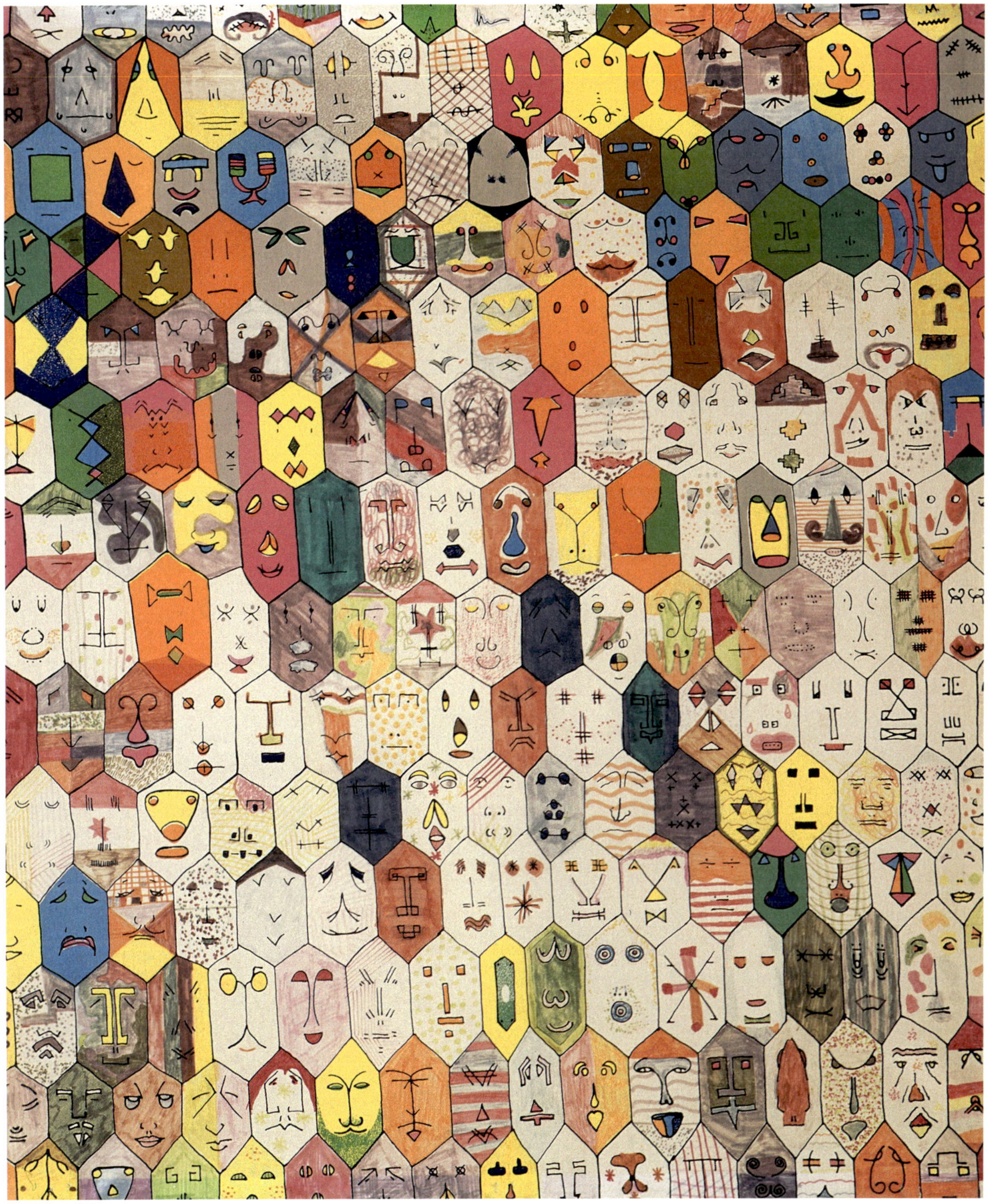

 Faccine (Little Faces), 1979

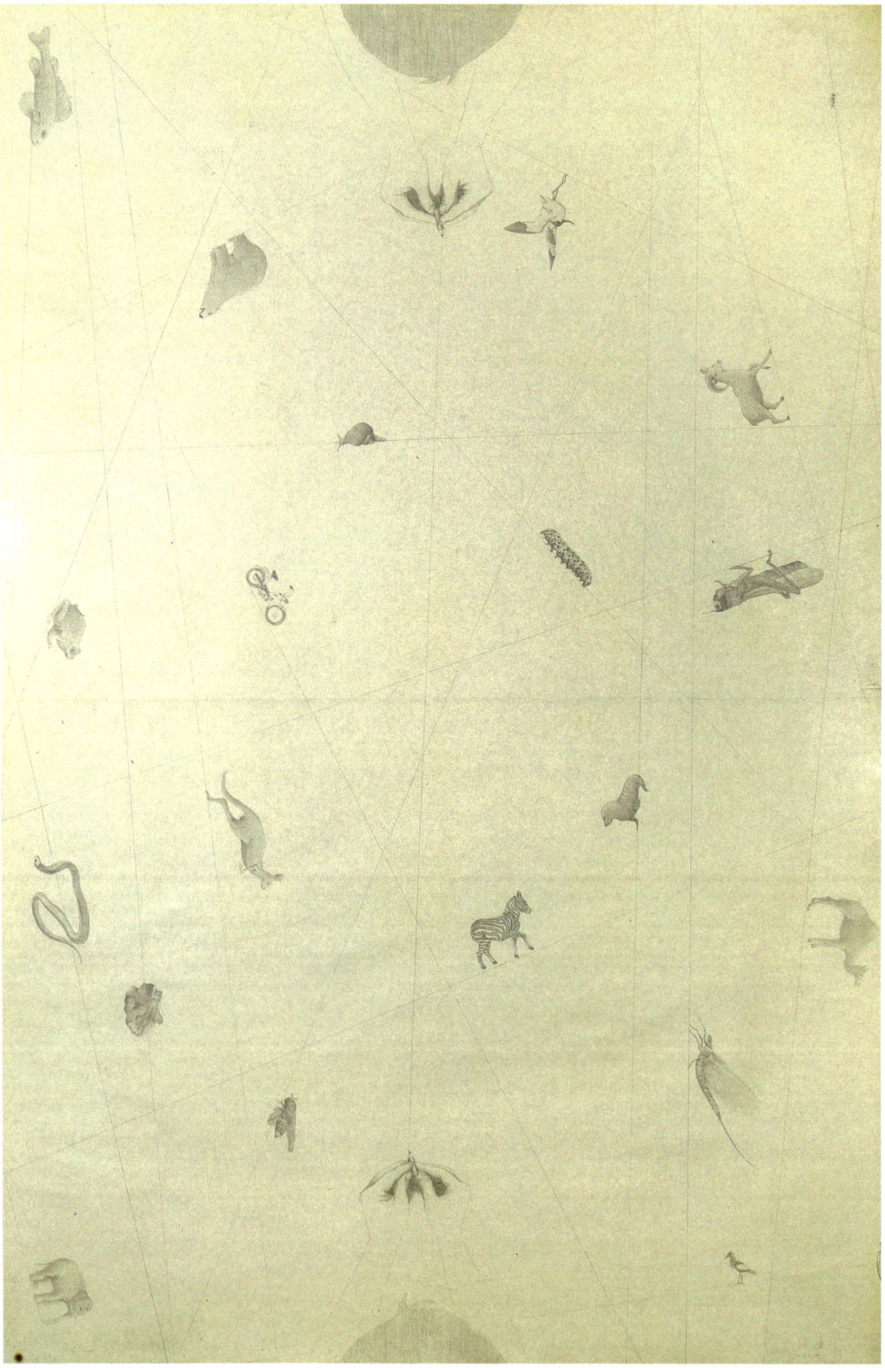

Regno animale (Animal Kingdom), 1978

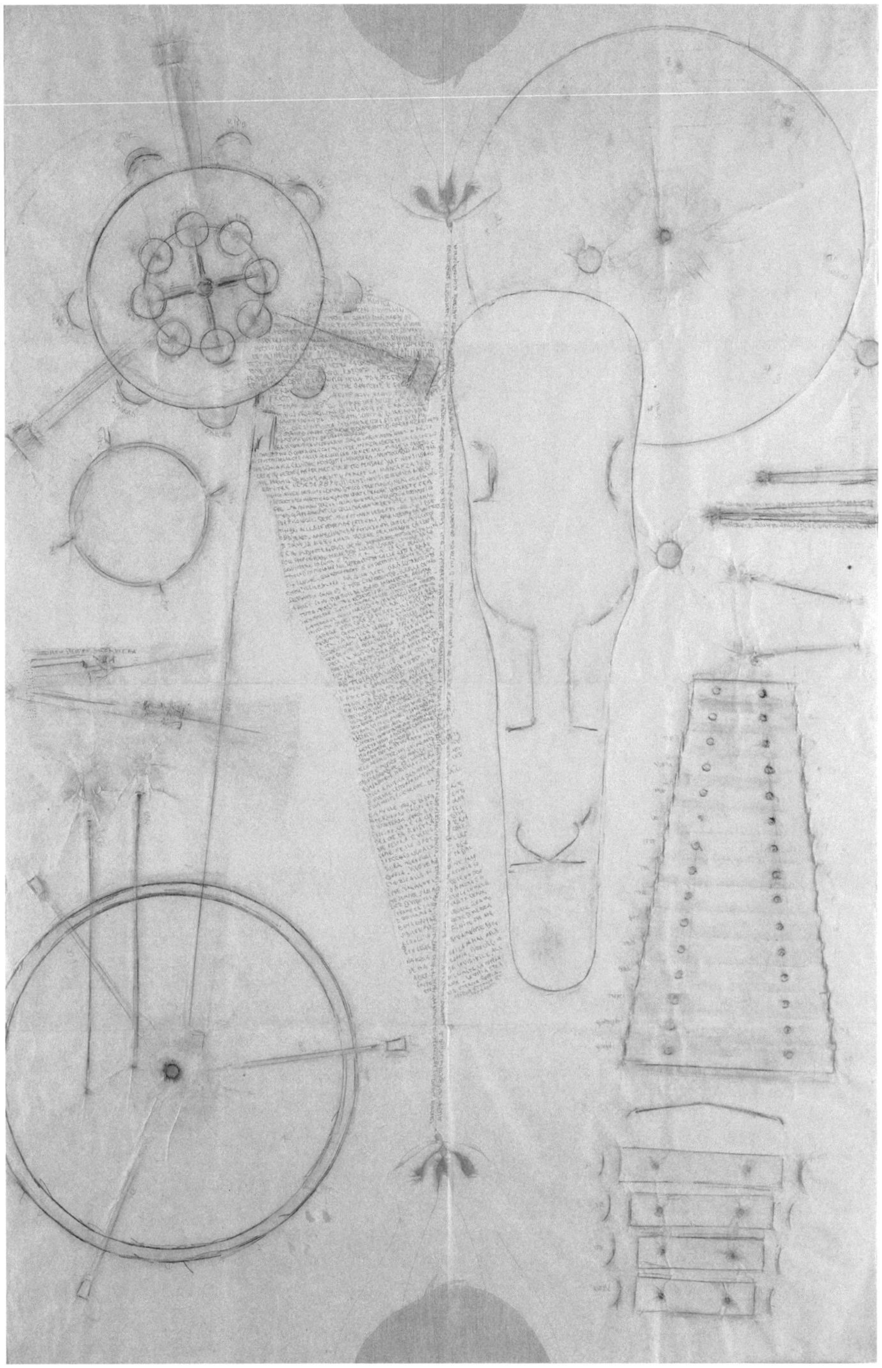

 Regno musicale (Music Kingdom), 1979

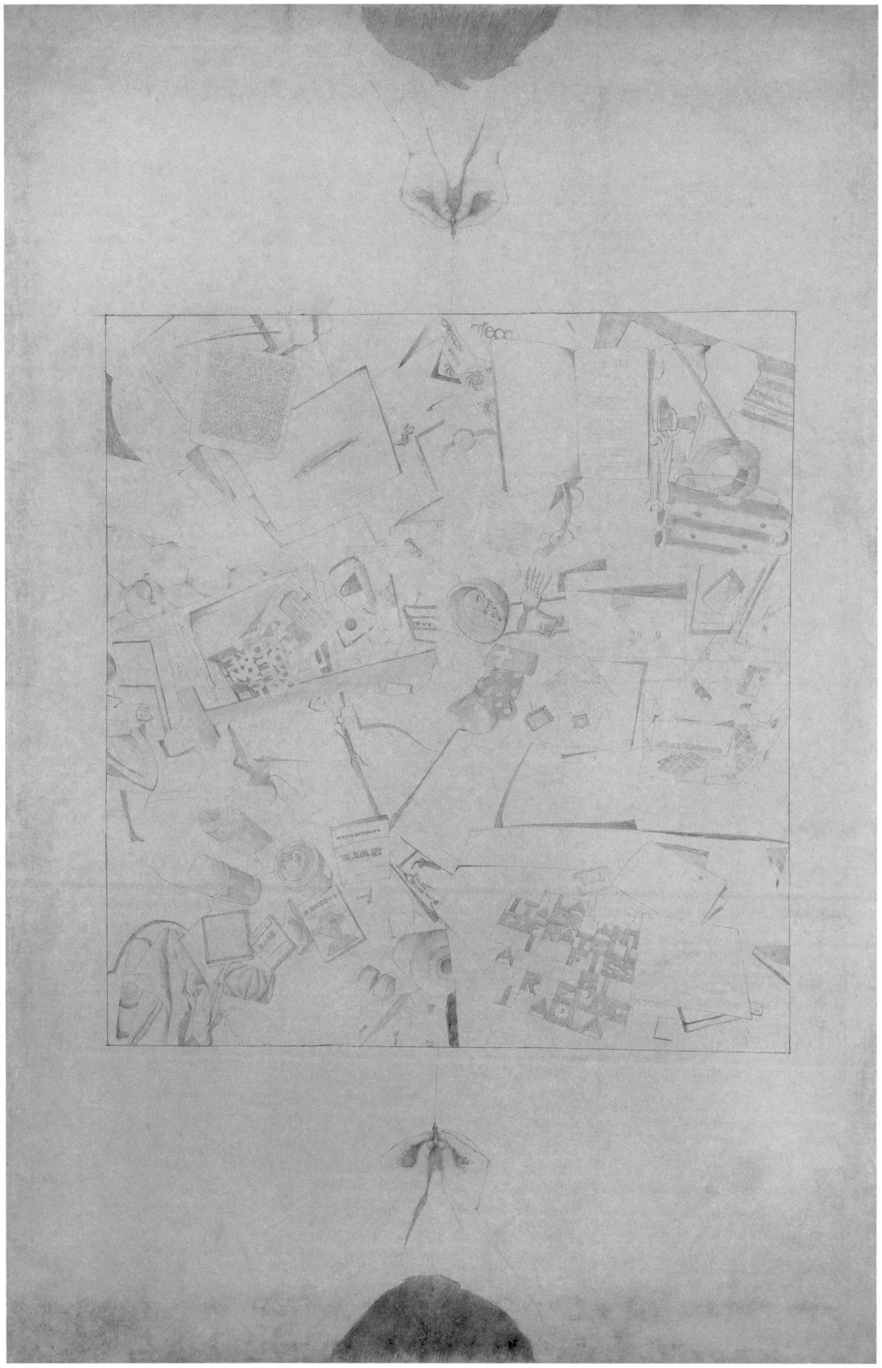

Regno delle carte (Paper Kingdom), 1979

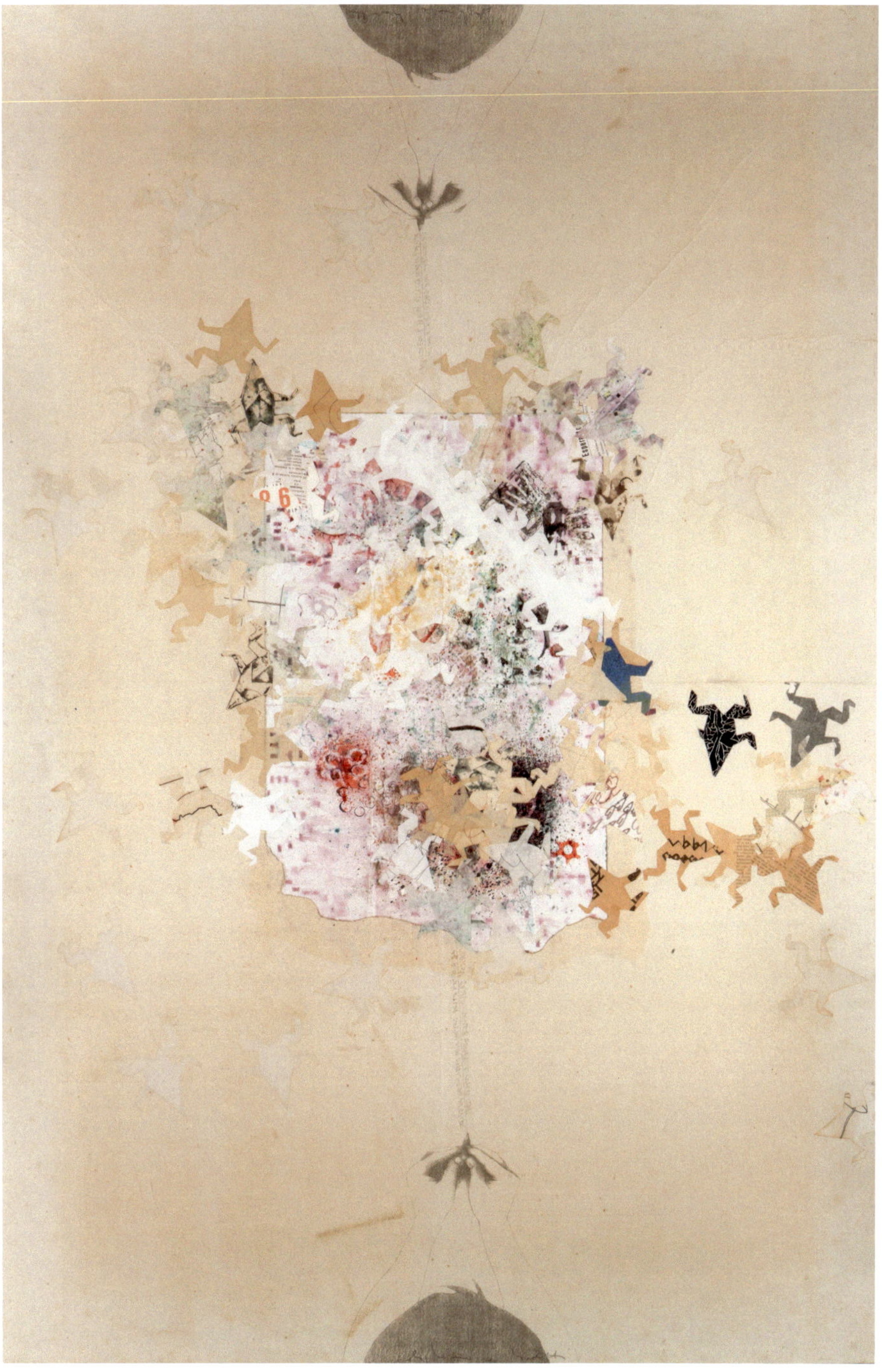

191 La natura, una faccenda ottusa (Nature, a Dull Affair), c. 1980

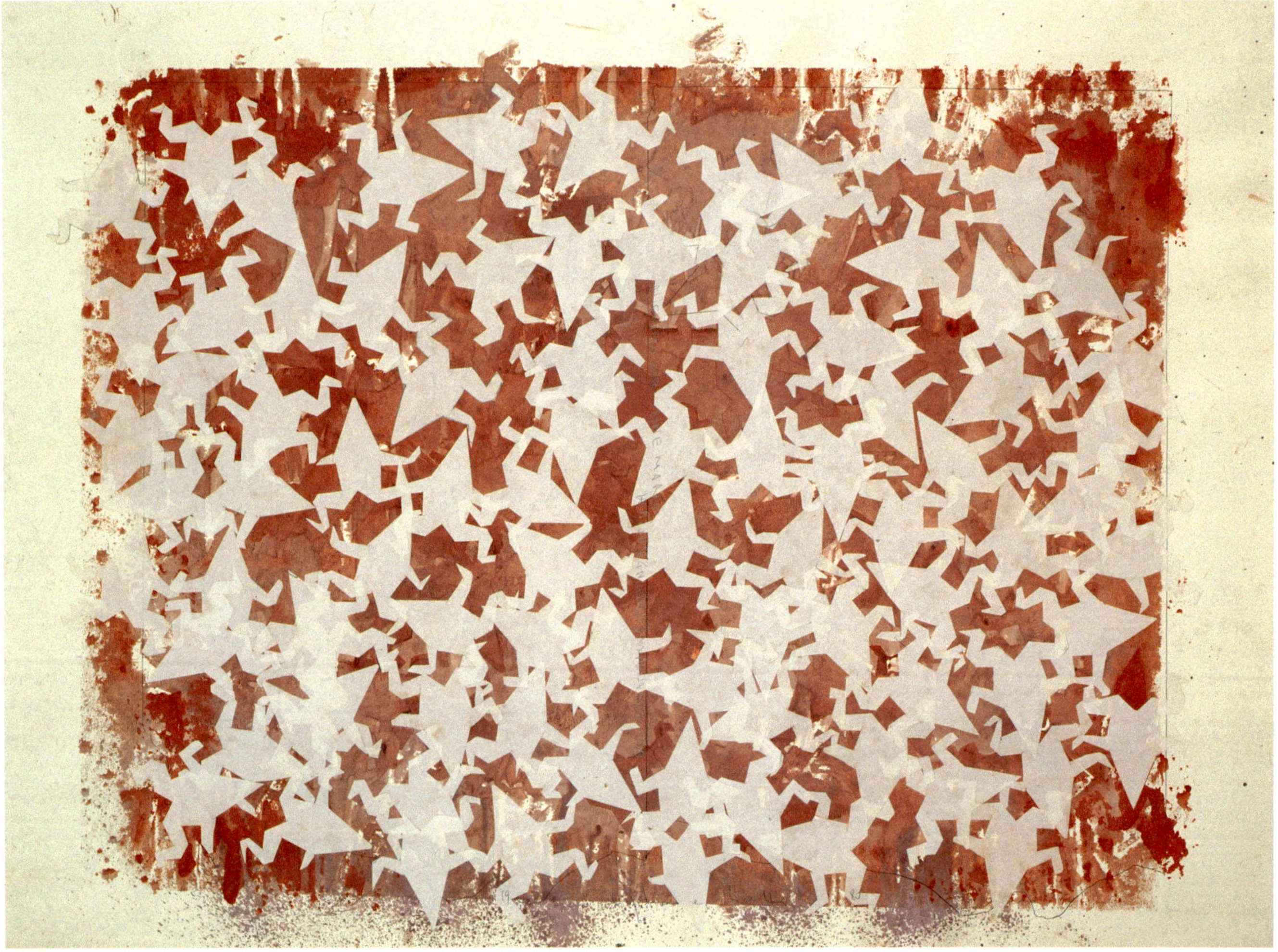

La natura, una faccenda ottusa (1) (Nature, a Dull Affair [1]), 1980

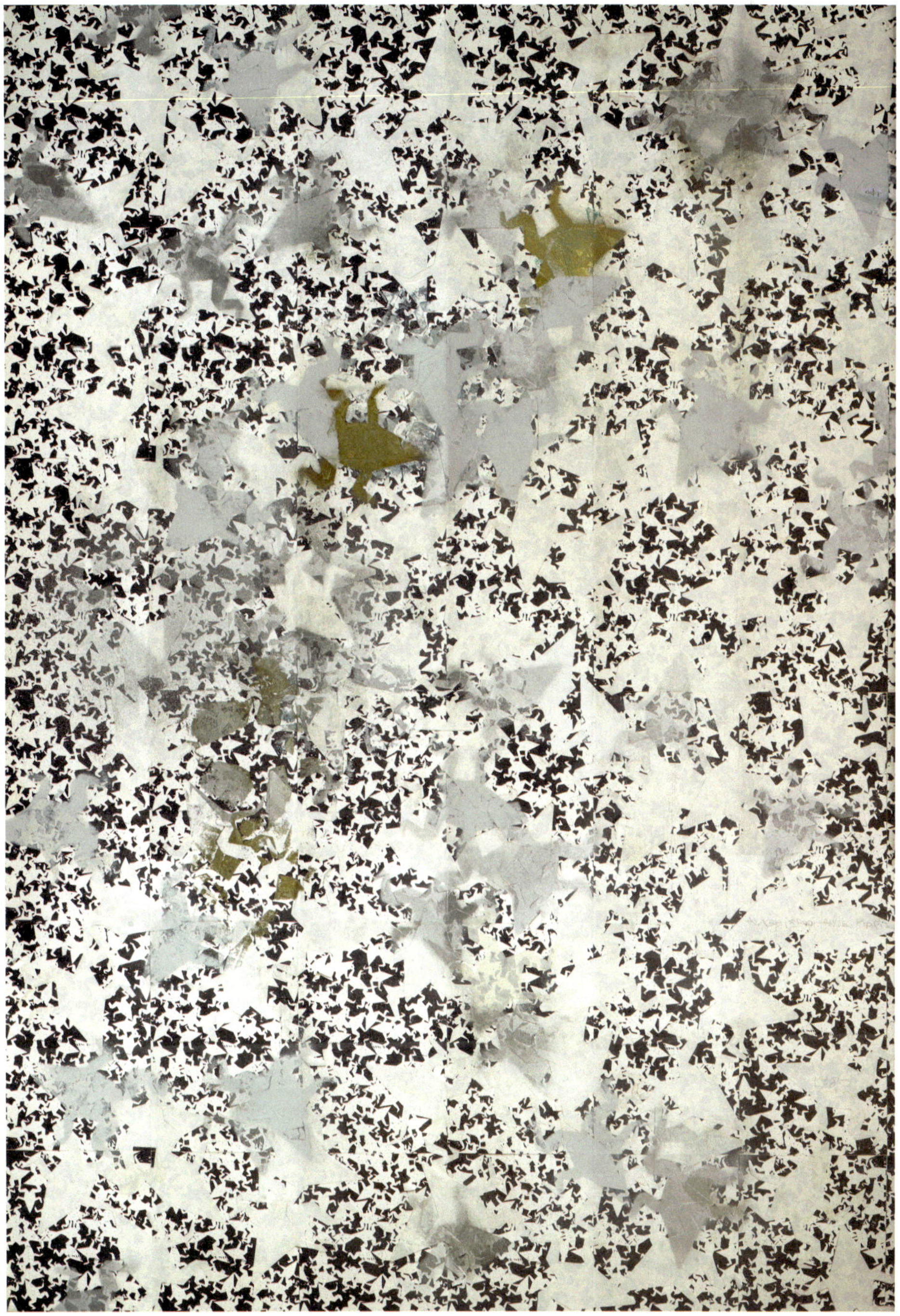

193 La natura, una faccenda ottusa (2) (Nature, a Dull Affair [2]), 1980

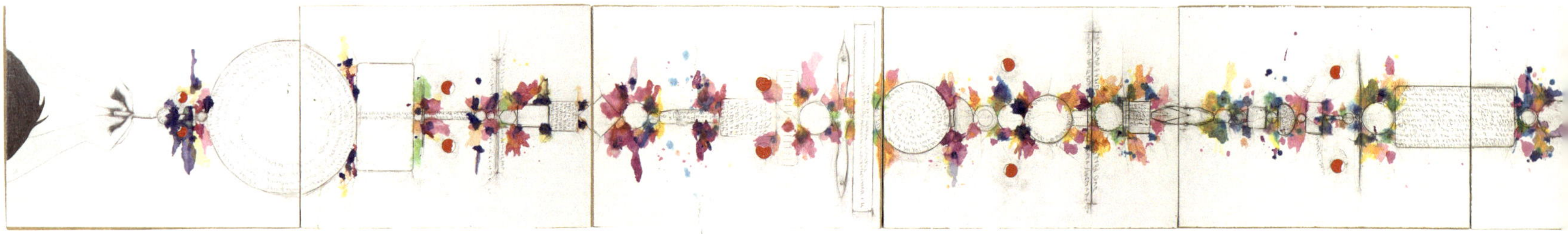

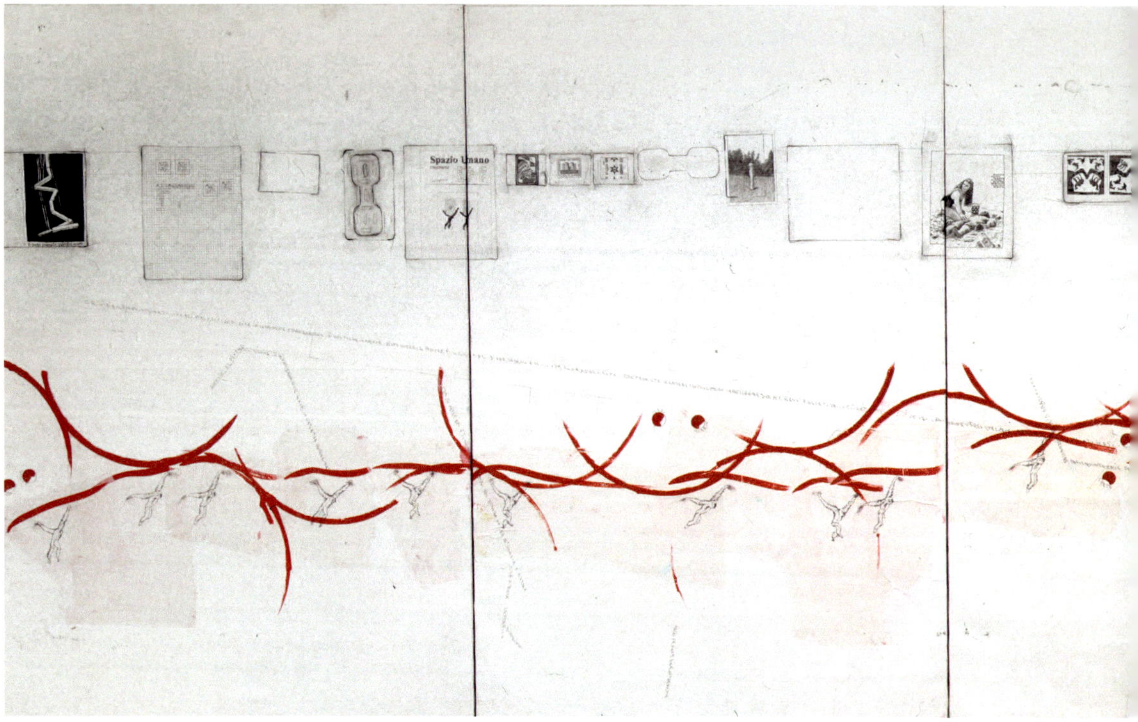

Tra sé e sé (Between Self and Self), 1987 (top)

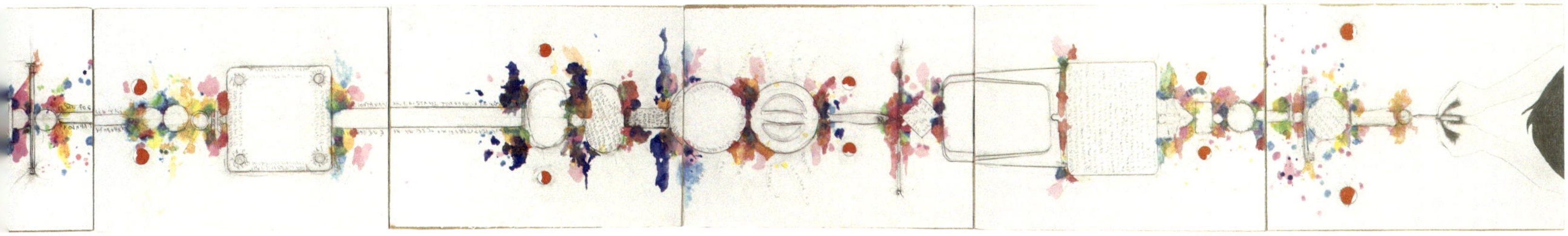

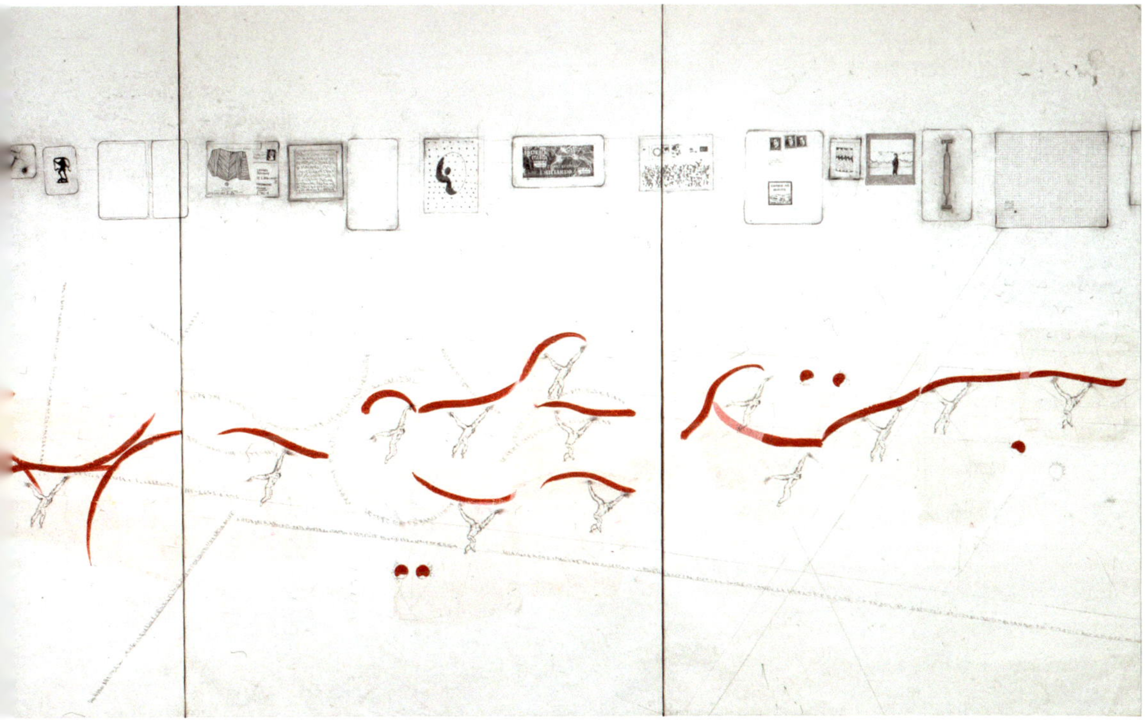

Untitled, 1987 (bottom)

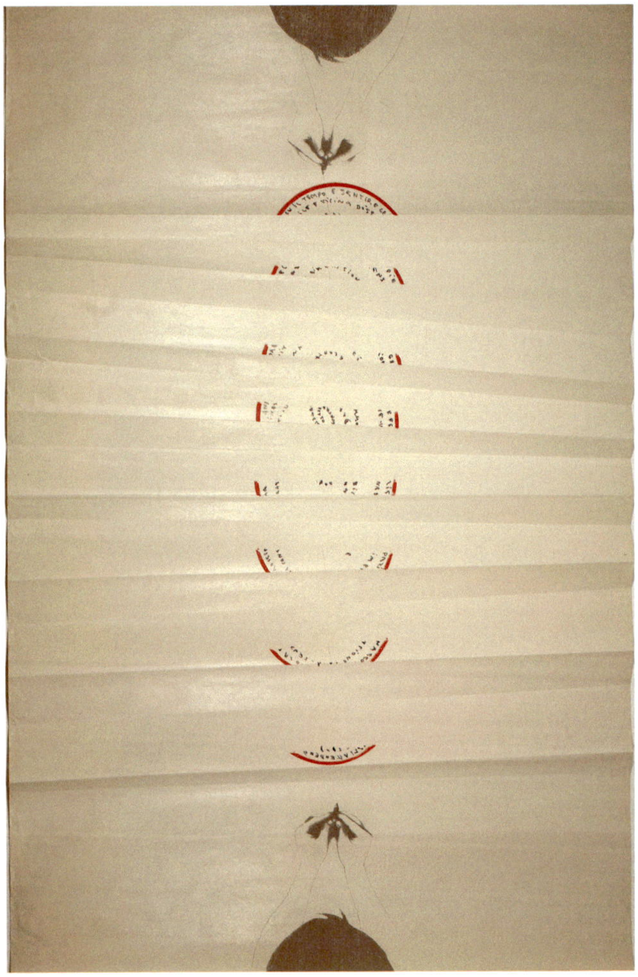

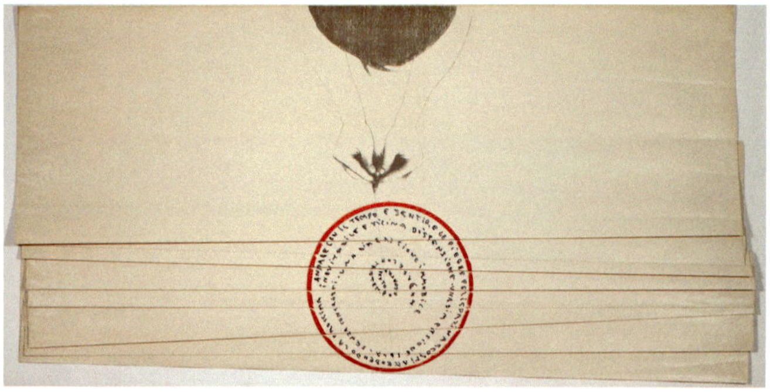

Tra sé e sé andare con il tempo (Between Self and Self Go with Time), 1985 (open and closed)

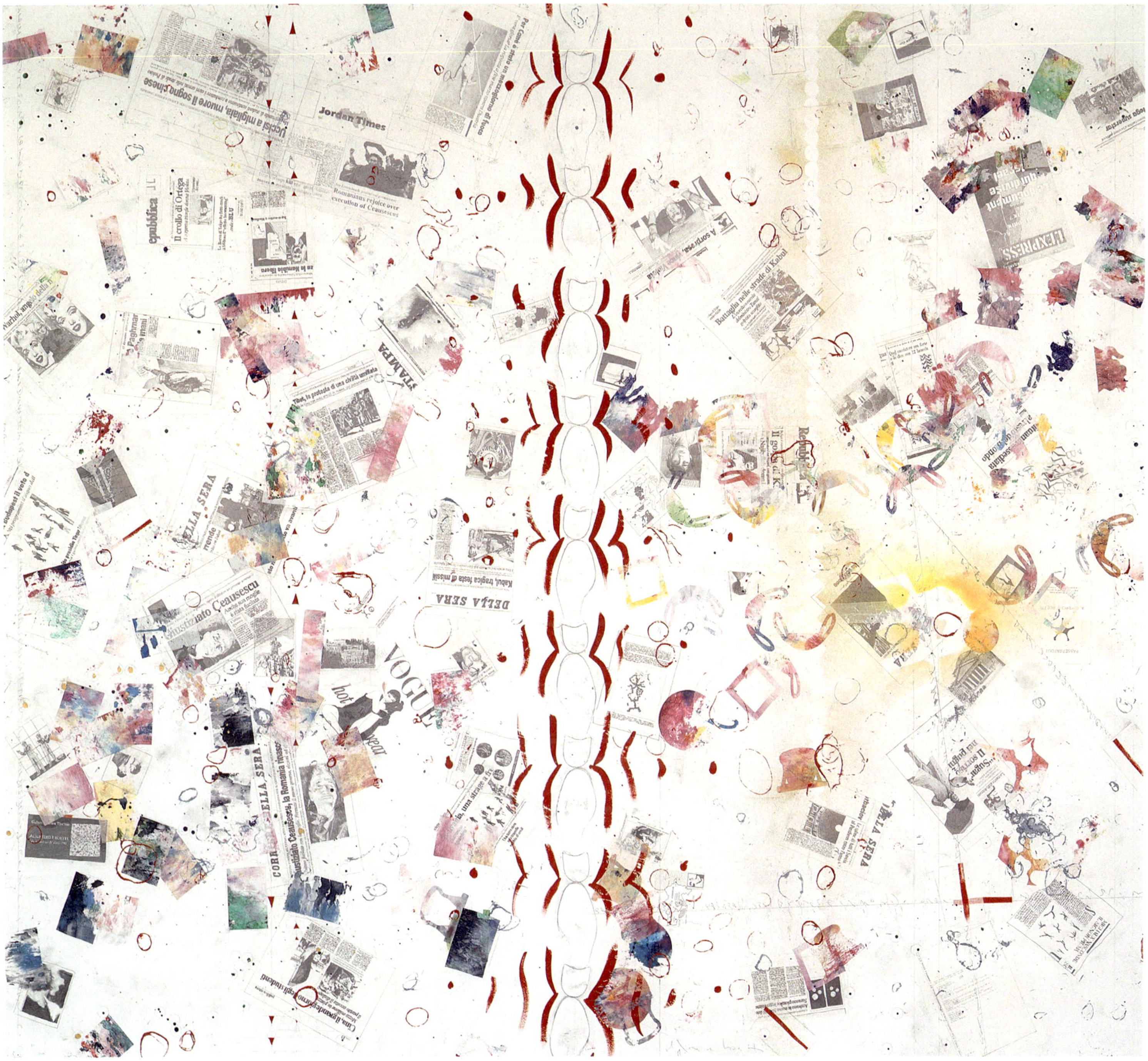

197 Orme (Footprints), 1990

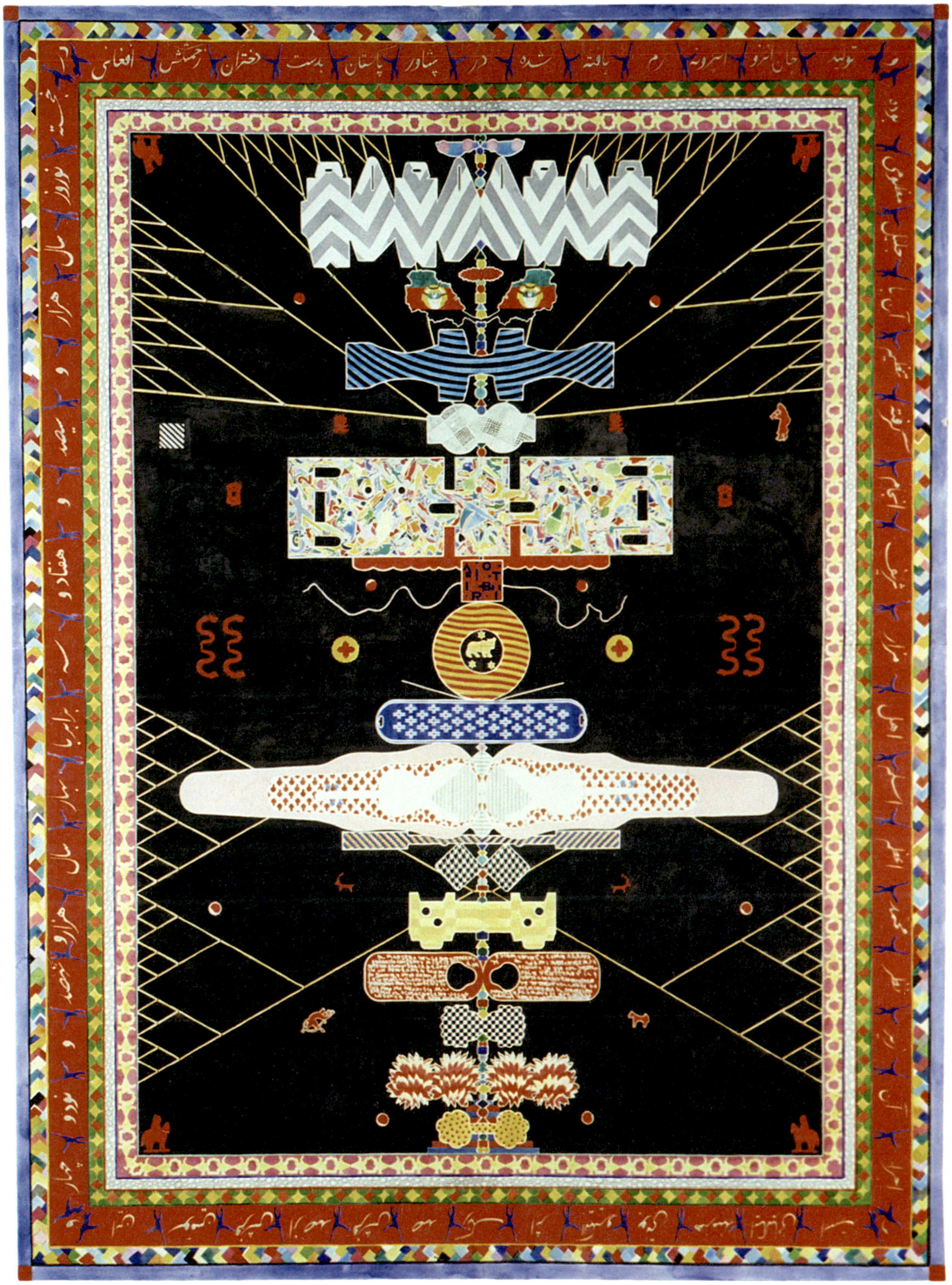

Untitled, 1994

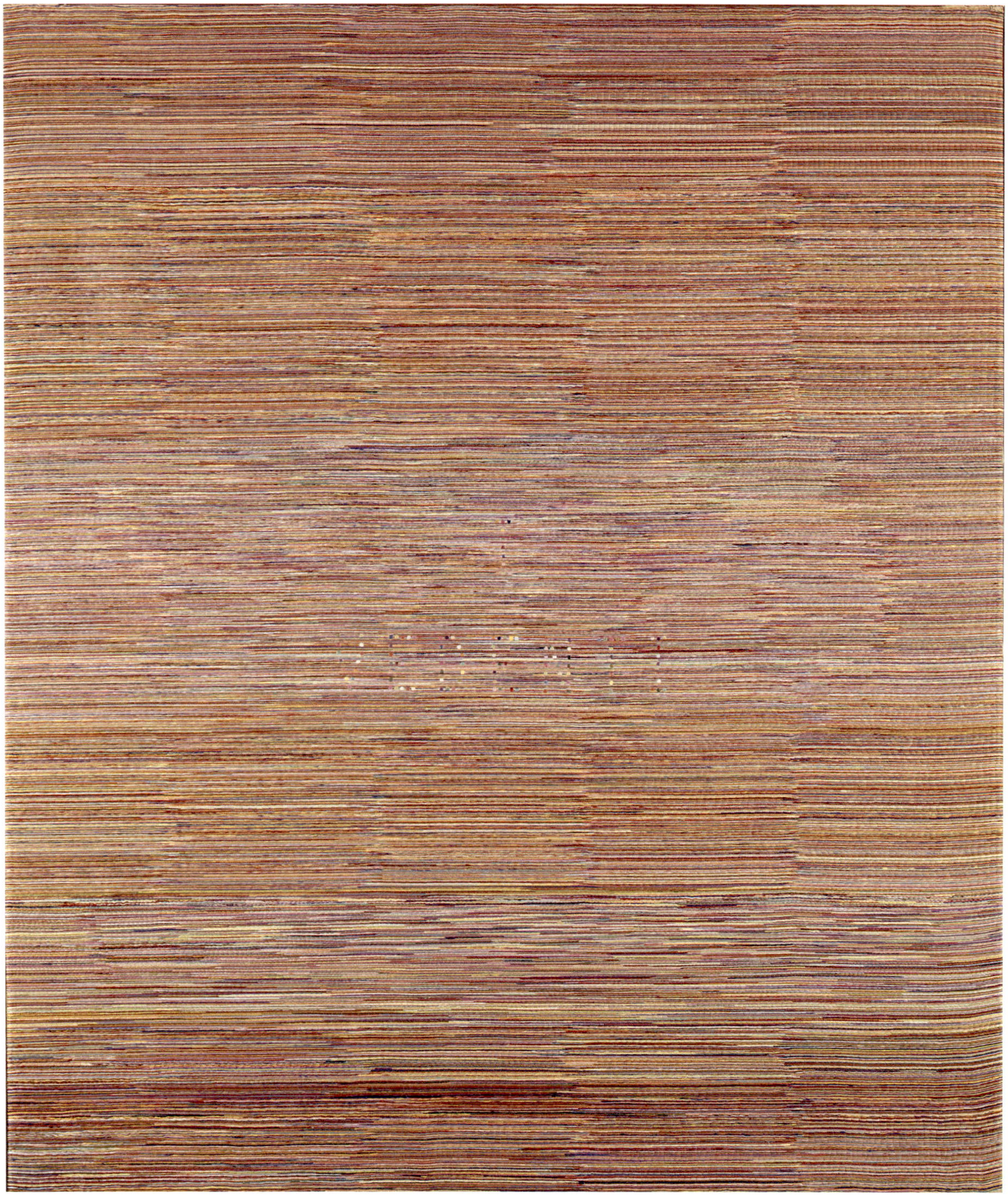

I VEDENTI (The Sighted), 1972–73

A drawing of flying thought

Bruno Corà in conversation with Alighiero Boetti

Q: A few years ago, we talked about the different aspects of perception. You talked to me about the "sixth sense" and I talked to you about Borges, the "poetic soothsayer," and during our chat—I don't recall the whys and wherefores now—your work titled *Collo rotto—braccia lunghe* (*Broken Neck—Long Arms*) came up.
A: *I'd produced that work thinking about someone capable of turning their neck 360 degrees—a broken neck, obviously—and I was also thinking of a blind man interviewed by Diderot about the problem of blindness. Diderot was obsessed by that problem and had written a book about blind people, interviewing them, asking them what a mirror is, and so on and so forth. He asked one person if he would have liked to see the moon, and the man answered no, but he would have liked to touch it—to have long, long hands to be able to touch it. Seeing it didn't matter to him—he wanted to touch it; which is why, in that work, there was the desire to touch from afar.*

Q: So you mean that it's the sixth sense that enables us to touch things that are a long way off? Well, when we started this conversation, you remembered, with regard to the five senses, an earlier example in art history: *Lo Spagnoletto* (The little Spaniard) the work by Ribera referred to by Roberto Longhi in an essay written after the discovery of one of the pieces making up Ribera's lost work on the five senses. The found work was the picture painted to illustrate "taste," while the other four, depicting *auditus*, *odoratus*, *tactus*, and *vissus* were lost. I asked you then what your impetus had been—the origin of your work on the senses. You replied that to understand the origin it was necessary to start from the concept of categories, in other words, of classifications—you'd brought a copy of the *I Mille fiumi più lunghi* (The Thousand Longest Rivers)—and from the fact that the world is seen as divided into animal kingdom, plant kingdom, and mineral kingdom, and that these classifications, in your view, were absurd, because, you said, "A plant is like an animal and a stone is the same, and then there are animals that pretend to be plants!" And so from that tendency towards a sort of homogenization, in the sense of making everything a single thing, like your "homonyms," came the idea of mixing things, including the alchemical criterion; then from that came the idea of "synchronism" and "happy coincidence." This is the story so far.

Recently, however, I've been very impressed by your latest *disegno* (drawing), and I've planned our dialogue based on this. Seeing it, I was very moved. I remember it as a work endowed with an extraordinary synthetic quality: it seems to me to encompass a series of aspects that recur in your work, such as, for example, the use of writing and the fact that, more than once, you've made a slash in the paper, like for example in the work *Raddoppiare dimezzando* (Double by Halving), which Giovan Battista Salerno talks about in his fine 1978 essay, even conjuring up death, which, like the slash, is in the middle: a shift from continuity to discontinuity. The magic of that work, when I saw it at Galleria Mario Diacono in June, just that one evening, seemed to me to have everything to do with the "minimum cause—maximum effect" concept, using the minimal means of pencil and paper. How did that work, with its extreme

ease of synthesis and the desire to scale the discourse down to minimal terms, come about?
A: *It came from the merger of three words:* clessidra/clepsydra (hour/water-glass), cerniera (hinge) *and* vice versa. *There are three different concepts: the* hour-glass *has to do with above and below, right and left; the* hinge *involves inside and outside, which is another concept, another direction;* vice versa *permits yet a further direction, even more absurd. In vice versa the word itself has a double meaning, a game in itself, while the hinge, on the other hand, refers more to a concept. These three things when merged together—with this "hole" and the paper folded by means of a hinge—mean that the hour-glass acts in the middle, because by turning the torn edges, what was right becomes left. At the same time, however, there are so many other directions involved in the phenomenon that an extraordinary thing emerges, which is that it is not logically possible to establish the position of the writing after certain operations, overturnings, and other similar things. This time, no binary process is triggered—like almost all the processes we've got used to, which is why the camera, where the right becomes left and the top becomes the bottom, is just fine, and the mirror, where you know that you're projected the other way round, is already established, and you understand it. If you look at the writings, it's only logical that what was written behind and upside down should now come out the right way up, and this is how it would be if there were just two elements. But there are several elements, several directions, which is why there's no longer any logical binary process. Or perhaps there will be a logical process, but I can no longer identify it because it continually changes position, and what you see is totally illogical. And I don't think anyone could identify it—though possibly a mathematician might be able to make an analysis of the movement that happens in that moment.*

Q: So this time, in this work, there's absolutely no recourse to the usual criterion of addition/subtraction?
A: *It's much more abstract.*

Q: It seems to me that the complexity of the *disegno* has to do instead with sidestepping the laws of logic.
A: *This is just one of so many elements that I'm experiencing in this work. For me, it's extraordinary because it's made with just paper and pencil and we could talk about it for years; it has a very troubling density. We've just talked about the fact of the tearing, about what happened: that a "hole" was made, pieces were torn off at random, they were folded in a certain way and put in certain positions. But there are also things to be said—and we tend to forget this—about the text and what's written in it. Here, too, oddly enough, there are some things that represent thought freely transcribed and, what's more, left-handedly. This involved quite a slow and tiring process, and much concentrating as a result. Then I started to think: "What should I write?" and I wrote: "What should I write?," because that's what I was thinking; then it emerged that it's tiring to write left-handed and then I wrote that, and then I started to play, I don't know, with a vowel, and I wrote* sinistro *(left),* da sinistra *(left-handed),* pauroso *(afraid), then* paura *(fear),* bagascia *(harlot), etc . . . and I kept on going like that: really expressing my thinking, which is the "sixth sense."*

Q: It seems to me that in this *disegno* the text, with all it contains, is an additional and important element.
A: *Then there's the visual fact of this "hole," which upsets so many things. And what's more, it too is double, because on the one hand it's orderly, in the shape of a rectangle, in which you see my gesture, and on the other, it's disorderly, and so there's a combination of new concepts, of order and disorder, and boundary. But one isn't more beautiful than the other; it's not that order is better than disorder, or that a tear is better than a straight line. The tear has the quality of a tear and the straight line has the quality of a straight line.*

Q: There's no hierarchy.
A: *Right. There's no hierarchy, even if a straight line may be more pleasing to you than a tear, or vice versa. I can't aesthetically maintain that a straight line is better than a torn sheet of paper. Each has its qualities, and this comes out too. In addition, there's the visual fact of the wall, of what's behind, which one day might be wallpaper.*

Q: It's including and excluding.
A: *An open space, let's say. After a while, you can feel this presence of the wall. It's a real presence. There's a rectangle of wall there, which is isolated by a large* passe-partout, *with small black pencil marks around it, like petals, and it almost*

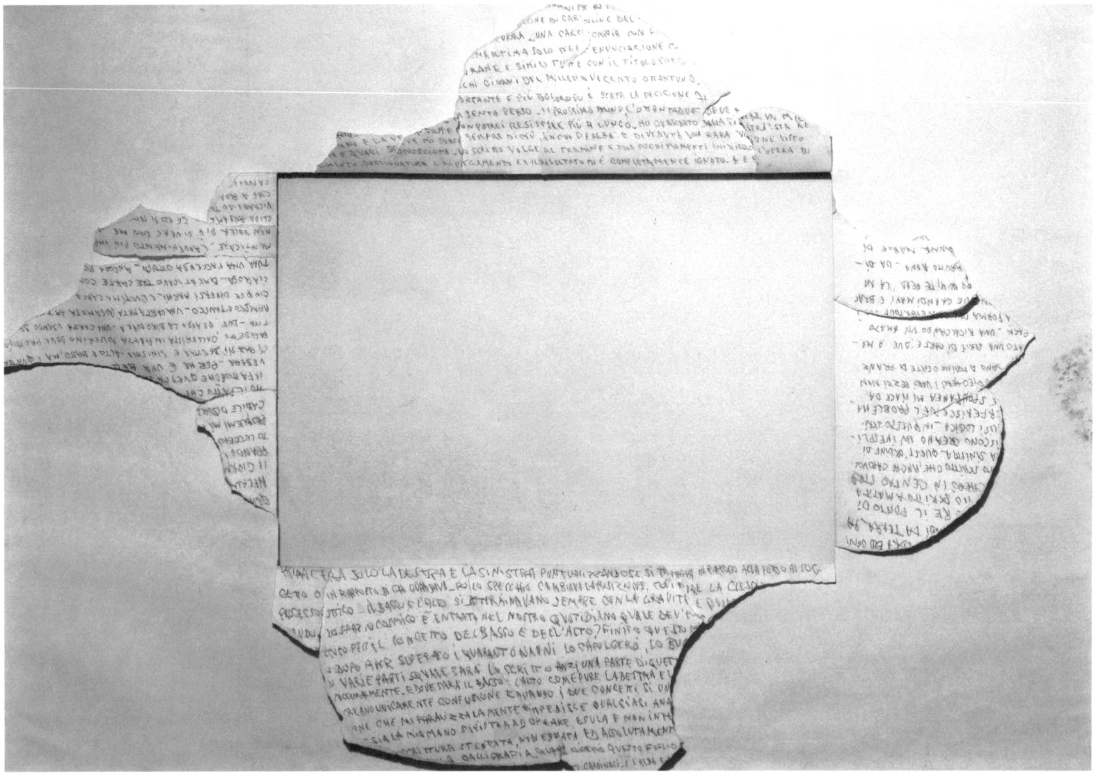

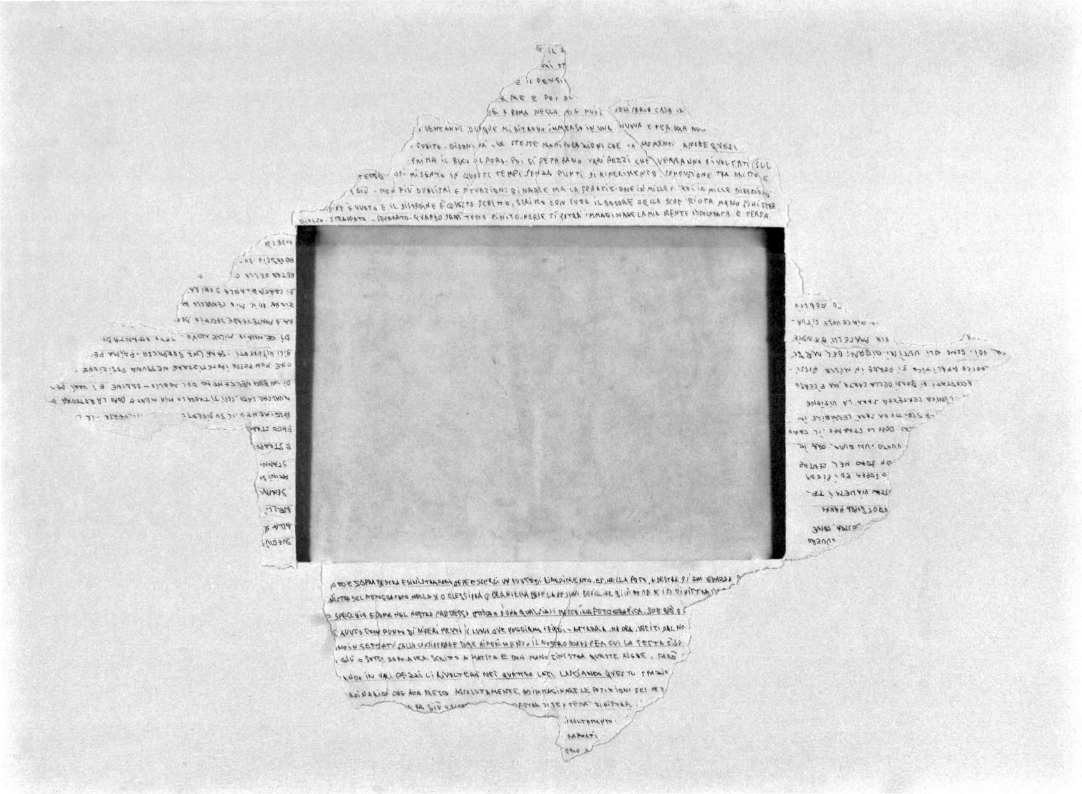

Clessidra, cerniera e viceversa (Hour-glass, Hinge and Vice Versa), 1982
Clessidra, cerniera e viceversa (Hour-glass, Hinge and Vice Versa), 1981 (bottom)

seems like something blossoming; and this "hole"—I don't like to call it a hole (buco), *since the word "buco" has a noise, while this isn't distressing or expressionist because it's made in an orderly way on one side and then left in disorder on the other. Had there been a totally fortuitous tear, there would have been too much disorder and what would have emerged would have been an almost symbolic expressionism, of the* "Scream" *type. Instead there's a rational zone, that of the straight line, which gives you a certain security and defines the visual outlines of what you see from the other side. But on the other hand, it overlays that film made of so many petals. So there's a visual part, then the text. In a show, I'd like to make three or four of these works, each one with a theme. And at this juncture, what you've written is important. Because there are four, if you want just one you can choose the theme you like best, exactly like a picture that you choose on the basis of the colors you like best: you choose the blue one rather than the pink. With the text, I do the same thing, and near the picture there's a sheet of paper with the transcript of what's written. The Chinese used to say that in a picture there should be the visual part, calligraphy, and poetry. In my work, all three of these ingredients are there, because a painter must also be a good poet. I don't know if I'm good or bad, but I do try to be a poet, too, writing in my own way. With this means, as a writer, I actually posit a fact of writing: my writing is about thinking that flies and floats, that jumps, that's also found its right pace and makes use of this tiring employment of the left hand, which is the most unusual means of execution.*

Q: I have the impression that this July *disegno* is a prelude to a new phase in your work. It seems to me that the complexity we're talking about, with regard to the writing, too, is a major component and it seems to be a real "re-invention of inventions." Added to which is the fact that a few weeks later there was that event, the car accident you had at San Bernardino. Talking about it—I remember you were convalescing—you told me straight out that the *disegno* had been a forewarning. That idea appears at least once in modern and contemporary art history: in De Chirico's work on Apollinaire, *Il ritratto premonitore di Apollinaire* (Premonitory Portrait of Apollinaire). But for you, what was that work a forewarning of? Did you realize afterwards that it was a particularly meaningful work from the viewpoint of existential fate?

A: *No, I suddenly realized that it might be my last work. And it would have been just fine as a last work; it would have had all the depth required. And to tell you the truth, it may well be that things end up like this, because I don't think I can make a more concentrated, denser, more diversified, more all-embracing thing—there's the calligraphy, the text, the poetry, this visual fact of the opening, of the shattering, of the tearing into so many bits and rediscovering unity in the negative, in the void; all these black pieces torn off and refolded are the scattered pieces of a rectangle, which is obvious in its absence; while its presence is shattered, its absence is total.*

Q: Calligraphy appears, as do shattering, chance, and also combinatory probability, etc. So where's this coming from? How does this type of poetic interest come into being? A few days ago, we were talking around this table about the initiation of your work, and what some of the early influences were; we talked about Herman Hesse. But now, things are coming about differently, because your work is completely autonomous in relation to that type of dimension. What is your real curiosity about, and your perception of reality?

A: *To get as close as possible to understanding this, I'd say "a western Zen," which is different from an eastern Zen, but it's still Zen. I'm involved in that particular dimension: very abstract, lots of thinking. Zen tales are the only tales that really make me laugh, and my laughter's like a little boy's, because those tales really are extraordinarily innocent and candid, and at the same time extraordinarily shrewd. There's never any rule; the rule is, "Make your own rules."*

Q: So in those tales, there's a definition of the world we're living in, the West, but with the spirit of the East.

A: *I've always liked the fact that in Chinese and Japanese pictures there was writing, which meant, for example, "How green is the meadow on the hill," or "You smell so sweet." That ideogram was lovely to see, and then there was also that sound factor. Like when I read: "I would like to live asleep / amid the gentle noise of life": that's an extraordinary poem by Sandro Penna. It's a western Zen poem. It's got nothing to do with Salvatore Quasimodo or Giuseppi Ungaretti; Penna is another* *of those truly Zen characters who have nothing to do with "making culture" or any of those things; they exist in terms of their sincerity and candor, in their extraordinary super-innocence. And we're made the way we're made. I say, there's no rule; there's just a need to be, like Penna. Penna existed in a western way, but he wrote poetry that could be a little Japanese Zen test.*

Q: And yet, as far as you're concerned, this apparently dreamlike dimension—living asleep within the gentle noise of life—seems to me to be an attitude that's constantly controlled by a scientific, mathematical system. It doesn't seen coincidental to me that, in your work, there's a continual appearance of numbers, in various forms. What value do you attach to numbers? What entity is a number for you?
A: *The number is the only real entity that exists in the world. Numbers are the only identities that exist in an autonomous way, in the sense that if it's true that, by convention, we've put B after A, there's nothing to say that it's by convention that we put 2 after 1, and 3 after 2: it's not a fact of language, whereas it is a fact of language that B comes after A—we could also have decided to do the opposite. On the other hand, the fact that 2 comes after 1 is a terrifying reality. So, for example, when I see a piece of quartz, I can't see it as something dead, I see it as a formula of numbers that at a certain moment—perhaps because a drop appears or some chemical procedure occurs—is released and, in a split second, this perfect, crystalline hexagon comes forth, these molecules that are perfectly embedded. So it comes forth like a mushroom. It is a mushroom. What difference is there between it and a mushroom? What does it mean that one is a plant and the other a mineral? Fibonacci taught us that the number of sunflower seeds develops on the basis of a precise series. So numbers are crazy entities, totally crazy. It's those numbers—for example, the periodic numbers—that end with a continuous three or four, which indicate the impossibility . . .*

Q: Of stopping them.
A: *Yes, of making a straight line. It never ends. You never manage to separate two things. I don't know, sometimes there are absurd supreme powers: the odd always wins over the even at the end of the day; there's a superiority of one over the other. So there's no symmetry in numbers. In fact, when I visualized the number 1,000, I suddenly realized that it's not a square; otherwise put: it's a square with irregularities. There's a series of prime numbers in which it's not possible to establish a sense. They're absurd, they're really crazy, but they have a very strong, concrete reality, and they block you, and at the same time, they can get you to visualize crazy things, in motion. Take a number with a comma or decimal point and a figure with the periodic sign: it's as if they were showing you a white line, which you're running continually in front of, but which never stops, and it goes on dividing, it goes on dividing, who knows what. If you divide a street, there's this line that has to separate it; it has a width, but a totally abstract width, because it might not exist. It doesn't take sides. If you divide 100, even if the line is 1, you don't get 49 and a half and 49 and a half and 1 for the line. No, you get 50 and 50. You don't count the line; the line is a total abstraction, but you can visualize it that way. A number is like the quartz: it's a numerical series, and it's like other things that put themselves in that particular position.*

Q: With regard to this, Celant wrote about a quality that seems to be there in your work: he said that it all comes about under the aegis of the "component," that is, of the association, of putting different things together, so that they form an organic whole. But this aspect seems to be organized on the plane of the rational, while, on the other hand, you continually say that numbers are crazy and so they can't be organized systematically or from the rational viewpoint. So is there something else? The number obviously triggers something else. What is this "something else"? Because it's this "something else" that makes your work poetic, which lends it that intangible quality, which is why it can't be read on the plane of rationality alone.
A: *Numbers have the quality of concepts. Every one has its individuality, its presence; I don't know: 3 is Mister 3, and 2 brings in the concept of dualism, of the double; 1 is unity; 4 is the earth, the four walls; 5 is the pentagon, and the terrible concept of war springs to mind; 6 is the hexagon, and that makes me think of bees. Then there are 10, 11, and 12. These are numbers with their own very personal story, which is why we need to prefer the one in the middle, 11, because it's the*

number that has already gone beyond 10 and hasn't yet reached 12. 10 represents a certain superficial completeness of the thing, a superficial splendor, very clear and dry. Then there's 11, which is very unstable, it's made up of a pair of numbers, like twins. 12, on the other hand, is a number that has a crazy historical load: think of the months, the signs of the Zodiac—everything's 12: the apostles; eggs are sold by the dozen, because they're a symbol of life; numerically, 12 is divisible by everything, by 2, by 3, by 4, by 6. 10 can only be divided by 2 and 5; 12 has a whole visual possibility, playing with 3 and 4, creating so many structures. There are structures like the triptych, you know, which come from the number 3; it's the concept of 3, which is then the concept of the Trinity. Numbers also have this aspect, as if they were statues and visions. In the time of the ancient Egyptians, there were those large animals, and men with animals' heads—there was a tendency to zoomorphism, which represented an idea, a concept almost always combined with numbers, too.

Q: Sticking with this entity—the number—I remember you once told me an eastern story. Vaguely, it involved grains of corn and a chessboard and you told me that, no sooner was the idea of numeration realized, than that idea became impossible and impracticable. In what sense? Can you explain in what way the idea becomes impracticable and impossible, based on the fact that it springs from numeration?
A: *Because the numeration of the power of 2, of doubling, is so speeded up that we can't keep up with it. While we do manage to reach infinity with a series of additions from 1 on (1 + 1 + 1 + 1 + 1 . . .), it's quite easy to arrive at colossal numbers, but this doubling series is impracticable, because, both as a power of two or a power of two billion, it has the same acceleration. After a split second from the start, which is slower, the acceleration is extremely powerful: just think that with one millimetre, after twenty doublings, you have a kilometer. It's incredible.*

Q: The aspect of the 1 + 1, of the 11, or the 1 alongside the 1, also calls to mind the problem of signature and identity. For years, you've been called Alighiero e Boetti, but this unity, which is the person, is in reality the conjunction between first name and surname. Hence the union between two hypothetical contrasts, with you nevertheless always representing the union. What role, in this sense, is played by the word "Alighiero," and what part does the word "Boetti" play? What does Alighiero Boetti bring to this union?
A: *Incredibly banal. The most banal thing in the world. Alighiero is the most childish, most extreme part, which dominates family things. Alighiero is what people I know call me. Boetti is more abstract, precisely because the surname is a category. While the first name is unique, the last name is already a category, a classification. This is something that affects us all. The first name offers certain sensations of familiarity, acquaintance, and intimacy. By the mere fact that Boetti is a surname means that it's already an abstraction, it's already a concept. If people see one of my works they say: "It's a Boetti" not "It's an Alighiero." "Have you got a Boetti to sell me?"—"How big d'you want it?"—"100 x 150." So it's a Boetti, not an Alighiero. Alighiero, on the other hand, is the one who kicks up a racket—more banal things.*

Q: Right, Alighiero, but the person who's talking about these two words is a third person, talking in a detached way, and at the same time he's the only thing, because he's the union of two opposites, or of the two parts that are joined. So since this aspect of identity is always being brought to the fore, what in your view is a subject, a person, during a period when a post-Nietzschean aesthetic in literature and philosophy is asserting the eclipse of the subject, the loss of the subject, the affirmation of objectivity and other aesthetic hypotheses? What do you think about the issue of identity and subject? As far as you're concerned, of course. Are you abdicating, the way a lot of philosophy seems to be claiming, from this identity as subject, or are you asserting it? People have written about this. Tomasso Trini said that in your work, there's the presentation—the staging—of the subject.
A: *There's also another concept in the criticism that I've happened to see, or an aesthetic category, that involves a "personal mythology." But as you know, it's not that I'm asserting anything, except the freedom to make one's own rules, and then afterwards everyone has the ability to play this game when the rules have been laid down. It's free, obviously, and it's egalitarian. And there's the person who plays well and the*

person who plays badly, the person who plays a little and the person who plays a lot. Here I feel a bit alien in the art world, because I go into it with my own rules. I'm not a painter, I don't use the rules of painting, and so they're all invented rules, which sometimes come up with good results. It's a bit like the rules of structure [in I Sei Sensi (The Six Senses)]—of commas, I mean—that fact of turning the word into a sign.

Q: A while ago you said that commas are the sign of temporariness and continuum.
A: *It's a fact that a word is transformed into a sign— this group of commas that signify something. There, that's a rule.*

Q: But here, too, these commas almost always helped to connote a name, a concept, an identity.
A: *There's one work of mine, made with a Biro, which is called* Seguire il filo del discorso (Following the Thread of the Discourse)*, where participants follow the thread made by these commas. Following the thread of the discourse is tautological and then, based on the rule, there's this structure that turns the word into a sign. It was necessary to visualize the comma as a fact of non-stability, of instability, and these little white dots were put on a certain background, that of the hatched Biro, the ground made by a different hand.*
Q: Here we have another thing I wanted to talk about. While on the one hand, you seem to be continuously asserting the subject, on the other, you contradict yourself, because in many of your works other hands, other subjectivities and other identities have found their way in, as actual operators even. Could you explain what you're after in this sense? In the art of the past twenty years, there have been creative work proposals made together with other people: Beuys' "collaborations," as he sometimes called them, and he wanted to get Pistoletto involved in those as well. In your case, what does this choice to work with others—your choice to shatter your own subjectivity along with other people's—involve?
A: *There's no contact with other people; there's just a visualization of so many "homonymous" realities—in the sense of nameless, but with the same name, which is to say that everyone has their own temperament, but without any form of collaboration, insomuch as there's their reality and there's mine. I've found a system whereby any kind of reality suits me. In other words, I don't make choices. This is also an important outcome—managing not to make choices.*

Q: We talked about this on another occasion. I wouldn't say it was fear, but definitely you expressed a desire not to make choices. Why this wish not to choose?
A: *Because if you go against the current in a river, at a certain moment you have to choose: you reach a tributary and you have to decide whether to go right or left. On the other hand, if you're going downstream, if you're going with the current, you never choose; you find yourself taking the same route. So I'd like to go with the flow, and never choose.*

Q: What is it that intrigues you? How come you let yourself go with the current? What is it that pushes you into a current?
A: *The pleasure of creativity, the pleasure of thinking. That huge pleasure that Penna's poetry gives you; for example, those two little disparaged lines—"I would like to live asleep / in the gentle noise of life"—that's a much greater pleasure than erotic pleasure, or the pleasure a friendship gives you. It's a truly dense pleasure, full of great things saying nothing. I don't know—this pleasure I get from making things and seeing other people's things. This is what draws me into the current. I like going along with other people who play with thought: mathematicians, logicians, theologians, or poets and musicians.*

Q: This work of yours seems more or less boundless, precisely because of the ways in which it likes to come across. Trini, again, talked in relation to your work about the "need for continual optical adjustment in our perceptions." For you, since there's no preparation of new dimensions to be offered, is there any arranging of the work beforehand? If there is, what's involved in this pre-arrangement of the work, given that there's no choice and there's an ongoing need to introduce an optical adjustment of perception? What's the ultimate rule that basically and invariably governs your work?
A: *The ultimate?*

Q: The last and the first, the one that's always there.
A: *It's managing to balance things.*

Q: It's a symmetrical conception of art and work? Among other things, balance has a symmetrical value.
A: *I see balance as forever taking a weight from one plate to another, in a quest for equilibrium; if there's more weight on the left, then you dash to the right and put something there, add a little bit more, and so on and so forth . . .*

Q: There's always a difference?
A: *Right, so there's no straight line that's the balancing factor. Continual motion exists, which is the "ping-pong" and the "vice versa."*

Q: Let's take a look at words—at the game that can be played with words. In these past few years, after Duchamp, frequent use has been made of tracing paper as a material for representing a concept or an image. In your work, on the other hand, it's seemed to me that there's a use of "re-tracing." What type of sign is "re-tracing"?
A: *Oddly enough, re-tracing is the aesthetic reality of a blind person who touches the paper and feels the edges, the outlines, following the drawing in a tangible way, in a physical way. To look at a Picasso drawing is to follow that line while he's making it, but re-tracing is seeing like blind people, by means of the edges. But then I've also used re-tracing more like a remedy—for example, that small drawing that was in the Mura Aureliane show,* Regno Musicale (Musical Kingdom)*, where these instruments appear that have been "massaged" in the middle of the paper with a bit of graphite, and they come out in a really physical way. It's another way of inventing the drawing; it's a drawing made by a human Xerox machine, a person, in a nutshell, who re-traces, who re-copies, but in a given way—so in this sense definitely not like a Xerox machine. That's one way of drawing, and then there's the classical way: taking a pencil in your hand, and then there's the fact of drawing and covering, filling, like in the Biro works. They're all ways of drawing. Everyone has their own way, their own certainty, their own temperament, their own shadows. And here, everyone has their own presence, which is beyond any possibility of choice. Everyone has their bodily self, their fullness; above all they've physically filled the sheet of paper. It's really a physical fact. So the works with the Biro are concentrates of time; for me, in a physical way, they give the sensation of a huge, expanded time frame.*

Q: And the embroideries too?
A: *And the embroideries too; and I'm really pleased that each embroidery takes five years to make. And oddly, I'm patient enough to wait for them. In fact, I don't wait for them. Then they arrive. There's a long time involved, and there's also uncertainty.*

Q: The element of contingency and eventuality was the hallmark of all your work in the 1960s, and seems to have had an influence on later artists. I'm thinking, for example, of Francesco Clemente, whom you pointed out to me when he was just starting out on his activities, which, incidentally, I dealt with in 1975–76 in the "Area" programmes. That factor, it seems to me, gave way to a series of other people's experiences, whose dimension seems redundant—exotic and forcedly expressionistic, rather than associated with faculties and split seconds of perception. As someone who's combined "happy coincidences" with the conception of a work that never renounces the qualities of intelligence and inventiveness, do you think there's still room at this time for such a dimension?
A: *Yes. In fact, this latest work is in this dimension. And then there's been a moment—and perhaps there'll also be others—when there's real pleasure in drawing, in working with colors, using scissors, sticking, overlaying, making carbon copies, massaging the paper, pulling it, squeezing it, anything you like. It's all okay, if there's the requisite communication.*

Q: How do you appraise your start as an artist in Turin? And what was the atmosphere like in Rome, where it seems you'd elected to live, during those years when your work was just getting underway? You renamed that 1969 work *Una vetrata*, "Nothing to See, Nothing to Hide," and thirteen years later, this drawing arrives, which seems to be saying: "Everything to see;" we can even see the wall behind. But as in *Una vetrata*—the window—once again there's "nothing to hide." It would seem that little has changed, and yet the environments have changed, the two realities. It's a story about halves. How did you experience that start and that arrival?
A: *First of all, there's the stance you have in relation to the city. There can be three positions: being a resident, paying a*

visit, or being a tourist. Now the best situation is undoubtedly that of the person visiting, because he has all the advantages of the resident and none of the disadvantages, meaning the familiarity. In Turin I lived as a resident: I lived the city and the city lived me. I lived with the other people living there, whereas here in Rome I'm a stranger. I'm somebody visiting, which is why I'm always aware of where I am. In Turin, at a certain moment, you can drown in the sea of familiarity.

Q: But with regard to the more strictly artistic aspect, the linguistic production, and relations with other artists, how do you see the two experiences?
A: *You know, the problem is meeting people and you can meet people both in Turin and in Rome. For me, relations and exchanges are always duets, meetings between two people. There's no group phenomenon as far as I'm concerned, but relations between two people, which are always much stronger, and which you can have anywhere.*

Q: Do you have somebody in mind right now?
A: *No.*

First published in *A.E.I.O.U.*, no. 6, December 1982
Translated from Italian by Simon Pleasance and Fronza Woods

Alighiero Boetti working with schoolchildren, 1992

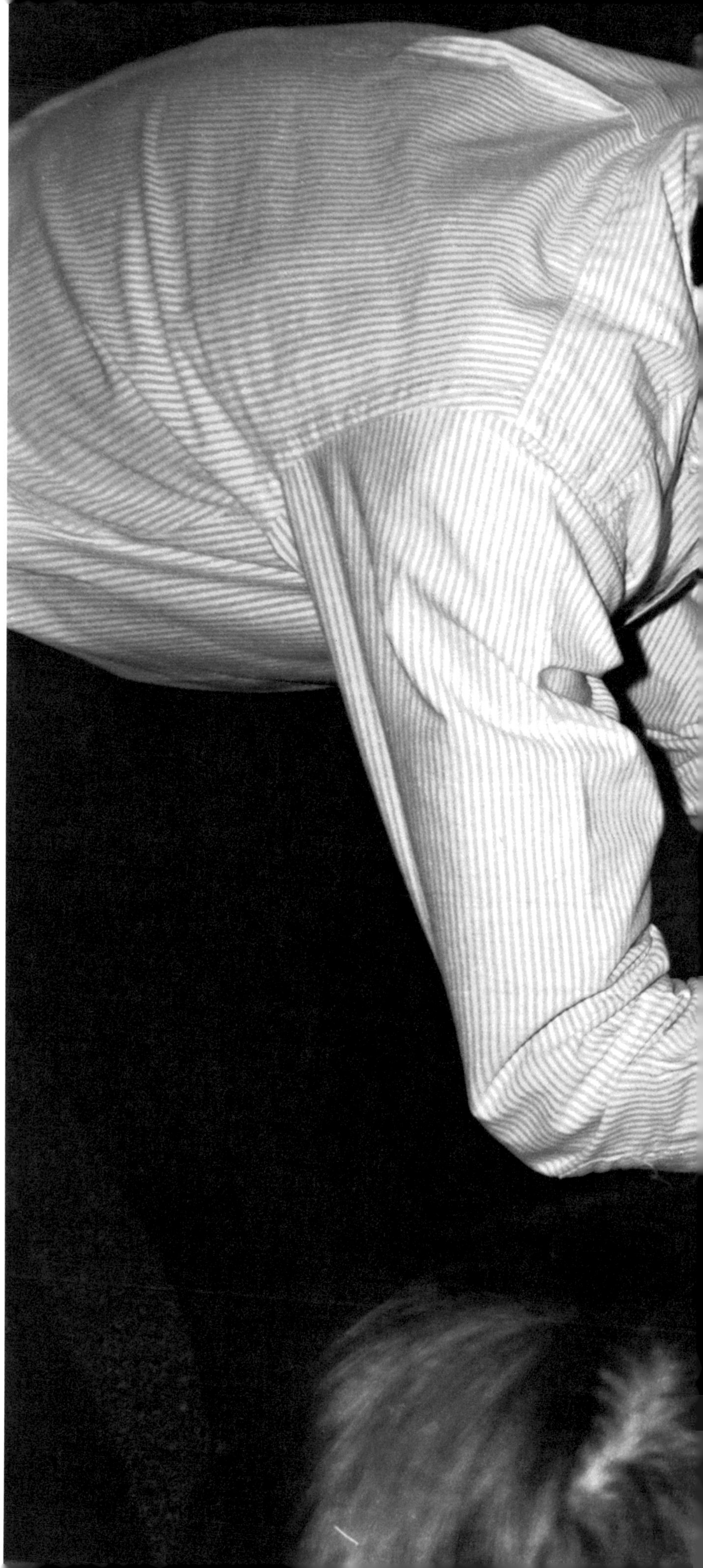

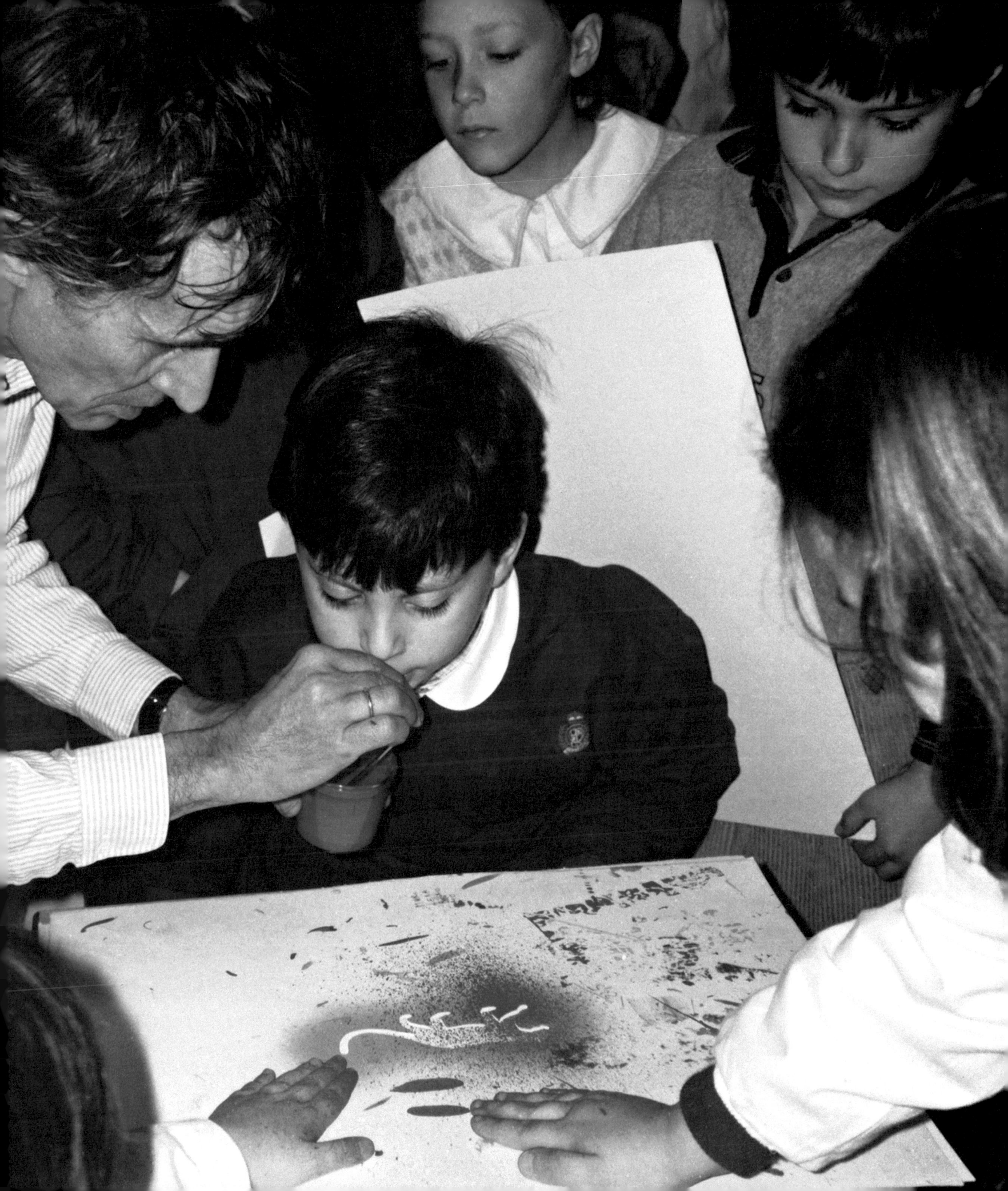

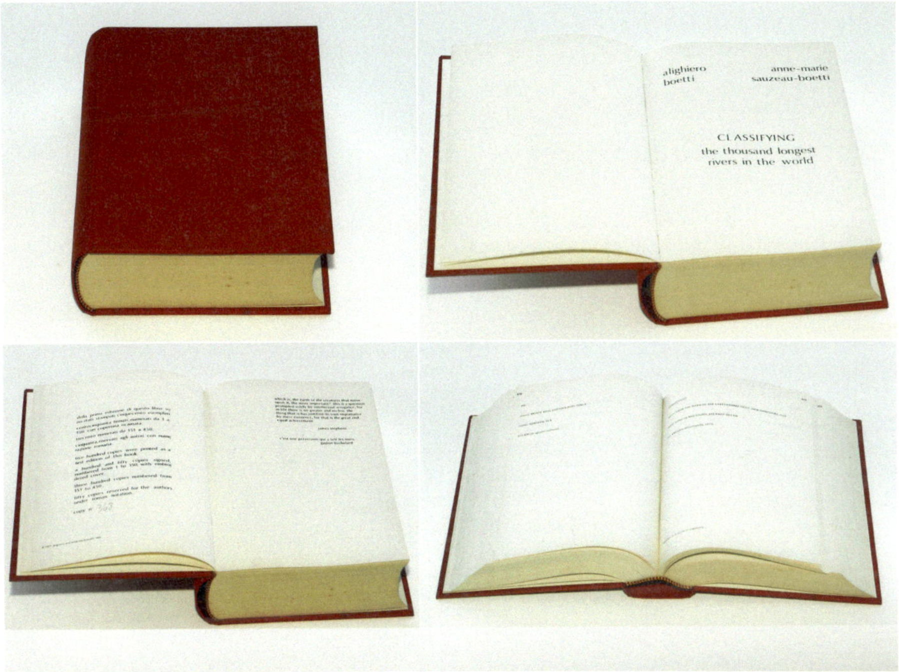

Classifying: The Thousand Longest Rivers in the World, 1977

1NILE-KAGERA.:2 RIO AMAZON-APURIMAC.:3 MISSI-MISSOURI.:4 YANGTZE-KIANG.:5 JENISEJ-SELENGA.:6 HUANG
FINLAY.:15 NIGER-JOLIBA.:16 MURRAY-DARLING.:17 VOLGA.:18 RIO JURUA.:19 RIO PURUS.:20 MADEIRA.:21 ZAMBEZI.:22 BRA
.:30 EUPHRATES.:31 DANUBE.:32 SYRDARYA.:33 SALWEEN.:34 GANGES.:35 VILJUJ.:36 TOCANTINS.:37 RIO ARAGUAIA.:38
.:46 DNIEPER.:47 ALDAN.:48 OLENEK.:49 COLORADO.:50 ORANGE.:51 TAPAJOS.:52 JAPURA.:53 TARIM-YARKAND.:54 RED-A
DEL NORTE.:63 COLUMBIA.:64 XINGU.:65 INDIGIRKA.:66 MAMORE.:67 WABE-SHEBELE.:68 URUGUAY.:69 UPPER MI
MAYO.:78 SENEGAL.:79 SIANG KIANG.:80 SONG KOI.:81 CULYM.:82 TIGRIS.:83 UPPER JENISEJ.:84 UPPER MURRAY
RIVER.:95 PLATTE RIVER.:96 RIO PILCOMAYO.:97 RIO MAGDALENA.:98 KURA.:99 OKA.:100 PECOS RIVER.:101 LA
.:110 COLORADO.:111 COOPER CREEK.:112 VAAL.:113 RIO BRANCO.:114 BRAZOS.:115 TENNESSEE RIVER.:116 JUMNA
RTHERN DVINA.:126 DESNA.:127 BENOUE.:128 RIO HUALLAGA.:129 GEORGINA.:130 ATBARA.:131 TISNA.:132
KATCHEVAN.:139 LIARD.:140 UDA.:141 AWASH.:142 CHENAB.:143 RIO DESAGUADERO.:144 HAN KANG.:145 JA
AK.:154 MARXA.:155 KANSAS.:156 GREEN RIVER.:157 ELBE.:158 CHINDWIN.:159 DEMJANKA.:160 WHITE RIVER
TIETE.:168 BANI.:169 RIO IRIRI.:170 CHU.:171 HARI RUD.:172 KIEN KIANG.:173 MADRE DE DIOS.:174 SAO
SUL.:182 KONDA.:183 TJUNG.:184 OM.:185 HAI-HUTO.:186 MAJA.:187 VISTULA.:188 VACJUGAN.:189 YELLOWSTO
BANDAMA.:198 MURRUMBIDGEE.:199 BARITO.:200 META.:201 KWILU.:202 RIO GRANDE BOLIVIA.:203 CUANDO
211 TAGUS.:212 MILK RIVER.:213 RIO ACRE.:214 CUNJA.:215 OUACHITA RIVER.:216 PARANAIBA.:217 TROMBE
.:225 SEVERN.:226 APURE.:227 RUKI.:228 BACK RIVER.:229 MEZEN.:230 FITZROY.:231 VAKH.:232 TISZA
VER.:240 RIO SANTIAGO.:241 TANANA.:242 UFA.:243 NEMAN.:244 OKA.:245 TYM.:246 MEUSE.:247 MACOUA
BIGHORN-WIND RIVER.:256 SABINE.:257 EBRO.:258 ODER.:259 SANAGA.:260 DIAMANTINA.:261 CH
8 DIGUL.:269 KUSKOKWIM RIVER.:270 VETLUGA.:271 KOKSOAK-KANIAPISKAU.:272 KUREJKA
LUAN HO.:280 RED RIVER OF THE NORTH.:281 KUBAN.:282 BARWON RIVER.:283 KAN KIANG.:284 KOK
92 RIO NEGRO.:293 HAY RIVER.:294 MURGAB.:295 CHEYENNE.:296 MAHANADI.:297 NAMOI RIVER.:298
306 FLINDERS.:307 GUADIANA.:308 FORT GEORGE.:309 ARAUCA.:310 CUIABA.:311 SAKARYA.:312 NOR
RIVER.:321 RIO CHUBUT.:322 PEND OREILLE.:323 WARTA.:324 TARA.:325 LINDE.:326 CONA.:327 APALACHICOLA
336 JEQUITINHONHA.:337 KOYUKUK.:338 LOMELA.:339 LUANGWA.:340 MIN KIANG.:341 NOSOB.:342 PARANAIBA
ITAPERCURU.:352 WASHITA.:353 PEARL.:354 SOKOTO.:355 INIRIDA.:356 SEFI RUD.:357 POWDER.:358 SEINE
369 RIO ROVUMA.:370 SAGUENAY.:371 SAINT FRANCIS.:372 SON.:373 WABASH.:374 WINNIPEG.:375 MURES.:376 KARUN
SKAT.:385 BUREJA.:386 GUADALUPE RIVER.:387 SIU SHUI.:388 TZUSHUI KIANG.:389 PARU DO OESTE.:390 KOCEC
RO.:398 SANTEE.:399 SOUTH PLATTE.:400 BOGAN RIVER.:401 MURAT.:402 REPUBLICAN RIVER.:403 COURANTYNE
413 NEOSHO.:414 OLIFANTS.:415 SOURIS RIVER.:416 TAPTI.:417 RIO JATUMA.:418 PRUT.:419 MUNA.:420 MANGOKY
429 JIPARAUA.:430 MOSKVA.:431 PERENE.:432 VICHADA.:433 PSEL.:434 SAINT JOHN RIVER.:435 CYM.:436 NIOBRARA
45 KENTUCKY.:446 NEPA.:447 BURDEKIN.:448 PEEL RIVER.:449 SALMON.:450 BOLSOJ IRGIZ.:451 BIG SIOUX.:452 GRE
C.:461 KANAWHA.:462 NECHES.:463 BELLE FOURCHE RIVER.:464 GWYDIR.:465 MUTAN HO.:466 INJA.:467 TAJAMURA
RIVER.:475 MOKSA.:476 TOMBIGBEE RIVER.:477 PO.:478 CONNECTICUT.:479 CAURA.:480 MUSI.:481 RAPTI.:482 GOR
491 GREAT FISH.:492 JAMUNDA.:493 KHOTAN.:494 NOATAK.:495 NOTTAWAY.:496 NYONG.:497 PARDO.:498 PASTAZA
HAZAL.:507 TURUHAN.:508 LOZVA.:509 SITTANG.:510 POLUJ.:511 BADULE.:512 RIO DULCE.:513 PATIA.:514 BHIMA
VER.:524 SREPOK.:525 SYLVA.:526 MOLODO.:527 CADOBETS.:528 BIJA.:529 EMBA.:530 MANJRA.:531 RED DEER.:53
AJA BAIKA.:541 RUPERT RIVER.:542 SHWELI.:543 RIO ATRATO.:544 PYSMA.:545 YGYATTA.:546 ASI.:547 COLVILLE.:5
55 GAZIMUR.:557 GREEN.:558 ORTON.:559 ILIM.:560 PING.:561 ALLAH.:562 GLOMMA.:563 BOLSOJ SALIM.:564 NJUK
3 WAINGANGA.:574 GARONNE.:575 SABUN.:576 IK.:577 TEMBENCI.:578 TOMPO.:579 TORNE.:580 ARGA-SALA.:581 DZI
1 CAPANAPARO.:592 CONCHOS.:593 CORRIENTES.:594 CUYUNI.:595 FAFAN.:596 FOW.:597 RIO DEL FUERTE.:598
NER.:607 PIDVIRI.:608 RAMGANGA.:609 SUNGEI REJANG.:610 SAO LOURENCO.:611 SEYHAN.:612 SILKA.:613 TAOU
KALADAN.:623 DAMODAR.:624 DINDER.:625 RIO LURIO.:626 MOSELLE.:627 PARAIBA DO NORTE.:628 RIO TIGRE
N.:639 LESSER ANYUI.:640 CASTLEREAGH.:641 JAMES RIVER.:642 KADUNA.:643 MOOSE.:644 PENGANGA.:645 SAN MI
URIO.:655 STIKINE.:656 DEMA.:657 ELKHORN.:658 BETSIBOKA.:659 KARASUK.:660 UNZA.:661 WHITE RIVER
K.:670 KOBDO.:671 LUNI.:672 MANA.:673 PAROO.:674 PELLY RIVER.:675 SAN JOAQUIN.:676 VAGA.:677 WHITE VO
AN.:686 TANAMA.:687 BATHA.:688 BEAS.:689 RIO CURUA.:690 DALALVEN.:691 ISET.:692 MARINGA.:693 SAINT
KAN.:702 AKHTUBA.:703 CUJA.:704 IJA.:705 INN.:706 IZHMA.:707 KABUL.:708 KASKASKIA.:709 KEMIJOKI.:710 OTI
SIDERTY.:721 COARI.:722 INDRAGIRI.:723 BOLSOJ TAP.:724 MONBOY.:725 VELMO.:726 CARCARANA.:727 BUUR.:728
JUAN.:737 SAVANNAH RIVER.:738 RIO VASA BARRIS.:739 JUCAR.:740 KENGA.:741 ARTIC.:RED RIVER.:742 BANAS
ERN BUG.:752 LEICHHARDT.:753 ALIMA.:754 ATREK.:755 BAYOU BARTHOLOMEW.:756 BOMOKANDI.:757 BOTOMA.:758 CA
SCOPPER.:766 CORUBAL.:767 CROSS.:768 DONGNAI.:769 EKWAN.:770 GANALE DORYA.:771 GASH.:772 GONGOLA
LUFIRA.:782 RIO LUGENDA.:783 MAE PING.:784 MUN.:785 MUND.:786 ORD.:787 OWYHEE.:788 PARAGUACU.:789
RNAREKHA.:797 SUSITNA.:798 TA-TUNG HO.:799 TONJ.:800 TUGELA.:801 YING HO.:802 TENASSERIM.:803 M BA
INISK.:811 YESILIRMAK.:812 HAN.:813 HUMBOLDT.:814 MAE KLONG.:815 MUSSELSHELL.:816 BERBICE.:817 LOBAY
826 DRINA.:827 ELILA.:828 SAINT JOHNS RIVER.:829 TSIENTANG.:830 BAHR KEITA.:831 MUR.:832 ANGERN
KA.:840 TUNDZA.:841 UDA.:842 CHARITON.:843 CHANDALAR.:844 NUSHAGAK.:845 NZI.:846 SAI.:847 OUED SE
CHI MAENAM.:857 DIYALA.:858 HORTON.:859 KOBUK.:860 LOA.:861 LOWA.:862 NAREW.:863 N GOUNIE.:864 PEMB
RIVER.:872 BURNETT RIVER.:873 HARTZ.:874 KALIX.:875 LARCH.:876 MU.:877 PARBATI.:878 QU APPELLE RIVER
887 RIO LIMAY.:888 LJUSNAN.:889 MONBOYO.:890 SAN JAVIER.:891 VENTUARI.:892 TALLAPOOSA.:893 MOLDAU
0.:902 INDALSALVEN.:903 RAHAD.:904 MANANARA.:905 ALSEK.:906 GAUJA.:907 GWAAI.:908 HUNYANI.:909 MORONA
18 MEKROU.:919 SKELLEFTE ALV.:920 WEST FORK OF WHITE RIVER.:921 SOMES.:922 TIBER.:923 MACLEAY.:924 AB
932 COPPENAME.:933 CORUMBA.:934 DIDESA.:935 DOLORES RIVER.:936 DUCK RIVER.:937 EREPECURU.:938 FRENCHMA
AN.:948 KUNAR.:949 KUNDUZ.:950 LINSSHUI.:951 LITTLE ZAB.:952 LUANG KIANG.:953 LUNG KIANG.:954 MAGALAKWIN.:95
4 PANGANI.:965 PANLUNG KIANG.:966 PA SAK.:967 RIO PIAUI.:968 RIET.:969 SABARMATI.:970 SAN PEDRO.:971 SARAMA
AND RIVER.:981 TAOERH HO.:982 TEBICUARY.:983 UDA.:984 WARDHA.:985 YAMPA.:986 SAN JORGE.:987 KUM.:988
EDONG.:995 VAH.:996 ZAB.:997 RIO SAN FRANCISCO.:998 VARDAR.:999 DIALE.:1000 AGUSAN

 I mille fiumi più lunghi del mondo (The Thousand Longest Rivers in the World), 1976–82

1 NILE-KAGERA · 2 RIO AMAZON-APURIMAC · 3 MISSI-MISSOURI-RED ROCK · 4 YANGTZE KIANG · 5 JENISEJ-SELENGA
TYSC · 14 MACKENZIE-FINLAY · 15 NIGER-JOLIBA · 16 MURRAY-DARLING · 17 VOLGA · 18 JURUA · 19 PURUS
7 RIO NEGRO · 28 NIZHNYAYA TUNGUNSKA · 29 YUKON · 30 EUPHRATES · 31 DANUBE · 32 SYRDARYA · 33 SALWEEN
VAN · 41 URAL · 42 CUBANGUI · 43 ISCIM · 44 OHIO-ALLEGHENY · 45 ARKANSAS · 46 DNIEPER · 47 ALDAN
YMA · 56 KASAI · 57 HSI KIANG-NAPAN · 58 LIMPOLO · 59 IRRAWADY · 60 ORINOCO · 61 KAMA · 62 SALADO DEL
DON · 71 PODKAMENNAYA TUNGUNSKA · 72 SUNGARI · 73 VITIM · 74 PECORA · 75 GUAPORE · 76 MARANON
PARNAIBA · 86 CHIARI · 87 BENI · 88 CUBANGO · 89 ABBAI · 90 SNAKE · 91 TOBOL · 92 KET · 93 RUKI
DIAN · 104 JUBA · 105 GODAVARI · 106 SUTLEJ · 107 OLEKMA · 108 BJELAJA · 109 LIAO HO · 110 COLORADO
AUCA · 120 GUAVIARE · 121 RHINE · 122 IGUAZU · 123 VJATKA · 124 NARMADA · 125 NORTHERN DVINA
ULEN · 135 ZEJA · 136 ATHABASKA · 137 NORTH CANADIAN · 138 NORTH SASKATCHEWAN · 139 LIARD · 140 UDA
9 CUMBERLAND · 150 KWANGO · 151 SANGHA · 152 NONNI · 153 KIZILIRMAK · 154 MARXA · 155 KANSAS
ES · 165 VOLTA · 166 RIO DAS VELHAS · 167 TIETE · 168 BANI · 169 IRIRI · 170 CHU · 171 HARI RUD
· 180 HUAI HO · 181 PARAIBA DO SUL · 182 KONDA · 183 TJUNG · 184 OM · 185 HAI-HUTO · 186 MAJA
195 PYASINA · 196 DONETS · 197 BANDAMA · 198 MURRUMBIDGEE · 199 BARITO · 200 META · 201 KWILI
10 BIRJUSA · 211 TAGUS · 212 MILK · 213 ACRE · 214 CUNJA · 215 OUACHITA · 216 PARNAIBA · 217 TROMBETAS
RN · 226 APURE · 227 RUKI · 228 BACK · 229 MEZEN · 230 FITZROY · 231 VAKH · 232 TISZA · 233 CUANZA
A · 242 UFA · 243 NEMAN · 244 OKA · 245 TYM · 246 MEUSE · 247 MACQUARIE · 248 ONON · 249 CUNENE
58 ODER · 259 SANAGA · 260 DIAMANTINA · 261 CHAMBAL · 262 KAPUAS · 263 LITTLE MISSOURI · 264 NARI-ANAMBAR
72 KUREJKA · 273 NAPO · 274 USSURI · 275 APAPORIS · 276 CHATTAHOOCHEE-APALACHICOLA · 277 FIMI
286 URUBAMBA · 287 IVAI · 288 COLORADO · 289 EASTERN ALEJ · 290 AMGUN · 291 CARA · 292 NEGRO · 293 HAY
AKAM · 303 PORCUPINE · 304 SASSANDRA · 305 TOM · 306 FLINDERS · 307 GUADIANA · 308 FORT GEORGE
318 RHONE · 319 UCUR · 320 WHITE · 321 CHUBUT · 322 PEND-OREILLE · 323 WARTA · 324 TARA · 325 LINDE
I KIANG · 335 ITAPICURU · 336 JEQUITINHONHA · 337 KOYUKUK · 338 LOMELA · 339 LUANGWA · 340 MIN KIANG
DES CYGNES · 350 WARREGO · 351 ITAPERCURU · 352 WASHITA · 353 PEARL · 354 SOKOTO · 355 INIRIDA
365 GANDAK · 366 KAVERI · 367 OMO · 368 RAVI · 369 ROVUMA · 370 SAGUENAY · 371 SAINT FRANCIS · 372 SON
N BUG · 382 KIRENGA · 383 MEDVEDITSA · 384 ATTAWAPISKAT · 385 BUREJA · 386 GUADALUPE · 387 SIU SHUI
HELIFF · 395 NZI · 396 JHELUM · 397 MANTARO · 398 SANTEE · 399 SOUTH PLATTE · 400 BOGAN · 401 MURAT
U · 411 MEGHNA · 412 RIO DAS MORTES · 413 NEOSHO · 414 OLIFANTS · 415 SOURIS · 416 TAPTI · 417 UATUMA
E · 427 BARGUZIN · 428 CAVALLY · 429 JAPARAUA · 430 MOSKVA · 431 PERENE · 432 VICHADA · 433 PSEL
GONAM · 444 KLJAZMA · 445 KENTUCKY · 446 NEPA · 447 BURDEKIN · 448 PEEL · 449 SALOMON · 450 BOLSOJ IRGIZ
MAENAM MUN · 460 POTOMAC · 461 KANAWHA · 462 NECHES · 463 BELLE FOURCHE · 464 GWYDIR · 465 MUTAN HO · 466 INJA
5 MOKSA · 476 TOMBIGBEE · 477 PO · 478 CONNECTICUT · 479 CAURA · 480 MUSI · 481 RAPTI · 482 GORIN · 483 SELEMDZA
MUNDA · 493 KHOTAN · 494 NOATAK · 495 NOTTAWAY · 496 NYONG · 497 PARDO · 498 PASTAZA · 499 RAMU · 500 ROOSEVELT
TANG · 510 POLUJ · 511 BALOVE · 512 DULCE · 513 PATIA · 514 BHIMA · 515 KAN · 516 SINJAJA · 517 KENKEME · 518 PARACATU
8 BIJA · 529 EMBA · 530 MANJRA · 531 RED DEER · 532 DESSEADO · 533 SACRAMENTO · 534 ROANOKE · 535 ILIMPEJA · 536 CURUA
46 ASI · 547 COLVILLE · 548 EASTMAIN · 549 MAPUTO · 550 PARANA · 551 TAPAUA · 552 TONLE SAP · 553 YUNGTING HO · 554
NJUKZA · 565 TROM-JUGAN · 566 DAWA · 567 PARAGUA · 568 MIN KIANG · 569 DOCE · 570 MAHI · 571 SIRET · 572 SKEENA
AS · 583 SCUCJA · 584 TES · 585 CLINCH · 586 BAKOYE · 587 ATHI · 588 BEAR · 589 BIKIN · 590 CANUMA · 591 CAPANAPARO
601 LUEMBE · 602 MAZARUNI · 603 MITCHELL · 604 SOUTH NAHANNI · 605 PEMBINA · 606 PENNER · 607 PIQUIRI · 608 RAMGANGA
· 618 GEORGE · 619 GOULBURN · 620 OUM ER ERBIA · 621 YOM · 622 KALADAN · 623 DAMODAR · 624 DINDER · 625 LURIO · 626
J · 636 WESER · 637 ABITIBI · 638 AGAN · 639 LESSER ANYUI · 640 CASTLEREAGH · 641 JAMES · 642 KADUNA · 643 MOOSE · 644
AT · 654 LURIO · 655 STIKINE · 656 DEMA · 657 ELKHORN · 658 BETSIBOKA · 659 KARASUK · 660 UNZA · 661 WHITE · 662 KUMA
3 PAROO · 674 PELLY · 675 SAN JOAQUIN · 676 VAGA · 677 WHITE VOLTA · 678 IOWA · 679 MARNE · 680 MYINGE · 681 TSIRIBI
LVEN · 691 ISET · 692 MARINGA · 693 SAINT MAURICE · 694 SEVIER · 695 SHEYENNE · 696 VORONEZ · 697 TUMEN · 698 KOVA
KEMIJOKI · 709 OTI · 710 PA SAK · 711 SIND · 712 WARBURTON · 713 CIZANKA · 714 KALAR · 715 JACUIPE · 716 TUBA · 717 TUJ
727 CEPTSA · 728 BUZI · 729 GILBERT · 730 ISANA · 731 LAS PIEDRAS · 732 LIU KIANG · 733 LOMELA · 734 MAPUERA · 735 SAN
HUDSON · 745 LO HO · 746 MARITSA · 747 BEAVER · 748 PORSUK · 749 THOMPSON · 750 WESTERN BUG · 751 LEICHHARDT · 752
ARCHAN DARYA · 761 CHINKO · 762 CHUNG KIANG · 763 RIO DAS CINZAS · 764 COPPER · 765 CORUBAL · 766 CROSS · 767 DONGNAI
I · 777 IKOPA · 778 LITTLE COLORADO · 779 LOT · 780 LUFIRA · 781 LUGENDA · 782 MAE PING · 783 MUN · 784 MUND · 785
· 795 SABARNAREKHA · 796 SUSITNA · 797 TA-TUNG HO · 798 TONJ · 799 TUGELA · 800 YING HO · 801 TENASSERIM · 802 M'BAM
O YESILIRMAK · 811 HAN · 812 HUMBOLDT · 813 MAE KLONG · 814 MUSSELSHELL · 815 BERBICE · 816 LOBAYE · 817 BULLOO · 818
JOHNS · 828 TSIENTANG · 829 BAHR KEITA · 830 MUR · 831 ANGERMAN ALV · 832 BRAHMANI · 833 CAMANA-MAJES · 834
AK · 844 NZI · 845 SAI · 846 OUED SEBOU · 847 STYR · 848 TAO HO · 849 VINDEL · 850 BLACK · 851 PORTUGUESA · 852 SAN
863 PEMBINA · 864 SUNGEI PERAK · 865 ROMAINE · 866 SIERRA LEONE · 867 NOTEC · 868 CURUCA · 869 AKOBO · 870 AUX OUTA
O USUMACINTA-CHIXOY · 881 CAGUAN · 882 DOUBS · 883 ESCAUT · 884 IPIXUNA · 885 KALIX ALV · 886 LIMAY · 887 LJUSNAN
KONDOMA · 897 MISSINAIBI · 898 YURYUZAN · 899 SHUNK · 900 CHICO · 901 INDALSALVEN · 902 RAHAD · 903 MANANARA · 904
4 ADIGE · 915 ALLIER · 916 SOUTH MAHAVADY · 917 MEKROU · 918 SKELLEFTE ALV · 919 WEST FORK OF WHITE RIVER · 920
RIMA · 929 BERSIMIS · 930 BIG BLUE · 931 COPPENAME · 932 CORUMBA · 933 DIDES · 934 DOLORES · 935 DUCK · 936
IALOMITA · 946 KAJAN · 947 KUNAR · 948 KUNDUZ · 949 LINSNUI · 950 LITTLE ZAB · 951 LUANGINGA · 952 LUNG KIANG
LY · 962 PAMPAS · 963 PANGANI · 964 PANLUNG KIANG · 965 PA SAK · 966 PIAUL · 967 RIET · 968 SABARMATI · 969 SAN
SI · 979 TANO · 980 TADERH HO · 981 TEBICUARY · 982 UDA · 983 WARDHA · 984 YAMPA · 985 SAN JORGE · 986 KUM · 987
SAO FRANCISCO · 997 VARDAR · 998 DIALE · 999 AGUSAN · 1000

 I mille fiumi più lunghi del mondo (The Thousand Longest Rivers in the World), 1976–82

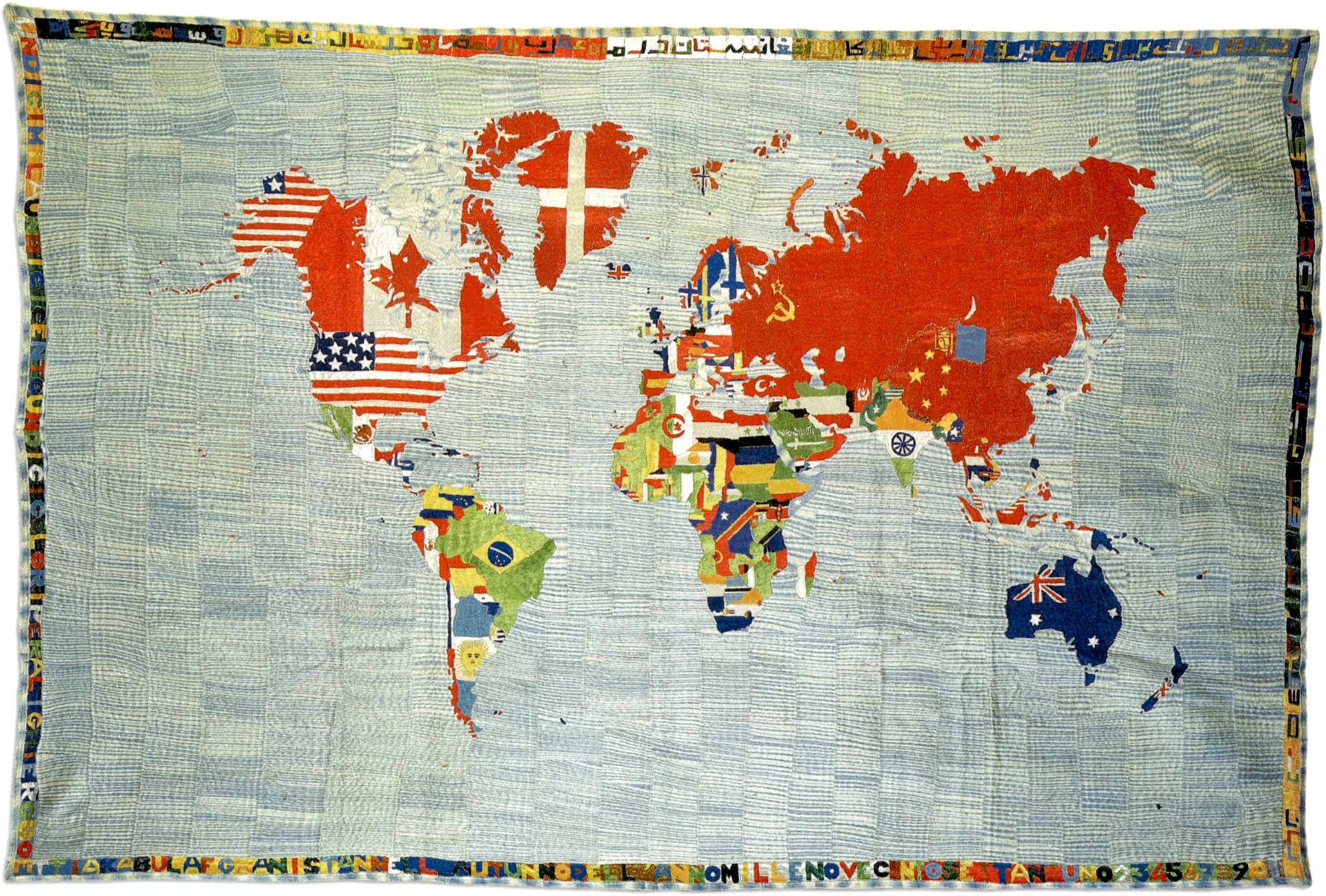

Mappa (Map), 1971–72

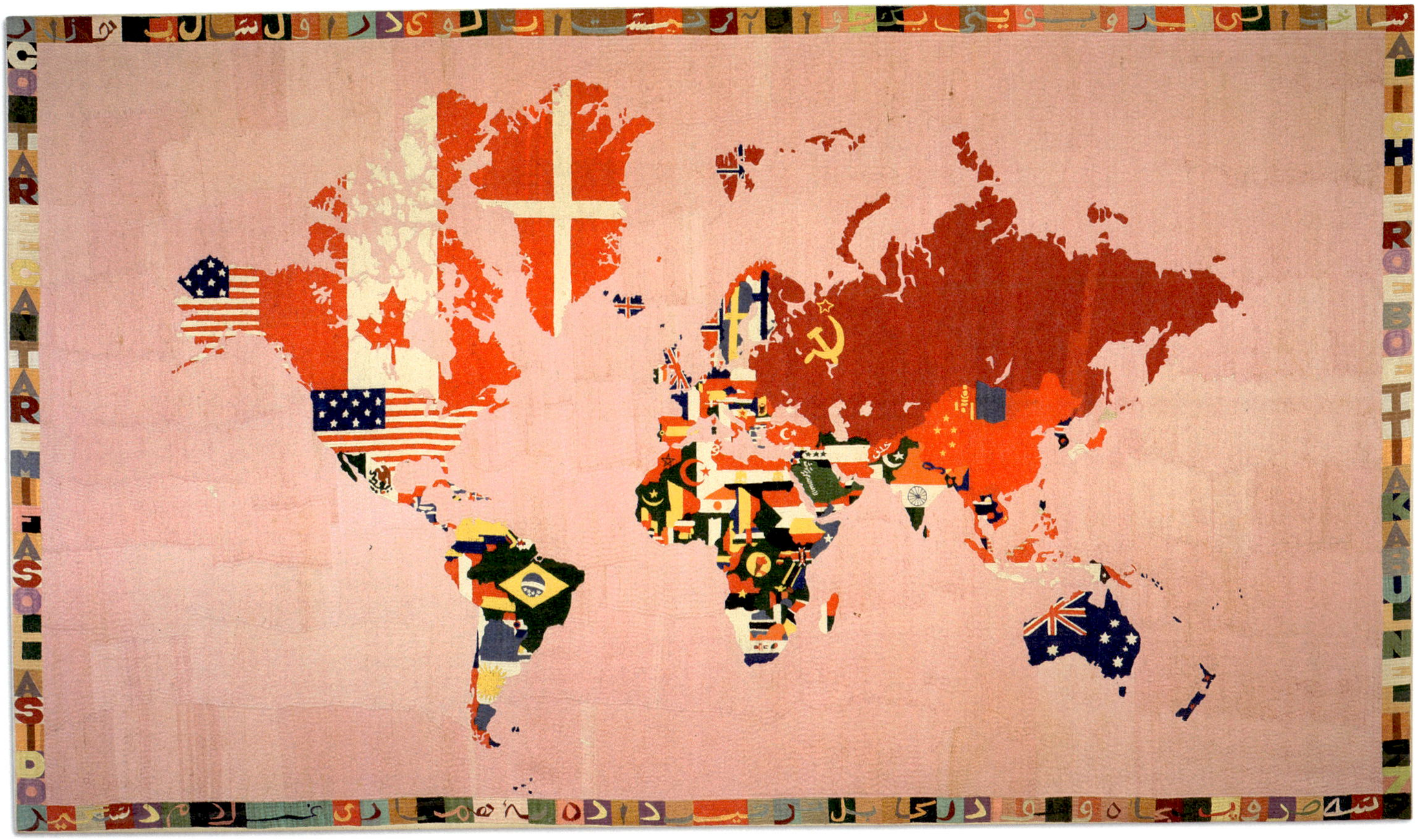

Mappa (Map), 1979

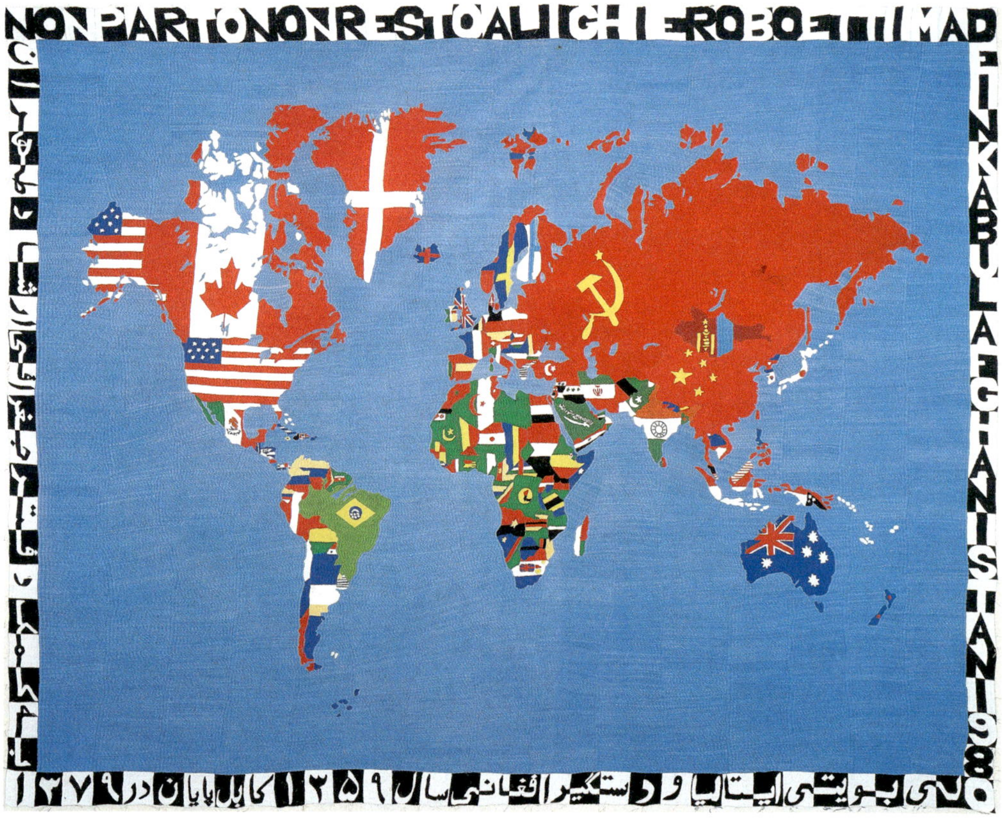

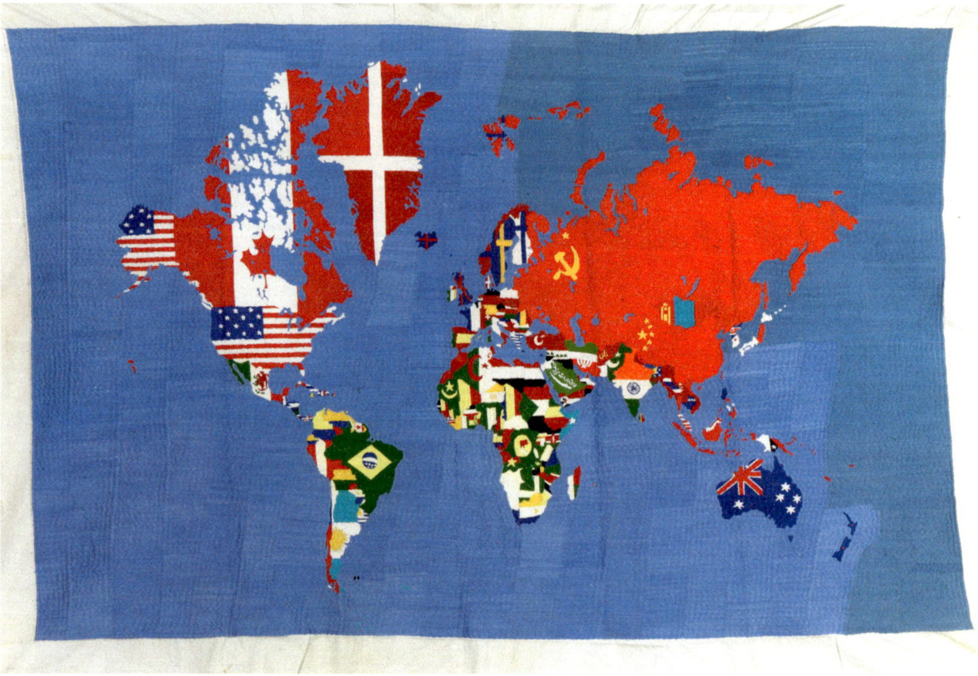

Mappa (Map), 1980 (top) : Mappa (Map), 1979–1983 (bottom)

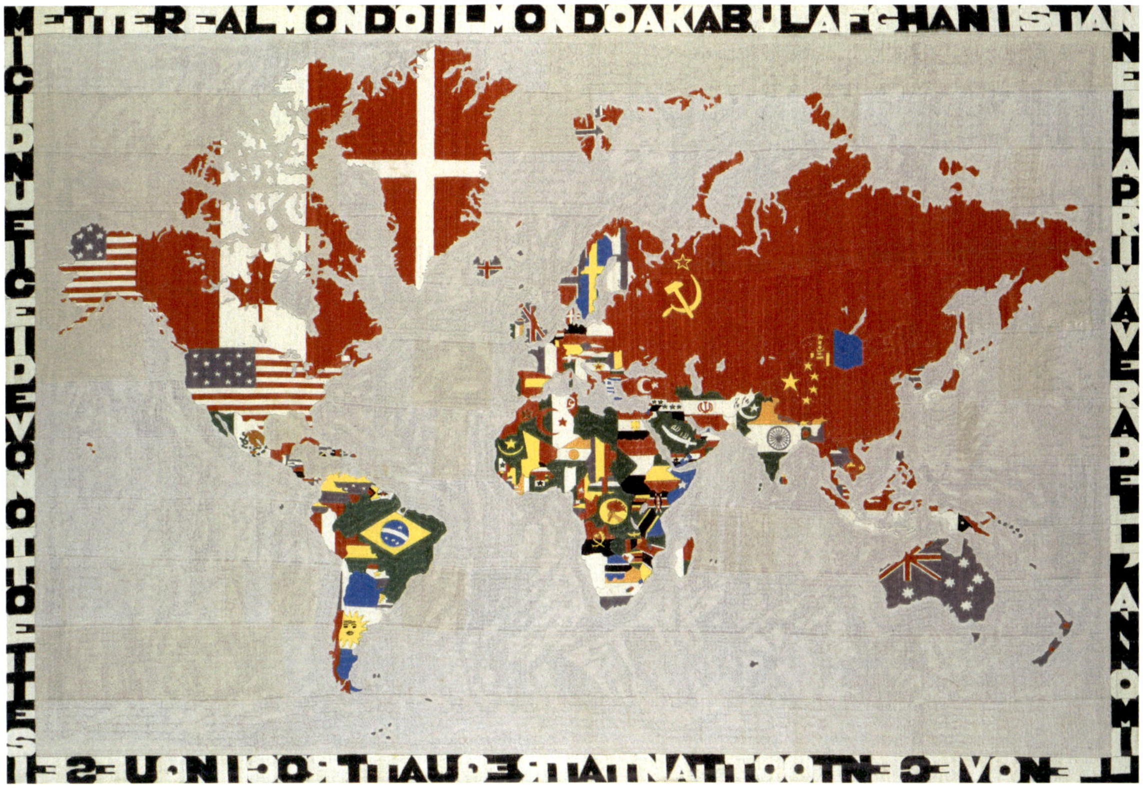

 Mappa (Map), 1983

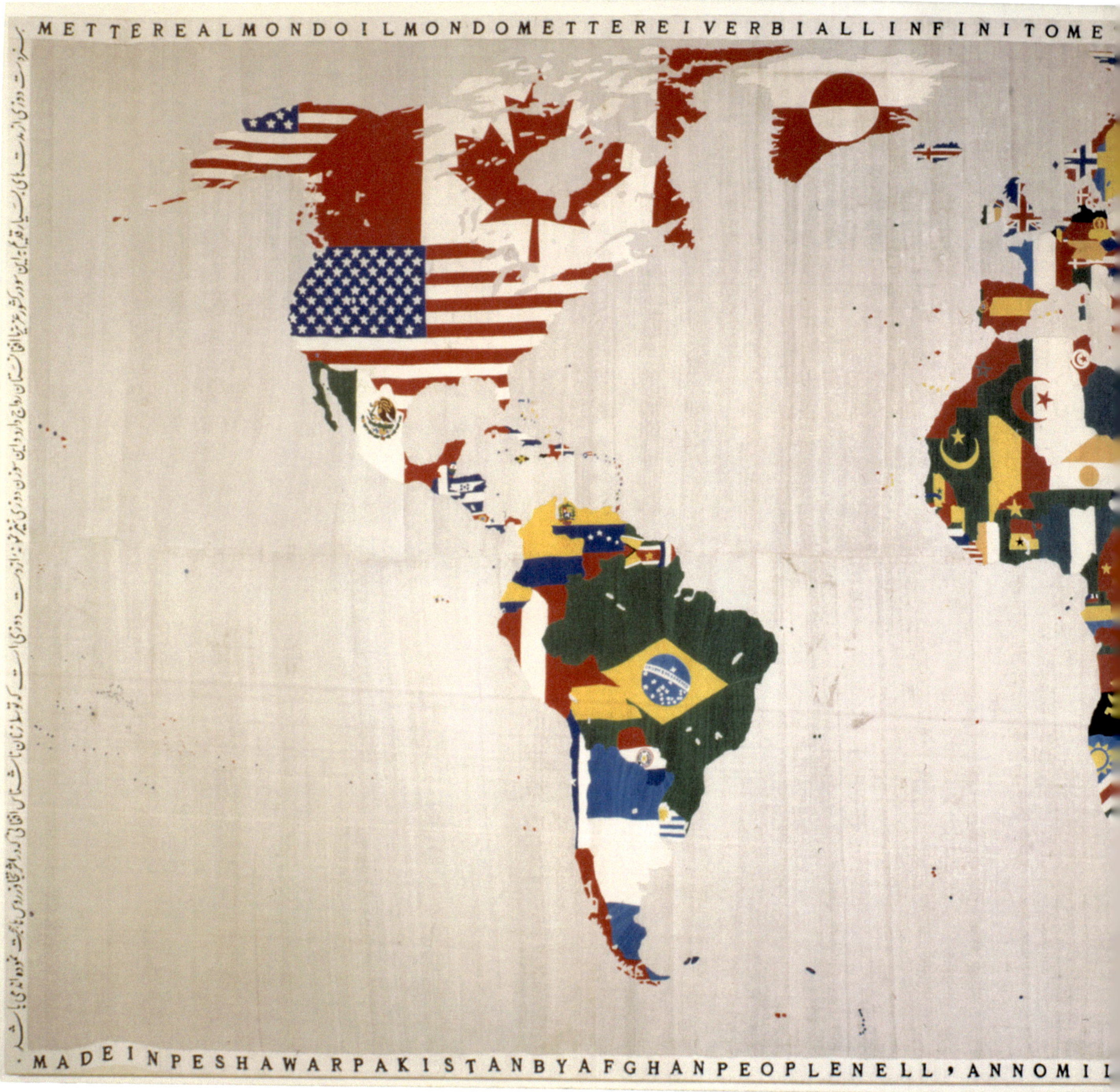
METTEREALMONDOILMONDOMETTEREIVERBIALLINFINITOME
MADEINPESHAWARPAKISTANBYAFGHANPEOPLENELL, ANNOMIL

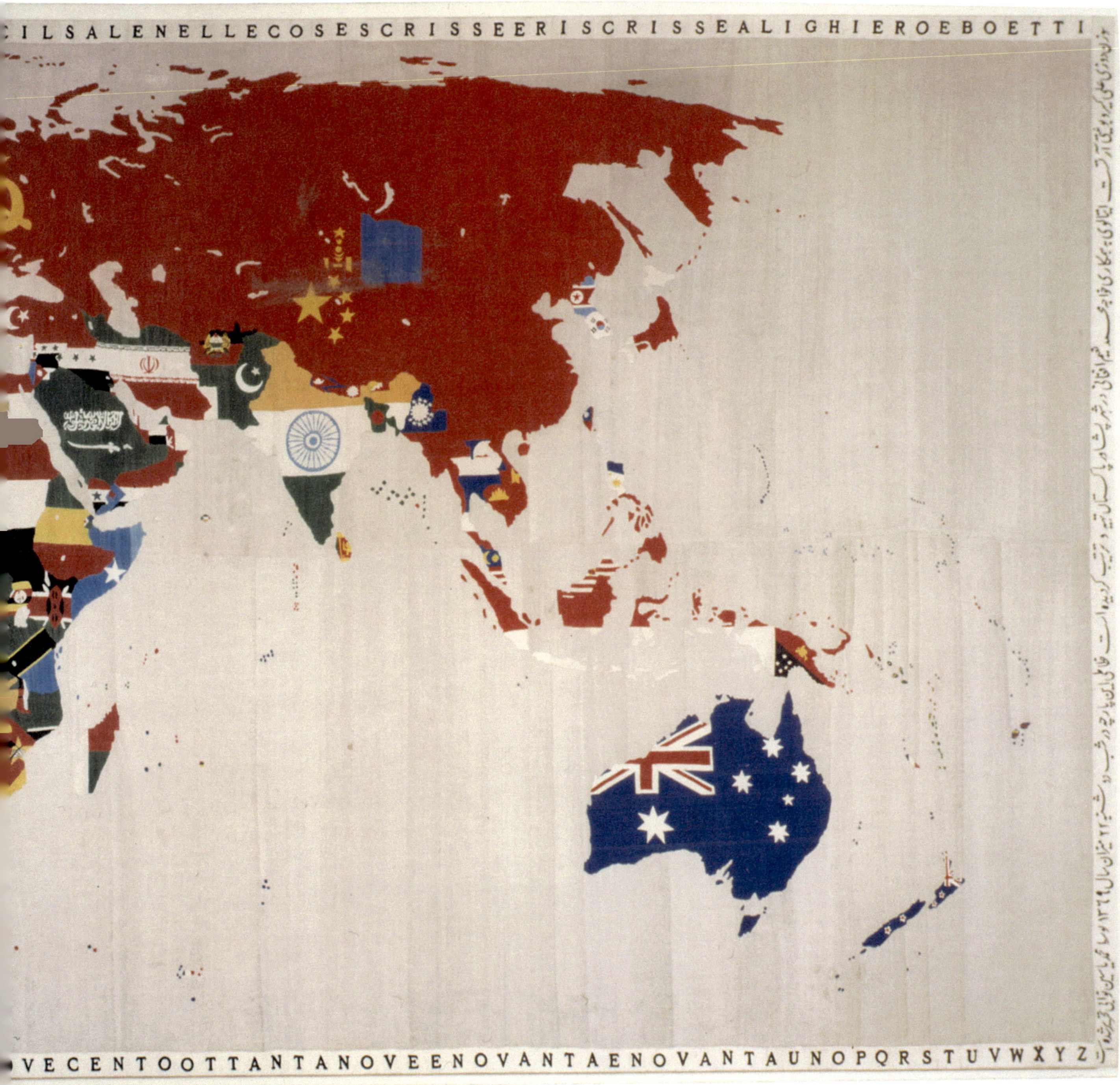

 Mappa (Map), 1989–91

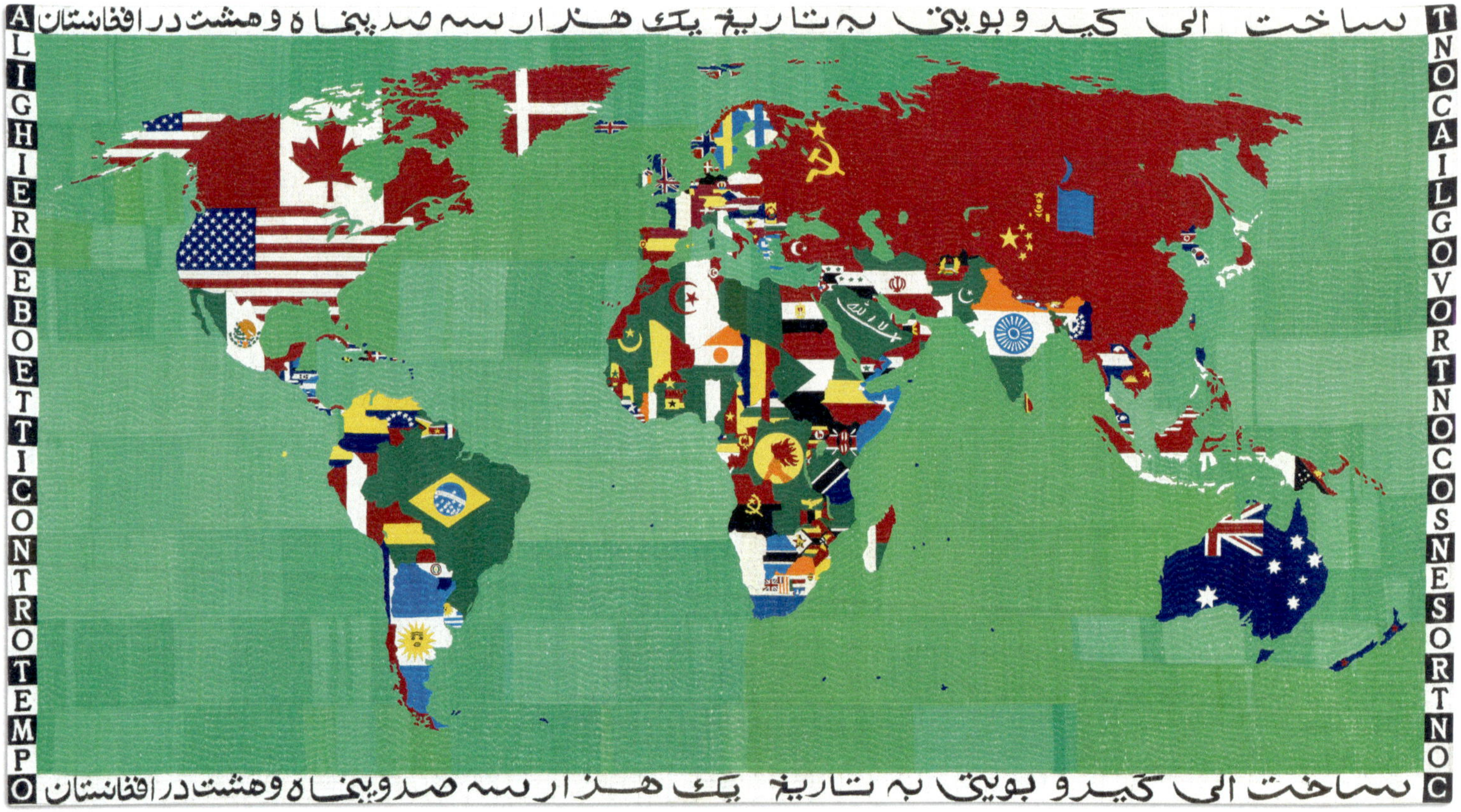

Mappa (Map), 1988

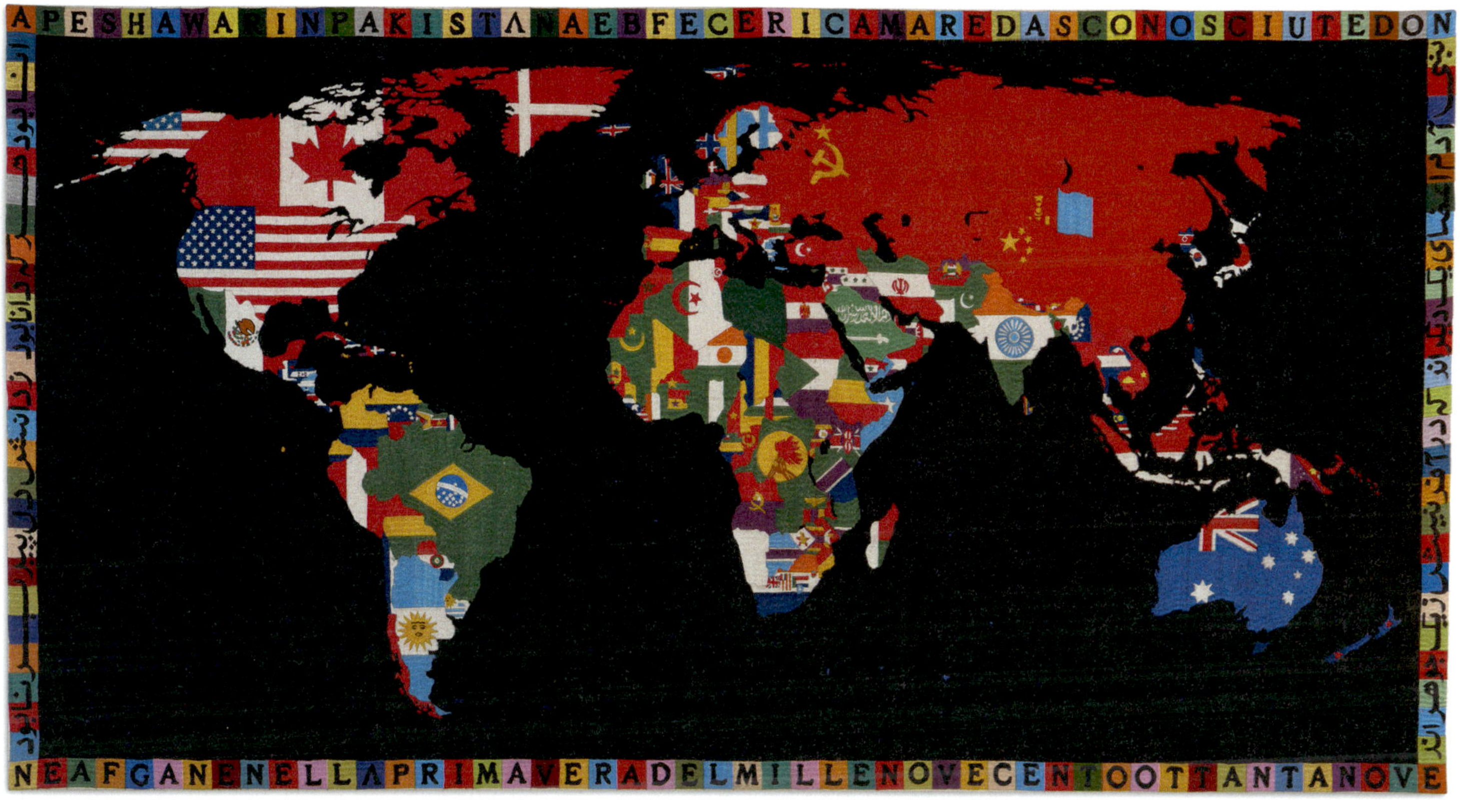

Mappa (Map), 1989

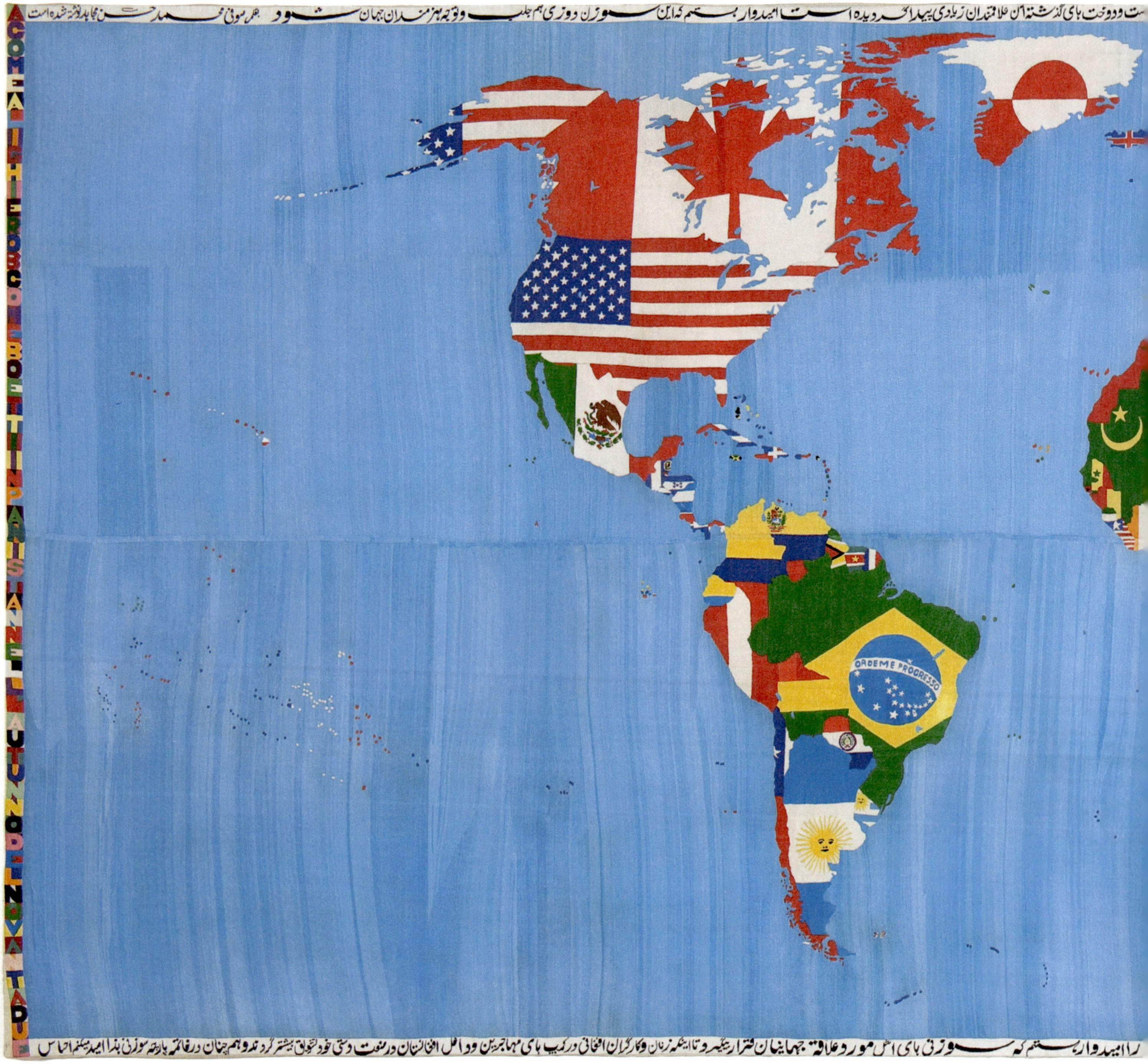
ORDEME PROGRESSO

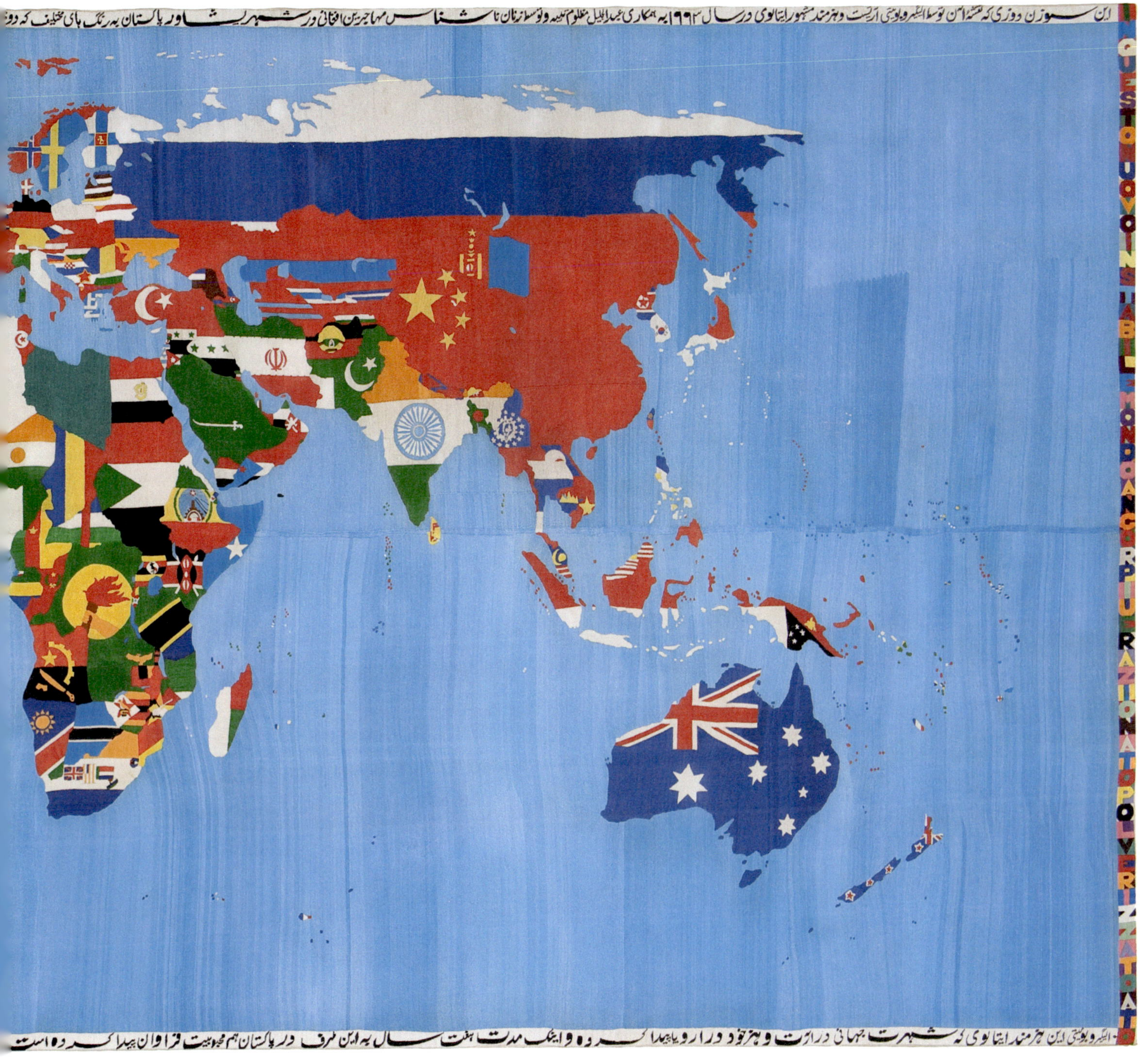

 Mappa (Map), 1989–94

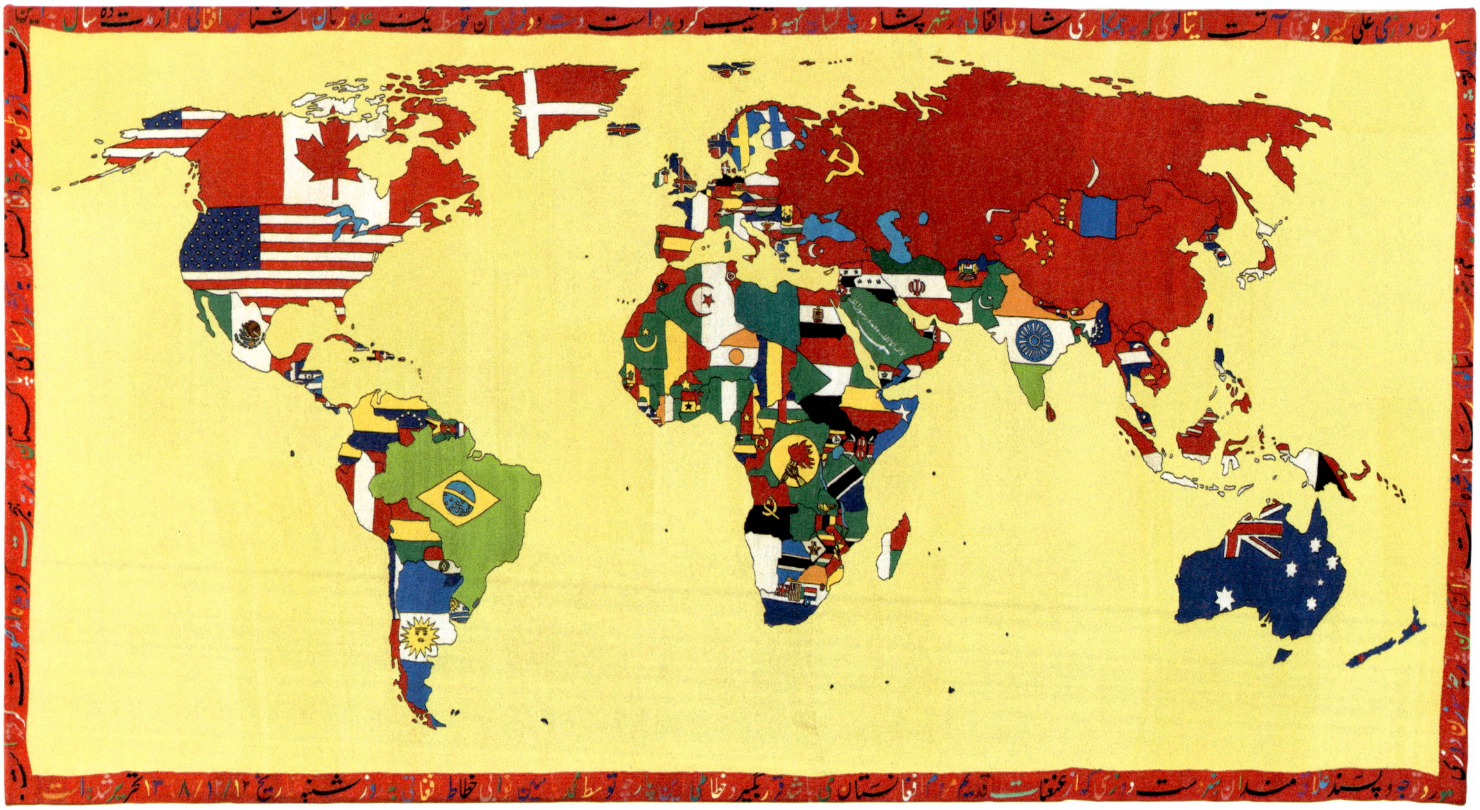

Mappa (Map), 1989

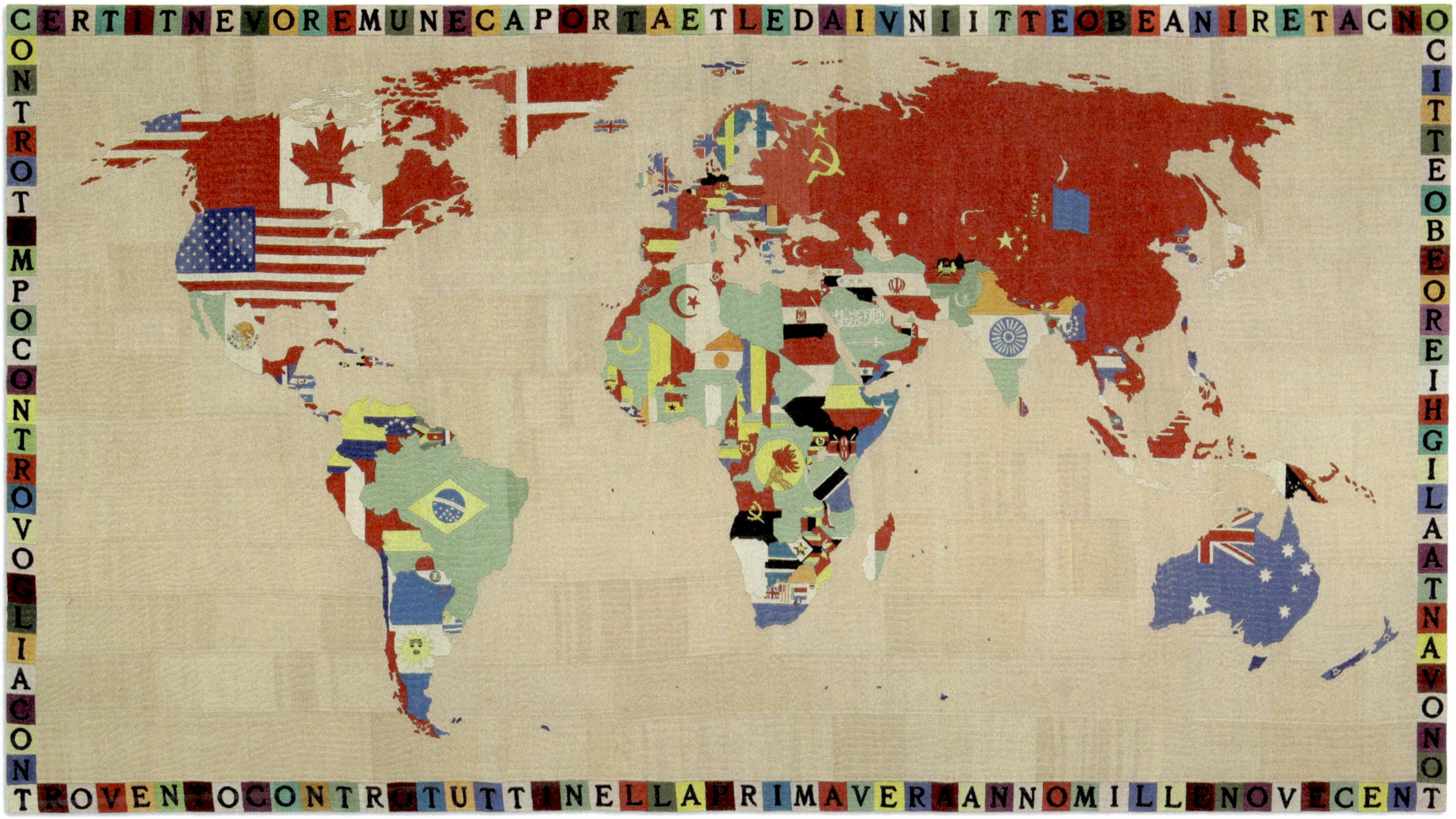

 Mappa (Map), 1990

Far quadrare tutto (Make Everything Fit In), 1979

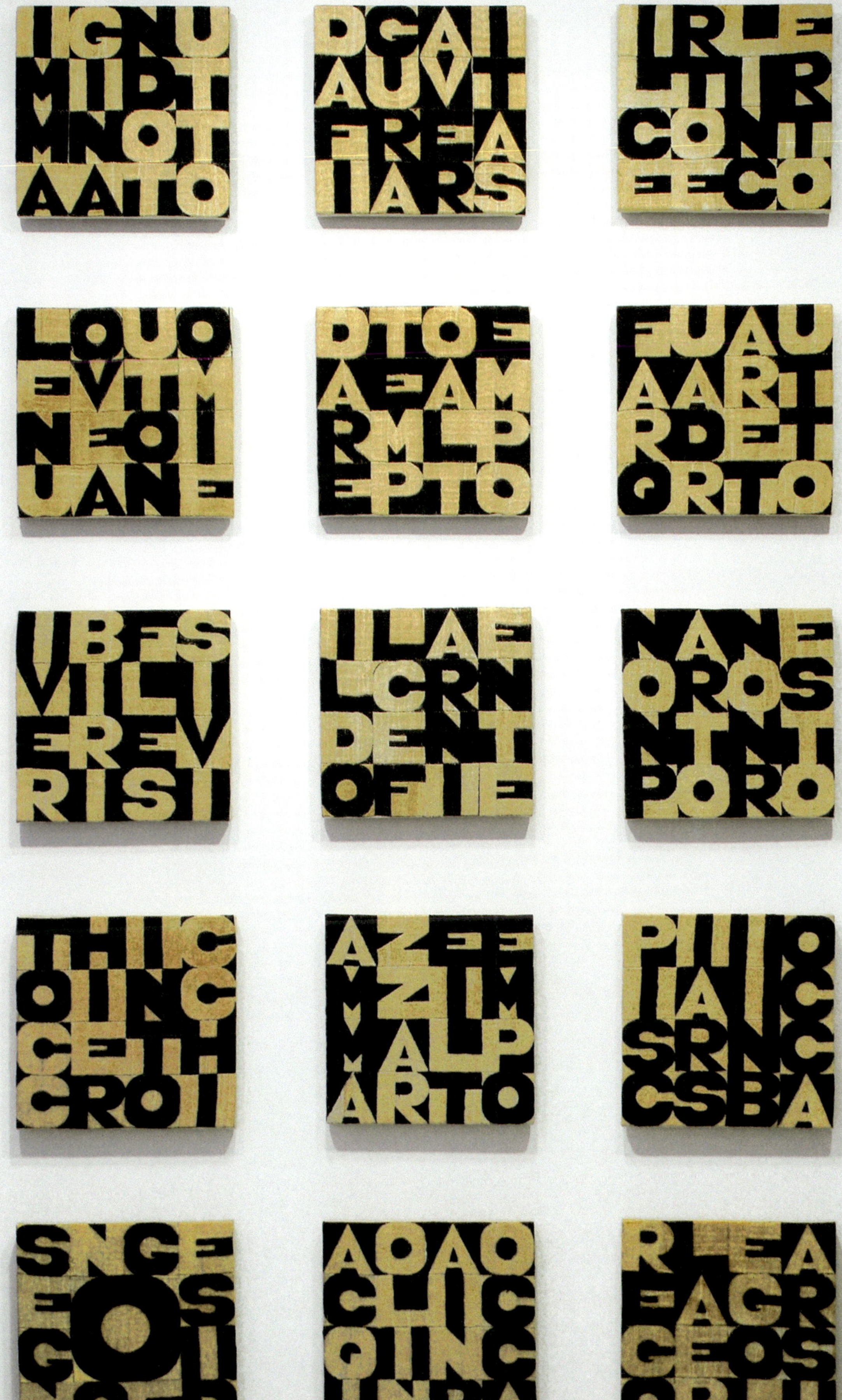

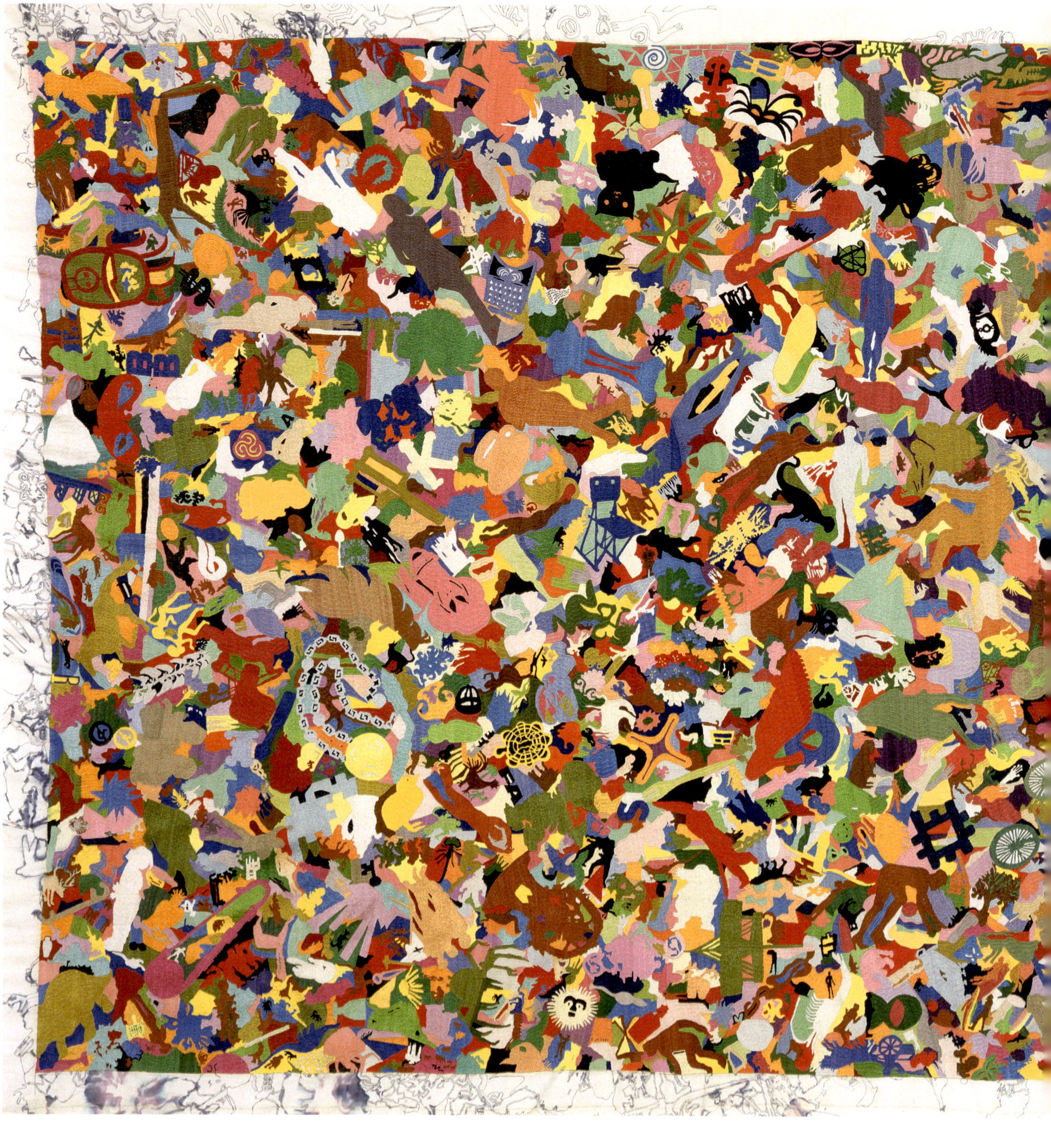

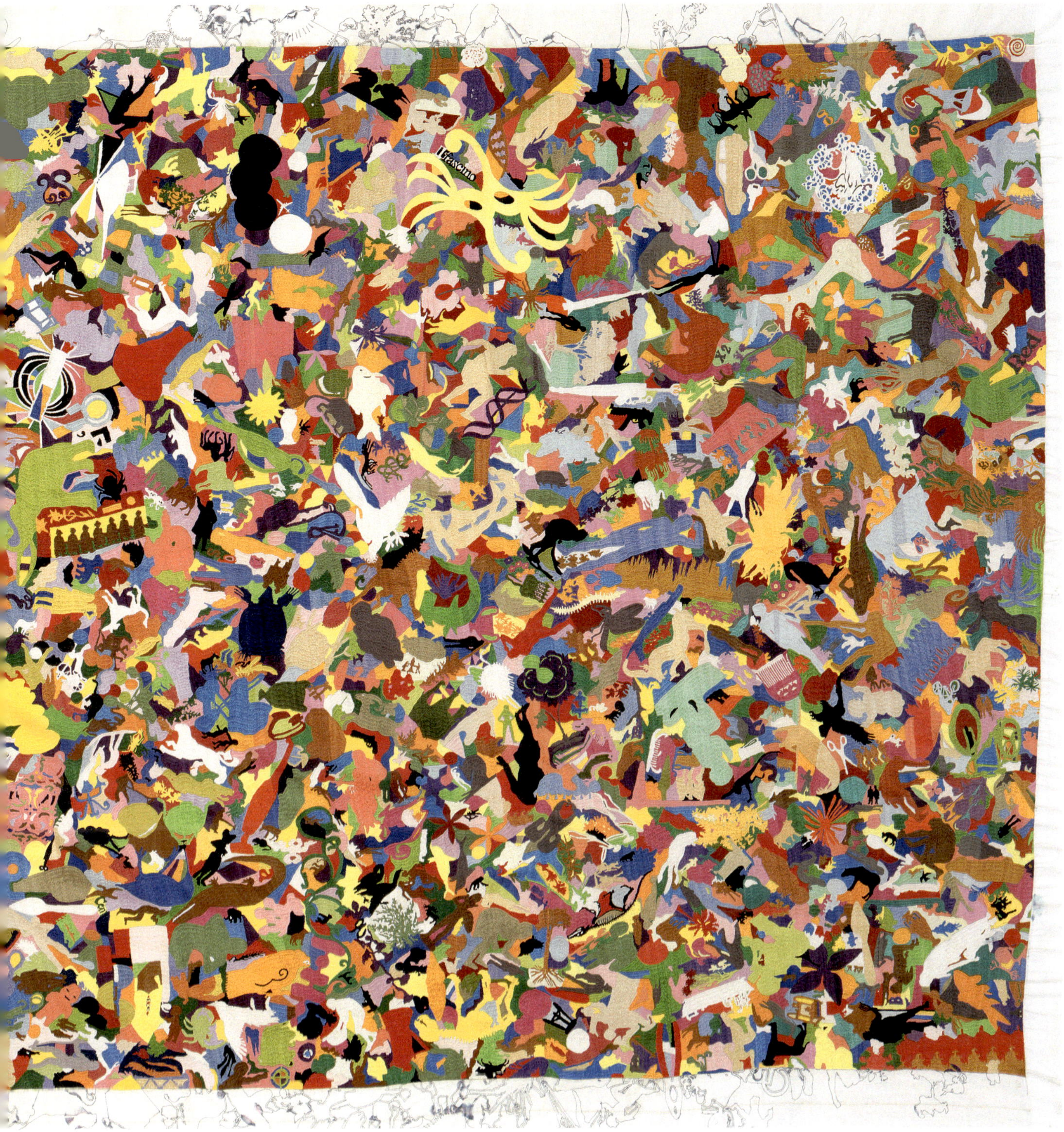

 Tutto (Everything), 1992–93

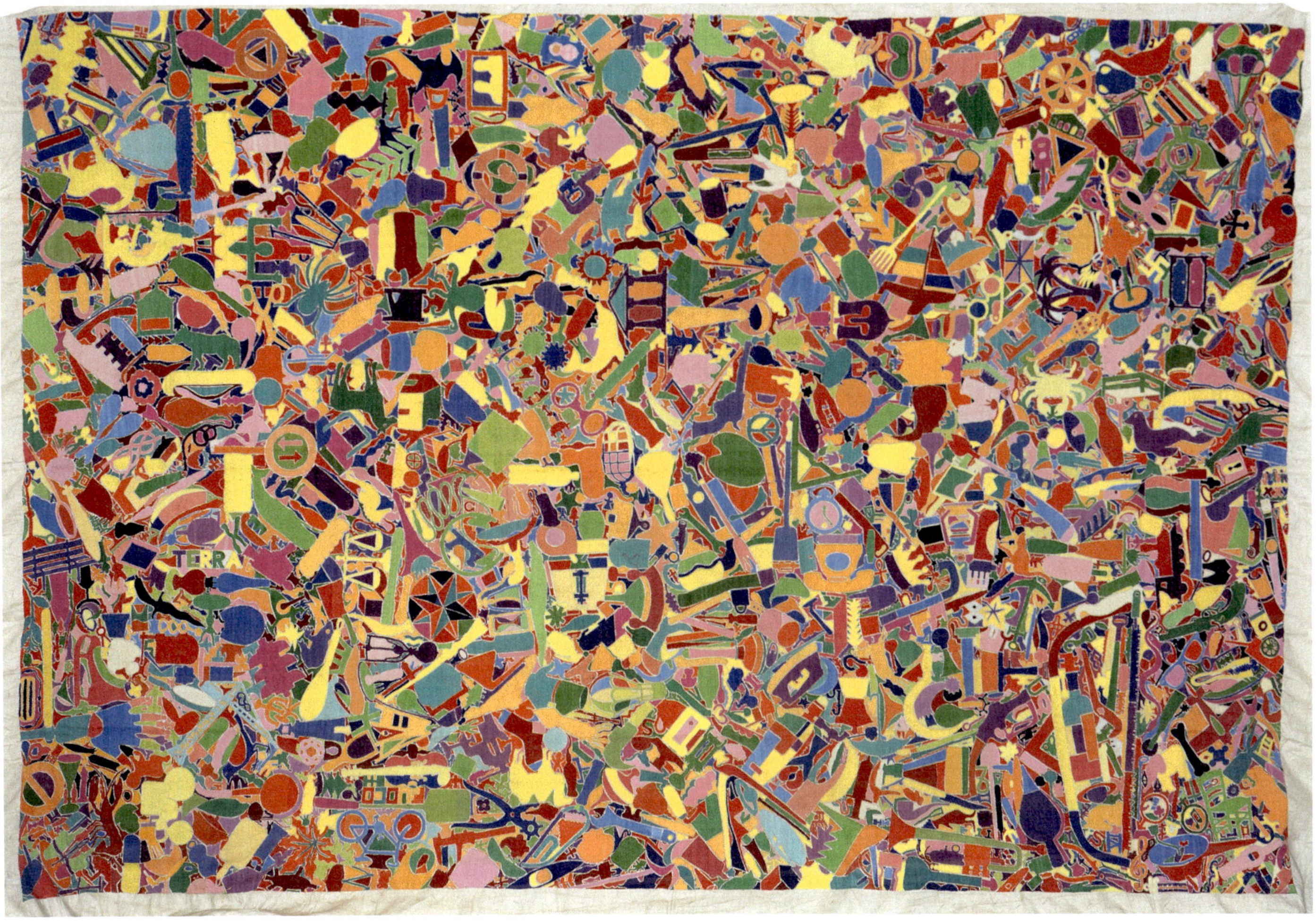

 Tutto (Everything), 1989

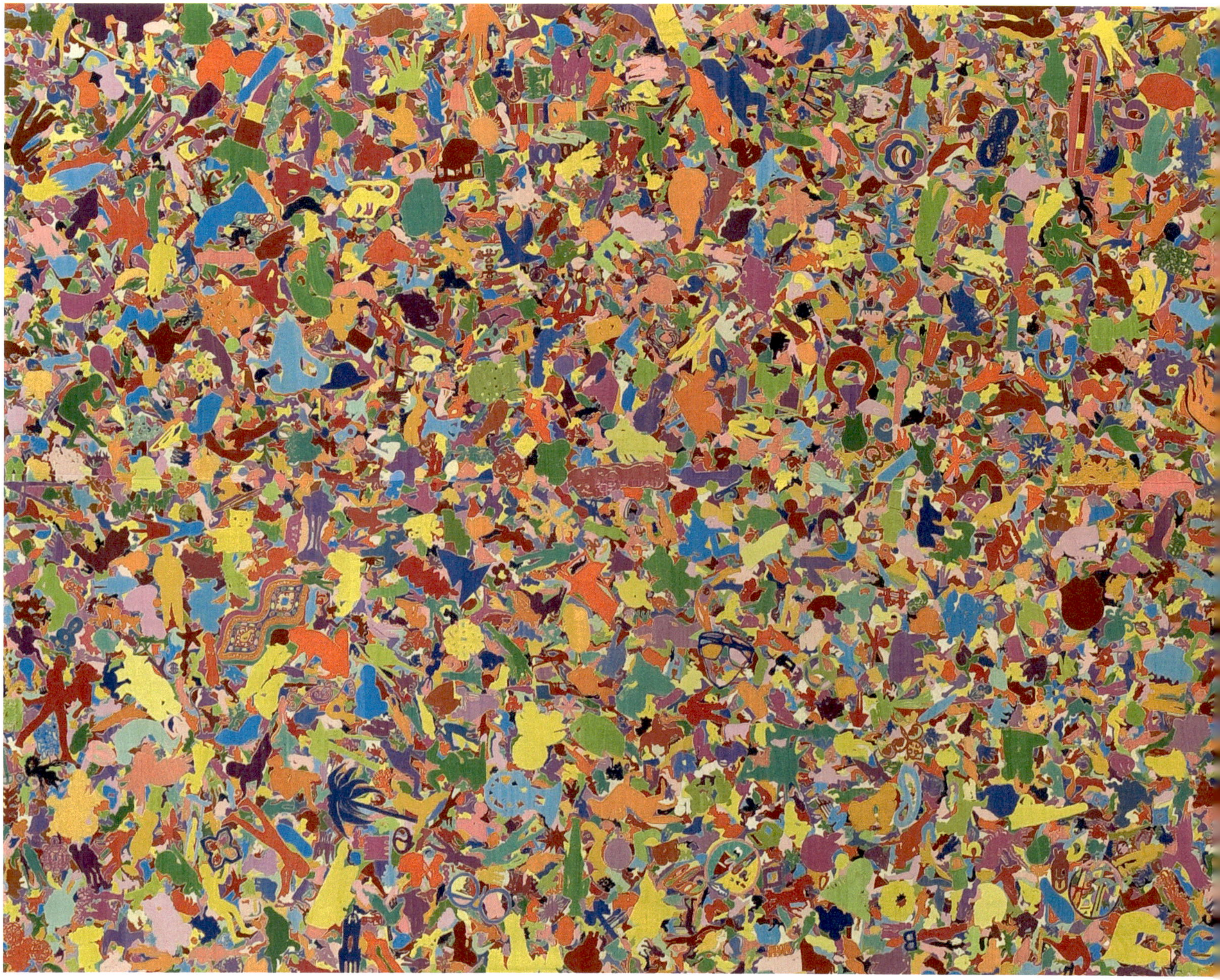

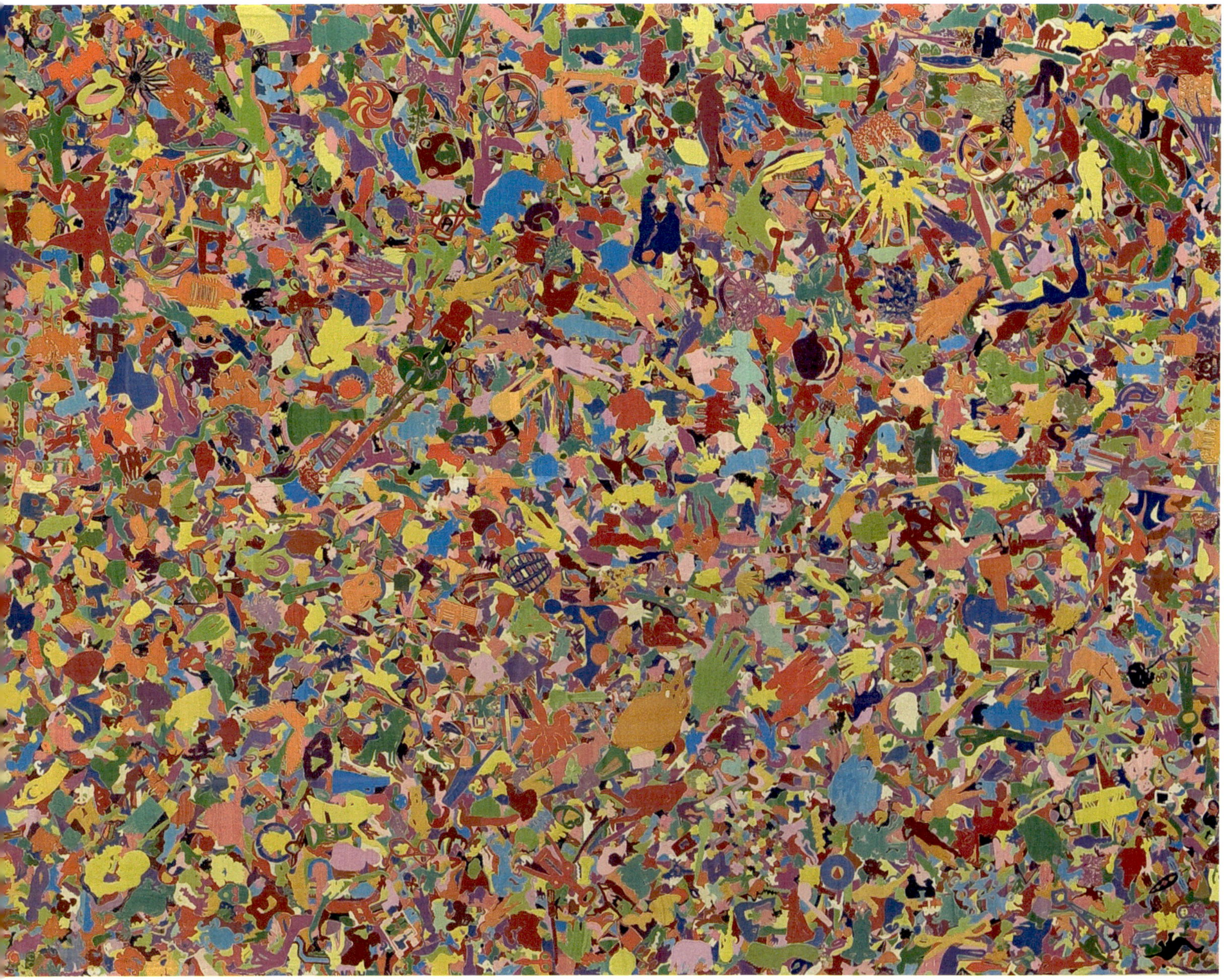

 Tutto (Everything), 1994

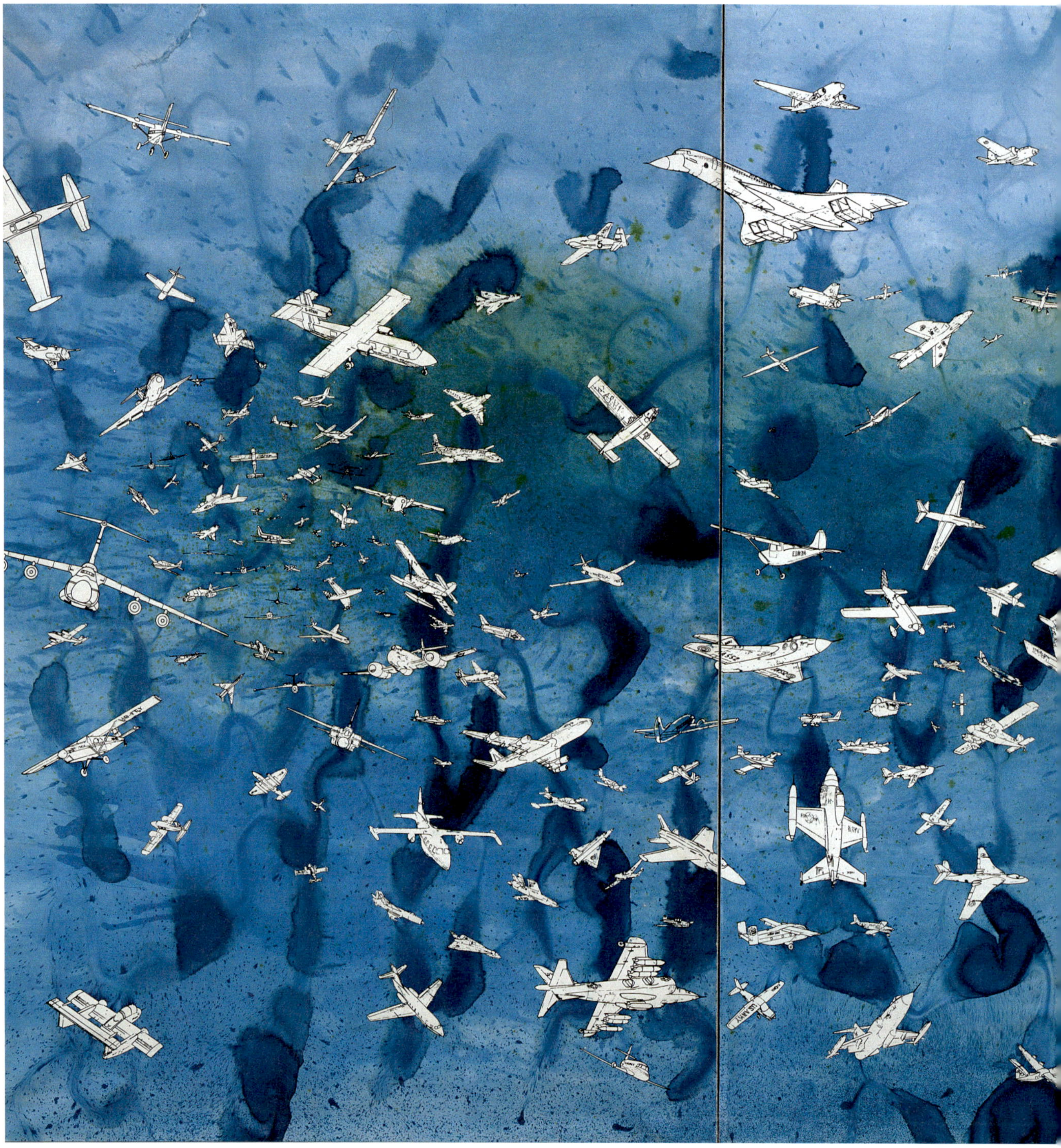

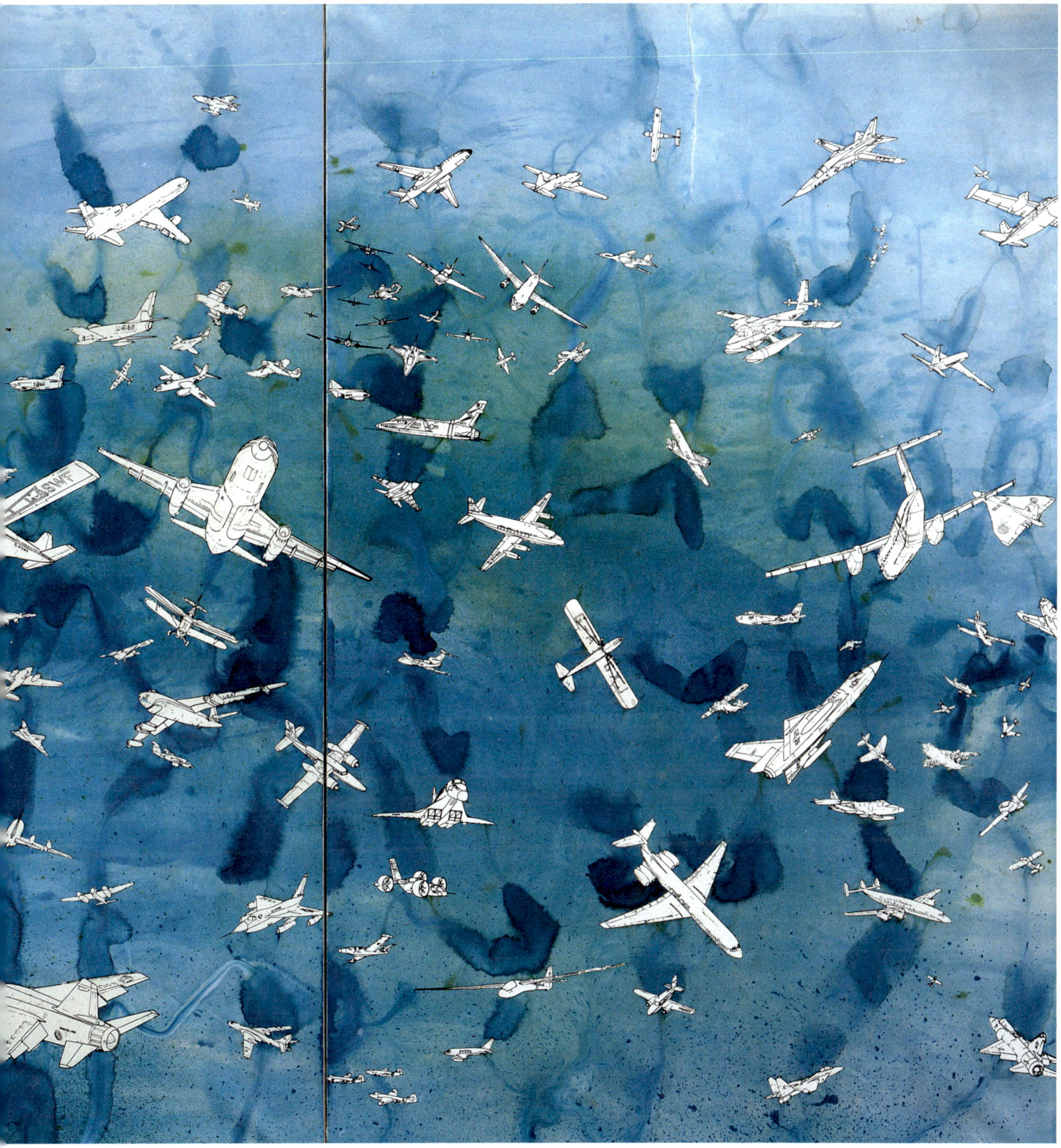

 Aerei (Aeroplanes), 1989

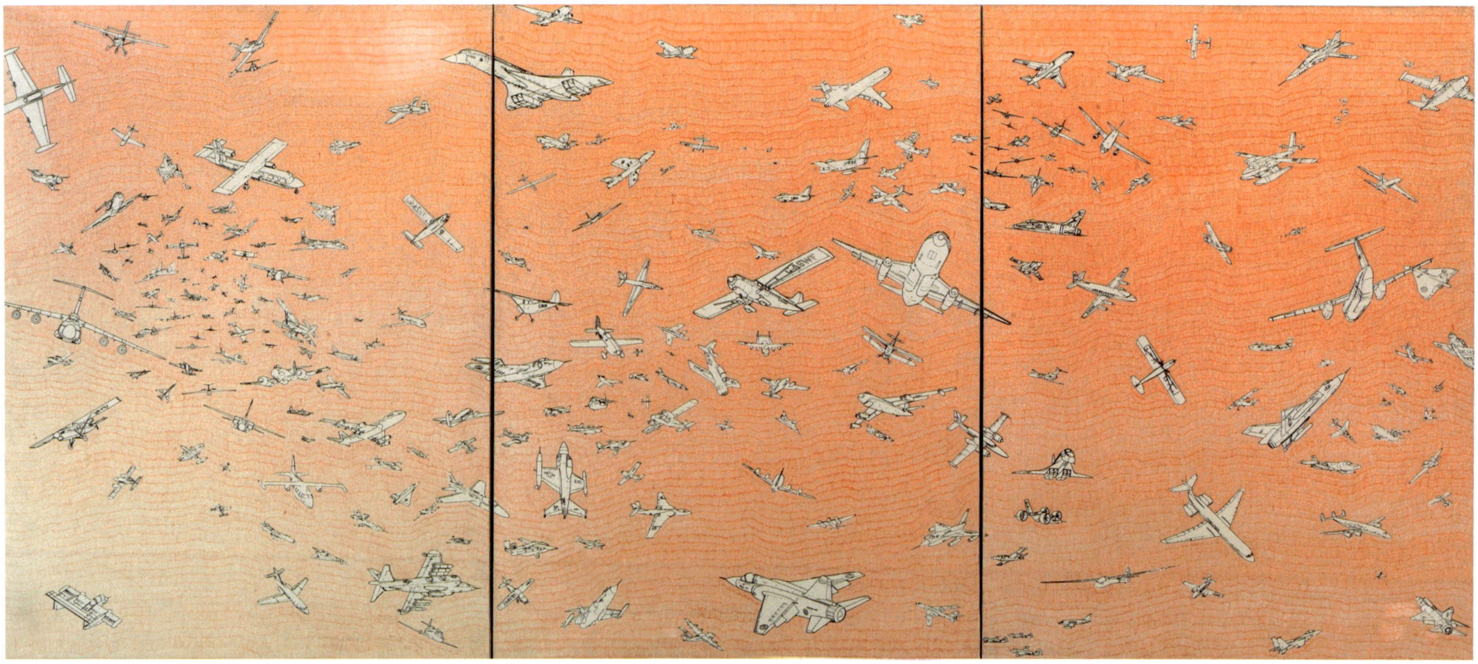

Aerei (Aeroplanes), 1984

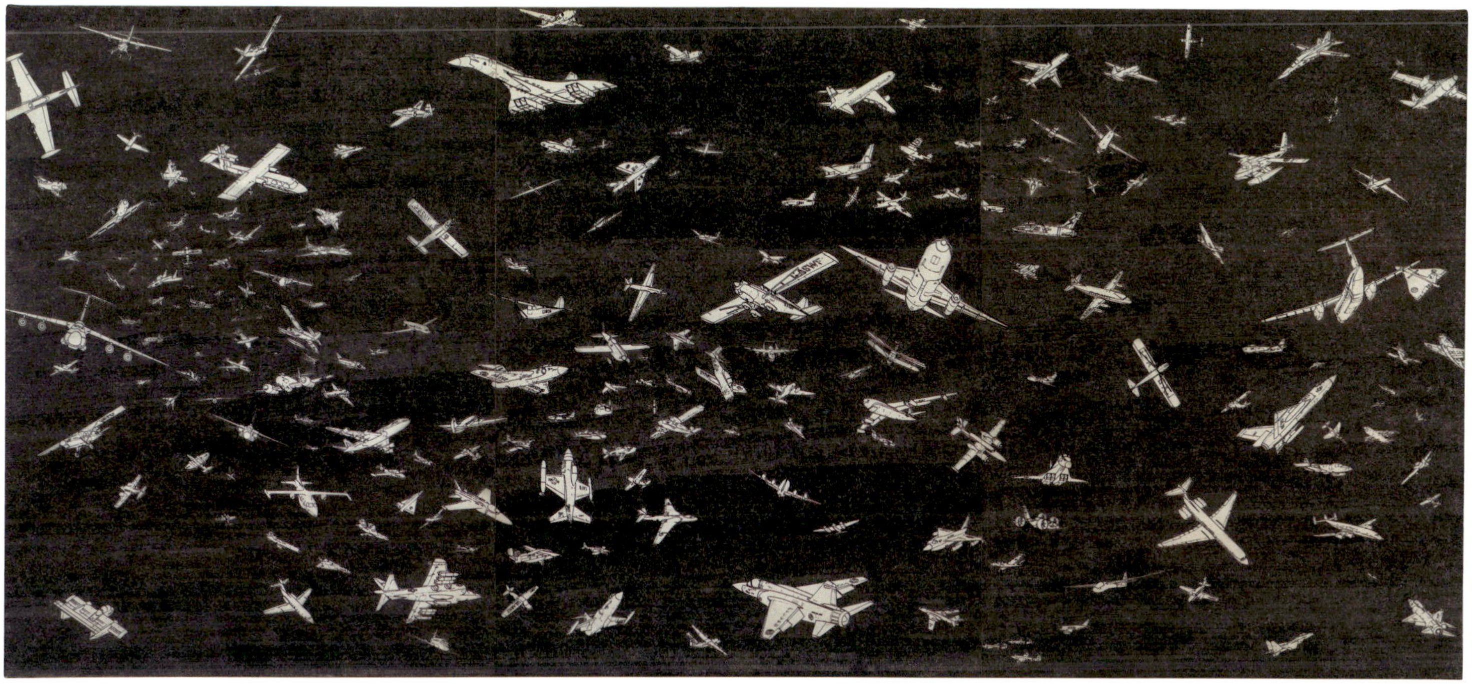

 Aerei (Aeroplanes), 1978

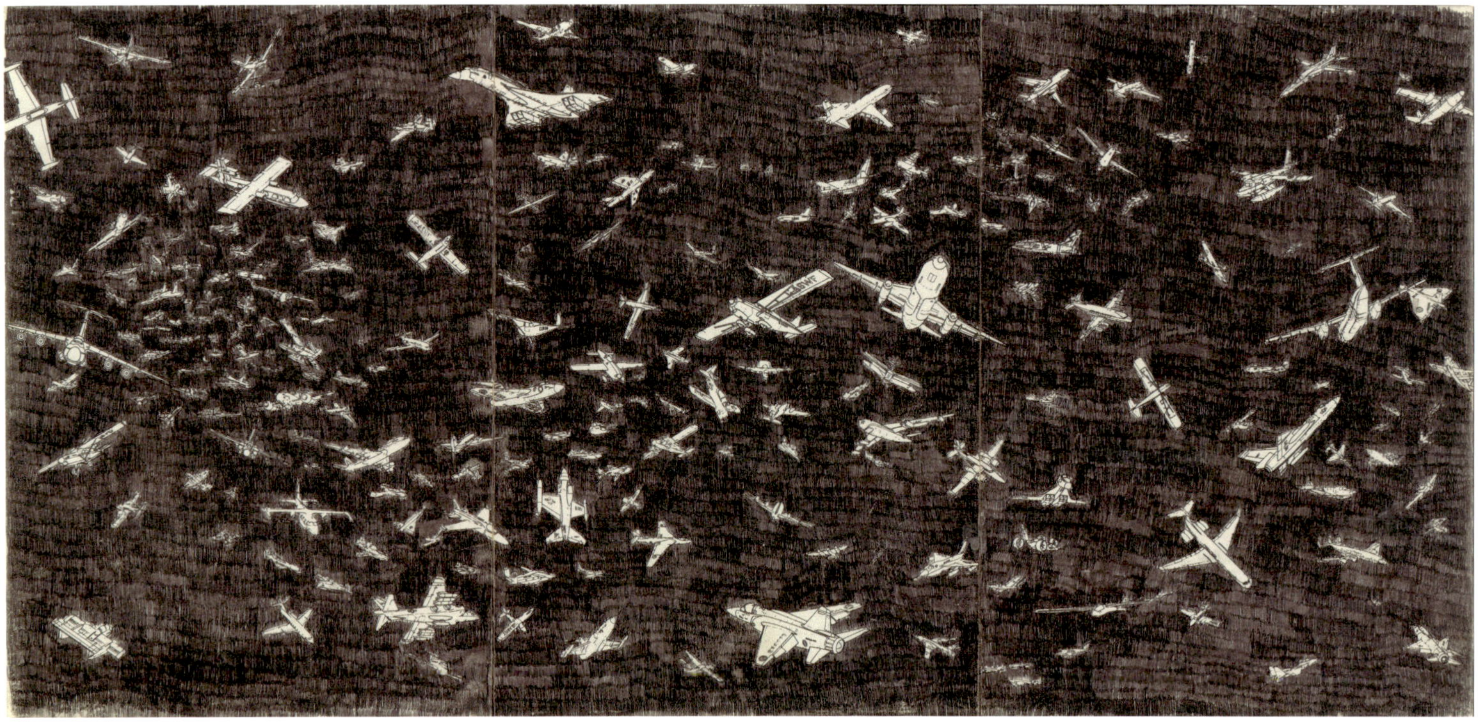

Aerei (Aeroplanes), 1983

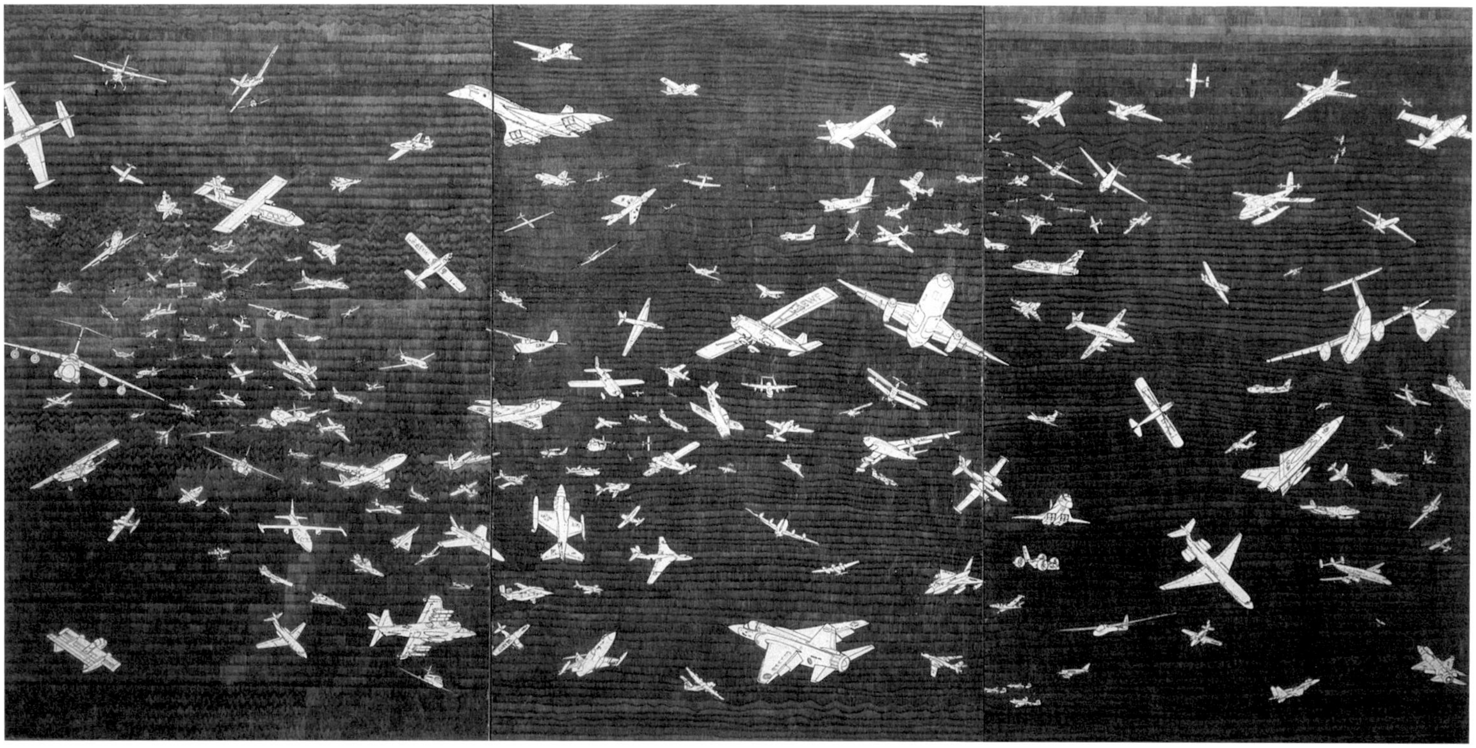

 Aerei (Aeroplanes), 1978

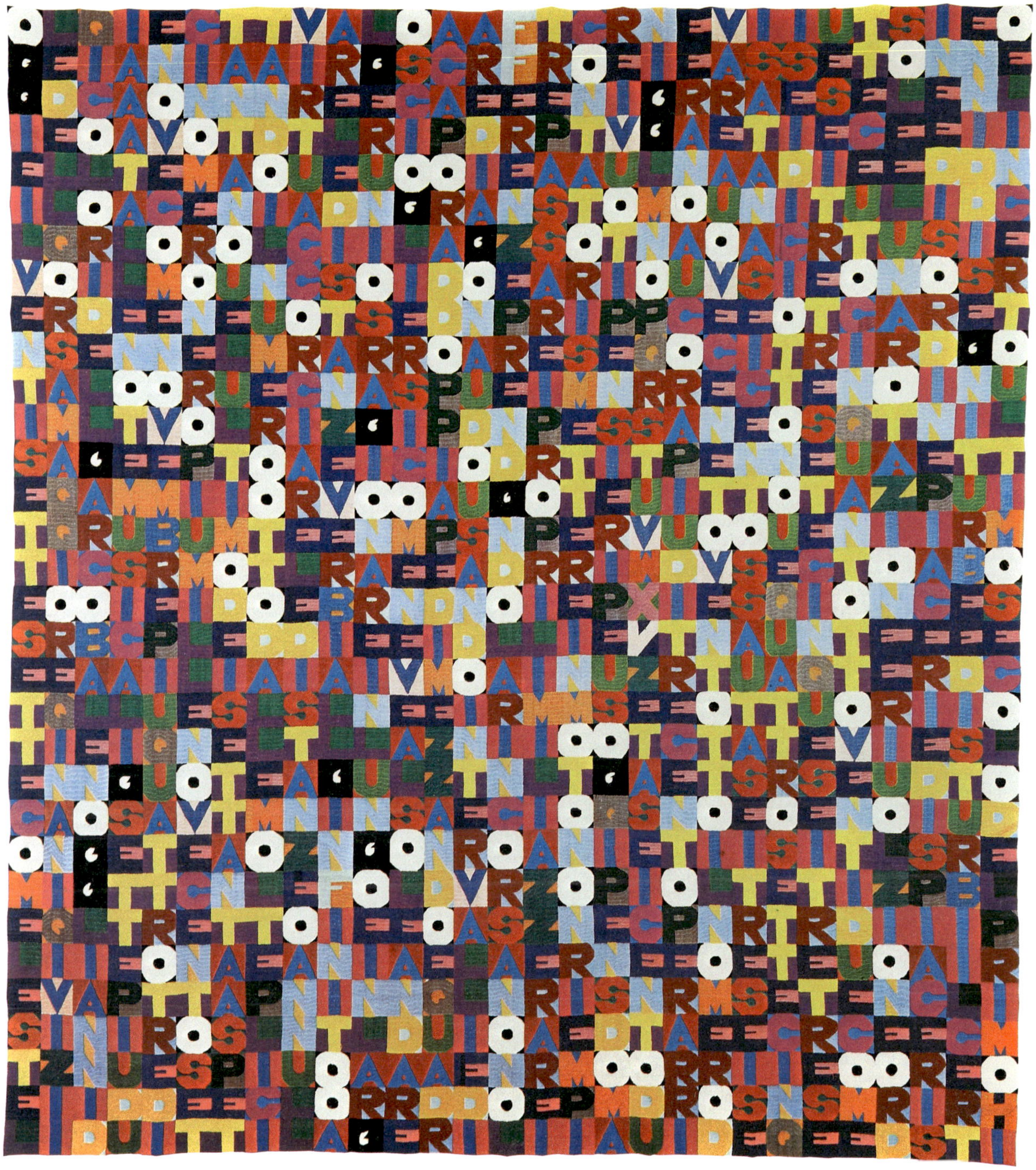

 Titoli (Titles), 1980

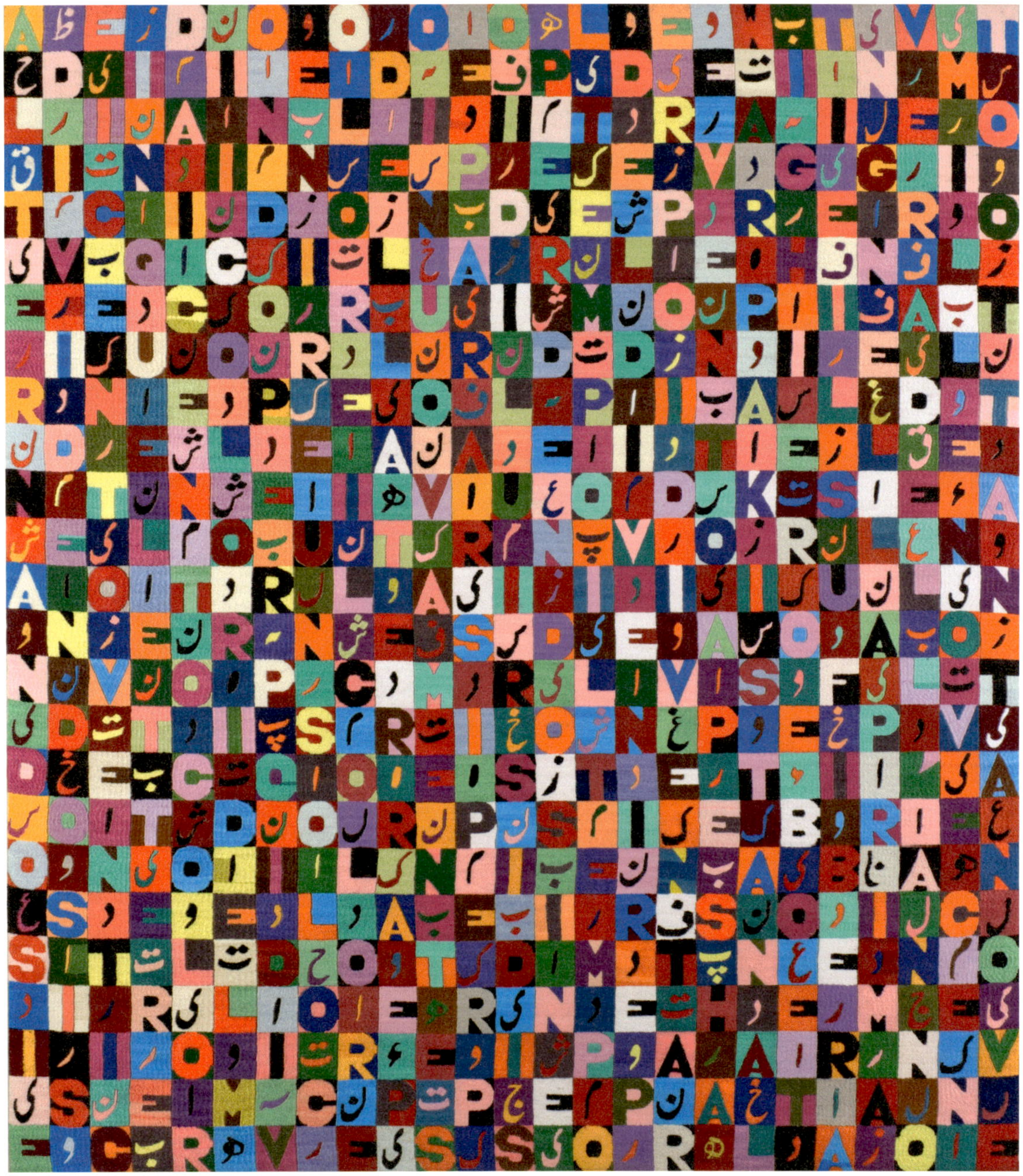

Untitled, 1989

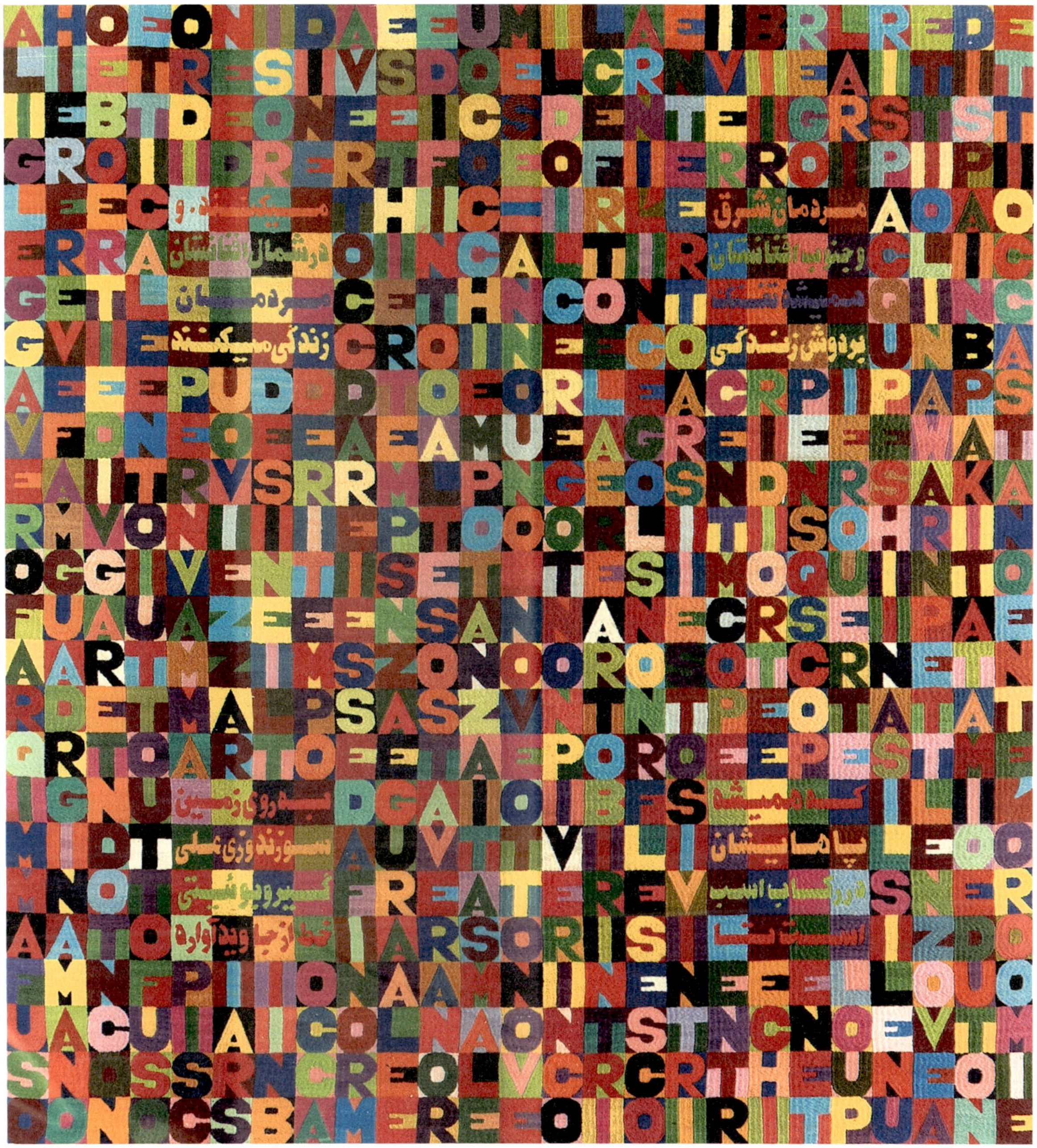

 27 maggio 1988 (May 27, 1988), 1988

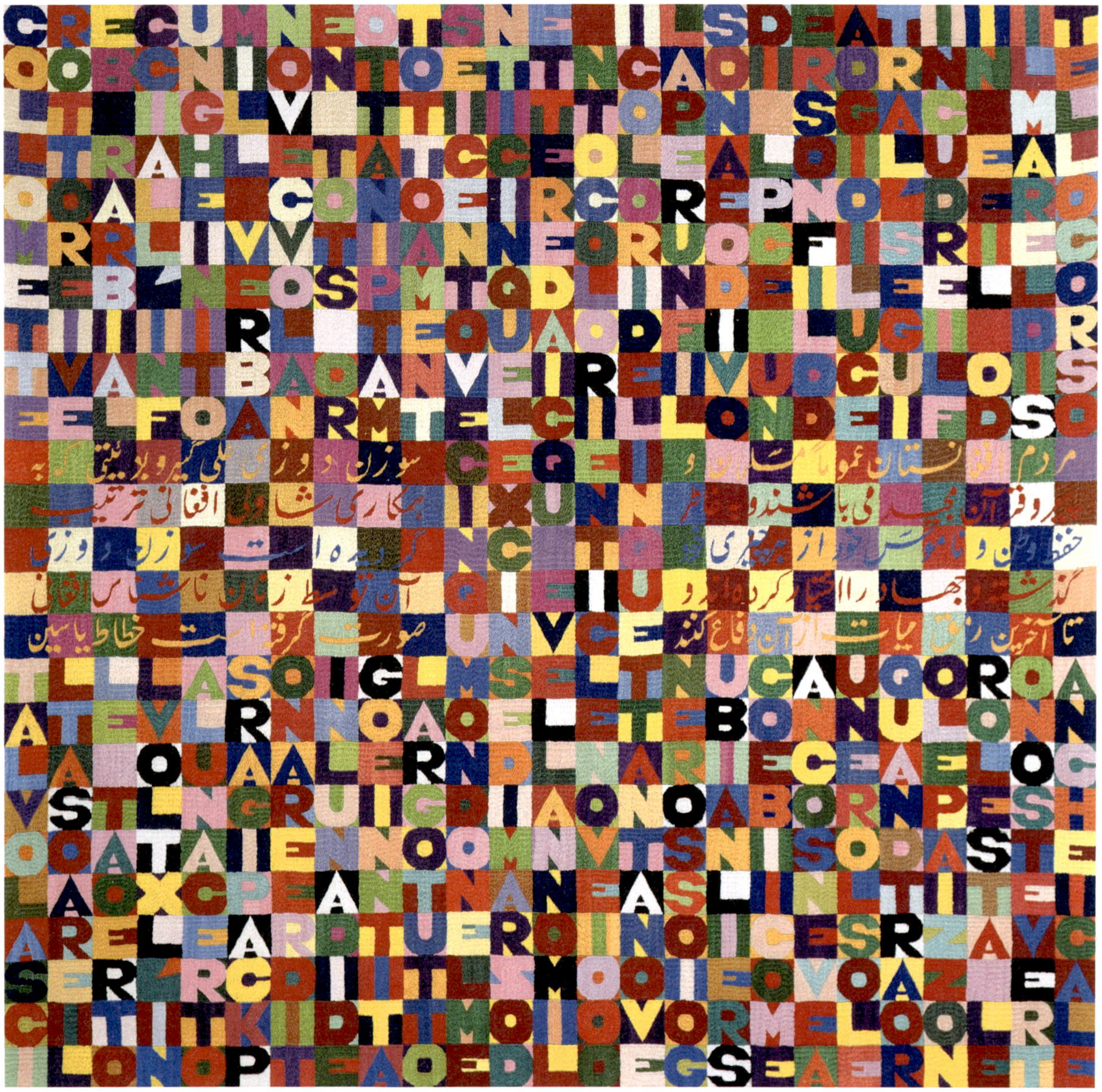

Senza titolo (Mese di marzo dell' anno mille nove 100 ottanta nove) (Untitled [The Month of March of the Year One Thousand Nine Hundred and Eighty-nine]), 1989

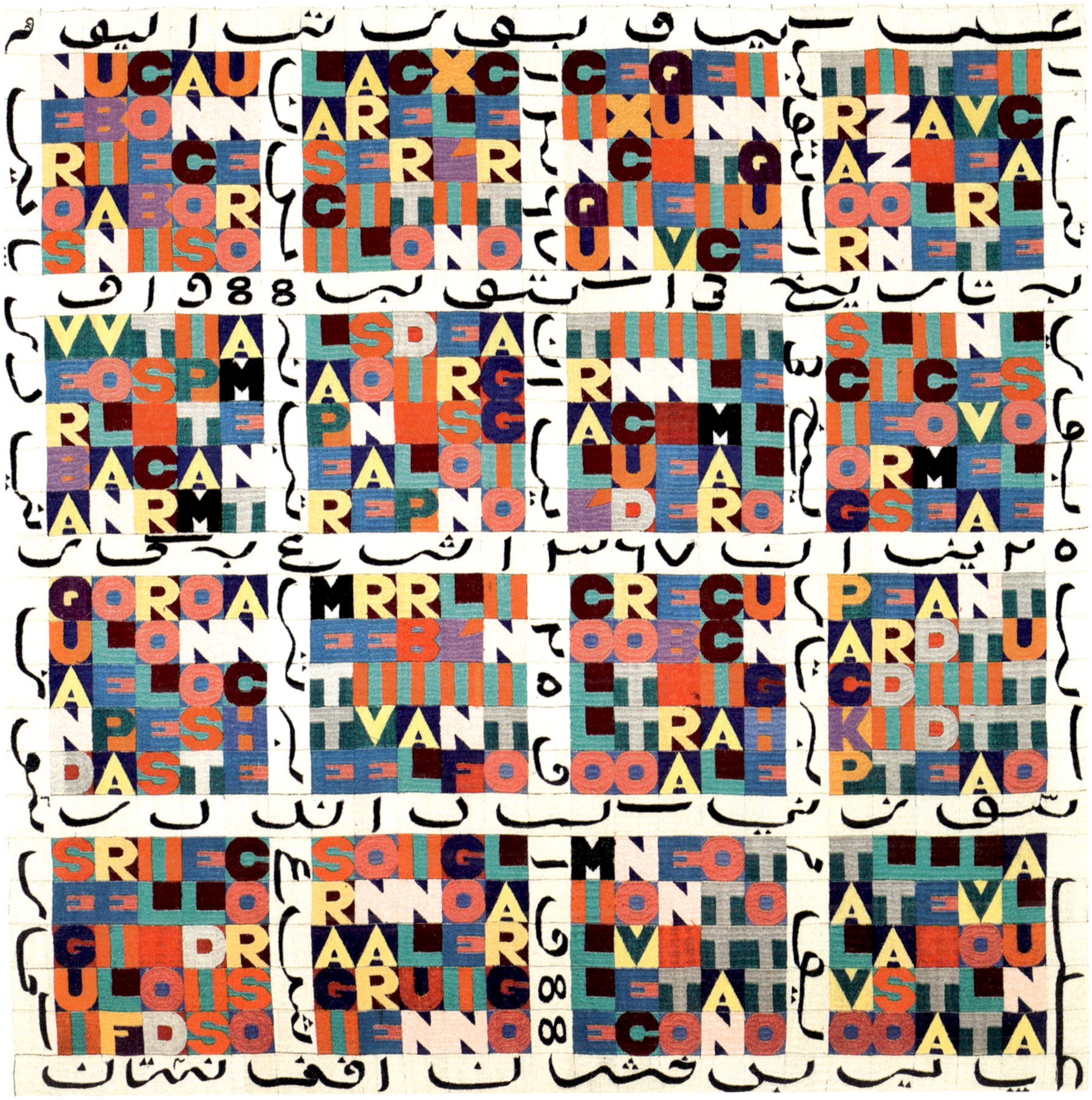

Senza titolo (nero su bianco, bianco su nero) (Untitled [Black on White, White on Black]), 1989

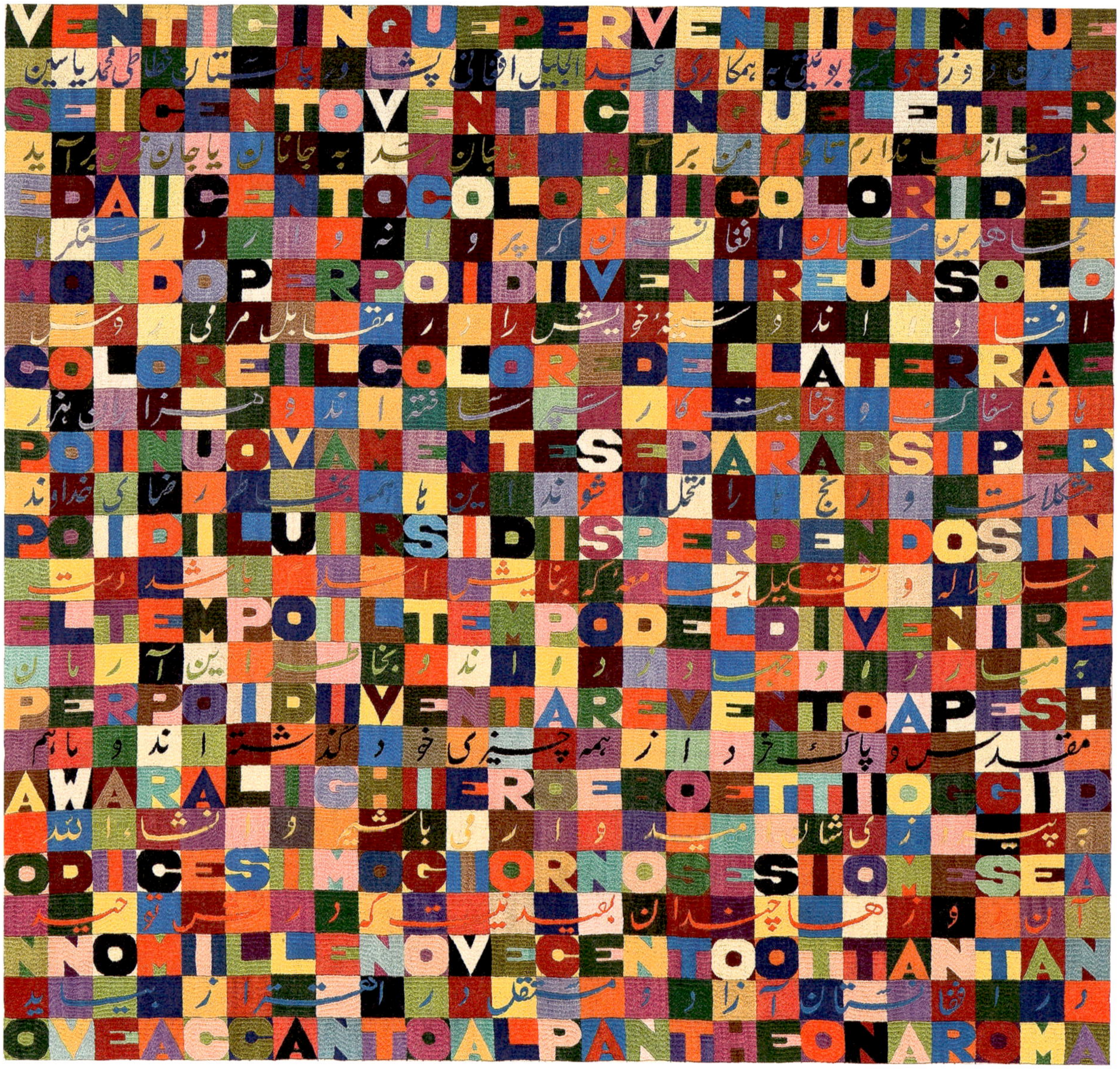

Oggi dodicesimo giorno sesto mese anno mille novecento ottantanove (Today the Twelfth Day of the Sixth Month of the Year One Thousand Nine Hundred and Eighty-nine), 1989

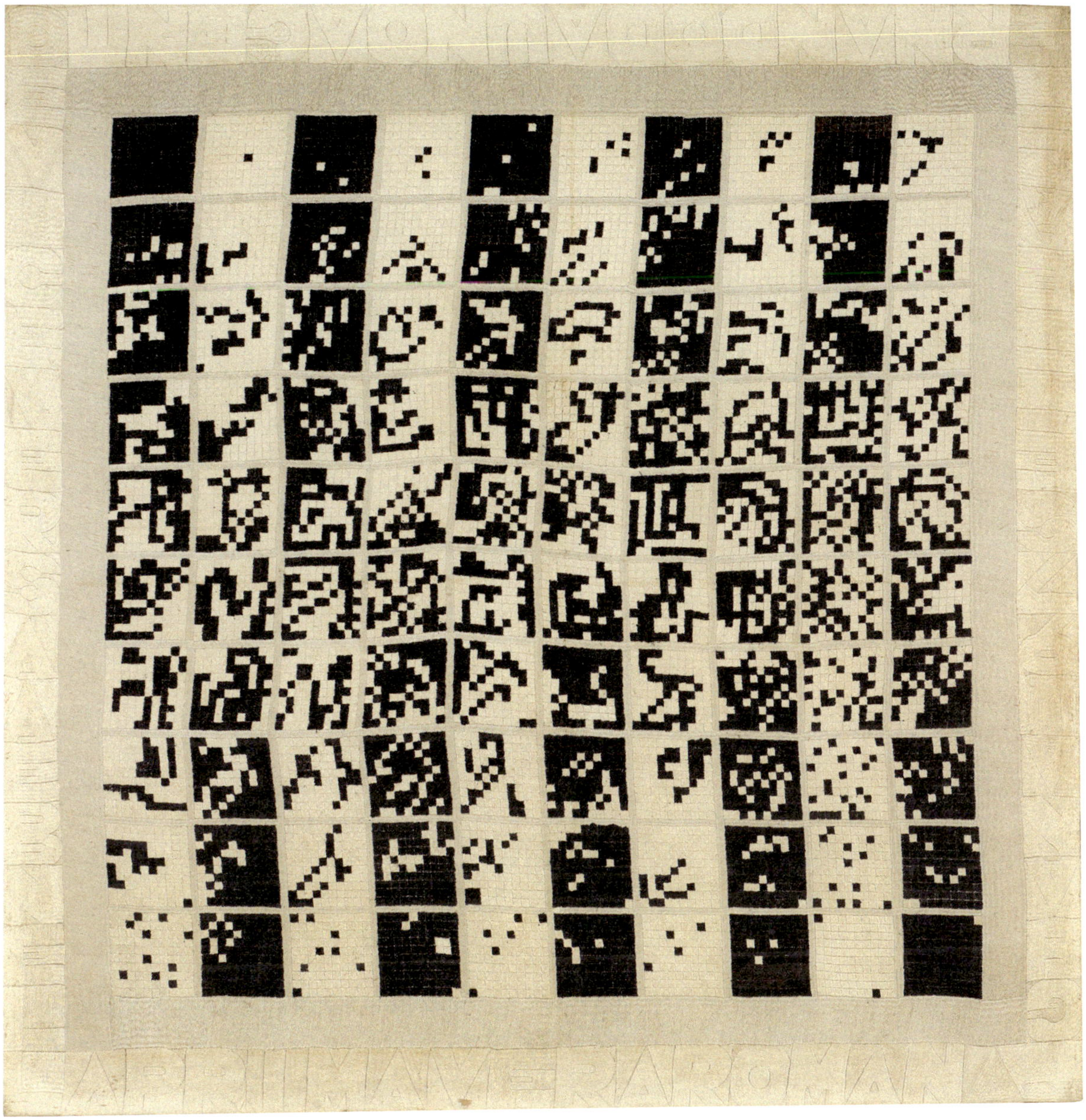

Alternando da uno a cento e viceversa (Alternating from One to One Hundred and Vice Versa), 1977–78

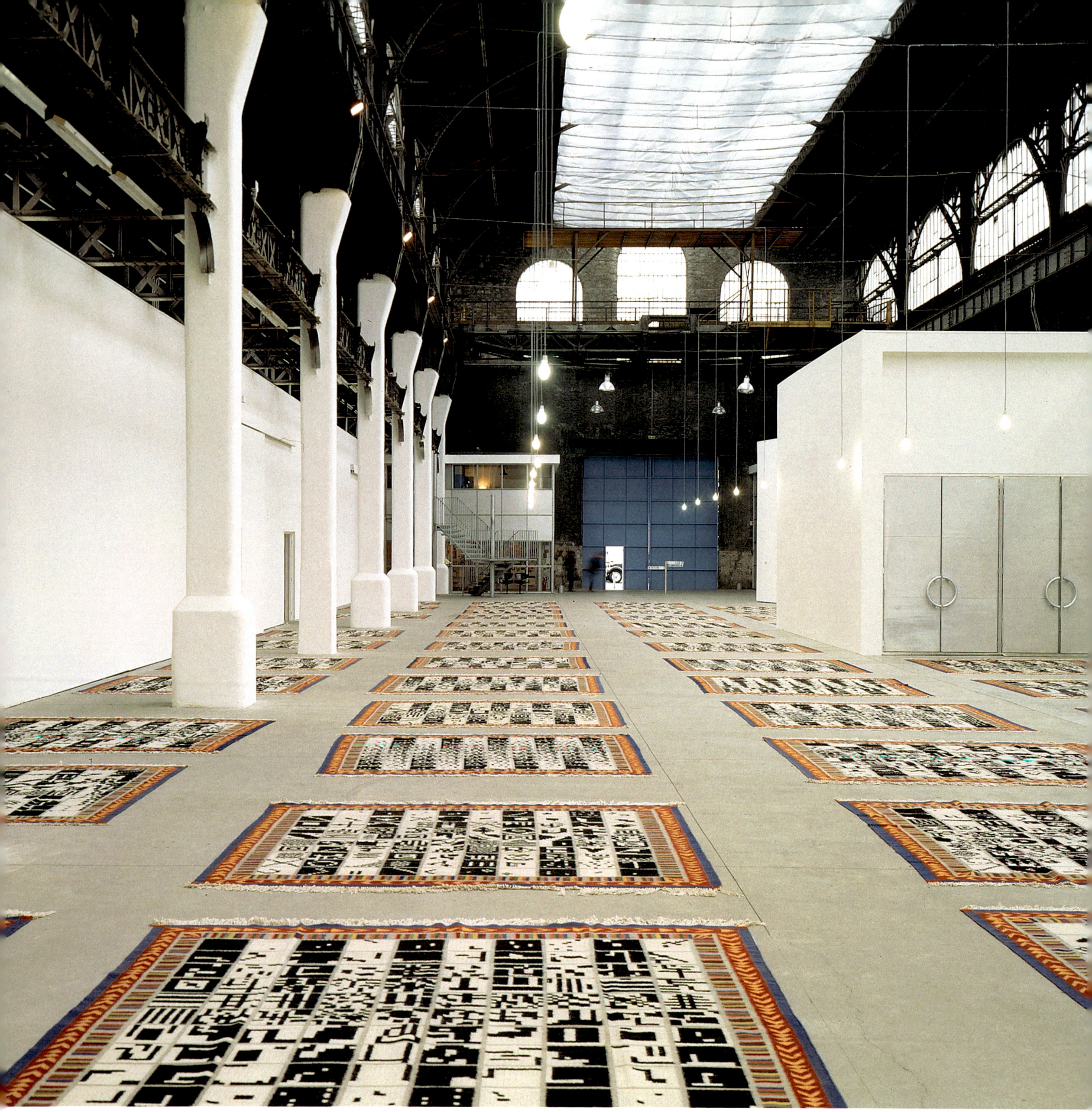

Alternando da uno a cento e viceversa (Alternating from One to a Hundred and Vice Versa), 1993

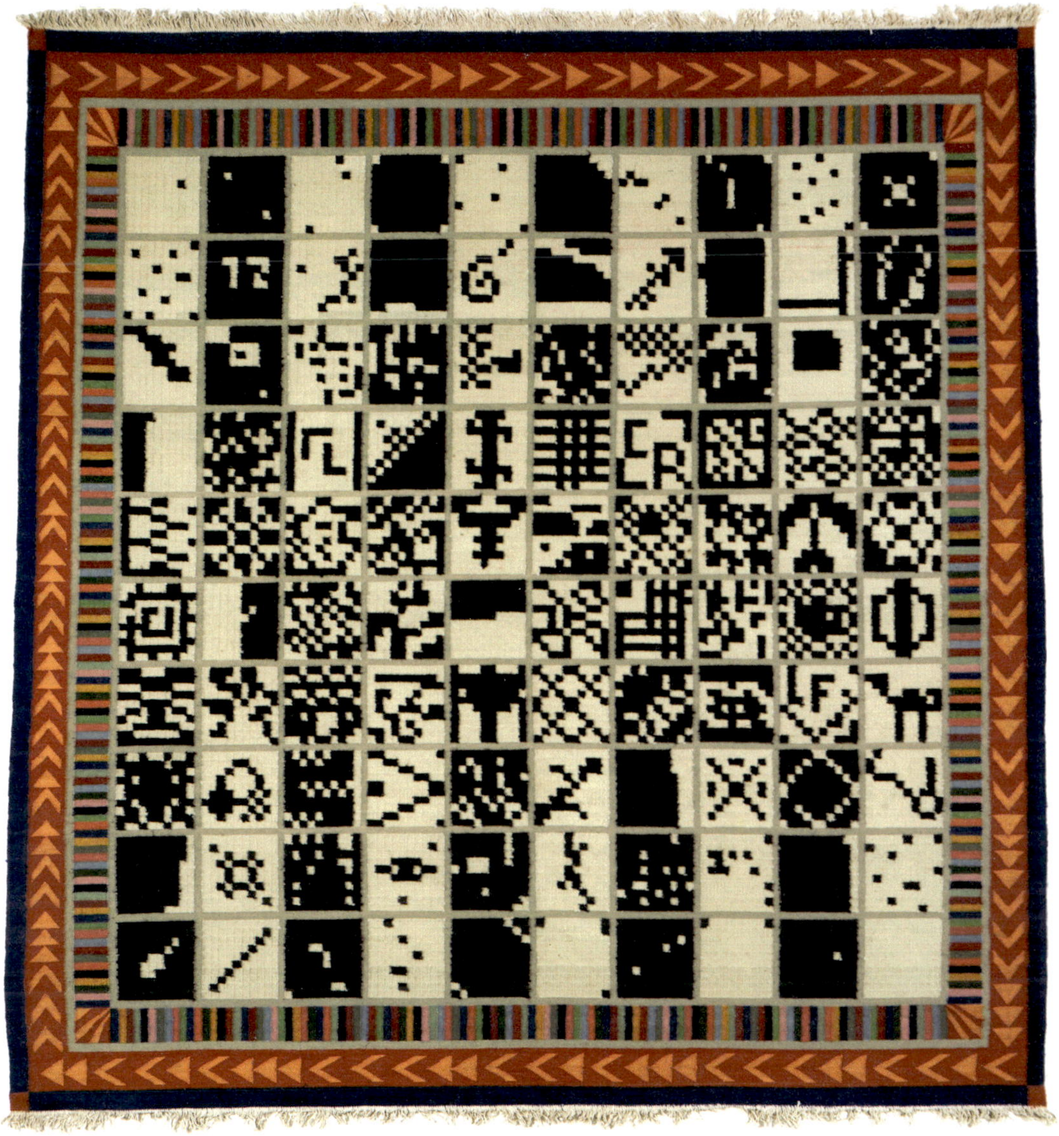

 Alternando da uno a cento e viceversa (Alternating from One to a Hundred and Vice Versa), 1993

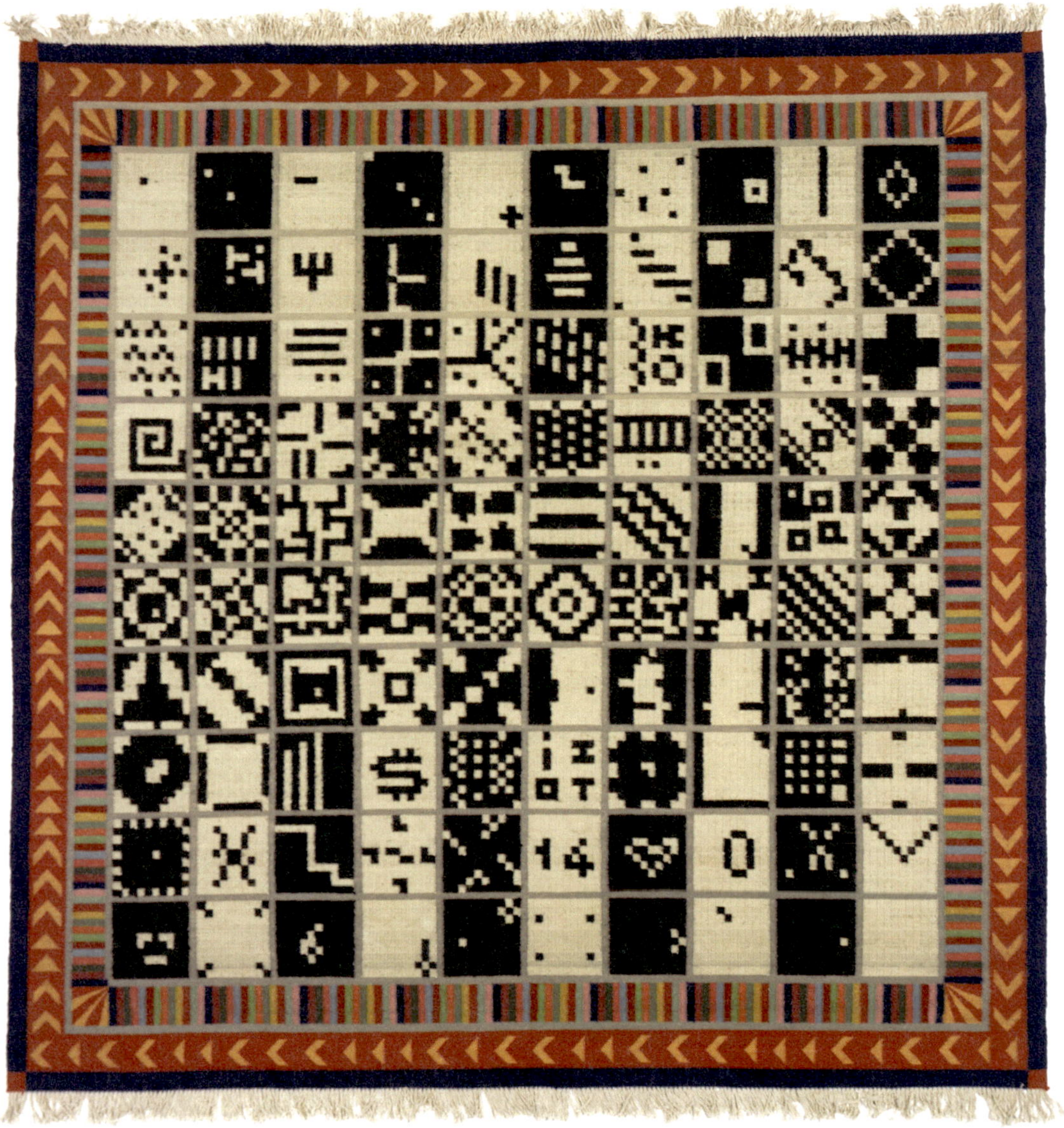

Alternando da uno a cento e viceversa (Alternating from One to a Hundred and Vice Versa), 1993

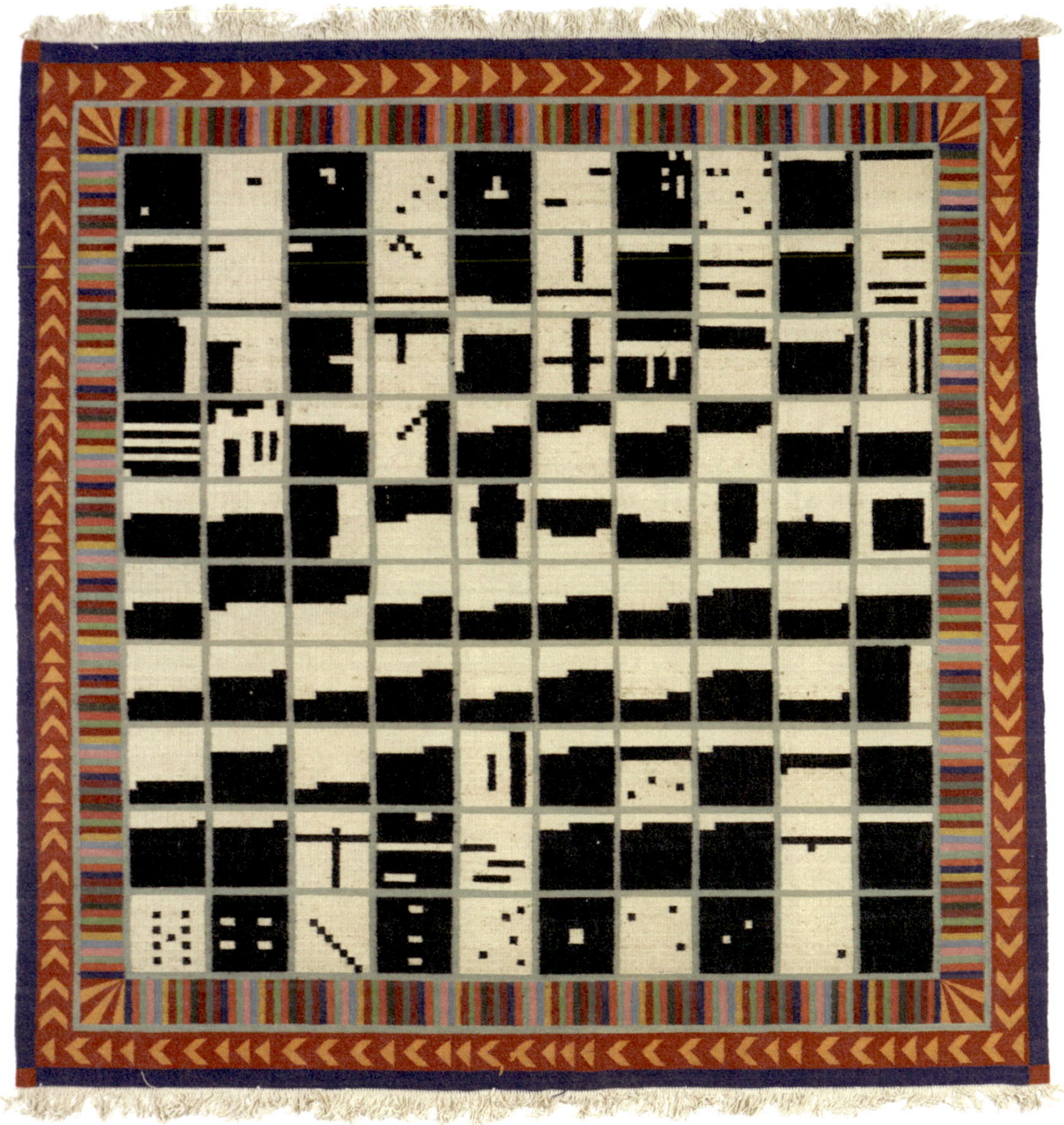

 Alternando da uno a cento e viceversa (Alternating from One to a Hundred and Vice Versa), 1993

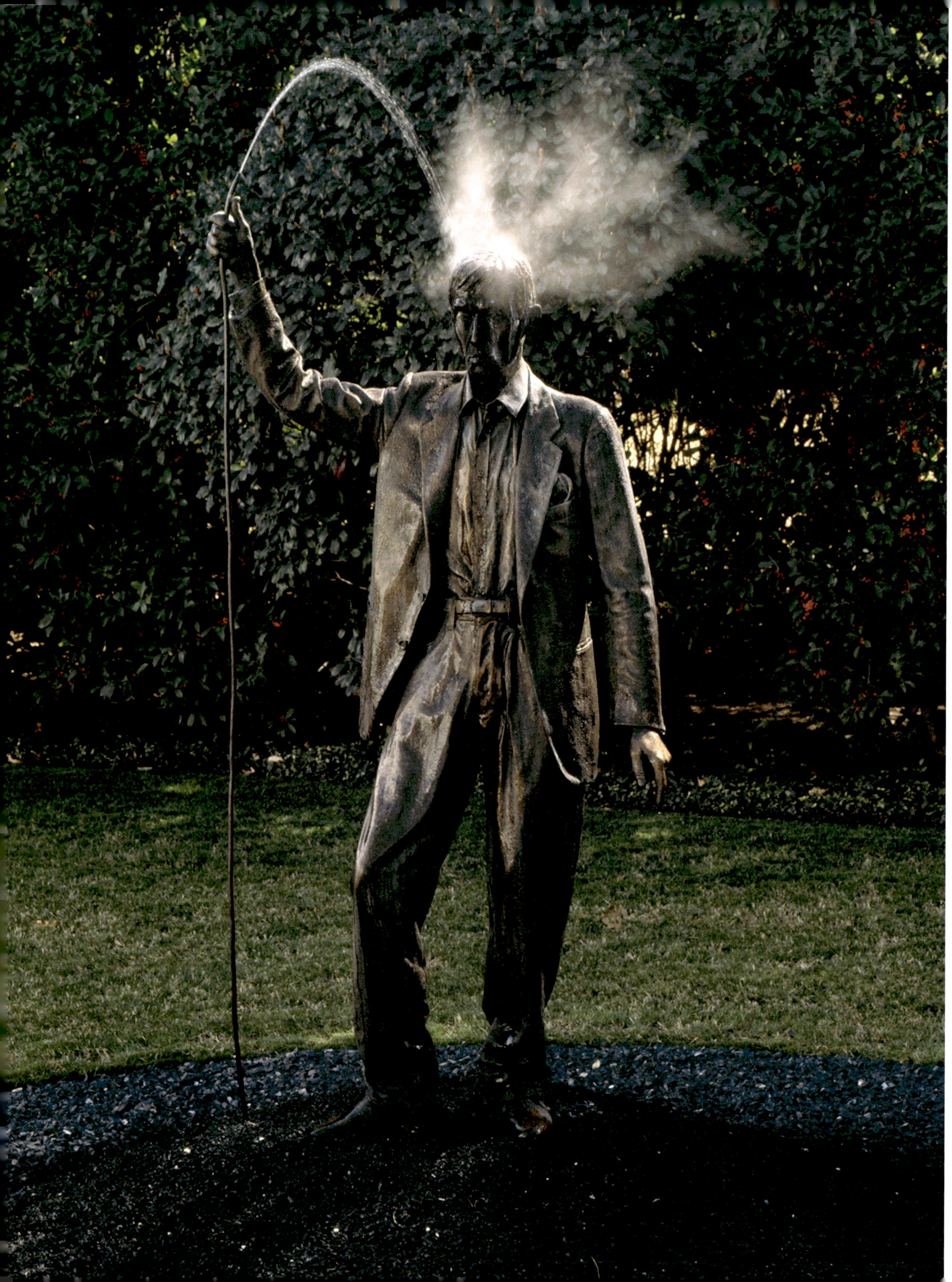

Selected Biography

1940
Born in Turin, December 16
Lived and worked in Turin and Rome

1994
Died in Rome, April 24

One-Person Exhibitions

1967
Christian Stein Gallery, Turin
La Bertesca Gallery, Genoa

1968
Christian Stein Gallery, Turin
"Shaman/Showman," De Nieubourg Gallery, Milan

1969
"Una vetrata – Io prendo il sole a Torino 24-2-1969 – Ritratto di Walter De Maria," Sperone Gallery, Turin

1970
"Besprechungsvortrag – Love's Body," Aktionsraum 1, Munich
"11 studi per 'Cimento dell'armonia e dell'invenzione'," Toselli Gallery, Milan
Sperone Gallery, Turin
Heiner Friedrich Gallery, Munich
Acme Gallery, Brescia
"Manifesto 1967," Toselli Gallery, Milan

1971
"16 Drawings," Konrad Fischer Gallery, Düsseldorf
"12 Forme dal 10 giugno 1967," Sperone Gallery, Turin

1972
Toselli Gallery, Milan
MTL Gallery, Brussels
Art & Project, Amsterdam

1973
"Il progressivo svanire della consuetudine," Marilena Bonomo Gallery, Bari
John Weber Gallery, New York
"Mettere al mondo il mondo," Sperone-Fischer Gallery, Rome
Toselli Gallery, Milan

1974
"Alighiero e Boetti," Kunstmuseum Luzern
Annemarie Verna Gallery, Zürich

1975
John Weber Gallery, New York
"Ein Werk fur einen Raum (Ononimo)," Kunstmuseum Luzern
"Zwei," Area Gallery, Munich
"Alighiero Boetti: Per una storia naturale della moltiplicazione," Sperone Gallery, Rome
Saman Gallery, Geneva
AREA Gallery, Florence
Pasquale TriSorio Gallery, Naples

1976
"Insicuro noncurante," Studio Marconi, Milan
"Quadrare diagonando," Banco Gallery/Massimo Mini, Brescia
Lia Rumma Gallery, Naples
"Insicuro noncurante," D'Alessandro-Ferranti Gallery, Rome

1977
"Orlogio annuale," Centre d'Art Contemporain, Geneva

1978
"Alighiero Boetti", Kunsthalle Basel

1983
"The Thousand Longest Rivers in the World," LP220 Gallery – Franz Paludetto, Turin

Autoritratto (Self-portrait), 1993

1984
Pinacoteca Communale Loggetta Lombardesca, Ravenna

1986
"Insicuro noncurante," Noveau Musée, Lyon; Villa Arson, Nice; Stedelijk Van Abbemuseum, Eindhoven

1989
Laure Genillard Gallery, London
Edward Totah Gallery, London

1990
XLIV Biennale di Venezia, Venice
Museo Casabianca, Malo

1991
John Weber Gallery, New York

1992
"Alighiero e Boetti, 1965–1992: Synchronizität als ein Prinzip akausaler Zusammenhänge," Kunstverein, Bonn; Westfälischer Kunstverein, Münster; Kunstmuseum Luzern

1993
"De bouche à oreille: En alternant de 1 a 100 et vice versa," MAGAZIN – Centre National d'Art Contemporain de Grenoble; The Museum of Contemporary Art, Los Angeles; P.S.1 Museum, New York

1994
"Alighiero e Boetti: Origine et Destination," Société des Expositions du Palais des Beaux-Arts de Bruxelles, Brussels
"De bouche à oreille: œuvre postale d'Alighiero e Boetti," Musée de la Poste, Paris
"Worlds Envisioned: Alighiero Boetti & Frédéric Bruly Bouabré," Dia Center for the Arts, New York; American Center, Paris

1995
John Weber Gallery, New York
Sperone Westwater, New York

1996
"Alighiero Boetti: 1965–1994," Galleria Civica d'Arte Moderna e Contemporanea, Turin; Musée d'Art Moderne, Villeneuve d'Ascq; Museum Moderner Kunst Stiftung Ludwig, Vienna
"Alighiero e Boetti: L'opera ultima," Galleria Nazionale d'Arte Moderna, Rome

1997
Esso Gallery, New York

1998
"Alighiero Boetti: Mettere al mondo il mondo," Museums für Moderne Kunst Galerie Jahrhunderthalle Hoechst, Frankfurt am Main
Lindig in Paludetto Gallery, Nürnberg

1999
"Boetti: The Maverick Spirit of Arte Povera," Whitechapel Art Gallery, London
Laure Genillard Gallery, London

2000
Gladstone Gallery, New York

2001
Gagosian Gallery, New York
Sperone Westwater, New York

2002
"'Alighiero Boetti. Untitled'–Victoria Boogie Woogie (1972) and selected early works," Sperone Westwater, New York
The Arts Club of Chicago, Chicago
"When 1 is 2: Alighiero Boetti," Contemporary Arts Museum, Houston

2003
Sprüth Magers Lee, London
"Alighiero Boetti. Ordre et désordre du monde: Œuvres 1967–1990," FRAC Bourgogne, Dijon

2004
"Alighiero Boetti. Quasi Tutto," Galleria d'Arte Moderna e Contemporanea, Bergamo; Fundación PROA, Buenos Aires
Gladstone Gallery, New York
"Alighiero Boetti. Tuttolibro," Galleria Nazionale d'Arte Moderna, Rome; Museo d'Arte Moderna e Contemporanea di Trento e Rovereto, Rovereto

2006
Ben Brown Fine Arts, London

2007
Gladstone Gallery, New York

2009
"Alighiero & Boetti: Mettere all'Arte il Mondo 1993–1962," MADRE, Museo de Arte Contemporanea DonnaRegina Napoli, Naples
Gladstone Gallery, New York

2010
Marta Cervera Gallery, Madrid
Tornabuoni Art, Paris

2011–2012
"Alighiero Boetti: Game Plan," Museo Nacional Centro de Arte Reina Sofía, Madrid; Tate Modern, London; The Museum of Modern Art, New York

Group Exhibitions

1967
"Arte Povera–Im spazio," La Bertesca Gallery, Genoa; University of Genoa
"Con temp l'azione," Christian Stein Gallery / Sperone Gallery / Il Punto Gallery, Turin

1968
"Arte Povera," De Foscherari Gallery, Bologna
"Arte Povera," Centro Arte Viva Feltrinelli, Trieste

"Il percorso," Arco d'Alibert Gallery, Rome
"Deposito d'Arte Presente," Turin
"RA3/Arte povera piu azione povere," Antichi Arsenali della Repubblica, Amalfi
Prospect 68, Stadtische Kunsthalle, Düsseldorf

1969
"When Attitudes Become Form," Kunsthalle, Bern; Museum Haus Lange, Krefeld; ICA, London
"Konzeption/Conception," Stadtisches Museum, Leverkusen
Prospect 69, Stadtische Kunsthalle, Düsseldorf

1970
"Identification," Videogalerie Schum, Hannover
"Conceptual Art/Arte Povera/Land Art," Galleria Civica d'Arte Moderna, Turin

1971
"Formulation," Addison Gallery of American Art, Phillips Academy, Andover, Massachusetts
"Arte povera," Kunstverein, Munich
"7e Biennale de Paris," Musée d'Art Moderne de la Ville de Paris

1972
Documenta 5, Kassel
XXXVI Biennale di Venezia, Venice
"420 West Broadway," Festival of Two Worlds, Spoleto
"Contemporanea," Parcheggio di Villa Borghese, Rome

1974
"Eight Contemporary Artists," The Museum of Modern Art, New York

1975
XIII Biennale de São Paolo, Sao Paulo

1976
"Prospectretrospect, Europa 1946–1976," Stadtische Kunsthalle, Düsseldorf

1977
"Contrasto apparente – 16 italiani," Museum Boymans Van Beuningen, Rotterdam

1978
XXXVIII Biennale di Venezia, Venice

1980
"Pier and Ocean," Hayward Gallery, London; Kröller-Müller Museum, Otterlo
XXXIX Biennale di Venezia, Venice

1981
Documenta 7, Kassel
"Identite Italienne, l'art en Italie depuis 1959," Centre Georges Pompidou, Paris

1983
"Eine Kunstgeschichte aus Turin 1965– 83," Kölnischer Kunstverein, Cologne

1984
"Il modo italiano," California State University, Los Angeles

1985
"Arte povera – dell'arte povera al 1985," Palacio de Velázquez, Palacio de Cristal, Parque del Retiro, Madrid
"Italienische Kunst," Castello di Rivoli
"The Knot: Arte Povera," P.S. 1, New York

1986
XLII Biennale di Venezia, Venice

1987
"Similia Dissimilia: Modes of Abstraction Today," Stadtische Kunsthalle, Düsseldorf; Leo Castelli Gallery and Sonnabend Gallery, New York

1989
"Les Magiciens de la terre," Centre Georges Pompidou, Paris
"L'art conceptual, une perspective," Musée d'Art Moderne de la Ville de Paris

1990
XLIV Biennale di Venezia, Venice

1993
Sonsbeek 93, Park Sonsbeek, Arnhem

1994
"Mapping," The Museum of Modern Art, New York
"The Italian Metamorphosis, 1943–1968," Solomon R. Guggenheim Museum, New York

1995
XLVI Biennale di Venezia, Venice

1996
"Jurassic Technologies Revisited: Tenth Biennale of Sydney," Sydney

1998
"Terra Incognita, Five Visionary Worlds," Neues Museum Weserburg, Bremen

2001
XLIX Biennale di Venezia: Italian Pavilion, Venice
"Zero to Infinity: Arte Povera," Tate Modern, London; Walker Art Center, Minneapolis; The Museum of Contemporary Art, Los Angeles; The Hirshhorn Museum, Washington

2005
"Open Systems: Rethinking Art c. 1970," Tate Modern, London

Selected Bibliography

Exhibition Catalogues and Monographs

Alighiero Boetti. Genoa: Galleria La Bertesca, 1967. Texts by Germano Celant, Henry Martin, Tommaso Trini.

Alighiero Boetti. Lucerne: Kunstmuseum Luzern, 1974. Text by Jean-Christophe Ammann.

Alighiero Boetti. Basel: Kunsthalle Basel, 1978. Text by Jean-Christophe Ammann.

Alighiero Boetti. In the series "Artisti contemponaei." Ravenna: Loggetta Lombardesca, Pinacoteca Comunale, 1984. Alberto Boatto (ed.). Includes anthology of previous essays on Boetti and interviews by the artist.

Alighiero & Boetti. Genoa: Galleria Chisel, 1985. Text by Tommaso Trini.

Alighiero e Boetti: Insicuro Noncurante. Villeurbanne: Nouveau Musée de Villeurbanne, 1986. Franz Kaiser (ed.). Texts by Giovan Battiste Salerno.

Alighiero e Boetti: Synchronizität als ein Prinzip akausaler Zusammenhänge. Bonn: Bonner Kunstverein; Westfälischer Kunstverein; Kunstmuseum Luzern. Basel/Stuttgart/Wien: Wiese Verlag, 1991. Annelie Pohlen (ed). Numerous contributors.

Alighiero e Boetti: De Bouche à oreille. Grenoble: Centre National d'Art Contemporain de Grenoble, 1993. Angela Vettese (ed.). Texts by Adelina von Fürstenberg, Giovan Battista Salerno, Angela Vettese.

Alighiero e Boetti: Œuvre Postale 1993 "De Bouche à oreille." Paris: Musée de la Poste, 1993. Angela Vettese (ed.).

Alighiero e Boetti / Frédéric Bruly Bouabré: Worlds Envisioned. Dia Center for the Arts, New York, 1995. Lynne Cooke and Karen Kelly (eds.). Texts by Lynne Cooke, Bice Curiger, Jean-Christophe Ammann, Francesco Clemente, Warren Niesluchowski, Kevin Power, Ramón Alejandro.

Alighiero Boetti 1965–1994. Turin: Galleria Civica d'Arte Moderna e Contemporanea, 1996. Texts by Jean-Christophe Ammann, Maria Teresa Roberto and Annemarie Sauzeau Boetti (eds.).

Alighiero e Boetti / Douglas Huebler: Origin and Destination. Brussels: Palais des Beaux-Arts, 1997. Marianne Van Leeuw and Anne Pontégnie (eds.). Numerous contributors.

Alighiero Boetti: Mettere al mondo il mondo. Frankfurt: Museum für Moderne Kunst, 1998. Rolf Lauter (ed.). Texts by Jean-Christophe Ammann and Rolf Lauter.

Alighiero e Boetti. London: Whitechapel Art Gallery, 1999. Text by Antonella Soldaini, Giovan Battista Salerno, Catherine Lampert.

Alighiero e Boetti. New York: Gagosian, 2001. Text by Norman Rosenthal and interview with Francesco Clemente by Louise Neri.

Alighiero Boetti – Works 1966–1988. Munich: Sprüth Magers Gallery, 2002. Text by Jean-Christophe Ammann.

When 1 is 2: The Art of Alighiero e Boetti. Houston: Contemporary Arts Museum, 2002. Paola Morsiani (ed.). Texts by Paola Morsiani and Barry Schwabsky.

Alighiero e Boetti: Shaman / Showman. Turin, Umberto Allemandi, 2003. Text by Annemarie Sauzeau Boetti.

Alighiero e Boetti: Shaman / Showman. Cologne: Buchhandlung Walther König, 2003. Text by Annemarie Sauzeau Boetti.

Alighiero Boetti: Quasi Tutto. Bergamo: Galleria d'Arte Moderna e Contemporanea, 2004. Giacinto di Pietrantonio and Corrado Levi (eds.). Texts by Laura Cherubini, Giacinto di Pietrantonio and Corrado Levi.

Alighiero e Boetti. Milan: Charta, 2004. Texts by Rolf Lauter and Andrea Marescalchi.

Alighiero e Boetti: Niente Tutto. Vaduz: Kunstmuseum Liechtenstein, 2005. Friedemann Malsch (ed.).

ALIGHIEROEBOETTI. Florence: Tornabuoni Arte and Cosenza: Palazzo Arnone, 2006. Text by Bruno Corà (ed.).

Alighiero e Boetti: Mappa. London: Afterall, 2008. Text by Luca Cerizza.

Alighiero & Boetti: Bringing the World into Art, 1993–1962. Naples: MADRE and Milan: Electa, 2009. Achille Bonito Oliva (ed.). Texts by Achille Bonito Oliva, Jean-Pierre Bordaz, Alain Cueff.

Alighiero Boetti Catalogo Generale – Tomo Primo. Jean-Christophe Ammann (ed.). Milan: Electa, 2009.

Alighiero e Boetti: Mappa. New York: Gladstone Gallery, 2010. Text by Jean-Christophe Ammann.

Alighiero Boetti. Paris: Tornabuoni Art, 2010. Text by Annemarie Sauzeau (ed.).

Alighiero e Boetti. New Haven and London: Yale University Press, 2011. Text by Mark Godfrey.

Interviews

Alighiero Boetti, "Intervento" (Interview), in *Bit*, vol. 1, no. 4, July 1967, pp. 9–10.

"Alighiero Boetti interviewed by Mirella Bandini in 1972," in *NAC*, no. 3, March 1973, pp. 2–18.

"Interview with Alighiero Boetti – Milan 1973," by Achille Bonito Oliva, originally published in *Dialoghi d'artista: incontri con l'arte contemporanea 1970–1984*, Achille Bonito Oliva, Milan: Electa, 1984, pp. 228–35.

"Alighiero Boetti, Dall'oggi al domani (From Today to Tomorrow)," interview by Sandro Lombardi, in *Dall'oggi al domani*, Brescia: Edizioni L'Obliquo, 1988

"Alighiero Boetti interviewed by Kazuo Akao Art Agency, Tokyo in 1980," first published in *Alighiero e Boetti*, (exh. cat.) Loggetta Lombardesca, Ravenna, 1990.

"Alighiero e Boetti – Un disegno del pensiero che va," interview by Bruno Corà, first published in *A.E.I.O.U.*, no. 6, Rome, December 1982

"Concept Boetti," interview, January 1991, by Mariuccia Casadio, first published in *Interview*.

"Dialogue with the artist," interview by Sergio Givone (1991), first published in Achille Bonito Oliva (ed.), *Alighiero & Boetti: Bringing the World into Art*, 1993–1962, Naples: MADRE and Milan: Electa, 2009, p. 41.

"Afghanistan," interview by Nicolas Bourriaud, in *Documents*, no. 1, October 1992, pp. 49–54.

Articles

Tommaso Trini, "Boetti o la riconstruzione con recostruita," *Domus*, no. 457, January 1967, pp. 29–30.

Tommaso Trini, "ABEEGHIIILOORTT," *Data*, no. 4, May 1972, p. 56.

Tommaso Trini, "Alighiero Boetti: I Primi Mille Fiumi Piu Lunghi del mondo – Dossier Postale," *Data*, [no. 11], Spring 1974, pp. 40–49.

Christopher Bennett, "Substantive Thoughts? The Early Work of Alighiero Boetti," *OCTOBER*, no. 124, Spring 2008, pp. 75–97.

Alex Potts, "Disencumbered Objects," *OCTOBER*, no. 124, Spring 2008, p. 169–189.

Tom Francis, "One Star is Enough to Make a Cosmos: Alighiero e Boetti and the One Hotel," *Bidoun* 19, 2009.

Mark Godfrey, "Divided Interests: The Art of Alighiero Boetti," *Artforum*, vol. 47 no. 9, May 2009, p. 204–213.

Additional References

Parkett, no. 24, 1990. Texts by Jean-Christophe Ammann, Giovan Battiste Salerno, Rainer Crone, David Moos, Friedemann Malsch et al.

Arte Povera. Phaidon, London, 1999. Carolyn Christov-Bakargiev (ed.).

Briony Fer, *The Infinite Line: Remaking Art After Modernism*. London and New Haven: Yale University Press, 2004.

Robert Lehman Lectures on Contemporary Art No. 2. Dia Center for the Arts, 2004. Essay by Sarat Maharaj.

Robert Lumley, *Arte Povera*. London: Tate Publishing, 2004.

Giovan Battista Salerno. Anthology of essays by Giovan Battista Salerno on Boetti. Milan: Galleria Massimo De Carlo, 2008. Luca Cerizza (ed.).

Germano Celant, *Arte Povera: History and Stories*. Milan: Electa, 2011.

List of Exhibited Works

Untitled, 1965
Chinese ink and pencil on paper
68.6 x 96.5 cm
(27 x 38″)
The Museum of Modern Art, New York.
The Judith Rothschild Foundation
Contemporary Drawing Collection Gift
(purchase, and gift, in part, of The Eileen
and Michael Cohen Collection), 2005
Accession number: 1329.2005
[Exhibited at Museo Reina Sofía and MoMA]
[p. 40]

Untitled, 1965
Chinese ink and pencil on paper
68 x 98 cm
(26 ¾ x 38 ¾″)
Private Collection, Houston, Texas
[Exhibited at Museo Reina Sofía and MoMA]
[p. 41]

Lampada annuale (Annual Lamp), 1966
Lacquered wood, electric device, metal, glass
76 x 37 x 37 cm
(29 ⅞ x 14 ¾ x 14 ¾″)
Private Collection
[p. 31]

Ping Pong, 1966
Wood, glass and electric device
Two elements: 50 x 50 x 20 cm
(19 ⅝ x 19 ⅝ x 7 ⅞″)
Goetz Collection, Munich
[p. 49, 50]

Pannello luminoso (Light Panel), 1966
Varnished wood and electric device
88 x 69 x 6 cm
(34 ⅝ x 27 ¼ x 2 ⅜″)
Courtesy Christian Stein Gallery, Milan
[p. 56]

Rotolo di cartone ondulato 2 (Roll of Corrugated Cardboard 2), 1986 (1966)
271 x 70 cm (diameter)
(106 ½ x 27 ½″)
Collection de l'Institut d'Art
Contemporain, Rhône-Alpes; Dépôt du
Nouveau Musée/ Collection Souvenir
[Different version illustrated p. 43]

Mazzo di tubi (Cluster of Tubes), 1966
PVC tubes
280 x 160 cm (diameter)
(110 ¼ x 63″)
Courtesy Christian Stein Gallery, Milan
[Exhibited at Museo Reina Sofía and MoMA]
[p. 45]

Mancorrente metri 2 (2 Meter Handrail), 1966
Iron, varnish, chrome
80 x 200 x 40 cm
(31 ½ x 78 ¾ x 15 ¾″)
Fondazione per l'Arte Moderna e
Contemporanea CRT on loan to Castello
di Rivoli Museo d'Arte Contemporanea,
Rivoli, Turin; GAM - Galleria Civica d'Arte
Moderna e Contemporanea, Turin
[p. 47]

the thin thumb, 1966
Industrial varnish, wood, cork letters
50 x 50 x 8 cm
(19 ⅞ x 19 ⅞ x 2 ¼″)
Collection Sprüth-Leccese
Courtesy: Sprüth Magers, Berlin–London
and Le Case D'Arte, Milan
[Exhibited at Museo Reina Sofía and Tate]
[p. 59]

frou frou, 1966
Industrial varnish, wood, cork letters
80 x 60 x 10 cm
(31 ½ x 23 ⅝ x 4″)
Gino Viliani Collection
[p. 58]

8,50 (Zig Zag), 1966
Aluminum and cloth
51.4 x 51.4 x 51.4 cm
(20 ¼ x 20 ¼ x 20 ¼″)
Fondazione per l'Arte Moderna e
Contemporanea CRT on loan to Castello di
Rivoli Museo d'Arte Contemporanea,
Rivoli, Turin; GAM – Galleria Civica d'Arte
Moderna e Contemporanea, Turin
[p. 52]

Scala (Ladder), 1966
Wood
173 x 111 x 48 cm
(68 x 43 ⅝ x 18 ⅞″)
Castello di Rivoli Museo d'Arte
Contemporanea, Rivoli, Turin; GAM -
Galleria Civica d'Arte Moderna e
Contemporanea, Turin
[Exhibited at Tate and MoMA]
[p. 46]

Mimetico (Camouflage), 1966
Printed cloth
170 x 291 cm
(66 ⅞ x 114 ½″)
Glenstone
[p. 44]

Untitled (Invitation), 1966–67
Mixed media on printed cardboard
24.8 x 21 cm
(9 ¾ x 8 ¼″)
The Museum of Modern Art, New York.
The Judith Rothschild Foundation
Contemporary Drawing Collection Gift
(purchase, and gift, in part, of The Eileen
and Michael Cohen Collection), 2005
Accession number: 1330.2005
[p. 32]

I VEDENTI (The Sighted), 1967
Plaster
60 x 60 x 6 cm
(23 ⅝ x 23 ⅝ x 2 ⅜″)
Viaindustriae / Private Collection, Foligno
[p. 70]

Dama (Checkerboard), 1967
Punched wood: 289 wooden blocks
97 x 97 x 5.5 cm
(38 ¼ x 38 ¼ x 2 ¼″)
Collection Gloria Molino
[p. 90]

Oro Longchamp 2 234 2288, 1967
Industrial enamel, cardboard and cork
letters and numbers
65 x 68 cm
(25 ½ x 27 ¾″)
Collection du Frac des Pays de la Loire

[Exhibited at Museo Reina Sofía and Tate]
[p. 57]

Rosso Palermo 511 52 27, 1967
Industrial enamel, cardboard, cork letters and numbers
65 x 68 cm
(25 ½ x 27 ¾″)
Collection du Frac des Pays de la Loire
[Exhibited at Museo Reina Sofía and Tate]
[p. 57]

ROSSO GILERA 60 1232 ROSSO GUZZI 60 1305, 1967
Enamel paint on iron
100 x 100 cm
(39 ⅜ x 39 ⅜″)
Private Collection, New York
[Exhibited at MoMA]
[p. 57]

Catasta (Stack), 1967
Eternit tubes 12 elements:
187 x 150 x 150 cm each
(173 ½ x 59 ⅛ x 59 ⅛″)
Collection François Pinault, Paris/Venice
[Exhibited at Tate and MoMA]
[p. 42]

Manifesto, 1967
Offset print on paper
100 x 70 cm
(39 ⅜ x 27 ¾″)
[Edition 14/50]
Private Collection
[p. 63]

Contatore (Counter), 1967
Collage on silkscreen
42.5 x 62.5 cm
(16 ¾ x 24 ½″)
[Edition X/123]
Private Collection
[Exhibited at Museo Reina Sofía and Tate]
[Edition no. 5 illustrated p. 128]

AB : AW = MD : L, 1967
Drawing on serigraphy
60 x 60 cm
(23 ⅝ x 23 ⅝″)
Private Collection
[Exhibited at Tate]
[p. 60]

Prefissi e progetti (Prefixes and Projects), 1967
Mixed media on paper
9 pieces:
a/ b/ h: 47.3 x 47.3 cm
(18 ⅝ x 18 ⅝″)
c/ e/ f/ g/ i: 57.8 x 57.8 cm
(22 ¾ x 27 ¾″)
d: 52 x 52 cm
(20 ½ x 20 ½″)
Collection Gian Enzo Sperone, New York
[Exhibited at Museo Reina Sofía and Tate]
[p. 53]

Ghise (ABoetti) (Cast Iron [ABoetti]), 1968
Cast iron
2 parts:
98 x 68 x 2.6 cm & 101 x 73 x 2.6 cm
(39 ⅝ x 23 ⅝ x 1″ & 38 ¾ x 23 ⅝ x ⅝″)
Courtesy 1000 Eventi Gallery, Milan
[p. 71]

Legnetti colorati (Little Colored Sticks), 1968
Wood, acrylic paint and elastic bands
35 x 160 cm (diameter)
(13 ¾ x 63″)
Private Collection
[p. 55]

Città di Torino (City of Turin), 1968
Pastel drawing on lithography
56 x 46 cm
(22 x 18 ⅛″)
Egidio Marzona Collection
[p. 61]

Cubo (Cube), 1968
Plexiglass container and various materials: wood, polystyrene, steel rods, aluminum, fiberglass, cardboard, plastic, glass, rubber, wire wool and glue
90 x 90 x 90 cm
(35 ⅜ x 35 ⅜ x 35 ⅜″)
Inhotim Collection. Minas Gerais, Brazil
[p. 54]

Colonna (Column), 1968
Scalloped-edged paper doilies and iron core
211 x 36 x 24 cm
(83 x 14 ⅛ x 9 ½″)
Colombo Collection, Milan
[p. 52]

Shaman/Showman, 1968
Lithography
70 x 50 cm
(27 ⅝ x 19 ⅝″)
Composti della Cà di Frá Collection – Milan
[Exhibited at Museo Reina Sofía and Tate]
[p. 64]

Gemelli (Twins), 1968
Photomontage
15 x 10 cm
(5 ⅞ x 3 ⅞″)
Private Collection
[p. 65]

Gemelli (Twins), 1968
Photomontage
15 x 10 cm
(5 ⅞ x 3 ⅞″)
Private Collection, Paris
[p. 66]

Per un uomo alienato (For an Alienated Man), 1968
Writing on quick-drying cement on wooden support
130 x 128.5 x 2.5 cm
(51 x 60 x ⅞″)
Galleria Nazionale d'Arte Moderna e Contemporanea, Rome
[p. 73]

Scrittura graffita (Graffito), 1968
Writing on quick-drying cement on wooden support
Ma faim Anne: 30 x 21 x 2 cm
(11 ¾ x 8 ⅝ x ¾″)
L'eau claire comme le sel des larmes d'enfance: 30 x 21 x 2 cm
(11 ¾ x 8 ⅝ x ¾″)
Private Collection
[Exhibited at Museo Reina Sofía and MoMA]
[p. 72]

Io che prendo il sole a Torino il 19 gennaio 1969, (Me Sunbathing in Turin 19 January 1969), 1969
111 pieces of concrete molded by hand, cabbage butterfly
c. 177 x 90 cm
(69 ⅝ x 35 ⅜″)
Private Collection, Turin
[p. 67]

Niente da vedere niente da nascondere (Nothing to See Nothing to Hide), 1969
Iron and glass
300 x 400 x 4 cm
(118 ⅛ x 157 ½ x 1 ½″)
Private Collection, London
[Exhibited at Tate and MoMA]
[p. 69]

Cimento dell'armonia e dell'invenzione (Contest of Harmony and Invention), 1969
Pencil on squared paper, metal frames
25 panels: 70 x 50 cm each
(27 ½ x 19 ⅝″)
Courtesy 1000 Eventi Gallery, Milan
[p. 80, 81]

Territori occupati (Occupied Territories), 1969
Cross stitch embroidery in wool on jute, circular wooden frame
120 x 127 cm (jute)
(47 ¼ x 50″)
15 x 4 cm diameter (frame)
(5 ⅞ x 1 ⅝″)
Regional Contemporary Art Fund of Burgundy (FRAC) Collection
[p. 79]

Autoritratto (Self-Portrait), 1969
Photocopy on Xerox paper (direct impression of the face on the photocopier)
12 elements: 32 x 20.5 cm each
(11 ¼ x 8 ¼″)
J.E. Van Praet
[p. 75]

Planisfero politico (Political Planisphere), 1969–70
Mixed media on map
78 x 125 cm
(30 ⅝ x 49 ⅛″)
Valerio de Paolis Collection
[p. 161]

Viaggi postali (Postal Voyages), 1969–70
19 stamped envelopes with stamps
Various measurements:
Smallest envelope: 11 x 22 cm
(4⅜ x 8 ⅝″);
largest envelope: 26 x 40 cm
(10 ¼ x 15 ¾″)
Collection Gian Enzo Sperone, New York
Courtesy Sperone Westwater, New York
[p. 116]

Dossier postale (Postal Dossier), 1969–70
181 cardboard folders (embossed and stamped) with print content
35 x 25.5 cm each folder
(13 ¾ x 10″)
Collection Gian Enzo Sperone, New York
Courtesy Sperone Westwater, New York
[p. 117]

Untitled, 1969
Ink and stickers on paper
200 x 200 cm
(78 ¾ x 78 ¾″)
Private Collection
[p. 91]

Iter-vallo, 1969/1986
Iron and tissue paper
54 x 54 x 1 cm
(21 ¼ x 21 ¼ x ⅝″)
Private Collection, London
[Exhibited at Museo Reina Sofía and Tate]
[Different version illustrated p. 93]

Strumento musicale (Musical Instrument), 1970
Photograph
50 x 60 cm
(19 ⅝ x 23 ⅝″)
Agata Boetti, Paris
[Exhibited at Museo Reina Sofía and Tate]
[p. 74]

Alfabeto (Scrittura a due mani (Alphabet [Writing with Two Hands]), 1970
Pencil on paper
66 x 48 cm
(25 ⅞ x 18 ⅞″)
Private Collection
[Exhibited at Museo Reina Sofía and Tate]
[p. 83]

EMME I ELLE ELLE E ..., 1970
Crocheted lace
27 x 27 cm
(10 ⅝ x 10 ⅝″)
Private collection
[p. 85]

EMME I ELLE ELLE E ... , 1970
Spray paint on wood
28 cm x 28 cm x 2 cm
(11 x 11 x ¾″)
Collection Sprüth-Leccese
Courtesy: Sprüth Magers, Berlin–London and Le Case D'Arte, Milan
[p. 87]

EMME I ELLE ELLE E ... (Green on Green), 1970
Pochoir
Irreg. composition: 55 x 54 cm
(21 ⅝ x 21 ¼″)
Sheet: 70 x 69.6 cm
(27 ½ x 27 ⅜″)
Publisher: Edizioni Multipli, Turin
The Museum of Modern Art, New York. Gift of the Associates of the Department of Prints and Illustrated Books
[Exhibited at MoMA]
[p. 86]

Lavoro postale (permutazione) (Postal Work [Permutation]), 1970
Six envelopes framed
30.5 x 20.5 cm
(12 x 8″)
Collection Agata and Matteo Boetti, Rome

[Exhibited at Tate and MoMA]
[p. 113]

La Mole Antonelliana, 1970–75
7 stamped postcards
15 x 10 cm each
(5 ⅞ x 4″)
Colombo Collection, Milan
[p. 115, recto/verso]

Per una storia naturale della misurazione (Towards a Natural History of Measurement), 1970
3 parts:
4 polaroids + stamped envelope:
36.5 x 63.5 cm
(14 ⅜ x 25″);
5 polaroids + stamped envelope:
45.5 x 67 cm
(18 x 26 ⅜″);
7 polaroids + stamped envelope:
43.5 x 76 cm
(17 ⅛ x 30″)
Private Collection
[p. 114]

Dodici forme dal 10 giugno 1967 (12 Forms from June 10, 1967), 1971
Engraving on copper
12 elements:
59 x 43 cm each
(23 ¼ x 17″)
Paolo and Alida Giuli, Malgrate-Lecco
[p. 78]

ABEEGHIIILOORT, 1971
Biro on paper
47.5 x 68.5 cm
(18 ¾ x 27″)
Private Collection, Turin
[Exhibited at Museo Reina Sofía and Tate]
[p. 102]

16 DICEMBRE 2040 – 11 LUGLIO 2023 (December 26, 2040 – July 11, 2023), 1971
Engraving on brass
2 elements: 40 x 40 cm each
(15 ¾ x 15 ¾″)
Private Collection, Houston, Texas
[pp. 122–123]

16 DICEMBRE 2040 – 11 LUGLIO 2023 (December 26, 2040 – July 11, 2023), 1971
Embroidery on fabric
2 elements: 60 x 60 cm each
(23 ⅝ x 23 ⅝″)
Private Collection, Houston, Texas
[pp. 124–125]

Serie di merli dispositi a intervalli regolari lungo gli spalti di una muraglia (A Row of Merlons Set at Regular Intervals Along the Ramparts of a Wall), 1971–93
13 telegrams in a vitrine
25 x 350 cm
(9 ⅞ x 137 ⅞″)
Collection Matteo Boetti, Rome
[pp. 126–127]

Mappa (Map), 1971–72
Embroidery on linen
200 x 360 cm
(78 ¾ x 141 ¾″)
Glenstone
[pp. 164–165]

Mappa (Map), 1971–72
Embroidery on linen
147 x 228 cm
(57 ⅞ x 89 ¾″)
Private Collection
[Exhibited at Museo Reina Sofía and Tate]
[p. 218]

I VEDENTI (The Sighted), 1972–73
Embroidery on fabric
174 x 150 cm
(68 ½ x 59″)
Gino Viliani Collection
[p. 200]

AELLEIGIACCAIEERREOBIOETITII, 1973
Biro on paper mounted on canvas
70 x 100 cm
(27 ½ x 39 ⅜″)
Courtesy of Ben Brown Fine Arts, London / Hong Kong
[Exhibited at Museo Reina Sofía and Tate]
[p. 101]

24 lettere dall'Afghanistan (24 Letters from Afghanistan), 1973
24 letters / 24 drawings
130 x 200 cm
(51 ⅛ x 78 ¾″)
Collection Gloria Molino
[pp. 120–121]

Ordine e Disordine, (Order and Disorder), 1973
Embroidery on fabric
100 elements:
17.5 x 17.5 cm each
(6 ⅞ x 6 ⅞)
Private Collection
[Different version illustrated pp. 95–97]

Mettere al mondo il mondo (Putting the World into the World), 1973–75
Biro on paper mounted on canvas
2 parts: 160 x 251 cm / 160 x 261.6 cm
(63 x 98 ⅞″ / 63 x 104″)
Glenstone
[pp. 104–105]

Sale e Zucchero (Salt and Sugar), c. 1973
Mixed Stamps and mixed media on paper
10 elements: 50 x 70 cm each
(19 ¾ x 27 ⅝″)
Private Collection, Germany
[p. 183]

Lavoro postale (Postal Work), 1974
1 panel of 4 envelopes in a 2 x 2 square
4 drawings in a 2 x 2 grid (GRID 1)
1 panel of 9 envelopes in a 3 x 3 square
9 drawings in a 3 x 3 grid (GRID 2)
1 panel of 16 envelopes in a 4 x 4 square
16 drawings in a 4 x 4 grid (GRID 3)
1 panel of 25 envelopes in a 5 x 5 square
25 drawings in a 5 x 5 grid. (GRID 4)
150 x 565 cm overall
(59 x 222″)
LWL-Landesmuseum für Kunst und Kulturgeschichte, Münster
[pp. 118–119]

Guatemala, 1974
4 photographs
29 x 22 cm each
(11 ½ x 8 ⅝″)
Collection Agata and Matteo Boetti, Rome
[p. 10]

I sei sensi (The Six Senses), 1974
Biro on paper mounted on canvas
161.7 x 477.4 x 5.2 cm
(63 ⅝ x 188 x 2″)
Private Collection
[Exhibited at Museo Reina Sofía and Tate]
[p. 103]

I sei sensi (The Six Senses), 1974–75
Biro on paper mounted on canvas
6 elements:
100.3 x 71.1 cm each
(39 ½ x 28″);
100.3 x 426.7 cm overall
(39 ½ x 168″)
The Museum of Modern Art, New York. The Judith Rothschild Foundation Contemporary Drawings Collection Gift
[Exhibited at MoMA]
[pp. 106–107]

Storia naturale della moltiplicazione (Natural History of Multiplication), 1975
Ink on graph paper
12 elements: 70 x 100 cm each
(27 ½ x 39 ⅜″)
Agata Boetti, Paris
[pp. 98–99]

Codice: Eritrea libera (Codex: Free Eritrea), 1975
Set of envelopes, framed
46 x 86 cm
(18 x 33 ⅞″)
Private Collection, Paris
[Exhibited at Tate]
[p. 145]

Insicuro Noncurante, 1975 (1966–75)
Mixed media
Portfolio with 81 plates
Edition of 41
56 x 46 cm each
(21 ⅝ x 17 ⅝″)
The Museum of Modern Art, New York. Committee on Prints and Illustrated Books Fund with support from Marie-Josée and Henry R. Kravis
[Exhibited at MoMA]
[pp. 178–179]

Gli anni della mia vita (The Years of My Life), 1976
Ink on paper using handmade stencils
102 x 80 cm
(40 x 31 ½″)
Collection Matteo Boetti, Rome
[p. 4]

I mille fiumi più lunghi del mondo (The Thousand Longest Rivers in the World), 1976–82
Embroidery on linen
251.5 x 535.9 cm
(8′ 3″ x 17′ 7″)
The Museum of Modern Art, New York. Gift of Jo Carole and Ronald S. Lauder, Jeanne C. Thayer Fund, The Bernhill Fund, Patricia Phelps de Cisneros Fund, Agnes Gund, and Barbara Jakobson Fund, 1993. Accession Number: 279.1993.1
[pp. 216–217]

I mille fiumi più lunghi del mondo (The Thousand Longest Rivers in the World), 1976–82
Embroidery on linen
280 x 460 cm
(110 ¼ x 181″)
MMK Museum für Moderne Kunst, Frankfurt am Main
[Exhibited at Museo Reina Sofía and Tate]
[pp. 214–215]

Classifying: The Thousand Longest Rivers in the World, 1977
Authors: Alighiero Boetti and Annemarie Sauzeau Boetti
Book, typographic print, 1000 pp.
21.5 x 16.5 x 5.5 cm
(8 ½ x 6 ½ x 2″)
Edition of 500 copies; 150 are with embroidered cover; 300 with red cloth binding, and 50 reserved for the authors
Edition nos.: 363 / 379 / 439
Caterina Boetti, Rome
[Exhibited at Museo Reina Sofia and Tate]

Classifying: The Thousand Longest Rivers in the World, 1977
Authors: Alighiero Boetti and Annemarie Sauzeau Boetti
Embroidered book
Edition 150/500
21.5 x 16.5 x 5.5 cm
(8 ½ x 6 ½ x 2″)
Private Collection, Paris
[Exhibited at Museo Reina Sofía and Tate]
[p. 213]

Alternando da uno a cento e viceversa (Alternating from One to One Hundred and Vice Versa), 1977–78
Embroidery on linen
127 x 129 cm
(50 x 50 ⅔″)
Paolo e Alida Giuli, Malgrate-Lecco
[p. 201]

Orologi annuali (Annual Watches), 1977–94
Paper and set of 16 watches in a vitrine
Vitrine: 41 x 83 cm
(16 ¼ x 32 ¼″)
The complete set, with interrupted production 1981/82
Agata Boetti, Paris
[Exhibited at Museo Reina Sofía and Tate]
[pp. 2, 129]

San Bernardino, 1968/1978
Photolithography
70 x 50 cm
(27 ½ x 19 ⅝″)
Courtesy Frittelli Arte Contemporanea, Florence
[Exhibited at Museo Reina Sofía and Tate]
[p. 77]

Untitled, 1978
Embroidery on cloth
93.7 x 94 cm
(37 x 37″)
Ben Brown Fine Arts, London
[Exhibited at Museo Reina Sofía]
[p. 89]

Mettere al mondo il mondo a Roma nella primavera dell'anno mille novecentosettantotto pensando a tutto tondo (Putting the World into the World in Rome in the Spring of the Year Nineteen Hundred and Seventy-eight Thinking in the Round), 1978
Biro on paper mounted on canvas
12 panels: 100.3 x 71.7 cm each
(39 ⅜ x 28 ¼″)
Ben Brown Fine Arts, London
[Exhibited at Museo Reina Sofía and Tate]
[pp. 108–109]

Calendari (Calendars) 1978–94
Collage on paper
17 sheets of various sizes: c. 27 x 37 cm each
(10 ⅝ x 14 ½″)
Collection Mariangelica De Gaetano
[Different version illustrated p. 130]

Aerei (Aeroplanes), 1978
Biro on canvas-backed paper
3 panels: 140 x 100 cm each
(55 ⅛ x 39 ⅜″)
Private Collection
[p. 243]

Aerei (Aeroplanes), 1978
Biro on paper mounted on canvas
93.5 x 209.1 cm
(36 ½ x 82 ¼″)
Glenstone
[Exhibited at Museo Reina Sofía and Tate]
[p. 241]

Regno animale (Animal Kingdom), 1978
Pencil on paper mounted on linen
150 x 100 cm
(59 x 39 ⅜″)
Private Collection, Paris
[p. 188]

Regno musicale (Music Kingdom), 1979
Pencil (drawing, writing, frottage) on paper
150 x 100 cm
(59 x 39 ⅜″)
Private Collection, Paris
[p. 189]

Regno delle carte (Paper Kingdom), 1979
Pencil on paper mounted on canvas
150 x 101.6 cm
(59 x 39 ⅜″)
Private Collection, Monza (Italy)
[p. 190]

Ordine e disordine (Order and Disorder), 1979
Embroidery on cloth
c. 186 x 205 cm
(73 ¼ x 80¾″)
Private Collection, New York
[Exhibited at Museo Reina Sofía]
[p. 94]

L'albero delle ore (The Hour Tree), 1979
Embroidery on linen
325 x 193 cm
(128 x 76″)
Dallas Museum of Art, fractional gift of the Rachofsky Collection
[p. 131]

Far quadrare tutto (Make Everything Fit In), 1979
Embroidery on fabric
15 panels: 22.5 x 24 cm each
(8 ⅞ x 9 ½″)
Private Collection
[p. 231]

Faccine (Little Faces), 1979
[Formerly know as Faccine colorate]
6 serigraph prints with felt-tipped pen
80.5 x 68.5 cm each
(31 ¾ x 27″)
Caterina Boetti, Rome
[pp. 86, 87]

Mappa (Map), 1979
Embroidery on linen
130.2 x 230 cm
(51 x 90 ½″)
Private Collection – La Spezia
[Exhibited at Museo Reina Sofía and Tate]
[p. 219]

Mappa (Map), 1979–83
Embroidery on linen
98 x 164 cm
(38 ⅝ x 64 ⅝″)
Tornabuoni Art, Paris
[Exhibited at Tate]
[p. 220]

Afghanistan, 1980
Mixed media on paper
150 x 100 cm
(59 x 39 ⅜″)
G. Aglietta, Biella
[p. 169]

La natura, una faccenda ottusa (Nature, a Dull Affair), c. 1980
Collage and Indian ink on paper
70 x 100 cm
(59 x 39 ⅜″)
Private Collection
[Exhibited at Museo Reina Sofía and Tate]
[p. 191]

La natura, una faccenda ottusa (1) (Nature, a Dull Affair [1]), 1980
Collage and ink on paper
70 x 100 cm
(27 ½ x 39 ⅜″)
Private Collection, Paris
[p. 192]

La natura, una faccenda ottusa (2) (Nature, a Dull Affair [2]), 1980
Collage and ink on paper
100 x 70 cm
(27 ½ x 39 ⅜″)
Private Collection, Paris
[p. 193]

Mappa (Map), 1980
Embroidery on linen
158 x 202 cm
(62 ¼ x 79 ½″)
Tornabuoni Art, Paris
[Exhibited at Tate]
[p. 220]

Titoli (Titles), 1980
Embroidery on cloth
215 x 218 cm
(84 ⅝ x 85 ⅞″)
Private Collection, Rome
[Exhibited at Museo Reina Sofía and Tate]
[p. 245]

Da uno a dieci (From One to Ten), 1980
Folder containing 20 boards
25 x 37 cm
(9 ⅞ x 14 ½″)
An edition published by Emme Edizioni, Milan, with a text by Gianni Jervis and graphic design by Rinaldo Rossi
Private Collection
[p. 23]

Clessidra, cerniera e viceversa (Hourglass, Hinge and Vice Versa), 1981
Pencil on paper
70 x 100 cm
(27 ½ x 39 ⅜″)
Alessandra Bonomo Gallery, Rome
[p. 203]

Da uno a dieci (giapponese) (From One to Ten [Japanese]), 1981
Watercolor on paper mounted on canvas
10 elements: 27.9 x 40.9 cm each
(11 ¾ x 19 ⅝″)
Private Collection – La Spezia
[Exhibited at Museo Reina Sofía and Tate]
[pp. 184–185]

Pier/Piet, 1982
Biro on paper
4 elements: 70 x 70 cm each
(27 ½ x 27 ½″)
Agata Boetti, Paris
[Exhibited at Museo Reina Sofía]
[p. 110–111]

Mappa (Map), 1983
Embroidery on linen
112 x 166 cm
(44 ⅛ x 65 ⅜″)
Alessandra Bonomo Gallery, Rome
[p. 221]

Dicembre 1983 (December 1983), 1983
Pencil on paper mounted on canvas
99.4 x 127 cm
(39 ⅛ x 50″)
The Museum of Modern Art, New York. The Judith Rothschild Foundation Contemporary Drawings Collection Gift
[Exhibited at MoMA]
[p. 182]

Aerei (Aeroplanes), 1983
Biro on paper mounted on canvas
23.2 x 48.9 cm
(9 ⅛ x 19 ¼″)
The Museum of Modern Art, New York. The Judith Rothschild Foundation Contemporary Drawings Collection Gift
[Exhibited at MoMA]
[p. 242]

Aerei (Aeroplanes), 1984
Biro on paper mounted on canvas
66 x 150 cm
(26 x 59″)
3 panels: 66 x 50 cm each
(26 x 19 ⅝″)
Roberto Casamonti
[Exhibited at Tate]
[p. 240]

Tra sé e sé andare con il tempo (Between Self and Self Go with Time), 1985
Pencil and Chinese ink on paper
79 x 114 cm
(31 ⅛ x 44 ⅞″)
Alessandra Bonomo Gallery, Rome
[Exhibited at Tate]
[p. 196]

Untitled, 1987
Pencil, ink and collage on paper on canvas
5 panels: 150 x 100 cm each
(59 x 39 ⅜″)
Alessandra Bonomo Gallery, Rome
[Exhibited at Museo Reina Sofía and Tate]
[pp. 194–195]

Tra sé e sé (Between Self and Self), 1987
Mixed media on paper mounted on hardboard
11 elements: 37.5 x 50 cm each
(14 ¾ x 19 ⅝″)
Giordano Boetti, Rome
[pp. 194–195]

27 maggio 1988 (May 27, 1988), 1988
Embroidery on linen
113 x 105 cm
(44 ½ x 41 ⅜″)
Meana Larrucea Collection
[p. 247]

Venticinque × venticinque seicento-venticinque lettere (Twenty-five × Twenty-five Six Hundred and Twenty-five Letters), 1988
Embroidery on fabric
100 x 100 cm
(39 ⅜ x 39 ⅜″)
Alessandra Bonomo Gallery, Rome
[p. 88]

Mappa (Map), 1988
Embroidery on linen
120 x 225 cm
(47 ¼ x 88 ⅝″)
Private Collection, London
[Exhibited at Museo Reina Sofía and Tate]
[p. 224]

Mappa (Map), 1989
Embroidery on linen
117.5 x 227.7 cm
(46 ¼″ x 7′ 3 ¾″ x 2″)
The Museum of Modern Art, New York. Scott Burton Fund, 1999. Accession number: 1253.1999
[p. 225]

Mappa (Map), 1989
Embroidery on linen
114.3 x 214.3 cm
(45 x 84 ⅜″)

Private Collection, London
[Exhibited at Museo Reina Sofía and Tate]
[p. 228]

Tutto (Everything), 1989
Embroidery on cloth
182 x 278 cm
(71 ⅝ x 109 ½″)
Stretched: 187 x 283
(73 ⅝ x 111 ⅜″)
Private Collection, Rome
[Exhibited at Museo Reina Sofía and Tate]
[pp. 235]

Aerei (Aeroplanes), 1989
Biro on photo-sensitive paper mounted on canvas
3 panels: 148 x 100 each
(58 ¼ x 39 ⅜″)
Carmignac Gestion Foundation
[Exhibited at Museo Reina Sofía and Tate]
[pp. 238–239]

Untitled, 1989
Embroidery on linen
105 x 105 cm
(41 ⅜ x 41 ⅜″)
Es Arte Deleitosa Collection
[Exhibited at Museo Reina Sofía]
[p. 246]

Senza titolo (Mese di marzo dell anno mille nove 100 ottanta nove) (Untitled [The Month of March of the Year One Thousand Nine Hundred and Eighty-nine]), 1989
Embroidery on cloth
105 x 109 cm
(41 ⅜ x 42 ⅞″)
Private Collection, Turin
[Exhibited at Tate]
[p. 248]

Oggi dodicesimo giorno sesto mese anno mille novecento ottantanove (Today the Twelfth Day of the Sixth Month of the Year One Thousand Nine Hundred and Eighty-nine), 1989
Embroidery on cloth
105 x 112 cm
(41 ⅜ x 44 ⅛″)
Francesco Riccio, Rome
[p. 250]

Senza titolo (nero su bianco, bianco su nero) (Untitled [Black on White, White on Black]), 1989
Embroidery on cloth
108 x 108 cm
(42 ½ x 42 ½″)
Alessandra Bonomo Gallery, Rome
[Exhibited at Museo Reina Sofía and Tate]
[p. 249]

Mappa (Map), 1989–91
Embroidery on linen
265 x 585 cm
(8′6″ x 19′2″)
Chiara and Francesco Carraro Collection, Venice
[p. 222–223]

Mappa (Map), 1989–94
Embroidery on cloth
254 x 588 cm
(3′2″ x 19′6″)
Giordano Boetti, Rome
[p. 226–227]

Mappa (Map), 1990
Embroidery on linen
123 x 228 cm
(48 ⅜ x 89 ¾″)
Caterina Boetti, Rome
[Exhibited at Museo Reina Sofía and Tate]
[p. 229]

Orme (Footprints), 1990
Mixed media on paper
270 x 300 cm
(6′25″ x 9′8″)
Collection Matteo Boetti, Rome
[Exhibited at Museo Reina Sofía and Tate]
[p. 197]

Anno 1990 (The Year 1990), 1990
Pencil on paper mounted on canvas stretched over frame; 12 parts
100 x 100 cm each
(39 ⅜″ x 39 ⅜″)
Private Collection, Rome
[Exhibited at Museo Reina Sofía and Tate]
[pp. 180–181]

Tutto (Everything), 1992–93
Embroidery on cloth
167 x 345 cm
(5′4 x 11′ 3″)
Including drawing: 193 x 375 cm
(5′4 x 11′ 3″)
Private Collection, Rome
[Exhibited at Museo Reina Sofía and Tate]
[pp. 232–233]

Alternando da uno a cento e viceversa (Alternating from One to a Hundred and Vice Versa), 1993
Wool and cotton kilims
13 of 50 examples
A variable number shown at each venue
Dimensions within a range:
largest: 290.8 x 276.9 cm (114 ½ x 109″)
/ smallest: 275 x 275 cm (112 x 110″)
Private Collection, Rome
[pp. 252–255]

Autoritratto (Self-portrait), 1993/1996
Bronze, electric elements and hydraulic components
205.1 x 90.2 x 58.4 cm
(80 ¾ x 35 ½ x 23″)
Edition 4/7
Private Collection, Rome
[Exhibited at Tate]

Autoritratto (Self-Portrait), 1993/1999
Bronze and electric and hydraulic components
205.1 x 90.2 x 58.4 cm
(80 ¾ x 35 ½ x 23″)
Rachofsky Collection, Houston
[Exhibited at MoMA]
[p. 256]

Untitled, 1993–95
Wool and cotton kilim
371 x 286 cm
(12′1″ x 9′3″)

Private Collection, Rome
[Exhibited at Museo Reina Sofía]
[Different version illustrated, p. 199]

Tutto (Everything), 1994
Embroidery on linen
245 x 657 x 3 cm
(8' x 21'5")
MMK Museum für Moderne Kunst, Frankfurt am Main
[pp. 236–237]

Untitled, 1994
Set of 6 jigsaws
27 x 20.5 cm each
(10 5/8 x 8")
6 jigsaw puzzles each published in 4000 copies
Private Collection
[p. 24]

Additional Illustrations

Una vetrata (A Window), 1969 at Sperone Gallery, Turin, 1969
Iron and glass
Materials and Dimensions unknown
Courtesy Sperone Gallery, New York
[p. 14]

Gilberto Zorio lying on Stones-bed, in Piero Gilardi's Turin studio, 1967
Polyurethene foam
199 x 100 cm
(78 1/4 x 39 1/4")
Photo courtesy the artist
[p. 14]

Pack, 1967
Eternit and cement
120 x c. 50 cm diameter
(47 1/4 x 19 5/8")
destroyed
Courtesy the Archivio Alighiero Boetti, Rome
[p. 23]

Enzo Mari, 16 animali (16 Animals), 1957
Wooden pieces
34.2 x 24.8 x 3 cm
(13 1/2 x 9 3/4")
Production by Danese. Photograph by Aldo and Marirosa Ballo, 1957
[p. 24]

Rotolo di cartone ondulato (Roll of Corrugated Card), 1966
Corrugated cardboard
195 x 70 cm (diameter)
(76 3/4 x 27 1/2")
GAM - Galleria Civica d'Arte Moderna e Contemporanea, Turin
[p. 43]

Gerry Schum, Identifications:
Alighiero Boetti, Untitled–Turin, September 24, 1970
16mm film, b/w, sound, 2:08 min
GAM – Galleria Civica d'Arte Moderna e Contemporanea, Torino
[p. 82]

Iter-vallo, 1969/1986
Iron and tissue paper
40 x 40 x 1 cm
(15 3/4 x 15 3/4 x 5/8")
Private Collection
[p. 93]

Order and Disorder, 1985–86
Embroidery on cloth
199 pieces
17.5 x 17.5 cm each
(6 7/8 x 6 7/8")
MMK Museum für Moderne Kunst, Frankfurt am Main
Installation view from, "Worlds Envisioned: Alighiero e Boetti and Frédéric Bruly Bouabré," Dia Center for the Arts, New York, 1994
[pp. 95–97]

Mettere al mondo il mondo (Putting the World into the World), 1973
Indian ink on squared paper mounted on paper
328 x 159 cm
(129 x 63")
Private Collection
[p. 100]

Colonne (Columns) 1968
Scalloped-edged paper doilies and iron core
5 elements:
Largest: 201.6 x 14 cm diameter
(79 x 5 1/2")
Smallest: 183 x 27.3 cm diameter
(72 x 10 3/4")
Collezione la Gaia, Cuneo
[p. 134]

Pino Pascali, Bachi da setola (Bristleworms), 1968
Acrylic brushes mounted on iron rods
Dimensions variable
Private Collection
Installation view of *Pino Pascali's final works 1967–1968* at Camden Arts Centre, London, 2011
[p. 134]

Pino Pascali, Testa di drago (Dragon's Head), 1966
Painted canvas over wood armature
152.4 x 85.1 x 55.9 cm
(60 x 33 1/2 x 22")
Courtesy Christie's London
[p. 135]

Pino Pascali, Ricostruzione del dinosauro (Reconstruction of the Dinosaur), 1966
White canvas stretched on wooden armature
16 elements: 1200 x 80 x 70 cm
(39'4 x 31 1/2 x 27 1/2") overall
Galleria Nazionale d'Arte Moderna e Contemporanea, Rome
Courtesy Claudio Abate
[p. 135]

Michelangelo Pistoletto
Uomo in camicia (Man with Shirt), 1962
Painted tissue paper on polished stainless steel mounted on canvas
130 x 100 cm
(51 x 39 3/8")
Nationalgalerie, Berlin
[p. 136]

Giulio Paolini, Disegno geometrico (Geometric Drawing), 1960,

Tempera and ink on canvas
40 x 60 cm
(15 ¾ x 23 ⅝")
Collection Anna Paolini Piva, Turin
[p. 136]

Michelangelo Pistoletto
Structure for Talking Standing Up – Minus Objects
(Struttura per parlare in piedi – Oggetti in meno), 1965–66
Varnished iron
120 x 200 x 200 cm
(47 ¼ x 78 ¾")
Collezione Fondazione Pistoletto-Cittadellarte, Biella
[p. 137]

Carl Andre, 144 Square Lead Unit, 1969
Lead
144 units: 1 x 367.8 x 367.8 cm overall
(⅜" x 12' x 12')
The Museum of Modern Art, New York. Advisory Committee Fund
[p. 139]

Legno Ferro (pavimento), (Wood Iron [Floor]) 1967
Wood and iron
7 x 50 x 50 cm
(2 ¾ x 19 ⅝ x 19 ⅝")
Private Collection, Lucca
[p. 139]

Gary Gilmore, 1977
Indian ink on paper
2 elements: 100 x 150 cm each
(59 x 39 ⅜")
Maramotti Foundation, Reggio Emilia
[p. 146]

Catasta (Stack), 1966
34 elements of Eternit:
192 x 100 x 100 cm
(75 ⅝ x 39 ⅜ x 39 ⅜")
Castello di Rivoli Museo d'Arte Contemporanea, Rivoli, Turin; GAM - Galleria Civica d'Arte Moderna e Contemporanea, Turin
[p. 149]

Eternit (pavimento) (Eternit (Floor)), 1967
14 elements of Eternit
22 x 227 x 149 cm
(8 ⅝ x 89 ¼ x 58 ⅝")
Courtesy Gallery Christian Stein, Milan
[p. 149]

Verde Ascot 1 288 6631, 1967
Industrial varnish, cardboard, cork letters and numbers
70 x 70 cm (27 ½ x 27 ½")
Private Collection, Turin
[p. 150]

Pavimento (Floor), 1967
Firebrick tiles
6 x 110 x 110 cm
(2 ¼ x 43 ¼ x 43 ¼")
Germano Celant. Genoa
[p. 150]

Dare tempo al tempo (To Give Time to Time), 1989
Embroidery on cloth
17 x 19 cm
(6 ¾ x 7 ½")
Private Collection
[p. 152]

One Hotel, Kabul (Afghanistan), 1971–1977
4 b/w photos: 30 x 40 cm each
(11 ¾ x 15 ¾")
3 colour photos: 9 x 7 cm each
(3 ½ x 2 ¾")
Courtesy Archivio Alighiero Boetti, Rome
[pp. 154, 158]

720 lettere dall'Afghanistan (720 Letters from Afghanistan), 1973–74
Postal work
720 envelopes in 6 panels:
165 x 120 cm each (65 x 47 ¼")
1 book of drawings mounted on a plinth
Book: 29 x 23 x 4 cm (11 ⅜ x 9 x 1 ⅝")
MUMOK, Museum Moderner Kunst Stiftung Ludwig Wien, Leihgabe der Österreichischen Ludwig Stiftung
[p. 159]

AEIOU, 1971
Embroidery on cloth
60 x 60 cm
(23 ⅝ x 23 ⅝")
Bruno Corà, Prato
[p. 162]

Vento (Wind), 1985
Ink on card
2 panels: 180 x 95 cm
(70 ⅞ x 37 ⅜")
Agata Boetti, Paris
[p. 171]

Poesie con il Sufi Berang (Poems with Sufi Berang), installed in the exhibition "Les Magiciens de la terre," Centre Georges Pompidou, Paris, 1989
Embroidery on cloth
51 panels
110.5 x 110.5 cm
(43 ½ x 43 ¼") each
[p. 172]

Untitled, 1994
Wool and cotton kilim
371 x 293 cm
(12'2 x 9'6")
Private Collection, Rome
[p. 199]

Clessidra, cerniera e viceversa (Hourglass, Hinge and Vice Versa), 1981
Pencil on paper
70 x 100 cm
(27 ½ x 39 ⅜")
Private Collection
[p. 203]

Alternando da uno a cento e viceversa (Alternating from one to a hundred and Vice Versa), 1993
Wool and cotton kilims
Dimensions variable
Installation view at MAGAZIN – Centre National d'Art Contemporain de Grenoble, 1993
[p. 250]

Authors

Lynne Cooke became Curator at Dia Center for the Arts in 1991. In 2008, she was appointed Chief Curator and Deputy Director of the Museo Nacional Centro de Arte Reina Sofía, Madrid. She was co-curator of the 1991 Carnegie International, Artistic Director of the 1996 Sydney Biennale, and has curated exhibitions in numerous venues in North America, Europe, and elsewhere. She has been on the faculty for Curatorial Studies at Bard College in addition to teaching as a visiting scholar in the Graduate Fine Art departments of several universities including Yale. Among her numerous publications are recent essays on the works of Roman Ondak, Rosa Barba, Francis Alÿs, Richard Serra, Agnes Martin, Josiah McElheny and Zoe Leonard.

Bruno Corà is a critic and art historian. Lecturer at the Academy of Fine Arts in Perugia (1979–1999), the University of Cassino (1999–2005) and Florence (2005–2008). Founder and editor of *AEIOU* (1980–1988). Director of the Museo Pecci (1995–2002); Palazzo Fabroni, Pistoia (1993–2001); CAMeC, La Spezia (2003–2007); Museo d'Arte, Lugano (2008–2010). Director of the Biennale di Carrara (2006) and La Spezia (2004 and 2006) and Commissioner for Italy of the Dakar Biennale (2002). Curator of numerous international exhibitions and author of publications including: Alberto Burri, Lucio Fontana, Antoni Tàpies, Piero Manzoni, Daniel Buren, Gerhard Richter, Pistoletto, Giulio Paolini, Alighiero Boetti, Luciano Fabro, Jannis Kounellis, Gilbert & George, Antony Gormley, Francesco Lo Savio, Jan Dibbets and others. Currently a member of the Executive Board of the Foundation Burri in Città di Castello.

Claire Gilman (Ph. D. Columbia University) is curator at The Drawing Center in New York where she recently organized the exhibition *Drawn from Photography*. Gilman has taught art history and critical theory at Columbia University; The Center for Curatorial Studies, Bard College; The Corcoran College for Art and Design; and the Museum of Modern Art. Her essays on postwar European and contemporary art have appeared in journals such as *Art Journal*, *CAA Reviews*, *Documents*, *Frieze* and *October* and in anthologies and exhibition catalogues including *Il confine evanescente. Arte italiana 1960-2010* (Rome: Electa, 2010) and *Michelangelo Pistoletto: From One to Many, 1956–1974* (The Philadelphia Museum of Art, 2010).

Mark Godfrey is a Curator at Tate Modern. He is the author of *Abstraction and the Holocaust* (2007) and *Alighiero e Boetti* (2011) both published by Yale University Press. At Tate he has curated "Roni Horn aka Roni Horn" (2009), "Francis Alÿs: A Story of Deception" (2010), and with Nicholas Serota, "Gerhard Richter: Panorama" (2011). He has contributed to *OCTOBER*, *Artforum*, *Parkett* and *Frieze*, and has recently written catalogue essays on artists including Christopher Williams, Sharon Lockhart, and Abraham Cruzvillegas.

Christian Rattemeyer joined The Museum of Modern Art in New York in 2007, where he curated *Lines, Grids, Stains, Words* (2007); *Compass in Hand: Selections from The Judith Rothschild Foundation Contemporary Drawings Collection* (2009); *I Am Still Alive: Politics and Everyday Life in Contemporary Drawing*; and *Projects 95: Runa Islam* (2011). From 2003 to 2007 he was the curator at Artists Space in New York. He has been on the faculty of the MFA Program and the Center for Curatorial Studies at Bard College. He has published widely on contemporary art, including his most recent book: *Exhibiting the New Art. "Op Losse Schroeven" and "When Attitudes Become Form" 1969* (London: Afterall, 2010).

Jason E. Smith is Assistant Professor in the Graduate Studies in Art Department at Art Center College of Design (Pasadena). He writes primarily on contemporary philosophy, political theory and contemporary art, and his work has recently appeared in *Artforum*, *Critical Inquiry*, *Grey Room*, *The Minnesota Review* and *Texte zur Kunst*. He is currently writing a book on the films of Guy Debord.

Tate Exhibition Credits

Curator
Mark Godfrey

Assistant Curator
Kasia Redzisz

Exhibition Registrar
Stephanie Bush

Exhibitions Touring Manager
Rachel Kent

Head of Exhibitions
Helen Sainsbury

Chief Curator
Sheena Wagstaff

Art Installation Manager
Phil Monk

Senior Art Handling Technician
Gary McDonald

Research Assistants
Teresa Kittler and Olimpia Isidori

The exhibition at Tate Modern has been supported by:
Mr and Mrs Oliver Bolitho
Mr and Mrs Ben Brown
Tornabuoni Art, Paris
Nina and Michael Zilkha
and the American Patrons of Tate

Copyright Credits

Photographic Credits

Courtesy Agata Boetti, Paris: 110–111 (Photo: Thomas Hennocques), 171
Courtesy Archivio Alighiero Boetti, Rome: II, 2, 10, 15 & 40–41 (Photos: Enrico Cattaneo), 23, 42, 43, 45, 47, 49, 50, 57, 59, 60, 61, 63, 64, 65, 66, 67, 69, 70, 73, 74, 78, 81, 83, 85, 93, 98–99, 113 (Photo: G. Benni), 116, 117, 119, 122–123, 124–125, 126–127 (Photo: Giorgio Colombo), 128, 129, 132, 134, 137, 139, 144, 146, 149, 150, 152, 154, 158 (Photo: Archivio Alighiero Boetti), 161, 162, 169, 174 [fig. 8] (Photo: Caterina Boetti), 176–177, 183, 188, 189 & 192–193 (Photo: Serge Veignant), 190, 197 (Photo: Giulia Putatura), 200, 203 (b&w), 210–211, 213 (Photo: Mimmo Capone), 218, 243, 252–255, 283, 284, 285, 286
Courtesy Alessandra Bonomo Gallery, Rome: 88 (Photo: Antonio Idini), 194–195 (Photo: Antonello Idini), 196 & 203 (Photos: Piero Cremonese), 221, 245, 250 (Photo: Antonello Idini)
Courtesy Ben Brown Fine Arts, London: 89, 101, 108–109, 287
Courtesy Camden Arts Centre. Photo: Andy Keate: 134 (bottom)
Courtesy Carmignac Gestion Foundation: 238–239
Courtesy Chiara and Francesco Carraro Collection, Venice: 222–223
Courtesy Castello di Rivoli Museo d'Arte Contemporanea, Rivoli, Turin; GAM - Galleria Civica d'Arte Moderna e Contemporanea, Turin. Photos: Paolo Pellion: 46, 52
Courtesy Centre Pompidou – MnamCci – Bibliothèque Kandinsky: 172
Courtesy of Christie's London: 54, 135 (bottom)
Courtesy Es Arte Deleitosa Collection. Photo: Jose Luis Municio: 246
Courtesy Collection du Frac des Pays de la Loire. Photo: Hugo Maertens: 57
Courtesy Collezione Fondazione Pistoletto-Cittadellarte, Biella: 136 (Photo: P. Bressano), 137 (Photo: P. Pellion)
Courtesy Paula Cooper Gallery, New York: 94
Courtesy Dia Center for the Arts, New York. Photos: Cathy Carver: 95–97
Courtesy Fondazione Alighiero e Boetti, Rome: 176–177, 180–181, (Photo Giorgio Benni), 186–187 (Photo: Giorgio Benni), 194–195 (Photo: Giorgio Benni), 232–233 (Photo: Claudio Abate), 235 (Photo: Giorgio Benni), 248 (Photo: Giorgio Benni), 253–255, 288 (Photo: Claudio Abate)
Courtesy Frac Bourgogne. Photo: André Morin, Paris: 79
Courtesy Frittelli Arte Contemporanea, Florence: 77
Courtesy Gagosian Gallery, New York: 253–255
Courtesy Paolo and Alida Giuli, Malgrate-Lecco: 251, 285
Courtesy Gladstone Gallery, New York: 199, 226–227, 229, 256
Courtesy Glenstone: IV, 44, 104–105, 164–165, 241, 283
Courtesy Paolo and Paola Levis. Photo: Tommaso Mattina: 102
Courtesy Liechtenstein Kunstmuseum, Vaduz: 71/ 80/ 103/ 282 (Photos: Stefan Altenburger); 72 (Photo: Reinhard Haider)
Courtesy LWL-Landesmuseum für Kunst und Kulturgeschichte Münster (Westfälisches Landesmuseum). Photo: Sabine Ahlbrand-Dornseif: 118
Courtesy Meana Larrucea Collection. Photo: Gestion Cultural: 247
Courtesy MMK Museum für Moderne Kunst, Frankfurt am Main: 214–215, 236–237
Courtesy Paola and Gloria Molino: 90 & 281 (Photos: Paolo Vandrasch, Milan), 120–121
Courtesy Museo Nacional Centro de Arte Reina Sofía, Madrid: 91
Courtesy The Museum of Modern Art, Department of Imaging Services: 32/ 40/ 106–107 (Photos: David Allison), 86, 139 (Photo: Kate Keller), 182, 225 (Photo: Paige Knight), 242, 178–179 (Photo: Peter Butler), 216–217 (Photo: Thomas Griesel)
Courtesy Jean-Edouard van Praet. Photo: Ken Paprocki: 75
Courtesy Private Collection. Photos: Tommaso Mattina: 31, 55
Courtesy Private Collection, La Spezia: 184–185, 219
Courtesy Private Collection, London. Photos: Todd White Photography: 224, 228
Courtesy Rachofsky Collection: 131
Courtesy Sperone Westwater, New York: 14, 53 (Photo: Tom Powel), 230
Courtesy Sprüth Magers, Berlin–London and Le Case D'Arte, Milan: 87, 130
Courtesy Francesco Riccio, Rome: 249
Courtesy Christian Stein Gallery, Milan. Photo: Peter Filé: 56
Courtesy Tornabuoni Art: 220, 240
Courtesy Gino Viliani Collection: 58
Photo © Claudio Abate: 135 (top)
Photo © Aldo and Marirosa Ballo. Courtesy Marirosa Toscani Ballo: 24
Photos © Bruce Chatwin / Trevillion Images: 156
Photos © Giorgio Colombo: 18, 28, 51, 115
Photo © Museum in Progress www.mip.at: 24
Photo © MUMOK, Museum Moderner Kunst Stiftung Ludwig Wien, Leihgabe der Österreichischen Ludwig Stiftung: 159
Photo © Paolo Mussat Sartor: 15
Photo © Archivio Giulio Paolini, Turin. Photo: Mario Sarotto: 136
Public domain: http://libcom.org/tags/fiat: 142
Photos © RMS Randi Malkin Steinberger: 12 (From: *Accanto al Pantheon*, Randi Malkin Steinberger, Milan: Prearo Editore, 1991), 174 (From: *Boetti by Afghan People, Peshawar, Pakistan, 1990: Photographs by Randi Malkin Steinberger*, Los Angeles: RAM Publications, 2011)
Photos © TATE: 178 (Photo (overview): David Lambert), 191 (Photo: David Lambert and Rod Tidnam)

Supporting Tate

Tate relies on a large number of supporters – individuals, foundations, companies and public funders – to enable it to deliver its programme of activities, both on and off its gallery sites. This support is essential in order for Tate to acquire works of art for the Collection, run education, outreach and exhibition programmes, care for the Collection in storage and enable art to be displayed, both digitally and physically, inside and outside Tate. Donations, of whatever size, are gratefully received, either to support particular areas of interest, or to contribute to general activity costs.

Tate would like to thank all the individuals and organisations who have so generously supported our work. We would particularly like to thank the following who have supported Tate Modern in the last year, and acknowledge the significant contribution of Tate Patrons, Tate International Council, Tate Asia-Pacific Acquisitions Committee, Tate Middle East and North African Acquisitions Committee, Tate Photography Acquisitions Committee, Tate North American Acquisitions Committee and the Tate Latin American Acquisitions Committee.

Tate Foundation Trustees
John C Botts, CBE
Carol Galley
Noam Gottesman
Scott Mead
Franck Petitgas (Chair)
Anthony Salz
Sir Nicholas Serota
Lord Stevenson of Coddenham, CBE

Tate Foundation Non-Executive Trustees
Victoria Barnsley, OBE
Mrs James Brice
The Lord Browne of Madingley, FRS, FREng
Susan Burns
Melanie Clore
Sir Howard Davies
Dame Vivien Duffield
Lady Lynn Forester de Rothschild
Mandy Moross
Paul Myners, CBE
Sir John Ritblat
Lady Ritblat
Mrs Theresa Sackler
The Rt Hon Sir Timothy Sainsbury
Peter Simon
Jon Snow
John J Studzinski, CBE
Anita Zabludowicz

Donors to the Tate Modern Project
We remain grateful to all those individuals and organisations who supported the creation of Tate Modern in 2000 as founding donors and sponsors. As we embark on the next stage of Tate Modern's development, we would like to pay particular thanks to the following donors who have supported the current Tate Modern Project.

Lauren and Mark Booth
Mr and Mrs James Brice
The Lord Browne of Madingley, FRS, FREng
John and Christina Chandris
James Chanos
Paul Cooke
Tiqui Atencio Demirdjian and Ago Demirdjian
Mala Gaonkar
Thomas Gibson in memory of Anthea Gibson
Lydia and Manfred Gorvy
Noam Gottesman
Maja Hoffmann/LUMA Foundation
Maxine Isaacs
Peter and Maria Kellner
Madeleine Kleinwort
Allison and Howard W. Lutnick
Donald B. Marron
Anthony and Deirdre Montagu
Alison and Paul Myners
Daniel and Elizabeth Peltz
Barrie and Emmanuel Roman
The Dr Mortimer and Theresa Sackler Foundation
John J Studzinski, CBE
Tate Members
Nina and Graham Williams
and those who wish to remain anonymous

Tate Modern Benefactors and Major Donors
29th May 1961 Charitable Trust
Alexander and Bonin Publishing, Inc.
Omar and Hind Alghanim
Francis Alÿs
American Patrons of Tate
Annenberg Foundation
Klaus Anschel
The Art Fund
Art Mentor Foundation Lucerne
The Arts & Humanities Research Council
Arts Council England
Charles Asprey
Marwan Assaf
Miroslaw Balka
The Estate of Frith Banbury
The Estate of Peter and Caroline Barker-Mill
Corinne Bellow Charity
Luis Benshimol
Big Lottery Fund
Billstone Foundation
Ronald Blythe
The Charlotte Bonham-Carter Charitable Trust
Mr Pontus Bonnier
Louise Bourgeois
Frances Bowes
Stuart Brisley, courtesy of England & Co
British Council
The Lord Browne of Madingley, FRS, FREng
John and Susan Burns
The Estate of Mrs Kathleen Bush
Mrs Simon Carter
John and Christina Chandris
James Chanos
Henry Christensen III
Patricia Phelps de Cisneros
Alvaro Clark and Sandro Brito
The Clore Duffield Foundation
The Clothworkers' Foundation
Ron Collins
Michael Craig-Martin
Douglas S Cramer
Martin Creed
Thomas Dane
Dimitris Daskalopoulos
Manny and Brigitta Davidson and the Family
Richard Deacon
Dedalus Foundation, Inc.
Tiqui Atencio Demirdjian and Ago Demirdjian
Department for Business, Innovation and Skills
Department for Culture, Media and Sport
Department for Education
Anthony d'Offay
Peter Doig
The Estate of Juan Downey
The D'Oyly Carte Charitable Trust
Jytte Dresing
Joakim Eneroth
European Union
Esmée Fairbairn Foundation
The Estate of Maurice Farquharson
Finnis Scott Foundation
First Light
Lady Lynn Forester de Rothschild

The Estate of Ann Forsdyke
Mildred and Martin Friedman
Larry Gagosian
Galerie Gebr. Lehmann
Henrietta Garnett
The Getty Foundation
The Glass-House Trust
Millie and Arne Glimcher
The Goss-Michael Foundation
The Great Britain Sasakawa Foundation
Konstantin Grigorishin
Arthur and Helen Grogan
Calouste Gulbenkian Foundation
Chloë and Paul Gunn
Viscount and Viscountess Hampden and Family
Hauser & Wirth
Janet Henderson
Heritage Lottery Fund
John Hewish Bequest
Anthony Hill
The Family of Klaus E Hinrichsen
The Hintze Family Charitable Foundation
Boris Hirmas Said
Damien Hirst
The Henry C Hoare Charitable Trust
Alan and Mary Hobart
David Hockney
Jenny Holzer
Stanley Honeyman
The Idlewild Trust
Cristina Iglesias
Institut Ramon Llull
Dakis and Lietta Joannou
Bharti Kher
Jack Kirkland
The Estate of RB Kitaj
Leon Kossoff
Jannis Kounellis
The Kreitman Foundation
Catherine and Pierre Lagrange
The Kirby Laing Foundation
David and Amanda Leathers
The Leche Trust
Legacy Trust UK
The Leverhulme Trust
Gemma Levine
The Estate of Barbara Lloyd
Doris J. Lockhart
Eugenio Lopez
Anne Lyles
John Lyon's Charity
Eykyn Maclean
The Estate of Sir Edwin Manton
Panos and Sandra Marinopoulos
The Paul Mellon Centre
Mexican Embassy to the United Kingdom
Michael Werner, Inc
Sir Geoffroy Millais
The Estate of Paul Edwin Millwood
The Monument Trust
Cynthia Moody
Donald Moore
The Henry Moore Foundation
Elisabeth Murdoch
Alison and Paul Myners
NADFAS
National Heritage Memorial Fund
Winston Ginsberg and Averill Ogden
Outset Contemporary Art Fund
Konstantinos Papageorgiou and Gregory Papadimitriou
Catherine and Franck Petitgas
PHG Cadbury Charitable Trust
The Pilgrim Trust
Jacqui Brantjes and Daniel Pittack
Heather and Tony Podesta Collection
Boyana Popova
Gilberto Pozzi
The Radcliffe Trust
Liz Gerring Radke and Kirk Radke
Maya and Ramzy Rasamny
The Family of Sir Norman Reid
The Estate of Karel and Betsy Reisz
Rootstein Hopkins Foundation
Edward Ruscha
The Estate of Simon Sainsbury
Doris Salcedo
Saloua Raouda Choucair Foundation, Beirut
Gerd Sander
Daman Sanders
Robin Saunders
Lilly Scarpetta and Roberto Pumarejo
The Search Foundation
Thomas J Sikorski Charitable Trust
Carla Emil and Richard Silverstein
Odyssia Skouras, New York
Candida and Rebecca Smith
Paul Smith Limited
The Office for Cultural and Scientific Affairs at the Embassy of Spain
The Spanish Tourist Office
Norah and Norman Stone
Tate Asia-Pacific Acquisitions Committee
Tate International Council
Tate Latin American Acquisitions Committee
Tate Members
Tate Middle East and North Africa Acquisitions Committee
Tate North American Acquisitions Committee
Tate Patrons
Tate Photography Acquisitions Committee
Terra Foundation for American Art
The Estate of Mr Nicholas Themans
Jannick Thiroux
The Sir Jules Thorn Charitable Trust
The Keith Vaughan Estate
Marc Vaux
VTB Capital
The Wates Foundation
White Cube
The Estate of Fred Williams
Jane and Michael Wilson
Iwan and Manuela Wirth
World Collections Programme
Poju and Anita Zabludowicz
and those who wish to remain anonymous

Tate Modern Corporate Supporters
Bank of America Merrill Lynch
Bloomberg LP
BP
British Land
Finsbury
Fundación Televisa
Goldman Sachs
Hildon Ltd
JCA Group
Le Méridien
Unilever
Vodafone
and those who wish to remain anonymous

Tate Modern Corporate Members
Accenture
Clifford Chance LLP
Deutsche Bank
EDF Energy
Freshfields Bruckhaus Deringer
Hanjin Shipping
HSBC Holdings plc
IPC Media
The John Lewis Partnership
Linklaters
Mace Group
Morgan Stanley
Native Land & Grosvenor
Nomura
Oliver Wyman
Pearson
Societe Generale
Thames & Hudson
UBS
Wolff Olins
and those who wish to remain anonymous

Curators' Acknowledgements

An exhibition on this ambitious scale devised for presentation in three far-flung institutions depends heavily on a large team for its realization. Collaborating closely over the past eighteen months, we three curators have benefitted greatly from the expertise and support of many individuals. Foremost among them is Annemarie Sauzeau Boetti whose unrivalled knowledge of the full span of Boetti's practice has proven invaluable. We are greatly indebted to Annemarie in her several roles: as Director of the Archivio Alighiero Boetti, she and her skilled team have provided detailed assistance in manifold ways; and as an expert and author on Boetti's art, she has offered sound counsel on numerous occasions.

We are also greatly indebted to Caterina Raganelli Boetti, the artist's widow and President of the Fondazione Alighiero e Boetti. With its excellent staff, the Fondazione has taken an active role in realizing this project. The artist's three children, Matteo, Agata and Giordano, have enthusiastically and generously supported the retrospective from its inception. Without the assistance and commitment of all of Boetti's extendend family, we could not have achieved our goals. Individually, we have each benefitted from the dedicated professional aid of a trio of remarkable assistants on this project: Soledad Liaño at the Museo Reina Sofía; Kasia Redzisz at Tate Modern; and Maura Lynch at MoMA. Among the many others whose contributions have been crucial we would like to single out Rosalind Horne who has skillfully organized the production of this catalogue and Filiep Tacq to whom we owe thanks for his beautiful design.

Without the generosity of lenders, private and institutional, major exhibitions of this kind would be impossible. We extend our sincere thanks to the individuals and institutions listed below who have lent works to the show:

1000 Eventi Gallery, Milan
G. Aglietta Collection, Biella
Caterina Boetti Collection, Rome
Giordano Boetti Collection, Rome
Alessandra Bonomo
Alessandra Bonomo Gallery, Rome
Paloma Botín
Ben Brown Fine Arts, London / Hong Kong
Carmignac Gestion Foundation
Chiara e Francesco Carraro Collection, Venice
Le Case D'Arte, Milan
Castello di Rivoli Museo d'Arte Contemporanea, Rivoli –Turin
Collection de l'Institut d'Art Contemporain, Rhône-Alpes
Collection du Frac des Pays de la Loire
Colombo Collection, Milan
Composti della Cadi Frá Collection, Milan
Dallas Museum of Art
Es Arte Deleitosa Collection
Fondazione per l'Arte Moderna e Contemporanea CRT, Turin
Frittelli Arte Contemporanea, Florence
Mariangelica De Gaetano Collection
GAM – Galleria Civica d'Arte Moderna e Contemporanea, Turin
GNAM, Galleria Nazionale d'Arte Moderna, Rome
Paolo and Alida Giuli Collection, Malgrate-Lecco
Goetz Collection, Munich
Inhotim Collection. Minas Gerais, Brazil
Egidio Marzona Collection
Kunstmuseum Liechtenstein
LWL – Landesmuseum für Kunst und Kulturgeschichte, Münster
Meana Larrucea Collection
Collection Gloria Molino
Valerio de Paolis Collection
François Pinault
Teresa Pomodoro
J.E. Van Praet Collection
Rachowsky Collection
Regional Contemporary Art Fund of Burgundy

Francesco Riccio, Rome
Alex Sainsbury
Collection Gian Enzo Sperone, New York
Coll. Sprüth-Leccese
Sprüth Magers, Berlin – London
Christian Stein Gallery, Milan
Gino Villani Collection
Viaindustriae / Private Collection, Foligno
As well as to those who wish to remain anonymous.

Special thanks to:

Howard and Cindy Rachofsky
Barbara Gladstone
Glenstone

In addition we are variously indebted to the following individuals for their kind assistance and support:

Salman Ali
Martin Angioni
Analisa Bacall
Chiara Bertola, Castello di Rivoli Museo d'Arte Contemporanea, Rivoli –Turin
Arianna Bonna
Melanie Bono, LWL-Landesmuseum für Kunst und Kulturgeschichte
Luca Cerizza
Laura Cherubini
Jeanne Chvosta, Rachofsky Collection
Mario Codognato
Marcos Corrales
Simone Cresci, Ilaria Giaccone and Arianna Mercanti, Archivio Alighiero Boetti, Rome
Tricia Dixon, Dallas Museum of Art
Danilo Eccher, GAM Galleria Civica d'Arte Moderna e Contemporanea, Torino
Pierpaolo Falone
Carlo Frittelli
Nathalie Gallon, Carmignac Gestion Foundation
María García Yelo
Marina Gargiulo
Stephen Gribbin
Beatriz Jordana
Robin Hemmer, Kunstmuseum Liechtenstein
Gelare Khoshgozaran
Renata Knes
Elizabeth Kujawski
Odile de Labouchère, Pinault Collection
Melissa Larner
Juan Gabriel López Guix
Carlos Martín García
Luisa Mensi
Valentina Pero
Paige Rozansky and Gaby Mizes
Elena Salza, Archive: Fondazione Alighiero e Boetti, Rome
Chantal Scotton, Regional Contemporary Art Fund of Burgundy
Elisa Sighicelli and Ruben Levi
Stephan Urbaschek, Goetz Collection

First published 2012 by order of the Tate Trustees
by Tate Publishing, a division of Tate Enterprises Ltd,
Millbank, London SW1P 4RG
www.tate.org.uk/publishing

on the occasion of the exhibition
Alighiero Boetti: Game Plan

organized by Tate Modern, London; The Museum of Modern Art, New York and the Museo Nacional Centro de Arte Reina Sofía, Madrid.

Museo Nacional Centro de Arte Reina Sofía
October 5, 2011 – February 5, 2012

Tate Modern
February 28 – May 27, 2012

The Museum of Modern Art
July 1 – October 1, 2012

Exhibition originated by Museo Nacional Centro de Arte Reina Sofía, Madrid

A catalogue record for this book is available from the British Library

ISBN 978 1 84976 008 9

Printed on sustainably sourced, certified paper

Printed and bound in Spain.

Measurements of artworks are given in centimetres and inches, height before width.

Cover: Alighiero Boetti, *Untitled*, 1969 (detail of plate, p. 91)

Exhibition

Curators
Lynne Cooke
Mark Godfrey
Christian Rattemeyer

Exhibition Co-ordinator at the Museo Reina Sofía
Soledad Liaño

Catalogue

Concept & Direction
Lynne Cooke

Editors
Lynne Cooke
Mark Godfrey
Christian Rattemeyer

Editorial Management
Rosalind Horne

Museo Nacional Centro de Arte Reina Sofía
Publications Department
Director
María Luisa Blanco
Coordination
Teresa Ochoa de Zabalegui

Graphic Design
Filiep Tacq

Translation
Duncan Brown (pp. 6–8)
Simon Pleasance (pp. 200–209)

Plates and Printing
Artes Gráficas Palermo, S.L.

Binding
Ramos

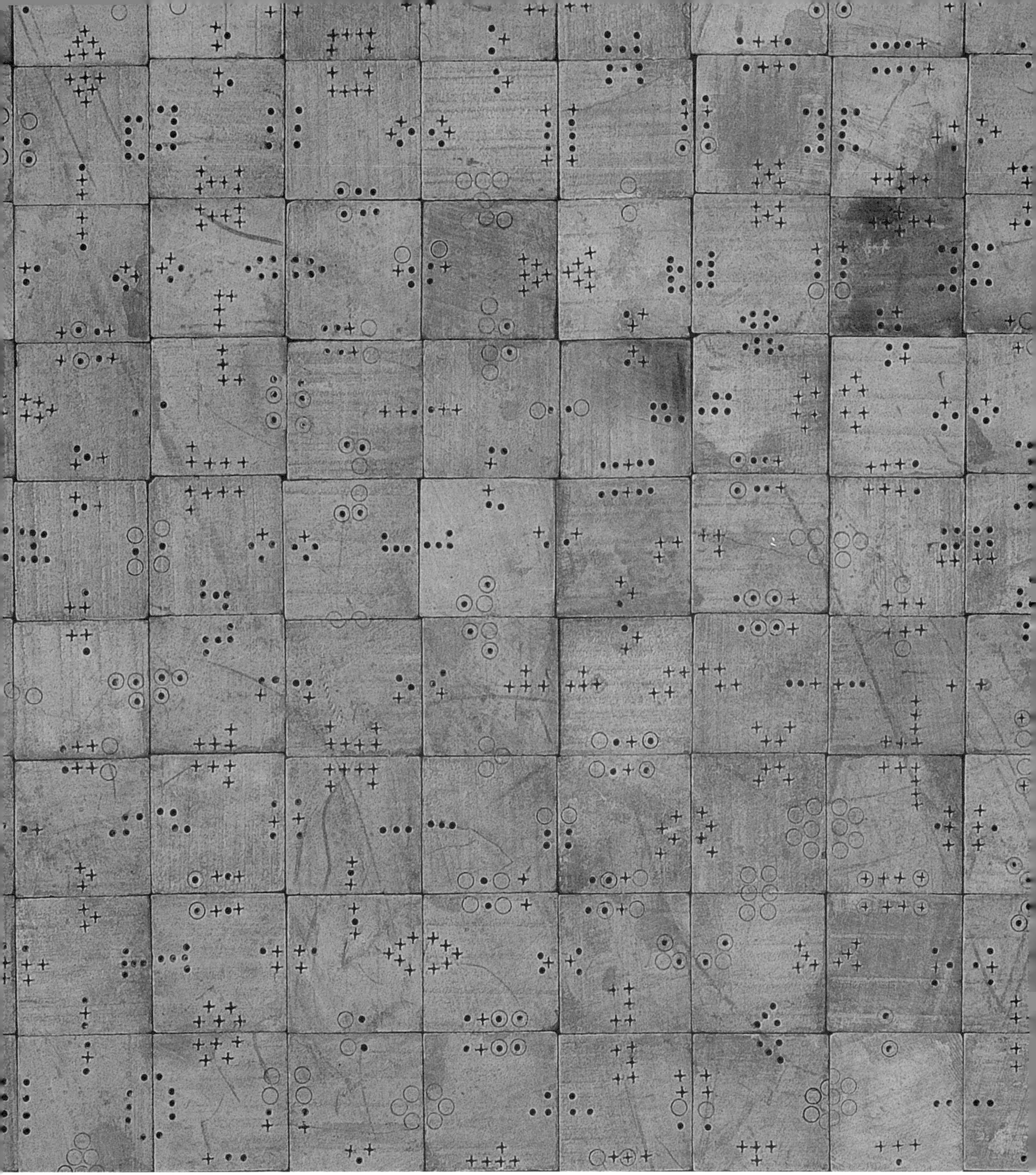

Dama (Checkerboard), 1967 (detail)

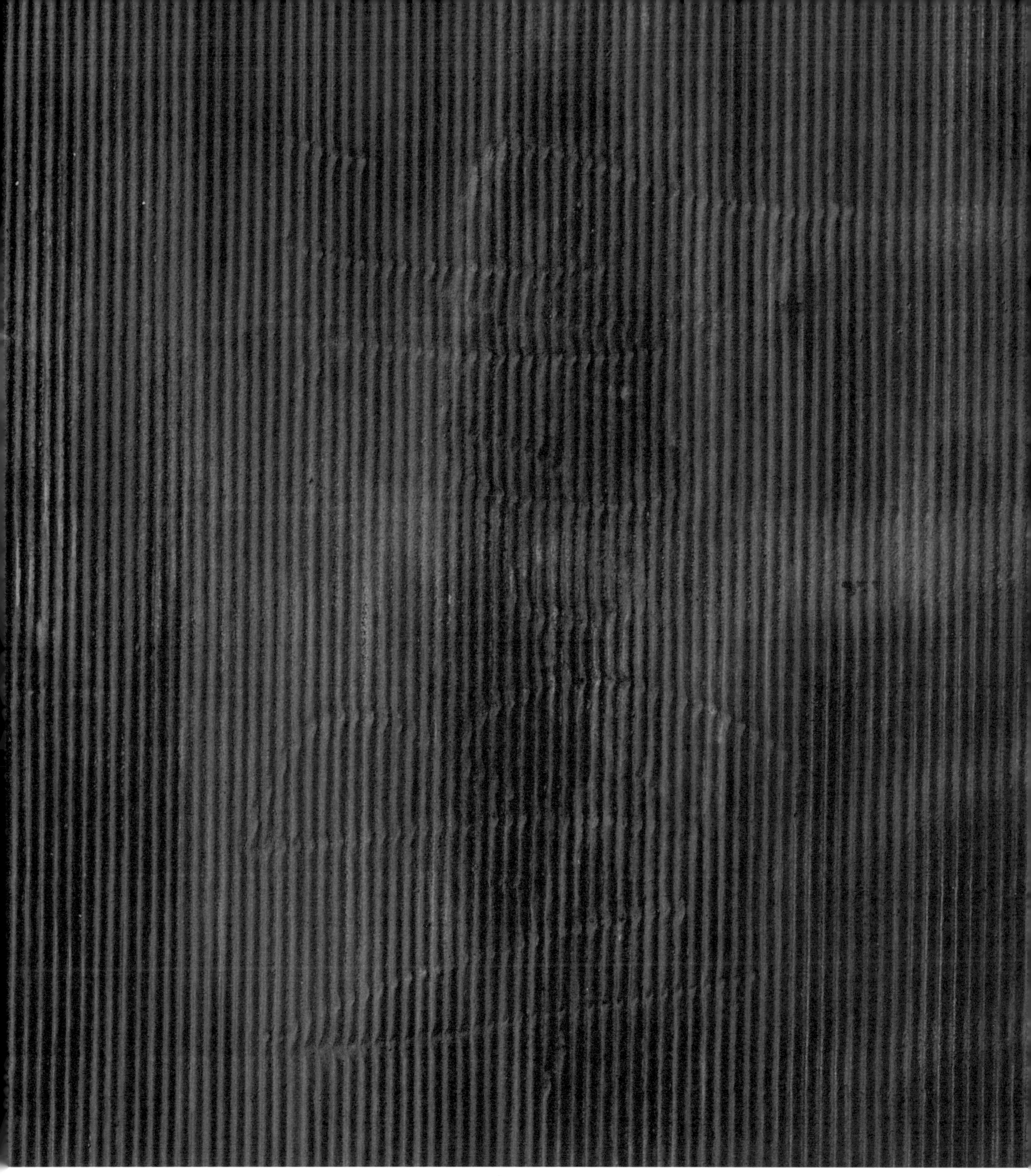

Ghise (ABoetti) (Cast Iron [ABoetti]), 1968 (detail)

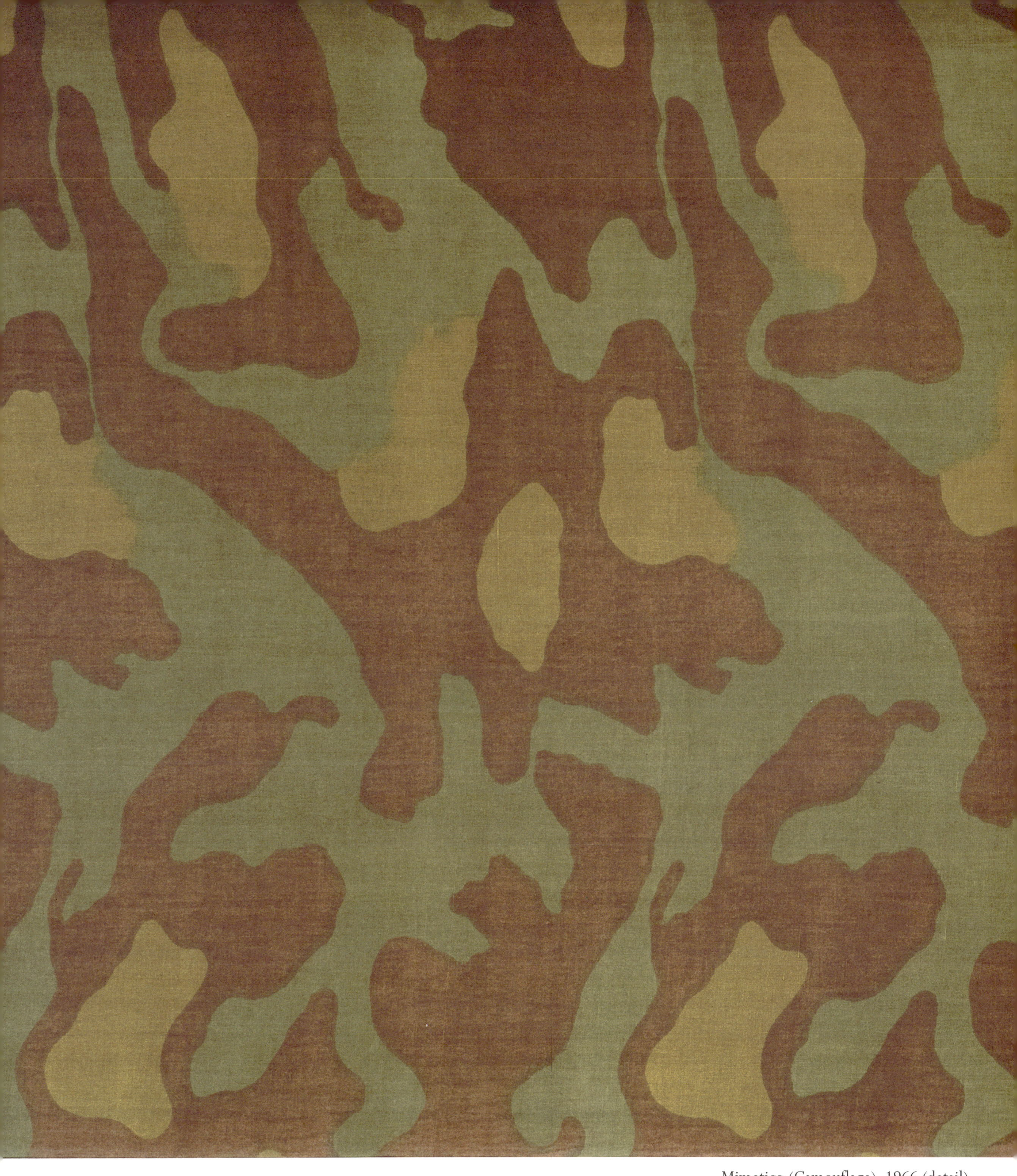

Mimetico (Camouflage), 1966 (detail)

Storia naturale della moltiplicazione (Natural History of Multiplication), 1975 (detail)

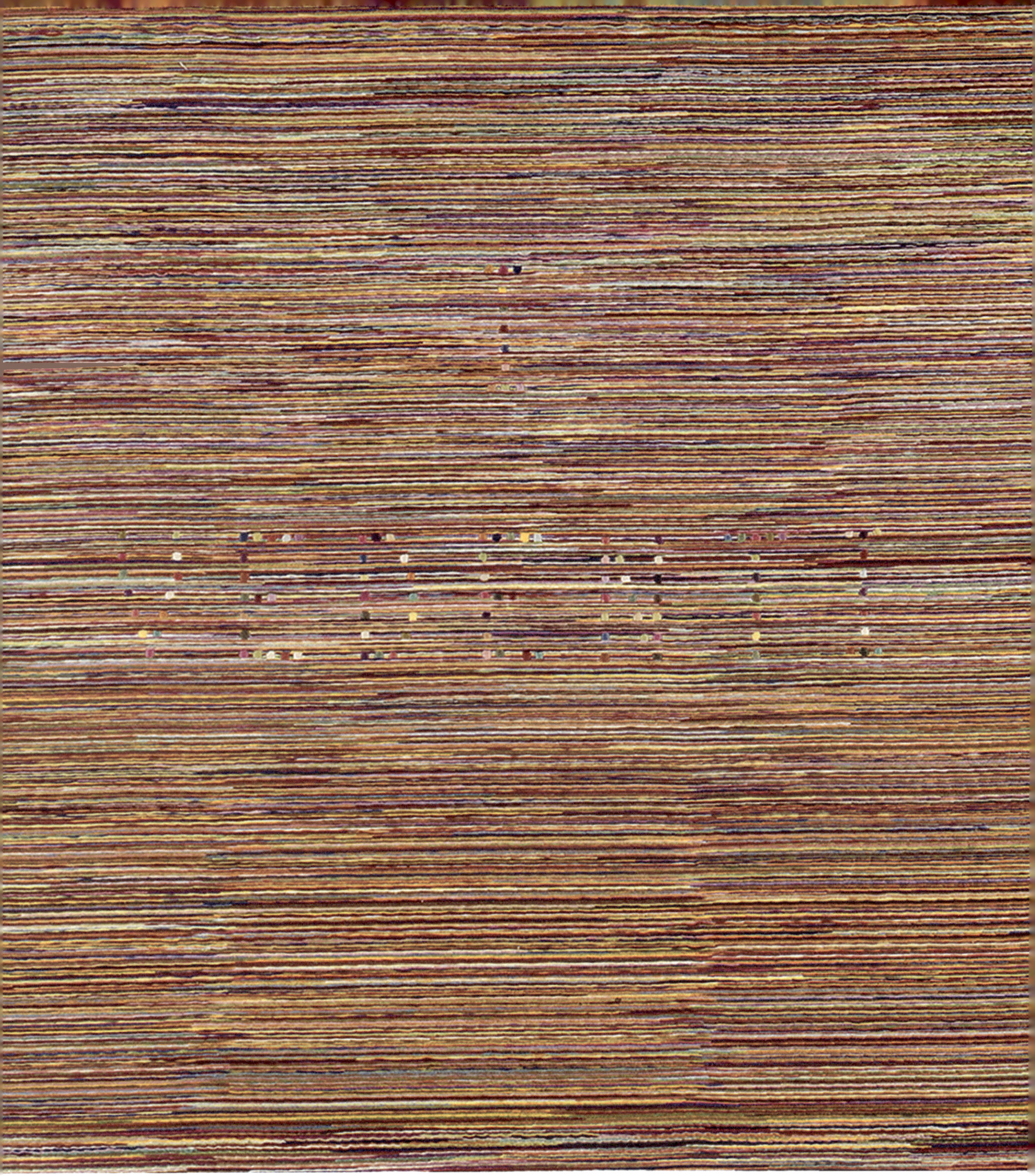

IVEDENTI (The Sighted), 1972–73 (detail)

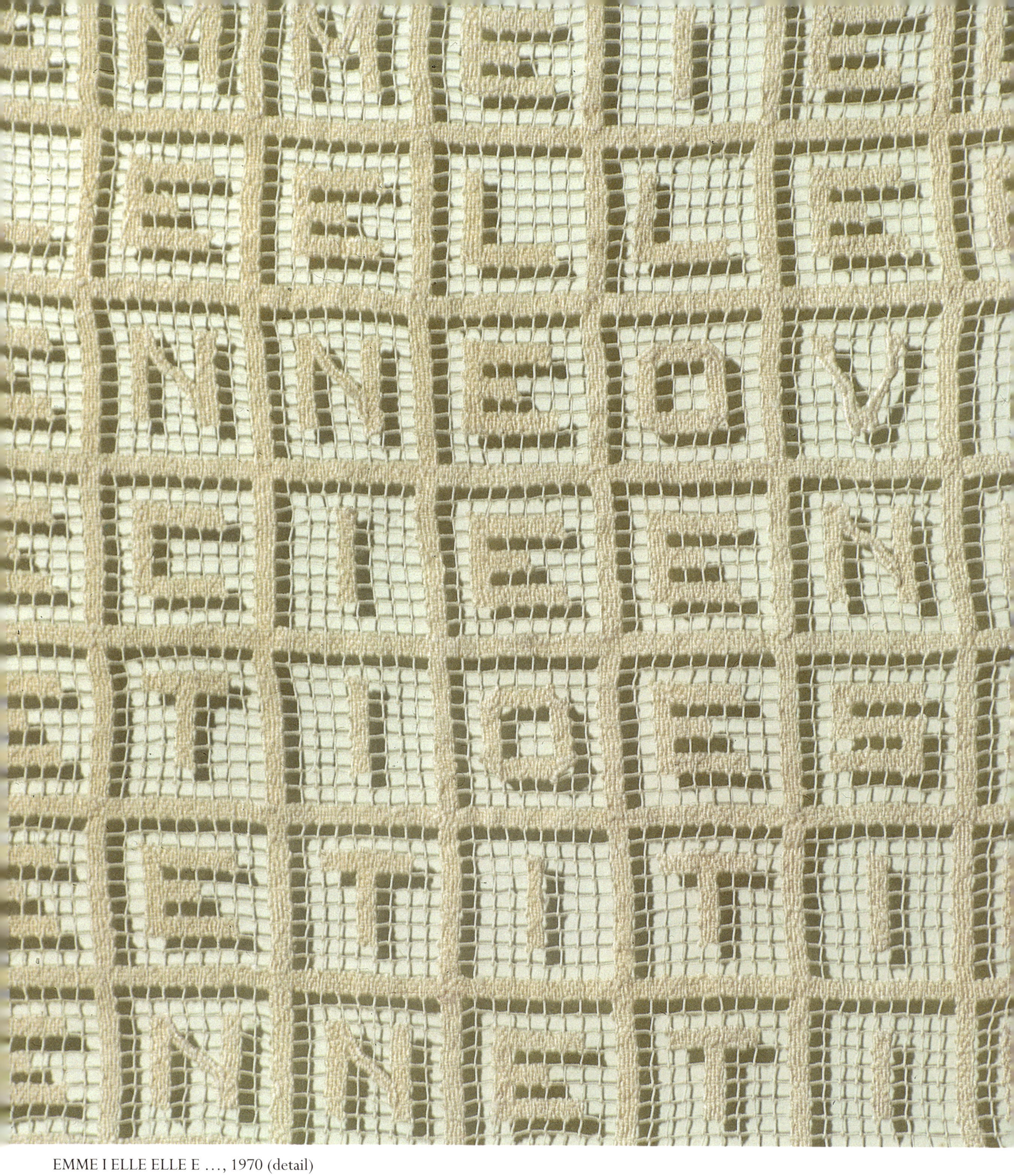

EMME I ELLE ELLE E …, 1970 (detail)

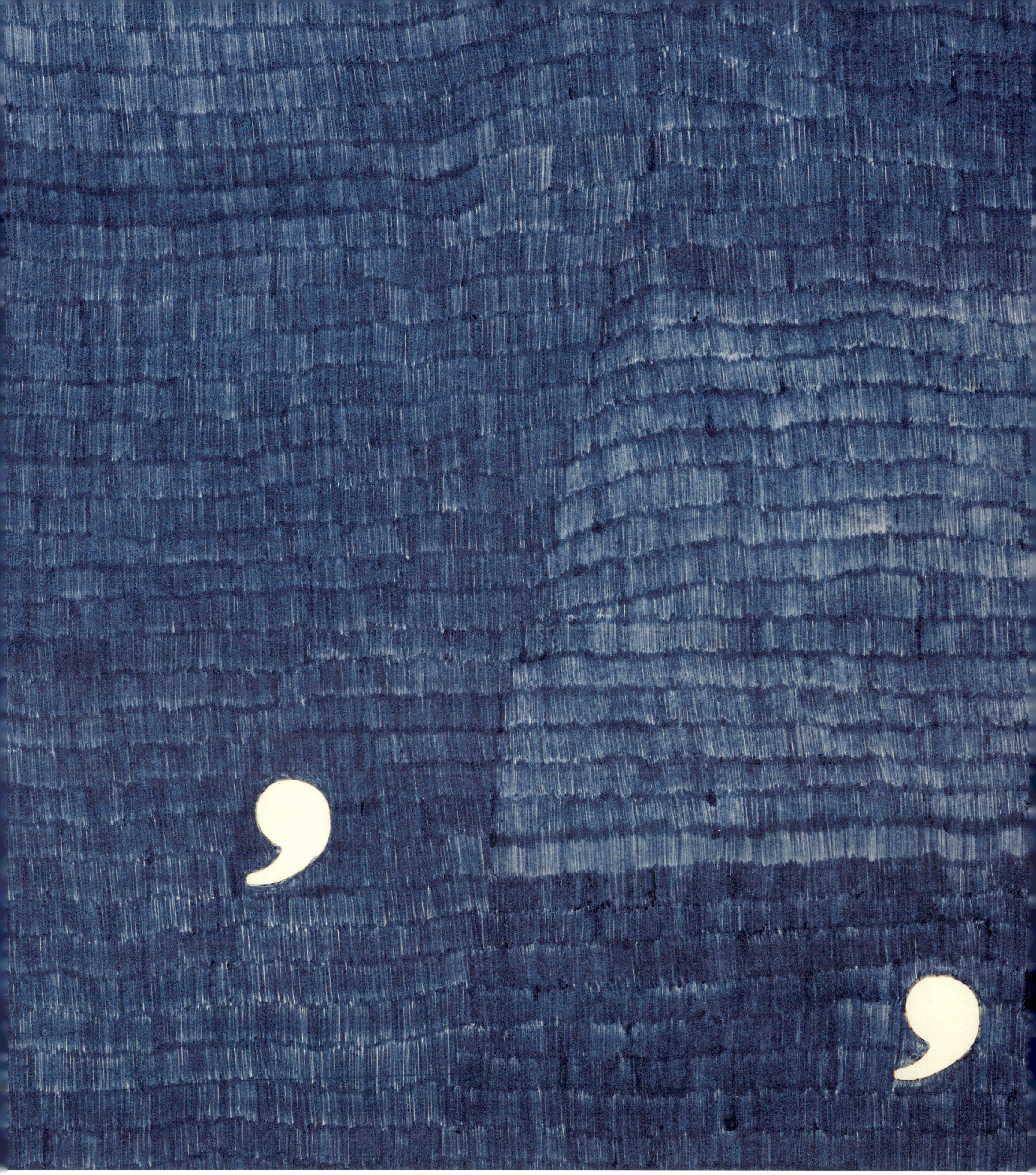

Mettere al mondo il mondo a Roma nella primavera dell'anno mille novecentosettantotto pensando a tutto tondo, 1978 (detail)

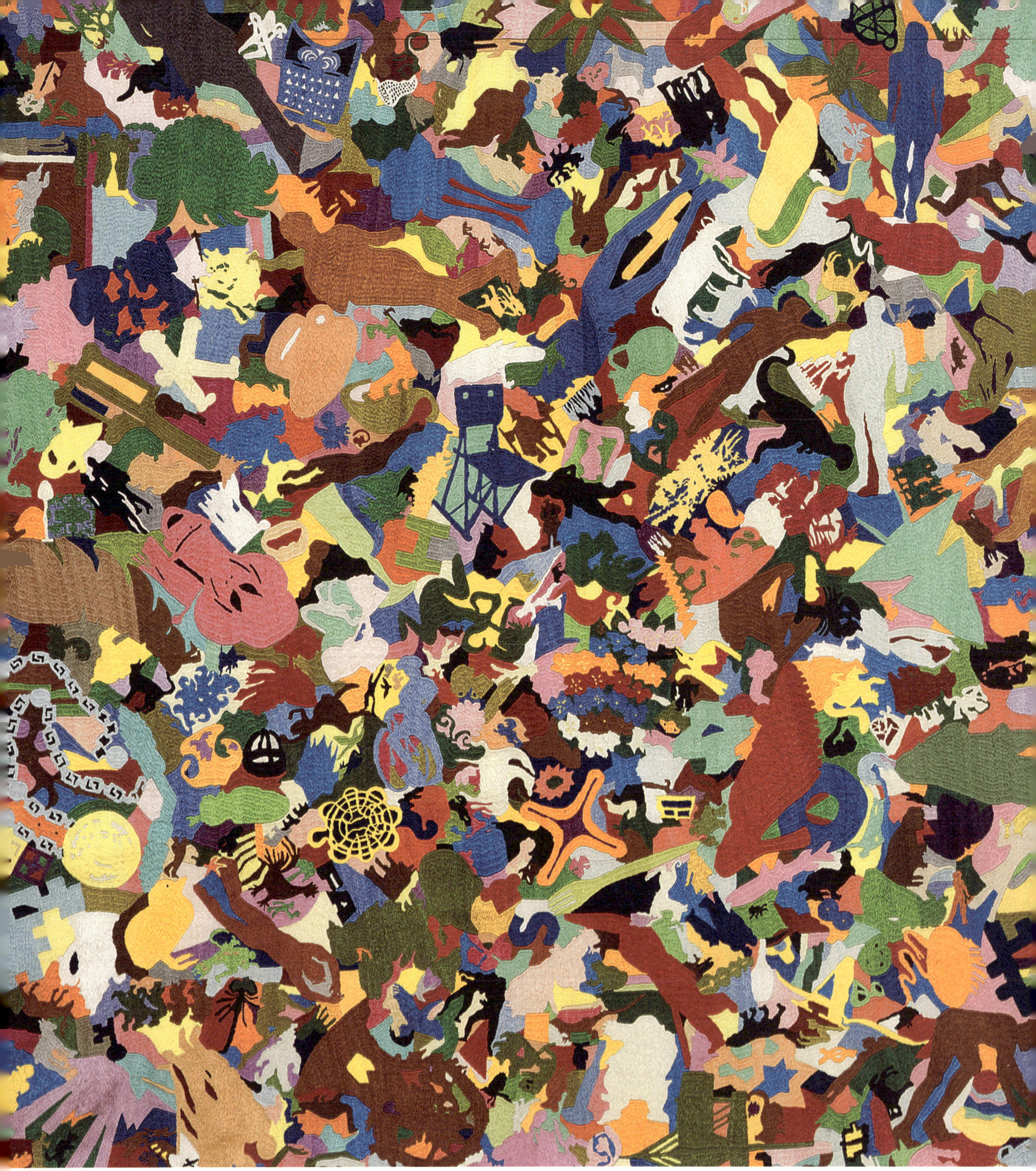

Tutto (Everything), 1992–93 (detail)

Alternando da uno a cento e viceversa (Alternating from One to One Hundred and Vice Versa), 1977–78 (detail)

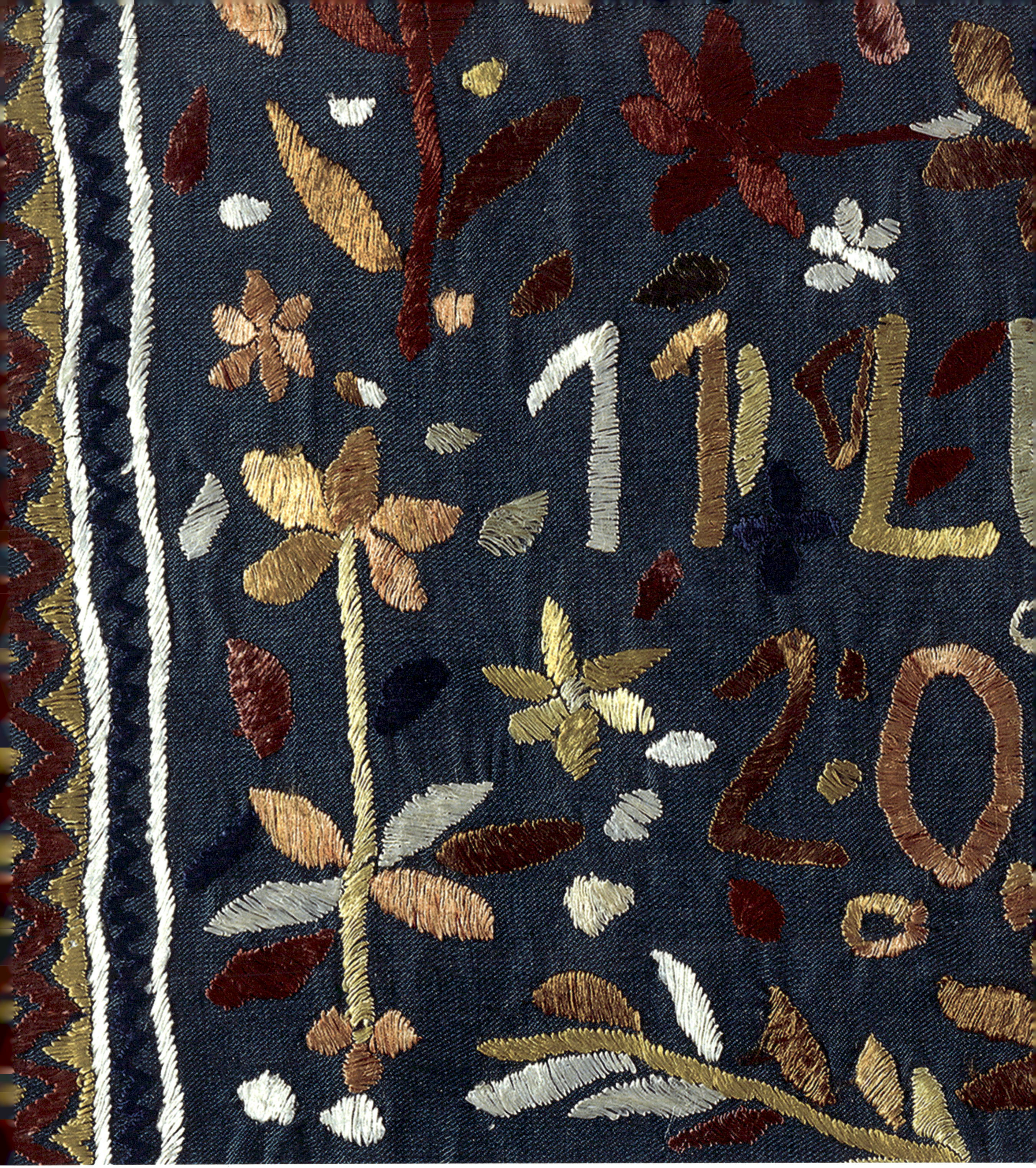